T0393149

Sustainable Urban Futures in Africa

Sustainable Urban Futures in Africa provides a variety of conventional and emerging theoretical frameworks to inform understandings and responses to critical urban development issues such as urbanisation, climate change, housing/slum, informality, urban sprawl, urban ecosystem services and urban poverty within the context of the sustainable development goals (SDGs) in Africa.

This book addresses topics including challenges to spatial urban development, how spatial planning is delivered, how different urbanisation variables influence the development of different forms of urban systems and settlements in Africa, how city authorities could use old and new methods of land administration to produce sustainable urban spaces in Africa, and the role of local activism in causing important changes in the built environment. Chapters are written by a diverse range of African scholars and practitioners in urban planning and policy, environmental science, sociology, agriculture, natural resources management, environmental law, and politics.

Urban Africa has huge resource potential – both human and natural resources – that can stimulate sustainable development when effectively harnessed. *Sustainable Urban Futures in Africa* provides support for the SDGs in urban Africa and will be of interest to students and researchers, professionals and policymakers, and readers of urban studies, spatial planning, geography, governance, and other social sciences.

Patrick Brandful Cobbinah is a senior lecturer in urban planning at the Melbourne School of Design and the Faculty of Architecture, Building and Planning at the University of Melbourne, Australia. He holds a PhD in Human Geography with emphasis on regional planning and resource conservation from Charles Sturt University, Australia. Patrick's background is in human geography with broad experience in urban and regional planning gained through teaching and research conducted at universities in Ghana and Australia.

Michael Addaney is a lecturer in environmental policy and planning at the Department of Planning and Sustainability of the University of Energy and Natural Resources, Ghana, and Senior Research Associate at the Centre for Public Management and Governance at the University of Johannesburg, South Africa. He is also a Research Fellow of the Earth System Governance Project at Utrecht University, The Netherlands. Michael is an environmental social scientist whose expertise and current research interests are in the multifaceted and embedded relationships between humans and the environment, whether facilitated by institutions or by local organisations/communities, and the effects of this on public policy and planning processes and outcomes, particularly in relation to notions of rights, justice, and equity. Michael holds a PhD in environment and natural resources law from the Wuhan University, China, and a BSc in Development Planning from the Kwame Nkrumah University of Science and Technology, Ghana.

Routledge Research in Planning and Urban Design

Routledge Research in Planning and Urban Design is a series of academic monographs for scholars working in these disciplines and the overlaps between them. Building on Routledge's history of academic rigour and cutting-edge research, the series contributes to the rapidly expanding literature in all areas of planning and urban design.

Economic Incentives in Sub-Saharan African Urban Planning
A Ghanaian Case Study
Kwasi Gyau Baffour Awuah

Street-Naming Cultures in Africa and Israel
Power Strategies and Place-Making Practices
Liora Bigon and Michel Ben Arrous

Identity in Post-Socialist Public Space
Urban Architecture in Kiev, Moscow, Berlin, and Warsaw
Bohdan Cherkes and Józef Hernik

Sustainable Urban Futures in Africa
Edited by Patrick Brandful Cobbinah and Michael Addaney

Smart Design
Disruption, Crisis, and the Reshaping of Urban Spaces
Richard Hu

Victorian Cemeteries and the Suburbs of London
Spatial Consequences to the Reordering of London's Burials in the Early 19th Century
Gian Luca Amadei

For more information about this series, please visit: www.routledge.com/Routledge-Research-in-Planning-and-Urban-Design/book-series/RRPUD

Sustainable Urban Futures in Africa

Edited by Patrick Brandful Cobbinah and Michael Addaney

Routledge
Taylor & Francis Group

NEW YORK AND LONDON

Cover image: Accra Metropolitan Assembly, Smart City Journal.

First published 2022
by Routledge
605 Third Avenue, New York, NY 10158

and by Routledge
4 Park Square, Milton Park, Abingdon, Oxon, OX14 4RN

Routledge is an imprint of the Taylor & Francis Group, an informa business

Library of Congress Cataloguing-in-Publication Data
A catalog record for this title has been requested

ISBN: 978-1-032-02016-7 (hbk)
ISBN: 978-1-032-02018-1 (pbk)
ISBN: 978-1-003-18148-4 (ebk)

DOI: 10.4324/9781003181484

Typeset in Sabon
by MPS Limited, Dehradun

Contents

Figures

x *Figures*

Tables

Abbreviations

ACC	Accra City Council
AMA	Accra Metropolitan Assembly
AMT	Akiba Mashinani Trust
ARPP	Aller River Pilot Project
ATT	Advanced Thermal Treatment
BAU	Business-as-usual
BMGF	Bill and Melinda Gates Foundation
BNG	Breaking New Ground policy
BREEAM	Building Research Establishment Environmental Assessment Method
CABs	Communal Ablution Blocks
CASELAP	Centre for the Advanced Studies in Environmental Law and Policy
CBD	Central Business District
CBEAs	Community-based Extension Agents
CEPIL	Centre for Public Interest Law
CMA	Catchment Management Agencies
COGTA	Cooperative Governance and Traditional Affairs
COHRE	Centre for Housing Right and Eviction
CRD	Centre for Reviews and Dissemination
DEA	Department of Environmental Affairs, South Africa
DEWATS	Decentralised Wastewater Treatment System
DHSWS	Department of Human Settlements, Water and Sanitation
DMOSS	Durban Metropolitan Open Space System
DRAP	Durban's Research Action Partnership
DWAF	Department of Water Affairs and Forestry
DWS	Department of Water and Sanitation
ECF	eThekwini Conservancies Forum
EFN	Ecological Footprint Network
EFT	Engineering Feld-Testing
EI	ecological infrastructure
EMA	eThekwini Metropolitan Area

EPCPD	Environmental Planning and Climate Protection Department
EWS	eThekwini Water and Sanitation Unit
GBCA	Green Building Council of Australia
GBCSA	Green Building Council of South Africa
GHGs	greenhouse gases
GIZ	Gesellschaft für Internationale Zusammenarbeit
GTM	Grounded Theory Methods
HUGSI	Husqvarna Urban Green Space Index
IAP	invasive alien plant
ICLEI	International Council for Local Environmental Initiatives
IDP	Integrated Development Plan
KENSUP	Kenya National Slum Upgrading Program
KISIP	Kenya Informal Settlements Improvement Project
KLERP	Korle Lagoon Ecological Restoration Project
LEED	Leadership in Energy and Environmental Design
LULC	land Use and Land Cover
MDGs	Millennium Development Goals
MGSP	Marlboro Gautrain Station Precinct
MSDF	eThekwini Municipality Municipal Spatial Development Frameworks
MSEs	micro and small enterprises
NCC	Nairobi City County
NDP	National Development Plan
NGO	Non-Governmental Organization
NSWMP	National Solid Waste Management Programme (of Egypt)
NUA	New Urban Agenda
ODA	official development assistance
PCRP	Palmiet Catchment Rehabilitation Project
PPPs	public-private partnerships
SDF	Spatial Development Framework
SDGs	Sustainable Development Goals
SDI	Slum Dwellers international
SEA	Strategic Environmental Assessment
SFDRR	Sendai Framework for Disaster Risk Reduction
SPA	Special Planning Area
SSA	Sub-Saharan Africa
SSP	Strategic Spatial Planning
UDDT	Urine Diversion Dehydration Toilet
UDDTs	Urine Diversion Dehydration Toilets
UDL	Urban Development Line
UEI	urban ecological infrastructure
UKZN	University of KwaZulu-Natal
UN	United Nations (Organisation)
UNA	urban natural assets

UNCTAD	United Nations Conference on Trade and Development
UNDESA	United Nations Department of Economic and Social Affairs
UNEP	United Nations Environment Programme
UNICEF	United Nations International Children's Emergency Fund
USGBC	US Green Building Council
VIPs	ventilated pit latrines
VUNA	Valorisation of Urine Nutrients in Africa
WASH R&D	Water, Sanitation, and Hygiene Research and Development Centre
WASH	water, sanitation and hygiene
WCED	World Commission on Environment and Development
WHO	World Health Organization
WMA	Water Management Areas
WRC	Water Research Commission
WSAs	Water Service Authorities
WSP	Water and sanitation Programme
WWWC	Wise Wayz Water Care

Contributors

Matthew Abunyewah is a workforce planning officer at the Industry Skills Advisory Council, Northern Territory, Australia and a Sessional Lecturer at the School of Architecture and Built Environment, University of Newcastle (Australia). He holds a PhD in Disaster Management from the same university. His research is broadly in the area of urban resilience and disaster management in cities of the Global South.

Millicent Awialie Akaateba is a senior lecturer in the Department of Planning, Faculty of Planning and Land Management of the Simon Diedong Dombo University of Business and Integrated Development Studies, Ghana. She had previously worked in private consultancy as an Urban/Transport Planner. Her general research interests cover issues relating to customary land administration and planning, bottom-up and insurgent planning practices, hybrid governance, critical urbanism and sustainable urban development in sub-Saharan Africa. Her PhD focused on the interface between customary land management and urban planning practice in Ghana with a specific focus on co-productive practices between traditional authorities and state actors in peri-urban land management.

Bernard Afiik Akanpabadai Akanbang is an associate professor in planning and head of the Department of Planning of the Simon Diedong Dombo University of Business and Integrated Development Studies, Ghana. He holds both Bachelor of Science and Master of Philosophy Degrees in Planning and a PhD in Development Studies. He is a reviewer for both local and international journals in the field of development studies, sustainable development and development evaluation. His research interests are in decentralized monitoring and evaluation systems; decentralized governance and planning systems; urbanization, land use and social change and urban planning capacity development; water and sanitation planning and management; and urban housing characterization and development.

Joseph Nyaaba Akongbangre is a technical advisor in geographic information systems and remote sensing expert for the German International Corporation-European Union's Resilience in Climate Change (EU-REACH) project in North-Western Ghana. He holds a Master of Philosophy in Environment and Resource Management from the University for Development Studies, Ghana. His research interests include spatial modelling of urban growth, landscape dynamics, change and management, and land use planning.

Desmond Ofosu Anim is a water resource engineer at Engeny Water Management, Melbourne, Australia. He holds an undergraduate degree in Geomatic Engineering from the Kwame Nkrumah University of Science and Technology, Ghana, and a master's degree in Environmental Engineering from Hohai University, China and a PhD in Environmental Engineering from the University of Melbourne, Australia. He is an environmental water resource engineer with experience primarily focused on ecohydrology and waterway management particularly in the context of physical and ecological management of freshwater systems with special interest on waterway health and rehabilitation. His research is focused on the environmental flows, ecohydraulics and management of waterways. He is a member of Engineers Australia and Stormwater Victoria.

Abena Boatemaa Asare-Ansah is a remote sensing and GIS analyst specialist at the Centre for Remote Sensing and Geographic Information Services, Department of Geography and Resource Development, University of Ghana. She holds an undergraduate degree in Geomatic Engineering from the Kwame Nkrumah University of Science and Technology, Ghana and a license in Radar Remote Sensing from the European Space Agency. Abena's research is focused on spatial modelling, vulnerability risk assessment, land and water resources appraisal and monitoring including rural and urban land use pattern and trend analysis.

Florence Abugtane Avogo is a lecturer at the Department of Planning at the SD Dombo University of Business and Integrated Development Studies, Wa-Ghana. She holds BSc Development Planning and MPhil Planning from Kwame Nkrumah University of Science and Technology, Ghana and an MSc in Urban Management and Development from the Institute of Housing Studies (HIS), Erasmus University, The Netherlands. Her research interests include urban planning, development controls, urban housing and livelihoods of the urban poor.

Marita Basson is an associate professor of urban design and planning and associate head of learning, teaching and student success at the University of Southern Queensland, Australia. Her disciplinary research interests include research on regional development, sense of place, government, and governance. Scholarship of learning and teaching interests include online learning and sense of belonginess.

Francis Diawuo Darko is an environmental researcher and educator. He holds a Master of Philosophy from the University for Development Studies, Ghana. He teaches Environmental Studies at the Institute of Distance and e-Learning (IDeL) of the University of Education, Sunyani Study Centre, on part-time basis. His research focuses on waste management, indigenous knowledge and belief systems, climate change adaptation and environmental change and human mobility.

Stephen Kofi Diko is a visiting assistant professor at the University of Memphis, USA. He holds a PhD in Urban and Regional Planning from the University of Cincinnati, Ohio, USA. His research examines sustainable urban development and policy from the aspects of climate change, green spaces and local economic development.

Michael Odei Erdiaw-Kwasie is an award-winning author and a Lecturer at the Asia Pacific College of Business and Law, Charles Darwin University, Australia. Michael works at the intersection of global development and business sustainability. For 10 years, in industry and academia, he has applied a multi-disciplinary lens to business sustainability and global development approaches to identify the tools, models, metrics and indicators that create the greatest value for businesses, society and the environment. Michael's research specialism covers Global Development, Circular Economy, Sustainability, and Digital Futures. He has produced a book, book chapters, journal articles, conference papers, industry reports as well as blogs on topics across these research themes.

Louis Kusi Frimpong recently completed his PhD in urban geography at the University of Ghana, Legon. His research focuses on safety and security in urban residential neighborhoods, social organisation and community mobilisation efforts for local development. He is currently the principal investigator of a funded project on the role of CBOs in post-pandemic community revitalisation in Freetown, Sierra Leone.

Eric Gaisie is a sessional academic at the Faculty of Architecture, Building, and Planning at the University of Melbourne in Australia, where he completed his PhD in Urban Planning. He previously held teaching and research positions at the Department of Planning, Kwame Nkrumah University of Science and Technology, Ghana and the Faculty of Economics, University of Rome, Tor Vergata, Italy. He is an affiliate member of the Planning Institute of Australia and a member of the Informal Urbanism Research Hub at the Melbourne School of Design. His research explores how urban planning could contribute to urban sustainability and resilience in a rapidly changing world.

Sylvia Hannan is a chief researcher at the Inclusive Economic Development Research Division of the Human Sciences Research Council, South Africa. She holds Masters in Geography and Environmental Science (cum laude) from the University of KwaZulu-Natal, South Africa. Her research focuses on sustainability and urban regeneration as well as science engagement and education.

Daniel Irurah is an associate professor of sustainable architecture and cities in the School of Architecture and Planning at the University of the Witwatersrand, where he conducts research and supervises masters and PhD studies in related fields and topics. He holds a BArch from the University of Nairobi, Kenya and MArch and MUP from University of Oregon, USA and PhD from University of Pretoria, South Africa. His PhD study focused on the application of the input-output model in the analyses of embodied energy of construction materials and buildings in South Africa. He is a registered Architect in Kenya and South Africa. He has previously served as a Member of the Board of Directors of the Green Building Council of South Africa where he chaired the Education Sub-Committee of the Board.

Kennedy Kariseb is a lecturer in law in the Department of Public Law and Jurisprudence, Faculty of Law, University of Namibia. He holds a doctor of laws and master of laws degrees from the University of Pretoria, South Africa. His areas of research include human rights in Africa and other public law aspects such as land reform, tenure security, environment and the law.

Michihiro Kita is a professor of planning and urban design at the Division of Global Architecture and the deputy director of the Social Solutions Initiative at Osaka University. He has researched extensively on neighbourhood planning, desig, and community-based management in Central European, Asian and African cities. His interest lies in contextual planning and improvement of urban communities.

Prosper Issahaku Korah is a lecturer at the Department of Planning, Faculty of Planning and Land Management at the Simon Diedong Dombo University of Business and Integrated Development Studies, Ghana. He holds PhD in Urban Studies and Planning from Griffith University, Australia. Prosper also holds MSc degree in Environmental and Infrastructure Planning from the University of Groningen, Netherlands. His research interests are in the areas of spatial transformation and governance, new cities, environmental planning, urban planning, climate change adaption and spatial analyses with Geographic Information System (GIS) and Remote Sensing (RS).

Enoch Akwasi Kosoe is a PhD candidate and a lecturer in the Department of Environment and Resource Studies (DERS) of the SDD University of

Business and Integrated Development Studies, Ghana. He holds MSc in Environmental Resource Management from the Kwame Nkrumah University of Science and Technology, Ghana and Bachelor of Arts in Integrated Development Studies from the University for Development Studies, Ghana.

Fanelesibonge Magwaza is a PhD candidate in development studies at the Howard College of the University of KwaZulu-Natal. He holds BSSc Housing and Master's degree in Town and Regional Planning from the University of KwaZulu-Natal, South Africa.

Roopanand Mahadew is a senior lecturer at the Department of Law, University of Mauritius and the current Head of Department. He holds an LLB (Hons) from University of Mauritius and an LLM in Human Rights and Democratisation in Africa from the University of Pretoria. He is an LLD candidate at the University of the Western Cape, South Africa.

Patrick Martel is a PhD candidate at the University of KwaZulu Natal, South Africa. He is part of a research team that is actively involved in a range of water and climate change-related action research projects in eTekwini. In terms of local river rehabilitation projects, Patrick was the lead author of the External Evaluation of the Aller River Pilot Project completed by UKZN for both phases of this collaborative project. In addition, he is part of the Community of Innovation for the Palmiet Catchment Rehabilitation Project. Patrick has attended several local and international workshops, fora and conferences, and has interacted with researchers from various backgrounds. His experiences have enabled him to engage with innovative projects and individuals, ranging from local and international academics, local government officials, communities and civil society.

Luckymore Matenga is a PhD candidate in the Department of Sociology and Social Anthropology at Stellenbosch University, South Africa. Luckymore focuses on the lived experiences of Zimbabwean migrant entrepreneurs during COVID-19 pandemic in the inner-city of Johannesburg. Luckymore holds BSc (Hons) degree in Social Anthropology from Great Zimbabwe University and Master of Urban Studies from the University of Witwatersrand, South Africa. He also holds Master of Social Anthropology from Stellenbosch University.

Bahle Mazeka is a PhD candidate and an urban geographer who is interested in, and works at the interface between socio-ecological systems with a focus on urbanization, human settlements, project management, and sustainable development. He received his junior degree at the University of KwaZulu-Natal (UKZN) where his interest in cities, urbanization and sustainability developed. He further pursued a B.Sc. Honours in Geographic Information System (GIS) at the Nelson

Mandela University, and later a Master of Housing at UKZN. Apart from lecturing, he has worked in several multi-disciplinary and stakeholder research projects including the position research coordinator at South African Research Chairs Initiative. He has delivered numerous academic seminars including at the Newcastle University (United Kingdom). He is working on his PhD with a focus on human socio-ecological relationships in urban spaces.

Seth Opoku Mensah is a graduate research student at the University of Technology Sydney, Australia. He holds BSc Development Planning from the Kwame Nkrumah University of Science and Technology, Ghana; MSc Development Studies from Lund University, Sweden and Master of Development Policy (Sustainable Development and Regional Development and Environment) from the Korea Development Institute (KDI), South Korea. He is an interdisciplinary development planner with experience and interests in local economic development, climate change and adaptive capacities, urban studies and resilience, and monitoring and evaluation. He is a member of the Ghana Institute of Planners (GIP), Commonwealth Association of Planners (CAP) and the Ghana Monitoring and Evaluation Forum (GMEF).

Anthony Odili is a PhD candidate in the School of Built Environment and Development Studies, University of KwaZulu-Natal, South Africa. His PhD thesis focuses on innovative sanitation technologies and their implications for a more inclusive and transformative sanitation governance in African cities. Anthony is a researcher in the Environmental Governance for Cities research portfolio. Anthony holds a master's degree in Development Studies and an Honours degree in Political Science from the University of KwaZulu-Natal. He also earned a Graduate Diploma in Sanitation from the Institute of Water Education, Delft and a Bachelor of Arts degree in Philosophy from St. Joseph's Theological Institute, Cedara.

Seth Asare Okyere is a development planner and assistant professor at the Graduate School of Engineering, Osaka University (Japan). He holds a PhD in Engineering with emphasis on urban development planning from Osaka University. His research interests and experiences emphasize interconnections between development planning, urbanism, and sustainable development in global south cities.

Collins Odote is a senior lecturer at the Centre for Advanced Studies in Environmental Law and Policy (CASELAP), University of Nairobi, Kenya, and an advocate of the High Court of Kenya. He has a PhD in Law from the University of Nairobi with a specialization in land and environmental law. His research interests span the areas of governance, elections, property theory, natural resource management and extractives.

Philip Olale is a town planner and outreach coordinator and research associate at the Center for Urban Research and Innovations University of Nairobi. He is a graduate of University of Nairobi with a BA (Hons) Urban and Regional Planning and holds a Masters in Environmental Law. He coordinated data collection and analysis for a project undertaken for the Kenya Informal Settlements Improvements Program (KISIP) by a consortium comprising Infrastructure Professionals Enterprise Private Limited (IPE Global) and Silverwind Consultants. He is also Research Assistant at the Centre for Urban Research and Innovations at the University of Nairobi.

Issaka Kanton Osumanu is a professor and the coordinator of graduate programmes of the Faculty of Integrated Development Studies at the Simon Diedong University of Business and Integrated Development Studies, Ghana. He holds a PhD in Urban Geography from the University of Ghana. His current research interests include urbanisation and development, environmental change and sustainable development, and natural resource governance.

Euridice Lurdes Jorge Pedrosa is a PhD candidate in urban planning and design lab at Division of Global Architecture, Osaka University, Japan. She is a trained architect and urban planner with Master of Engineering (Urban Planning) from the same university. Her research explores the planning and management of urban neighborhoods drawing on the relationship between the social and the spatial dimensions. Her current project is on the availability, accessibility and significance of informal green spaces in the peripheral areas of Luanda, Angola.

Kwanele Phinzi is a PhD candidate in geography at the University of Debrecen, Hungary. He holds MSc in Environmental Science from the University of KwaZulu-Natal, South Africa and certificate in Drones for Agriculture from the Wageningen University, The Netherlands. Mr. Phinzi has extensive experience in spatial data processing and analysis using Geographic Information System (GIS) and remote sensing software packages, i.e. ArcMap, Quantum GIS, SAGA, ERDAS and ENVI.

Vipua Rukambe is a PhD candidate in Architecture with a scholarship from the Wits/TU Berlin Urban Lab Programme, a partnership between the University of Witwatersrand and the Technische Universität of Berlin. The Urban Lab Collaboration seeks to contribute to the implementation of the Sustainable Development Goals (SDGs) of 2015 and the New Urban Agenda (NUA) of 2016 on the Sub-Saharan African continent. Vipua's research focuses on filling critical gaps in sustainable city transitioning towards capacitating African cities to re-envision their futures with specific anchoring on the temporal dimension.

Catherine Sutherland is a professor and an urban geographer in the School of Built Environment and Development Studies at the University of KwaZulu-Natal, Durban, South Africa whose research focuses on water and climate governance, informal settlement upgrading and sustainability and environmental governance in peri-urban areas.

Ivone Tjilale is currently a PhD candidate in the Faculty of Economics and Management Sciences at the University of Namibia. She holds a BTech degree in Public Management from the University of South Africa and a Master's degree in Public Administration from the University of Namibia. Her research and publications broadly focus on public policy, housing and urbanization.

Preface

The pattern of urban development across Africa is described variously as distinctive, problematic and, in some cases, a threat to sustainable development due to its inconsistency with global trends. While it is true that urban Africa is faced with mounting critical infrastructure and management challenges, the continent also offers hope, optimism and opportunities for many who live and derive their livelihoods from its cities. Balancing the act of providing opportunities and addressing development concerns remains a critical issue in urban development dispensation across African cities, as the continent is faced with rapid urbanisation challenges and increasing threats of climate change. Efforts towards sustainable development are therefore urgently required and their adoption undebatable. The introduction of the sustainable development goals (SDGs) in 2015 was timely and remains one of the surest ways of improving the future state of urban Africa as these goals possess transformative power to addressing key urbanisation and climate change challenges. Since the introduction and promulgation of the SDGs across the world, African cities have and continue to make various strides towards achieving them, but challenges remain. One critical hurdle relates to the limited appreciation of the spatial manifestation of the SDGs across the continent and the implications for the future of African cities in terms of how the goals are spatially manifesting. In response, this book, *Sustainable Urban Futures in Africa*, takes the position that the fundamental question is not the number of goals or targets of the SDGs that is achieved in African cities, but rather how these goals translate and find expression in the urban space of a rapidly urbanising continent. This book, therefore, provides a space for a variety of conventional and emerging theoretical and imaginary frameworks to inform understandings and responses to critical urban development issues that threaten and contribute to sustainable futures, such as urbanisation, climate change, informality, urban sprawl, urban ecosystem services, and urban poverty. Chapters in this book are written by established and emerging scholars and offer a contemporary and multi-disciplinary overview of a significant sub-field within urban studies. The chapters in the book have undergone a rigorous two-stage double-blind peer-review process to ensure quality and originality. Drawing from over 35 internationally recognised scholars from across Africa, the book provides a pioneering understanding of Africa's urban future, benefitting enormously from diverse disciplines. This book is an authoritative volume and remains an essential resource across a range of disciplines, including African studies, climate science, environmental studies, human geography, planning, sustainability science and urban studies.

Patrick Brandful Cobbinah, Melbourne, Australia &
Michael Addaney, Sunyani, Ghana

Acknowledgements

This book is a culmination of many years of work that would not have been possible without the effort and patience of all the contributing authors – we are grateful to you for your commitment to and involvement in the project. We are also grateful to the editors at Routledge and the anonymous reviewers who provided timely and constructive feedback that refined the ideas, design, and overall development of the book.

Part I

Conceptual and Theoretical Foundations

1 Sustainable Urban Futures in Africa: Concepts, Practices and Prospects

Patrick Brandful Cobbinah and Michael Addaney

Introduction

The importance of understanding and taking actions towards sustainable development in rapidly urbanising Africa cannot be overemphasised in the 21st century. History and current patterns of urban development in Africa hold many lessons for the future. To be certain, early urban studies scholars and practitioners encountered and attempted to resolve some of the same kind of urban development and management challenges confronting Africa today (e.g. Parnell & Mabin, 1995; Mabogunje, 1990; Simon, 1985). Therefore, it makes much sense, in terms of time, geography and other resources that can potentially be managed, to simply learn lessons of experience from predecessors. There is no denying, as previous literature indicates, that African countries have been largely incapable of learning from history as they are fated to repeating past urban development and management challenges (Harrison, 2006; Kamete, 2013). A synonymous situation relates to the unplanned rapid rate of African urbanisation since the 1960s, and understanding this urban phenomenon is essential to accurately plan and manage the continent's urban future in a sustainable pathway (Addaney & Cobbinah, 2019; Cobbinah et al., 2015). The history of urban development in Africa is very rich, and consequently holds many potentially useful lessons for sustainable urban futures. This chapter provides a theoretical foundation on sustainable development and how that influences Africa's urban development. The chapter further summarises and discusses the urban realities and patterns in Africa. Additionally, the chapter introduces subsequent chapters and lays out a plan for the rest of the book.

Theoretical Foundation of Sustainable Development in Africa's Urban Futures

The emergence and popularisation of the sustainable development notion in the 1980s was in response to the disregard for the natural environment in development processes (World Commission on Environment and

DOI: 10.4324/9781003181484-1

Development [WCED], 1987). With its foundation on environmental protection, the meaning of sustainable development as a concept has evolved to foster adaptive capabilities and to generate opportunities that maintain a balance coalescence of economic, social and ecological structures for the current and emerging generations (Cobbinah et al., 2011). By its very nature, sustainable development is by no means a simple concept to define or an easy enterprise to achieve but should be regarded as a potential pathway for advancing environmental protection and fostering socio-economic development at all levels particularly in urban areas.

With its integration in national, regional and international development policies (e.g SDGs, New Urban Agenda), there are promising benefits of sustainable development, particularly serving as a framework for promoting a balance between socio-economic development and environmental conservation worldwide. Yet, Cobbinah et al. (2015) note that these claims of benefits are limited in urban Africa with increasing disillusionment among practitioners and stakeholders. Research has identified urbanisation and climate change as principal factors that have a potential to advance or limit sustainable development in Africa. To support improved urban living and human wellbeing, there are calls by stakeholders for sustainable development to move beyond environmental protection and poverty alleviation and ensure consistency of overall human development with sustainable use of natural and environmental resources (Boadi et al., 2005). Such interpretation of sustainable development has the potential to promote community welfare, guarantee positive urban management and safeguard the natural environment in Africa that provides habitat for significant ecological species.

Emerging debates indicate that sustainable development and urbanisation are compatible. For example, economic development is a critical requirement and feature for both sustainable development and urbanisation (UNDESA/PD, 2012; WCED, 1987). The process of urban growth produces cities as engines of economic growth and hubs for generation of ideas, innovation and technologies required for sustainable and productive use of resources (United Nations Human Settlements Programme [UN-Habitat], 2012). Evidence of sustainable development compatibility in developing countries include China where there is improved economic development. In such countries, urbanisation produces clustering of productive activities in industry and service resulting in improved urban living due to low production costs and improved benefits (UN-Habitat, 2012). Despite these compatibility prospects, the fast-paced urbanisation in Africa has been characterised as a threat to sustainable development with some arguments indicating that sustainable development is not always compatible with urbanisation (Cobbinah et al., 2015). Many African cities have demonstrated increasing failure to manage severe, unplanned and haphazard urbanisation perceived to be diminishing the socio-economic and environmental gains linked with urbanisation and sustainable development. The incapacity of

African cities to manage, for example, flood events, transport challenges, rising numbers of urban poor, slum formation and proliferation, urban sprawl and inadequate housing remains fundamental threats to sustainable development.

Despite this gloomy truth, sustainable development is a critical tool for the international community to stimulate economic and social development initiatives and environmental protection in Africa (United Nations Environment Programme [UNEP], 2011). The establishment of UN agencies such as UNEP, UN-Habitat and UNDP since 1980s to advance sustainable development in developing countries particularly those in Africa is an indication of the importance of sustainable development in Africa's urban future. It is perhaps reasonable to argue that, regardless of the activities of these UN agencies, urban Africa is still trailing in terms of meaningful improvements in the urban space and living as the continent continues to experience the threats of urbanisation such as unemployment, poverty, and water and sanitation challenges (see Boadi et al., 2005). While this argument is true to some extent, there is a limited number of studies on the potential and real usefulness of the sustainable development thinking in shaping the current and future urban pathways of Africa. The chapters in this book provide further analysis of Africa's urban future within the framework of sustainable development, highlighting the complexities, cases of successes and areas requiring improvement.

Africa's Urbanisation Processes and Urban Futures

As the regional share of people who live in urban areas continues to grow, understanding urban dynamics is increasingly important with respect to land use, socio-demographics, human health, prosperity, social equity and environmental sustainability. The purpose of this section is to provide a theoretical understanding of urban, urbanity and urbanisation, and how this understanding influences sustainable futures in African cities. There is an ongoing dialogue on the definition of an urban area including comparatively straightforward accounts such as using the administrative unit with a defined number of inhabitants (McIntyre et al., 2000). Urban areas and regions can be described in many other ways including by population density, built-up area and travelling distance (Haase & Schwarz, 2016). There are further debates on the need for new concepts to characterise the "urban." The concept of urbanity was proposed and defined by "the magnitude and qualities of livelihoods, lifestyles, connectivity, and place that creates 'urban-ness' of intertwined human experiences and land configurations" (Boone et al., 2014: 314). The concept of urbanity originates from an increasing consensus that the archetypal urban vs. rural ordering of labelling land is inadequate for research or practice. Importantly, the concept of urbanity is a continuum which is potentially applicable to external administrative boundaries of cities and their environs and thus can extend to multiple dimensions, such as livelihoods, land uses, and economies. Schwarz (2010) contends that the spatial form of an urban area such as its density or compactness is a significant factor for quality of life and environmental sustainability.

On the other hand, urbanisation remains a demographic process characterised by increasing number of people concentrating in urban regions (Haase & Schwarz, 2016). The UN-Habitat (2010) conceptualises urbanisation as a spatial and land use process that predominantly leads to the physical expansion of built-up areas, either horizontal or vertical. The UNDESA (2014) has projected that by 2050, 65% of the population in developing countries will reside in urban areas. Thus, in the future, urbanisation will continue and the percentage of people living in urban areas will further grow. It is estimated that most of this urban growth will occur in Asia and Africa with population growth rates of between 3% and 5% annually (UNDESA, 2014). Regions with younger urbanisation, such as Africa, are predicted to develop less-compact cities but with a pronounced dense central business districts (CBD) grounded in less dense counter-urbanised environs (Haase & Schwarz, 2016). This has been characterised as urban sprawl, describing the expansion of settlements away from central urban areas into rural environs (Cobbinah et al. 2015). Compounding the urbanisation threat of urban sprawl are issues of climate change, endemic poverty, poor infrastructure, health pandemics and inadequate services, particularly in informal settlements (Addaney & Cobbinah, 2019).

Similarly, contemporary urbanisation in Africa has led to the growth of megacities (over ten million inhabitants) and rapidly growing smaller towns and cities across Africa. In 2000, only one megacity existed on the continent; Cairo (Egypt). By 2019, this number increased to three (Cairo, Kinshasa and Lagos), each with a population of over 15 million inhabitants. Kinshasa's population had grown 70 times over the past seven decades; the population of Lagos has increased about 50 times from 300,000 in 1950 to an estimated 21.2 million in 2019. Other cosmopolitan cities such as Johannesburg (South Africa), Mogadishu (Somalia), Dar es Salaam (Tanzania), Alexandria (Egypt) and Abidjan (Ivory Coast), have high population density levels ranging from 20,000 to 30,000 people per square kilometer, implying novel, idiosyncratic settlement patterns and urban forms. Despite the general trend of increase in, and issues (e.g. growth of informal settlements, and slums) of urbanisation, the dynamics are different and varied. Each city in Africa has distinct characteristics and faces distinctive challenges (Anderson et al., 2013) that make them different from cities in other regions of the world (Guneralp et al., 2017). This book explores in detail and with interesting case studies the distinctiveness of urbanisation and urban development across African cities.

The analysis in this book is grounded in multiple urbanisation theories to reflect the diversity of African urbanisation experiences. A combination of Pacione's (2005) argument of cities attracting migrants by offering employment and income opportunities and improved health, education and social services, and Peng et al.'s (2000) discussion on the influence of natural population increase are used to theorise urbanisation experiences in Africa. Supporting this, Fischer et al. (2012) note that, as the population of urban areas increases naturally, surrounding land areas initially reserved for ecological security, climatic control and peri-urban agriculture are turned into residential, commercial or industrial land areas. These changes modify the spatial and ecological quality as well as the economic patterns of African cities including Lagos, Johannesburg, Harare, Addis Ababa, Nairobi and Cairo (Potts, 2012). Regions that are less urbanised (e.g. West and Eastern Africa) are currently urbanising faster than those with already high share of urban population (North and Southern Africa). In this sense, exploring Africa's urban futures is imperative to understanding and responding to urban patterns and processes. Ultimately, Africa's urbanisation is without a doubt a driver of societal transformation, but more exploration into how African societies can effectively transition towards more livable and desirable resilient futures is required. This book addresses this gap in African urbanisation and sustainable development literature.

Reflections on Urban Development Agenda in Africa

Spatial urban development is becoming more topical in urbanisation discourse and particularly with sustainable development narratives (Nunbogu et al., 2018). Sustainable development enterprises controlled and dominated by spatial definition of urban futures include the Sustainable Development Goals, particularly Goal 11, the New Urban Agenda and other regional characterisations such as the Africa Urban Agenda. These sustainable development undertakings are largely a response to the spread and impact of rapid urbanisation particularly in developing countries, including those in Africa. As presented in Figures 1.1 and 1.2, Africa is rapidly urbanising. Urban land and economic opportunities are frequently the main attraction for migrants seeking improved opportunities in African cities including Accra, Cape Town, Lagos, Luanda and Nairobi (see Bakewell & Jónsson, 2011). Indeed, history of African urban planning suggests that planning efforts largely revolve around major urban spaces with little or no attention to secondary and small cities (Bolay, 2015; Silva, 2015). In this regard, it is only expected that these cities have become prime target for most migrants across the continent. Urbanisation benefits such as economic opportunities, industrialisation and urban growth are a drawcard for migrants (Cobbinah et al., 2015). Unfortunately, urbanisation in many African cities is still occurring without these economic benefits, leading to haphazard urban development, unplanned physical growth, increased poverty, inequality and marginalisation. With the lack of needed industrialisation, some have characterised urbanisation in Africa as unplanned, pre-matured and poverty driven (see Obeng-Odoom, 2010). Migrants and urban residents who

The population in Sub-Saharan Africa is projected to grow 10-fold between 1960 and 2050

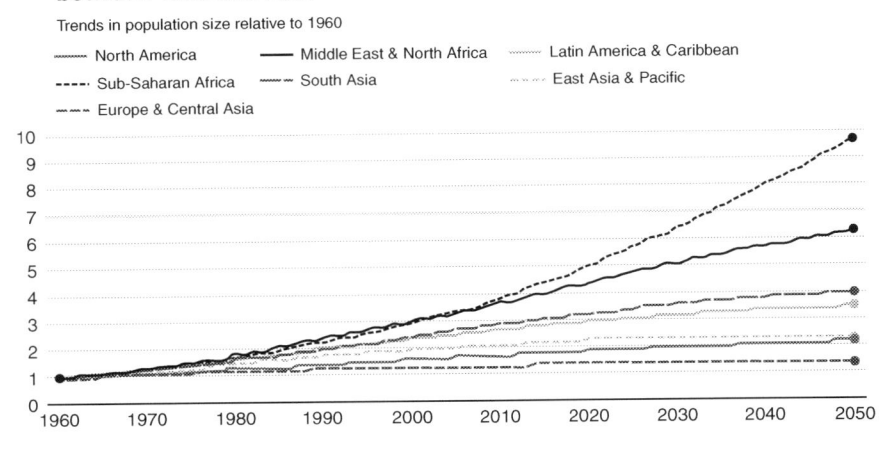

Figure 1.1 Population in Sub-Saharan Africa from 1960 to 2050 (projected).

Source: World Bank (2021). This is an adaptation of an original work by (World Bank Group member institution name). Responsibility for the views and opinions expressed in the adaptation rests solely with the author or authors of the adaptation and are not endorsed by any member institution of the World Bank Group.

encounter the reality of African urban growth phenomenon are increasingly resorting to the "survival extinct," a situation that is contributing to slum formation and expansion, crime and violence and destruction of the urban ecological integrity of cities (Mugisha et al., 2003; Owusu et al., 2008).

Most of Africa's urban development since the 1950s have been subjected to poor monitoring and loose planning following independence from European colonisation (see Mabogunje, 1990). African governments have played less influential role in determining the patterns and rate of urban transformations occurring in their cities (Bolay, 2015). The political economy of most urban countries following independence did not attend to improving African planning and design, urban morphologies and changing land use transformation (Silva, 2015). By the end of European colonisation between 1950s and 1990s, an even spatial economy, although limited to urban centers, was evident across major African cities (Cobbinah & Darkwah, 2017). The product of the introduction of urban planning by the Europeans during colonisation remains evident in African cities, such as Accra, Cape Town, Dakar, Harare, Nairobi, and Luanda. It is reasonable to argue that urbanisation level at the time of colonisation was low compared with recent rapid rate of Africa's urbanisation (UNDESA/PD, 2012). While urbanisation rate is unprecedented in the continent, industrialisation, urban renovation and critical urban infrastructural projects required to meet and transform the evolving spatial order of African cities are largely limited (see Cobbinah et al., 2015).

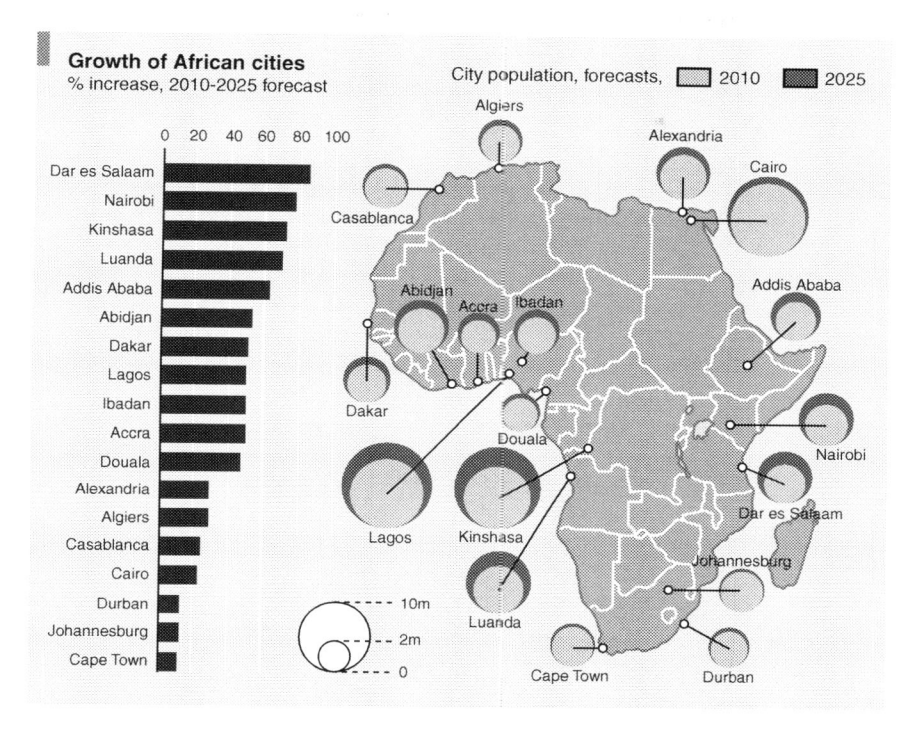

Figure 1.2 Urban and rural population of the world, 1950–2050.

Note: Data are from the United Nations' World Urbanization Prospects (2018, Revision).

The spread of rapid urbanisation across Africa often coincides with widespread practice of unsustainable land use planning and development (see Sumari et al., 2020). Particularly, cities that are overwhelmed with population growth but lack the capacity to provide decent basic essential services, such as housing for residents, demonstrate stark urban realities of segregation in terms of planning responses. On the one hand, the rich and political elites live in relatively well-planned zones within the cityscape with improved basic services (e.g. housing, sanitation, roads, etc.). On the other hand, the same city is epitomised by uncontrolled informality and growing slum proliferation serving as home to many urban residents. Cities with such characterisation in Africa include Cape Town, Johannesburg, Kampala, Nairobi, Accra, Freetown and Lagos where they are defined by the interface of slum vs. well planned neighborhoods, sustainable vs. un-sustainable land uses, green space destruction vs. management systems, limited employment vs. growing unemployment alleyways and religion vs. corruption practices. On the contrary, small cities with improved urbani-sation strategy and strong institutions, particularly in Rwanda (e.g. Kigali), are also a growing focus for sustainable development in the continent.

Environmental, cultural, economic, spatial, social, political and institutional aspects of urban life are integral to developing sustainable futures and are featured in sustainable urban development discourse globally. In this case, a renewed optimism expressed in management enterprises across African cities are frequently proposed by researchers to be the way of improving the urban fortunes in the continent. Land use planning is also a growing focus for sustainable urban development in Africa and other developing regions. For example, the city of Morogoro in Tanzania is experiencing rapid urban expansion more than double the rate of population growth (Sumari et al., 2020), highlighting the importance of land use planning in stimulating urban growth and directing future pathways. In these African countries, chaotic and unsustainable urban development patterns are also found in the growing religiosity that is sweeping over the continent. In Ghana, many urban residents and professionals in Kumasi – the second largest city – were reported to have disregarded urban planning and management regulations because of religious reasons (Cobbinah & Korah, 2016).

Globally, there is greater public awareness of both the environmental and socio-economic impacts of rapid urbanisation on cities. Sustainable urban development recognises the important links between the economy, culture, environment, space (land), institution and politics. A growing rural-urban migration in the continent further coincides with urban residents need for new economic opportunities (e.g. industries, service sector improvement) deriving income and livelihood from sustainable use and development of resources (e.g. land) that reduce negative environmental gearing, promote healthy urban living and protect the integrity of future generational needs. This global trend is reflected in the SDGs, local content development in the continent (e.g. Africa Urban Agenda), and the opening of regional cities to help reduce population influx into major cities. These regional and secondary cities are usually in peripheral areas, away from mainstream city development agenda, where urban development is relatively on sustainable development footing due to low urbanisation levels, relatively less pressure on land resources and have maintained ecosystem integrity and otherwise endangered biodiversity. While secondary cities in the continent are dependent and vulnerable to increased accessibility and contact with major cities (Bolay, 2015), sustainable urban development is seen as one way to maintain ecosystems and provide livelihood options to migrants. This contributes to reducing population pressures on large cities. Unfortunately, there is evidence of limited attention on secondary cities in Africa in terms of development support (Bolay, 2015; Cobbinah et al., 2020). Many of them, for instance, are witnessing a decline in their green spaces (McConnachie et al., 2008).

With greater legal recognition, institutional strengthening and residents' involvement in urban planning and development, many cities across the continent are determining appropriate sustainable urban development future pathways. As well as being migrant attraction centers, African cities are increasingly the owners, managers, and joint partners in sustainable urban development narratives. Examples of such narratives include the Rockefeller Foundation's 100 Resilient Cities and the City Resilience Index launched in 2013, with Dakar (Senegal) being the first African city to produce a resilience strategy in partnership with 100 Resilient Cities (Ville De Dakar and 100 Resilient Cities, 2016). Similarly, another initiative relates to the Urban ARK – Urban Africa: Risk Knowledge – a research and policy agenda for risk management in urban Africa by the UK's Department for International Development and the Economic and Social Research Council (UN-Habitat 2020). Therefore, there is a real potential for African cities to chart their development course on a sustainable development footing to generate optimum outcomes from urbanisation, support socio-economic drive and strengthen environmental and ecosystem services. This understanding of urban development in growing cities, often in developing countries, is increasingly reflected in sustainable development initiatives. For African cities, sustainable urban development has become an absolute requisite for managing urbanisation and safeguarding the future. Mushrooming cases of urban blight, land tenure conflicts, corruption, institutional inadequacies, political distortions and haphazard development are pathologies that impede African cities from benefiting from the fruits of traditional urbanisation, through sustainable urban development interventions. Unfortunately, research on sustainable urban futures in Africa has been isolated, singularised and incomprehensive. However, to position African cities to reap the benefits of urban growth while producing sustainable urban spaces requires comprehensive understanding and analysis of the various variables that limit sustainable urban development in Africa today, and explore how they can become catalyst for defining the sustainable urban future of the continent. It is within the foregoing context that this book is based.

Urbanisation and Sustainable Development in Africa: Critical Evolving Integrative Inquiry

The contributors to this book encountered an important responsibility of having to establish and set the context for future urban research agenda in the African continent. In the case of sustainable futures, this is a particularly difficult task since the knowledge base is emerging, and no consensus currently exists as to the evolution and role of, for example urbanisation, in Africa's urban development. Yet, even in this atmosphere of conceptual dearth, chapters in this book perform the extremely useful function of pointing out the debates, disputes, shortfalls and ambiguities that characterise urban development patterns in African countries which is, after all, still only in its infancy. Moreover, where warranted, the authors suggest areas in which some degree of consensus or cohesion may be emerging; an indication, perhaps, that research on Africa's urban agenda is moving towards a higher level of maturity. Particularly, in this volume, 16 essays focus on the current and future aspects of urbanisation, urban planning, and environmental sustainability in African cities. The editors and contributors are Africans located and researching in three out of the five main geopolitical blocks in Africa (Western, Eastern and Southern Africa) and include reviews of national case studies from Angola, Ghana, Kenya, Mauritius, Namibia and South Africa.

Regional contributions are also discussed, making this edited volume a comprehensive collection of African voices on urbanisation, urban planning and sustainable futures. Blending the use of case studies and pluralistic approaches, the chapters espouse the transformations in and of urban studies, urban planning, and environmental sustainability in Africa and their future positioning from the perspectives of home-grown African scholars, policymakers and practitioners. The editors and contributors recognise and admit differences across the continent and express collectively in general terms as it is necessary here; however, with restraint. By recognising the uniqueness of African cities, an attempt is made to map out the common African experiments and opportunities towards informing collective action, which partly include the amplification of new in-depth case studies, that would both communicate to macro-scale observations and enlighten city-specific understandings. This, it is argued, is a significant first step towards developing alternative sustainable pathways that can potentially build resilient futures and guarantee well-being in Africa's urban areas, especially, traditional and emerging cities. This book is organised into three sections. Each section addresses an important aspect of the interconnections between urbanisation and sustainable development in the African context.

Part I: Conceptual and Theoretical Foundations

The chapters in this section examine urbanisation trends and how different urbanisation variables influence the development of different forms of urban systems and settlements in Africa. Chapter 1 provides a contextual understanding of the urban development experiences, realities and trends in Africa in relation to sustainable development. It further offers theoretical foundation to ground the analysis and arguments in the successive chapters. It considers the environmental, cultural, social, economic, spatial, institutional and political realities that have defined and continue to shape Africa's urban development fortunes and highlights the limitations in current research on urban Africa. In Chapter 2, Cobbinah and colleagues highlight why achieving sustainable development in Africa is a challenge from the theoretical perspective with some concrete cases. They establish a positive theoretical and strong complementary relationship between sustainable development and spatial planning, both normative and distributive aims. Key to the discussion is how the manifestation of the theoretical and complementary relationship between sustainable development and spatial planning produces urban space in Africa that is characterised by poor local content as a result of, *inter alia*, limited state agency commitment, colonial legacy impediments and the influence and agenda of international organisations.

Building on the previous chapter on the challenge of sustainable development, in Chapter 3, Akanbang and colleagues discuss how institutions could use old and new methods of land administration to produce sustainable urban spaces in Africa. Drawing on extensive literature analysis and evidence from Ghanaian towns, the authors argue that the creation of sustainable urban spaces in an African country largely involves resolving the problem of urban sprawl and protecting tenure security in urban contexts. Chapter 4 offers theoretical and practical insights into local activism and how it can cause important changes in the built environment, using climate change and adaptive response measures as an example. Matenga builds on the findings and arguments in Chapter 3 by demonstrating that not only old and new institutions can potentially work to generate new sustainable development outcomes (in terms of land use) but local activism is also critical for achieving sustainable development (in the context of climate change). After a careful examination of institutions and local activism in the context of urbanisation and environmental sustainability, Rukambe and Irurah explore further by analysing architecture tools for reimagining the future in Chapter 5 by providing a form of futuristic architecture perspective in transitioning into sustainable city. The authors argue that the prevailing inertia in transforming African cities towards sustainable-city futures (including the expedited pursuit of the SDGs) is due to lack of domain-specific futurity-tools and communities-of-practice for sustainable city transitioning from their undesirable status quo to desirable futures. They address this gap through futures-studies as the central knowledge-field coupled with a figurative linkage of architecture (a practice-driven discipline) to backcasting (a newly emerged transitioning-studies field) in order to overcome the inertia. They convincingly argue that for backcasting to become an effective practice towards accelerated sustainable city transitioning, there is a need for its unique tools of liminality and communities-of-practice to coherently guide the growth in the prerequisite knowledge and practice of the field. Embedded in these discussions are the fundamental issues of how and under what conditions rapid urbanisation and socio-economic interactions alter global, regional and local ecological systems.

Part II: Land Use and Ecological Integrity

Part II of the book examines ways in which land use systems, forms and practices modulate and reshape urbanity and urbanisation processes in Africa. Land use planning and its expressions have a wide spectrum of effects on urban growth and processes. There are, however, many pathways through which land use planning and regulations affect urban systems in Africa. Resilience of socio-ecological systems and places as well as the capacity of formal and informal institutions to advance urban transformation is contingent on land use planning and regulations. The chapters in Part II collectively address pathways through which land uses and forms affect the integrity of urban ecological systems and ultimately human well-being. Core to the conversation on land use and ecological integrity, Chapter 6 examines how liquid waste and storm water often create problems in Africa by underscoring the importance of storm water management in protecting the ecological integrity of cities using flood events as examples. This chapter presents a case for reconsidering the current urban drainage approaches to storm waterlogging in sub-Saharan African cities towards more sustainable management approaches that enhance resilience and support sustainable urban living. Anim and colleagues introduce a robust *"eco-sustainable"* approach based on sustainable urban drainage systems as a viable alternative for urban stormwater management. The authors argue that integrating these sustainable management practices and principles into urban planning and water management has significant potential for mitigating urban storm waterlogging and flood risk as well as providing benefits that improve general living in urban areas. Building on the argument and findings in the previous chapter, Mazeka, Phinzi and Sutherland provide specific examples of the socio-ecological relations in urban environment in the context of land use in Durban, South Africa. The authors use eThekwini Municipality as a reflective lens through transformative and experimental learning on contemporary urbanisation to generate a novel understanding of the role of urbanisation in landscape-level transformation in urban environments. They achieved this through land use and land cover method to quantify and analyse the highly dynamic socio-natural relationship in the Municipality from 1991 to 2017. The chapter concludes that urbanisation process involves relationalities that encompass the transformation of biophysical and material entities in the making of urban environments.

Chapters in Part II also examine the interactions between competing urban land uses and ecosystem services and their spatial manifestations at different scales. In Chapter 8, Pedrosa and colleagues argue that even green spaces that are informal offer benefits to the ecology of the place but pose some challenges to both land use and the ecological integrity. The authors examine the perception and significance of informal green space from residents in Funda commune, Luanda, to underscore its potential for improving residents' access to urban green space. Through in-depth interviews, this chapter reveals that in the absence of well-planned urban green space, there is a high dependence on informal green space for ecosystem services with its inherent wildness, ecosystem disservices, and lack of formal planning recognition constraining its potentials. The discussions offer residents' collective management, formal planning recognition and support for informal green space to improve access to greenspaces and to contribute to urban sustainability in low-income communities. Chapter 9 examines how ecological integrity could be improved through collaborative spatial planning as an agent. Martel and colleagues explore the value of river rehabilitation projects and associated ecological infrastructure in supporting sustainable development across the social, economic, environmental and governance landscapes of Durban in South Africa. The chapter examines the projects' value as emergent spatial "sustainable development" pathways in the city drawing on empirical research conducted on four river rehabilitation projects. They argue that by supporting built infrastructure and social learning and by providing ecosystem services to urban residents at multiple scales, these spatial projects which integrate the social, economic, environmental and political dimensions of life in the city reflect a new form of planning for sustainability in cities in Africa.

In Chapter 10, Addaney, Avogo and Mensah take the debate forward by providing how regulation in land use if properly or improperly applied can yield positive or negative outcomes, using Ghana as a case. The authors analyse the legal and institutional contexts of land use and spatial plan formulation, levels of adherence to physical control procedures and assessment of capacities of key planning and land institutions responsible for achieving sustainable and inclusive physical development in Ghana. They conclude that achieving target 11.3 of Sustainable Development Goal 11 would be difficult considering the prevailing physical development systems and practices, and accordingly, advocate for inclusive, participatory and multi-approach to physical development in Ghana. Taking a different approach, Chapter 11 examines how waste management has become a critical issue in African cities particularly in informal communities and underscores why its management is central to sustainable development. Using a systematic and inclusive literature review, the chapter highlights that rapid urbanisation, rise in middle-income households and the attendant rise in living standards and consumption, have led to many cities in Africa generating large quantities of solid waste which has become a development challenge. The authors argue that the lack of clear policy strategies in sustainably managing waste is an issue in many African countries because governments are not fully prepared to integrate waste management into their sustainable urban development priority goals. The authors conclude that the future of solid waste management in African cities will remain a challenge without efforts to discover and apply locally-appropriate technologies that incorporate the principle of "reduce, reuse, recycle, recover and dispose." Part II concludes with a discussion on how sustainable land use can be realised and the ecological integrity protected with the introduction of efficient transport network/system using Mauritius as a case study. Mahadew and colleagues underscore that such projects are important for promoting social and economic development of a developing country in Chapter 12. They argue that it is even more essential that urban transportation systems are designed and implemented by infusing principles of spatial planning and sustainable development. By highlighting critical issues such as the impact of traffic congestion, the use of feeder buses as an operational component of the MEP and traveling cost being below international standards, the MEP reveals the failure of the planning authority to integrate sustainability and spatial planning requirements in the design and implementation of the project.

Part III: Urban Informality, Regeneration and Tenure Security

The final part of the book focuses on urban action on informality including urban regeneration and land tenure security. Here, it is argued that how urban systems respond to urban sprawl and informality largely depends on existing interactions between socio-economic and geopolitical processes and the built environment. And in turn, urban form and function transform local ecologies and influence human behaviour. In addition, urban built environments and communities have different capacities in coping, adapting and responding to the impacts of urban environmental change. Okyere and colleagues explore the lived experiences of people in informal settlements and how it impacts sustainable developments goals in Chapter 13. By using in-depth interviews with residents of old Fadama, the largest informal settlement in Accra, the authors consider the everyday struggles of residents in relation to the SDGs. They contend that transforming the lives of informal settlement residents will help cities attain the SDGs beyond SDG 11 that focuses primarily on promoting sustainable cities. Additionally, they suggest the need for participatory actionable initiatives that mainstream multiple elements of the SDGs and residents' everyday realities for a truly sustainable and inclusive urban development agenda that leaves no one behind.

In advancing arguments in the previous chapter, Kosoe and colleagues explore the combined effects of urbanisation and climate change on the sustainable urban futures of Tamale, a rapidly urbanising and largest city in northern Ghana, in Chapter 14. They examine three key issues, namely, the extent of spatial expansion of the city, flood vulnerability zones in the city, and the geography of warming areas across the cityscape and wind variation zones. The chapter argues that rapid urbanisation and climate change have altered the city-scape considerably with land cover change doubling in less than a decade. Chapter 15 offers optimism for improving functionality of informal communities in terms of security through flexible land arrangement mechanisms. Kariseb and Tjilale use Namibia's flexible land tenure system as a case reflection to analyse the prospects and shortcomings of flexible tenure arrangements in providing security of tenure to peri-urban and urban settlers.

This is undertaken against the backdrop of providing possible lessons and insight into such tenure systems for African countries, especially those contemplating reforms in their urban and peri-urban informal settlements. A key argument in this chapter is that flexible land tenure arrangements in practice fail to provide security of tenure predominantly because of the informal and relaxed nature of such arrangements. Chapter 16 examines methods with which sanitation management can be enhanced across cities, using South Africa as a case. In this chapter, Sutherland and Odili raise concerns about how African cities of the future hope to attain SDG 6: provide adequate and safely managed water and sanitation services for all. They analyse the changing sanitation landscape of the city of Durban using a governmentality framework. The findings reveal the emergence of a transformative sanitation framework, which is more diverse, context specific and flexible, and which is deepening the engagement of the local state with people, the environment, and innovative technology. Finally, in Chapter 17, the authors provide ways of transforming informal communities applying adaptive spatial planning and regularisation using Kenya as a case. Odote and Olale note that despite the formal-informal dichotomy that characterises development in African cities, there is a need for transformation in urban governance that requires reconceptualisation of the effectiveness of spatial planning either as a tool for integration and inclusivity or as an agent of seclusion. Using published literature, policy and case law, this chapter analyses existing approaches in upgrading and regularising informal settlements that have been applied in Kenya. The authors argue for adaptive spatial planning as an inclusive planning approach towards incremental transformation of urban informal settlements that can support tenure regularisation and promote the realisation of SDG 11 on making cities and human settlements inclusive, safe, resilient and sustainable.

Conclusion

Each chapter offers a rich and valuable contribution towards building a more systematic agenda for Africa's urban futures. Such an agenda could contemplate not only fundamental thematic issues that are presently underexplored (such as urbanisation trends, forms of urban governance and participation, future urban economies, future urban lifestyles, urban culture) but also strategic spatial planning and futuristic urban studies that consider the landscape of cities as complex, evolving, and diverse systems. This implies that various urban typologies, actors, functions, and interconnections must be examined, and evolutions and/or adaptations towards achieving context-relevant methods and approaches are of importance. A further consideration for the agenda might also engage with more epistemological issues with the aim of bringing together diverse approaches to support the development of novel knowledge and understanding.

References

Addaney, M., & Cobbinah, P. B. (2019). Climate change, urban planning and sustainable development in Africa: the difference worth appreciating. In Cobbinah, P.B. & Addaney, M. *The geography of climate change adaptation in urban Africa* (pp. 3–26). Cham: Palgrave Macmillan.

Anderson, P., Brown-Luthango, M., Cartwright, A., Farouk, I., & Smit, W. (2013). Brokering communities of knowledge and practice: Reflections on the African Centre for Cities' CityLab programme. *Cities, 32*, 1–10.

Bakewell, O., & Jónsson, G. (2011). *Migration, mobility and the African city*. Oxford, UK: International Migration Institute.

Boadi, K., Kuitunen, M., Raheem, K., & Hanninen, K. (2005). Urbanisation without development: Environmental and health implications in African cities. *Environment, Development and Sustainability, 7*(4), 465–500.

Bolay, J. C. (2015). Urban Planning in Africa: Which alternative for poor cities? The case of Koudougou in Burkina Faso. *Current Urban Studies, 3*, 413–431.

Boone, C., Redman, C. L., Blanco, H., Haase, D., Koch, J., Lwasa, S., Nagendra, H., Pauleit, S., Pickett, S. T. A., Seto, K. C., & Yokohari, M. (2014). Reconceptualising urban land use. In K. Seto & A. Reenberg (Eds.), *Rethinking global land use in an urban era*. Cambridge, MA: MIT Press.

Cobbinah, P. B., Black, R., & Thwaites, R. (2011). Reflections on six decades of the concept of development: Evaluation and future research. *Journal of Sustainable Development in Africa, 13*(7), 134–149.

Cobbinah, P. B., & Darkwah, R. M. (2017). Toward a more desirable form of sustainable urban development in Africa. *African Geographical Review, 36*(3), 262–285.

Cobbinah, P. B., Erdiaw-Kwasie, E., & Adams, E. A. (2020). COVID-19: Can it transform urban planning in Africa? *Cities & Health*, 10.1080/23748834.2020.1812329.

Cobbinah, P. B., Erdiaw-Kwasie, M. O., & Amoateng, P. (2015). Africa's urbanisation: Implications for sustainable development. *Cities, 47*, 62–72.

Cobbinah, P. B., & Korah, P. I. (2016). Religion gnaws urban planning: The geography of places of worship in Kumasi, Ghana. *International Journal of Urban Sustainable Development, 8*, 93–109.

Fischer, G., Winiwarter, W., Cao, G. Y., Ermolieva. T., Hizsnyik, E., Klimont, Z., Wiberg, D., & Zheng, X. Y. (2012). Implications of population growth and urbanisation on agricultural risks in China. *Population and Environment, 33*(2–3), 243–258.

Guneralp, B., Lwasa, S., Masundire, H., Parnell, S., & Seto, K. C. (2017). Urbanization in Africa: Challenges and opportunities for conservation. *Environmental Research Letter, 13*, 1.

Haase, D., & Schwarz, N. (2016). Urban land use in the global context. In K. C. Seto, W. D. Solecki, & C. A. Griffith (Eds.), *The Routledge handbook of urbanisation and global environmental change*. London/New York: Routledge.

Harrison, P. (2006). On the edge of reason: Planning and urban futures in Africa. *Urban Studies, 43*(2), 319–335.

Kamete, A. Y. (2013). Missing the point? Urban planning and the normalisation of 'pathological' spaces in southern Africa. *Transactions of the Institute of British Geographers, 38*(4), 639–651.

Mabogunje, A. L. (1990). Urban planning and the post-colonial state in Africa: A Research Overview 1. *African Studies Review*, 33(2), 121–203.

McConnachie, M. M., Shackleton, C. M., & McGregor, G. K. (2008). The extent of public green space and alien plant species in 10 small towns of the Sub-Tropical Thicket Biome, South Africa. *Urban Forestry & Urban Greening*, 7(1), 1–13.

McIntyre, N. E., Knowles-Yanez, K., & Hope, D. (2000). Urban ecology as an interdisciplinary field: Differences in the use of 'urban' between the social and natural sciences. *Urban Ecosystems*, 4, 5–24.

Mugisha, F., Arinaitwe-Mugisha, J., & Hagembe, B. O. (2003). Alcohol, substance and drug use among urban slum adolescents in Nairobi, Kenya. *Cities*, 20(4), 231–240.

Nunbogu, A. M., Korah, P. I., Cobbinah, P. B., & Poku-Boansi, M. (2018). Doing it 'ourselves': Civic initiative and self-governance in spatial planning. *Cities*, 74, 32–41.

Obeng-Odoom, F. (2010). 'Abnormal' urbanization in Africa: A dissenting view. *African Geographical Review*, 29(2).

Owusu, G., Agyei-Mensah, S., & Lund, R. (2008). Slums of hope and slums of despair: Mobility and livelihoods in Nima, Accra. *Norsk Geografisk Tidsskrift-Norwegian Journal of Geography*, 62(3), 180–190.

Pacione, M. (2005). *Urban geography: A global perspective*. New York: Routledge.

Parnell, S., & Mabin, A. (1995). Rethinking urban South Africa. *Journal of Southern African Studies*, 21(1), 39–61.

Peng, X., Chen, X., & Cheng, Y. (2000). *Urbanisation and its consequences*. http://www.eolss.net/sample-chapters/c04/e6-147-18.pdf.

Potts, D. (2012). *Rural–urban and urban-rural migration flows as indicators of economic opportunity in sub-Saharan Africa: What does the data tell us?* A paper presented at the conference on urbanisation and rural–urban migration in sub-Saharan Africa held 26–27th November in Nairobi, Kenya.

Schwarz, N. (2010). Urban form revisited – selecting indicators for characterizing European cities. *Landscapes and Urban Planning*, 96, 29–47.

Silva, C. N. (2015). *Urban planning in Sub-Saharan Africa: Colonial and post-colonial planning cultures*. New York and London: Routledge.

Simon, D. (1985). Independence and social transformation: Urban planning problems and priorities for Namibia. *Third World Planning Review*, 7(2), 99.

Sumari, N. S., Cobbinah, P. B., Ujoh, F., & Xu, G. (2020). On the absurdity of rapid urbanization: Spatio-temporal analysis of land-use changes in Morogoro, Tanzania. *Cities*, 107, 102876.

UNDESA. (2014). *World urbanisation prospects: The 2014 revision, highlights (ST/ESA/SER.A/352)*. UN Department of Economic and Social Affairs, Population Division.

UNDESA/PD. (2012). *World urbanisation prospects: The 2011 revision*. New York: United Nations.

UN-Habitat. (2010). *2010/11 state of the world's cities report, 'bridging the urban divide.'* Nairobi: United Nations Human Settlement Programme.

UN-Habitat. (2012). *State of the world's cities 2010/2011: Bridging the urban divide*. London, UK: Earthscan.

UN-Habitat. (2020). Breaking cycles of risk accumulation in African cities. UN-Habitat. https://www.urbanark.org/sites/default/files/resources/UN%20Report%202019%20eBook%20HIGH.pdf. Accessed 24 February 2020.

UNEP. (2011). *Towards a green economy: Pathways to sustainable development and poverty eradication.* UNEP.

United Nations Department of Economic and Social Affairs (UNDESA), Population Division. (2018). *World Urbanization Prospects: The 2018 Revision.* Online Edition.

UN. (2018). *World urbanization prospects: The 2018 Revision.* New York: United Nations Department of Economic and Social Affairs/Population Division. https://esa.un.org/unpd/wup/Download/ (7 March 2021).

Ville De Dakar and 100 Resilient Cities. (2016). *Dakar resilience strategy.* http://www.100resilientcities.org/wp-content/uploads/2017/07/Dakar_Resilience_ Strategy.pdf. Accessed 9 January 2020.

WCED. (1987). *Our common future.* Report of the Brundtland Commission. UK: Oxford University Press.

2 Deconstructing Africa's Urban Space: Sustainable Development and Spatial Planning Challenge

*Patrick Brandful Cobbinah,
Michael Odei Erdiaw-Kwasie,
and Marita Basson*

Introduction

Sustainable development and spatial planning, including urban and regional planning, and strategic spatial planning are intrinsically linked. Sustainable development has the potential to contribute to managing the pressures of rapid urbanisation, poverty, climate change and the haphazard development characterising African cities (see Cobbinah et al., 2015). However, sustainable development is also a concept that depends on spatial organisation – the use and management of land which is essential to guarantee sustainable development outcomes in African cities (Watson, 2016). In this regard, initiatives by scholars, governments, and international development organisations to promote a better understanding of the relationship between sustainable development and spatial planning are critical.

The document, "The Future We Want" from the United Nations Conference on Sustainable Development (Rio+20) in June 2012, emphasised that urban development that is well planned, implemented and managed, can make considerable contribution to sustainable development, particularly in developing countries where urban problems seem insurmountable (Adams et al., 2019; Cobbinah & Addaney, 2019). Sustainable urban development, in this context, includes promotion of controlled land development, protection of ecologically sensitive areas, and development of resilient city-scapes, which are central to the post-2015 sustainable development agenda. The UN Sustainable Development Goals (SDGs), particularly goals 11 and 13, emphasise the importance of creating safe and resilient human settlements and combating climate change in a rapidly evolving world. While commitment to combat climate change, create safe human habitats and minimise disruptions to ecosystem services is integral to the SDGs and the Rio+20 Conference outcome, spatial planning is critical in these sustainability initiatives (see section "Theoretical understandings of sustainable development and spatial planning" for a detailed explanation on spatial planning). As argued by Chigudu and Chirisa (2020) and Nogués et al. (2019), the objective of

DOI: 10.4324/9781003181484-22

spatial planning is to create sustainable cities and communities, and it remains paramount to the attainment of the SDGs. For this reason, the Rio+20 further called for improved support for urban (spatial) planning activities and capacity building in developing countries where the threats of rapid unplanned urbanisation and climate change are most severe (see Cobbinah, 2021; Silva, 2015).

Building on the outcome of the Rio+20 and efforts to actualise the SDGs in developing countries, the United Nations Conference on Housing and Sustainable Urban Development (Habitat III) has been working closely with UN-Habitat to advance sustainable development in the context of spatial planning and in the adoption of the New Urban Agenda (NUA). The NUA represents a shared vision for a more sustainable future by providing people with equal rights and access to the benefits cities provide and setting urban systems and forms as international priority areas. The NUA presents an opportunity to re-evaluate governance regimes and to enhance the significance of urban planning and sustainability in national and city-level development agendas (Dahiya & Das, 2020; Sietchiping et al., 2016). Unfortunately, this relationship between spatial planning and sustainable development is dimly appreciated in African cities with several case studies reporting on the failure of urban Africa to respond appropriately and adequately to existing (e.g. poverty) and emerging threats (e.g. climate change, urbanisation) (see for example, Cobbinah & Addaney, 2019; Fuseini & Kemp, 2015). However, to put urban Africa on a sustainable development footing, it is pressing and tenable to improve understanding of the inseparable relationship between spatial planning and sustainable development.

This chapter addresses the potential role that improved understandings of the relationship between spatial planning and sustainable development could play in charting sustainable future pathways for African cities. It contributes to the achievement of sustainable development initiatives, particularly the SDGs and the NUA. It establishes the theoretical relationship between the two concepts and relates their relevance to the future of the urban space in Africa as well as implications for future research in this area. In doing this, the chapter explores the emerged and the emerging notions of sustainable development and spatial planning with an African focus and further reviews theories and regional and national case studies. The chapter is organised into five sections. The next section analyses the theoretical understandings of sustainable development and spatial planning and their relationship thereof. This is followed by an evaluation of urban Africa's development experience, exploring the implications for sustainable development and spatial planning. Further, discussions on ways of integrating sustainable development and spatial planning initiatives are presented. The concluding section highlights the major takeaways from this chapter and suggests areas requiring further research.

Theoretical Understandings of Sustainable Development and Spatial Planning

This section first presents theoretical understandings of both "sustainable development" and "spatial planning," attempting to ascertain the relationship between the concepts. It then proceeds to discuss the characteristics of sustainable development and spatial planning, such as the normative nature of both, before analysing the impact of the government-governance nexus in which spatial planning occurs. Next, global initiatives to promote sustainable development are contrasted with the role of spatial planning in attaining sustainable development on the ground.

Evolution of Sustainable Development and Spatial Planning

The concept of sustainable development originated from 1960s systems theory wherein environment, society and economy were deemed inter-related elements of a larger system (Magis & Shinn, 2009). Apart from the well-known 1987 Brundtland Report definition of sustainable development, there has been no generally agreed upon definition of the concept (Alexander, 2016). Its conceptual ambiguity and fuzziness remain (see Cobbinah & Darkwah, 2016; Orenstein & Shach-Pinsley, 2017). On the other hand, a 1983 definition of spatial planning by the European Regional/Spatial Planning Charter states that spatial planning gives spatial expression to the economic, social, cultural, and ecological policies of society, and that, it is simultaneously a scientific discipline, an administrative technique, and a policy (Reimer et al., 2014). Alexander (2016) builds on this view of spatial planning by stating that it operates at a variety of abstraction levels and geographic scales; an argument that disputes simply viewing spatial planning at a specific geographic level espoused by others such as Wong (2011) who argues that spatial planning remains an intervention with the intent to shape the development outcomes of a specific area. Segura and Pedregal (2017) highlight the visionary element of spatial planning which is implemented through land use plans to attain sustainable spatial development.

In general, there appears to be a strong focus in spatial planning on sustainable development goals (Chigudu & Chirisa, 2020; Nogués et al., 2019). Sustainable development is a societal aim across local, regional and global geographical scales, whereas spatial planning occurs at different geographical scales from the local to the regional, to the state and in some cases a conglomeration of states. The definitions of sustainable development and spatial planning provide the first layer for a theoretical analysis of each concept and the relationship between them, but the characteristics embedded in each concept further inform the analysis.

The Normative Nature of Sustainable Development and Spatial Planning

Spatial planning and sustainable development exhibit normative and distributive aims (Alexander, 2016). Sustainable development is a normative principle that is part of the response of developing countries to the limits of the growth narrative in the late 1960s and early 1970s. Inherent in this discourse, is the notion of distributive ethics (Fukuda-Parr and Muchhala, 2020). Sustainable development deals with the social, environment and economic domains, but recently, there has been an "ethical turn" in the discourse on sustainable development (Holden et al., 2017, p. 214). Sustainable development has become a much more prominent goal in spatial planning over the past three decades (Orenstein & Shach-Pinsley, 2017). Spatial planning is an important tool for achieving sustainable development, which means that spatial planning principles become sustainable by default (Persson, 2013). Like spatial planning, sustainable development is mediated through physical spaces and built form.

Depending on the institutional and policy context, development can steer us towards either a more virtuous circle of development or the reverse. Holden et al. (2017, p. 214) argue that the "moral imperatives of needs, equity and limits" should guide policy making on sustainable development. The same applies to spatial planning which always occurs within the framework of government structure and its accompanying forms of governance, including policy making (Alexander, 2016; Erdiaw-Kwasie & Basson, 2018). According to the Brundtland Commission, sustainable development requires a political system that can secure its citizens' real influence on decisions through functional democracy and governance processes.

Government and governance are linked, through spatial planning, to sustainable development. As spatial planning is inherently normative, institutional, and legal frameworks guiding spatial planning should benefit future generations (Alexander, 2016). The bottom lines (economic development, environmental sustainability, and social inclusion) proposed earlier by Sachs (2012) as a means of classifying sustainable development goals strongly depend on good governance at all levels – local, national, regional and global. Orenstein and Shach-Pinsley (2017) state that sustainable development and the notion it represents has endured and found its way into every discipline dealing with the environment, resources, and land use. This is particularly true for spatial planning which is now strongly focused on sustainable development. How sustainable development has made its way into so many disciplines and agendas can be related to the main drivers for sustainable development – the global sustainable development agendas.

Global Sustainable Development Agendas: How they Link with
Spatial Planning

Various globally agreed sustainable development agendas, such as the Millennium Development Goals (MDGs), Sustainable Development Goals (SDGs) and Local Agenda 21, have attempted to address sustainable development issues. The SDGs are part of the UN's Agenda 2030 (2016–2030) and were adopted by the United Nations Member States in 2015 to eradicate poverty, protect the planet and ensure universal prosperity (UN, 2020). The SDGs provide guidelines on frameworks to ensure sustainable development and has gained prominence due to the urgency of sustainable planetary development (Valencia et al., 2019). Not all global agendas have the same focus or aim, with the MDGs essentially being improvement targets for the poor countries with assistance expected from affluent countries (Fakuda-Parr & Muchhala, 2020). However, the SDGs apply to all countries – an approach which underscores the understanding that rich and poor countries must all aspire to achieve sustainable development (Klopp & Petretta, 2017). The SDGs were formulated through a comprehensive global participatory process. Top-down spatial planning practices were heavily criticised almost three decades ago, resulting in an enduring communicative turn in spatial planning (Healey, 1996).

The New Urban Agenda (NUA) was adopted by government leaders at the Habitat III summit in 2016. The global focus on sustainable development agendas, described above, have resulted in initiatives in spatial planning to attain sustainable development but there is no manual for operationalising the goals of sustainable development of which the NUA is an example (Orenstein & Shach-Pinsley, 2017; Satterthwaite, 2016; Schindler, 2017; Turok & Scheba, 2019). Lacking implementation frameworks do not prevent these initiatives from being viewed as an opportunity to reassess governance systems and to elevate the importance of sustainable development on spatial planning agendas (Sietchiping et al., 2016). Initiatives such as the SDG and the NUA are regarded to be progressive and to have the potential to reconceptualise spatial planning and sustainable development (Valencia et al., 2019). Strong links are commonly observed between sustainable development and spatial planning; first based on the need for effective governance and secondly through refocusing spatial planning on sustainable development goals.

Unlike the global initiatives, spatial planning has strong local implementation frameworks such as master plans, local development plans, and planning schemes. Despite cautions and criticisms about the link between spatial planning and sustainable development outcomes (Berke & Conroy, 2000; Holden et al., 2017). Oliveira Tobias and Hersperger (2018) in their review found that spatial planning has been increasingly practised globally to achieve sustainable development. In fact, sustainable development remains a core objective of spatial planning in recent years.

Their study has revealed shifts in the aims of spatial planning. Given that there might not be anything inherent in spatial planning that steers it towards sustainable development, the existence of frameworks and guides to operationalise sustainable development agendas and evaluation of sustainable development goals deserve to be mentioned (Chigudu & Chirisa, 2020).

Sustainable Development and Spatial Planning Interventions

How sustainable development aims, embedded in frameworks and structures, are actualised at a local level is addressed in the literature. For instance, Jenks and Jones (2010) argue that urban form is a consideration in the attainment of sustainable development; with compact city development being a desired urban form. Valencia et al. (2019) conducted a comparison between seven global cities to assess what planning practitioners will need to localise the SDGs and the NUA. In this research, links were drawn between spatial planning, communicative and consultative planning, and sustainable development.

In this section, clear relationships, similarities, and disparities have been demonstrated between spatial planning and sustainable development. These include the normative nature of both, with the aim of a more sustainable, equitable society firmly embedded in both concepts. In addition, both spatial planning and sustainable development occur over different geographical scales. However, spatial planning practice might further result in improved frameworks for action that are more focused on the local, regional and national level outcomes, although it takes cognisance of global trends and issues (Alexander, 2016; Jenks & Jones, 2010). Both sustainable development and spatial planning are commonly built on the social, economic and environmental pillars of sustainability (Erdiaw-Kwasie & Basson, 2018) but spatial planning is impacted heavily by governance as a fourth pillar of sustainability. In addition, both sustainable development and spatial planning outcomes can suffer from top-down regimes, lacking in public consultation.

Urban Africa's Development Experience: Locating Sustainable Development and Spatial Planning

Research indicates that achieving sustainable development in cities entails the integration of social development, economic development and environmental management (Cobbinah et al., 2015). Progress by African cities towards achieving these development goals varies (Lubida et al., 2018); while some cities are progressing towards meeting these global goals, others are recovering, and many are lagging. This section of the chapter therefore focuses on discussing how African cities are faring with global development goals under these mentioned sustainable development pillars.

Social Development

Social development efforts across cities and countries are based on the principle of leaving no person behind – education; access to clean water, sanitation, health services and wellbeing; and zero hunger and poverty for all. Africa's transformation into the urban age is without precedent in its swiftness (UN-Habitat, 2018). However, unplanned urban growth produces social problems; with many African cities grappling with its spatial implications. According to the Africa Sustainable Development Report (2018), access to safe drinking water and improved sanitation remains low in the continent by global standards, despite sub-Saharan Africa receiving the world's largest proportion of official development assistance (ODA) for water supply and sanitation. Rapid unplanned urban growth in Sub-Saharan Africa has led to large volumes of water extraction (Adams et al., 2019; Stren & White, 2019). The influx of water plus the increase in human waste in many African cities has outpaced wastewater management systems – which are usually centrally planned and implemented and fail to connect the population to water and sanitation services. Some attribute the disjunction between spatial plans and water and sanitation projects to a lack of coordination between planners, budget officials and project implementers (Cameron & Katzschner, 2017; Hersperger et al., 2018). Others associate the failure to political interference and the prioritisation of cheap and easy projects (Emenike et al., 2017; Keeton & Nijhuis, 2019). The World Bank's (2018) report on water supply and sanitation in selected African countries shows that cities such as Luanda (Angola), Bamako (Mali), Kampala (Uganda), Lagos (Nigeria), Niamey (Niger) and Accra (Ghana) are in water and sanitation stress zones.

Understanding of the actual urban governance processes and how different actors interact to make and operationalise decisions is lacking but important (Basson et al., 2018; Cobbinah & Erdiaw-Kwasie, 2018). Thus, these cities are unable to keep pace with change and unable to provide residents with adequate water and sanitation infrastructure services. Compounding the situation further, many African cities continue to show unsustainable water and waste management, worsening poverty, hunger, children's malnutrition and unemployment and endangered human wellbeing (Cosgrove & Loucks, 2015; Kubanza & Simatele, 2016; Omisore, 2018). In Burkina Faso, for example, almost half (8.4 million people) of the population live without clean water and three in four people (14 million people) do not have a functional toilet (see Figure 2.1).

In addition, more than 4,500 children under five years old die annually from diarrhoea due to dirty water and poor toilet facilities (WaterAid report, 2018). Consistent with this is Newborne and Tucker's (2015) finding that Ouagadougou, the capital city of Burkina Faso, draws its main water supply from the heavily polluted Loumbila Dam, with the city continuously facing water shortage.

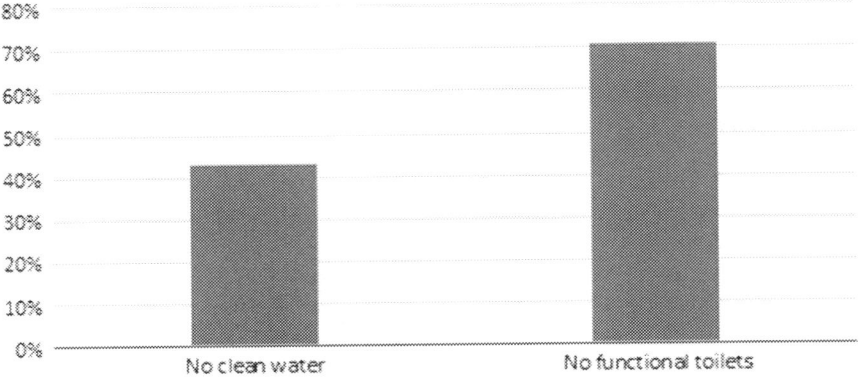

Figure 2.1 Water and sanitation stress in Burkina Faso in 2018.

Source: Created from the World Bank Report (2018).

Similarly, rapid population growth in African cities contributes to informal settlements ("slums") which are usually characterised by poverty, tenure insecurity, overcrowded dwellings and inadequate infrastructure and services, coupled with elevated rates of diseases (Cobbinah & Darkwah, 2016; Corburn & Sverdlik, 2019; Forster & Ammann, 2018). Davis (cited in Forster & Ammann, 2018) explains that Global South cities are dominated by informal settlements/slums. An example is the slums in Maputo, Mozambique, where three-quarters of the city's population lack adequate housing, access to piped water and sewage systems (Chiodelli & Mazzolini, 2019; Zehra et al., 2019). However, several African cities (e.g. Harare, Zimbabwe) are addressing the issue of slums through inclusive municipal governance and slum upgrading (Muchadenyika, 2015). The Harare Slum Upgrade Programme engaged and applied local knowledge through planning and its success is associated with a spatial planning governance model that responds to the needs and aspirations of residents. Such programmes support the assertion that involving the local people in the plan-making process is important (Healy, 2010; Lane, 2006). In contrast, the problem has been approached in a top-down, "technocratic" and "neo-liberal" style across majority of African cities, where slum residents are disempowered by and disengaged from slum improvement initiatives (Erdiaw-Kwasie et al., 2020; Habib et al., 2019). Although improved public participation in spatial planning is critical to address challenges, it is frequently ignored by governments and state agencies as it is time-consuming and financially intensive. In this situation, It is unclear whether conscious effort to promote public participation in spatial planning, and the delivery of the anticipated sustainable development results will be a mirage (Curry, 2012; Pacioni, 2019).

Environmental Management and Development

African countries are projected to experience changing rainfall patterns, rising sea levels and higher temperatures that will affect food security, agricultural production, water availability, and public health (Giugni et al., 2015; Kogo et al., 2020). Considering the actual and potential impacts of climate change threatening vulnerable sectors and human populations, African cities are already taking actions (Akukwe, 2019; Satterthwaite et al., 2019), including the City of Johannesburg's first green bond ever from a C40 city; the City of Dakar's Vivre avec l'eau investment in infrastructure and partnerships to address flash flooding; and 11 C40 African cities committing to produce climate action plans that are compliant with the Paris Agreement by the end of 2020 (UN-Habitat, 2018). Nevertheless, as shown in Figure 2.2, 84 of the world's 100 fastest-growing cities are at extreme risk from the impacts of a warming planet, with 79 of them in Africa (UN-Habitat, 2018). These include Kinshasa (Democratic Republic of Congo), Lagos (Nigeria), Dar es Salaam (Tanzania) and Luanda (Angola) (Owolabi, 2017; Udelsmann, 2019).

Climate change exacerbates the vulnerability of the urban poor (Satterthwaite et al., 2019). In 2018, for example, flooding in Sub-Saharan Africa destroyed more than 10,000 homes and affected more than 2 million people (Adaawen et al., 2019; Grasham et al., 2019). Flooding in Lagos has increased city-wide poverty as farmlands are destroyed and essential services are interrupted. The impacts include displacement from

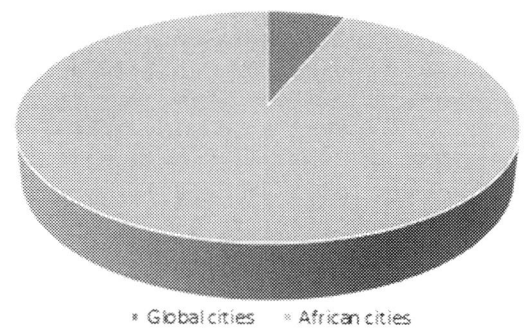

Percentage of world's largest cities at extreme risk of global warming (n=100)

⋅ Global cities   ⋅ African cities

Figure 2.2 Proportion of fastest-growing cities facing risk of global warming.

Source: Created from the UN Habitat Report (2018).

homes, mortality, physical injuries, disruption of economic activities and destruction of urban infrastructure (Aluko et al., 2019). Similarly, Kinshasa, with about 15 million people, is exposed to impacts from extreme weather, including flooding, which disrupt food and water supplies (Ahmed & Ogunola, 2016; Lebailly & Muteba, 2011). In such a case, strategic retreat is often the only solution, but in many cases it is a volatile political intervention (Broto, 2017; Funder et al., 2018). Efforts to pursue the SDGs are gaining momentum, however, are outpaced by African population growth (Satterthwaite et al., 2019; Stren & White, 2019). Two-thirds of the urban population across Africa do not have access to electricity while the remaining one-third experience intermittent electricity power supply (Aidoo & Briggs, 2019; Lotsu et al., 2019). For example, in Accra, despite access to electricity increasing from 24% of the population to 79% between 1990 and 2016 (World Bank 2018), electricity supply from the national grid has not matched the rapid growth in demand (Addae et al., 2019; Kemausuor & Ackom, 2017). This is due to technical losses from outdated equipment and a reliance on hydroelectric generation (Cobbinah & Adams, 2018; Kumi 2017; Mensah et al., 2014). As a result, since 2011, the city has continued to experience electricity power rationing impacting living and livelihood options. Without effective spatial planning and governance practices, many African countries are unlikely to meet emerging energy challenges and jeopardise efforts towards meeting the SGD 7 on clean energy access.

Economic Development

Economic development has caused improved living conditions in many cities across the globe. Some African countries are making progress towards ending poverty. For example, Ethiopia, Africa's second most populous country, is projected to lift 22 million people out of extreme poverty by 2030, reducing the percentage of Ethiopians living in extreme poverty from 25.6% today to 3.9%. As illustrated in Figure 2.3, 5.3 million of citizens in Côte d'Ivoire are projected to be lifted out of poverty, bringing down the percentage of citizens living in extreme poverty from 17.2% today to 4.9% (UN-Habitat, 2018).

However, as cities generally function as sources of economic development and human progress, there has not been greater economic dynamism in African cities (Rogerson & Rogerson, 2015; Turok, 2010). African cities have failed to drive economic development for its residents because programmes aimed more directly at economic development have been fragmented and ineffective. However, an emerging example of an approach to economic development that is embedded in spatial planning approaches is observed in Zanzibar, where the potential for tourism development has led to the development of the Zanzibar Strategy for Growth and Reduction of Poverty (Lubida et al., 2018). Here, spatial planning is used to balance

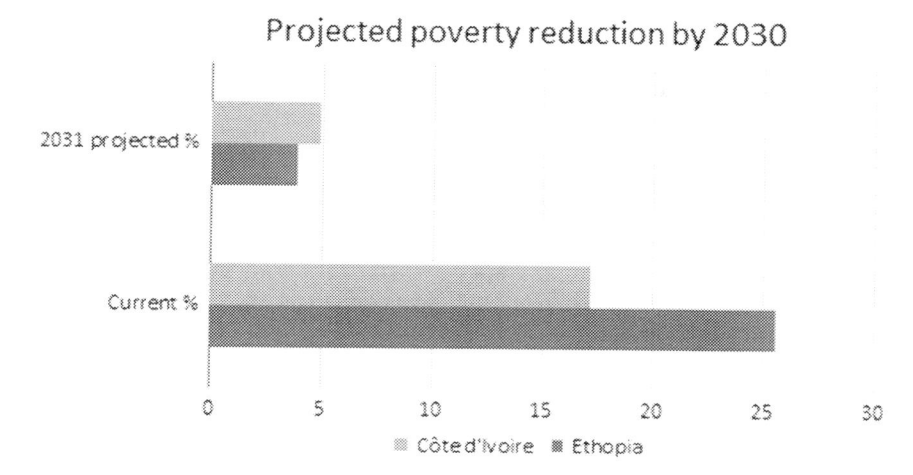

Figure 2.3 Projected poverty reduction by 2030.
Source: Created from the UN Habitat Report (2018).

conflicting social, economic, and environmental interests, with the overall aim of sustainable development.

Historically, rapid population increases have been associated with economic transformation in many African cities – declining agricultural employment; a shift in economic activity from rural to urban areas; and the rise of the modern industrial and service economy (UN Habitat, 2012). However, the inadequacy of infrastructure and services such as road and rail networks, energy, and telecommunication is undermining the economic performance of many African cities. When compared with other regions such as Asia, urban-based economic activities in Africa (i.e. industry and services) have performed poorly and the link between urban incomes and local economic performance has remained weak (Becker & Frankema, 2019; Pieterse et al., 2018). The poor economic infrastructure in Harare, Kinshasa, Abidjan and Antananarivo has contributed to high production costs for businesses, raising unit production costs and making these cities uncompetitive.

Towards the Future: Marrying Sustainable Development and Spatial Planning

The foregoing discussion supports the criticism that spatial planning in Africa is superficial, weak and lacks political commitment in implementation (Berrisford, 2011; Okpala, 2009); and, like the sustainable development concept, does not at present serve as an authoritative foundation for policy development and institutional efficiency in the Anthropocene.

However, spatial planning remains highly relevant to today's sustainable development initiatives across urban Africa because it offers a robust platform for effecting sustainable development policy and stimulating a new planning agenda (Korah et al., 2017). There is evidence of spatial planning across African cities and many city authorities are gradually embracing sustainable development – particularly the sustainable development goals – but many have only a superficial understanding and application of how to translate the sustainable development ideals into practical spatial planning outcomes (Fuseini & Kemp, 2015; Silva, 2015). This is primarily because sustainable development initiatives do not take a spatially balanced and holistic approach to urban development. Instead, these sustainable development initiatives focus narrowly on creating spatially resilient cities and more orderly urban morphologies. Many scholars (e.g. Cobbinah & Poku-Boansi, 2018; Mabogunje, 1990; Okpala, 2009) have argued that the disconnect between sustainable development and spatial planning across African cities results from the foundational ambiguity and overshadowing interest of international organisations. They argue that both spatial planning and sustainable development, and their associated interventions (e.g. sustainable development goals) in Africa, are largely dictated and dominated by international organisations (e.g. UN, UN-Habitat), colonialism and multilateral organisations (e.g. World Bank), with little or no evidence of local aspirations, knowledge and strategies.

Within this context, it is understandable that sustainable development initiatives at the local city levels are developed to reflect international interest while spatial planning remains largely a remnant of colonialism (Fuseini & Kemp, 2015; Salm & Falola, 2009). As a consequence, major sustainable development and planning practice across several African countries have not developed beyond the traditional aspects of meeting international requirements, gaining international recognition and receiving international support (e.g. financial and technical), and reflecting colonial origins to local pressing deliverables (e.g. poverty, homelessness, disaster management, climate adaptability, informal economic activities) necessary for the survival of city residents (Cobbinah et al., 2015). A typical African city today is characterised by, *inter alia*, slum proliferation (e.g. Nairobi, Cape Town), poor transport infrastructure and services (e.g. Lagos), limited social services (e.g. Addis Ababa), traffic congestion (e.g. Accra, Lagos), deteriorating sanitation conditions (e.g. Monrovia) and unplanned and haphazard spatial development (e.g. Kumasi) (see for example Kamete, 2013).

The apparent foreign nature of spatial planning (Diaw et al., 2002; Okpala, 2009; Silva, 2015), coupled with international dominance in the production of sustainable development discourse may have contributed to the weak relationship between sustainable development and spatial planning in the African urban landscape. This, of course, is not to argue that foreignism of the concepts and international dominance are the only reasons accounting for the poor relationship between spatial planning and sustainable development in Africa. In fact, others argue that it has been decades following the introduction of both sustainable development and spatial planning in Africa, and that, presently, foreignism or international dominance should not be the basis for poor performance as emergence of modern cities preceded colonisation (Coquery-Vidrovitch, 2005). Similarly, urban Africa's population explosion intensified at the turn of the 21st century, and African city authorities should go beyond the narrative of foreignism and international dominance to spur economic growth and manage their urban spaces sustainably. Unfortunately, this is not the situation across urban Africa. The urban experience in Africa is characterised by pathologies in urban forms, distortions in land governance regimes, conflicting power relations, undue political interference, and nonchalant residents' behaviour towards urban living (Cobbinah & Darkwah, 2017; Okpala, 2009).

Moving forward, promoting spatially grounded sustainable development in African cities is by no means guaranteed. This chapter makes recommendations to support locally-driven sustainable spatial planning efforts across African cities. First is education. Both sustainable development and spatial planning are imported concepts with limited local content. However, with recent worrying African statistics on climate change and urbanisation, education on the two concepts is critical in developing urban resilience pathways. This chapter argues that urban planning schools in Africa should develop and teach planning content that reflects more of the local situation rather than Western models – such as understanding growth patterns in African cities rather than tagging it as informal; relying on local knowledge and strategies to map out sustainable development projects; and involving local stakeholders in sustainable development and planning discourse (see, for example, Odendaal, 2012). Similarly, city planning authorities and professional planning bodies across the continent should be educated on local and practical approaches to credentialing the sustainable development and spatial planning concepts via workshops, seminars, and training sessions, with considerable emphasis on their relevance in these changing times. Additionally, urban residents should be informed on urban planning and sustainable development matters via media and social media platforms to create an informed citizenry. By this endorsement, city planning authorities, planning institutions and student planners would develop an understanding of ways of integrating sustainability into spatial planning and vice versa (see Brown, 2011), as well as an appreciation of their implementation weaknesses, and identify ways of contextualising them in every African city.

Second, localising African urbanism is important. Analysis presented in this chapter shows that sustainable development, spatial planning and urban experiences in Africa are evaluated and compared with Western ideals and criteria. However, an emerging body of literature indicates that

African urbanism is unique and needs to be recognised as such. The frequent application of Western criteria to understanding African urbanism limits incorporation of local content and initiatives, as do increasing efforts that are focused on modelling African cities on Western designs, planning and management models. This commendation does not argue that consideration and evaluation of Western ways of doing sustainable development in Africa should not be encouraged. It explains that best practices can be integrated into locally defined and engineered sustainable spatial planning initiatives – e.g. local interpretation of growth patterns; socio-cultural characteristics such as family systems, housing preferences, and nature of economic activities – instead of wholesale adoption as it is occurring in many African cities. The process of localising African urbanism also ensures local sustainable solutions are prescribed for urban issues, as often activities spurring sustainable growth of African cities (e.g. informal economic activities) are tagged as informal or nuisance-based following Western standards and are ignored in spatial planning practice (Kamete, 2013). Localising African urbanism may further improve the image of spatial planning and sustainable development as it would be reflected in policies and reality.

In summary, sustainable development and spatial planning have become highly recognised concepts in public policy discourse in Africa. These concepts have been characterised as all-embracing pathways for delivering sustainable outcomes in cities and for managing threats of urbanisation, climate change and poverty in the region (Cobbinah et al., 2015; Salm & Falola, 2009). The task ahead is to address the disconnect between sustainable development and spatial planning in practice with local content. This chapter is a first step in carrying out this task in an African context – it explains that city planning authorities in Africa should go beyond an emblematic blame-game of colonisation and international dominance in sustainable development and spatial planning concepts to comprehensively develop a local narrative that integrates both concepts, reflects local aspirations and draws on local knowledge and strategies. The chapter recommends ways in which sustainable development and spatial planning can be integrated to promote African urbanism that foster local ownership and leadership of the urban space. However, caution needs to be exercised, acknowledging that the pathway to realising sustainable spatial planning is an involved, complicated and difficult one, with no easy remedies.

Conclusion

This chapter has demonstrated that spatial planning is inherently reflected in the global development agenda (e.g. SDGs) and drives international dialogue (e.g. New Urban Agenda). However, this dialogue is characterised by some dissenting voices and some doubts are being expressed about the state of sustainable development and spatial planning occurring in

Africa. For some, the concept of spatial planning offers a potential "win–win" solution to the current urban development, and socio-economic and environmental crises facing the continent; whereas, for others, the prevailing sustainable development rhetoric and experience in African cities do not go far enough in advocating improvement in the current spatial planning system to produce sustainable urban futures.

This chapter has further established that there is clearly enormous potential for Africa if its development agenda is founded on the intersection between spatial planning and sustainable development. To realise this objective, several significant hurdles will need to be overcome, particularly relating to the role and influence of international and local agencies in sustainable development and spatial planning initiatives, which invariably determine the extent of success in relation to the management of unplanned urbanisation, climate change impacts and urban poverty. As discussed earlier, urbanisation in Africa is happening at unprecedented rates, but governments, planners and governance models are not equipped to deal with the influx of citizens into the urban environment, despite funding from global organisations being available to, for example, provide infrastructure. Part of the reason for this lack of preparedness is the legacy of the Eurocentric, and particularly British and French, town planning systems which many countries in Africa inherited. These systems do not necessarily reflect the need, nature and desire of the communities they are currently regulating. African cities tend to be polycentric, while these systems promote monocentric cities. In this case, sustainable development will not be achieved until spatial planning is aligned with the realities of the cities and the people that it is serving.

Successful integration of sustainable development and spatial planning concepts in Africa's development agenda will require education of local authorities and residents and redefinition of the role and influence of international organisations in urban development. As profiled here, the introduction, development and publication of both concepts have been informed by a wide variety of different international perspectives (e.g. colonisation) and organisations (e.g. UN), around which there is still considerable debate. A central issue that remains contentious in Africa is whether sustainable development initiatives should be integrated into spatial planning. Despite the lack of clarity on ways of integrating the two concepts, there is a widespread agreement that these concepts can potentially make a positive contribution to Africa's urban futures if they are carefully considered and integrated. Realisation of this potential will require strong and effective institutions, renewed optimism in spatial planning practice that reflects local ideals and aspirations, and spatial reflections of sustainable development initiatives. The motivation to achieve this potential lies in the anticipated national and local governments' intervention, to provide appropriate investments and policies and to support appropriate planning and development strategies.

References

Adaawen, S., Rademacher-Schulz, C., Schraven, B., & Segadlo, N. (2019). Drought, migration, and conflict in sub-Saharan Africa: What are the links and policy options? *Current Directions in Water Scarcity Research, 2,* 15–31.

Adams, E. A., Price, H., & Stoler, J. B. (2019). Urban slums, drinking water, and health: Trends and lessons from Sub-Saharan Africa. In Vojnovic, I., Pearson, G. A., DeVerteuil, G., & Allen, A. (Eds.), *Handbook of global urban health* (pp. 533–552). New York: Routledge. 10.4324/9781315465456-34

Addae, B. A., Zhang, L., Zhou, P., & Wang, F. (2019). Analyzing barriers of Smart Energy City in Accra with two-step fuzzy DEMATEL. *Cities, 89,* 218–227.

Addaney, M., & Cobbinah, P. B. (2019). Climate change, urban planning and sustainable development in Africa: The difference worth appreciating. In Cobbinah, P. B., & Addaney, M. (Eds.), The geography of climate change adaptation in urban Africa (pp. 3-26). Cham: Palgrave Macmillan. https://doi.org/10.1007/978-3-030-04873-0_1

African Union, African Development Bank and United Nations Development Programme. (2018). *Africa sustainable development report.* Retrieved from https://www.africa.undp.org/content/rba/en/home/library/reports/africa-sustainable-development-report-2018.html

Ahmed, O. O., & Ogunola, S. O. (2016). Climate change: Effects and adaptive measures in Africa. *Journal of Geography, Environment and Earth Science International, 8*(1), 1–13.

Aidoo, K., & Briggs, R. C. (2019). Underpowered: Rolling blackouts in Africa disproportionately hurt the poor. *African Studies Review, 62*(3), 112–131.

Akukwe, T. I. (2019). *Spatial analysis of the effects of flooding on food security in Agrarian communities of South Eastern Nigeria* (Doctoral dissertation). Nairobi: University of Nairobi.

Alexander, E. R. (2016). There is no planning – only planning practices: Notes for spatial planning theories. *Planning Theory, 15*(1), 91–103.

Aluko, O. J., Bobadoye, A. O., & Adejumo, A. A. (2019). Perceived effects of damage caused by flood on change in livelihood security along gender line in Ido local government of Oyo State, Nigeria. *Journal of Sustainable Environmental Management, 11,* 47–55.

Basson, M., van Rensburg, H., Cuthill, M., & Erdiaw-Kwasie, M. O. (2018). Is regional government-governance nexus delivering on social sustainability promises? Empirical evidence from Moranbah in Australia. *Local Government Studies, 44*(6), 826–847.

Becker, F., & Frankema, E. (2019). Poverty in Africa. In Greve, B. (Ed.), *Routledge International Handbook of Poverty (pp. 203-216).* London: Routledge.

Berke, P. R., & Conroy, M. M. (2000). Are we planning for sustainable development? *Journal of the American Planning Association, 66*(1), 21–33. doi:10.1080/01944360008976081

Berrisford, S. (2011, September). Unravelling apartheid spatial planning legislation in South Africa. *Urban Forum, 22*(3), 247–263.

Broto, V. C. (2017). Urban governance and the politics of climate change. *World Development, 93,* 1–15.

Brown, D. (2011). Making the linkages between climate change adaptation and spatial planning in Malawi. *Environmental Science & Policy, 14*(8), 940–949.

Cameron, R., & Katzschner, T. (2017). Every last drop: The role of spatial planning in enhancing integrated urban water management in the City of Cape Town. *South African Geographical Journal*, 99(2), 196–216.

Chigudu, A., & Chirisa, I. (2020). The quest for a sustainable spatial planning framework in Zimbabwe and Zambia. *Land Use Policy*, 92(2020), 1–7. doi:10.1016/j.landusepol.2019.104442

Chiodelli, F., & Mazzolini, A. (2019). Inverse planning in the cracks of formal land use regulation: The bottom-up regularisation of informal settlements in Maputo, Mozambique. *Planning Theory & Practice*, 20(2), 165–181.

Cobbinah, P. B. (2021). Urban resilience in climate change hotspot. *Land Use Policy*, 100, 104948.

Cobbinah, P. B., & Adams, E. A. (2018). Urbanization and electric power crisis in Ghana: Trends, policies, and socio-economic implications. In Benna, I., & Benna, U. G. (Eds.), *Urbanization and its impact on socio-economic growth in developing regions* (pp. 262–284). Hershey, PA. USA: IGI Global.

Cobbinah, P. B., & Addaney, M. (Eds.). (2019). *The geography of climate change adaptation in Urban Africa*. Cham: Palgrave Macmillan.

Cobbinah, P. B., & Darkwah, R. M. (2016). Toward a more desirable form of sustainable urban development in Africa. *African Geographical Review*. doi: 10.1080/1937681.2016.1208770

Cobbinah, P. B., & Darkwah, R. M. (2017). Urban planning and politics in Ghana. *GeoJournal*, 82(6), 1229–1245.

Cobbinah, P. B., & Erdiaw-Kwasie, M. O. (2018). Urbanization in Ghana: Insights and implications for urban governance. In Information Resources Management Association (Ed.), *E-planning and collaboration: Concepts, methodologies, tools, and applications* (pp. 256–278). Hershey, PA, USA: IGI Global.

Cobbinah, P. B., Erdiaw-Kwasie, M. O., & Amoateng, P. (2015). Africa's urbanisation: Implications for sustainable development. *Cities*, 47, 62–72. doi:10.1016/j.cities.2015.03.013

Cobbinah, P. B., & Poku-Boansi, M. (2018). Towards resilient cities in Ghana: Insights and strategies. *Futures*, 101(2018), 55–66.

Coquery-Vidrovitch, C. (2005). African urban spaces. In Steven J. Salm, Toyin Falola (Eds.), *African urban spaces in historical perspective*. Rochester, NY. USA: University of Rochester Press.

Corburn, J., & Sverdlik, A. (2019). Informal settlements and human health. In *Integrating Human Health into Urban and Transport Planning* (pp. 155–171). Cham: Springer.

Cosgrove, W. J., & Loucks, D. P. (2015). Water management: Current and future challenges and research directions. *Water Resources Research*, 51(6), 4823–4839.

Curry, N. (2012). Community participation in spatial planning: exploring relationships between professional and lay stakeholders. *Local Government Studies*, 38(3), 345–366.

Dahiya, B., & Das, A. (2020). New Urban Agenda in Asia-Pacific: governance for sustainable and inclusive cities. In *New urban agenda in Asia-Pacific* (pp. 3–36). Singapore: Springer.

Diaw, K., Nnkya, T., & Watson, V. (2002). Planning education in sub-Saharan Africa: Responding to the demands of a changing context. *Planning Practice and Research*, 17(3), 337–348.

Emenike, C. P., Tenebe, I. T., Omole, D. O., Ngene, B. U., Oniemayin, B. I., Maxwell, O., & Onoka, B. I. (2017). Accessing safe drinking water in sub-Saharan Africa: Issues and challenges in South–West Nigeria. *Sustainable Cities and Society, 30*, 263–272.

Erdiaw-Kwasie, M. O., & Basson, M. (2018). Reimagining socio-spatial planning: Towards a synthesis between sense of place and social sustainability approaches. *Planning Theory, 17*(4), 514–532.

Erdiaw-Kwasie, M. O., Abunyewah, M., Edusei, J., & Alimo, E. B. (2020). Citizen participation dilemmas in water governance: An empirical case of Kumasi, Ghana. *World Development Perspectives, 20*, 100242.

Forster, T., & Ammann, C. (2018). African cities and the development conundrum. *International Development Policy, 10*, 3–25.

Fukuda-Parr, S., & Muchhala, B. (2020). The Southern origins of sustainable development goals: Ideas, actors, aspirations. *World Development, 126*. 10.1016/j.worlddev.2019.104706.

Funder, M., Mweemba, C., & Nyambe, I. (2018). The politics of climate change adaptation in development: Authority, resource control and state intervention in rural Zambia. *The Journal of Development Studies, 54*(1), 30–46.

Fuseini, I., & Kemp, J. (2015). A review of spatial planning in Ghana's socio-economic development trajectory: A sustainable development perspective. *Land Use Policy, 47*, 309–320.

Giugni, M., Simonis, I., Bucchignani, E., Capuano, P., De Paola, F., Engelbrecht, F., Mercogliano, P. & Topa, M. (2015). The impacts of climate change on African cities. In: Pauleit S. et al. (Eds.), *Urban Vulnerability and Climate Change in Africa*. Cham: Springer.

Grasham, C. F., Korzenevica, M., & Charles, K. J. (2019). On considering climate resilience in urban water security: A review of the vulnerability of the urban poor in sub-Saharan Africa. *Wiley Interdisciplinary Reviews: Water, 6*(3), e1344.

Habib, S., Jamil, M., & Ahmed, E. (2019). Slums: Prevalence, prevention and solutions. *WALIA journal 35*(1), 146-153

Healey, P. (1996). The communicative turn in planning theory and its implications for spatial strategy formation. *Environment and Planning B, 23*(2), 217–234. 10.1068%2Fb230217

Healey, P. (2010). *Making better places: The planning project in the twenty-first century*. London: Macmillan International Higher Education.

Hersperger, A. M., Oliveira, E., Pagliarin, S., Palka, G., Verburg, P., Bolliger, J., & Grădinaru, S. (2018). Urban land-use change: The role of strategic spatial planning. *Global Environmental Change, 51*, 32–42.

Holden, E., Linnerud, K., & Banister, D. (2017). The imperatives of sustainable development. *Sustainable Development, 25*(2017), 213–226.

Jenks, M., & Jones, C. A. (2010). Issues and concepts. In M. Jenks, & C. Jones (Eds.), *Dimensions ofthe sustainable city* (pp. 1–19). Dordrecht, Heidelberg, London and New York: Springer.

Kamete, A. Y. (2013). Missing the point? Urban planning and the normalisation of 'pathological' spaces in southern Africa. *Transactions of the Institute of British Geographers, 38*(4), 639–651.

Keeton, R., & Nijhuis, S. (2019). Spatial challenges in contemporary African New Towns and potentials for alternative planning strategies. *International Planning Studies*, *24*(3-4), 218–234.

Kemausuor, F., & Ackom, E. (2017). Toward universal electrification in Ghana. *Wiley Interdisciplinary Reviews: Energy and Environment*, *6*(1), e225.

Klopp, J. M., & Petretta, D. L. (2017). The urban sustainable development goal: Indicators, complexity and the politics of measuring cities. *Cities*, *63*(2017), 92–97.

Kogo, B. K., Kumar, L., & Koech, R. (2020). Climate change and variability in Kenya: A review of impacts on agriculture and food security. *Environment, Development and Sustainability*, *23*(1), 23-43..

Korah, P. I., Cobbinah, P. B., & Nunbogu, A. M. (2017). Spatial planning in Ghana: Exploring the contradictions. *Planning Practice & Research*, *32*(4), 361–384.

Kubanza, N. S., & Simatele, D. (2016). Social and environmental injustices in solid waste management in sub-Saharan Africa: a study of Kinshasa, the Democratic Republic of Congo. *Local Environment*, *21*(7), 866–882.

Kumi, E. N. (2017). *The electricity situation in Ghana: Challenges and opportunities*. Washington, DC: Center for Global Development.

Lane, M. B. (2006). Public participation in planning: an intellectual history. *Australian Geographer*, *36*(3), 283–299.

Lebailly, P., & Muteba, D. (2011). Characteristics of urban food insecurity: The Case of Kinshasa. *African Review of economics and finance*, *3*(1), 58–68

Lotsu, S., Yoshida, Y., Fukuda, K., & He, B. (2019). Effectiveness of a power factor correction policy in improving the energy efficiency of large-scale electricity users in Ghana. *Energies*, *12*(13), 10.3390/en12132582

Lubida, A., Veysipanah, M., Liesjo, P., & Mansourian, A. (2018). Land-use planning for sustainable urban development in Africa: A spatial and multi-objective optimization approach. *Geodesy and Cartography*, *45*(1), 1–15.

Mabogunje, A. L. (1990). Urban planning and the post-colonial state in Africa: A research overview 1. *African Studies Review*, *33*(2), 121–203.

Magis, K., & Shinn, C. (2009). Emergent themes of social sustainability. In J. Dillard, V. Dujon, & M. King (Eds.), *Understanding the social aspect of sustainability* (pp. 97–121). New York: Routledge.

Mensah, G. S., Kemausuor, F., & Brew-Hammond, A. (2014). Energy access indicators and trends in Ghana. *Renewable and Sustainable Energy Reviews*, *30*, 317–323.

Muchadenyika, D. (2015). Slum upgrading and inclusive municipal governance in Harare, Zimbabwe: New perspectives for the urban poor. *Habitat International 2015*, *48*, 1–10.

Newborne, P., & Tucker, J. (2015). *The urban–rural Water interface: A preliminary study in Burkina Faso*. PRISE working paper. https://www.odi.org/sites/odi.org.

Nogués, S., González-González, E., & Cordera, R. (2019). Planning regional sustainability: An index-based framework to assess spatial plans. Application to the region of Cantabria (Spain). *Journal of Cleaner Production*, *225*, 510–523. doi:10.1016/j.jclepro.2019.03.328

Odendaal, N. (2012). Reality check: Planning education in the African urban century. *Cities*, 29(3), 174–182.

Okpala, D. (2009). Regional overview of the status of urban planning and planning practice in Anglophone (Sub-Saharan) African countries. In: Mutizwa-Mangiza, N. D. (Ed.), *United Nations Human Settlement Programme, Regional study for Global Report on Human Settlement, Nairobi*. UN-Habitat.

Oliveira, E., Tobias, S., & Hersperger, A. M. (2018). Can strategic spatial planning contribute to land degradation reduction in urban regions? State of the art and future research. *Sustainability*, 10(4), 949.

Omisore, A. G. (2018). Attaining sustainable development goals in sub-Saharan Africa; the need to address environmental challenges. *Environmental Development*, 25, 138–145.

Orenstein, D. E., & Shach-Pinsley, D. (2017). A Comparative framework for assessing sustainability initiatives at the regional scale. *World Development*, 98, 245–256. doi:10.1016/j.worlddev.2017.04.030

Owolabi, A. (2017). Increasing population, urbanization and climatic factors in Lagos State, Nigeria: The nexus and implications on water demand and supply. *Journal of Global Initiatives: Policy, Pedagogy, Perspective*, 11(2), 6.

Pacioni, M. (2019). The rhetoric and reality of public participation in planning. *Urban Development Issues*, 63(1). 10.2478/udi-2019-0012

Persson, C. (2013). Deliberation or doctrine? Land use and spatial planning for sustainable development in Sweden. *Land Use Policy*, 34(2013), 301–313. doi:10.1016/j.landusepol.2013.04.007

Pieterse, E., Parnell, S., & Haysom, G. (2018). African dreams: Locating urban infrastructure in the 2030 sustainable developmental agenda. *Area Development and Policy*, 3(2), 149–169.

Reimer, M., Getimis, P., & Blotevogel, H. (2014). *Spatial planning systems and practices in Europe*. London: Routledge.

Rogerson, C. M., & Rogerson, J. M. (2015). Johannesburg 2030: The economic contours of a "linking global city". *American Behavioral Scientist*, 59(3), 347–368

Sachs, J. D. (2012). From millennium development goals to sustainable development goals. *The Lancet*, 379(9832), 2206–2211.

Salm, S. J., & Falola, T. (Eds.). (2009). *African urban spaces in historical perspective* (Vol. 21). Rochester, NY. USA: University Rochester Press.

Satterthwaite, D. (2016). A new urban agenda? *Environment and Urbanization*, 28(1), 3–12. doi:10.1177/0956247816637501

Satterthwaite, D., Sverdlik, A., & Brown, D. (2019). Revealing and responding to multiple health risks in informal settlements in sub-Saharan African cities. *Journal of Urban Health*, 96(1), 112–122.

Segura, S., & Pedregal, B. (2017). Monitoring and Evaluation Framework for Spatial Plans: A Spanish Case Study. *Sustainability*, 2017(9). doi:10.3390/su9101706

Schindler, S. (2017). The New Urban Agenda in an era of unprecedented global challenges. *International Development Planning Review*, 39, 349–374.

Sietchiping, R., Reid, J., & Omwamba, J. (2016). Implementing the SDGs and the New Urban Agenda. *Environment and Urbanization ASIA*, 7(2), x–xii. doi:10.1177/0975425316660664

Silva, C. N. (2015). *Urban planning in Sub-Saharan Africa: Colonial and post-colonial planning cultures*. London: Taylor & Francis.

Stren, R. E. & White, R. R. (Eds.). (2019). *African cities in crisis: Managing rapid urban growth*. New York: Routledge.

Turok, I. (2010). The prospects for African urban economies. *Urban Research & Practice*, 3(1), 12–24

Turok, I., & Scheba, A. (2019). 'Right to the city' and the New Urban Agenda: Learning from the right to housing. *Territory, Politics, Governance*, 7(4), 494–510.

Udelsmann R. C. (2019). Climate change and DIY urbanism in Luanda and Maputo: New urban strategies? *International Journal of Urban Sustainable Development*, 11(3), 319–331.

Un-Habitat. (2012). *State of the World's Cities 2008/9: Harmonious Cities*. London and New York: Routledge.

UN-Habitat. (2018). *Annual report 2012*. (Annual Progress Report). Retrieved from https://unhabitat.org/un-habitat-annual-report-2012

UN-Habitat. (2018). *Working for a better future*. (Annual Progress Report). Retrieved from https://unhabitat.org/annual-progress-report-2018.

Valencia, S. C., Simon, D., Croese, S., Nordqvist, J., Oloko, M., Sharma, T., Taylor, N., & Versace, I. (2019) Adapting the Sustainable Development Goals and the New Urban Agenda to the city level: Initial reflections from a comparative research project. *International Journal of Urban Sustainable Development*, 11(1), 4–23. doi: 10.1080/19463138.2019.1573172

WaterAid Australia. (2018). *Annual report 2018–19*. Retrieved from https://www.wateraid.org/au/wateraid-australia-annual-report-2018-19

Watson, V. (2016). Locating planning in the New Urban Agenda of the urban sustainable development goal. *Planning Theory*, 15, 435–448.

Wong, C. (2011). Decision-making and problem solving: turning indicators into a double-loop evaluation framework. In A. Hull, E. R. Alexander, A. Khakee, & J. Wolhuter (Eds.), *Evaluation for participation and sustainability in planning* (pp. 14–31). London and New York: Routledge.

World Bank. (2018). *Annual report*. Retrieved from http://documents1.worldbank.org/curated/en/630671538158537244/pdf/The-World-Bank-Annual-Report-2018.pdf

Zehra, D., Mbatha, S., Campos, L. C., Queface, A., Beleza, A., Cavoli, C., … & Parikh, P. (2019). Rapid flood risk assessment of informal urban settlements in Maputo, Mozambique: The case of Maxaquene A. *International Journal of Disaster Risk Reduction*, 40, 101270.

3 Tradition Meets Modernity: Creation of Sustainable Urban Spaces in Africa

Bernard Afiik Akanpabadai Akanbang,
Millicent Awialie Akaateba, and
Prosper Issahaku Korah

Introduction

The relevance of integrating traditional and modern land governance systems and institutions in the production of sustainable urban spaces in sub-Saharan African cities has gained prominence. In Africa, where much of the urban transformations of the 21st century is predicted to occur, land management has become a major challenge due to the existence of plural land tenure systems. Under neoliberal conditions, there has been a shift in how land is governed including but not limited to the commodification of land with outcomes such as social differentiation, increasing inequality and exclusion of the urban poor in land use decisions (Chimhowu & Woodhouse, 2006). Yet, social inclusiveness is recognised as an important pillar in the quest towards achieving sustainable urban development in Africa. Land administration is thus a critical development issue as land serves multiple purposes: as a source of income, food, employment, export earnings, a place of settlement, burial sites, sacred woodlands, and spiritual life (Commission for Africa, 2005; Cotula et al., 2004; Kameri-Mbote, 2016). Access to land and the ability to make effective use of it are therefore critical to the welfare of people. The growing commodification of land caused by population growth; the rising value of real estate and the expansion of urban residential areas; the development of new commercial export agricultural sectors; the extinction of remaining agricultural frontiers; and increasing inequity in the face of land shortage have together highlighted the importance of developing policies and academic discourses on land and land reform agendas across the continent (Abudulai, 2002).

Land use planning is a tool to generate sustainable evolution of human settlements in the face of rapid urbanisation, globalisation and neoliberalisation (UN-Habitat, 2009). Yet effective land use planning – the ability of planning to regulate land uses to achieve harmony, curtail urban sprawl and ensure sustainability (Berke & Conroy, 2000) – especially in Africa remains a dream rather than a reality. One of the critical challenges of Africa today is how to deal with the problem of rapidly increasing unplanned urban settlements particularly in contexts of customary land tenure

DOI: 10.4324/9781003181484-3

systems (Chigbu et al., 2019). This increasing unplanned growth is partly associated with a unique phenomenon where formal/modern institutions – planning departments, prepare land use plans with the expectation of implementing them on customary lands which are controlled by traditional authorities (Kleemann et al., 2017; Yeboah & Shaw, 2013). Thus, many land use plans are either not implemented or ignored because of weak intuitional capacities of formal planning institutions and poor coordination between state institutions and non-state institutions in the administration of land resulting in uncontrolled and unsustainable urban development patterns (Akaateba et al., 2018; Yeboah & Shaw, 2013). Where there is no clarity on the difference between ownership of land and prescribed use of land, it creates fundamental problems for physical planning authorities. Besides, the fact that the use of a parcel of land affects other adjoining parcels makes its ownership systems and administration critical to the success of physical planning which is needed for the creation of sustainable spaces and inclusive cities as envisaged by SDG 11 and the New Urban Agenda. Sustainable urban spaces as used in this chapter refer to the use of urban spaces in a manner that leads to a balance between the built and natural environments in line with population growth patterns.

Various reforms have been undertaken in the land sector in Africa (Cotula et al., 2004; Kameri-Mbote, 2016). Unfortunately, even though much research has gone into examining the effectiveness of these reforms (Cotula et al., 2004), not many, with the exception of Sim et al. (2018) and Akaateba (2018), have holistically examined the influence of the "adaptation approach" to land governance in Africa. "Adaptation approach" as used in this chapter refers to the integration of traditional and modern systems of land administration in land use planning and sustainable urban space development. Effective land administration and land use planning enable the transfer of different land use rights from one party to another permissible by zoning and local plan provisions. Thus, effective land administration recognises the role of planning authorities in the determination of the use of land. The role of governance and legislation in ensuring harmony between land administration and land use planning is thus critical to the realisation of the goals of physical planning. A comprehensive understanding of this link is critical if land use planning is to achieve its primary objective of promoting sustainable human settlements development based on the principles of efficiency, orderliness, safety and healthy growth of communities. This chapter aims at answering two critical questions. First, what is the nature of relationships between traditional and modern land institutions in land use planning in urban Africa? And second, how do the existing relationships facilitate or constrain the creation of sustainable urban spaces?

In what follows is an overview of the method and research design for the online literature search and the empirical case study. Section 3 examines the evolution of customary land administration systems in sub-Saharan Africa (SSA). Section 4 presents land use planning and sustainable urbanisation in Africa. Section 5 is about the interface between hybrid land administration and the creation of sustainable spaces in Africa. Section 6 presents the conclusion with recommendations for future research and policy in order to produce sustainable built environments across Africa.

Methods and Research Design

Scholarly electronic databases were searched to identify research articles published in English language journals related to land governance and spatial development in SSA focusing on Anglophone countries. The scope of the search was limited to countries in Africa with dual land tenure systems. The search was conducted in the following dominant scholarly databases: Scopus, ScienceDirect, ProQuest, Sage, and Google Scholar. The search terms were "urban spatial development in Africa" and a combination of terms including: "land administration," "customary land tenure," "urbanisation," "governance," "spatial planning," "land use planning," "sustainability" and "land reforms." In the process of downloading lead searched articles, suggested related articles were downloaded. This was the case for articles downloaded from the Science Direct database. Additional papers were identified from the reference list of those research papers downloaded through the database search. To capture the changing dynamics of customary tenure systems across SSA, the literature search covered the period from the late 1980s to 2020. Key issues from the downloaded papers were then extracted and organised under various themes of the Chapter.

In addition to the literature review, results of a study conducted in 2017 by the first author in Wa (Ghana) were reported in this Chapter. Relevant interview quotes from this study were added to support some of the evidence reported in the literature. The study investigated the problems associated with growing fragmentation in land administration and draws implications for planning and development of Wa. In terms of methodology, the study deployed qualitative data gathering (i.e. interviews with key informants such as Tindanas and officials of land administration institutions) and observation. Wa is the capital of the Wa Municipality, one of the 11 Local Authorities that make up the Upper West Region of Ghana. Wa also doubles as the Regional Capital of the Upper West Region. The Wa Municipality has a population of 107,214 people, representing 15% of the population of the Upper West Region (Ghana Statistical Service, 2014). Presently, Wa is experiencing a radial and concentric growth pattern although this is under check by the administrative boundary and the Billi Dam to the North and the Forest Reserve to the East (stretching from Wa Senior High School to Tampaalipaani). Housing development is increasing at a fast rate particularly along the Wa-Kumasi road (where the University for Development Studies now SD Dombo University of Business and

Integrated Development Studies is also located), the Wa-Kpongu road and the SSNIT Flats-Bamahu belt. Land administration in Wa has evolved from being under the control of one Tindana to a fragmented ownership consisting of multiple Tindanas, families and individuals. The fragmented land administration and management structures coupled with the increasing pace of physical development (with limited planning) makes Wa an important reference for grounding the discussion on the creation of sustainable urban spaces under plural land tenure systems in Ghana and other secondary cities in SSA. To contextualise the study within the broader Ghanaian land ownership context, case study data were also drawn from an earlier study conducted and reported in (Akaateba, 2018, 2019) in the secondary towns of Tamale and Techiman, Ghana where chiefs rather than Tindanas are the main custodians of land. The next section examines the evolution of customary land administration in SSA.

The Evolution of Customary Land Administration Systems in SSA

Land for a greater part of SSA has been held under customary tenure for generations and remains today a significant type of tenure (Chigbu et al., 2019; Cotula et al., 2004; Kameri-Mbote, 2016). While it is possible to identify some major trends in customary land administration across SSA, it is worth emphasising that customary rights to land are dynamic and diverse, and largely depend on localised historical, geographical, economic, social, political and cultural factors (Cotula et al., 2004; Kasanga & Kotey, 2001). As such, a generalisation of customary tenure systems in Africa is problematic. Largely, however, customary rights to land are understood as general rights to use land without depriving others of access to it, except by prior and continuing use. Lentz (2006) revealed that customary tenure in Africa is characterised by the presence of a "bundle of owners" of land from a property-holding group which has fuzzy geographical boundaries. She argues that under customary tenure, multiple layers of rights and interests can exist in a given piece of land making customary land tenure systems across SSA to be continuously evolving.

Customary land tenure is deeply embedded in culture and the values contained in culture (Chigbu et al., 2019; Cotula et al., 2004). A key tenet of customary land tenure is that land is held in trust on behalf of the community or family. That is, "land belongs to a vast family of which many are dead, few are living and countless numbers are still unborn" (Chanock 1991, p. 64 cited in Chimhowu & Woodhouse, 2006; Kasanga & Kotey, 2001). Land rights are vested in current tribal or lineage leadership by virtue of lineage ancestors' claims on land through first clearance and settlement, or conquest (Cotula et al., 2004). The process by which land rights are transmitted are through inheritance or succession or donation, long occupation or market transaction (Toulmin, 2009). Individuals claim usufruct rights to land through membership of lineages with such rights normally being inherited by sons or nephews. In some cases, these rights are transferable to heirs or can be sold; in others, consent must be sought from the underlying rights-holder (Toulmin, 2009). Land is also inalienable from the lineage, reverting to the control of lineage leaders in the absence of individuals to exercise inheritance rights. The inalienability and re-allocation processes within customary tenure protect access to land for poorer members of lineages in a flexible and efficient way without the need of land registry or cadastral surveys (Chimhowu & Woodhouse, 2006).

Over the years, indigenous land tenure arrangements in the sub-region have proven to be considerably flexible and allow for multiple ownership systems – individual, family and communal rights to coexist. Land in Wa, for instance, is owned by Tindana,[1] family and individuals as identified from a field survey in 2017 and depicted in Table 3.1.

Land in the past was mostly not for sale, and monetary value was not attached to land (Kasanga & Kotey, 2001). A Tindana in Wa buttressed the non-commodification of land in the past as follows:

> In ancient days, an individual, whether a native or an in-migrant, was required to provide only cola-nut and one bottle of schnapps and two fowls to acquire land for settlement. No financial commitment was required to settle people, and there was no documentation done, but the people respected the customs and traditions of their settlers and paid homage to them annually through the provision of new foodstuffs such as tubers of yam and first millet harvested just to let their settlers know that they recognise them as people who gave them the land to settle (Interview with Tindana, July 2017).

The value of land was high but not in economic terms, even though it has always been a source of livelihood for the people. It was more in terms of the spiritual significance, which is not devoid of economics, because land was perceived as the god that provided the people with their social and economic needs. For community leaders and kingdoms, it was seen as a status symbol as it denotes the size and importance of one's kingdom. The colonial period witnessed some level of urbanisation in SSA. Thus, growing population

Table 3.1 Type of land ownership

Type of Grantors	Frequency	Percentage
Tindana	42	42.4
Private Individuals	30	30.3
Family Land	17	17.2
Others	10	10.1
Total	99	100

pressures and increasing urbanisation birthed a gradual but significant change in land tenure practices (Kasanga & Kotey, 2001). Enhanced individualisation of tenure for exclusive use, increased incidence of land sale and monetary transactions in land characterised the tenure practices of the period. Outright sale of land, though often redeemable to the seller, also began to take place, running counter to one of the most deeply rooted customary limitations on land use. At first, sales were sanctioned only among members of the group (of common descent or residence), then to outsiders with approval of the group or its head, and now without such consent. In addition, sales may be initially subject to a right of pre-emption by family members or to a right of repurchase by the seller (Bruce, 1998).

The post-independence era witnessed an acceleration of individualisation and monetisation in customary land tenure, conflicts, larger-scale acquisitions, and enactment of laws on customary land (Kasanga & Kotey, 2001). An indigene in Tamale Ghana, in a study by Akaateba (2019, p. 5), revealed the monetisation and commodification of customary lands in peri-urban areas in the following statement:

> "In the olden days, if you wanted a plot to develop, you buy kolanuts and go and pay homage to the chief. The 'Wulana' would lead you to the chief to beg for land. Those days, they were not selling lands in this community, but now things have changed. Therefore, if you want a plot of land, but have no money, whether you are a native or whatever, the chiefs would not give you. They sell plots to everybody regardless of your relationship with them. Everything about land in this community is now a money matter" (In-depth interview, Indigene, Tamale, October 2015).

Likewise, a narrative by an informant shows how commodification and monetisation of land is the source of land conflicts in Wa.

> These conflicts started when land began to be seen as a commodity. Initial settlers began having problems with later day settlers over boundary delineations because when land was given, there were no defined boundaries. With increasing population and expansion of settlements the issue of where each settlement and communal boundary ended became an issue" (Interview with Tindana, July 2017, Wa)

The integration of rural areas into the market economy and increasing population accounted for such changes in the customary land tenure. There has been a move away from family and share cropping arrangements to short-term rental and hiring arrangements. This has introduced increased insecurity and reduced investment incentives on land. The inalienability of land by individuals through commercial sales, rentals, or credit-related pledging was, however, resilient to the change (Malton, 1994). African tenure systems have dynamic arrangements which continue to recognise both individualised and group rights even under the pressure of rising land values. As such, "they can best be thought of as systems in which individual rights are maturing" (Land Tenure Center, 1990, p. 1). In the words of Bruce, the changes that have taken place have often not required radical revision of older tenure arrangements, nor have they often involved a conscious decision (Bruce, 1988, p. 33) by the community: instead, change has come in an unfolding of the internal logic of indigenous tenure systems in response to new circumstances (Bruce, 1988, p. 33). Customary land tenure has been perceived as a more legitimate "non-state" alternative that promises equity and security of access to land for the poor; and that it gives officially invisible, off-register rights that often form the basis for multiple livelihood strategies and therefore supports the modern view of land as an economic asset. Ubink (2008) and Akaateba (2018) have however questioned the equity, transparency and accountability issues with customary land tenure and assert that they provide avenues for exploitation by a few to enrich themselves. Customary land tenure has also been criticised for obscuring the multiple interests people have in land and, therefore, undermining the effectiveness and productivity in the use of land (Alcock & Hornby, 2004). De Soto (2000) identifies ambiguity and negotiability of rights under customary tenure as characteristics that lead to low rates of productivity-enhancing investment or land becoming a "dead capital" (Chimhowu & Woodhouse, 2006; De Soto, 2000).

These criticisms notwithstanding, customary tenure remains a dominant mode of land acquisition in many African cities. It exists alongside state land administration systems, thus creating a hybrid system of land administration where both traditional and modern rules of land management become intertwined. Due to the individualisation and fragmentation of land under customary tenure today, this hybrid arrangement means that state planning authorities do have to deal with diverse individuals with interest in land as well as custodians of the land-owning community when planning for urban development. This has undermined the ease in terms of cooperation between customary land owners and planning agencies required for effective creation of sustainable spaces in urban areas. Besides, the commodification of land has come with it flourishing land markets in urban and peri-urban areas resulting in a trend in which physical development is ahead of institutionalised planning (Akaateba, 2019; Kasanga & Kotey, 2001; Korah, Nunbogu, & Akanbang, 2018). This trend presents huge challenges to orderly physical development and planners appear incapacitated in bringing development under control. The rising trend in litigations and conflicts related to customary land tenure thus has challenges for controlled development by planning authorities. This is because the needed cooperation required for planning authorities to prepare schemes to regulate the use of urban spaces is seriously affected under such situations, thus undermining the effectiveness of land use planning in promoting sustainable urban development.

Land Use Planning and Sustainable Urbanisation in Africa

As cities in Africa become centres of population growth and economic activity, they expand in size to accommodate the increasing demand for housing, transport, land and other activities. This expansion in physical and demographic terms has been linked to unsustainable urbanisation patterns in different contexts driven by various factors, including unrestrained production and consumption practices, globalisation, privatisation, unplanned urban growth, and weakening state regulatory powers among others (Cobbinah et al., 2015; Korah et al., 2019; UN Habitat, 2016).

Land use planning is considered one of the key mechanisms towards promoting the creation of sustainable cities in Africa (UN-Habitat, 2009). In recent times, there is a growing consensus that the evolution of cities depends on the way in which they are planned and managed, particularly if they are to become sustainable. The United Nations (UN) Habitat is championing a renewed effort at planning and governing cities to make them sustainable, resilient and inclusive via its Sustainable Development Goal (SDG) 11 and the New Urban Agenda. Renewed interest in the planning of cities is necessary in the wake of climate change and its impacts on urban areas such as flooding and extreme heatwaves. Sustainable urban planning and development is essential and necessary not only for creating safe and liveable cities but also for protecting natural areas and farmlands, which provide essential ecosystem benefits and livelihoods, respectively (Van Lier, 1998). Sustainable planning as used in this chapter, refers to a combination of knowledge, science and creativity to formulate, implement and evaluate a set of justified actions and activities within the public domain to achieve the three major dimensions of sustainability: environmental, economic and social. Sustainable urban development concerns the use of land in a manner that leads to the realisation of economic and social development, and environmental protection goals (Berke & Conroy, 2000).

As one of the approaches through which sustainable urban development can be achieved, land use planning is mostly used to regulate the use of land in order to curtail urban sprawl, protect the natural environment and farmlands, minimise flooding, reduce transportation cost, improve productivity, prevent land use conflicts, reduce exposure to pollutants, mitigate urban heat island and improve the quality of places, among others (Huxley, 2006; Jusuf et al., 2007; Van Lier, 1998). A review of the relationship between land use planning and health by Barton (2009) showed that while not discounting the role of individual factors in shaping health outcomes, there was a growing consensus in the literature that urban environment alleviates or worsens "well-being outcomes." Particularly, active travel such as cycling and walking are influenced by the level of access to outdoor recreational facilities, including parks and green spaces. Access to parks for socialising as observed by Barton (2009) is a determinant of mental-wellbeing. In Ghana, Awuah et al. (2014) found that land use planning generates substantial benefits for residential areas. Specifically, they found that tarred roads, availability of utility (water and electricity), concrete drain and formalised titles generate significant benefits for residential neighbourhoods.

Given the benefits associated with land use planning as described above, and specifically its role in contributing towards achieving SDG 11 and some of the principles and commitments of the New Urban Agenda, it is surprising that effective land use planning and regulation is limited in many African countries. Scholars have criticised the nature of land use planning in Africa, which is typically based on western planning ideals with little reference to local socio-economic conditions (Andersen et al., 2015; Korah et al., 2017; Watson, 2006). Andersen et al. (2015), based on an examination of the land use planning and development process in Maputo, Mozambique, found that the state's land use plans were often too detailed and impractical due to a failure to incorporate local conditions, a situation that leads to spontaneous structuring of urban land uses by inhabitants. Similarly, Sim et al (2018), observed that in the areas in eThekwini Municipality, South Africa, where traditional authorities exercise control over land allocation and governance, the municipality finds it challenging to fulfil its mandate of producing spatial development plans and enforcing those plans to protect green areas. In Wa, Ghana, the dominance of customary land administration has resulted in uncoordinated processes of documenting land transactions. As a result, formal documentation of land transactions is limited. Field studies conducted in 2017 revealed that only about 25% of lands were registered with the Lands commission with about 41% of land transactions not documented and the remaining 34% under various forms of customary documentation. The failure to document some land transactions in Wa has implications for the quality of physical planning and development control. Some areas in Wa have witnessed significant development without recourse to any planning scheme resulting in encroachment of open spaces and reservations for schools and sanitation areas. A respondent from the physical planning department complained about the difficulties involved in planning and controlling development under such a context.

> It is almost an impossibility to plan and enforce orderly physical development because developers would not seek authorisation before developing. The few who seek authorisation especially in areas without planning schemes, a note and plotting is made of the land and it is used at the office for the purposes of subsequent planning (Interview with Physical Planner, Wa, June 2017).

The above challenges with land use planning and development are not limited to Wa nor Ghanaian cities but are widespread across SSA cities such as Maputo (Andersen et al., 2015) and eThekwini Municipality, South Africa (Sim et al., 2018) as indicated earlier. In Nigeria, Aribigbola (2008) found that land use planning in the city of Akure was exclusively concerned with granting permits for the use of land for various purposes without adequate development control. Without adequate development control and enforcement of land use plans, gains such as sprawl reduction, flood risks minimisation, protection of the natural environment, mitigation against pollutants and natural disasters that are associated with land use planning would be missed.

Several factors underlie the ineffectiveness of land use planning in Africa, among which include the nature of land tenure regime (Gough & Yankson, 2000; Larbi, 1996; Yeboah & Shaw, 2013), lack of local citizen participation (Kleemann et al., 2017), failure to incorporate local socioeconomic conditions (Andersen et al., 2015), and institutional inadequacies leading to non-enforcement of land use plans (Aribigbola, 2008; Cobbinah & Korah, 2016). In many African cities that are experiencing unguided spatial expansion, green areas and prime agricultural lands are being replaced by urban uses (Cobbinah & Amoako, 2012; Korah et al., 2018). In addition, political interference, inadequate staffing, and limited financial resources mean that the land use planning departments in many African countries are unable to monitor and guide development outcomes (Aribigbola, 2008; Cobbinah & Korah, 2016). Consequently, the unfolding patterns of spatial development in most African cities become disjointed, fragmented, and highly unsustainable (Cobbinah et al., 2015; Korah et al., 2019; Sumari et al., 2019). Across many cities in Africa, dual land tenure regimes comprising both traditional and modern systems of land administration that have established separate inisitutional arrangements for land ownership and modernist planning have often been linked to the failure of land use planning to generate sustainable urban development (Goodfellow & Lindemann, 2013; Nnkya, 2007; Owusu-Ansah & Braimah, 2013; Simelane, 2016). For instance, in Ghana, more than 80% of land is owned and controlled by individuals, families and chiefs with less than 20% possessed by the state (Gough & Yankson, 2000). This land ownership arrangement implies that families and chiefs constitute the major source of land release for developmental purposes across Ghanaian towns and cities (Larbi et al., 2003). Thus, land use plans are often prepared with the expectation of implementing them on mainly private land. Distortions in the land market create a phenomenon of unguided physical development without appropriate land use planning schemes (Owusu-Ansah & Braimah, 2013; Siiba et al., 2017). Consequently, many land use planning related challenges such as unplanned urban developments, flooding, land speculation, sprawling urban developments, limited documentation of land transactions, land commodification and land tenure security which should be addressed by planning authorities are entirely beyond their control as they have no control over the lands they manage. The discussion here is situated in the discourse on the land-tenure induced planning challenges in Africa by unearthing how these problems of hybrid land administration systems negatively affect the creation of sustainable urban spaces in Africa.

The Interface Between Hybrid Land Administration and the Creation of Sustainable Spaces in Africa

In Africa, the urban land question is one of the main challenges to sustainable urbanisation. Consequently, governments and international development actors have grappled with issues of land ownership, tenure and security. The issue of land administration is compounded in SSA by the non-homogeneous land ownership structure (Antwi & Adams, 2003; Arko-Adjei, 2011; Nnkya, 2007). This has generated clear and practicable distinctions between land ownership and land use rights, which tend to undermine sustainable land use planning. For instance, in Ghana, despite the passing of the Land Use and Spatial Planning Act, 2016 (Act 925) to integrate the spatial and socio-economic aspects of planning and to serve as a linchpin for strengthening the land use planning system in the country, the Act has not been able to address the complex challenges surrounding the dual (statutory and customary) land management system in the country (Akaateba, 2018). Therefore, the dual but interrelated mandate of who owns land and who controls the use to which land is put has become the bane of sustainable land use planning in SSA. This is because, in contexts of rapid urbanisation, chiefs and other customary land custodians have assumed pseudo-land use rights positions, re-interpreting customary land rights and usurping the planning roles of the formal planning authorities; creating and exacerbating the trend of development leading planning. For instance, a planning officer in Tamale, Ghana bemoaned:

> ... here in the Northern Region, the chiefs are so powerful that they have managed to (...) ... eeer ..., to suppress the people who are there. For instance, if I am made a chief of a particular community and there is a piece of land that people have been farming on, I can just give it to somebody to build on without even consulting the person who is getting his sustenance from that place. (In-depth interview, Senior Planner, Tamale; September 2015) cited in Akaateba (2018, p. 5)

In Wa, it was found that about 87%, 75% and 74% of respondents acquired lands that were not accessible by road, did not have potable water and electricity, respectively. Likewise, in other Ghanaian towns, customary land owners through informal collaborative arrangements with land sector institutions or unilaterally, prepare and or alter land use subdivision plans and allocate customary lands without planning approval, thus altering planning schemes (Barry & Danso, 2014; Kuusaana & Eledi, 2015; Siiba et al., 2017; Yeboah & Shaw, 2013). For instance, Barry and

Danso (2014, p. 364) bemoaned how in Accra Ghana, chiefs allocate farmlands for residential development without planning approval: "it is surprising that land disposals may be surveyed and registered on the edge of a large city without land use planning approval by state planning agencies and verification that new sub-division parcels comply with a land use plan". Likewise, in many rapidly urbanising Ghanaian towns and cities, agricultural uses are seldom given priority in local plans by chiefs (Ayambire et al., 2019; Korah et al., 2018; Kuusaana & Eledi, 2015), hence urban agriculture is unable to compete with other land uses such as residential and commercial. This coupled with increasing land values due to rapid urbanisation and the weak resource capacities of the local planning authorities to enforce development controls in many African cities (Arimah & Adeagbo, 2000; Chome & McCall, 2005; Nkurunziza, 2006; Nnkya, 2007; Onyebueke & Ikejiofor, 2017; Yeboah & Shaw, 2013) have made the creation of sustainable urban spaces a distant reality. This is because planning authorities are unable to ensure efficient and planned urban development in order to achieve the balance of social, economic and environmental interests.

Besides the challenges posed by the land ownership systems, the challenges of limited documentation of land transactions reported in many African countries (Bennett et al., 2013; Boamah, 2013; Mahama & Antwi, 2006; Oluwadare & Kufoniyi, 2019) have significant implications on sustainable urban development. Within customary tenure systems where a given piece of land has a "bundle of owners" and multiple interests and rights associated with it, the limited documentation of land transactions is often associated with multiple land sales/transactions (Boamah, 2013; Lavigne Delville, 2004; Toulmin, 2009). This has led to land litigations and conflicts and tenure insecurity on the continent, which have not only claimed lives but affected livelihoods. Land conflicts and litigations associated with customary land acquisitions, peri-urban land conversions and land use planning have variously been reported for various peri-urban towns in Tanzania (Magigi & Drescher, 2010; Nnkya, 2007), Mali (Neimark et al., 2018; Rakodi & Leduka, 2004), Lesotho (Leduka, 2006), Zambia (Tembo & Sommerville, 2018) and Ghana (Ubink, 2008). These litigations and conflicts associated with land administration undermine the process of sustainable land use planning.

In Wa, an informant revealed succinctly the effect of land conflicts and litigations on land use planning process in the following remarks:

The development of planning schemes is abandoned midway because of conflicts in relation to ownership rights. This is because once the land is under litigation, it becomes very dangerous to go into such lands to take data because the conflicting parties each view you as being in bed with the other party. Under such circumstances, while the planning authority pauses the development of the scheme, the conflict parties go ahead to parcel and sell out plots to trustees who proceed to develop the lands without registering them and or acquiring building permit (Interview with Physical Planning Department, June 2017, Wa).

The COVID 19 Pandemic has heightened the importance and necessity of open spaces in cities as isolation and treatment centres; hence the need for open spaces to be created and protected in African cities cannot be over-emphasised. This notwithstanding, the creation and sustainability of open spaces in Ghanaian towns remains problematic. Akaateba (2018) reports for Tamale and Techiman Ghana that because lands designated as open spaces are not economically rewarding, chiefs often covert them to commercial and residential land uses which are more profitable, thus undermining the effectiveness of formal land use plans. A planner in the following remarks lamented on the practice:

> Here in Tamale, planners are grappling with the unauthorised conversion of lands designated for open spaces into residential uses. Within the plan, we allocate areas on the plan for public open spaces but the Assembly does not take the initiative to compensate the land owners and acquire such lands. When it happens this way and later on the chiefs realise that the area has been engulfed with development, and it is lying fallow in the community, they start doing illegal rezoning (In-depth interview, Planner, Techiman, August 2016).

A chief confirmed this practice of re-zoning public land with the following explanation:

> After spending money to prepare a Local Plan, I think it is incumbent upon the Assembly to acquire some of the land allocated for public uses in the plan and pay compensation to us the land owners. However, this is where the Assembly is falling short. ... Therefore, if the areas become developed and we see bushes where people are leaving, the chiefs feel the Assembly does not need it. So, we apply for rezoning of the area and sometimes we do the rezoning ourselves leading lands earmarked for public use turning into residential use. (In-depth interview, Divisional Chief, Techiman, October 2015) cited in Akaateba (2018, p. 65)

Besides challenges associated with the management of public and green spaces, urban sprawl characterised by sparse low dense developments in peri-urban areas and land speculation in African cities is yet another set of urban sustainability challenges that have variously been associated with the ineffectiveness of the hybrid land administration systems in Africa (Cobbinah & Aboagye, 2017; Olujimi, 2009; Zevenbergen et al., 2015). In many countries, there is an increasing, scramble for land and speculative land buying (Benjaminsen et al., 2008), which is largely responsible for the phenomenon described in many African countries as "planning following development rather than development following planning." Some speculative developers acquire parcels of land and live them undeveloped leading to agricultural land scarcity and sprawling urban development and hence inefficiencies in land use planning. Thus land speculation, characterised by large parcels of undeveloped or partially developed land is perhaps the major challenge to urban sustainability that urban planners are grappling with in Africa (Bugri, 2012; Obeng-Odoom, 2016). In Wa, an informant captured the effect of speculative buying of land on the creation of sustainable urban spaces in the following:

> The result of speculative buying is that these areas have witnessed demarcation and parceling of land ahead of the areas being declared planned areas. Land owners in a bit to cash in on demand, parcel out land without recourse to the appropriate planning agency and in the process create problems for the orderly development of such neighborhoods (Interview with Physical Planning Department, July 2017).

The situation is compounded in most African cities because of the huge deficit in housing supply. The gap between supply and demand for housing has created a huge market for private estate developers who acquire large prime agriculture land for housing development. Even though such areas have a planning scheme, it undermines equitable and inclusive spatial development. The problem of land speculation is also heightened by the absence of explicit policies to control land speculation. Property taxes, for instance, in many countries in SSA, are only levied on buildings and not undeveloped land and the payment of annual ground rents is difficult to enforce as most land transactions and interests in land are not formally documented with legislated institutions. As a result, there is no deterring policy to prevent people from speculating in land. This coupled with uncontrolled urbanisation processes have made land use planning unable to manage urban growth resulting in sprawling urban developments which are problematic when it comes to infrastructure delivery. Sustainable land use planning is therefore threatened as land speculation induces urban sprawl which thwarts dense urban settlement development.

Alongside urban sprawl, land commodification as a result of rapid urbanisation and hybrid planning practices in many African cities is among the major issues that impede the creation of sustainable cities in Africa. This is because land commodification is shown to limit access to land by indigenous people, especially in urban and peri-urban areas (Akaateba, 2019; Kameri-Mbote, 2016; Ubink, 2008). Although a key feature of customary land tenure in Africa is that it is embedded in culture, the integration of modern and indigenous systems of land administration has fuelled the erosion of traditional values in land administration. This has weakened the communal land ownership where land is held in trust by an allodial title holder for the community and created in its place fragmentation of land (Kameri-Mbote, 2016; Ntihinyurwa et al., 2019) resulting in commodification and individualisation of land rights and their attendant consequences for land use planning. Thus, rather than land use planning securing the land use rights of peri-urban dwellers in Africa, in many hybrid planning situations, land use planning benefits public bureaucrats and traditional authorities and dispossesses indigenes who depend on land for various resources and livelihoods as planned customary land gains increased value and becomes commodified (Akaateba et al., 2018; Leduka, 2006; Ubink, 2007). Tenure responsive planning is however essential for sustainable development as it promotes inclusive and socially just cities. Besides, with the fragmentation and individualisation of land, acquisition of land for public use becomes problematic in terms of payment of compensation as well as negotiating with different people when a large tract of land is required. Similarly, the planning authority has so many people to collaborate with during the plan preparation process. The limited financial resources plaguing and undermining the abilities of planning authorities to proactively execute their development control functions is worsened further under a fragmented land ownership regime where the planning authorities have to deal with varied actors with diverse interests in land (Akaateba et al., 2018; Nnkya, 2007; Rakodi & Leduka, 2004; Yeboah & Obeng-Odoom, 2010).

Conclusion

Urbanisation is an irreversible phenomena and present enormous potential for poverty reduction. The creation of sustainable urban spaces is critical to tapping the potential urbanisation presents in the African continent. This chapter has shown that the creation of sustainable urban spaces in an African context largely involves resolving the problem of urban sprawl and protecting tenure security in urban contexts. In addition, the erosion of cultural values associated with land, the commodification and individualisation of land rights as well as the creation of a dual system where ownership and user rights reside in different people with unbalanced power create serious problems for planning for the creation of sustainable urban spaces. This coupled with the diverse interests – private and public in hybrid land use planning require that there is a strong regulatory and enforcement environment to manage the diverse interests in land if Africa is to be able to create urban spaces that are sustainable, equitable and inclusive. Even though a strong regulatory environment has been created for land governance, administration and management, enforcement is a prerequisite for laws to achieve their objectives. There should be open discussions and conclusions reached on how to in accord harmoniously implement the provisions in the laws that give ownership rights to allodial title holders and use rights to planning authorities. Detailed and comparative research and analysis of the different forms of hybrid planning practice within the dual land management relationship and their implications is needed to give further insight into which of the hybrid planning practices support the development of sustainable urban spaces.

Note

1 Landlord.

References

Abudulai, S. (2002). Land rights, land-use dynamics and policy in peri-urban Tamale, Ghana. In C. Toulmin, P. Lavigne Delville, & S. Traoré (Eds.), *The dynamics of resource tenure in West Africa* (pp. 72–85). London: James Currey, IIED.

Akaateba, M. A. (2018). *Urban planning practice under neo-customary land tenure: The interface between government agencies and traditional authorities in peri-urban Ghana* (Doctoral Dissertation). Berlin: Technische Universität Berlin.

Akaateba, M. A. (2019). The politics of customary land rights transformation in peri-urban Ghana: Powers of exclusion in the era of land commodification. *Land Use Policy, 88,* 104197.

Akaateba, M. A., Huang, H., & Adumpo, E. A. (2018). Between co-production and institutional hybridity in land delivery: Insights from local planning practice in peri-urban Tamale, Ghana. *Land Use Policy, 72,* 215–226.

Alcock, R., & Hornby, D. (2004). *Traditional land matters: A look into land administration in tribal areas in KwaZulu-Natal.* Legal Entity Assessment Project.

Andersen, J. E., Jenkins, P., & Nielsen, M. (2015). Who plans the African city? A case study of Maputo: Part 1 – the structural context. *International Development Planning Review, 37*(3), 329–350.

Antwi, A., & Adams, J. (2003). Economic rationality and informal urban land transactions in Accra, Ghana. *Journal of Property Research, 20*(1), 67–90.

Aribigbola, A. (2008). Imroving urban land use planning and management in Nigeria: The case of Akure. *Cercetări Practice Şi Teoretice În Managementul Urban, 3*(9), 1–14.

Arimah, B. C., & Adeagbo, D. (2000). Compliance with urban development and planning regulations in Ibadan, Nigeria. *Habitat International, 24*(3), 279–294.

Arko-Adjei, A. (2011). *Adapting land administration to the institutional framework of customary tenure: The case of peri-urban Ghana* (Doctoral dissertation). TU Delft: Delft University of Technology.

Awuah, K. G. B., Hammond, F. N., Lamond, J. E., & Booth, C. (2014). Benefits of urban land use planning in Ghana. *Geoforum, 51,* 37–46.

Ayambire, R. A., Amponsah, O., Peprah, C., & Takyi, S. A. (2019). A review of practices for sustaining urban and peri-urban agriculture: Implications for land use planning in rapidly urbanising Ghanaian cities. *Land Use Policy, 84,* 260–277.

Barry, M., & Danso, E. K. (2014). Tenure security, land registration and customary tenure in a peri-urban Accra community. *Land Use Policy, 39,* 358–365.

Barton, H. (2009). Land use planning and health and well-being. *Land Use Policy, 26,* S115–S123.

Benjaminsen, T. A., Holden, S., Lund, C., & Sjaastad, E. (2008). Formalisation of land rights: Some empirical evidence from Mali, Niger and South Africa. *Land Use Policy, 26*(1), 28–35.

Bennett, R. M., Van Gils, H., Zevenbergen, J., Lemmen, C., & Wallace, J. (2013, April 8). *Continuing to bridge the cadastral divide* (pp. 8–11). Washington DC.

Berke, P. R., & Conroy, M. M. (2000). Are we planning for sustainable development? An evaluation of 30 comprehensive plans. *Journal of the American Planning Association, 66*(1), 21–33.

Boamah, N. A. (2013). Urban land market in Ghana: A study of the Wa Municipality. *Urban Forum, 24*(1), 105–118.

Bruce, J. W. (1988). A perspective on indigenous land tenure systems and land concentration. In R. E. Downs & S. P. Reyna (Eds.), *Land and society in contemporary Africa* (pp. 23–52). Hanover and London: University Press of New England.

Bruce, J. W. (Ed.). (1998). *Country profiles of land tenure: Africa, 1996* (LTC Research Paper 130). Madison: Land Tenure Center, University of Wisconsin.

Bugri, J. T. (2012). *Improving land sector governance in Ghana: Implementation of the Land Governance Assessment Framework (LGAF) – Final report (English)* (Working Paper No. 119604). Washington, DC: World Bank. Retrieved from World Bank website: http://documents.worldbank.org/curated/en/201121504 860579264/Improving-land-sector-governance-in-Ghana-implementation-of-the-Land-Governance-Assessment-Framework-LGAF-final-report

Chigbu, U. E., Ntihinyurwa, P. D., de Vries, W. T., & Ngenzi, E. I. (2019). Why tenure responsive land-use planning matters: Insights for land use consolidation for food security in Rwanda. *International Journal of Environmental Research and Public Health, 16*(8), 1354.

Chimhowu, A., & Woodhouse, P. (2006). Customary vs private property rights? Dynamics and trajectories of vernacular land markets in sub-Saharan Africa. *Journal of Agrarian Change, 6*(3), 346–371.

Chome, J., & McCall, M. K. (2005). Neo-customary title registration in informal settlements: The case of Blantyre, Malawi. *International Development Planning Review, 27*(4), 451–477.

Cobbinah, P. B., & Aboagye, H. N. (2017). A Ghanaian twist to urban sprawl. *Land Use Policy, 61,* 231–241.

Cobbinah, P. B., & Amoako, C. (2012). Urban sprawl and the loss of peri-urban land in Kumasi, Ghana. *International Journal of Social and Human Sciences, 6*(388), e397.

Cobbinah, P. B., Erdiaw-Kwasie, M. O., & Amoateng, P. (2015). Africa's urbanisation: Implications for sustainable development. *Cities, 47,* 62–72.

Cobbinah, P. B., & Darkwah, R. M. (2017). Toward a more desirable form of sustainable urban development in Africa. *African Geographical Review, 36,* 262–285.

Cobbinah, P. B., & Korah, P. I. (2016). Religion gnaws urban planning: The geography of places of worship in Kumasi, Ghana. *International Journal of Urban Sustainable Development*, 8(2), 93–109.

Commission for Africa. (2005). *Our common interest: Report of the Commission for Africa*. London: Commision for Africa.

Cotula, L., Toulmin, C., & Hesse, C. (2004). *Land tenure and administration in Africa: Lessons of experience and emerging issues*. London: IIED.

De Soto, H. (2000). *The mystery of capital: Why capitalism triumphs in the West and fails everywhere else*. London: Bantam Press.

Goodfellow, T., & Lindemann, S. (2013). The clash of institutions: Traditional authority, conflict and the failure of 'hybridity'in Buganda. *Commonwealth & Comparative Politics*, 51(1), 3–26.

Gough, K. V., & Yankson, P. W. (2000). Land markets in African cities: The case of peri-urban Accra, Ghana. *Urban Studies*, 37(13), 2485–2500.

Huxley, M. (2006). Spatial rationalities: Order, environment, evolution and government. *Social & Cultural Geography*, 7(5), 771–787.

Jusuf, S. K., Wong, N. H., Hagen, E., Anggoro, R., & Hong, Y. (2007). The influence of land use on the urban heat island in Singapore. *Habitat International*, 31(2), 232–242.

Kameri-Mbote, P. (2016). *Kenya Land Governance Assessment Report*. Washington DC: World Bank. 10.1596/28502

Kasanga, K., & Kotey, N. A. (2001). *Land management in Ghana: Building on tradition and modernity*. London: International Institute for Environment and Development.

Kleemann, J., Inkoom, J. N., Thiel, M., Shankar, S., Lautenbach, S., & Fürst, C. (2017). Peri-urban land use pattern and its relation to land use planning in Ghana, West Africa. *Landscape and Urban Planning*, 165, 280–294.

Korah, P. I., Cobbinah, P. B., Nunbogu, A. M., & Gyogluu, S. (2017). Spatial plans and urban development trajectory in Kumasi, Ghana. *GeoJournal*, 82(6), 1113–1134.

Korah, P. I., Matthews, T., & Tomerini, D. (2019). Characterising spatial and temporal patterns of urban evolution in Sub-Saharan Africa: The case of Accra, Ghana. *Land Use Policy*, 87, 104049.

Korah, P. I., Nunbogu, A. M., & Akanbang, B. A. A. (2018). Spatio-temporal dynamics and livelihoods transformation in Wa, Ghana. *Land Use Policy*, 77, 174–185.

Kuusaana, E. D., & Eledi, J. A. (2015). Customary land allocation, urbanization and land use planning in Ghana: Implications for food systems in the Wa Municipality. *Land Use Policy*, 48, 454–466.

Land Tenure Center. (1990). *Security of tenure in Africa*. Madison: University of Madison-Wisconsin, Land Tenure Center.

Larbi, W. O. (1996). Spatial planning and urban fragmentation in Accra. *Third World Planning Review*, 18(2), 193.

Larbi, W. O., Antwi, A., & Olomolaiye, P. (2003). Land valorisation processes and state intervention in land management in peri-urban Accra, Ghana. *International Development Planning Review*, 25(4), 355–371.

Lavigne Delville, P. (2004). Registering and administering customary land rights; current innovations and questions in French-speaking West Africa.

Presented at the *Proceedings of the Expert Group Meeting on secure land tenure: new legal frameworks and tools*, UN-Gigiri in Nairobi, Kenya, 10–12 November, 2004.

Leduka, R. C. (2006). Chiefs, civil servants and the city council: State–society relations in evolving land delivery processes in Maseru, Lesotho. *International Development Planning Review*, 28(2), 181–208.

Lentz, C. (2006). Land and the politics of belonging in West Africa: An introduction. In R. Kuba & C. Lentz (Eds.), *Land and the politics of belonging in West Africa* (pp. 1–34). Leiden: Brill Academic Pub.

Magigi, W., & Drescher, A. (2010). The dynamics of land use change and tenure systems in Sub-Saharan Africa cities; learning from Himo community protest, conflict and interest in urban planning practice in Tanzania. *Habitat International*, 34(2), 154–164.

Mahama, C., & Antwi, A. (2006). *Land and property markets in Ghana*. Presented at the Discussion Paper, Prepared by Royal Institution of Chattered Surveyors, World Urban Forum III.

Malton, P. (1994). Indigenous land use systems and investments in soil fertility in Burkina Faso. In J. W. Bruce & S. E. Migot-Adholla (Eds.), *Searching for land tenure security in Africa* (pp. 41–69). Washington, DC: The World Bank.

Neimark, B., Toulmin, C., & Batterbury, S. (2018). Peri-urban land grabbing? Dilemmas of formalising tenure and land acquisitions around the cities of Bamako and Ségou, Mali. *Journal of Land Use Science*, 13(3), 319–324.

Nkurunziza, E. (2006). Two states, one city?: Conflict and accommodation in land delivery in Kampala, Uganda. *International Development Planning Review*, 28(2), 159–180.

Nnkya, T. J. (2007). *Why planning does not work? Land use planning and residents' rights in Tanzania*. Dar es Salaam: Mkuki na Nyota Publishers Ltd.

Ntihinyurwa, P. D., de Vries, W. T., Chigbu, U. E., & Dukwiyimpuhwe, P. A. (2019). The positive impacts of farm land fragmentation in Rwanda. *Land Use Policy*, 81, 565–581.

Obeng-Odoom, F. (2016). Understanding land reform in Ghana: A critical postcolonial institutional approach. *Review of Radical Political Economics*, 48(4), 661–680.

Olujimi, J. (2009). Evolving a planning strategy for managing urban sprawl in Nigeria. *Journal of Human Ecology*, 25(3), 201–208.

Oluwadare, C. O., & Kufoniyi, O. (2019). Space-enhanced systematic land titling and registration: A stride at resuscitating Nigeria's 'dead capital'. *African Journal on Land Policy and Geospatial Sciences*, 2(2), 88–99.

Onyebueke, V., & Ikejiofor, C. (2017). Neo-customary land delivery systems and the rise of community-mediated settlements in peri-urban Enugu, Nigeria. *International Development Planning Review*, 39(3), 319–340.

Owusu-Ansah, J. K., & Braimah, I. (2013). The dual land management systems as an influence on physical development outcomes around Kumasi, Ghana. *Journal of Housing and the Built Environment*, 28(4), 689–703.

Rakodi, C., & Leduka, C. (2004). *Informal land delivery processes and access to land for the poor: A comparative study of six African cities* [Policy Brief 6]. International Development Department, University of Birmingham/Department of Geography, National University of Lesotho.

Siiba, A., Adams, E. A., & Cobbinah, P. B. (2017). Chieftaincy and sustainable urban land use planning in Yendi, Ghana: Towards congruence. *Cities*, *73*, 96–105.

Sim, V., Sutherland, C., Buthelezi, S., & Khumalo, D. (2018). *Possibilities for a hybrid approach to planning and governance at the interface of the administrative and traditional authority systems in Durban*. 29(4), 351–368. Springer.

Simelane, H. (2016). Urban land management and its discontents: A case study of the Swaziland Urban Development Project (SUDP). *The Journal of Development Studies*, *52*(6), 797–812.

Sumari, N. S., Xu, G., Ujoh, F., Korah, P. I., Ebohon, O. J., & Lyimo, N. N. (2019). A geospatial approach to sustainable urban planning: Lessons for Morogoro Municipal Council, Tanzania. *Sustainability*, *11*(22), 6508.

Tembo, E., & Sommerville, M. (2018). Land tenure dynamics in peri-urban Zambia. *USAID Policy Brief*. Retrieved from https://land-links.org/wp-content/uploads/2018/04/USAID_Land_Tenure_Peri-urban_Zambia-Brief_-1.pdf

Toulmin, C. (2009). Securing land and property rights in sub-Saharan Africa: The role of local institutions. *Land Use Policy*, *26*(1), 10–19.

Ubink, J. M. (2007). Tenure security: Wishful policy thinking or reality? A case from peri-urban Ghana. *Journal of African Law*, *51*(02), 215–248.

Ubink, J. M. (2008). *In the Land of the Chiefs: Customary Law, Land conflicts, and the role of the State in Peri-Urban Ghana*. Leiden: Leiden University Press.

UN Habitat. (2016). World cities report 2016: Urbanization and development: Emerging futures. Nairobi: UN Habitat.

UN-Habitat. (2009). *Global report on human settlements 2009: Planning sustainable cities*. London: Earthscan.

Van Lier, H. N. (1998). The role of land use planning in sustainable rural systems. *Landscape and Urban Planning*, *41*(2), 83–91.

Watson, V. (2006). Deep difference: Diversity, planning and ethics. *Planning Theory*, *5*(1), 31–50.

Yeboah, E., & Obeng-Odoom, F. (2010). "We are not the only ones to blame": District assemblies' perspectives on the state of planning in Ghana. *Commonwealth Journal of Local Governance*, (7), 78–98.

Yeboah, E., & Shaw, D. P. (2013). Customary land tenure practices in Ghana: Examining the relationship with land-use planning delivery. *International Development Planning Review*, *35*(1), 21–39.

Zevenbergen, J., De Vries, W., & Bennett, R. M. (2015). *Advances in responsible land administration*. New York: CRC Press.

4 Local Activism and Climate Action in Africa: Protecting the Environment as a Social Justice Imperative

Luckymore Matenga

Introduction

Climate change is an interminable conundrum to the international community particularly in Africa. Indeed, climate change affects almost all sectors in societies including agriculture and livestock, food and water, energy, housing and transportation (Cobbinah and Addaney). Climate change refers to any extended change in the distribution of weather patterns (Solomon et al. 2007; Brazier, 2015). It is an explicit target of the global village regardless of boundaries, race and ethnicity. The main characteristics of climate change in Africa include excessive temperatures, heatwave, decline of productive agricultural land, droughts and changing rainfall patterns (Matenga, 2019). These characteristics, "... have far – reaching implications, and no country is immune, whether rich or poor, big or small, strong or weak, although the degree of impacts varies" (Addaney & Cobbinah, 2019, pp. 3–4). It is argued that extreme temperatures, heatwaves and unpredictable rainfall impact on "climate – sensitive sectors such as hydropower electricity, agriculture, water and fisheries" (ibid.). Recurrent climate change conundrums in access to water, energy and food, livelihoods and natural systems rigorously challenge efforts to achieve the Sustainable Development Goals, in Africa (Addaney & Cobbinah, 2019).

As a result, researchers, policymakers, environmental scientists, community-based organisations and other specialists have identified casual factors and have also provided adaptive strategies. Scholarly analysis has led to challenging explicatory replicas mostly accentuating urbanisation[1] and/or modernisation[2] being the major factors for climate change. Urbanisation explanations emphasise population growth and competition over scarce resources in cities as the foremost lashing factor in this era of modernisation and digitalisation (Shamasundari, 2017). Following Africa's efforts in eradicating poverty and to meet the needs of citizens, a lot of people are migrating from rural to urban areas in search of employment which results in congestion, pollution and poor sanitation in urban areas (Matenga, 2019). It is estimated that "by 2050, more than 1.2 billion Africans will live in cities; this figure is

DOI: 10.4324/9781003181484-4

more than the total urban and rural population of the western hemisphere" (Addaney & Cobbinah, 2019, p. 7). According to World Bank, "… megacities (cities with more than ten million people) increased from one (Cairo: 11.9 million) in 2007 to three in 2017 – Lagos (21 million), Cairo (20.4 million), and Kinshasa (15 million)" (Addaney & Cobbinah, 2019, p. 7). However, voluminous increase of the populace in cities is associated with uncontrolled growth of informal settlement which adds pressure to the already endangered environment (ibid.).

The act of pulling people out of poverty and into more developed nations, unfortunately comes at the expense of the environment and ecosystems (Shamasundari, 2017). Although climate change is a global issue, developed nations are the chief culprits of endangering the environment at the expense of developing nations. According to Ogwu (2019), developing countries with Green House Gas emissions of 3.8% are the least contributors to global warming in both absolute and per capita terms but the most vulnerable to climate change effects (Addaney & Cobbinah, 2019, p. 32). UNFCCC (2006) reported that developing countries and particularly Africa is experiencing an increase of about "0.7-degree Celsius temperature which has caused a decrease in food production, increased flooding and inundation of coastal zones and deltas, the spread of diseases, changes in natural ecosystems, and biodiversity decline" (ibid.). Unfortunately, Africa's harmful emissions which range from deforestation and the use of fossil fuel for electricity and other related pertinent issues are less than the emissions for a single country including India, Russia, China and the United States of America (Ogwu, 2019). The factors often mentioned here include the legacy of modernisation which is a linear path towards a developed industrial society (Groh, 2019). Economic development through industrial transformation, a colonial legacy, would lead to economic growth, allowing developing countries to catch up with developed countries but it leads to potential environmental consequences if not guided by smart and sustainable policies (Shamasundari, 2017). For example, China's increasing urban population, modernisation and continuous economic growth led to a rapid increase in resource consumption and sustainable development crisis (Bao & Chen, 2015 in Addaney & Cobbinah, 2019). Tramel (2018, p. 1293) argues that capitalism and modernity have been continually underpinned by a fear of nature and desire to dominate it – and since Europeans associated non-European "others" with nature, they too became the subjects of systemic fear and domination.

To make matters worse, globalisation enables developed nations to dump clichéd products in developing countries which most of them pose environmental threats. If done poorly, massive urban sprawling also brings about more deforestation, habitat destruction and greenhouse gas or carbon emissions (Shamasundari, 2017). Addaney Cobbinah (2019) cite cities of the Global South as the most vulnerable areas to climate change. Within this context, it is not a surreptitious that developing countries are more exposed to the impacts of climate change in comparison to developed countries (Schellnhuber, 2013). Drawing from the above, climate change threatens human security namely, food, water, environmental and economic security in Africa (United Nations Development Programme, [UNDP], 1994; Adger et al., 2003). African countries especially on the Sub-Sahara region is more vulnerable because they heavily depend on natural resources and rainfall (Matenga, 2019). Accordingly, climate change is a, "'… threat multiplier' of existing global human security challenges such as food insecurity, water and other resource scarcity, natural disasters, desertification, and disease" in Africa (Jegede & Mokoena, 2019, p. 332). Furthermore, climate change is a menace to humanoid security because it disturbs communities' and individuals' capacity to adjust to changing temperatures and rainfall patterns usually by proliferating existing or producing new – fangled stresses on human livelihoods particularly in Africa whose livelihoods are depended on natural resources and rainfall (ibid.).

Being an ongoing catastrophe, UNDP (2018, p. 18) indicates that, "temperatures in Africa are projected to rise faster than the global average during the 21st Century, with temperature extremes breaching levels experienced today by 2°C by 2050 and 4–6°C by the end of the 21st Century in tropical western Africa and the Sahel." Increasing temperatures and changing rainfall patterns negatively affect agricultural activities and food security in with estimates of additional amount of between 5 and 170 million people at risk of hunger by the year 2080 (Statistical Review on World Energy, 2016). Dry spell frequencies, rainfall intensity and changing of rainfall patterns such as duration and the onset, have been noticed in the southern and eastern region of Africa (UNDP, 2018). It is further noted that, "East Africa has experienced intense rainfall and drought more frequently in recent decades during the spring and summer seasons, and southern Africa is experiencing more droughts" (ibid, 17). Moreover, 2017 droughts in Eastern Africa created food insecurity and famines, "and propelled a global spike in malnutrition – the first time in over a decade that we have fallen back on targets to end hunger by 2030" (UNDP, 2018, p. 17). Atapattu (2016) notes that climate change causes indescribable devastation and suffering such as loss of life. Heatwaves, significantly impacts on health that can be worsened by both drought conditions and high humidity (Addaney & Cobbinah, 2019). And developing countries are more vulnerable to heat related child mortality and escalated adults' sickness and death (Kenny et al., 2010; Oudin Astrom et al., 2013; Egondi et al., 2012). Heat waves may result in intensified levels of illness and death by discrediting the body's ability to regulate its temperature or by inducing direct or indirect health complications (Addaney & Cobbinah, 2019).

Also, natural disasters such as floods and cyclones are said to be consequences of the changing climate (Addaney & Cobbinah, 2019).

For instance, Freetown located in Sierra Leone was hit by mudsliding in 2017; Accra, Ghana was affected by floods in June 2015 whereby an estimated of more than 150 people died and properties worth millions were destroyed (ibid.). In the Sahel region, prolonged droughts exacerbate desertification while the rise in sea levels in the coastal cities of West Africa, from Ghana to Benin, is ravaging farming and fishing communities (Africa Renewal, 2019). Apart from that, Cyclone Idai, one of the worst long-lived storm on record in March 2019 which affected African countries such as Malawi, Mozambique and Zimbabwe leaving more than 1,300 people dead and many more missing (Yuhas, 2019). With these cases, the cost of overwhelming consequences of climate change is likely to increase encompassing mass loss of life, dislocation of the populace and pronounced decrease in the quality of life (Addaney & Cobbinah, 2019, p. 480).

Climate justice action being a set of connections and a key to advocacy is crucial in coming up with sustainable environmental measures and the attainment of sustainable development goals (Bond, 2012). Faced with the reality of climate change, the United Nations through sustainable development goals urges the international communities to join hands towards climate change justice action so that the future generation will use the same climate (UNDP 2007; Atapattu, 2016; Mayer, 2018; Addaney & Cobbinah, 2019). This will ensure sustainable development for the future generations in an environmentally friendly world particularly in Africa. Contemporaneously, Article 4(8) (d)–(f) of the United Nations Framework Convention on Climate Change (UNFCCC) urges parties to take into consideration necessary actions to meet the adverse effects of climate change and response measures in countries prone to natural disasters, liable to drought and desertification, and with areas of high urban atmospheric pollution (see, for example, Jegede & Mokoena, 2019, p. 332). Moreover, the preface of the Paris Agreement also points out the necessity to "safeguard food security owing to the adverse impacts of climate change" (ibid.). The 2015, aegis of the UN meeting emphasised that "positive climate change action within the UNSC would strengthen peace throughout the developing world and mitigate risks to the stability of regions where freshwater, land use, and access to food are all endangered by rising sea levels" (Jegede & Mokoena, 2019, p. 332).

While much has been documented on the factors, vulnerability to and challenges of climate change, little has been done on the role of local environmental activism in promoting environmental justice in Africa. Using a desk research method, this chapter explores new perspectives on trends and the role of environmental activism in the form of community protests and demonstrations in promoting environmental justice and climate change mitigation strategies in Africa. This chapter is of significant standing in academic literature because it is multidimensional, crosscutting a gamut of theoretical issues of the role of environmental activism, a subject which has hitherto received a paucity of research dedication, management of the environment and climate change where much attention has been placed and local environmental activists' urgency defined as community participation by virtue of its major assumptions which has received little attention. Moreover, local environmental activists are recognised as collective actors and mobilisers who use their urgency to call for environmental justice and climate change mitigation strategies across the globe in general and Africa in particular. On the flipside, this chapter argues that, environmental justice is challenging in Africa because there is no assimilation and integration between developed and developing countries to combat climate change and promotion of environmental justice. Therefore, there is a need for a bottom up approach and integration of all countries from both poles (North and South), communities and individuals towards attaining sustainable development goals and in climate change adaptation efforts. In the following section, the chapter delves into the climate change and environmental injustice in Africa. It then follows a section which offers adaptation measures to climate change in Africa. Finally, the third section explores emerging local environmental activism in Africa towards promoting environmental as social justice; leading a conclusion.

Climate Change and Environmental Injustice in Africa: Nexus between Developed and Developing Countries

One argumentative subject around climate change injustice is the extent to which capitalism is regarded as the major root cause of climate change. This question regularly leads to fundamental arguments between liberals on the one hand and conservative environmental groups and, on the other, leftist and radical organisations (Building Bridges Collective, 2010). While the former often tend to blame the excesses of neoliberalism for climate change and argue in favour of market-based reform, the latter view capitalism with its exploitative traits as the underlying central issue in Africa (ibid.). From the scheme of things, African countries that are least responsible for causing climate change are the ones suffering most from its effects, especially regarding food insecurity and nutrient deficiencies (DW, 2019). Climate change is a direct product of the sociopathic greediness and bias of the capitalist system (New Flame, 2019). Developed countries have built their power and wealth on the basis of industrialisation and modernisation. Faced with a choice between catastrophe and a safer future for humanity, the elites have chosen to throw the rest of the world into the deep maw of climate mayhem (New Flame, 2019).

Against this backdrop, scientists and environmentalists have been warning that the least developed nations with very low carbon footprints are bearing the brunt of carbon dioxide emissions in the wealthy world (New Flame, 2019). Concurrently, what makes this particular unjust is that the people who are suffering from these impacts are the least responsible for their plight (Ware & Kramer, 2019, p. 4). The problem with developed countries is that they know that they are responsible for climate change catastrophes but their responsibility has become rich from a carbon intensive development route by using developing countries as dumping areas (ibid.). Referring to developed nations, Ware and Kramer (2019, p. 4) note that "it is their responsibility to make major emissions cuts in their own countries to reverse climate change and to invest in the global efforts to move to a net zero carbon pathway." A recent report by Christian Aid brings the drama of inequality into light:

> the recent meetings of the UNFCCC, both in Katowice, Poland in December 2018 and in Bonn in June 2019, high emitting countries such as Russia, the USA and Saudi Arabia not only failed to commit to slashing their emissions in support of those low emitting climate vulnerable countries, but they also blocked the adoption of the IPCC's 1.5C report by the other countries in attendance (Ware & Kramer, 2019, p. 4).

The injustice of this is inevitable because developed countries heavily invest and rely on industrialisation which is costly to the environment (Addaney & Cobbinah, 2019). Of course, industrialisation and urbanisation enhance poverty reduction efforts and improves people's standards of living through employment creation, however, these conditions negatively affect environmental sustainability (African Growth Initiative, 2017). Toxic gases emitted by industries exacerbate global warming. Hence changing rainfall patterns and increasing temperatures affect African countries as they heavily rely on agricultural activities (ibid.). In addition, African countries especially from the Southern region frequently receive an unequal portion of climate change relief and recovery aid (Cooley , 2012). Also, these countries normally have less voice and involvement in decision-making, political, and legal processes that relate to climate change and the natural environment (ibid.). Developed countries yield power and voice to determine issues related to climate change as demonstrated by Russia, the USA and Saudi Arabia when they failed to commit to slashing their emissions and also blocked the adoption of the IPCC's 1.5C report by countries in attendance (Cooley et al., 2012). Consequently, the impacts of climate change accelerate the increase of food insecurity and hunger while development is also strained. Ironically, Africa is top in the hierarchy of underdevelopment, for example, "Burundi and DR Congo emit less carbon emissions in the world but are the most food insecure" (Ware & Kramer, 2019, p. 6). It has been noted that Burundi, DR Congo, Madagascar, Yemen, Sierra Leone, Chad, Malawi, Haiti, Niger and Zambia are the top ten utmost nations at jeopardy which emit less than half a tonne of carbon dioxide per capita (ibid.) [see Figure 1.1]. In proportional terms these African countries produce a collective 0.08% of entire international carbon dioxide (Ware & Kramer, 2019).

In contrast, most developed countries responsible for climate change (Ware & Kramer, 2019). In the same vein, Ware and Kramer (2019, p. 6) demonstrate that:

> Russia contributes 12.3 tonnes of CO_2 per person, the United States 15.7 tonnes and Saudi Arabia 19.4 tonnes. The data also reveals the current responsibility of other more developed countries such as the UK at 5.7 tonnes, China at 7.7, South Africa at 8.2, Poland at 8.4, Germany at 9.7, Japan at 10.4, South Korea at 13.2, Australia at 16.5 and Canada at 16.9 tonnes. That means that the average person in the UK generates as much CO_2 as 212 Burundians. A Russian generates as much CO_2 as 454 Burundians, an American 581 and a Saudi 719 [see Figure 1.2].

Failure to respond with urgency to climate change has already resulted in the reversal of development gains for the poorest and most vulnerable African countries, an erosion of biodiversity, and ever-increasing difficulties in providing food and shelter. The imbalance between the developed and developing nation about who causes and who suffers from the impacts of climate change need to be assessed in the manner that benefit and affect both poles. Moreover, "if the world is going to mitigate climate change, … it is vital that countries recognise and act on the scientific evidence that demonstrates an ongoing and intensifying climate and environment emergency" (Ware & Kramer, 2019, p. 4). Regardless of environmental injustice, the following section discusses responses and adaptation strategies to climate change used by developing countries in Africa.

Alternatives to Sustainable Climate Change Adaptation in Africa

While much has been documented about climate change mitigation, adaptation and resilient strategies in Africa, this chapter examines some of adaptation strategies used by communities in Africa to generate a rich understanding of the emerging fundamental actors involved in dealing with climate change. The section dwell much on the sociological and anthropological perspective to frame a critical argument about climate change mitigation strategies. Primary adaptation schemes in Africa were largely focused in small-scale options such as modernising agricultural technologies and practices to cope with changing rainfall cycles, however, current adaptation programmes focus on large efforts that address varied sectoral entries and make better use of collaborations (UNDP, 2018). The idea is to work with communities and governments in reducing vulnerability and delivering growth in the context of climate change (ibid.). Being the most vulnerable to climate change, African countries are the "least able to adapt" as they lack finance and "institutional capacity to identify the best ways to build resilience" (UNDP, 2018, p. 5). Therefore, with the help of donors such as the Global Environment Least Developed Countries Fund (GEF-LDCF), developing countries embraces the largest set of adaptation schemes (ibid.). Also, by implementing sustainable urban management models, communities can be reflected in "building adaptable cities that support positive economic, social, and environmental progress" (Addaney & Cobbinah, 2019, p. 6). In Zimbabwe, UNDP-supported a project which improves food security and "income diversification and levels for project beneficiaries, thereby improving resilience to climate change in Chiredzi district project areas" (UNDP, 2018, p. 23).

Furthermore, inventions in "developing seasonal weather forecasts under another project offer great promise for Zimbabwe where use rates of the current weather forecasts among farmers and confidence in the information provided are low" (UNDP, 2018, p. 23). The project is sustainable and brought consistent forecasting methods in Zimbabwe (ibid.). Also, the government through the Environmental Management Agency (EMA) "control and regulate urban wetlands in a conservative way by preserving them to make sure that wetlands are free and safe from human threats" (Matenga, 2019, p. 173). In the same vein, the Ugandan government approved the "Building Resilient Communities, Wetland Ecosystems and Associated Catchments" project to "restore wetlands and their eco-system services, based on the wise-use principles and guidelines outlined by the Ramsar Convention on Wetlands" (UNDP, 2018, p. 23). The project is programmed to "reduce pressure on wetlands and to support sustainable land management practices and reforestation, resilient rural and urban agricultural practices and alternative livelihoods for communities living in these areas" (ibid.). In 2011, Ethiopia established the National Adaptation Plan (NAP) for Climate Resilient Green Economy (CRGE) strategy to diminish vulnerability to the impacts of climate change by building adaptive capacity and resilience (FDRE, 2011). With an average of US$ 3 million Green Climate Fund (GCF), countries such as Malawi, Niger, DR Congo, Liberia and Zambia with NAPs projects aimed at "facilitating the mainstreaming of adaptation at planning level, creating the framework for integrated approaches that leverage the innovations from projects and planning processes" (UNDP, 2018, p. 23). Therefore, adaptation systems which enable African cities to navigate the brunt of climate change are crucial to the continent's sustainable development and achieving the United Nations sustainable development goals (Addaney & Cobbinah, 2019).

In Malawi, through the, "Saving Lives and Protecting Agriculture Based Livelihoods in Malawi: Scaling up the Use of Modernised Climate Information and Early Warning Systems" (M-Climes), NAP improved livelihoods and saved lives at jeopardy from climate-related tragedies, reaching an estimated three million people (UNDP, 2018, pp. 23–24). The scheme directs Malawi's "access barriers related to weather and climate information" which will be addressed by "enhancing hydro-meteorological early warnings and forecasting systems; developing and disseminating tailored products for different actors including smallholder farmers and fishers; and strengthening capacities of communities to respond to climate-related disasters" (ibid.). In Guinea, the government used the municipality and community integration strategy to clear out silt and sedimentation in Kakossa, Kaback, Kito and Koba stone dykes (UNDP, 2018). The strategy salvaged 879 hectares of agrarian land that had been abandoned due to saline foray (ibid.). In 2009, through engaging traditional chiefs, Namibia improvised livestock farming and growing of traditional crops which helped agriculturalists to adapt to changing climate by distributing enhanced seeds and livestock (UNDP, 2018).

Given these adaptation measures to climate change, co-production strengthens good governance by sharing decisions made on how to adapt to the changing climate (UNDP, 2018; Matenga, 2019). It is noted that the involvement of different stakeholders also develops confidence, transparency and equitable use of public resources (UNDP, 2018). In addition, collaboration between communities and governments "improves the identification of the adaptation strategy, promotes ownership, spurs innovation and learning, and develops change agents" (ibid, p. 44). Therefore, there is a need for different stakeholders to work hand in glove in promoting measures that controls climate change effects. This also improves sustainability, acceleration and mainstreaming of the changing climate adaptation schemes (UNDP, 2018).

Data Collection and Methods

This examines the role of local environmental activism in Africa through a qualitative research design and particularly, through a review of existing literature, reports of international organisations and secondary data. Literature (for example, Bond & Dorsey, 2010; Shamasundari, 2017; Rathzel et al., 2018; Tramel, 2018) provided a significant knowledge about factors driving local environmental activism in Africa and consequences thereof. The study is situated in African countries including South Africa, Senegal, Mali, Kenya and Zimbabwe. Moreover, the chapter considered data gathered through international organisations reports and websites such as the Human Rights Watch on protesting against the government and harassments of environmental activists in South Africa; the Open Society Foundation on organising for climate justice in Africa. Policy reports used in this chapter include the UNDP (2018) on Climate Change Adaptation in Africa, Synthesis of Experiences and Recommendations 2000–2015; the United Nations (2015) report on Sustainable Development; Network of Peasant Organisations and Agricultural Producers (ROPPA); Mali's National Coordination of Peasant Organisations (CNOP) on land and water grievances and United Nations International Children Educational Fund (UNICEF) (2020) on young people participation in decision makings on climate change mitigation strategies. From these sources, the chapter managed to gather holistic findings around environmental injustice and the effectiveness of local environmental activism in Africa. Archival and website information helped to augment that there is a need for strong engagements of all communities, that is, from the North to the South Pole to create sustainable urban environments globally. The following section discusses the role of activism through protests or social movements in promoting environmental justice and climate change mitigation strategies in Africa.

Towards Environmental Justice: Local Environmental Activism in Africa

This section explores the role of activism in promoting environmental justice and climate change mitigation strategies in Africa. Presentations and discussions proffered here contribute to achieving the United Nations SDGs, "especially Goals 11 and 13 on sustainable and resilient human settlements, and climate change action" (Addaney & Cobbinah, 2019, p. 11). As explored earlier, scholars such as Ware and Kramer (2019) have provided rich literature around the challenge of climate change which include droughts, shifting rainfall patterns and temperature increases; some cited disasters related to climate change. Other scholars such as Cobbinah and Addaney (2019) and Chitongo (2019) identified adaptive strategies to climate change and environmental threats. However, little is known about the repertoires of activism as a progressive prevalent technique to hold the world to consider climate change justice in Africa. To analyse the role of activists in lobbying for environmental justice, it is argued that, power is ubiquitous, and it can be exercised by anyone or any organisation with the capacity to influence change in societies and/or towards environmental justice.

Being the most vulnerable continent, individuals and communities in Africa mobilise themselves to fight against climate change and its effects. Communities in Africa agitate for climate change action, igniting a revolutionary spark against capitalism in the battle for the present and future (New Frame, 2019). On Friday 20 September 2019, millions of people took part in a first Global Climate Change Strike, taking to the streets to protest the inaction of their governments on global warming (ibid.). More specifically, in South Africa, there was a trade union-led picket outside the Department of Mineral Resources and Energy in Tshwane (New Frame, 2019). Undisclosed environmental activists on that day, added their voice and advocated for the South African government to address the ecological, social and economic downsides of mining (New Frame, 2019). This followed an extremely unequal and stagnant economy which is based on letting the capitalists enjoy by extractive mining industry while the poor die from the effects posed by climate change (Shamasundari, 2017; Tramel, 2018; New Frame, 2019). The New Frame (2019) and Bond and Dorsey (2010) demonstrate that the movement was against the government's vacillation on renewables as exemplified by Eskom, a dysfunctional company which continues to run toxic coal while not being able to keep the lights on all the time. Eskom's power stations in Mpumalanga have the highest level of air pollution in the world (New Flame, 2019). Although Eskom plays a significant role in generating electricity for the country, it built its supremacy and wealth on the base of fossil fuels. Faced with a choice between disaster and a safer future for humankind, capitalists have chosen to throw communities into the gaping maw of climate chaos (New Frame, 2019). An activist was quoted blaming the government for being ignorant and blind in responding to climate change. He lamented that;

> President Cyril Ramaphosa may make pretty speeches about the environment, but in practice his government continues to push fossil fuel expansion. The South African state has no credible response to the climate crisis, and this dismal reality will persist until it is forced to act by the citizenry. Corporate polluters will not stop ravaging our air and water until their operations are forced to a halt (New Frame, 2019).

Given the continued environmental threats, capitalism is an apocalypse by the elite's disorder manifesting gluttony and bias at the expense of the environment and consequently impacting negatively on the need of the poor who depend on the environment. Faced with an unprecedented existential threat, humanity is locked into an economic system based on endless growth and consumption (New Frame, 2019). The situatedness of South Africans in environmental threats and climate change is best captured by devastating environmental collapse which is already disentanglement wealth creation by the elites.

In South Africa, there is evidence of engagement of diverse trade unions, with workers mobilising themselves to protest the lack of action on climate change and demanding transition from polluting coal, oil and gas towards renewable energy (New Frame, 2019). The South African Federation of Trade Unions (SAFTU) and the General Industries Workers Union of South Africa (GIWUSA) led the demonstration in partnership with climate justice advocacy group. While the protest was small, its significance was not because the protest represented an emerging alliance between trade unions and the climate justice movement (New Frame, 2019). The emerging engagements and union support showed a growing recognition that indecision on climate change represents one of the severest threats to workers' jobs and livelihoods and that with union leadership, climate action can protect workers and ensure a more just and prosperous future (Rathzel et al., 2018; New Frame, 2019). The new emerging trend of engagement of different parties to fight environmental justice, transformed alliances can potentially open the government ears and bid for a sustainable action towards environmental protection and fighting for social justice. This is in tandem with SDG 13 which encourage countries to engage at different scales to circumvent the challenge of climate change in the world (UN, 2015).

The youth are also becoming vocal about climate justice in Africa. A 17-year-old Ayakha Melithafa from Eerste River in Cape Town joined Greta Thunberg and 14 other climate activists from around the world in signing a legal complaint with the United Nations Convention on the Rights of the Child on 23 September 2018 (Daily Maverick, 2019). Through joining the Project 90 by 2030 – an NGO working to cut the country's carbon emissions by 90% by 2030,

Ayakha Melithafa was quoted lamenting about Cyclone Idai. She said that:

> The people that are often affected the most often don't cause the problem. I want people to know that not only privileged people are aware of climate change. They aren't the only ones that experience problems. (Daily Maverick, 2019)

In Senegal, where the economy is mainly dependent on the environment, and where climate change eventually exacerbates poverty and further contributes to inequality by promoting estate conflicts, rural exoduses and clandestine immigration, Mariama Diallo, a climate justice activist has been influential in advocating for climate justice (Open Society Foundations [OSFs], 2019). During an interview with the Open Society Foundations, she explained what pioneered her to participate in such movement;

> I decided to get involved because I believe that climate change puts Africa's economic and human development at risk; and because I worry that, unless they participate in designing global policy re-sponses to climate change, African countries could become "out-siders" who effectively don't control their own economies – or even their people's access to food. The good news is that this is not inevitable; we can make changes to create fairer and more sustainable societies. That means the fight for climate justice in Africa is not only important for those who care about the environment, it is important to everyone who wants Africa to be a prosperous, free, and self-sufficient continent (Open Society Foundations OSFs, 2019).

On 25 May, 2018, 35 environmental activists led a peaceful protest in Lamu town, Kenya. The activists, staff of the environmental groups, Save Lamu and Lamu Youth Alliance, were protesting the government's deci-sion to proceed with construction of a power plant despite environmental and health concerns (Human Rights Watch, 2018). As the Kenyan gov-ernment moves ahead with implementation of the Lamu Port project, communities on the coast and organisations supporting them have become increasingly vocal about the adverse health and environmental impacts of the projects (Ibid.). They campaigned especially loudly against a planned coal-fired power plant, saying it will pollute the air and water, affecting the livelihoods of local communities. However, the State authorities responded in a radical way by deploying police and the military officers who arrested two activists during the protest but they failed as activists continued with their struggle (Human Rights Watch, 2018). The argument by activists was that the power plant will emit smoke that contains hazardous particulate matter, discharge waste effluents into the sea that could kill fish and other sea animals, and further emit coal dust that poses serious health risks to those residing near coal plants, including cancer to people who live nearby (ibid.). They also contended that the port construction will destroy mangrove forests and breeding grounds for fish and other marine animals (Human Rights Watch, 2018). The activists further expressed concerns over the government's taking of farmland, with most of it yet to result in compensation, risks of water pollution from waste discharge and climate change brought about by greenhouse gas emissions (Human Rights Watch, 2018). The Government's response to these activists was a test case for Kenya to uphold and protect rights in the context of large-scale development projects but the executive director at the National Coalition of Human Rights Defenders – Kenya, Kamau Ngugi, was quoted arguing that, "Kenyan authorities have an obligation to respect the role of activists and to uphold the rights outlined in international treaties" (ibid.).

Since independence, Zimbabwean youth, in schools have been advocating for climate change crisis to be given attention (UNICEF, 2020). Through collaborations with international organisations such as UNICEF, a 17-year-old Nkosilathi Nyathi, on 17 November, 2020, was appointed as a UNICEF Youth Climate Change Advocacy to advance the climate change and environment agenda in Zimbabwe and mobilise other young people to join the fight against climate change. The appointment came as UNICEF commemorates World Children's Day on November 20, under the theme "Reimagining a greener more sustainable future, for every child" (UNICEF, 2020). Through interviewees with local newspapers, Nkosilathi exposed that he has been lending a voice for the youth around climate change because they are the future. In his own remarks, Nkosilathi said that;

> I live it, my family and friends live it too. I stand in solidarity with countless young people who want their voices to be heard and acted upon for climate change action. We are becoming more certain that we will be heard and those in power will listen (UNICEF, 2020).

In this regard, inclusion of the youth, the future generation and with the support from international organisations is significant when dealing with climate change. Participation in climate change action programmes of the youth who are and who will continue suffering from the brunt of climate change is significant because "climate change is a child rights issue and it very important that awareness is raised among young people, by young people to drive hope for a better future – one with a safe and secure environment" (UNICEF, 2020). Furthermore, inclusion in the management of climate change is problematic in Africa – there is need for countries to involve all countries, sectors in governments and NGOs towards sustainable environmental issues.

During the 6th African Regional Forum on Sustainable Development in Victoria Falls, Nkosilathi Nyathi raised concerns around lack of inclusion of young people when dealing with climate change conundrums. In Spain, he made a plea to involve the young people – the voices and opinions of children and young people – in making decisions and policies about climate change and the environment. In his own words, he noted that;

> We are here. We are smart. We are activists. We have solutions. Involve us, he said to a clearly roused audience at the Sustainable Development Goals Forum.

As inclusion is credited in Zimbabwe, it is therefore reasonable, environmentally and politically just and sustainable for other African countries to act more decisively on youth participation and inclusion and take advantage of their knowledge to curb climate change. Inclusion is all about engagement of different stakeholder from all angles, gender sensitive and youths and contributions especially from urban residents in addressing the ongoing climate change catastrophe (Cobbinah & Darkwah, 2016). The COVID-19 pandemic has also dealt a blow to collective efforts to drive awareness and advocacy to fight climate change (UNICEF, 2020). Countries from both poles have completely focused on the pandemic. However, African countries such as Mozambique and Zimbabwe have taken the climate change fight online and digitally because their voices matter (ibid.). Young people have been noticed participating in several series of virtual meetings organised at both international and national level (UNICEF, 2020). For instance, Nkosilathi Nyathi noted that, during the lockdown period he participated and represented other young people from Africa in the UNICEF group of friends for SDGs meeting featuring the UNICEF executive director, Henrietta Fore (UNICEF, 2020). As a result, young people are also agents of the change and the fight is not on the horizon, whereas the fight is right in front of everyone so everyone should make the voice louder towards sustainable environmental development.

In West Africa, the Network of Peasant Organizations and Agricultural Producers (ROPPA) and Mali's National Coordination of Peasant Organisations (CNOP) through the food sovereignty forum held at Nyeleni in 2007 ... have predominately engaged with the framework of food sovereignty to articulate their grievances against land and water grabbing (Tramel, 2018, p. 1292). Also, under the Agrarian Justice Movement, fishers, small-scale farmers and pastoralist "use food sovereignty as a way to express their position, which is starkly opposed to that of mere hunger reduction through food security as promoted by mainstream policies" (ibid.). The contribution of this social movement is positive in West Africa, its affiliates combined the global convergence of land and Water Struggles ... "environmental/climate change justice into the new movement's political platform that is focused on putting a stop to natural resource grabbing" (Tramel, 2018, p. 1292). As argued by Tilly (1986), "the whole set of means that a group has for making claims of different kinds on different individuals or groups" is essential.

In the same vein, Tramel (2018, p. 1294) argues that "since radical agrarian and environmental movements are converging on the broad basis of system change, the protest devices within their repertoires of contention can be assembled in accordance with political opportunities." In addition, such social movements in West Africa diversify the participation in intercontinental political spaces. For example, they are increasingly drawing from not only environmental but also agrarian and fisheries protests within their repertoire of contention" (ibid.). In theory, collective action result in good governance[3] which is instrumental in dealing with societal (Tilly & Tarrow, 2015) and environmental or climate change issues. These engagements promote inclusivity by promoting citizen participation which contribute to a concrete system of democratic and good governance in dealing with climate change (UNDP, 2018).

Conclusion

This explored how local environmental activists protest and promote environmental justice in Africa. Climate change is a serious concern with developing countries and particularly Africa being the most vulnerable continent in the world. Whenever temperatures increase or decrease, or rainfall patterns change or shift for a prolonged period of time, crops will wilt leading to famine and hunger. Analysis in this chapter reveals that modernisation and urbanisation are the major factors leading to climate change in the world through population growth over scarce resources, that threatens the environment. As culprits of environmental injustice, developed countries through modernity and capitalism desire to dominate the world by promoting their legacy at the expense of the environment. Western dominance destroys the environment which is the chief source of Africa's livelihood sustenance as noted by Tramel (2018). Also, globalisation permits developed countries to use developing nations and Africa as dumping sites of hazardous products which pose environmental catastrophe. Following these developments, it will be difficult to achieve environmental justice in the world, therefore there is a need for countries from the North and South to engage and collaborate on an equal basis and work together in promoting environmental justice for the benefit of the future generation worldwide. Anthropologically, if the inequality and environmental injustice persist, development in Africa will remain in quagmire as the gap will be widened by taking Africa for granted when it comes to environmental justice.

To curtail this, local environmental activists in Africa must mobilise with urgency and advocate against environmental injustice as demonstrated in South Africa, Kenya, Senegal and Zimbabwe among others. The value of environmental activism calls for inclusivity and citizen participation in environmental protection decision makings. The usage corresponds with what Tilly (1986) calls "collective action," that is, individuals or organisations engage to promote good governance and environmental justice. This chapter argues that there is need for strong engagements of communities in decisions that affect their economic and social life of the people. Failure to achieve integration and/or inclusion between developed and developing countries impinges on climate change mitigation strategies, therefore there is a need for countries from both the North and South to work towards sustainability and resilient to climate change management as urged by goal numbers 11 and 13 of the United Nations Sustainable Development Goals.

Notes

1 Urbanisation is an extension of urban areas and the rapid increase of the general population in urban areas (see Kantakumar et al., 2011).
2 Modernisation refers to a model of a progressive transition from a "pre-modern" or "traditional" to a "modern" society (see Bernstein, 1971).
3 The understanding that the State does not govern alone, but policy decisions are also influenced by non-state actors (civil society and business).

References

Addaney, M., & Cobbinah, P. B. (2019). Climate change, urban planning and sustainable development in Africa: The difference worth appreciating. In Cobbinah P., & Addaney M. (Eds.), *The geography of climate change adaptation in urban Africa*. Cham: Palgrave Macmillan.

Adger, N. W., Huq, S., Brown, K., Conwaya, D., & Hulmea, M. (2003). Adaptation to climate change in the developing world. *Progress in Development Studies*, 3(3), 179–195.

Africa Renewal. (2019). *Taking action on climate change*. New York: United Nations.

Åström, D. O., Forsberg, B., Ebi, K. L., & Rocklöv, J. (2013). Attributing mortality from extreme temperatures to climate change in Stockholm, Sweden. *Nature Climate Change*, 3(12), 1050–1054.

Atapattu, S. A. (2016). Climate change, human rights, and COP 21: One step forward and two steps back or vice versa? *Georgetown Journal of International Affairs*, 17(2), 47–55.

Bao, C., & Chen, X. (2015). The driving effects of urbanization on economic growth and water use change in China: A provincial-level analysis in 1997-2011. *Journal of Geographical Sciences, 25*(5), 530–544.

Bernstein, H. (1971). "Modernization theory and the sociological study of development". *Journal of Development Studies, 7*(2), 141–160.

Bond, P. (2012). *The politics of climate justice paralysis above*. Pietermaritzburg, South Africa: University of KwaZulu-Natal Press.

Bond, P., & Dorsey, M. (2010). Anatomies of environmental knowledge and resistance: Diverse climate justice movements and waning eco-neoliberalism. *Journal of Australian Political Economy* (66), 286–316.

Brändlin, A. (2019). *The global injustice of the climate crisis*. Germany: DW. Retrieved 7 October 2021 from: https://www.dw.com/en/the-global-injustice-of-the-climate-crisis-food-insecurity-carbon-emissions-nutrients-a-49966854/a-49966854

Brazier, A. (2015). *Climate change in Zimbabwe, facts for planners and decision makers*. Harare: Konrad Adenauer Stiftung.

Building Bridges Collective (2010). *Space for Movement? Reflections from Bolivia on Climate Justice, Social Movements and the State*. Leeds: Footprint Workers Co-op.

Chitongo, L. (2019). Rural livelihood resilience strategies in the face of harsh climatic conditions. The case of ward 11-Gwanda, South, Zimbabwe. *Cogent Social Sciences, 5*, 1617090.

Christian-Smith, J., Gleick, P.H., & Cooley, H. (2012). *A twenty-first century US water policy*. Oxford: Oxford University Press.

Cobbinah, P. B., & Darkwah, R. M. (2016). Toward a More Desirable Form of Sustainable Urban Development in Africa. *African Geographical Review*. DOI: 10.1080/19376812.2016.1208770

Cooley, H., & Pacific Institute (2012). *Social vulnerability to climate change in California*. Sacramento, CA: California Energy Commission.

Egondi, T., Kyobutungi, C., Kovats, S., Muindi, K., Ettarh, R., & Rocklöv, J. (2012). Time-series analysis of weather and mortality patterns in Nairobias informal settlements. *Global Health Action, 5*(1), 19065.

FDRE. (2011). *Ethiopia's Climate-Resilient Green Economy Green economy strategy*. Ethiopia: Addis Ababa.

Groh, A. (2019). *Theories of culture*. London: Routledge.

Human Rights Watch. (2018). *Kenya: Harassment of Environmental Activists. Arrested, Interrogated, Detained*. Retrieved 7 October 2021 from: https://www.hrw.org/news/2018/12/17/kenya-harassment-environmental-activists

Jegede A.O., & Mokoena U.C. (2019). Thinking into the future: Constructing social security law as climate change adaptation strategy in urban South Africa. In Cobbinah P., & Addaney M. (Eds.), *The geography of climate change adaptation in urban Africa*. Cham: Palgrave Macmillan. 10.1007/978-3-030-04873-0_12

Kantakumar, L.N., Sawant, N.G., & Kumar, S. (2011). Forecasting urban growth based on GIS, RS and SLEUTH model in Pune metropolitan area. *International journal of geomatics and geosciences, 2*(2), 568.

Kenny, R., Law, C., & Pearce, J. M. (2010). Towards real energy economics: energy policy driven by life-cycle carbon emission. *Energy Policy, 38*(4), 1969–1978.

Knight, T. (2019). *Cape Town teen climate activist Ayakha Melithafa takes drought to the UN*. Maverick Citizen, 26 September.

Matenga L. (2019) Placing climate change in wetland conservation and urban agriculture contestations in Harare, Zimbabwe. In Cobbinah P., & Addaney M. (Eds.), *The geography of climate change adaptation in urban Africa*. Cham: Palgrave Macmillan.

Mayer, B. (2018). *The International Law on Climate Change*. Cambridge: Cambridge University Press.

New Flame. (2019). *If we burn, you burn with us*. Retrieved 7 October 2021 from: https://www.newframe.com/if-we-burn-you-burn-with-us/

Lenferna, A. (2019). *Why climate activists and unions should team up*. New Frame. Retrieved 7 October 2021 from: https://www.newframe.com/why-climate-activists-and-unions-should-team-up/

Ogwu, M. C. (2019). Towards sustainable development in Africa: the challenge of urbanization and climate change adaptation. In Cobbinah, P. B. & Addaney, M. (eds.), *The geography of climate change adaptation in Urban Africa* (pp. 29–55). Cham: Palgrave Macmillan.

Open Society Foundations [OSFs]. (2019). Q&A: Organizing for climate justice in sub-Saharan Africa. *The Voices*. Retrieved 7 October 2021 from: https://www.opensocietyfoundations.org/voices/q-and-a-organizing-for-climate-justice-in-sub-saharan-africa

Rathzel, N., Cock, J., & Uzzell, D. (2018). Beyond the nature–labour divide: Trade union responses to climate change in South Africa. *Taylor & Francis Online*, 15(4), 504–519.

Schellnhuber, H. J. (2013). *Turn down the heat: Climate extremes, regional impacts, and the case for resilience*. A Report for the World Bank by the Potsdam Institute for Climate Impact Research and Climate Analytics.

Shamasundari, R. (2017). *Climate change dilemma driven by urbanisation*. The ASEAN Post (daily), 26 August 2017.

Tilly, C. (1986). *The Contentious French*. Cambridge: Belknap Press of Harvard University Press.

Tilly, C., & Tarrow, G. S. (2015). *Contentious Politics*. Oxford: Oxford University Press.

Tramel, S. (2018). Convergence as political strategy: Social justice movements, natural resources and climate change. *Third World Quarterly*, 39(7), 1290–1307.

UNDP. (2018). *Climate Change Adaptation in Africa*. UNDP Synthesis of Experiences and Recommendations 2000–2015.

UNFCCC. (2006). *United Nations Fact Sheet on Climate. Africa Is Particularly Vulnerable to the Expected Impact of Global warming*. Nairobi: UN Climate Change Conference.

Nyathi, N. (2020). *Covid-19, tackling imminent danger of climate change*. Zimbabwe: UNICEF. Retrieved 7 October 2021 from: https://www.unicef.org/zimbabwe/stories/covid-19-tackling-imminent-danger-climate-change

Mupfumira, E.. (2020). *Young people rally world leaders to act on climate change and sustainable development*. Zimbabwe: UNICEF. Retrieved 7 October 2021 from: https://www.unicef.org/zimbabwe/stories/young-people-rally-world-leaders-act-climate-change-and-sustainable-development

Solomon, S., Manning, M., Marquis, M., & Qin, D. (2007). *Climate change 2007-the physical science basis: Working group I contribution to the fourth assessment report of the IPCC* (Vol. 4). Cambridge University Press

UNICEF. (2020). *UNICEF appoints young Zimbabwean as youth climate change advocate.*

Ware, J., & Kramer, K. (2019). *Hunger strike: The climate and food vulnerability index*. London: Christian Aid.

Yuhas, A. (2019). *Cyclone Idai May Be 'One of the Worst' Disasters in the Southern Hemisphere*. New York Times.

5 Memories of Futures-Past and Visions of Future-Futures: An Architecture-to-Backcasting Metaphor Approach Towards Tools and Practices for Sustainable City Transitioning in Africa

Vipua Rukambe and Daniel Irurah

Introduction

Due to increasing rates of urbanisation in the developing world, African cities are rapidly becoming the critical contexts influencing our futures especially in relation to mitigation and adaptation responses to climate change, biodiversity loss, escalating poverty and socio-economic inequalities. Even though the underlying drivers of these challenges have been primarily global, the need for sustainable city transitioning is most drastic in Sub-Saharan African cities which are only now experiencing the most intense waves of urbanisation. However, with regard to knowledge and understanding, transitioning towards sustainable cities has largely remained as an academic pursuit focusing on cities in the developed world with minimal translation into tools and communities-of-practice for effecting the necessary transitioning. The chapter argues that the prevailing theoretical focus has not been translated into systematic transitioning tools and practices globally and more specifically for African cities.

The chapter addresses this gap based on the significance and application of metaphor as a cognitive-bridging tool commonly applied towards a better understanding of an "unknown-domain" (the *metaphrand*) through correlating it to a similar but more familiar domain (the *metaphier*) (Jaynes, 2000; Lakoff & Johnson, 2003). The initial section appraises the critical shortfalls of sustainable city transitioning studies and especially flaws arising from the overdependence on approaches anchored on the prevailing reductionist paradigm. The section concludes with the observation that transitioning towards sustainable cities (as the desirable futures) for African cities now calls for the systematic evolution of tools and communities-of-practice which can systematically effect the required transformation. Subsequent sections explore the cognitive significance of *metaphor* followed by a presentation of a process of evolving

DOI: 10.4324/9781003181484-5

more relevant and effective transitioning tools through a metaphorical mapping of architecture (as the *metaphier* or known practice-domain) to backcasting (as the *metaphrand* or unknown practice-domain) with futures-studies as the overarching multi-disciplinary field.

Structure, Logic and Process Across the Theoretical Foundations

Arising from the motivation and objective of facilitating the evolution of tools and communities-of-practice towards expediting sustainable city transitioning for African cities, the chapter is inevitably multi-disciplinary in nature and is therefore grounded within numerous theoretical fields from a wide range of disciplines. Sustainable city transitioning is therefore the core theoretical field from which the chapter springs and feeds back into (see for example Byrne et al., 2017; Robinson et al., 2011; Swilling et al., 2017). With transitioning in mind, the chapter prioritises backcasting approach and mental-time-travel as the additional sub-fields of immediate interest. The three fields (transitioning, backcasting and mental-time-travel) inevitably locate the chapter within the broader multi-disciplinary field of futures-studies which is kept at a peripheral even though it is one of the most systematically developed to date (see for example, Jancsary, 2016; Van den Berg & Ganzevoort, 2014).

In order to convincingly engage with backcasting, the scientific-domain of neuroscience and the philosophy-domain of phenomenology are introduced through an integrated subfield of neurophenomenology which emerged from neuroscience over two decades ago. This allows the analysis to highlight the rarely acknowledged cognitive competencies needed to underpin backcasting in sustainable city transitioning with a focus on mental-time-travel as the primary cognitive competence (see Section 3 for sample readings). Although architecture as a discipline and practice is also intensely referenced in the chapter, the primary interest is its hypothesised temporal similarity with backcasting which in turn allows for a *metaphor approach* as the overall method of the chapter. Architecture closely resembles backcasting in that both are future-oriented – in a technical sense, they are both *projective* domains (they entail goals set for realisation within set future-time horizons). It is within this logic that the two fields can be metaphorically be linked (with architecture as the *metaphier* and backcasting as the *metaphrand*) and both can therefore be contextualised within futures-studies. It is also within this logic that the metaphor sub-field is adopted as the overall method of the chapter based on insights from Jaynes (2000) as briefly appraised in Section 4.

With architecture as the *metaphier* (the known knowledge-domain), it is prioritised as the primary informant towards the evolution of responsive tools and communities-of-practice which are deemed to be missing in backcasting. Given that the key competence in architecture is based on our cognitive capacity of bringing "*other-worlds*" into materialisation in the form of buildings, the field of *liminality* becomes crucial towards an understanding of this cognitive competence. However, the analysis clearly notes the extent to which the competence is distributed across diverse disciplines as elaborated on in Section 4. It is on this basis that similar liminality-tools for the "*making-of-other-worlds*" through backcasting can be envisaged.

Finally, the argument presented in the chapter entails enormous novelty of thought and envisaged practice which radically challenges our prevailing understanding of reality. In particular, the idea that we have agency to influence the future we will experience (and thus the overall efficacy of backcasting itself) is likely to be dismissed as "wishful thinking" and even possibly as time wasting. It is in view of this inertia/constraint that the chapter engages with the field of paradigm shifting well before getting into the substantive sections. Even though paradigm shifting has been systematically studied across multiple fields, our main reference and source of insights is Kuhn (1996). It is within this concern that we have engaged a comparative appraisal of essentialism (as the prevailing paradigm of reality where human agency over the futures we face is deemed to be negligible) vs. constructivism (as the newly emerging paradigm of reality where our agency is fully acknowledged and exercised). Without such a paradigm shift, actors and stakeholders are likely to find it extremely frustrating when engaging with sustainable city transitioning through a backcasting process, especially because they are likely to misunderstand it as "wishful thinking" or "mere fantasy" which would inevitably entail a negative emotion due to the concern about wasted time. The schedule below presents a summary of the main fields engaged in the chapter (Table 5.1).

The Status Quo and Forecasted Futures for African Cities

The Critical Drivers Calling for Sustainable City Transitioning

Arising from the urgent need for expedited realisation of sustainable cities, and especially through the implementation of sustainable development goals (SDGs), transitioning (as a time-focused field of knowledge on how cities transform over time) has gained increasing attention. In particular, the emergent field focuses on the processes which drive intended and spontaneous change which in turn transform cities over time. Understanding the dynamics of past and ongoing transitions is crucial as it guides the co-evolution of the key drivers such as economic, cultural, technological, ecological, and institutional sub-systems which co-evolve in many ways and reinforce each other in the transition process (Grin et al., 2010). The co-evolutionary aspect of transitioning also calls for co-evolutionary approaches of managing transitions where envisioning, experimenting and learning co-evolve in cyclical, co-creative, prototyped, iterative processes that reflect ongoing adaptations to feedback loops over time (Kemp et al., 2007). In contrast to the global shift towards urban futures, African cities

Table 5.1 Summary of theoretical domains/fields engaged in the chapter

Core/Primary Level Fields	Key Sources Appraised for the Insights Engaged in the Chapter
Sustainable city transitioning Architecture Futures-studies Backcasting	Swilling et al., (2017), Robinson et al. (2011), Byrne et al. (2017), Condia (1991), Frascari (2011), Robinson and Pallasmaa (2015), Jancsary (2016), Van den Berg and Ganzevoort (2014), Robinson et al. (2011), Wangel (2011), Daisy (2011)
Complementary/Secondary Level Fields Mental-time-travel Neurophenomenology (Neuroscience and Phenomenology)Metaphor	Addis et al. (2007), Varela et al. (1991), Van den Berg and Ganzevoort (2014), Varela et al. (1991), Varela (1996), Laughlin and Throop (2009), Robinson and Pallasmaa, (2015), Jaynes (2000), Lakoff and Johnson (2003)
Tertiary Level Fields Paradigm shifting (essentialism vs. constructivism)Liminality Quantum science	Kuhn (1996), Harper (2008), Metzner (1994), Barret (2017), Maape (2013, 2016), Bohm (1980), Armstrong (2010), Ingold (2013), Turner (1969, 1974), Weisbrode (2012), Winkelman (2000), Bohm (1980)

remain preoccupied with legacy challenges inherited from colonial and apartheid planning principles based on power and dominance by one race over the others. This also entailed superimposition of ideologically motivated and self-serving western notions such as incremental modernisation and progress for communities that the west deemed to be "primitive" or "backward" (see Rist (2014) and de Rivero (2010).

This colonial origin of most African cities was antithetical to the creation of proper communities, living and working in humane urban environments. From the start, African cities were therefore "conceived" and developed within a fundamental tension of conflicting and inhumane rationalities and especially between the logic of imperialism through racial segregation vs. the logic of basic survival for those drawn to them without access to formal systems of education and livelihoods (UN Habitat, 2014). Metaphorically, their origin was therefore anchored on illegitimate "conception" especially when one considers the flawed visions of their founding. During the neo-colonial period, urban planning theory and practice for African cities remains predominately rooted on theories primarily responding to western city opportunities and challenges which have continued to serve as universal models to date. As a result, African cities continue to be measured according to the historically distortional metrics centered around western values and interests (Myers, 2011).

Arising from this legacy, this section appraises prioritised readings to elaborate on how this historical origin has contributed to the undesirable status quo of our cities as well as the key approaches that have been applied towards mitigating the resultant crises. In particular, the appraisal focuses on the prioritisation of forecasting approaches (the extrapolation of past and present trends into the future) towards the pursuit of city-futures such that current and historical trends become prioritised as the dominant informants of the envisaged futures (Daisy, 2011). As part of setting the context for the chapter, the section argues that forecasting-based planning for cities undergoing rapid change entails a highly passive approach that perpetuates the undesirable status quo, thus leaving us ill prepared for the fast-approaching futures.

Based on forecasted urbanisation scenarios, Bello-Schünemann (2018) states that by 2035, more than 810 million Africans will be living in cities, megacities and towns of different sizes, thus resulting in 348 million more urban-dwellers compared to the present. In particular, Sub-Saharan Africa is expected to account for close to a quarter of the global urban population growth over the next 15 years. Bello-Schünemann (2018) thus concludes that sub-Saharan Africa's urban transition is now in full swing, and its urban population is growing the fastest globally. However, Alaazi and Aganah (2019) note that by 2014, slum-dweller population in sub-Saharan Africa cities was estimated to be 55% of the urban population. Their study further questions the common neoliberal-guided approach of slum clearance which most city and national authorities default to as a response to the challenge.

In order to confront such enormous backlogs in urban housing, infrastructure and services, Swilling et al. (2017) project that by 2050, material infrastructure will need to have been implemented for five billion new urban dwellers. From a forecasting-oriented perspective, Bello-Schünemann, (2018) also notes that "defining the future of Africa's brave new world" should start with 2035 as a time horizon to work towards and should be guided by the following strategic questions: *what are the key characteristics of urbanisation in sub-Saharan Africa? What does the future hold? Is the urbanisation in Sub-Saharan Africa likely to translate into increased prosperity? Lastly, what should government look like to capitalise on the opportunities brought about by urbanisation?* (Bello-Schünemann, 2018, p. 13). Bello-Schünemann (2018) further substantiates on the status quo through a comparison of what was historically done in the context of urbanisation in the West vs. what is currently manifesting in African cities. The western approach was to simultaneously implement large-scale industrialisation and economic diversification as a means of pursuing their city-futures. The difference in approach is one of the significant gaps contributing to Africa's ill-preparedness in facing its urbanised futures.

Faced with the mega-trend of rapid urbanisation and having failed to rapidly factor in similar responsive economic programmes, Africa now faces its urbanisation crisis as a complex of multi-faceted crises such as pervasive poverty, inequality, unemployment for large proportions of the youth populations and a general deficit of economic opportunities as well as infrastructure and services. Based on a business-as-usual (BAU) trajectory, the study further elaborates on the need for policymakers to find interventions that improve people's lives in the short-term while also ensuring strategic investments targeting long-term returns to underpin sustainability. This approach emphasises the critical significance of explicitly engaging the temporal dimension in the pursuit of sustainable urban futures for African cities.

Focusing on South Africa, Everatt (2018) addresses the prior whites-only utopia under apartheid that has now soured into the country's status quo of poverty and infrastructure/services backlogs in face of the ongoing rapid urbanisation especially for the black population. The study further argues that since the end of apartheid the central issue of the democratic government should have been to re-think the political economy of cities. Given that such a strategy was not systematically conceived or implemented during the democracy-era, the dystopia of segregated and dysfunctional cities has become deeply embedded in the infrastructural, spatial and social fabric of South Africa's cities. Everatt (2018) thus focuses on attempts to develop policies towards mitigating the dystopia of what H.F. Verwoerd (the infamous *"architect-of-apartheid,"*Kenney, 2016) once conceived, crafted and materialised as a utopia of his time and for his white-race-only beneficiaries. This signifies a prior future vision/utopia which has soured over time to become our status-quo (post-apartheid) nightmare. This scenario demonstrates a memory of a prior desirable future(s) or utopia whose legacy now continues as our status quo dystopia. The overall argument anchoring this discussion thus takes a similar perspective as in Everatt (2018), especially where the author attributes the current urban crises in African cities to the absence of *"the vision,"* particularly among those who hold the crucial power to effect the required transformation.

Key insights from the selected literature on the escalating urbanisation and the resultant crises in African cities indicate that the critical relevance of understanding and working with futures (the temporal perspective) is neither systematically acknowledged nor evenly applied. In the few instances where futures are acknowledged, no systematic differentiation is drawn between forecasting (projection of historical or status quo trends and trajectories) vs. backcasting (envisioning and pursuing desirable futures) approaches even though it is now clear that the two approaches draw from entirely different paradigms. The prevailing challenges facing African cities thus primarily stem from the dominance of a forecasting approach in urban planning, development and governance, especially when anchored on a mechanistic paradigm (or essentialist worldview of reality) which inadequately allows for agency and control among human actors at multiple levels towards envisioning and pursuing their own context-informed desirable futures. It is within this temporal-gap that participatory backcasting has emerged and evolved (see elaboration in the next section).

Backcasting as a Transformative Approach to Sustainable Cities

Moving into the 21st century, futures studies have shifted from the more formalistic futures-thinking in Europe and USA in the 20th century in favour of looking elsewhere for inspiration towards desirable futures we can collaboratively aspire to. In the process, backcasting has emerged as one of the key approaches in futures-studies and is rapidly being adopted as an effective approach to sustainable city transitioning (Wangel, 2011). The core argument substantiated in this chapter is therefore premised on backcasting as the primary approach as it presents a significant advantage over the other tools of future-knowing. In particular, it is a target-driven and goal-oriented approach based on backcasted images (*visions*) of the desirable future such that the images in turn can serve as pathway-indicators towards the desired future.

As indicated in Figures 5.1 and 5.2, backcasting is thus used to envision the future state the stakeholders would like to head towards over the long-term

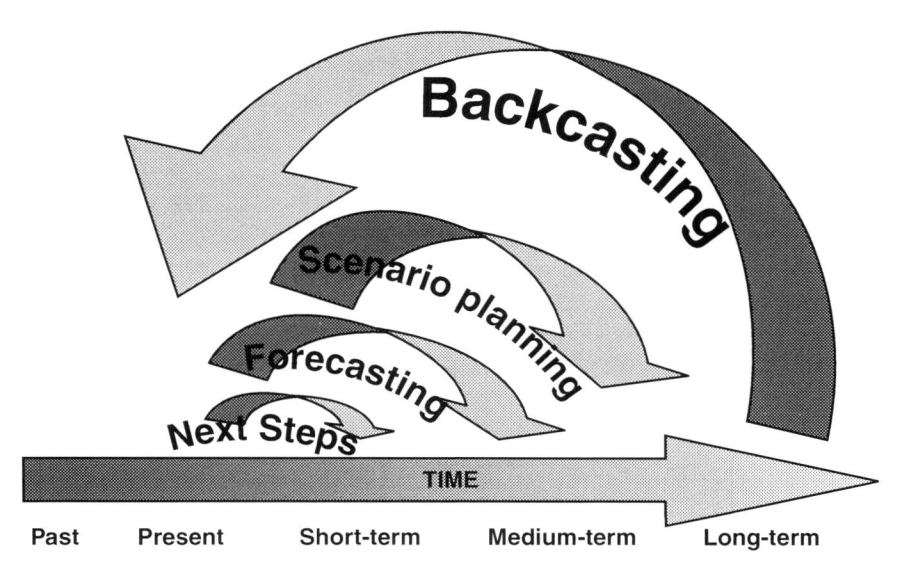

Figure 5.1 Backcasting vs. forecasting and scenario-planning as key approaches in futures-studies.

Source: Daisy, 2011.

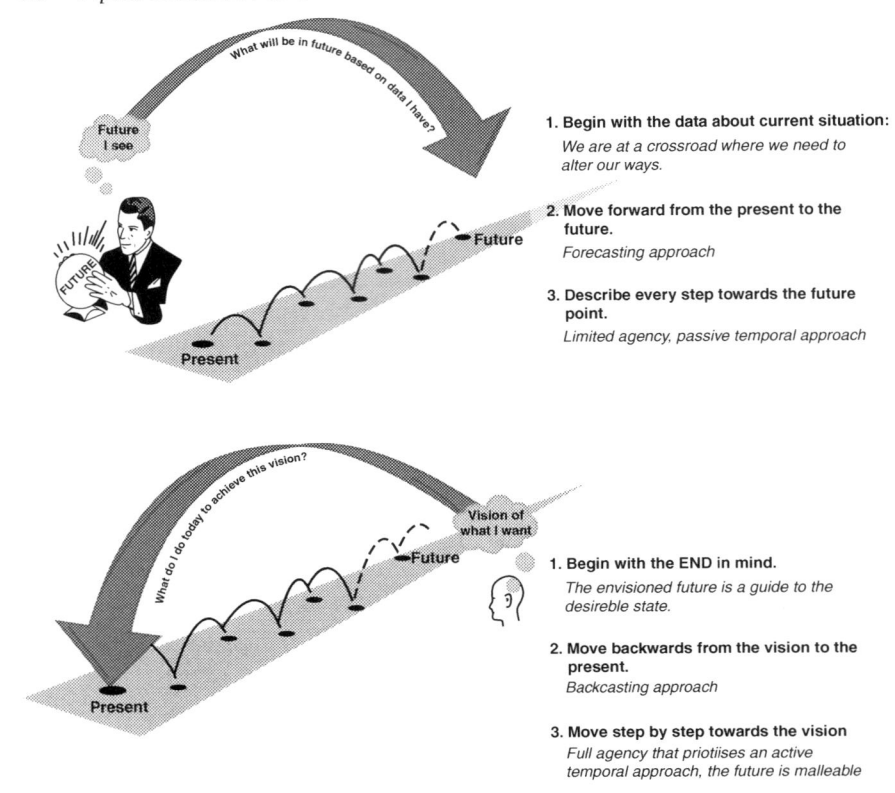

Figure 5.2 Temporal perspective: contrasting forecasting vs. backcasting.

horizon, as well as realistic pathway towards the vision. The approach is therefore more advantageous in tackling sustainability challenges as it deals with acting on the status quo from a radically different mindset compared to the projection of historical-trends as commonly applied in forecasting or scenario-planning. The key element in backcasting for sustainable city transitioning is the *prioritisation of the vision*. Through an envisioning process and the resultant vision(s) of the desirable futures, backcasting thus directly targets transformative change at both individual and collective levels as the means for pursuing the more radical future as envisioned. Taking the SDGs 2030 as an example, they clearly stipulate the envisioned outcomes by 2030 as the envisioning time-horizon. However, the transitioning pathway(s) for the pursuit of the vision is left to the discretion of diverse parties who are expected to subsume the goals within their priority areas of interest as opposed to prioritising the goals as the cohering force of their visions.

The prioritisation of a backcasting approach changes the fundamental question in sustainability transitioning such that attention on *how* and *what* get transformed to other questions that are rarely included in forecasting or even under alternative sustainability transitioning approaches. In particular, the additional question of *who* is to change now becomes crucial (Wangel, 2011). The transformative power of prioritising backcasting thus resides in its leveraging of change within societal structures

as an inevitable strategy in sustainable city transitioning. This intentional transformation from one state (an undesirable *now*) to another (the *desirable-future*) for the same city over time is therefore metaphorically re-imagined as a journey-in-time in a manner similar to transiting through space when we undertake spatial journeys with a clear start-point and destination.

It is however important to note that in sustainable city transitioning studies so far, even when a clear backcasting perspective is applied, the approach typically takes a rationally-motivated conceptualisation of the desirable future (the *vision*). The pathways to the desirable futures are therefore inevitably dominated by the rational mindset as opposed to the more malleable creative approaches. While Daisy (2011) states that backcasting is an opportunity to "*let go*" of the current reality for a moment and "*freely imagine*" what could be possible, the rationally-motivated backcasting approach still entails a limited understanding of future-making and crafting mainly because stakeholders and practitioners have no responsive methods and tools on how to "*let go*" of the present in order to "*freely imagine*" a more radically different desirable future without the fear of falling into a "*wishful-thinking*" trap. Even when the more enhanced participatory backcasting approach is prioritised (see for example Robinson et al., 2011), it still lacks the critical *cognitive* insights which would enrich its tools and processes for *visioning* and *action* in pursuit of the resultant visions. Such critical insights, knowledge, skills and tools are commonly associated with *liminality-driven*disciplines or practices which focus on the "*making-of-other-worlds*" or "*other realities*" (with examples such as literature, music, film, drama/dance, *shamanism* and to some extent mathematics and architecture). The key insight from prevailing studies to date therefore indicate that backcasting has fallen far short of its promised efficacy both in theory and more so in practice.

The crucial competence of liminality-disciplines is their affordances for respective knowers and practitioners to access and inhabit "*two* or *more worlds*" simultaneously. This includes the affordance to operate in the two realms of a *present* and a *future* that is yet to emerge. As an approach in future-knowing (knowledge and crafting of futures as well as the tools and means to pursue such futures), backcasting still lacks proven and credible tools or methods of practice for "*accessing other worlds*" as well as tools of translating affordances so-accessed towards manifestation in our everyday realities. Figure 5.3 shows an initial liminality aspect in architecture. What is most crucial in this depiction is that, unlike in Figures 5.1 and 5.2, the future and present are co-present in the architect's mind at all times throughout the process of an architect's project.

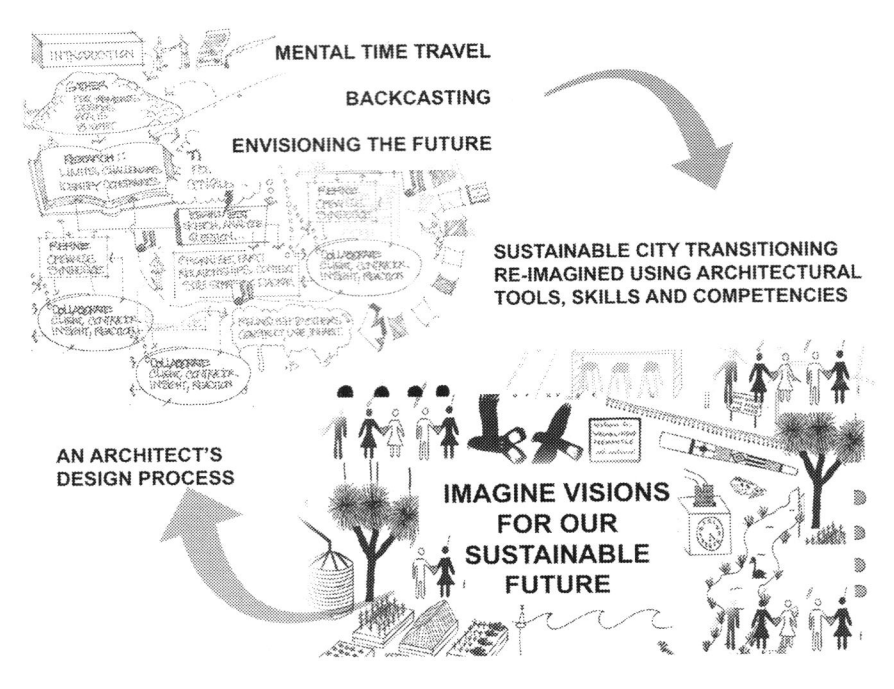

Figure 5.3 Liminality in architecture.
Source: Author, 2018.

The second reason why backcasting falls short in effecting the change is the lack of compelling communities-of-practice where groups of like-minded, interacting actors filter, amplify, invest and provide, convene, build, learn and facilitate each other to ensure ongoing co-creation and sharing of knowledge in their domain (Serrat, 2017). Key examples in recent emergence of communities-of-practice in sustainability transitioning include the various entities which operate the diverse but mainly voluntary, green building rating schemes which include the World Green Building Council (World Green Building Council, 2020); Leadership in Energy and Environmental Design – LEED in US and Canada (LEED rating system – USGBC, 2020); Building Research Establishment Environmental Assessment Method – BREEAM in UK (BREEAM, 2020); Green Star in Australia (Green Building Council of Australia (2020); and in South Africa (GBCSA, 2020). However, a key transitioning-disadvantage of these communities-of-practice is that they mainly focus on the evaluation stage of the process based on measurement tools they have evolved. While an entity such as the Ecological Footprint Network (EFN) (Ecological Footprint Network, 2020) also operates in a manner similar to a community-of-practice, its focus has been primarily on knowledge stand-alone bio-capacity demand data with limited opportunities for application in practice among the relevant city actors.

As elaborated on in Section 4, architecture as a discipline and a field of practice enjoys a strong presence of communities-of-practice over and above its strong history as a liminality-driven discipline. It is on this account that architecturehas been prioritised as the metaphier-domain for interrogating the critical shortfalls which render future studies in general, and backcasting in particular, ineffective towards our pursuit for sustainable city transitioning. In order to evolve more effective understanding and tools, Figure 5.4 reflects the hypothesised metaphorical mapping with future studies as a bridging discipline. The future-focus of architecture and sustainable city transitioning thus informs their metaphorical relationship which in turn allows architecture (*metaphier*) to help us develop more refined understanding and tools as well as communities-of-practice for sustainable city transitioning (*metaphrand*) as elaborated in subsequent sections.

However, it is the unique contribution of neuroscience, and especially the newly emerged sub-field of neurophenomenology, which has added immense impetus to the liminality-disciplines and in turn opened up new opportunities for backcasting to re-invent itself. This motivates for the prioritisation of a neurophenomenological approach based on neuroscience insights where cognition, mind and consciousness are understood as embodied and also embedded to the respective environment of the knowing-brain (Depraz, Varela & Vermersch, 2002). Varela et al. (1991) provide a crucial bridging based on insights from neuroscience of perception and cognition. Varela (1996) further clarifies on neurophenomenology as the point of intersection between phenomenology as commonly investigated in

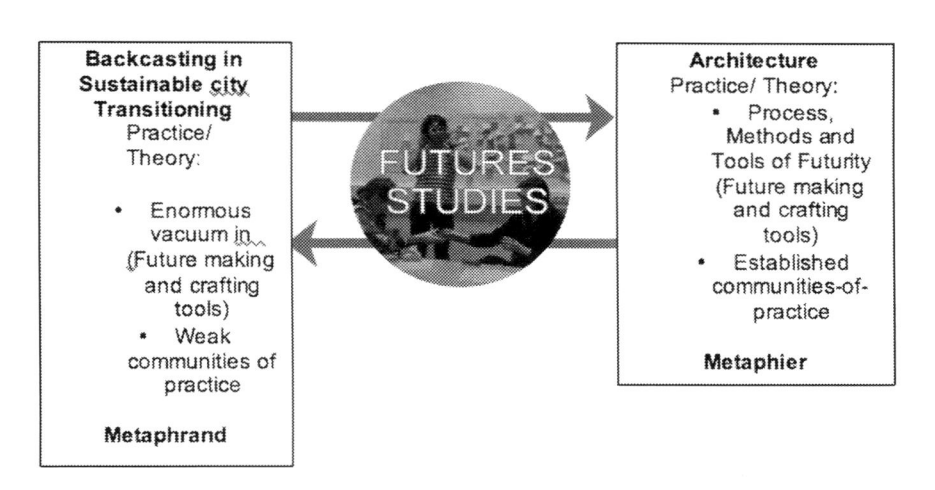

Figure 5.4 Bridging from backcasting to architecture through futures-studies.

philosophy (see for example Merleau Ponty, 1962, 1968) and mainstream neuroscience. This is substantiated further in the next section focusing on neuroscience studies in relation to mental-time-travel, paradigm-shifting and unlearning as the key pillars towards a constructivist worldview.

Constructivism, Neurophenomenology and the Temporal Dimension

In all the sustainability transitioning studies accessed so far, none of them have engaged with the significance of neurophenomenological insights, especially towards disrupting our obsolete understanding of how the reality – we perceive is constituted through our perceptual processes. To further clarify the link of neuroscience studies in mental-time-travel and futures-studies, as well as its relevance to the argument of this chapter, it is crucial to grasp an insight on neuro-mechanisms which support our cognitive competence for mental-time-travel. Van den Berg and Ganzevoort (2014) explain that mental-time-travel is supported by the same brain structures that help us connect our past actions and experiences to the present and thus housing the action programmes for future behaviour and cognition. Metaphorically, neural networks of behaviour and cognition of the past, present and future are "housed in the same room" in our brains from where they can be interactively recalled and rehearsed, both virtually as well as in mock-scenarios before they manifest in real action, and hence Ingvar (1985) provocative allusion to "memories of the future."

The ability to consciously or sub-consciously draw on memories from the past into the present, and thus re-live them, as well as the ability to apply this in the simulation of alternative future scenarios that have not yet manifested is all a part of our species' temporal-cognition competence which thus anchors our capacity for seemingly-effortless mental-time-travel. Suddendorf et al. (2009) define mental-time-travel in relation to *episodic memory* that supports the remembering of personal experiences. Addis et al. (2007, p. 11) affirm that mental-time-travel is also understood to share similar "core neural networks with the simulation of future episodes, enabling mental time travel into both the past and the future." This cognitive capacity to imagine and rehearse future scenarios before they materialise is what underpins the concept of "mental time travel" (Suddendorf et al., 2009). Addis et al. (2007) demonstrate that memory, especially episodic memory, also allow us to engage in "mental time travel" into both the past and the future and is crucial in our ability to mentally process non-existent events, especially towards simulating future happenings before they manifest. Suddendorf et al. (2009) further elaborates on the strong "overlap in brain activity between backward and forward mental time travel," which serves as mediation between the past, the present and the future through memories and visions. This highlights the significance of neurophenomenology in the argument developed in this chapter.

Their study further explored the neuro-mechanisms of mental time travel and then argued that it is possibly one of our most formidable cognitive competencies, and a uniquely human capability.

The key motivation for factoring neurophenomenology insights in the chapter is that, in the absence of such scientific evidence, most of us are likely to underestimate our enormous capacity for agency over the reality we experience at an individual and collective scale. It is this enhanced sense of our own agency coupled with the paradigm-shift to a more malleable reality which renders backcasting approach to sustainable city transitioning a worthwhile pursuit. However, this promise of neurophenomenology in transitioning cannot materialise without a radical paradigm shift as explored in the next section.

Paradigm Shifting from Essentialism to Constructivism

The glaring contradiction between sustainability and historical western mindset of progress, growth and development (see Rist, 2014 and de Rivero (2010) links the argument of this chapter to paradigm-shifting studies where "inner-changes" in terms of prevailing "ideation-systems" reciprocally drive the more significant structural and outwardly-visible changes especially in behaviour as well as the techno-spatial transformations we are hoping to see in our sustainable city futures. Commenting on this imperative, Byrne et al. (2017, p. 44) asserts that what constraints our sustainability responses "is that we are trying to solve all the apparent problems of the world, large and small by using the modernistic frame of thinking and acting that created the meta-problem of un-sustainability."

To understand why paradigm shifting is essential, we need an understanding of the prevailing world-views guiding most of the actors involved in the envisaged transitions. This is commonly captured under diverse terms such as "*modernist paradigm*," "*Cartesian*," "*mechanistic*" (as primarily informed by Newtonian mechanics), "*industrial-technological*," "*enlightenment*" and "*essentialist*." As Metzner (1994) explains, this worldview emerged out of a unique way of comprehending our world based on a combination of critical drivers in western culture such as the scientific revolution, renaissance and enlightenment as well as the resultant industrial revolution. With specific reference to the essentialist paradigm, Harper (2008) argues that it is anchored on key ideas which have gained increasing dominance since the enlightenment period in the West and has therefore become embedded in the beliefs and values of most actors in our cities at various levels.

Towards the end of the 19th century, the paradigm began to unravel as new sets of anomalies and contradicting ideas slowly began to take root. By the 1960s and 1970s, the new ideas had gained broader public support, with the specific example where "it became clearer that ideas of natural resource abundance to fuel unlimited material growth no longer fitted society" (Harper, 2008, p. 4). Having been historically embraced in the pursuit of progress and development, the promise of utopia under essentialism/enlightenment started morphing into our status quo nightmare and dystopia.

Among the emerging knowledge fields contending for alternative ways of construing our realities, neuroscience as well as mind/consciousness studies now guide us towards a reality where perpetual-flux and inter-dependency, as well as a "co-emerging of being" (better understood as a perpetual "becoming" rather than a mere passive "being"), constitutes the primary foundation of our reality. The "*I*" or "*self*" should thus be understood as a perpetual becoming as well as an emergence out of the dynamic interactions between body, mind and environment. The worldview anchored on this insight is commonly termed as "*constructivism.*" It is characterised as an interplay between our belief systems, meaning-making and environmental-stimuli, and our resultant feelings/emotions, responses and actions, which thus integrate into our perception and a construction of the reality we experience. If the components (belief systems and meaning-making) in this dynamic interaction change, the nature of our perception also changes and as a result the reality we perceive changes as well. It is on this basis that the sense of "agency of self" arises, which in turn translates to the experience of an "empowered-being" ready to act according to meaning arising from the emergent perception and experience. This stands in strong contrast to "*essentialism*" which continues to perpetuate the legacy of Newtonian/mechanistic science, especially through a positivistic and supposedly objective approach commonly termed as reductionism (Maape, 2013, 2016). Essentialism is also anchored on an obsolete belief system of a pre-existing "objective" reality that independently exists externally relative to the knower/observer, such that the observer has no means of influencing it, especially with the goal of pursuing alternative future outcomes. It is also anchored on a temporal view where the observer passively experiences the future as it unfolds and therefore has no means of influencing the manner in which such futures plays out.

Under constructivism, reality emerges as a co-creation, which is informed by or constituted out of our perceptions and experiences as well as the meanings we infer on such experiences. Reality is thus perceived as a perpetual dialogue between the "external" and "internal" realms of the self, between the perceiving and sensing subject or self and her reciprocative environment when all is understood as an integral whole. This section thus substantiates on the relevance and significance of neurophenomenological insights of mental time travel (especially when anchored on a constructivist worldview as opposed to essentialism) as a critical theoretical field in backcasting. It is within such an integrated and constructivist worldview that the hidden significance of architecture has started to emerge (see Section 4). However, it is crucial to factor in an additional scientific theory (implicate vs. explicate orders) which further explains our experience of reality.

Implicate vs. Explicate Order in Our Perception of Reality

Similar to *obduracy and affordance* theory by Jancsary (2016) and Laughlin and Throop (2009), implicate order is an ontological concept (concerns our understanding of nature of-being) from quantum theory as developed over half a century by the quantum physicist, David Bohm. In particular, Bohm (1980) argues that the reality we perceive entails an interplay between two orders or levels of reality – an *unfolding/explicate* and an *enfolding/implicate* order. The explicate order constitutes the order-level that is manifest to our senses as our everyday reality while the implicate order is an order-level that remains latent and hidden from our everyday reality. The implicate order is thus the domain of the integrated whole where the diverse explicate-orders are co-present at once and from where explicate order springs from. The simplest way of articulating this metaphorically would be the common saying that the sculpture is already within the marble even before the sculptor starts her sculpting and the sculpting is merely a process of making explicit (unfolding) what is already there at an implicate (enfolding) order level.

There are two orders to conceptualise complementary frameworks towards understanding a phenomenon or aspect of reality (Bohm 1980). At the level of *implicate order reality,* everything is related to each other and everything contains everything else. He constantly makes use of the *hologram* as the closest metaphor for facilitating comprehension. Only at the level of *explicate order reality* can phenomenon be perceived as separate or differentiated and relatively independent as commonly assumed under reductionism which currently drives conventional science as well as in our everyday experience. The implicate order level is therefore the enfolded reality which contains everything inseparably within itself (an integrated whole) and this unfolds into the explicate order reality within which we sense phenomena as separately ordered, categorisable and thus reducible towards a rational method of knowing. Within the implicate order, the future, the present and the past are all enfolded into a *singular super-reality* with a vast range of potentialities which can be unfolded into *diverse explicate orders* (Bohm, 1980).

Architecture in Relation to Tools and Communities-of-Practice for Sustainable City Transitioning

Architecture (as the *metaphier*) is metaphorically mapped to backcasting (as the *metaphrand*) based on their common features when viewed as disciplines and practices within futures studies. Guided by such a mapping, the chapter argues for metaphorically-guided enhancement of knowledge and know-how through connecting from that "*which-we-know*" (with architecture being the authors' background and primary knowledge field) to that *"which-we-aspire-to-understand"* (with backcasting as our prospective field). In a manner similar to (Jaynes, 2000; Lakoff & Johnson, 2003), the fundamentals of this mapping are represented in Figure 5.3. Similar to holistic fields under humanities such as mathematics, arts, music, film, drama and literature, architecture is strongly rooted in the knowledge and practice of the *"making-of-other-worlds/realities"* (the making of *other places* and *other times*) and therefore explicitly engages with the temporal dimension as a primary affordance or resource. Beyond the authors' intensive reflective knowing in this field, the chapter prioritises architecture due to its well-evolved complementary knowledge and tools that support the *making-of-other-worlds* as well as its well-established communities-of-practice which are engaged in the process of materialising such *"other worlds"* through buildings as the ultimate manifestation.

Liminality and Neurophenomenology in Architecture

Besides our capacity for mental time travel, the crafting of other realities entails the cognitive capacity for liminality as the competence/skill of *being-in* and *inhabiting* two or more worlds simultaneously. The closest term in everyday language which aligns with liminality is *ambivalence* (see for example, Weisbrode, 2012). In the past, liminality has been more systematically studied in psychology and anthropology and especially in relation to ritual practices among indigenous communities (see for example Ingold, 2013; Turner, 1969, 1974). Within anthropology in particular, one of the commonly studied ritual fields on liminality is *shamanism* (see for example, Armstrong, 2010; Winkelman, 2000). In recent neuroscience studies (over the last ten to twenty years), the competence for liminality has been closely associated with creativity across multiple disciplines, including the arts and architecture, as well as in paradigm-shifting moments in mainstream sciences such as physics, chemistry and biology. Such neuroscience insights are challenging architecture to systematically bridge from its prior anchoring in phenomenology (as commonly studied in philosophy) to the newly emerging multi-disciplinary field of neurophenomenology as pioneered by cognition and consciousness scholars such as Varela and Thompson (see for example, Varela, 1996; Varela et al., 1991). One of recent studies linking architecture to neurophenomenology is Robinson and Pallasmaa (2015).

Since its origin as an academic and practice discipline, architecture prepares the architect primarily for the *"hard labour"* of tackling the perverse obduracy of our everyday common-sense reality in order to access and render-manifest *new-worlds/realities* where buildings constitute the key outcome we commonly associate with architecture. In their strife to access other worlds, architects inevitably leave traces and memory-tracks which allow a perspective into how they access and bring forth these *other-worlds* to manifest in reality (Frascari, 2011). Such traces include the architect's doodling, sketching and building models. In addition, the discipline has legendary anecdotes of recurring episodes of agitation and anxiety, cycles of sleepless nights and lucid-dreaming, reverie, as well as fluency and deep-sense of metaphor (yet another marker of ambivalence and keeping oneself in "suspense over a viable duration" for the metaphor to stabilise and manifest). Ingold (2013, p. 71) further elaborates on the designer's journey of liminality and ambivalence from an anthropological perspective.

Contrary to modern-day understanding, the architect is therefore not merely an *"imagineering-machine"* for buildings but rather more of a *"medium"* which mediates between the present *"world-without-the-building"* and a future *"world-with-the-building."* Figure 5.1 demonstrates such a mediumship model for facilitating *"other-worlds/realities"* which rests on *tools of liminality* which facilitates the capacity momentarily in-habiting two or more worlds simultaneously. Borrowing from the language of future studies, the architect's ability to simultaneously operate within these two seemingly independent mental states (the undesirable present – *world-without-the-building*, and a desirable future – *world-with-the-building-manifested*) is primarily anchored on the competence of the architect as a medium for a new reality to manifest. Liminality is therefore an essential mediumship-competence which underpins and drives the architect's "mediation between the two worlds."

The term *"medium"* is used here in a dual sense. First, it denotes the architect herself as a transformed being capable of accessing other worlds such that she becomes the channel of exchange connecting to a *hidden reality* and its affordances in a manner similar to a *shaman* as elaborated in Condia (1991) and Armstrong (2010). In particular, Condia (1991) furthers this notion of the *architect-as-a-shaman* by stating that at the level of her professional role, she senses herself operating as a medium offering herself as a prototype for a new creative mode, that of a self without estrangement, able to transcend the world without negating it. The second sense is that of information flow by which affordances from the hidden realm (similar to Bohm, 1980) implicate order level) are rendered manifest into everyday reality. These two perspectives of "channel" and "information-flow" constitute the liminality component in archi-tecture specifically in relation to the materialisation of buildings as op-posed to other fields of practice (such as poetry or film) where similar materialisations take different modes of manifestation.

Besides liminality in conventional architecture, this chapter primarily applies a metaphor-approach to argue for a crucial role of the *meta-phorical architect* as applied in everyday language to capture the essence of *any actor* who serves as a *mastermind of any* radical social-political or economic transformation. Inspired by neurophenomenological in-sights and provoked by the technocratic aspirations in backcasting, the chapter therefore argues that *"architecture"* can be understood to denote the *"vital-"* or *"transformative-force"* within any *"projected future goal"* of an individual or collective and *"not solely"* a trade, profession or discipline for the realisation of a building or engineering project as commonly understood and practiced today. Within a neuro-phenomenological and constructivist paradigm, Barret (2017) extensively elaborates on such an understanding of agency which allows us to be the *"architects"* of our own experiences and hence the *crafters* of our own realities (Barret, 2017, p. 57). Neuroscience and neurophenomenology in particular therefore strongly affirm a new insight on the agency we need to build new realities as we engage with our futures, especially through *re-meaning* our perceptions in order to change behaviour in our present so as to optimally align them with our desirable future as it unfolds (becomes explicate). Liminality in architecture therefore only becomes necessary in illustrating a down-to-earth sense of one unique way in which such agency continues to manifest in our modern reality. Metaphorically, architecture can therefore be viewed as an ongoing manifestation of historical *shamanism* as understood and practiced among indigenous communities till now, even though the tools, methods and motives of practice may differ significantly.

This fluidity of the term *"architect"* thus allows for a broader metaphorical exploration in other domains which entail liminality such as *"ritual master as architect"* as commonly experienced in rituals by indigenous communities especially in Africa (Rukambe, 2016). Within this perspective, transformational leadership in Africa and globally can be equally viewed as entailing the *crafting of other-worlds* and *realities with liminality* as a crucial attribute for both the leader(s) and those whose efforts are to be cohered for the successful manifestation of their transformational goal. Leaders ready to shoulder such enormous responsibilities can therefore be understood to be serving as *"architects"* of their own and of their community's futures. This perspective of the architect as more than a mere *"imagineering* machine" for buildings thus facilitate the diverse range of actors to view and deploy themselves as the *"architects"* of their city-realities, in a manner that endows efficacy into their agency towards pursuing desirable futures for themselves rather than leaving that responsibility solely to transitioning experts and especially those currently wielding agency merely based on their conventionally narrow and reductionist-based know-how (technocratic, economic, environmental or political). The chapter therefore argues for the leveraging of architecture competence and tools to revitalise sustainable city transitioning studies and practice in general while also re-anchoring the study and practice of architecture within a broader range of principles, skills, and competencies, more firmly guided by the emerging understanding from neuroscience and consciousness studies. The key categories of relevant architect's tools can now be summarised as follows:

- tools for liminality – How architects develop and apply their competence for accessing and inhabiting two or more worlds (*other places, other times*) simultaneously;
- tools of capturing and stabilising alternative realities – This entails tools for regular entering-and-emerging from liminality with implicate-order affordances which get translated into explicate order building realities (concept, design-development, construction);
- tools of sharing/imparting the "totality/holistic" alternative realities among a broader range of actors within a communities-of-practice (concept, design-development, construction);
- tools of cohering efforts towards the pursuit of the prioritised "other world/reality" across diverse actors within communities-of-practice; and
- tools of reinforcing and adapting experiences within the new-worlds/ buildings once they manifest in the future.

Conclusion

Emerging from the insights on the key discussion points above, Figure 5.5 depicts the consolidation of the metaphorical relationship envisaged in the argument of the chapter. Since its origin as a craft in prehistoric era, and more recently as an academic/professional discipline, the practice of architecture has remained rooted in our species' competence of accessing and inhabiting other worlds/realities with "accessing-alternative-futures" as a key competence of the craft/profession. This competence can be attributed to the fact that fully skilled and adept architects are able

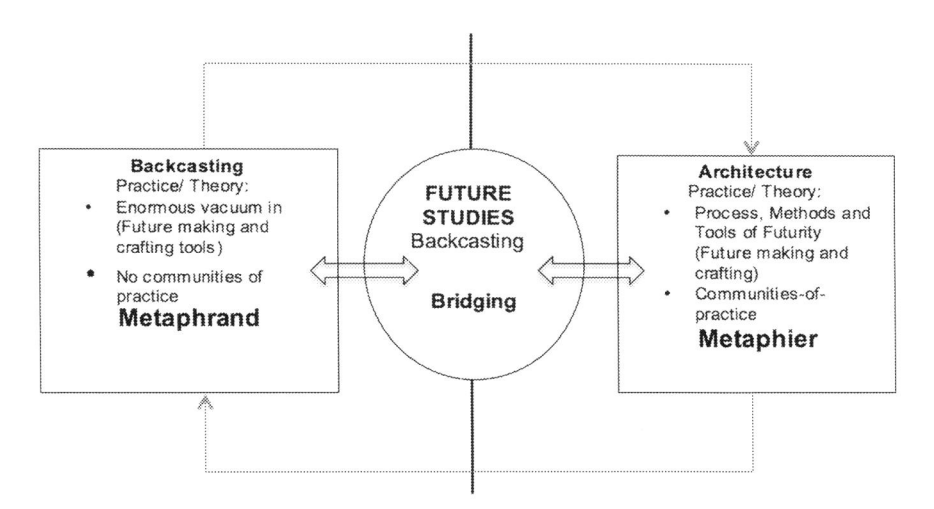

Figure 5.5 Consolidation of the metaphor principle in architecture and backcasting.

to access the *implicate order* in order to bring-forth new worlds as our *explicate order* reality.

Given the strong resonance to the argument in this chapter, Bohm's theory (the "*whole as enfolded within the implicate order*" and manifesting through unfolding into the *explicate order* level) further substantiates the significance of architecture as a practice of *accessing the implicate order reality* so as to influence how the *explicate order reality* unfolds and thus manifest into our future prospects. In the context of architecture and sustainable city transitioning, Figure 5.6 presents the two temporal periods (present/status quo and future state) as *explicate order levels of reality* which manifest in contrast to the *implicate order level of reality* which encompasses and thus transcends the explicate order duality of present vs. future.

In the practice of architecture, skilled architects can access the implicate order (the non-local state) directly without remaining trapped within the two discrete states at explicate order level where the present and the future are sensed as separate. It is in this sense that the chapter attributes the absence of futurity (explicit study of futures as understood and pursued in future-studies) as an explicit body of knowledge in architecture compared to its growing visibility in studies on sustainable city transitioning and backcasting in particular. In relation to the awareness of

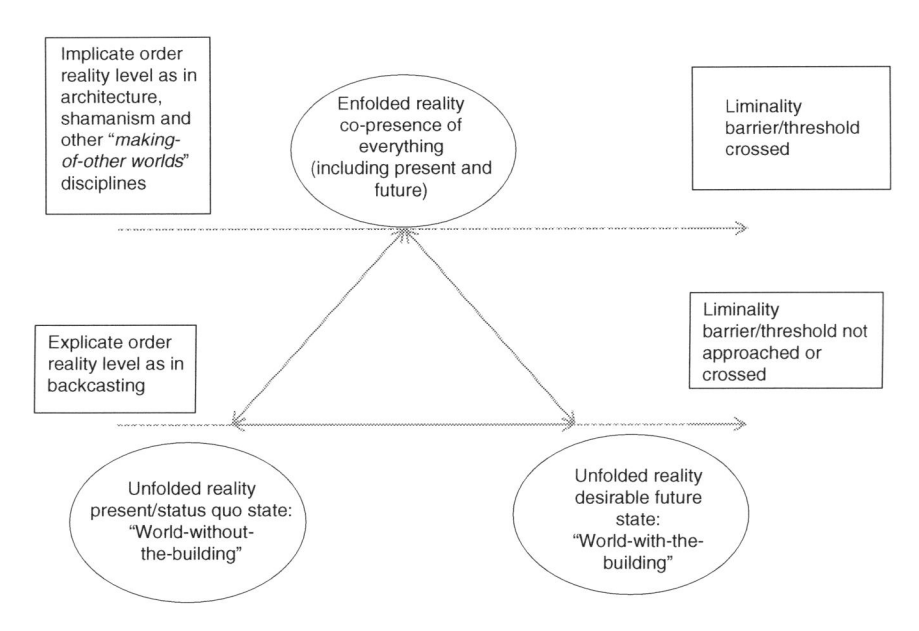

Figure 5.6 Explicate order levels as in futures studies and backcasting vs. implicate order level as in architecture.

the lower level explicate order (*"world-without-the-building"* as status quo state and *"world-with-the-building"* as the future state) vs. awareness of the higher level *implicate order* (where both time states are co-present and co-existing enfolded into each other), this chapter argues that, unlike in backcasting where the status quo and future states are sensed purely at explicate order level as oppositional binaries (present vs. future states remain as discrete and separate points on a timeline), skilled architects, possibly in similar manner to skilled *shamans*, can access the implicate order level awareness directly without remaining trapped in the explicate order level. This improved understanding is demonstrated through a comparison of Figures 5.3 and 5.6. Figure 5.6 therefore represents the newly synthesised articulation of the argument of the chapter within the context of architecture. For backcasting to become a more effective approach, it requires to adapt tools of liminality in order to facilitate a more transformative foundation for envisioning desirable futures and also evolve its own base of communities of-practice who can translate the visions into explicate reality through an unfolding process similar to the process by which the architect's blue-prints underpin the materialisation of the envisioned building.

An initial approach to translate and prototype the hypothesised tools elaborated in this chapter had envisaged a face-to-face design/planning charrette for the Marlboro Gautrain Station Precinct (MGSP) in Johannesburg, South Africa. However, due to Covid-19 restrictions, the prototype is now undergoing modification to allow for implementation through gamification within an online digital platform with a diverse range of purposefully selected participants from the case study precinct. This will entail participants remotely working together collaboratively in teams towards co-creating their desirable future(s) as well as the means for cohering efforts towards the pursuit of the prioritised "other world/reality" as a means towards prototyping a responsive communities-of-practice perspective.

References

Addis, D. R., Wong, A. T. & Schacter, D. L. (2007). Remembering the past and imagining the future: Common and distinct neural substrates during event construction and elaboration. *Neuropsychologia*, *45*(4), 1363–1377. Retrieved from: doi: 10.1016/j.neuropsychologia.2006.10.016.

Alaazi, D. A., &. Aganah, G. A. (2019). Understanding the slum–health conundrum in sub-Saharan Africa: A proposal for a rights-based approach to health promotion in slums. *Global Health Promotion* 1757–9759, *27*(3), 65–72. Retrieved from: 10.1177/1757975919856273

Armstrong, J. F. (2010). *Dambudzo Marachera as shamanistic "doppelganger": His shamanistic sensibility in his life and works* (Doctoral dissertation). Australia: The University of the Western Australia. Retrieved from: https://research-repository.uwa.edu.au/en/publications/dambudzo-marechera-as-shamanistic-doppelganger-his-shamanistic-se

Barret, L. F. (2017). *How emotions are made*. London: Macmillan.

Bello-Schünemann, J. (2018). Defining the future of Africa's brave new world. *Africa in fact: The quarterly journal of good governance Africa, 45*(4), 13–18.

Bohm, D. (1980). *Wholeness and the implicate order*. New York: Routledge.

Building Research Energy and Environmental Assessment Method-BREEAM. (2020). Retrieved from https://www.breeam.com/

Byrne, E., Mullally, G., & Sage, G. (2017). *Trans-disciplinary perspectives to transitions to sustainability*. New York: Routledge.

Condia, R. (1991). *The architect as shaman*. Retrieved from 10.4148/2378-5 853.1224

Daisy. (2011). *Backcasting – first, get clear on your vision of success*. [Blog post]. Retrieved from http://green-changemakers.blogspot.com/2011/06/backcasting.html

Depraz, N., Varela, F. J. & Vermersch, P. (Eds.). (2002). *On becoming aware: A pragmatics of experiencing*. Netherlands: John Benjamin Publishing.

de Rivero, O. (2010). *The myth of development: Non-viable economies and the crisis of civilization*. London: Zed Books.

Ecological Footprint Network. (2020). Retrieved from https://www.footprintnetwork. org/resources/data/

Everatt, D. (2018). Sidelined by policy makers. *Africa in Fact: The Quarterly Journal of Good Governance Africa, 45*(4), 69–75.

Frascari, M. (2011). *Eleven exercises in the art of architectural drawing: slow food for the architect's imagination*. New York: Routledge.

Green Building Council of Australia (2020). Retrieved from https://new.gbca. org.au/

Green Building Council of South Africa. (2020). Retrieved from https://gbcsa. org.za.

Grin, J., Rotmans, J. Schot, J., Geels, F. & Loorbach, D. (2010). *Transitions to sustainable development: New directions in the study of long term transformative change*. New York: Routledge.

Harper, S. A. (2008). *Towards the development of a "green" worldview, and criteria to assess the "green-ness" of a text: Namibia Vision 2030 as example* (Doctoral dissertation). Pretoria, South Africa: The University of Pretoria. Retrieved from https://www.ajol.info/index.php/sajee/article/viewFile/122814/ 112354

Ingold, T. (2013). *Making: Anthropology, archeology, art and architecture*. New York: Routledge.

Ingvar, D. H. (1985). "Memory of the future": an essay on the temporal organization of conscious awareness. *Human Neurobiology, 4*, 127–136.

Jancsary, J. (2016). The future as an undefined and open time: A Bergsonian approach. *Axiomathes, 2019*(29), 61–80. Retrieved from 10.1007/s10516-017-93 64-0

Jaynes, J. (2000). *The origin of consciousness in the breakdown of the bicameral mind*. Boston, New York: Mariner Books.

Kemp, R., Loorbach, D., and Rotmans, J. (2007) Transition management as a model for managing processes of co-evolution towards sustainable development. *International Journal of Sustainable Development and World Ecology, 14*, 1–15.

Kenney, H. (2016). *Verwoerd: Architect of apartheid*. Johannesburg: Jonathan Ball Publishers.

Kuhn, T. S. (1996). *The structure of scientific revolutions*. Chicago: University of Chicago Press.

Lakoff, G. & Johnson, M. (2003). *Metaphors we live by*. Chicago: The University of Chicago Press.

Laughlin, C. D. & Throop, C. J. (2009). Husserlian meditations and anthropological reflections: Toward a cultural neurophenomenology of experience and reality. *Anthropology of Consciousness*, 20(2), 130–170. Retrieved from 10.1111/j.1556-3537.2009.01015

Maape, S. (2013). *Dialogues with place in the indigenous communities of Kuruman during the Holocene period* (Doctoral dissertation Proposal). Johannesburg, South Africa: The University of the Witwatersrand.

Maape, S. (2016). *Architecture for resilience: Dialogues with place in the indigenous communities of Kuruman during the Holocene period* (Doctoral dissertation). Johannesburg, South Africa: The University of the Witwatersrand.

Merleau Ponty, M. (1962). *Phenomenology of perception*. New York: Humanities Press.

Merleau Ponty, M. (1968). *The visible and the invisible*. Evanston: Northwestern University Press.

Metzner, R. (1994). The emerging ecological worldview. In M. E. Tucker, & J. A. Grim (Eds.), *Worldviews and ecology: Religion, philosophy and the environment* (pp. 163–172). Maryknoll: Orbis Books.

Myers, G. (2011). *African Cities: Alternative visions of urban theory and practice*. London: Zed Books.

Rist, G. (2014). *The history of development: From western origins to global faith* (4th ed.). London: Zed Books.

Robinson, J., Burch, S., Talwar, S., O'Shea, M., & Walsh, M. (2011). Envisioning sustainability: Recent progress in the use of participatory backcasting approaches for sustainability research. *Technological forecasting and social change* 78(5), 756–786.

Robinson, S., & Pallasmaa, J. (2015). *Mind in architecture: Neuroscience, embodiment, and the future of design*. Massachusetts: MIT Press.

Rukambe, V. (2016). A rite of passage: An exploration of cultural catalytic spaces in the urban context (Masters mini dissertation). The University of Pretoria, Pretoria, South Africa. Retrieved from https://repository.up.ac.za/handle/2263/60199.

Serrat, O. (2017). Asian development bank. *Knowledge solutions*. Retrieved from DOI 10.1007/978-981-10-0983-9_61

Suddendorf, T., Addis, D. R. & Corballis, M. C. (2009). Mental time travel and the shaping of the human mind. *The Royal Society*, 20(364), 1317–1324.

Swilling, M., Musango, J., Robinson, B., & Peter, C. (2017). Flows, infrastructures and the African urban transition. (Eds.), *Urban sustainability transitions* (pp. 311–328). New York: Routledge

The Natural Step. (2009). *The natural step*. City of Madison, Wisconsin. Retrieved from http://www.cityofmadison.com/sustainability/naturalStep/

Turner, V. (1969). *The ritual process: Structure and anti-structure*. Middlesex: Penguin.

Turner, V. (1974). *Dramas, fields and metaphors: Symbolic action in human society*. New York: Cornell University Press.

UN Habitat. (2014). *State of African cities: Reimagining sustainable urban transitions*. Kenya: UN Habitat.

United States Green Building Council – USGBC. (2020). *LEED rating system*. Retrieved from https://www.usgbc.org/leed.

Van den Berg, G. A. & Ganzevoort, R. R. (2014). The art of creating futures – practical theology and strategic research sensitivity for the future. *Acta Theologica*, *34*(2), 166–185.

Varela, F. J. (1996). A methodological remedy for the hard problem. *Journal of Consciousness Studies*, *3*(4), 330–349. Retrieved from https://unstable.nl/andreas/ai/langcog/part3/varela_npmrhp.

Varela, F. J., Thompson, E., & Rosch, E. (1991). *The embodied mind: Cognitive science and human experience*. Cambridge, MA: The MIT Press.

Wangel, J. (2011). Exploring social structures and agency in backcasting studies for sustainable development. *Futures*, *78*(2011), 872–882. Retrieved from https://www.sciencedirect.com/science/article/pii/S0040162511000588

Weisbrode, K. (2012). *On ambivalence: The problems and pleasures of having it both ways*. Massachusetts: The MIT Press.

Winkelman, M. (2000). *Shamanism: The neural ecology of consciousness and healing*. Westport: Bergin and Garvey.

World Green Building Council. (2020). Retrieved from https://worldgbc.org/

Part II
Land Use and Ecological Integrity

6 Towards Sustainable and Resilient Urban Development: Rethinking Stormwater Management in Sub-Saharan African Cities

Desmond Ofosu Anim, Eric Gaisie, and Abena Boatemaa Asare-Ansah

Introduction

Global population is projected to rise to over nine billion by 2050, and more of this will be concentrated in urban areas at unprecedented rate (Cohen, 2003). Interestingly, most of the population growth is expected to occur in the developing world with the fastest urban growth currently occurring in Sub-Saharan Africa (SSA) (Förster & Ammann, 2018). The United Nations estimate that the total urban population in SSA will more than triple not only due to rural-urban migration but also natural increase (Un-Habitat, 2011). However, this rapid urbanisation is usually associated with unplanned urban expansion (Mguni et al., 2016). Research indicates that the rapid urban change in SSA is characterised by haphazard infill development of urban green areas and uncontrolled expansion into peripheral areas, posing debilitating effects on the remaining natural ecosystems resources (Marshall, 2007; Anim et al., 2013). Thus, increased urbanisation results in the alteration of urban and peri-urban landscapes, particularly manifesting in the increase in the land areas covered by impervious surfaces such as buildings, roads and other paved areas (Anim et al., 2018). This consequently leads to drastic changes of the hydrological cycle with an increased portion of rainfall becoming surface stormwater runoff and escalating the risks of urban storm waterlogging (USWL) and flooding which threatens public infrastructure and populations (Yao et al., 2016).

The risk is further exacerbated by recent trends of climate variability and consequent rise in droughts, intensified precipitation and rising sea levels. According to Mora et al. (2013), the impacts of climate change will be enormously experienced in low-income tropical countries heightening the vulnerability of urban infrastructural systems and populations in SSA cities. Thus, the existing trends of haphazard development, uncontrolled expansion and present manifestations of climate change threaten the resilience and sustainable development of cities in SSA. The foregoing, coupled with

DOI: 10.4324/9781003181484-6

persistent challenges such as limited institutional and financial capacities, socio-cultural practices, and environmental attitudes, render the challenge for managing stormwater and waterlogging to be more complicated than ever before. This calls for the need for a robust adaptation options that have a primary objective of supporting sustainable urban development as well as improving the resilience of urban systems to climate change.

Generally, in most SSA cities, the management of USWL relies mainly on conventional stormwater management practices typically characterised by constructing stormwater drainage pipe and sewage networks (Le Jallé et al., 2013). However, increasing evidence suggests that conventional pipe-based approach poses significant threats to urban systems, particularly the surrounding waterways which is seen as a new class of environmental problem (Walsh et al., 2012; Prudencio & Null, 2018). The conventional stormwater management approaches primarily focus on disaster elimination through flood control and do not promote the overall ecosystem sustainability of urban areas. Sadly, urban waterways and associated wetlands are directly impacted by the current trend of urban growth and management of USWL (Azous & Horner, 2000; Anim et al., 2018). Moreover, conventional stormwater management is linked to economic and technical constraints which questions its sustainability, particularly in SSA where there are concerns of growing infrastructure deficit (Mguni et al., 2016). There is increasing global recognition by urban planners and water management professionals for a shift towards more sustainable urban water management due to the debilitating environmental impacts linked with the conventional approach of managing urban water (Brown & Farrelly, 2009; Losco, 2014; Kooy et al., 2019).

A robust "eco-sustainable" approach using sustainable urban drainage systems (SUDS) has received increased recognition by many scholars for being an effective adaptation option for managing urban stormwater because of the ability to drive increased resilience of urban areas and support sustainable urban living (Duffy et al., 2013; Walsh et al., 2016; Anim et al., 2019). "*Eco-sustainable*" approach is characterised by the use of green infrastructure to manage stormwater runoff in urban areas. Such an approach comprises the use of green elements such as rain gardens, infiltration basins, retention ponds, bioretention units and wetlands which relies solely on natural systems and processes to manage urban stormwater using the urban landscape (Li, 2012; Fletcher et al., 2014). Several studies have explored the suitability of "*eco-sustainable*" approaches to urban cities which are mainly based in Europe, Asia, the USA and Australia (Figure 6.1) and have reported the different elements such as biophysical processes, social, technological, and institutional elements as well as the associated multiple benefits to urban systems and populations (see Akinyemi, 2009; Ashley et al., 2010; Backhaus & Fryd, 2013; Fletcher et al., 2015). However, there is a limited exploration on its applicability and adaptation in SSA which is characterised by unplanned development, drainage network deficits and poor ecosystem service delivery (Adegun 2017).

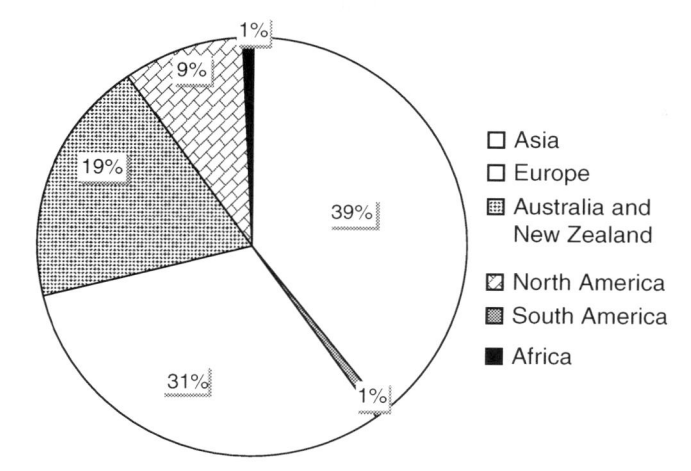

Figure 6.1 Origin of research on sustainable urban water management (data adapted from Haaland & van Den Bosch, 2015).

The purpose of this chapter is to explore the feasibility of SUDS as a practicable adaptation option for urban stormwater management (USM) in SSA cities. The analysis draws extensively on the review of secondary data from sources including journal articles, books, and published reports, towards understanding the current state of stormwater management in SSA and explore the potential of SUDs for mitigating key urban challenges. While there is abundant research on urban drainage and stormwater management, there is limited consideration of SUDS and its potential as a sustainable option for holistic urban water management in the midst of urbanisation wave and climate change impact. Assessing the applicability of SUDS in SSA cities will provide valuable perspectives to the present debate on the potential for sustainable urban water management in more challenging contexts. To this end, the chapter describes the context of urban water management and USWL in SSA cities and analyse the limitations of conventional approaches to addressing it. We then introduce and discuss the application of an eco-sustainable and alternative USM approach using SUDS. The concepts and framework of systematic application of SUDS coupled with best management practices (BMPs) and principles are proposed.

Stormwater Management in African Cities

Conventional Urban Stormwater Management

The pace of urbanisation in SSA presently tops the rate in other regions of the world (Förster & Ammann, 2018). A peculiar feature of urban change in Africa is an increased density of existing areas combined with the expansion of existing urban areas into new areas (Un-Habitat, 2011). New dwellings are being built at a rapid rate and more than half of these occurs in greenfield sites. The consequent increase of surface imperviousness associated with intense development changes the urban water balance of catchments which results in dramatic rise in urban stormwater runoff (Burns et al., 2012; see Figure 6.2). Urban communities consider stormwater as "unwanted water" that need to be eliminated to minimise their impacts especially urban flooding. To mitigate flood risk and protect public infrastructure and hygiene, stormwater managers and city planners and engineers build drainage networks typically characterised by concrete gutters, kerbs, drainage pipes and stormwater pits to efficiently remove excess stormwater runoff when it rains (Brown et al., 2009; Barbosa et al., 2012). Generally, most impervious surfaces are connected to these drainage systems such that nearly all runoff generated are routed quickly from the urban area.

As urban stormwater is usually seen as a nuisance, the design of conventional urban drainage system takes little or no consideration for water quality issues, its amenity or recreational social values. Recent studies (e.g. Burns et al., 2012; Vietz et al., 2014) have discussed the negative effects of

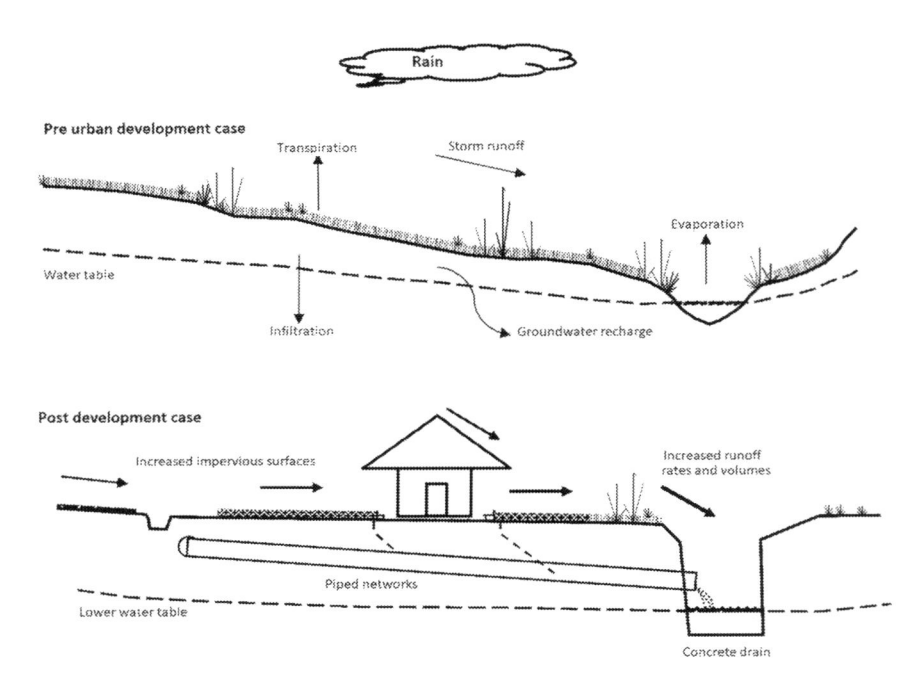

Figure 6.2 Typical before and after urban development scenario with the conventional approach to stormwater management using pipe-based drainage networks.

this traditional urban drainage approach of managing urban stormwater, emphasising the threats to life, the environment and properties due to associated increased volumes of flow, faster arriving and higher peak flows, which raises serious concerns about the sustainability of urban environments. Some researchers (e.g. Fletcher et al., 2014; Anim et al., 2019) have examined the impacts on receiving waterways and reported that the runoff draining to waterways are mostly polluted which causes water quality impairment as well as hydrological disturbance leading to ecological degradation of important waterways in urban areas. In addition to the environmental concerns, the conventional urban drainage network is usually made up of huge structural network of concrete pipes and underground basins which require enormous time and resources for construction, installation and restoration (Davis & Naumann, 2017). Moreover, they have to be built in bits and pieces in most places limiting the flexibility to adapt to critical situations (Krebs & Larsen, 1997).

Until now, this conventional approach has remained the fundamental stormwater management action in SSA cities where huge amounts of money and effort are channelled to achieve public hygiene and flood protection (Amoako & Inkoom, 2018; Richmond et al., 2018). However, its effectiveness to manage flood risk is limited and there are mounting criticisms about the long-term sustainability. In the face of climate variability and urbanisation, there are concerns about the ability of conventional pipe-based stormwater management to adequately manage the projected precipitation and hydrological alterations. Under these conditions, the usual approach of expanding drainage piping systems have become untenable and fail to meet the general criteria of sustainability (Hellström et al., 2000). This calls for a paradigm shift from conventional approaches to stormwater management towards alternative decentralised approaches which, in addition to core stormwater management goals, are capable of addressing water supply, flood risk and public health challenges, as well as contribute additional benefits of improved resilience and overall sustainability of African cities.

Urban Water Management and Storm Waterlogging Problem in SSA

Several factors influence the challenges of urban stormwater management in African cities, but these have been recently compounded by rapid urbanisation and climate variability. According to Brikké and Vairavamoorthy (2016), urban water management in SSA cities faces constraints such as infrastructure deficit, limited institutional, technical and policy capacities, as well as unsupportive attitudes of government agencies and local residents. For example, inadequate investments in stormwater drainage networks and poor water management over time have driven USWL – the phenomenon where water disasters in urban areas are caused by heavy or continuous rainfall that exceeds the drainage capacity – in many cities. The capacity of institutions to provide the required drainage systems is continuously outpaced by the rapid urban development and its associated demand (Mguni et al., 2016). Unfortunately, the existing infrastructure is also outstretched with the current trends of unplanned urbanisation (Hove et al., 2013). As a result, there is a huge infrastructure deficit where the existing structures persistently fall below their design capacities and are inflexible to allow any alteration to meet the changing conditions. This widespread phenomenon in SSA has led to a common urban crisis primarily driven by the lack of access to urban drainage and sanitation services (Hove et al., 2013; Dodman et al., 2017; Moretto et al., 2018).

The limited infrastructure capacities are further aggravated by local attitudes towards waste management. In many African cities, significant proportions of waste generated are not properly collected and treated but rather exposed directly to the environment. A typical strategy has involved indiscriminately dumping refuse into open drains which silts and limits the design capacities of the limited drainage infrastructure to carry stormwater volume. For instance, in Accra, Ghana, only 55% of the daily generated waste is collected for treatment, with the rest improperly disposed (Gaisie, et al., 2019). Similarly, in most urban cities in South Africa (e.g. Johannesburg, Cape Town), a substantial proportion of generated solid waste enter the drainage system reaching surrounding waterways and the sea (Armitage, 2007; Weideman et al., 2020). This rampant indiscriminate waste disposal is a major source of environmental hazards such as flooding, pollution, and health risks as well as presenting existential threats to the urban waterway ecosystem with significant implications on human health (Helmer et al., 1997; Ferronato & Torretta, 2019).

The problems of urban stormwater management are further compounded by weak institutional capacity and lack of effective governmental responses. Aside the limited fiscal and technical capacities, research indicates a lack of political will to pursue investments in alternative UWM strategies affecting stormwater management in SSA cities. To date, many cities continue to adopt conventional physical drainage infrastructure as a viable strategy despite the inability to meet the growing demand for greater capacities. The inefficacy of response is further compounded by unclear governance systems and lack of coordination among the different institutions responsible for urban water management (Frick-Trzebitzky, 2017). According to Lindell (2008), the several levels of power and contestation operating at different scales in many African cities hinder governance initiatives particularly with respect to infrastructure delivery. The unclear institutional responsibilities for repairs and maintenance have often led to urban service failures. Sadly, such institutional fragmentations also delay implementation of reforms even when significant amounts have been spent on policy reforms (Dos Santos et al., 2017).

The rapid and unplanned urban development presents a daunting challenge to UWM and USWL in many SSA urban cities. Large scale proliferation of informal settlements characterised by haphazard land-use conversions has seen a rise in encroachment into natural vegetation areas, limiting the capacities of existing natural stormwater pathways and the overall capacities of local authorities to address the issue. A prominent feature of this widespread informalisation is the lack of access to essential urban services like drainage (Herslund et al., 2016; Mguni et al., 2016). As a result, communities and locals seek a suite of survival approaches outside of formal drainage networks designed and built to engineering standards to ease the risk of UWSL. In addition, unguided urban development has led to widespread settlement in environmentally precarious areas such as wetlands, floodplain corridors, and steep slopes exposing dwellers to stormwater runoff-related disasters and hazards (Adegun, 2014). Such developmental patterns with associated environmental degradation make the cities vulnerable to climate changes effects.

The foregoing issues coupled with the lack of effective management policies and socio-economic constraints in SSA cities present limited opportunities for UWM reforms. In such context, it is not surprising that the effectiveness of conventional urban drainage approach has been questioned particularly under expected climate variability. Thus, addressing such a multi-dimensional problem in UWM and USWL in SSA cities requires urban planners and water managers to adopt alternative strategies that tackle multiple objectives simultaneously. The next section, therefore, explores the potential of "eco-sustainable" approach to stormwater management with the application of SUDS as a viable option for addressing deficits and deficiencies of drainage infrastructure in African cities.

"Eco-sustainable" Approach – the Application of SUDS as an Alternative for Stormwater Management

Sustainable or green infrastructure is a set of systems that relies on ecological models to support lives and to attain a multiplicity of objectives including environmental, social, and economic health (Benedict & McMahon, 2012). This section examines, against the backdrop of rapid urbanisation, high drainage infrastructure deficits, environmental pollution and imminent impacts from climate change, how eco-sustainable approaches are valuable for stormwater management in SSA cities.

Concept and Principles

The emerging approach regarding sustainable stormwater management is founded on the notion that urban waters are the lifeline of cities and may result in greener, more sustainable and resilient urban environments if managed in an integrated and decentralised manner (Novotny, 2008; Mguni, 2015).

This approach considers green developments and strategies at the micro-scale and connects them with larger catchment-scale management of infrastructure for water supply and sewerage services. In particular, it emphasises the concept of total water cycle management grounded on the ideas of environmental protection and sustainability, and generally draw linkages among the urban water system, green infrastructure, and land use planning (Fletcher et al., 2015). It is also regarded as one of the methods for achieving water sensitive urban futures in which cities form a water supply catchment, provide ecosystem services as well as encompass elements that progressively lead to environmentally sustainable development.

Sustainable stormwater management approaches have evolved over the years and been described by concepts generally reflecting the practices and principles of sustainable urban drainage (Table 6.1). These concepts include SUDS (adopted in this chapter), BMPs, Low Impact Development (LID) and Water Sensitive Urban Design (WSUD) among others based on different geographical contexts (Fletcher et al., 2015). The central theme in these approaches involved the implementation of green elements such as green roofs and rain gardens, among others and mainly rely on pre-development catchment hydrological processes of infiltration, evaporation, conveyance and retention of stormwater.

SUDS Approaches

In contrast with the conventional perceptions that see stormwater as a nuisance that needs to be gotten rid of, SUDS approaches view it as resource offering opportunities for integrated management of the urban water cycle (Novotny et al., 2010; Short et al., 2019). It consists of management systems that simulate the pre-development urban hydrological cycle processes by incorporating the city's green infrastructure for infiltration, storage, detention, retention, evaporation, conveyance and treatment of stormwater (Charlesworth et al., 2003; Mguni, 2015). It is centred on developing drainage networks that complement and connect green spaces with built infrastructure and can be incorporated into new developments.

The SUDS concept seeks to achieve threefold objectives, including: (i) attenuate and minimise stormwater runoff quantity via source control; (ii) enhance runoff quality by passively treating the captured water before discharge into receiving waterways or land and (iii) improve amenity and maintain ecosystem biodiversity (Cettner et al., 2013) (see Figure 6.3). By these objectives, SUDS provide principal avenues for sustainable urban development. It applies structural and non-structural components at site-scale (e.g. green roofs and walls, rainwater tanks, permeable paving etc.) and catchment-scale (e.g. swales, wetlands, retention ponds, infiltration systems) (Charlesworth et al., 2003) (Figures 6.4). The SUDS framework principally involves the following:

Table 6.1 Evolution of the sustainable urban stormwater management terms associated with urban drainage

Concept	Geographic Focus	Principles	Reference
Low Impact Development (LID)	North America, New Zealand	• Attempts to minimise the cost of stormwater management by taking a design with a nature-based approach. • Achieve a "natural" hydrology using site layout and integrated measures. • Characterised by smaller scale stormwater treatment devices such as bioretention systems, green roofs and swales located at or near the source of surface runoff.	(Barlow et al., 1977)
Water Sensitive Urban Design (WSUD)	Australia	• Urban planning and design approach that aims to reduce the hydrological impacts of urban development on the surrounding environment. • It is directed at providing flood control, flow management, water quality improvements and opportunities to harvest stormwater to supplement mains water for non-potable uses.	(Mouritz, 1996)
Integrated Urban Water Management (IUWM)	France	• Involves the integrated management of all parts of the water cycle in a catchment considering water supply, groundwater, wastewater and stormwater. • Considers the roles and interactions of the various institutions involved in urban water cycle management.	(Geldof, 1995)
Sustainable Urban Drainage System (SUDS)	United Kingdom	• Replicate as closely as possible, the natural, pre-development drainage from a catchment, consistent with LID principles. • Typically configured as a sequence of stormwater practices and technologies that work together to form a management train.	(Butler & Parkinson, 1997)
Best Management Practices (BMPs)	North America (particularly the United States and Canada)	• Focused on activities that reduce pollutant content in stormwater drainage. • Based on the management of wastewater treatment processes and primarily focused on non-structural measures	(Ice, 2004)

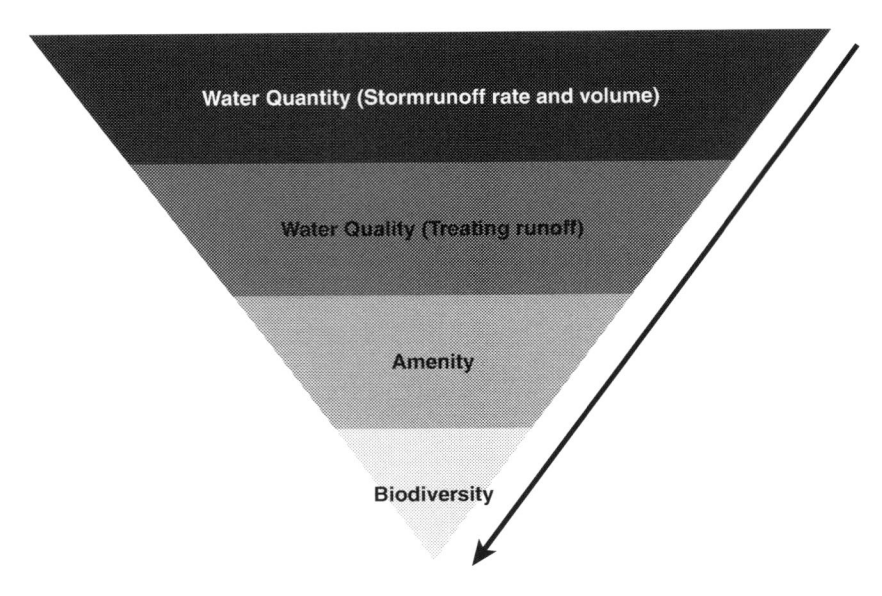

Figure 6.3 The sustainable urban stormwater design hierarchy
Source: Authors.

i   *prevention:* attenuation of harmful pollutants, disposing of solid waste, recycling of wastewater for reuse;
ii   *source controls:* managing surface runoff near source via rainwater harvesting using tanks, green roofs, permeable pavements;
iii *localised management:* of water using elements like infiltration systems, swales and bioretention ponds; and
iv   *catchment-wide controls:* managing stormwater runoff from several areas using wetlands, retention and detention ponds (see Ashley et al., 2010 for more details).

SUDS help to achieve the triple bottom line of sustainability by facilitating the attainment of economic, environmental and social goals within cities. Implementing SUDS does not only involve technical considerations but also an understanding of the socio-economic, institutional and bio-physical contexts of the region in question (Mguni, 2015). Thus, SUDS yield inter-disciplinary solutions to stormwater management problems drawing on a wide range of professionals including engineers, urban planners, hydrologists, architects and social scientists. The decentralised nature also implies that the participation of end-users is very essential to achieve the full potential of eco-sustainability and enhance the implementation and maintenance of SUDS.

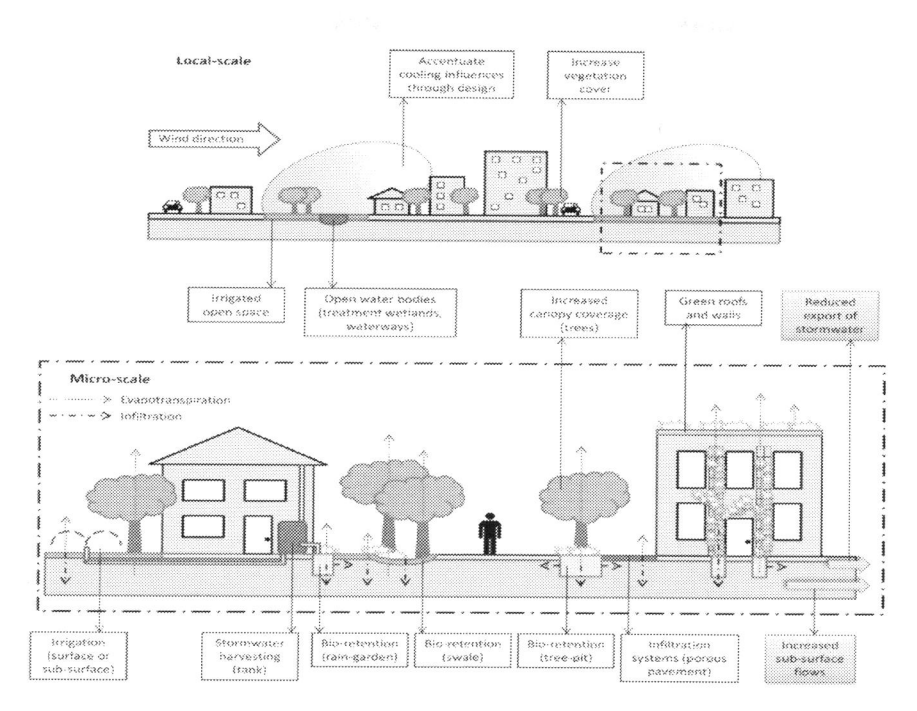

Figure 6.4 Schematic demonstration of widespread implementation of SUDS components in urban space.

Source: Coutts et al. (2013).

The Potential Benefits of SUDS for SSA Cities

As an eco-sustainable-based solution, SUDS present a more holistic approach to addressing UWM offering opportunities to connect the urban water balance loop via stormwater recycling (Novotny et al., 2010). In the context of developing countries, SUDS is capable of yielding benefits of controlling water quantity and quality as well as contribute to biodiversity and amenity. These benefits are attained at two broad levels, including (i) urban catchment and (ii) aquatic ecosystem downstream of the catchment, as explained below. In SSA, the simultaneous attainment of these benefits within cities can facilitate progress with resilient and sustainable development as indicated by Goal 11 of the sustainable development goals (SDGs).

Urban Catchment Benefits

Flood Mitigation

Flooding has become a perennial phenomenon in many SSA cities causing devastating impacts on lives, properties and resulting in huge economic loss

Table 6.2 Major flood events and their impacts in selected African countries

Country	Year	Number of Deaths	Number of People Displaced	Population Affected (Millions)	Properties Damaged (Million US$)
South Africa	1987	506	N/A	0.065	0.765
Malawi	1991	472	174,000	0.64	0.024
Mozambique	2000	800	463,000	4.5	0.42
Ethiopia	2006	705	100,000	N/A	0.32
Kenya	2006	114	723,000	0.72	N/A
Sudan	2007	64	750,000	0.56	0.3
Nigeria	2012	363	2,100,000	7.7	16.9
Ghana	2015	154	N/A	0.1	55.0

Note: N/A – not available.
Source: compiled by authors from multiple sources.

(see Table 6.2). For instance, in the 2000–2010 decade, flooding alone accounted for 80% of all disaster-related deaths and 70% of economic losses in the sub-region (Ndaruzaniye et al., 2010). In West Africa alone, Salami et al. (2017) estimated that up to 500,000 people are affected by flooding each year. While fluvial flooding is very common in African cities, the high occupancy of residents in floodplains subjects many cities to high fluvial flooding risk (Adelekan & Asiyanbi, 2016; Smith et al., 2019). For instance, research indicates that more than half of the population of Accra, Ghana live on the floodplains of River Densu and its tributaries (Karley, 2009). This is also the case in the Zambezi River basin in southern Africa including Zambia, Zimbabwe, Botswana and Angola (Kirchhoff & Bulkley, 2008; Lumbroso, 2020). Along with this situation, recent trends of climate variability underscore the urgent need for an effective means for flood mitigation and adaptation.

One of the primary benefits of SUDS is the ability to minimise urban flood risk. Contrary to the conventional USM approach of removing excess stormwater runoff from urban areas, SUDS mitigate flood risk by minimising and/or attenuating runoff via storage in the ground or elsewhere thereby ensuring low peak flows. Studies (e.g. Burns et al., 2012; Viavattene & Ellis, 2013; Fletcher et al., 2014; Anim et al., 2019) have demonstrated that SUDS elements like green roofs, infiltration systems, rainwater tanks, porous pavement reduced runoff volume by up to about 40% depending on the size, duration of event and placement. It is worth noting that while the influences may be little, theoretically even a small reduction (5%) from each development could have enormous consequences for inundation. More so, flood mitigation benefits of SUDS are even highly likely when implemented at the catchment scale (Burns et al., 2015).

Table 6.3 Trends in water stress and scarcity in selected African countries (2000–2019)

Country	Proportion of Population in Water Stress and Scarce Areas (%)					
	2000		2010		2019	
	Stress	Scarce	Stress	Scarce	Stress	Scarce
Ghana	14.1	2.6	12.2	9.5	13.5	4.5
Nigeria	13.2	6.2	17.5	9.3	19.7	9.5
South Africa	8.2	9.5	8.8	9.2	7.4	13.1
Botswana	9.9	18.9	9.8	24.5	9.2	27.5
Kenya	7.4	13.8	14.5	14.1	19.0	20.9
Ethiopia	13.8	6.5	14.0	9.8	18.5	13.3
Rwanda	21.8	15.4	18.9	37.8	20.2	17.6

Notes: Population living in water scarcity (i.e. with less than 1000 m^3 per capita per year) and stress (i.e. with less than 1,500 m^3 per capita per year) in selected SSA countries. Water scarcity reflects the lack of sufficient available water resources to meet the demand of usage within a region whereas water stress refers to the inability to meet the human and ecological demand for water.
Data extracted from World Data Lab (https://worldwater.io/about.php; Accessed on 13 February 2020).

Water Supply Augmentation

Water scarcity recognised as a global challenge in Target 6.4. of the SDGs affects many countries and cities in SSA where water resources are generally known to be unevenly distributed with limited chance of finding new water sources (Kakonge, 2002) (Table 6.3). With the water demand pressures from rapid population growth and urban expansion, there is an urgent need to increase the efficiency of use by implementing strategies for improving the conservation of available water. For example, the 2016 severe drought in South Africa, considered one of the worst in decades caused most urban areas of the country with limited access to water, which also affected food production (Fisher-Jeffes et al., 2017). To avert future water crisis, SSA countries need to not only conserve water supplies but also minimise the reliance on traditional sources and consider alternative sources of water supply (Armitage, 2020). This is particularly timelier today considering expectations that water shortage will worsen due to climate change and risk of droughts causing the decline of water levels of dam and freshwater supply sources (e.g. lakes, rivers) (Naik, 2017).

The storage capacities of SUDS through strategies like rainwater harvesting could be used for capturing stormwater and used as alternative sources of water supply to augment the limited supplies received from main water supply systems. Research (e.g. Cobbinah et al., 2016) has shown that alternative water sources provide up to 37% of water needs in African cities; and hence, harvested stormwater could augment this capacity that has proven especially useful for low-risk domestic purposes such as washing, bathing, irrigation and flushing toilets. In addition, SUDS approaches that apply bioretention technique (i.e. uses soil, plants and microbes to biologically treat stormwater) can help to recharge groundwater supplies by raising the water table which adds to the potential sources of water for many households in SSA cities (Heiberger, 2013).

In addition, using SUDS through strategies like rainwater harvesting provide alternative sources which becomes valuable in future crisis or pandemics such as the current COVID-19 pandemic (Anim & Ofori-Asenso, 2020). Indeed, access to water is a key determinant for infectious disease control and prevention; thus, limited access creates a challenge for transmission control (WHO, 2019). However, across many SSA countries where inequalities in access to safe water are pervasive (Kakonge, 2002), there is a need to be concerned in light of the pandemic. For instance, in Ghana (CitiTube, 2020) and Kenya (Natarajan, 2020), it was challenging to comply with the directive to "frequently wash hands under running water" in many urban households as a result of the water rationing. Kalra et al. (2014) reported that poorly developed water supply and sanitation systems were central in the rapid spread of the 2014 Ebola outbreak, and was a fundamental factor in the high number of deaths. Green or nature-based solutions can help to reduce the over-reliance on conventional surface water schemes and improve water storage and supply, thus increasing water availability even in a crisis.

Economic Cost, Social Amenity and Thermal Comfort

Research (e.g. Ashley et al., 2010) indicates that SUDS approaches provide huge economic savings as compared with a more traditional stormwater management approach. These savings are made from capital and operating costs as well as economic gains from ecosystem, making SUDS a cheaper option for stormwater management in the long run. For instance, Ossa-Moreno et al. (2017) extensively examined the economic cost-benefits analyses of multiple SUDS schemes in Decoy Brook catchment in London, UK and revealed it provided significant savings. For example, as a climate change adaptation strategy, the city of Copenhagen saved about USD 1 billion by implementing a series of SUDS schemes instead of expanding conventional drainage system. Moreover, the implementation of SUDS schemes yielded land use benefits in Australia by making houses more desirable for home buyers, thereby increasing land values (Water by Design, 2010). The economic savings from SUDS are also derived in substantial volumes at household levels through, for example, water savings from rainwater harvesting systems (Brandes et al., 2006).

The integration of green elements of SUDS techniques (e.g. rain gardens, street trees, and bioswales) adds aesthetic value to public and private spaces and create recreational benefits while promoting biodiversity by creating habitat for biota (e.g. bees, birds and butterflies) (Figure 6.5).

Figure 6.5 Some examples of local implementation of SUDS technologies in urban
       areas.
Source: Costa, 2014.

Moreover, active usage of such inherent green spaces provided through
SUDS has been reported to create better urban communities through social cohesion and improved quality of life (Maas et al., 2009). SUDS approaches also enhance urban form as it is based on multifunctional and
connected infrastructure provide opportunity for transitioning into water
sensitive urbanisation (Brown et al., 2010). With significant environmental challenges from changing climate (e.g. urban heat waves), SUDS
elements that retain water in the urban landscape through infiltration,
harvesting and increased vegetation cover can provide human thermal
comfort and health, improve soil moisture and can deliver energy savings
benefits (Coutts et al., 2013).

Benefits to Downstream Aquatic Environment

Conventional approaches to stormwater management mainly focus on
managing the risk to people and infrastructure safety without considering
the downstream influence to surrounding waterways. Polluted stormwater

runoff quickly routed to surrounding waterways via conventional urban drainage systems degrade aquatic ecosystems and expose many urbanites to significant health threats. However, eco-sustainable approaches of SUDS generate enormous benefits to the downstream aquatic environment through the following means.

Controlled Fluvial Flooding

When urban stormwater runoff is directed into aquatic ecosystem, it increases the risk of flooding as these streams experience increased frequent peak flows input (Anim et al., 2018). The major hydro-geomorphic impact from frequently increased flows and morphological degradation through erosion result in ecological degradation (Vietz et al., 2016). However, SUDS techniques involving retention or detention, infiltration and harvesting can reduce the frequency of stormwater runoff inputs, thereby reducing the volumes of runoff that reach the aquatic systems (Burns et al., 2015; Li et al., 2017; Anim et al., 2019). The collective gains of reduced runoff distributed across the urban catchment prevent localised flood damage to properties along the corridors of the aquatic systems.

Aquatic Ecosystem Water Quality and Biodiversity Damage

The quality of water in aquatic systems such as streams and rivers are very important for ecological benefits. When polluted stormwater runoff is directed into these systems, it impairs the water quality which degrades ecosystem health, reduces biota diversity and aggravates loss of species (Anim et al., 2019). Applying SUDS involving infiltration and bioretention can retain, filter and treat polluted stormwater runoff before they are released (Davis et al., 2012; Hunt et al., 2012).

Aquatic Ecosystem Channel and Riparian Structure

Aquatic ecosystem draining urban areas have been commonly reported to damage channel and riparian structure (Vietz et al., 2016). As land use changes occur through urbanisation, increased impervious surface eventually lead to decreased sediment supply. Together with increased flows from connected urban drains, channels are degraded where they typically get enlarged and incised, as well as change in sediment supply, losing its morphological diversity (Vietz et al., 2014). This threatens infrastructure like bridges and buildings close to them. SUDS that significantly reduce stormwater flows can prevent such unwarranted cost. Also, the loss of riparian vegetation especially at the floodplain of the aquatic channels leads to bank instability and eventual loss of habitat to biota that can be averted through SUDS (Fletcher et al., 2014).

Challenges for Implementation of SUDS in SSA Cities

The foregoing analysis indicates that eco-sustainable-based SUDS holds promising pathways to achieve sustainable stormwater management in SSA cities. However, its implementation faces critical limitations that ought to be overcome to guarantee its success. First, a paradigm shift towards these alternative sustainable scenarios is challenged by financial and technical constraints. The initial cost and risk of failure associated with a complete shift to innovative and high-tech SUDS approaches vis-à-vis the conventional urban drainage systems can undermine their adoption in SSA. However, using market mechanisms (e.g. voluntary offset incentive programmes such as free maintenance) to encourage implementation at the site and local levels is a viable strategy that can draw support for a successful application as has been promoted in several other developed countries (e.g. USA, Australia) (Barbosa et al., 2012). Using economic feasibility assessments at the initial stage of the adoption process to illustrate the immense economic benefits from SUDS could inspire its acceptance and adoption by households, businesses and public authorities (Johnson & Geisendorf, 2019). This assessment must involve the technical requirements of operations and maintenance to understand the available skillset and what capacity development is required for the skills that are not readily available within specific countries. Ashley et al. (2010) highlighted that the lack of skills and knowledge required to implement SUDS usually result in failures in realising the full benefits. However, recent increasing concern of the general public for environmental quality, especially in relation to water resources protection in SSA could be capitalised upon to promote public acceptance and/or adoption for SUDS and particularly be incorporated in the planning and design of new developments rather as an add-on.

The weak institutional authority and lack of spatial governance coordination in most SSA cities that has overseen the chaotic and unplanned urban environments could be another major hindrance to the successful implementation of sustainable USM (Pastore, 2015; Gaisie et al., 2019). However, previous studies reveal that a strong long-term commitment by all actors is needed to ensure policy continuity for the provision of sustainable basic facilities like SUDS (Walker et al., 2012). Unlocking the potentials of sustainable USM in SSA cities will need active institutional guidance and leadership to accelerate urban resilience and sustainability. In addition, the increased complexity surrounding multi-stakeholder and interdisciplinary decision-making of SUDS can pose a challenge. Parallel expert views and divergent stakeholder interests elongate the process of strategising for SUDS, which could make it less desirable in the context of SSA cities which are mostly characterised by highly fragmented and chaotic institutional setup. Hence, operating and managing SUDS will require a high level of coordination and cooperation between the different institutions especially when city-wide implementation is envisioned. Lastly, SUDS are linked with open spaces which continue to be increasingly dissipated in many African cities (Cobbinah et al., 2020). As spatial constraints are usually cited as a reason for not incorporating them into urban drainage strategies, there is a need to integrate SUDS in strategic land use planning of African cities going forward.

Conclusion

Planning for sustainable cities is a complex process that requires improving the economic, environmental and social benefits of development. However, fostering development that equitably facilitates all these dimensions remain a daunting challenge in developing countries, particularly in SSA. In highly urbanised contexts like Africa cities, it is true that the implementation of SUDS will involve different avenues of departure from cities in developed countries (Mguni, 2015). In most developed countries, integrating SUDS in cities primarily hinges on retrofitting them into the larger infrastructure systems within the existing urban fabric. With widening infrastructure and environmental deficits in SSA cities, the foremost challenge centres on how to address these current deficits while leapfrogging with technological advancements available today and effectively spearheaded by developed cities (Cettner et al., 2013).

Moving towards sustainable USM solutions such as SUDS in SSA should not void present efforts towards achieving universal centralised water infrastructure under the Water Sanitation and Hygiene (WASH) initiative (WHO, 2017). However, it is contended that the unswerving focus for achieving WASH goals within the water sectors could unwittingly disable the considerations for more integrated UWM approaches such as eco-sustainable SUDS approach. Although most UWM strategies in the developing world operate under vigorous constraints, there seems to be a lack of reflexivity to try alternative methods outside the conventional paradigm (Barbosa et al., 2012). An initial action is, perhaps, for urban planners and water managers in developing cities to consent that the target for developing urban areas may no longer be to just achieve the modern infrastructure ideal of centralised conventional (pipe-based) drainage networks and services but instead to aim for suitable and sustainable infrastructure. If SSA cities could have any chance to catch up and move towards sustainable UWM, they must begin to explore alternative configurations for not only water service infrastructure but a holistically integrated urban infrastructure system. Any explorations should acknowledge the fiscal and environmental costs of centralised systems and incorporate co-production in urban water infrastructure provision and management (Mguni, 2015) to promote and validate community initiatives involving non-governmental actors like residents, households, NGOs and site-scale independent infrastructure suppliers.

Moreover, exploration with SUDS approaches from the perspectives of local authorities or the public sector will require changes in the way urban infrastructural systems are governed. It has been suggested that water management issues are predominantly governance problems than lack of resources or technology (Barbosa et al., 2012; Hagemann & Kirschke, 2017). Thus, transitions towards sustainable management options like SUDS implementation must address inherent societal concerns and not just the environmental and infrastructural problems. As argued by Swilling (2019), in cities where infrastructure deficits reflect historical discrimination and persistent inequality, it is important for any transitions to focus on social justice as well. By this, moving towards sustainable UWM in SSA should be anchored on adaptive governance that highlights inclusive innovations and strives for public participation. After all, successful transitioning towards sustainability approaches require the support and views of the community to shape adaptation preferences (Baptiste et al., 2015).

Lastly, the adoption and implementation in SSA cities should evolve in a strategic and realistic manner. With limited resources and structural developmental deficits, it is crucial to be strategic in starting small and choosing measures less susceptible to failure. SUDS may best be initially approached as experiments at local scales to provide evidence-based understanding or lessons which will inform upscaling implementation efforts. It is noted that a careful rollout of eco-sustainable-based SUDS that addresses these deficiencies will facilitate effective stormwater management, ameliorate structural challenges like flooding, water scarcity and ecosystem degradation and propel African cities towards sustainable and resilient futures.

References

Adegun, O. B. (2014). Coping with stormwater in a Johannesburg, South Africa informal settlement. *Proceedings of the Institution of Civil Engineers-Municipal Engineer*, 167(2), 89–98.

Adegun, O. B. (2017). Green infrastructure in relation to informal urban settlements. *Journal of Architecture and Urbanism*, 41(1), 22–33.

Adelekan, I. O., & Asiyanbi, A. P. (2016). Flood risk perception in flood-affected communities in Lagos, Nigeria. *Natural Hazards*, 80(1), 445–469.

Akinyemi, E. (2009). International experiences with low impact development (LID). In *Low impact development for urban ecosystem and habitat protection*. Seattle, Washington, United States, pp. 1–10. 10.1061/41009(333)66.

Amoako, C., & Inkoom, D. K. B. (2018). The production of flood vulnerability in Accra, Ghana: Re-thinking flooding and informal urbanisation. *Urban Studies*, 55(13), 2903–2922.

Anim, D. O., Fletcher, T. D., Pasternack, G. B., Vietz, G. J., Duncan, H. P., & Burns, M. J. (2019). Can catchment-scale urban stormwater management measures benefit the stream hydraulic environment? *Journal of Environmental Management*, 233, 1–11.

Anim, D. O., Fletcher, T. D., Vietz, G. J., Pasternack, G. B., & Burns, M. J. (2018). Effect of urbanization on stream hydraulics. *River Research and Applications*, 34(7), 661–674. doi:10.1002/rra.3293.

Anim, D. O., Fletcher, T. D., Vietz, G. J., Pasternack, G. B., & Burns, M. J. (2019). Restoring in-stream habitat in urban catchments: Modify flow or the channel? *Ecohydrology*, 12(1), doi: 10.1002/eco.2050.

Anim, D. O., Li, Y., Agadzi, A. K., & Nkrumah, P. N. (2013). Environmental issues of Lake Bosomtwe impact crater in Ghana (West Africa) and its impact on ecotourism potential. *International Journal of Scientific & Engineering Research*, 4(1), 1–9.

Anim, D. O. , & Ofori-Asenso, R. (2020). Water scarcity and COVID-19 in sub-Saharan Africa. *The Journal of Infection*, 81(2), e108.

Armitage, N. (2007). The reduction of urban litter in the stormwater drains of South Africa. *Urban Water Journal*, 4(3), 151–172.

Armitage, N. (2020). Harvesting a valuable resource. *Water & Sanitation Africa*, 15(2), 28–29.

Ashley, R., Newman, R., Walker, L., & Nowell, R. (2010). Changing a Culture: Managing Stormwater Sustainably in the UK City of the Future – Learning from the USA and Australia. In *Low impact development 2010: Redefining water in the city* (pp. 1571–1584). 10.1061/41099(367)135.

Azous, A., & Horner, R. R. (2000). *Wetlands and urbanization: Implications for the future*. CRC Press., University of Washington, Seattle, WA

Backhaus, A., & Fryd, O. (2013). The aesthetic performance of urban landscape-based stormwater management systems: A review of twenty projects in Northern Europe. *Journal of Landscape Architecture*, 8(2), 52–63.

Baptiste, A. K., Foley, C., & Smardon, R. (2015). Understanding urban neighborhood differences in willingness to implement green infrastructure measures: A case study of Syracuse, NY. *Landscape and Urban Planning*, 136, 1–12.

Barbosa, A. E., Fernandes, J. N., & David, L. M. (2012). Key issues for sustainable urban stormwater management. *Water Research*, 46(20), 6787–6798.

Barlow, D., Burrill, G., & Nolfi, J. (1977). *Research report on developing a community level natural resource inventory system*. Center for Studies in Food Self-Sufficiency, Vermont Institute of Community Involvement.

Benedict, M. A., & McMahon, E. T. (2012). *Green infrastructure: Linking landscapes and communities*. Island Press, Washington, D.C, USA.

Brandes, O. M., Maas, T., & Reynolds, E. (2006). *Thinking beyond pipes and pumps: Top 10 ways communities can save water and money*. POLIS Project on Ecological Governance, University of Victoria.

Brikké, F., & Vairavamoorthy, K. (2016). Managing change to implement integrated urban water management in African cities. *Aquatic Procedia*, 6, 3–14.

Brown, P., Ahern, J., & Novotny, V. (2010). *Water centric sustainable communities: Planning, retrofitting and building the next urban environment*. Hoboken, New Jersey, USA: John Wiley & Sons.

Brown, R. R., & Farrelly, M. A. (2009). Delivering sustainable urban water management: A review of the hurdles we face. *Water Science and Technology*, 59(5), 839–846.

Brown, R. R., Keath, N., & Wong, T. H. (2009). Urban water management in cities: Historical, current and future regimes. *Water Science and Technology*, 59(5), 847–855.

Burns, M. J., Fletcher, T. D., Walsh, C. J., Ladson, A. R., & Hatt, B. E. (2012). Hydrologic shortcomings of conventional urban stormwater management and opportunities for reform. *Landscape and Urban Planning*, 105(3), 230–240. doi:10.1016/j.landurbplan.2011.12.012.

Burns, M. J., Fletcher, T. D., Walsh, C. J., Ladson, A. R., & Hatt, B. E. (2015). Flow-regime management at the urban land-parcel scale: Test of feasibility. *Journal of Hydrologic Engineering*, 20(12), 04015037.

Butler, D., & Parkinson, J. (1997). Towards sustainable urban drainage. *Water Science and Technology*, 35(9), 53–63.

Cettner, A., Ashley, R., Viklander, M., & Nilsson, K. (2013). Stormwater management and urban planning: Lessons from 40 years of innovation. *Journal of Environmental Planning and Management*, 56(6), 786–801.

Charlesworth, S., Harker, E., & Rickard, S. (2003). A review of sustainable drainage systems (SuDS): A soft option for hard drainage questions? *Geography*, 88(2) 99–107.

CitiTube. (2020). *Residents of Accra fear high risk of Coronavirus infection amidst water rationing*. Retrieved from https://www.youtube.com/watch?v=Kl5V8A8ToYg.

Cobbinah, P. B., Gaisie, E., Oppong-Yeboah, N. Y., & Anim, D. O. (2020). Kumasi: Towards a sustainable and resilient cityscape. *Cities*, 97, 102567.

Cobbinah, P. B., Okyere, D. K., & Gaisie, E. (2016). Population growth and water supply: The future of Ghanaian cities. In *Population growth and rapid urbanization in the developing world* (pp. 231–252). Hershey PA: IGI Global.

Cohen, J. E. (2003). Human population: The next half century. *Science*, 302(5648), 1172–1175.

Costa, J. P., De Sousa, J. F., Silva, M. M., & Nouri, A. S. (2014). Climate change adaptation and urbanism: A developing agenda for Lisbon within th6.6

Coutts, A. M., Tapper, N. J., Beringer, J., Loughnan, M., & Demuzere, M. (2013). Watering our cities: The capacity for Water Sensitive Urban Design to support urban cooling and improve human thermal comfort in the Australian context. *Progress in Physical Geography*, 37(1), 2–28.

Davis, A. P., Traver, R. G., Hunt, W. F., Lee, R., Brown, R. A., & Olszewski, J. M. (2012). Hydrologic performance of bioretention storm-water control measures. *Journal of Hydrologic Engineering*, 17(5), 604–614.

Davis, M., & Naumann, S. (2017). Making the case for sustainable urban drainage systems as a nature-based solution to urban flooding. In N. Kabisch, H. Korn, J. Stadler, & A. Bonn (Eds.), *Nature-based solutions to climate change adaptation in urban areas* (pp. 123–137). Springer Nature Switzerland AG.

Dodman, D., Leck, H., Rusca, M., & Colenbrander, S. (2017). African urbanisation and urbanism: Implications for risk accumulation and reduction. *International Journal of Disaster Risk Reduction*, 26, 7–15.

Dos Santos, S., Adams, E., Neville, G., Wada, Y., De Sherbinin, A., Bernhardt, E. M., & Adamo, S. (2017). Urban growth and water access in sub-Saharan Africa: Progress, challenges, and emerging research directions. *Science of the Total Environment*, 607, 497–508.

Duffy, A., D'Arcy, B., Berwick, N., Wade, R., & Jose, R. (2013). *Source control SUDS delivery on a global scale and in Scotland including approach by responsible organisations and professional groups*. Scotland's Centre of Expertise for Waters (CREW), Urban Water Technology Centre, University of Abertay Dundee, DD1 1HG.

Ferronato, N., & Torretta, V. (2019). Waste mismanagement in developing countries: A review of global issues. *International Journal of Environmental Research and Public Health*, 16(6), 1060.

Fletcher, T. D., Shuster, W., Hunt, W. F., Ashley, R., Butler, D., Arthur, S., ... Bertrand-Krajewski, J.-L. (2015). SUDS, LID, BMPs, WSUD and more–The evolution and application of terminology surrounding urban drainage. *Urban Water Journal*, 12(7), 525–542.

Fletcher, T. D., Vietz, G., & Walsh, C. J. (2014). Protection of stream ecosystems from urban stormwater runoff: The multiple benefits of an ecohydrological approach. *Progress in Physical Geography*, 38(5), 543–555.

Fisher-Jeffes, L., Carden, K., Armitage, N. P., & Winter, K. (2017). Stormwater harvesting: Improving water security in South Africa's urban areas. *South African Journal of Science*, 113(1–2), 1–4.

Förster, T., & Ammann, C. (2018). African cities and the development conundrum: Actors and agency in the urban grey zone. In C. Ammann & T. Förster (Eds.), *African cities and the development conundrum* (pp. 3–25). International Development Policy Series 10: Brill.

Frick-Trzebitzky, F. (2017). Crafting adaptive capacity: Institutional bricolage in adaptation to urban flooding in Greater Accra. *Water Alternatives*, 10(2), 625–647.

Gaisie, E., Kim, H. M., & Han, S. S. (2019). Accra towards a city-region: Devolution, spatial development and urban challenges. *Cities*, 95, 102398. doi:10.1016/j.cities.2019.102398.

Geldof, G. D. (1995). Adaptive water management: Integrated water management on the edge of chaos. *Water Science and Technology*, 32(1), 7–13.

Haaland, C., & van Den Bosch, C. K. (2015). Challenges and strategies for urban green-space planning in cities undergoing densification: A review. *Urban Forestry & Urban Greening*, 14(4), 760–771.

Hagemann, N., & Kirschke, S. (2017). Key issues of interdisciplinary NEXUS governance analyses: Lessons learned from research on integrated water resources management. *Resources*, 6(1), 9. doi:10.3390/resources6010009

Heiberger, J. R. (2013). *Infiltration and Potential groundwater recharge performance of stormwater bioretention designed for semiarid climates*. Department of Civil and Environmental Engineering, University of Utah.

Hellström, D., Jeppsson, U., & Kärrman, E. (2000). A framework for systems analysis of sustainable urban water management. *Environmental Impact Assessment Review*, 20(3), 311–321.

Helmer, R., Hespanhol, I., & Organization, W. H. (1997). *Water pollution control: A guide to the use of water quality management principles*. CRC Press, Boca Raton, Florida.

Herslund, L. B., Jalayer, F., Jean-Baptiste, N., Jørgensen, G., Kabisch, S., Kombe, W., ... Printz, A. (2016). A multi-dimensional assessment of urban vulnerability to climate change in Sub-Saharan Africa. *Natural Hazards*, 82(2), 149–172.

Hove, M., Ngwerume, E. T., & Muchemwa, C. (2013). *The urban crisis in Sub-Saharan Africa: A threat to human security and sustainable development. Stability*, 2(1), 1–14.

Hunt, W. F., Davis, A. P., & Traver, R. G. (2012). Meeting hydrologic and water quality goals through targeted bioretention design. *Journal of Environmental Engineering*, 138(6), 698–707.

Ice, G. (2004). History of innovative best management practice development and its role in addressing water quality limited waterbodies. *Journal of Environmental Engineering*, 130(6), 684–689.

Johnson, D., & Geisendorf, S. (2019). Are neighborhood-level SUDS worth it? An assessment of the economic value of sustainable urban drainage system scenarios using cost-benefit analyses. *Ecological Economics*, 158, 194–205.

Kakonge, J. O. (2002). Water scarcity and related environmental problems in parts of Sub-Saharan Africa: The role of the transboundary environmental impact assessment convention. *Impact Assessment and Project Appraisal*, 20(1), 49–59.

Kalra S., Kelkar D., Galwankar S.C., Papadimos T.J., Stawicki S.P., Arquilla B., Hoey B.A., Sharpe R.P., Sabol D., & Jahre J.A. (2014). The emergence of Ebola as a global health security threat: From 'lessons learned' to coordinated multilateral containment efforts. *Journal of Global Infectious Diseases*, 6(4),164–177.

Karley, N. K. (2009). Flooding and physical planning in urban areas in West Africa: Situational analysis of Accra, Ghana. *Theoretical and Empirical Researches in Urban Management*, 4(13), 25–41.

Kirchhoff, C. J., & Bulkley, J. W. (2008). Sustainable water management in the Zambezi River Basin. *Journal of the International Institute*, 15(2), 10.

Kooy, M., Furlong, K., & Lamb, V. (2019). Nature Based Solutions for urban water management in Asian cities: Integrating vulnerability into sustainable design. *International Development Planning Review*,(3), 381–390.

Krebs, P., & Larsen, T. A. (1997). Guiding the development of urban drainage systems by sustainability criteria. *Water science and technology*, 35(9), 89–98.

Le Jallé, C., Désille, D., & Burkhardt, G. (2013). Urban stormwater management in developing countries. *NOVATECH 2013*.

Li, C. (2012). Ecohydrology and good urban design for urban storm water-logging in Beijing, China. *Ecohydrology & Hydrobiology*, 12(4), 287–300.

Li, C., Fletcher, T. D., Duncan, H. P., & Burns, M. J. (2017). Can stormwater control measures restore altered urban flow regimes at the catchment scale? *Journal of Hydrology*, 549, 631–653.

Lindell, I. (2008). The multiple sites of urban governance: Insights from an African city. *Urban Studies*, 45(9), 1879–1901.

Losco, S. (2014). Water Sensitive Urban Design-WSUD-Principles and Inspiration for Sustainable Stormwater Management in the City of the Future-AA. VV. *CSE-City Safety Energy*, 1, 102–103.

Lumbroso, D. (2020). Flood risk management in Africa. *Journal of Flood Risk Management*, 13(3), 1–5.

Maas, J., Van Dillen, S. M., Verheij, R. A., & Groenewegen, P. P. (2009). Social contacts as a possible mechanism behind the relation between green space and health. *Health & Place*, 15(2), 586–595.

Marshall, J. D. (2007). Urban land area and population growth: A new scaling relationship for metropolitan expansion. *Urban Studies*, 44(10), 1889–1904.

Mguni, P. (2015). *Sustainability Transitions in the Developing World: Exploring the Potential for Integrating Sustainable Urban Drainage Systems in the Sub-Saharan Cities*. University of Copenhagen, Denmark.

Mguni, P., Herslund, L., & Jensen, M. B. (2016). Sustainable urban drainage systems: Examining the potential for green infrastructure-based stormwater management for Sub-Saharan cities. *Natural Hazards*, 82(2), 241–257.

Mora, C., Frazier, A. G., Longman, R. J., Dacks, R. S., Walton, M. M., Tong, E. J., ... Anderson, J. M. (2013). The projected timing of climate departure from recent variability. *Nature, 502*(7470), 183.

Moretto, L., Faldi, G., Ranzato, M., Rosati, F. N., Ilito Boozi, J.-P., & Teller, J. (2018). Challenges of water and sanitation service co-production in the global South. *Environment and Urbanization, 30*(2), 425–443.

Mouritz, M. (1996). *Sustainable urban water systems: Policy and professional praxis*. Murdoch University, Perth, Western Australia

Naik, P. K. (2017). Water crisis in Africa: Myth or reality? *International journal of water resources development, 33*(2), 326–339.

Natarajan, S. (2020). *Coronavirus: Why washing hands is difficult in some countries*. Retrieved from https://www.bbc.com/news/world-51929598

Ndaruzaniye, V., Lipper, L., Fiott, D., Flavell, A., & Clover, J. (2010). Climate change and security in Africa: Vulnerability discussion paper. *Africa Climate Change Environment and Security (ACCES)*, 3–9.

Novotny, V. (2008). Sustainable urban water management. In J. Feyen, K. Shannon, & M. Neville (Eds.), *Water and urban development paradigms* (pp. 19–31). CRC Press, USA.

Novotny, V., Ahern, J., & Brown, P. (2010). *Water centric sustainable communities: Planning, retrofitting, and building the next urban environment*. John Wiley & Sons, USA.

Ossa-Moreno, J., Smith, K. M., & Mijic, A. (2017). Economic analysis of wider benefits to facilitate SuDS uptake in London, UK. *Sustainable Cities and Society, 28*, 411–419.

Pastore, M. C. (2015). Reworking the relation between sanitation and the city in Dar es Salaam, Tanzania. *Environment and Urbanization, 27*(2), 473–488.

Prudencio, L., & Null, S. E. (2018). Stormwater management and ecosystem services: A review. *Environmental Research Letters, 13*(3), 033002.

Richmond, A., Myers, I., & Namuli, H. (2018). Urban informality and vulnerability: A case study in Kampala, Uganda. *Urban Science, 2*(1), 22.

Salami, R. O., Von Meding, J. K., & Giggins, H. (2017). Urban settlements' vulnerability to flood risks in African cities: A conceptual framework. *Jàmbá: Journal of Disaster Risk Studies, 9*(1), 1–9.

Short, C., Clarke, L., Carnelli, F., Uttley, C., & Smith, B. (2019). Capturing the multiple benefits associated with nature-based solutions: Lessons from a natural flood management project in the Cotswolds, UK. *Land Degradation & Development, 30*(3), 241–252.

Smith, A., Bates, P. D., Wing, O., Sampson, C., Quinn, N., & Neal, J. (2019). New estimates of flood exposure in developing countries using high-resolution population data. *Nature Communications, 10*(1), 1–7.

Swilling, M. (2019). *The age of sustainability: Just transitions in a complex world*: Routledge, UK.

Un-Habitat. (2011). *Cities and climate change: Global report on human settlements 2011*: Routledge.

Viavattene, C., & Ellis, J. B. (2013). The management of urban surface water flood risks: SUDS performance in flood reduction from extreme events. *Water Science and Technology, 67*(1), 99–108.

Vietz, G. J., Rutherfurd, I. D., Walsh, C. J., Chee, Y. E., & Hatt, B. E. (2014). *The unaccounted costs of conventional urban development: Protecting stream systems in an age of urban sprawl.* Paper presented at the Proceedings of the Australian Stream Management Conference, Townsville, QLD, Australia.

Vietz, G. J., Walsh, C. J., & Fletcher, T. D. (2016). Urban hydrogeomorphology and the urban stream syndrome: Treating the symptoms and causes of geomorphic change. *Progress in Physical Geography, 40*(3), 480–492.

Walker, L., Ashley, R., Nowell, R., Gersonius, B., & Evans, T. (2012). *Surface water management and urban green infrastructure in the UK: A review of benefits and challenges.* Paper presented at the WSUD 2012: Water sensitive urban design; Building the water sensitive community; 7th international conference on water sensitive urban design.

Walsh, C. J., Booth, D. B., Burns, M. J., Fletcher, T. D., Hale, R. L., Hoang, L. N., … Wallace, A. (2016). Principles for urban stormwater management to protect stream ecosystems. *Freshwater Science, 35*(1), 398–411. doi:10.1086/685284

Walsh, C. J., Fletcher, T. D., & Burns, M. J. (2012). Urban stormwater runoff: A new class of environmental flow problem. *PLoS One, 7*(9), e45814.

Water by Design. (2010). *A business case for best practice urban stormwater management (Version 1.1).* Brisbane: South East Queensland Healthy Waterways Partnership.

Weideman, E. A., Perold, V., Arnold, G., & Ryan, P. G. (2020). Quantifying changes in litter loads in urban stormwater run-off from Cape Town, South Africa, over the last two decades. *Science of The Total Environment, 724,* 138310.

WHO, U. (2017). *Progress on drinking water, sanitation and hygiene: 2017 update and SDG baselines.* Geneva.

WHO. (2019). United Nations Children's Fund (UNICEF) and World Health Organization; New York: 2019. *Progress on household drinking water, sanitation and hygiene 2000–2017. Special focus on inequalities.* https://www.who.int/ water_sanitation_health/publications/jmp-report-2019/en/

Yao, L., Wei, W., & Chen, L. (2016). How does imperviousness impact the urban rainfall-runoff process under various storm cases? *Ecological Indicators, 60,* 893–905.

7 Monitoring Changing Land Use-Land Cover Change to Reflect the Impact of Urbanisation on Environmental Assets in Durban, South Africa

Bahle Mazeka, Kwanele Phinzi, and Catherine Sutherland

Introduction

African cities are rapidly urbanising, which is transforming urban landscapes and placing pressure on planning, housing and service provision and environmental sustainability. Determining the pace and scale of land use change, and its spatiality, using land use and land cover (LULC) maps, can support policy-makers in the future development, planning and risk management of cities. This chapter identifies LULC change in Durban, South Africa from 1991 to 2017. Durban has experienced rapid socio-spatial transformation post-apartheid. The expansion of the land area of the Durban Functional Region by 68% in 2000, as part of the national municipal demarcation process, led to the formation of the eThekwini Municipal Area (EMA). Through this process, peri-urban and rural areas were added to Durban's periphery, increasing the amount of green open space in the city. Since 2007, the rural periphery of the city has been rapidly urbanising and densifying, which is impacting on the provision of ecosystem services in a municipality which has based its response to climate change, resilience and sustainability on the protection and wise use of these services. This chapter identifies the scale and location of land use change in the EMA with a particular focus on the built environment and vegetation cover. It explains this change through the urban processes that are shaping urban development in Durban.

Urban Development and Land Cover Change

Cities are a nexus of complex socio-economic, political and environmental relationships, shaped by the forms of governance employed to govern them (Heynen et al., 2006). These relationships determine land use patterns and land use change, as cities both grow and transform within national and local development trajectories and urban development frameworks. African cities are experiencing rapid urbanisation which is undermining their ability

DOI: 10.4324/9781003181484-7

to achieve sustainable urban planning and development (Cobbinah & Darwah, 2016; Ellis, 2013; Seto et al., 2012). Undertaking research on urban land use change in African cities and the processes underpinning this change is important for urban policy making in the face of rapid urbanisation (Odindi and Mhangara, 2011). Given the critical role played by urban green spaces in building resilience and ensuring the sustainability of cities, this study applies the LULC method to determine changes in vegetation cover and built up areas in Durban. It then presents reasons for the changes in land cover based on urban processes evident in the city. The study shows the value of using remote sensing as a tool to provide information for socio-ecological and development planning in achieving more sustainable cities in rapidly changing urban environments (Gairola & Noresah, 2010; Odindi et al., & Mhangara, 2012; Shao et al., 2008).

By 2019, 55.7% of the world's population were living in cities. The developed world has a higher share of urban population, 80.5%, with 51.1% of the developing world's population living in cities (Unctad, 20182021). Asia and Oceania have experienced the greatest increase in rates of urbanisation, with Africa rapidly urbanising in the last decade. The share of urban population in Africa is expected to increase from 43.1% in 2019 to 59.1% by 2050 (UNCTAD, 2021). South Africa is one the most urbanised countries in Africa with more than 60% of its population (56,5 million) residing in urban environments. This is projected to increase to 72% in 2030 and 80% in 2050 (COGTA, 2016; Turok, 2012).

Urbanisation can be understood as the growing share of the population residing in urban settlements (Poston & Bouvier, 2010) as a result of a rural to urban transition which includes changes in economic activity, population distribution, land use and culture (McGranahan & Satterthwaite, 2014). The reasons for urbanisation are well documented, recognising that processes of urbanisation vary from one context to another, producing different types of urban challenges (Cohen, 2004; Cobbinah et al., 2015; Fay & Opal, 2000; Fox, 2012; Huchzermeyer, 2011; IOM, 2013; Osman et al., 2016; Parnell & Mabin, 1995; Simon, 2010; UN-Habitat, 2016). One of the impacts of urbanisation is an increase in land cover of the built environment and a subsequent decrease in the amount of vegetation present in cities. Given the recent focus on using ecological infrastructure and its associated ecosystem services in building urban resilience, the loss of green open spaces or vegetation in cities is of concern, particularly in relation to climate change (Gómez-Baggethun et al., 2013; Kaczorowska, 2014; Roberts et al., 2012; World Bank, 2016).

The rapid rate of urbanisation continues to transform society and the environment at a "pace that renders formal urban planning processes and capacity insufficient" (Braathen et al., 2016, p. 1; Roy, 2011; Wu & Murray, 2003) and which undermines urban sustainability. African cities are rapidly urbanising, which is transforming urban landscapes and placing pressure on planning, housing and service provision and environmental sustainability. Urban processes which lead to urban development are not equally distributed which leads to the production of uneven urban landscapes that benefit some social groups while disadvantaging others (Swyngedouw, 2004; Swyngedouw & Heynen, 2003). Determining the pace and scale of land use change, and its spatiality, using LULC maps, can support policy-makers in the future development, planning and risk management of cities. This chapter identifies LULC change in Durban, South Africa from 1991 to 2017. Durban has experienced rapid socio-spatial transformation post-apartheid. The expansion of the land area of the Durban Functional Region by 68% in 2000, as part of the national municipal demarcation process, led to the formation of the EMA. Through this process, peri-urban and rural areas were added to Durban's periphery, increasing the amount of green open space in the city. Since 2007, the rural periphery of the city has been rapidly urbanising and densifying which is impacting on the provision of ecosystem services in a municipality which has based its response to climate change, resilience and sustainability on the protection and wise use of these services. This chapter identifies the scale and location of land use change in the EMA with a particular focus on the built environment and vegetation cover. It explains this change through the urban processes that are shaping urban development in Durban. The study has revealed that since 1991 the built up area of Durban, and its hinterland prior to 2000, has increased by 16.92% at the expense of vegetation cover loss of 24.8%, which has implications for the future sustainability of the city, given the municipality's ongoing commitment to support the value of ecosystem services for sustainable development.

In South Africa, rapid urbanisation is occurring as an additional layer to apartheid's spatial planning legacy, which remains a core spatial structure of South African cities, which is further exacerbating poverty and inequality (Spinks, 2001). LULC in South African and other African cities is being transformed by a wide range of socio-economic and political factors. This includes the development of edge cities, megaproject and infrastructural development, the development of higher density middle and upper income gated estates, suburbanisation, growing informality, evident in the rapid growth of informal settlements and peri-urban densification under traditional communal land tenure (Blakely & Snyder, 1997; Braathen et al., 2016; Cobbinah et al., 2015; Garreau, 1991; Sim et al., 2016; Zeilhofer & Topanotti, 2008). This is leading to increasing urban sprawl and the loss of valuable ecosystem services (Cartwright et al, 2012; World Bank, 2016).

The primary purpose of this chapter is to understand the role of urbanisation and the processes underpinning urban development in landscape-level transformation of urban environments. This is achieved through applying the LULC methodology to quantify and analyse the dynamic socio-natural relationship in eThekwini Municipality from 1991 to 2017. LULC is a pragmatic method, which offers the opportunity to understand complex socio-ecological relations (Ishtiaque et al., 2017). Traditionally,

LULC was derived from mapping techniques (such as field surveys and aerial photography) which proved to be expensive, time consuming and difficult (Wu et al., 2013). Remote sensing has transformed LULC as it has increased its ability to quantify and monitor urban growth (Xiao et al., 2006) through integrating it with Geographic Information Systems (GIS). This has enhanced the identification of LULC changes using relatively simple methodologies (Weng, 2002).

Land Use and Land Cover Change

The definition of LULC change remains contentious due to its multi-disciplinary use and application. There is however consensus that land cover is considered to be the biophysical state of the earth's surface and it's features such as natural topography, vegetation, waterbodies, and anthro-pogenic structures. On the other hand, land use is the human utilisation and management of the earth's surface, including agriculture, forestry and urban activities which lead to land cover modification (Lillesand et al., 2008; Schulze, 2000; al., 2017). Anthropogenic activities are usually de-rived from agriculture expansion, human settlements, infrastructural expansion, deforestation and mining, driven by production and consumption (Iqbal et al., 2013). These activities coupled with rapid urbanisation are influential in the shaping and reshaping of the biophysical surface.

Globally and locally, there is scarcity of adequately located developable land (Fourie, 2002) which consequently has led to competition and conflict for resources such as agriculture and urban development (Wu et al., 2013). As the demand for land grows, ecosystems and ecologies are transformed and disrupted with significant consequences (Aspinall & Hill, 2008). This includes increased pressure on natural resources consequent deforestation and depletion of forest species (Meyfroidt et al., 2013) which results in a decline of natural available habitats, species competition for new habitats, and loss of biodiversity (Foley et al., 2005). On the other hand, there is increased pressure on hydrological resources with natural cycle's disrupted due to increased evapotranspiration (Sterling et al., 2013) which has implications for agricultural productivity (Foley et al., 2005) thus affecting food security. Moreover, soil sediment deposits and pollution (Wu, 2008) transforms hydrological systems (such as rivers) and affects the functioning of ecosystems once dependent of specific water quantities and quality (Olang & Kundu, 2011). Sustainable urban development becomes com-promised by increased demands for land exacerbated by unprecedented rapid population growth (Smith et al., 2010). The urban environment is characterised by uneven and unequal socio-ecological relations which are choreographed by different power relations that exist between humans and the environment in different political, social and economic contexts. This results in different environmental outcomes for citizens of the city depending on where they live and on their socio-economic context

(Swyngedouw, 2015). The loss of ecosystem services in urban areas therefore impacts on society in different ways.

Urban Development in Durban

EThekwini municipality (Figure 7.1) is located on the east coast of South Africa with a municipal surface area of 2,555 square kilometers (eThekwini Municipality, 2017; Roma et al., 2013). It is extending between –29°18'58.36" S and –30°17'36.27" S and 30°25'05.42" E and 31°01'20.72" E. It lies within the Maputaland-Pondoland-Albany region, a biodiversity hotspot with 25% of its species endemic to the region (eThekwini Municipality, 2017). The topography is generally undulating with elevation ranging from 1m to 870m above sea level; the central business district (CBD) occupies a relatively flat topography with mean elevation of 35 m; and it has a relatively high annual rainfall for South Africa, of 550mm to 1200mm (Institute of Natural Resources, 2004). Furthermore, the EMA has a subtropical climate with natural vegetation including grassland, thicket and bushland.

Durban is a sprawling city, with urbanisation continuing to transform the EMA and its landscape. The municipality's Durban Metropolitan Open Space System (D'MOSS) which covers an area of 78,000 hectares (30% of the total municipal area) remains a progressive land-use management and planning tool in the face of rapid urbanisation, demand for housing and development, increasing pollution, invasive alien species, habitat fragmentation, and climate change with its associated impacts (eThekwini Municipality, 2017). Durban is home to an estimated population of 3.7 million people (eThekwini Municipality, 2017). The EMA has a fragmented spatial structure with a dense urban core. It sprawls outwards to less dense peri-urban and rural periphery. The municipality has to address multiple social, economic and environmental challenges within these different contexts which includes unemployment, poverty, growing informality and the need for sustainable economic growth and development (eThekwini Municipality, 2017).

Durban does not have the same level of migration as the two other major cities in South Africa, Cape Town and Johannesburg, but it continues to grow as approximately 150,000 migrants move in to the city each year (Posel, 2017; Statistics South Africa, 2011). Rather than constant immigration in to the urban area, Durban experiences patterns of circular migration as residents move between their rural and urban homes. The majority of migrants coming into the city are poor and find their way in to the 566 informal settlements that have been established in the city or obtain land through the traditional authority. Due to the pressure of rapid urban population growth, through natural increases and immigration, there is significant landscape transformation and competition for resources. This chapter presents a method for identifying and understanding urban

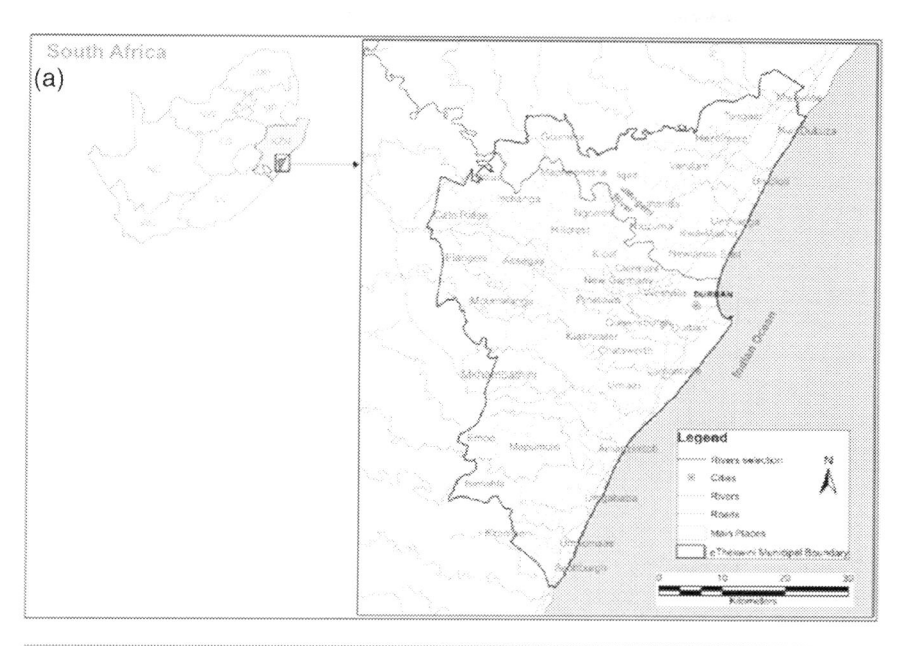

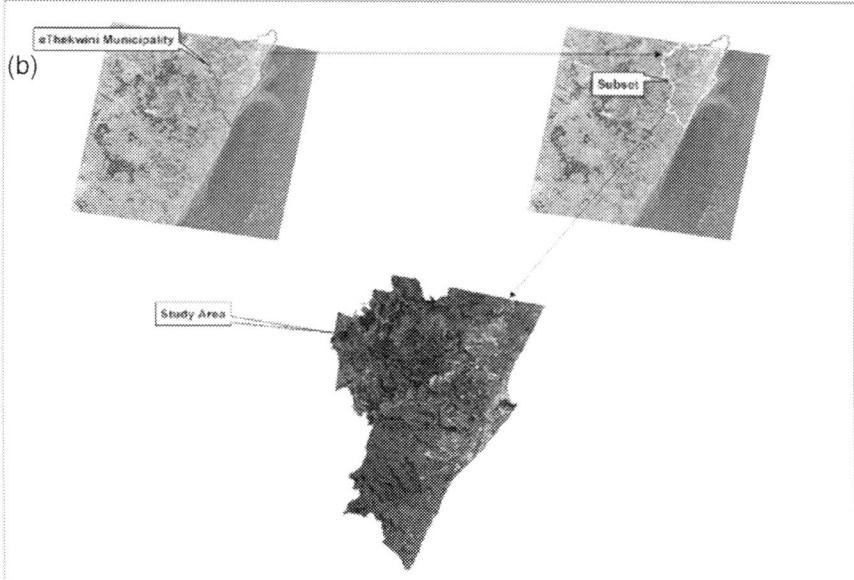

Figure 7.1 Geographical location of the study area.

land level transformation and its relationship to urban processes in the city which provides an opportunity to reflect on contemporary African urbanism and its spatial impacts.

The development of Durban, or the EMA, with its administrative entity eThekwini Municipality has been shaped by post-apartheid transformation, pro-growth development planning, rapid urbanisation and increasing informality (Freund & Padayachee, 2002; Sutherland et al., 2018). It is a unique metropolitan municipality in South Africa as its spatial management and governance is complicated by the existence of dual governance system (Sutherland et al., 2016). An estimated 43.8% of the EMA comprises of Ingonyama Trust land which is governed by both eThekwini Municipality and traditional councils. The Ingonyama Trust was established in 1994 (as a product of political negotiations at the end of apartheid) by the former KwaZulu homeland government through the *KwaZulu Ingonyama Trust Act*, 3 KwaZulu-Natal of 1994, to hold the land previously held in trust by the KwaZulu homeland government (ITB, 2014). Primarily, the mandate of the Ingonyama Trust is to be the custodian of land jointly administered by the traditional councils and ITB, for communities living on the land. Within the Municipality, land allocation process on Ingonyama Trust land are responsible for land transformation and rapid urban densification, which has significant impact on urban management (Sim et al., 2018). The administration of customary law/traditional land by traditional leaders does not align with the eThekwini Municipality's strategic spatial plans, the Spatial Development Frameworks (SDF), which leads to challenges of land management, mainly in the periphery of the city where Ingonyama Trust land is predominantly located (Sim et al., 2018).

The eThekwini Municipality's SDF, which forms part of a suite of Integrated Development Plans, was first drafted in 2002. One of the main features of the 2002 SDF was an urban edge which demarcated an urban core, and a peri-urban and rural periphery (Sim et al., 2016). The overall intention was to promote sustainable development within the municipality through initiatives targeting the densification of the urban core and protecting ecological infrastructure and its associated ecosystem services in the rural periphery. In 2010, the Urban Development Line (UDL), a planning instrument used to define rural and urban development zones in the city was introduced to supersede the urban edge. The UDL was developed to improve social, economic, and environmental sustainability within the Municipality. It defined urban and rural zones which receive different levels of services with the EMA. It also demarcates areas of urban densification (Sim et al., 2016). The line has shifted since its inception in 2010 to accommodate economic growth nodes in the EMA which reveals the power of pro-growth discourses in the city (Sim et al., 2016). However, to date, the UDL conceptually holds the notion that the rural periphery contains the largest areas of open space and ecological infrastructure in the EMA; which is valuable and needs to be protected for the future resilience and sustainability of Durban (World Bank, 2016). The impact of land use change in the periphery of the city as a result of the dual governance system and land allocation processes is reflected in its inclusion as one of the two pillars of Durban's Resilience Strategy (Roberts et al., 2020).

Despite dealing with complex land-level transformations, eThekwini Municipality has received global recognition for its innovative and progressive efforts towards sustainable development (Sutherland et al., 2018). EThekwini Municipality adopts a pro-poor approach in the management of its ecosystem services, as reflected in its community ecosystem based adaptation programme (Roberts et al., 2012) which are led by the Environmental Planning and Climate Protection Department (EPCPD). This includes selection as one of 100 Resilience Cities first 32 resilient cities (Sutherland et al., 2019) and the Palmiet Catchment Rehabilitation Project (PCRP) in an attempt develop an innovative governance model built on water resilience and increase adaptive capacity (Martel & Sutherland, 2019; Vogel et al., 2016). Durban's efforts are reflective of experimental urban governance and management of African cities in the face of rapid urbanisation and the need for continuous exploration to find participatory development planning approaches which support sustainable development.

Methods of Data Collection and Research Design

Multi-temporal remote sensing datasets were used to investigate the LULC change from the period 1991 to 2017 in Durban. Four Landsat scenes (path 168, row 81) were downloaded from the United States Geological Survey (USGS) website (https://earthexplorer.usgs.gov/). In an attempt to avoid excessive cloud cover, the images with minimal or no cloud cover were acquired outside of the rainfall season. More specifically, all the images were acquired in April, except a 2000 image which was acquired in June due to unavailability in April. The images included Landsat-5 Thematic Mapper (TM) acquired on 09 April, 1991, Landsat-7 Enhanced TM plus (ETM+) acquired on 28 June, 2000, Landsat-5 TM acquired on 13 April, 2010, and Landsat-8 Operational Land Imager (OLI) acquired on 16 April, 2017. The obtained Landsat images were already projected to the Universal Traverse Mercator (UTM), zone 35 South (S), and referenced to the World Geodetic System 1984 (WGS84) datum. With a spatial resolution of 30m and the longest data archive, Landsat imagery was preferred in the current study. In addition to spatial and temporal resolutions, the high spectral resolution also makes Landsat imagery attractive to LULC analysis. However, in this study, only the visible red (Red) and near-infrared (NIR) spectral channels were considered for LULC classification.

The area of the EMA in 2017 is far larger (by 68%) than the area of the Durban Functional Region of 1991. Prior to 1994, large areas of the periphery of the EMA were located in KwaZulu homeland, a product of apartheid spatial engineering. These areas were relatively densely settled as African households attempted to move as close to the city of Durban as was legally possible so as to gain access to urban opportunities. They could not easily reside in Durban as a result of the Group Areas Act of 1950. These peripheral areas were incorporated in to the EMA in 2000 as a result of the national municipal demarcation process. For the purpose of this study, so as to show the change in land cover over a 25-year period, the current boundaries of the EMA have been used across the full time period from 1991 to 2017.

Preprocessing

All the preprocessing steps including image enhancement and radiometric calibration were carried out within the ArcMap 10.4 environment. The "Apparent Reflectance Function" located within the Image Analysis tool was used to convert digital numbers (DN) to top of atmosphere reflectance. Geometric calibration was not performed since Level 1 Landsat products have been geometrically corrected. Topographic normalisation was also not considered given that the study area is mostly urban with relatively flat topography. Subsequent to necessary preprocessing steps, all the Landsat scenes for different years were spatially subset to the extent of the study area. Since the images were already projected to the desired coordinate system by the USGS (e.g. WGS84 UTM 35S), all the other datasets including shapefile demarcating the study area were projected to this coordinate system.

Image Classification

In this study, the USGS-based broad LULC classification scheme was adopted to classify LULC within the study area. Many LULC classification techniques exist and can be broadly grouped into supervised and unsupervised. Amongst such techniques, vegetation indices are increasingly recognised and have proven useful for feature extraction as evidenced by the previous studies (Bhandari et al., 2012; Phinzi & Ngetar, 2017). One advantage of using vegetation indices in LULC change research is their ability to minimise the effects of sun angle, shadow and topography (Lu et al., 2004). Although a wide variety of vegetation indices now exist, the Normalised Different Vegetation Index (NDVI) developed by Rouse et al. (1973) remains the most widely used vegetation index. In this study, NDVI was used to derive LULC classes as detailed below. NDVI can be mathematically expressed as follows:

$$NDVI = \frac{(NIR - Red)}{(NIR + Red)} \tag{7.1}$$

where *NIR* is the near-infrared reflectance and *Red* is the visible red reflectance. It is worth noting that NIR is band 4 and Red is band 3 in Landsat TM/ETM+. In Landsat OLI, NIR and Red represent bands 5 and 4, respectively. Using this equation [7.1], the NDVI for each year (1991, 2000, 2010 and 2017) was manually computed within the "Image Analysis" module in ArcMap 10.4. NDVI was used to extract different LULC classes. The "identify" tool allowed for the identification of the minimum and maximum NDVI values for various LULC classes. Upon identifying the minimum and maximum NDVI values, suitable NDVI classification thresholds were determined after a series of trial runs (Phinzi & Ngetar, 2017). Within the "Raster Calculator" suitable NDVI thresholds were keyed in using conditional statements (e.g. "Con" tool) and five LULC classes were derived ranging from water, built-up areas, bare surface, poor vegetation cover and strong vegetation cover. Such LULC classes together with their relevant NDVI classification thresholds are presented in Table 7.1.

Accuracy Assessment

Accuracy assessment is a prerequisite for any LULC map derived from a remote sensing product. Contingency table or error matrix is the most commonly used and preferred method of expressing accuracy. For these well-known reasons, error matrix was used in this study to assess the accuracy of LULC maps. Fifty randomly selected accuracy assessment points were generated in ArcMap 10.2 using the "Create Accuracy Assessment Points" tool. Within the tool dialog box, the "Equalized Stratified Random" option was selected as a sampling strategy to ensure that each class is assigned the same number of points, *viz.* ten points per class. The resulting random points were then converted to KML (keyhole makeup language) format and exported to Google Earth for ground truth. In Google Earth, the LULC classes with corresponding points were manually identified. After updating the points using the "Update Accuracy Assessment Points" tool, the "Compute Confusion Matrix" tool was used to generate the error matrix table.

Results

NDVI-Based LULC Classification

In general, NDVI values range from –1 to +1, with the former representing non-reflective features such as water or shadows whereas the latter commonly denotes maximum vegetation. Presented in Figure 7.2 is the NDVI for 1991, 2000, 2010 and 2017 while Figure 7.3 illustrates corresponding LULC maps. Of all the years, the year 2000 recorded the least NDVI reflectance values ranging from –1.17 to 0.85. If low NDVI values are illustrative of low vegetation biomass, one plausible explanation for this could be that the image was acquired in June which represents a dry month in the study area. On the other

Table 7.1 LULC classes and their respective NDVI classification thresholds for different years (1991–2017)

LULC Class	Description	NDVI 1991	NDVI 2000	NDVI 2010	NDVI 2017
Water	Surface water bodies including rivers, dams, and lakes.	0 <	0 <	0 <	0 <
Built-up Areas	Residential (rural and urban), industrial, and commercial areas including roads, and other impervious surface features.	0.01–0.40	0.01–0.31	0.01–0.37	0.01–0.51
Bare Surface	Areas with no vegetation cover such as bare soil, sand bars/dunes, exposed rocks, uncultivated agricultural land and open mines.	0.41–0.42	0.32–0.38	0.38–0.46	0.52–0.59
Poor vegetation	Areas with minimal, sparse, or partially dry vegetation cover, e.g. shrubs and grassland.	0.43–0.54	0.39–0.45	0.47–0.50	0.60–0.65
Strong Vegetation	Green, photosynthetic, and dense vegetation cover such as trees.	0.55–0.87	0.46–0.85	0.51–0.89	0.66–088

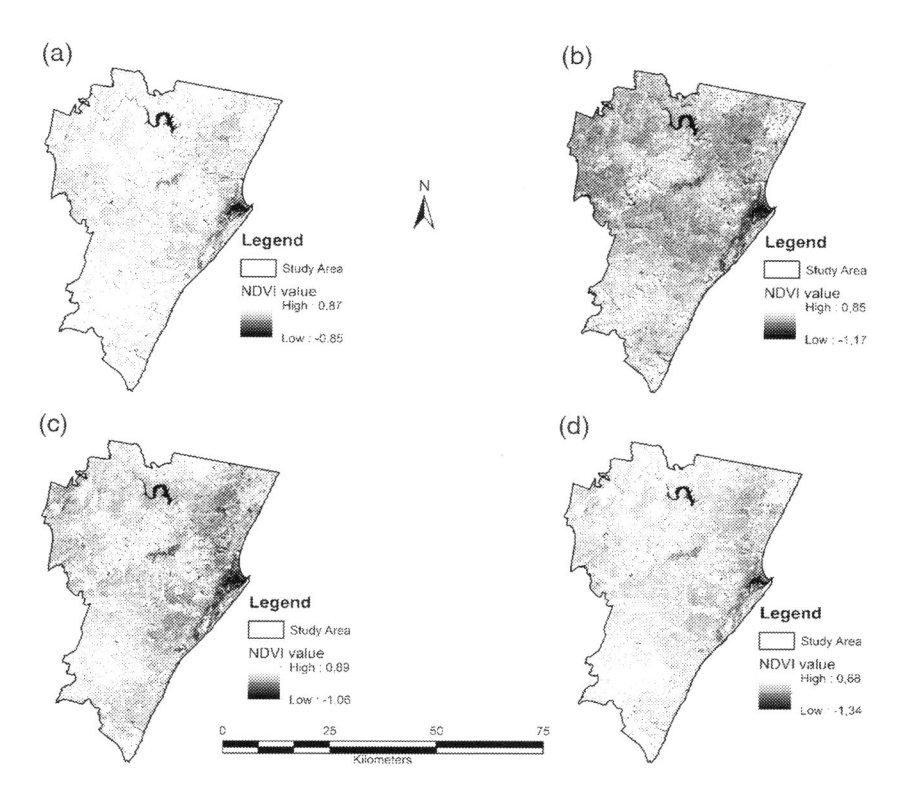

Figure 7.2 NDVI maps: 1991 (a), 2000 (b), 2010 (c) and 2017 (d).

hand, the NDVI values were slightly different for 1991 (–0.85 to 0.87), 2010 (–1.08 to 0.89) and 2017 (–1.34 to 0.88) albeit the images for these years were acquired in the same month, e.g. April. In Figure 7.4, it can be observed that the mean NDVI values for LULC classes have been fluctuating over different years. In the main, such fluctuation of NDVI values could be ascribed to varying rainfall regimes between 1991 and 2017, which is expected given the cycles of drought experienced in eThekwini Municipality. Based on qualitative assessment, it appears that the most pronounced LULC change occurred in built-up and vegetation categories as can be observed in Figure 7.3. A more detailed and quantitative assessment of LULC change is presented in a subsequent section.

LULC Change

Vegetation, particularly, strong (photosynthetic) vegetation cover occupies a significant portion of the study area contributing 68.70% in 1991, 46.63% in 2000, 47.51% in 2010 and 43.91% in 2017 of the total coverage (Figure 7.5). However, there has been a sharp decrease in vegetation coverage

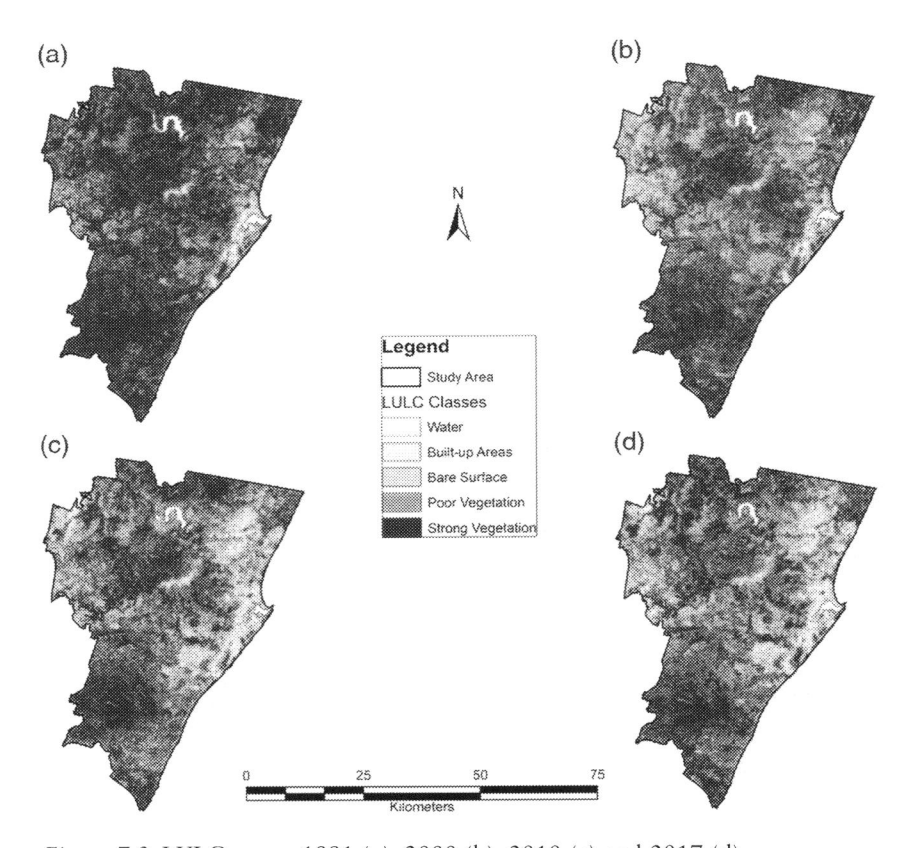

Figure 7.3 LULC maps: 1991 (a), 2000 (b), 2010 (c) and 2017 (d).

between 1991 and 2000, although a slight increase can be observed between 2000 and 2010. As vegetation coverage decreases, there is a corresponding increase in built-up areas and bare surface coverage. For instance, the built-up areas constituted only 8.85% of the entire study area in 1991 and increased to 17.69% in 2000, 21.17% in 2010 and 25.77% in 2017. Overall, 24.80% of green space (strong vegetation) has been lost between 1991 and 2017 whereas the built-up area has increased by 16.92% in the same period (Table 7.2). Bare surface and poor vegetation cover gained about 6.43% and 1.48%, respectively. There is no significant change in water bodies. As indicated in Table 7.2, a mere 0.03% of water surface was lost between 1991 and 2017.

Accuracy Assessment

Table 7.3 presents accuracy assessment results for 1991, 2000, 2010 and 2017 NDVI-derived LULC classifications. Within the confusion matrix, the

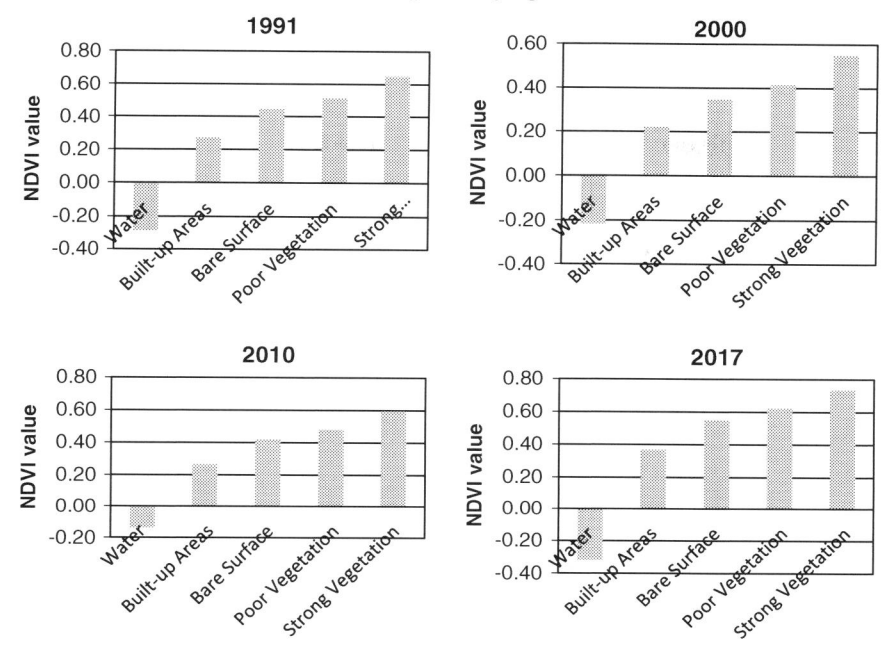

Figure 7.4 Mean NDVI reflectance values for different LULC classes.

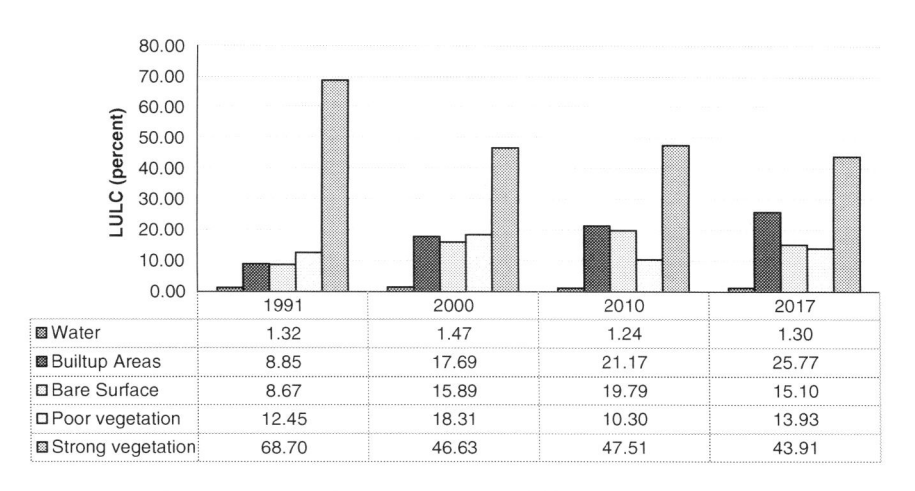

	1991	2000	2010	2017
Water	1.32	1.47	1.24	1.30
Builtup Areas	8.85	17.69	21.17	25.77
Bare Surface	8.67	15.89	19.79	15.10
Poor vegetation	12.45	18.31	10.30	13.93
Strong vegetation	68.70	46.63	47.51	43.91

Figure 7.5 The proportion of LULC classes in different years (1991–2017).

Table 7.2 Overall LULC change between 1991 and 2017

LULC Class	1991			2017			LULC Change (%)
	Count[a]	Area (km²)	Area (%)	Count	Area (km²)	Area (%)	
Water	34866	31.38	1.32	34138	30.72	1.30	−0.03
Builtup Areas	232826	209.54	8.85	678103	610.29	25.77	16.92
Bare Surface	228250	205.43	8.67	397456	357.71	15.10	6.43
Poor Vegetation	327651	294.89	12.45	366562	329.91	13.93	1.48
Strong Vegetation	1808108	1627.30	68.70	1155472	1039.92	43.91	−24.80
Total	2631701	2369	100	2631731	2369	100	0.00

Note:
a The count column represents the total number of cells in each LULC polygon.

Table 7.3 Confusion matrices for 1991, 2000, 2010 and 2017 LULC maps

LULC Class 1991	Water	Built-up Areas	Bare Surface	Poor Vegetation	Strong Vegetation	Total	User's Accuracy	Kappa
Water	10	0	0	0	0	10	1	0
Built-up Areas	1	8	1	0	0	10	0.8	0
Bare Surface	0	0	6	4	0	10	0.6	0
Poor Vegetation	0	0	1	9	0	10	0.9	0
Strong Vegetation	0	0	0	0	10	10	1	0
Total	11	8	8	13	10	50	0	0
Producer's Accuracy	0.9	1	0.8	0.7	1	0	0.9	0
Kappa	0	0	0	0	0	0	0	0.8
LULC Class 2000								
Water	10	0	0	0	0	10	1	0
Built-up Areas	0	6	4	0	0	10	0.6	0
Bare Surface	0	2	6	2	0	10	0.6	0
Poor Vegetation	0	0	0	10	0	10	1	0
Strong Vegetation	0	0	0	0	10	10	1	0
Total	10	8	10	12	10	50	0	0
Producer's Accuracy	1	0.8	0.6	0.8	1	0	0.8	0
Kappa	0	0	0	0	0	0	0.00	0.8
LULC Class 2010								
Water	9	1	0	0	0	10	0.9	0
Built-up Areas	0	8	2	0	0	10	0.8	0
Bare Surface	0	2	5	3	0	10	0.5	0
Poor Vegetation	0	0	0	10	0	10	1	0
Strong Vegetation	0	0	0	0	10	10	1	0
Total	9	11	7	13	10	50	0	0
Producer's Accuracy	1	0.7	0.7	0.8	1	0	0.8	0
Kappa	0	0	0	0	0	0	0	0.8

(Continued)

Table 7.3 (Continued)

LULC Class 1991	Water	Built-up Areas	Bare Surface	Poor Vegetation	Strong Vegetation	Total	User's Accuracy	Kappa
LULC Class 2017								
Water	8	2	0	0	0	10	0.8	0
Built-up Areas	0	6	3	1	0	10	0.6	0
Bare Surface	0	2	6	2	0	10	0.6	0
Poor Vegetation	0	0	1	8	1	10	0.8	0
Strong Vegetation	0	0	0	0	10	10	1	0
Total	8	10	10	11	11	50	0	0
Producer's Accuracy	1	0.6	0.6	0.7	0.9	0	0.8	0
Kappa	0	0	0	0	0	0	0	0.7

accuracy of a particular LULC class is assessed in terms of the user's accuracy, producer's accuracy and kappa's coefficient. The latter is probably the most important indicator of accuracy. The kappa's coefficient value ranges from 0 to 1. The closer the value to 0, the lesser the accuracy can be obtained, and the closer the value to 1, the greater the accuracy can be achieved. The 1991, 2000 and 2010 LULC maps recorded the kappa's coefficient of 0.8 suggesting the highest accuracy. Of all the years, the LULC map of 2017 yielded the least kappa's coefficient, namely 0.7 indicating the lowest accuracy. Altogether, the accuracy achieved by the NDVI-derived LULC maps including the 2017 map is adequate for the purpose of this study.

Analysis and Discussion

There has been a continuous decline of vegetation coverage and an increase of the built-up area of the EMA and the previous DFA and its rural hinterland from 1991 to 2017. The study has revealed that since 1991 the built up area of Durban and its hinterland prior to 2000 has increased by 16.92% at the expense of vegetation cover loss of 24.8%; which has implications for the future sustainability of the city given the municipality's ongoing commitment to support the value of ecosystem services for sustainable development. Ongoing urbanisation of the EMA is likely to sustain this trend which is of concern to a municipality which has focused much of its efforts around resilience and sustainability on its ecosystem services (SANBI, 2009; Sutherland et al., 2018). The main urban processes responsible for this change are identified as being rapid urbanisation, investment in large scale development projects (or megaprojects), the growth in human settlements, peri-urban densification under a dual governance system, and investment in open spaces and ecosystem services (see Table 7.4).

Conclusion

This chapter has quantified land-level transformation of the EMA between 1991 and 2017, demonstrating the value of LULC change method in urban planning and governance. The results of the chapter indicate a consistent decline in vegetation coverage, while showing a persistent increase in the built-up area, which is a well-established dialectical relationship between cities and nature. This supports the argument that urbanisation is more than the growing share of the population residing in urban environments. It includes the significant transformation of natural land cover and hence socio-ecological relationships. Urbanisation is a complex process of cultural, social, economic, political and environmental change, which includes the transformation of biophysical and material entities in the making of urban environments which impacts on the resources available to support

Table 7.4 Summary of urbanization relationalities

Urban Process	Characteristics (Durban)	Impact
Urbanisation		Increasing demand for land for economic development, housing, services and social facilities.
Investment in large scale development projects of megaprojects	eThekwini Municipality has embarked on a number of catalytic and mega projects that are responsible for land-level transformations, as they lead to new urban development nodes within the EMA. The majority of these have been developed through public private partnerships. The development of Dube Tradeport and King Shaka Airport in 2010 has led to significant growth in the north of the city, and the shifting of the UDL (Hannan & Sutherland, 2015; Robbin, 2010; Sim et al., 2016).	Development of new urban nodes and development corridors that have led to significant development in the north of the EMA.
Growth in human settlements	Rapid densification of peri-urban areas under traditional authority governance outside of administrative planning and building controls (Dlamini et al., 2014; Mbatha & Mchunu, 2016; Sim et al., 2016). Growth in informality, with many of Durban's informal settlements being located along rivers, which produces social and environmental risk (Williams et al., 2018). Large scale development of gated estates on the periphery of the city, driven by "white flight." The development of an edge city, Umhlanga/Gateway/ Cornubia (Michel & Scott, 2005), and other urban development nodes, for decentralised economic growth with their associated housing developments.	Increasing demand for land. Increase in the built environment, infrastructure and hard surfaces through the development of a wide range of human settlements including high income gates estates, densification of middle income suburbs, low cost housing projects, peri-urban housing development and informal settlements. Large areas of sugar cane, which does not represent ecological infrastructure, but is open space, has been transformed in to human settlements across the EMA since the early 1990s.

Peri-urban densification under a dual governance system	The dual governance system which is present in 43% of the EMA, creates a complex system of land use management as traditional councils are responsible for land allocation, while the eThekwini Municipality, is responsible land use management, services and environmental protection (Sim et al., 2016). Land allocation processes in the traditional authority areas are providing access to affordable land, which is resulting in the city being built from below (Sutherland et al., 2018).	Rapid densification of the peri-urban and rural periphery outside the UDL, which is undertaken outside of administrative planning and building controls, and which takes not take adequate cognizance of the value of environmental resources and ecosystem services (Sutherland et al., 2016). The UDL is ineffective and politically contested as a planning instrument.
Investment in open spaces and ecosystem services	DMOSS as a layer in the EMA's SDF, which identifies land which contains valuable ecological infrastructure and associated ecosystem services. Open spaces are protected under different levels of regulatory controls (World Bank, 2016). Development of Durban's community ecosystem based adaptation programme, including the Buffelsdraai community reforestation project (Archer et al., 2014; Douwes et al., 2016; Roberts et al., 2012) as part of its climate response. Investment in Durban's Transformative Riverine Management Programme, which focuses on participatory and community based river rehabilitation to build resilience, address poverty, reduce risk and ensure sustainability (Martel & Sutherland, 2019).	Positive impact on protecting vegetation and ecological infrastructure in the EMA through the use of planning instruments such as DMOSS, and investment in community ecosystem based adaptation which addresses poverty and supports climate adaptation. Ongoing investment in river rehabilitation projects in Durban, which is having positive impacts on urban sustainability (Martel, et al., 2021). These projects which drive urban sprawl are developed in contract to progressive urban densification projects in the EMA which support the urban poor due t their focus on informality. This includes the innovative and socially transformative Warwick Junction Urban Renewal Project in the urban core, located in the city's busiest transport hub, which has received global recognition. The project ensures the integration of street traders into and supports informal markets in the life of the city (Dobson & Skinner, 2009).

sustainability (Lawhon et al., 2014). LULC change is evident, and it reflects a decrease in vegetation cover, which is of concernas the municipality focuses on the value of ecological infrastructure in supporting the future resilience and sustainability of its city. Progressive planning instruments such as DMOSS, and climate response programmes such as Durban's Community Ecosystem Based Adaption programme and the newly established Transformative Riverine Management Programme continue to support the protection of the EMA's valuable ecological infrastructure. However, as this chapter has shown, rapid urbanisation and pro-growth urban development, continue to place pressure on the city's natural resources. This challenge is evident in other African cities. What is required is an approach to planning and development that focuses on the value of environmental assets, given their rapid decline as a result of urbanisation.

Acknowledgements

The financial assistance of the National Institute for the Humanities and Social Sciences, in collaboration with the South African Humanities Deans Association towards this research is hereby acknowledged. Opinions expressed and conclusions arrived at are those of the author and are not necessarily to be attributed to the NIHSS and SAHUDA. *Declaration of conflicting interests*: the authors declared no potential conflicts of interest with respect to the research, authorship and/or publication of this article.

References

Addaney, M., & Cobbinah, P. B. (2019). Climate change, urban planning and sustainable development in Africa: The difference worth appreciating. In P. B. Cobbinah & M. Addaney (Eds.), *The geography of climate change adaptation in urban Africa* (pp. 3–26). Cham: Palgrave Macmillan.

Archer, D., Almansi, F., DiGregorio, M., Roberts, D., Sharma, D., & Syam, D. (2014). Moving towards inclusive urban adaptation: Approaches to integrating community-based adaptation to climate change at city and national scale. *Climate and Development*, 64(4), 345–356.

Aspinall, R. J., & Hill, M. J. (2008). *Land use change: Science, policy and management*. Boca Raton: Taylor & Francis.

Bhandari, A. K., Kumar, A., & Sigh, G. K. (2012), Feature extraction using nomarlised difference vegetation index (NDVI): A case study of Jabalpur city. In *2nd International Conference on Communication, Computing & Security (ICCCS-2012), Procedia Technology* (Vol. 6, pp. 612–621).

Blakely, E. J., & Snyder, M. G. (1997). *Fortress America: Gated communities in the United States*. Washington, D.C.: Brookings Institution Press.

Braathen, E., Dupont, V. J.-L., & Sutherland, C. (2016). Situating the politics of slum within the 'urban turn'. In V. Dupont, D. Jordhus-Lier, C. Sutherland, & B. Einar (Eds.), *The politics of slums in the global south: Urban informality in Brazil, India, South Africa and Peru* (pp. 1–29). New York: Routledge.

Cartwright, A., Parnell, S., & Oelefse, G., eds. (2012). *Climate Change at the City Scale: Impacts, Mitigation and Adaptation in Cape Town*. Oxford: Routledge, pp. 263–270.

Cobbinah, P. B., Erdiaw-Kwasie, M. O., & Amoateng, P. (2015). Africa's urbanisation: Implications for sustainable development. *Cities*, 47(1), 62–72.

Cobbinah, P., & Darkwah, R. M. (2016). Toward a more desirable form of sustainable urban development in Africa. *African Geographical Review*, 36(3), 262–285.

COGTA (2016). Integrated Urban Development Framework: A New Deal for South African Cities and Towns. Available at: http://www.cogta.gov.za/cgta_2016/wp-content/uploads/2016/05/eJZWfa-IUDF-2016_WEB.pdf (accessed 30 October 2020).

Cohen, S., (2004). Social relationships and health. *American Psychologist*, 59(8), 676–684.

Dlamini, S., Akombelwa, M., & Chilufya, M., 2014; Exploring spatial growth pattern of settlements in customary land – a study of Adams Rural, *KwaZulu-Natal in Proceedings of the AfricaGEO* 2014, Cape Town, South Africa.

Dobson, R., & Skinner, C. (2009). *Working in Warwick: Including street traders in urban plans, UKZN School of Development Studies*. University of KwaZulu-Natal. In Durban.

Douwes, E., Rouget, M., Diederichs, N., O'Donoghue, S. H., Roy, K., & Roberts, D. (2016). The Buffelsdraai Landfill Site Community Reforestation Project. *Unasylva*, 67(247/248), 12–19.

Ellis, E. (2013). *Land-use and land-cover change*. http://www.ecotope.org/people/ellis/papers/ellis_eoe_lulcc_2007.pdf Accessed 26 June 2020

eThekwini Municipality. (2002). *eThekwini municipal area spatial development framework – Spatial response to long term development framework and integrated development plan*. Draft discussion document, May 2002. Durban: eThekwini Municipality.

eThekwini Municipality. (2012). *Spatial development framework SDF report, 2012/2013*. Durban: eThekwini Municipality.

eThekwini Municipality. (2017) *eThekwini Municipality Integrated Development Plan, 2012/13 to 2016/17, Annual Review 2016/2017*. Durban: eThekwini Municipality.

eThekwini Municipality. (2017) *Municipal Spatial Development Framework*, 2017/2018–2021/2022. Durban: eThekwini Municipality.

Fay, M., & Opal, C. (2000). *Urbanization without growth: A not so uncommon phenomenon, Policy Research Working Paper no. 2412*. Washington DC: The World Bank.

Foley, J. A., DeFries, R., Asner, G. P., Barford, C., Bonan, G., Carpenter, S. R., Chapin, F. S., Coe, M., Daily, g. C., Gibbs, H., Hleowski., Holloway, T., Howard, A., Kucharik, C. J., Monfreda, C., Patz, J., Prentice, C., Ramankutty, N., & Snyder, P. (2005). Global consequences of land use. *Science*, 309(5734), 570–574.

Fourie, C. (2002). Land management, land administration and geospatial data: exploring the conceptual linkages in the developing world. *Geomatica*, 56(4), 351–361.

Fox, S. (2012). Urbanization as a global historical process: Theory and evidence from sub-Saharan Africa. *Population and Development Review*, 38(2), 285–310.

Freund, B., & Padayachee, V. (2002). *Urban vortex: South African city in transition*. Pietermaritzburg: University of Natal Press.

Gairola, S., & Noresah, M. S. (2010). Emerging trend of urban green space research and the implications for safeguarding biodiversity: A viewpoint. *Nature and Science*, 8(7), 43–49.

Garreau, J. (1991). *'Edge City': Life on the New Frontier*. New York: Double Day.

Gómez-Baggethun, E., Gren, Å., Barton, D., Langemeyer, J., McPhearson, T., O'Farrell, P., Andersson, E., Hamstead, Z., Kremer, P., Elmqvist, T., Fragkias, M., Goodness, J., Güneralp, B., Marcotullio, P. J., McDonald, R. I., Parnell, S., Schewenius, M., Sendstad, M., Seto, K. C., & Wilkinson, C., eds. (2013). *Urbanization, Biodiversity and Ecosystem Services: Challenges and Opportunities*. Dordrecht Heidelberg New York London: Springer, pp. 175–252.

Hannan, S., & Sutherland, C., 2015. Mega-projects and sustainability in Durban, South Africa: Convergent or divergent agendas? *Habitat International*, 45, 205–212.

HDA. (2013) *KwaZulu-Natal: Informal settlements status*. Johannesburg: The Housing Development Agency (HDA).

Hellberg, S. (2014). Water, life and politics: Exploring the contested case of eThekwini municipality through a governmentality lens. *Geoforum*, 56, 226–236.

Heynen, N. (2014). Urban political ecology I: The urban century. *Progress in Human Geography*, 38(4), 598–604.

Heynen, N., Kaika, M., & Swyngedouw, E. (2006). In *In the nature of cities: Urban political ecology and the politics of urban metabolism*. Abingdon: Routledge.

Heynen, N., Perkins, H. A., & Roy, P. (2006). The political ecology of uneven urban green space: The impact of political economy on race and ethnicity in producing environmental inequality in Milwaukee. *Urban Affairs Review*, 42(1), 3–25.

Iqbal, M. F., Khan, M. R., & Malik, A. H. (2013). Land use change detection in the limestone exploitation area of Margalla Hills National Park (MHNP), Islamabad, Pakistan using geo-spatial techniques. *Journal of Himalayan Earth Sciences*, 46(1), 89–98.

Ingonyama Trust Board (ITB). (2014), *Ingonyama Trust Board annual report 2013/ 2014*, Pietermaritzburg: Ingonyama Trust Board.

Institute of Natural Resources. (2004), *Rural agricultural land potential assessment and agribusiness policy for eThekwini*. Viewed 23 January 2018, http://www.durban.gov.za/Documents/City_Government/IDP_Policy/05percent 20Statuspercent20quo.pdf

Ishtiaque, A., Shrestha, M., & Chhetri, N. (2017). Rapid urban growth in the Kathmandu Valley, Nepal: Monitoring land use land cover dynamics of a Himalayan City with Landsat Imageries. *Environments*, 4(72), 1–16.

Kaczorowska, A. (2014). Ecosystem Services and Urban Resilience. 50th ISOCARP Congress, Conference paper, pp. 1–9

Lawhon, M., Ernstson, H. & Silver, J. (2014). Provincializing urban political ecology: Towards a situated UPE through African urbanism. *Antipode*, 46(2), 497–516.

Lillesand, T. M., Kiefer, R. W., & Chipman, J. W. (2008). *Remote sensing and image interpretation*. Hoboken: John Wiley & Sons Ltd.

Lu, D., Mausel, P., Brondízio, E., & Moran, E. (2004), Change detection techniques. *International Journal of Remote Sensing*, 25(12), 2365–2407.

Mabin, A. (2017). Grounding southern city urban theory in time and place. In S. Parnell & S. Oldfield (Eds.), *The Routledge handbook on cities in the global south* (pp. 21–36). London: Routledge.

Maharaj, B., & Ramballi, K. (1998). Local economic development strategies in an emerging democracy: The case of Durban in South Afiica. *Urban Studies*, 35(1), 131–148.

Martel, P., & Sutherland, C. (2019). Governing river rehabilitation for climate adaptation and water security in Durban, South Africa. In P. Cobbinah & M. Addaney (Eds.), *The geography of climate change adaptation in urban Africa* (pp. 355–387). Cham: Palgrave Macmillan.

Mazeka, B., Sutherland, C., Buthelezi, S., & Khumalo D. (2019). Community-based mapping methodology for climate change adaptation: A case study of quarry road west informal settlement, Durban, South Africa. In P. Cobbinah & M. Addaney (Eds.), *The geography of climate change adaptation in urban Africa* (pp. 57–88). Cham: Palgrave Macmillan.

Mbatha, S., & Mchunu, K. (2016). Tracking peri-urban changes in eThekwini Municipality – beyond the 'poor–rich' dichotomy. *Urban Research & Practice*, 9(3), 1–15.

McGranahan, G., & Satterthwaite, D. (2014) *Urbanisation concepts and trends. IIED Working Paper*. London: IIED.

Meyfroidt, P., Lambin, E., Erb. K., & Hertel, T. H. (2013). Globalization of land use: Distant drivers of land change and geographic displacement of land use. *Current Opinion in Environmental Sustainability*, 5(1), 438–444.

Michel, D. P., & Scott, D. (2005). The La Lucia-Umhlanga Ridge as an emerging "Edge City". *South African Geographical Journal*, 87(2), 104–114.

Odindi, J., Mhangara, P., & Kakembo, V. (2012). Remote sensing land-cover change in Port Elizabeth during South Africa's democratic transition. South African Journal of Science, 108(5/6), 1–7.

Olang L. O., & Kundu P. M. (2011). Land degradation of the Mau forest complex in Eastern Africa: A review for management and restoration planning. In E. Ekundayo, eds. *Environmental Monitoring*. IntechOpen, pp. 254–262.

Osman, T., Divigalpitiya, P., & Arima, T. (2016). Quantifying the driving forces of informal urbanization in the western part of the greater Cairo Metropolitan Region. *Environments*, 3(13), 1–17.

Otunga, C., Odindi, J., & Mutanga, O. (2014). Land use land cover change in the fringe of eThekwini Municipality: Implications for urban green spaces using remote sensing. *South African Journal of Geomatics*, 3(2), 145–162.

Parnell, S., & Mabin, A. (1995). Rethinking urban South Africa. *Journal of Southern African Studies*, 21(1), 39–61.

Phinzi, K., & Ngetar, N. S. (2017), Mapping soil erosion in a quaternary catchment in Eastern Cape using geographic information system and remote sensing. *South African Journal of Geomatics*, 6(1), 11–29.

Posel, D. (2017). Enriching economics in South Africa: interdisciplinary collaboration and the value of quantitative – qualitative exchanges. *Journal of Economic Methodology*, 24(2), 119–133.

Poston, D. L., & Bouvier, L. F. (2010). *Population and society: An introduction to demography*. New York: Cambridge University Press.

Robbins, G. (2010). Beyond local economic development? Exploring municipality-supported job creation in a South Africa city . *Development Southern Africa*, 27(4), 531–546.

Roberts, D., Boon, R., Diederichs, N., Douwes, E., Govender, N., Mcinnes, A., Mclean, C., O' Donoghue, S., & Spires, M. (2012). Exploring ecosystem-based adaptation in Durban, South Africa: "Learning-bydoing" at the local government coal face. *Environment and Urbanisation*, 24(1), 167–195.

Roma, E. et al. (2013). User perceptions of urine diversion dehydration toilets: Experiences from a cross-sectional study in eThekwini Municipality. *Water SA*, 39(2), 305–312.

Rouse, J. W., Haas, R. H., Schell, J. A., & Deering, D. W. (1973). Monitoring vegetation systems in the Great Plains with ERTS. In *3rd ERTS Symposium*. Washington DC: NASA.

Roy, A. (2011). Slumdog cities: Rethinking subaltern urbanism. *International Journal of Urban and Regional Research*, 35(2), 223–238.

SANBI. (2009) *STEP: Conservation priority status. Mega-conservancy networks*, Pretoria.

Schulze, R. E. (2000). Modelling hydrological responses to land use and climate change: A southern African perspective. *Ambio*, 29(1), 12–22.

Scott, D., Sutherland, C., Sim, V., & Robbins, G. (2015). Pro-growth challenges to sustainability in South Africa. In A. Hansen & U. Wethal (Eds.), *Emerging economies and challenges to sustainability. Theories*,strategies, local realities (pp. 204–217). London: Routledge.

Seto, k., Reenberg, A., Boone, C., Fragkias, M., Haase, D., Langanke, T., Marcotullio, P., Munroe, D., Olah, B., & Simon, D. (2012). Urban land teleconnections and sustainability. *Proceedings of the National Academy of Sciences*, 109, 7687–7692.

Shao, H., Chu, L., Jaleel, C. A., & Zhao, C. (2008). Water-deficit stress-induced anatomical changes in higher plants. *Comptes Rendus Biologies*, 331(3), 215–225.

Sim, V., Sutherland, C., & Scott, D. (2016). Pushing the boundaries – urban edge challenges in eThekwini Municipality. *South African Geographical Journal*, 98(1), 37–60.

Sim, V., Sutherland, C., Buthelezi, S., & Khumalo, D. (2018). Possibilities for a Hybrid Approach to Planning and Governance at the Interface of the Administrative and Traditional Authority Systems in Durban. *Urban Forum*, 29(1), 351–368.

Simon, D. (2010). The challenges of global environmental change for urban Africa. *Urban Forum*, 21(1), 235–248.

Smith P., Gregory P. J., van Vuuren, D., Obersteiner, M., Havlik, P., Rounsevell, M., Woods, J., Stehfest, E., Bellarby, J. (2010). Competition for land. *Philosophical Transactions of the Royal Society B: Biological Sciences*, 365(1554), 2941–2957.

Sutherland, C., Hordijk, M., Lewis, B., Meyer, C., & Buthelezi, B. (2014). Water and sanitation delivery in eThekwini municipality: A spatially differentiated approach. *Environment & Urbanisation*, 26(2), 469–488.

Sutherland, C., Roberts, D., & Douwes, J. (2019). Constructing resilience at three scales: The 100 Resilient Cities programme, resilience journey and water resilience in the Palmiet Catchment. *Human Geography, 12*(1), 33–49.

Sutherland, C., Sim, V., Buthelezi, S., & Khumalo, D. (2016). Social constructions of environmental services in a rapidly densifying peri-urban area under dual governance in Durban, South Africa. *African Biodiversity and Conservation, 46*(2), 1–12.

Statistics South Africa. (2011). eThekwini municipality. Viewed 23 January 2018, http://www.statssa.gov.za/?page_id=993&id=ethekwini-municipality.

Stats S. A. (2017) *Mid-year population estimates*. Pretoria: South African Statistics.

Sterling, S. M., Ducharne, A., & Polcher, J. (2013). The impact of global land-cover change on the terrestrial water cycle. *Nature Climate Change 3*(4), 385–390.

Swyngedouw, E. (2004). *Social Power and the Urbanization of Water: Flows of Power*. Oxford: Oxford University Press.

Swyngedouw, E. (2015). Urbanization and environmental futures: Politicizing urban political ecologies. In T. Perreault, G. Bridge, & J. McCathy (Eds.), *Handbook of* political ecology (pp. 609–619). London, New York: Routledge.

Swyngedouw, E., & Heynen, N. (2003). Urban political ecology, justice and the politics of scale. *Antipode, 35*(1), 898–918.

Turok, I. (2012) Urbanisation and development in South Africa: Economic imperatives, spatial distortions and strategic responses. *International Institute for Environment and Development, United Nations Population Fund Urbanization and Emerging Population Issues Working Paper*. London: IIED.

UNCTAD. (2018). Total and urban population. https://stats.unctad.org/handbook/Population/Total.html Accessed 15 January 2021.

UN-Habitat. (2016) *World cities report: Urbanisation and development: Emerging futures*, Nairobi: UN-Habitat.

United Nations, Department of Economic and Social Affairs, Population Division. (2014). *World urbanization prospects: The 2014 revision, highlights (ST/ESA/SER.A/352)*.

Vogel, C., Scott, D., Culwick, C., & Sutherland, C. (2016). Environmental problem solving in South Africa: Harnessing creative imaginaries to address 'wicked' challenges and opportunities. *South African Geographical Journal, 98*(3), 515–530.

Ward, K. (2003). Entrepreneurial urbanism, state restructuring and civilizing 'New' East Manchester. *Area, 35*(2), 116–127.

Watson, V. (2013). African urban fantasies: Dreams or nightmares. *Environment and Urbanization, 26*(1), 1–17.

Woodruff, S. C. (2016). Planning for an unknowable future: Uncertainty in climate change adaptation planning. *Climatic Change, 139*(3-4), 445–459.

World Bank. (2016) *Promoting Green Urban Development in African Cities, Urban Environmental Profile for eThekwini South Africa*. Washington DC: The World Bank Group.

World Health Organisation. (2016) *Health as the Pulse of the New Urban Agenda: United Nations Conference on Housing and Sustainable Urban Development*. Geneva: WHO.

Weng, Q. (2002). Land use change analysis in the Zhujiang Delta of China using satellite remote sensing, GIS and stochastic modelling. *Journal of Environmental Management, 64*(3), 273–284.

Wu, J. (2008). Land use changes: Economic, social and environmental impacts. *Choices, 23*(4), 6–10.

Wu, C., & Murray, A. T. (2003). Estimating impervious surface distribution by spectral mixture analysis. *Remote Sensing and Environment, 84*(1), 493–505.

Wu, K.-y., Xin-Yue, Y., Qi, Z.-f., & Zhang, H. (2013). Impacts of land use/land cover change and socioeconomic development on regional ecosystem services: The case of fast-growing Hangzhou metropolitan area, China. *Cities, 31*, 276–284.

Xiao, J. et al. (2006). Evaluating urban expansion and land use change in Shijiazhuang, China, by using GIS and remote sensing. *Lanndscape and Urban Planning, 75*(1-2), 69–80.

Zeilhofer, P., & Topanotti, V. P. (2008). GIS and ordination techniques for evaluation of environmental impacts in informal settlements: A case study from Cuiaba', central Brazil. *Applied Geography, 28*(1), 1–15.

8 Informal Greenspaces in Peripheral Luanda, Angola: Benefits and Challenges

Euridice Lurdes Jorge Pedrosa,
Seth Asare Okyere, Stephen Kofi Diko,
and Michihiro Kita

Introduction

Urban green spaces (UGS) contribute significantly to the resilience and sustainability of cities (Venter et al., 2020). The ecosystem services they provide such as air purification, noise reduction, temperature regulation and recreation are key components of urban dwellers wellbeing and quality of life (Du Toit et al., 2018). Green spaces also improve residents' physical and psychological health, sense of place, social bonding and livelihoods (Du Toit et al., 2018). Given the immense benefits they offer to urban areas, the consensus is that UGS should be considered a common good (Sikorska et al., 2020). Yet, substantial evidence across the world shows that the problem of insufficient and inequitable distribution of UGS has reached alarming proportions (Wolch et al., 2014; Cobbinah & Darkwah, 2016; Rigolon et al., 2018). This is more acute in Africa and Latin America where there is a strong dependence on UGS and their related ecosystem services (Haase et al., 2014).

Unfortunately, the persistent decline in UGS and their limited access by low-income urban dwellers – resulting from poor planning and management and deplorable conditions of existing UGS – constitute some of the persistent sustainability challenges in cities of the Global South, especially Sub-Saharan Africa (Angel et al., 2011; Cobbinah & Darkwah, 2016; Du Toit et al., 2018). UGS often occupy a small part of many African cities (Adjei Mensah, 2014). For instance, urban green space constitutes less than 3% of the city of Lagos landmass. Similarly, the urban landscape of Ghana's second largest city, once called the Garden City of West Africa, does not currently reflect its accolade due to significant declines in UGS (Adjei Mensah, 2014; Diko & Palazzo, 2018). Furthermore, countries such as South Africa (McConnachie et al., 2008), Kenya (M'Ikiugu et al., 2012) and Ethiopia (Girma et al., 2019) have experienced substantial decline in UGS over the years.

In Africa, strong evidence of rapid urbanisation (Cobbinah et al., 2015; Cobbinah & Darkwah, 2016), unplanned and uncontrolled urban growth (Cobbinah et al., 2015; Pieterse, 2017) due to poor land use planning and

DOI: 10.4324/9781003181484-8

management (Adjei Mensah, 2014; Diko & Palazzo, 2018), dispossessive land accumulation driven by neoliberal urban development (Gillespie, 2016) have resulted in significant land cover and land use changes. According to Güneralp et al. (2017), urban land in Africa is expected to increase by almost 600% between 2000 and 2030. Falling population densities and high rate of land use and expansive land cover changes have placed pressure on natural habitats in urban areas. These have occasioned losses in ecological spaces and left African cities at the crossroad of urban transition and its implications for sustainable urban development (McGranahan et al., 2009; Angel et al., 2011; Güneralp et al., 2017). Together, these factors undermine efforts to plan and conserve UGS on the continent (Adjei Mensah et al., 2018; Diko & Palazzo, 2018).

From a sustainable urban development perspective, the decline in UGS in African cities is troubling given the documented ecological, economic, socio-cultural and health benefits of UGS (Cilliers et al., 2013; Shackleton et al., 2018). This realisation is what led the Africa countries to successfully push a territorial dimension of cities and the management of urban expansion in the Habitat III process and eventually the New Urban Agenda (Güneralp et al., 2017). This is also captured in the Sustainable Development Goals, specifically SDG 11, Target 7: universal access to safe, inclusive, and accessible UGS (UNDESA, 2015). Both claim the mantra of "leaving no one behind" and ensuring every citizen's equal right to live and benefit from a sustainable city. However, in the context of UGS, this is far from reality.

There are significant inequities in the distribution and access to well managed UGS in African cities. For example, in South Africa, low-income communities had lower areas of public UGS relative to affluent areas (McConnachie & Shackleton, 2010; Gwedla & Shackleton, 2017). Nero (2017) also makes similar findings in the Kumasi Metropolis of Ghana. On the one hand, manicured UGS dot high-class residential areas and are often closed off to the public, while in low-income communities, there exist poorly managed or non-existent UGS (Kuruneri-Chitepo & Shackleton, 2011; Shackleton et al., 2014). This is problematic as the latter is where majority of the urban population reside (Okyere and Kita, 2015; Okyere et al., 2017). Besides, low density urban expansion, sprawling satellite towns and new low-cost housing development in peripheral areas of African cities have missed opportunities for integrating UGS (Shackleton et al., 2014).

In fact, studies demonstrate that not only are UGS in sharp decline but also their conditions are often deplorable, especially in low-income communities of African cities (Cobbinah & Darkwah, 2016; Nero, 2017; Du Toit et al., 2018). Unfortunately, while there has been significant attention to the protection and management of formal UGS (e.g. urban parks, forests, city gardens), spontaneous vegetation, street verges, lots, gaps, waterside, tree rings, brownfields, and microsite green areas – commonly referred to as

IGS – have been ignored in UGS planning and management (Adegun, 2017; Shackleton et al., 2018). Thus, in spite of efforts to enrich the discourse on UGS to include those outside formal classifications and to work towards effective management systems (Adegun, 2019), IGS have been considered marginal, liminal, and ambivalent landscapes yet to be fully recognized by stakeholders in urban planning (Kim et al., 2018). As Adegun (2017) intimates, this is problematic, in view of the sheer number of Africa's urban population living in low-income settlements; their strong intersections with IGS; and inadequate access to formal UGS.

Furthermore, in a COVID-19 pandemic era, emerging evidence shows that restrictions on social gathering and workplace closures have limited access to indoor recreational spaces but increased visits to community parks for physical, mental and social wellbeing (Geng et al., 2020). More than ever, therefore, access to IGS is needed to support low-income residents traverse the severe impact of the COVID-19 pandemic. The above evidence notwithstanding, Rupprecht et al. (2015) note that there is limited understanding of IGS in the African context. This chapter subsequently explores the distribution, use, perception and significance of IGS from the perspective of residents in Funda – a low-income community on the periphery of Luanda. It presents IGS as a potential that can enable urban planners to contribute to the discourse on improving access to UGS in African cities within the broader debate on sustainable urban development and eventually progress towards the achievement of SDGs 11 target 7.

Literature Review: Informal Green Space

UGS are used as an encompassing term for all areas of land that consist predominantly of unsealed, permeable surfaces (e.g. soil, grass or shrubs), irrespective of whether they are publicly accessible or managed – including parks, playgrounds and others intended for recreational use, among others (Swanwick et al., 2003; Du Toit et al., 2018). Similarly, Adjei Mensah (2014) uses the term to denote spaces that cover all public and private open spaces in urban areas predominantly covered by vegetation that are directly or indirectly available for use. Chen and Hu (2015, p. 33) provide a broader definition of UGS "as all land covered by vegetation within the urban environment." While a plethora of definitions exist, it is generally agreed that UGS constitute two broad aspects – UGS such as parks, botanical gardens, playgrounds and pockets of (semi) natural vegetation) owned by public authorities; and UGS such as domestic gardens and allotments privately owned and restricted (Lategan & Cilliers, 2016).

More recently, a third dimension has emerged that include vacant lots, railway sidings, utility easements, spontaneous vegetation and others generally unconsidered in green space classifications (Lategan & Cilliers, 2016, Rupprecht & Byrne, 2014a). A growing body of work now emphasises the distinctiveness of the different forms of UGS that are unique in their management, planning and spontaneous patterns of growth, often embedded into the socio-spatial and economic differences within and between diverse residential geographies (Ward Thompson, 2002; Rupprecht & Byrne, 2014a; Rupprecht et al., 2015). These have been framed as formal and informal UGS. According to Rupprecht et al. (2015), formal UGS includes public and private highly managed vegetated landscapes or spaces in urban areas. On the other hand, IGS embody spontaneous vegetation that are mostly not considered in the planning or ecological regime. For the purposes of this chapter and also given the disproportionate attention to formal green space in both research and practice, what follows primarily focuses on urban IGS.

Informal green spaces are an inherent natural element of many cities, especially African cities, but only recently have they occupied the research agenda of urban scholars. Literature on IGS is limited as urban green space studies are skewed towards "formal" UGS (Rupprecht et al., 2015). However, there is growing scholarly evidence that IGS have enormous potential for urban conservation and preservation of biodiversity (Adegun, 2017, Del Tredici, 2010). Some quantitative studies estimate that IGS occupy 5% of cities (Rupprecht et al., 2015). Rupprecht et al. (2015) note that IGS, being neoteric, face a conceptual challenge due to a lack of agreed approach to define them as well as geographical and contextual differences. Nonetheless, IGS can be defined as spaces with a history of strong artificial disturbance and spontaneous vegetation occupying part of or an entire space (Rupprecht & Byrne, 2014a). As socio-ecological entities, they have recreational and transitional importance to urban residents rather than just cultural or biological (Rupprecht & Byrne 2014b). IGS encompasses any urban space that is partly covered with non-remnant vegetation but also not recognised by government institutions and thus their use (recreation, agriculture, environmental protection) is primarily informal or transitional (Del Tredici, 2010a; Rupprecht & Byrne 2014b). Instone and Sweeney (2014) also refer to them as liminal ecologies, in the sense that culture and nature is disrupted and division between private/public, controlled/neglected is often blurred. In other words, such spaces are generally characterised by interfaces of informality and emergence (Imai, 2013). Others have identified IGS as ambivalent landscapes where uncertainty characterises land tenure, conservation, maintenance regimes, use, regulation and legitimacy (McLain et al., 2014). In most stances, the management of IGS is non-existing, but if present, occurs at the community level by individuals or community actors. State support is often absent with no recognition of such spaces in urban planning (Adegun, 2017).

In terms of classification, Rupprecht and Byrne (2014a) provide a comprehensive nine-subtype typology of IGS. This topology is defined based on factors such as management, land use, site history, scale and shape, soil characteristics and local urban context. These subtypes developed are considered not exclusive and include street verge, lot, gap, railway, brownfield, waterside, structural, microsite and power lines (Table 8.1).

Table 8.1 Classification of IGS

IGS	Examples	Description	Common Substrates
Street verges	Roadside verges, roundabouts, tree rings, informal trails and footpaths	Vegetated area within 5 m from street not in another IGS category; mostly maintained to prevent high and dense vegetation growth other than street trees; public access unrestricted, use restricted.	Soil, gravel, stone, concrete, asphalt
Lots	Vacant lots, abandoned lots	Vegetated lot presently not used for residential or commercial purposes; if maintained, usually vegetation removed to ground cover; public access and use restricted.	Soil, gravel, bricks
Gap	Gap between walls or fences	Vegetated area between two walls, fences or at their base; maintenance can be absent or intense; public access and use often restricted.	Soil, gravel
Railway	Rail tracks, verges, stations	Vegetated area within 10 m adjacent to railway tracks not in another IGS category; usually herbicide maintenance to prevent vegetation encroachment on tracks; public access and use mostly restricted.	Soil, gravel, stone
Brownfields	Landfill, post-use factory grounds, industrial park	Vegetated area presently not used for industrial or commercial purposes; usually no or very infrequent vegetation removal and maintenance; public access and use mostly restricted.	Soil, gravel, concrete, asphalt
Waterside	Rivers, canals, water reservoir edges	Vegetated area within 10 m of water body not in another IGS category; occasional removal of vegetation to maintain flood protection and structural integrity; public access and use often possible with some restrictions.	Soil, stone, concrete, bricks

(*Continued*)

Table 8.1 (Continued)

IGS	Examples	Description	Common Substrates
Structural	Walls, fences, roofs, buildings	Overgrown human artefacts; often vertical; occasional removal of vegetation to maintain structural integrity; public access and use mostly restricted.	Soil, stone, gravel, wood, metal
Microsite	Vegetation in cracks or holes	Vegetation assemblages in cracks, may develop into structural IGS; maintenance can be absent or intense	Deposits, soil, stone, concrete
Power line	Powerline rights of way	Vegetated corridor under and within 25 m of power lines not in another IGS category; vegetation removed periodically to prevent high growth; public access and use mostly unrestricted.	Soil
Kitchen garden	Small farm around a residence	A kitchen garden is where herbs and vegetables are grown around the house for household use. Since early times a small plot near to the house has been used for growing a variety of vegetables according to the season	Soil
Open Camp	Open spaces	Wide open spaces usually formally covered by grass that constant use or drought make them plan for different ludic kind of activities	Soil

Source: Adapted from Rupprecht and Byrne (2014a).

This typology provides a useful analytical framework to understand the categories, distribution and use of IGS. Informal green spaces offer a number of benefits to urban residents. In the existing literature, such benefits are framed around the ecosystem services (Millennium Ecosystem Assessment, 2003) namely: provisioning, regulating, socio-cultural and supporting services (Adegun, 2017). Provisioning concerns services such as food and water while regulating services includes flood mitigation, climate moderation and air quality regulation. Cultural services denote recreational, religious, aesthetic and cultural fulfilment. Supporting services include soil formation, infiltration, retention and groundwater recharge (Adegun, 2013, 2017; Vollmer & Gret-Regamey, 2013; Kaoma & Shackleton 2014). In the informal settlements of Pretoria for example, Adegun (2017) reports that more than half of residents rely on IGS as a major source of provisioning services. This is particularly the case for many informal settlements where residents have limited access to well-managed UGS (Dubbeling 2011; Gallaher et al. 2013).

In a study of Bangalore, Gopal (2011) shows that IGS positively affects the surrounding climate with a reported decrease in temperature of 3–5 degrees Celsius in the summer season. Trees also play a key role in decreasing the air pollutant components. Additionally, IGS also provided informal spaces for various types of activities such as leisure, domestic work and informal economic activities (Gopal & Nagendra 2014). But IGS can have downsides as well. Studies have shown that IGS can become spots for criminality and predatory attacks by dangerous and wild animals (Adegun, 2017, 2019). In sum, the literature review reveals a growing body of work on IGS directed at documenting its potential to improve access to the benefits of UGS especially in low-income communities or areas where UGS are in poor conditions. The extant literature signals three criticalities. First, IGS is mostly conceived as spontaneous and informal without the particular engagement of their significance or potential benefits. Second, these so-called spontaneous entities can provide important ecological services similar to formal UGS. Third, although IGS are common in low-income communities, formal planning regimes, especially in African cities, are not prioritising or planning for their effective management. In this context, studying IGS in low-income communities can provide a micro-level understanding of their importance and benefits to local people and the need for their protection and proper management as part of the localization of SDG 11-Target 7.

Methods, Data Collection and Study Setting

Study Context

This research was conducted in Funda, a peri-urban settlement in the province of Luanda (the capital of Angola). Funda was selected due to the vast expanse of green space, IGS, compared with other areas of Metropolitan Luanda (Luanda Urban Planning and Management Institute, 2015). This is recognised in the Lunda Master plan, which underscores the importance of UGS for the city's sustainable development but unfortunately fails to emphasise the potential and significance of IGS to improving access to UGS in low-income areas. Geographically, Funda is bounded to the south by the municipalities of Viana and Cazenga, to the west by the Atlantic Ocean and municipality of Luanda and to the north and east by the municipality of Dande (Figures 8.1 and 8.2). The community, together with

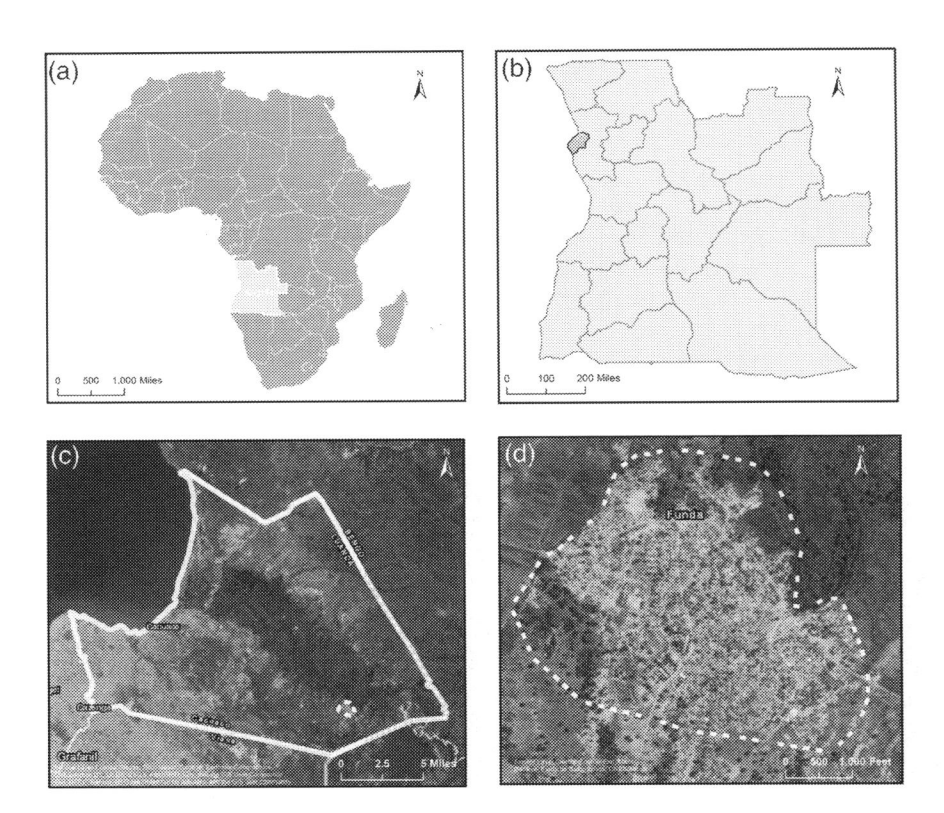

Figure 8.1 (A) Luanda in Africa and national context; (B) Funda In Cacuaco
Municipality of Luanda Province (*Source*: UPMLI, 2019); (C) Funda
Municipality (Google satellite Image, Google Earth 2019).

four other urban districts (Kikolo, Cacuaco, Mulenvos Baixo and Sequele)
constitute Cacuaco Municipality.

Funda is about 18 km North of Luanda city center. There are industrial,
agricultural and piscatorial activities in this part of the province. Many
people from provinces such as Huambo, Benguela, Kwanza-Norte settled at
Funda due to its favorable and large area for agriculture. During the years
of the Angola civil war beginning in 1975, the population increased significantly and it became one of the largest settlements in the municipality of
Cacuaco. Available statistics show that Funda has 209,387 inhabitants
(National Statistical Institute of Angola, 2014). Funda is considered the
green belt of Luanda because it has a very strong agricultural potential and
is a source of agricultural products for one of the largest informal markets
in Luanda called "Sabadão." This settlement receives limited municipal
services. The Luanda province provides water through communal stand-
pipes only in few areas. There are no sewer and drainage systems. Due to its

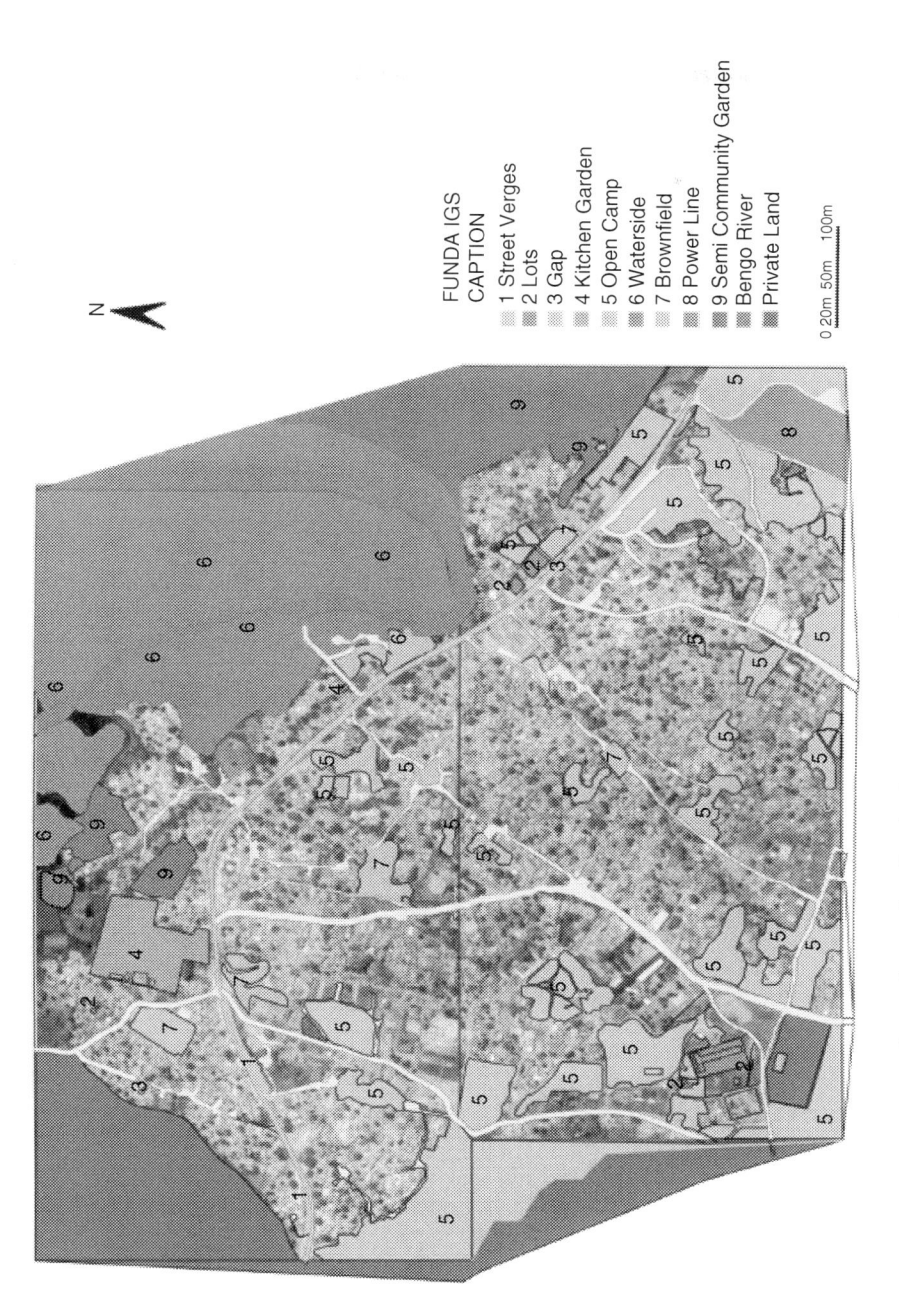

FUNDA IGS
CAPTION

1 Street Verges
2 Lots
3 Gap
4 Kitchen Garden
5 Open Camp
6 Waterside
7 Brownfield
8 Power Line
9 Semi Community Garden
Bengo River
Private Land

0 20m 50m 100m

N

Figure 8.2 Distribution of IGS observed at Funda Community.

undulating terrain, when it rains, most of the water and detritus flow into the Bengo River located in the lower part of the settlement.

Research Approach

This chapter forms part of ongoing research on IGS in peri-urban areas of the province of Luanda. A case study design was adopted focusing on residents' use and perceptions of significance and challenges of IGS in Funda. The adoption of the case study for this research was based on its strength to focus on specific contexts, draw on diverse sources of data and the ability to show relationships between elements and processes (Babbie, 2015). Qualitative research methods of field observations and semi-structured interviews were used to obtain data on residents' use and perceptions of IGS. Institutional semi-structured interviews were conducted with officials at four agencies based on their knowledge, experience, and institutional interest in urban planning practice, UGS and land use management. Three officials from the Urban Planning Institute and one official from the Municipality's Land use agency were engaged in conversations on: (i) UGS management regime; (ii) the urban planning and peri-urbanisation in Luanda; and (iii) awareness, significance and use of IGS in local communities.

At the community level, three main approaches were utilised in collecting data namely (i) observation, (ii) residents' interviews and (iii) mapping. Data collection began with a one-day preliminary visit and transect walk to observe the area in terms of the distribution of IGS and their "everyday" use. Local leaders and opinion leaders were informed, and their consent sought as part of community entry processes. Upon their consent and willingness to cooperate, they informed local residents of the objective and purpose of the research. Local leadership provided a list of 50 residents who showed interest in the study. Following this, 23 residents who were willing and available to participate were interviewed. Twenty-three residents were engaged as the pattern of saturation had clearly emerged from the insights gained from participants (Gibbs, 2007). Among resident participants, five additional in-depth interviews were conducted with opinion leaders (2), community elders (2) and a local environmental activist (1). Pictures of IGS taken during the transect walk were shown to residents during the interviews to enable them to respond adequately to the interview questions. The main items considered during the interviews comprised (i) residents' awareness of the benefits and challenges of IGS; (ii) perception and use of IGS; and (iii) management of IGS. Interviews were conducted in Portuguese and lasted an average of 40 minutes. All interviews were translated and transcribed into English.

In addition, the transect walks and direct observations allowed for verification of IGS and helped ascertain their characteristics. For community residents, the main defining criteria of IGS is in its "spontaneity," "lack of recognition" and "planning and control" (see Rupprecht & Byrne, 2014a). Spontaneous in the sense that they are natural growth that emerged at specific locations without any deliberate or purposeful planning or activity on their use. Recognition entails respondents' perception that these are not afforded the same value as formally planned UGS that usually dominate other planned neighborhoods or communities of Luanda. Informal green spaces in the study area were also mapped. Colored photos of the settlement were captured on Google Earth 2016. This was used to physically map and categorise the IGS using the typology by Rupprecht et al. (2015). Observations were also done to document the use and condition of these spaces. Transcripts were coded and analysed using thematic content analysis, a form of descriptive analysis that opens up our understanding of perception, use and benefits of IGS as well as challenges constraining its potential (Gibbs, 2007). Salient quotations were collated to identify themes and interrelationships for discussion and theorising. The analysis, therefore, followed a pattern; main theme, insights and supporting quotations; as typical of the qualitative research community (see Gibbs, 2007; Seguin et al., 2018)

Results

Typology of Informal Green Spaces in Funda

The results show that there are diverse IGS in Funda. The main types of IGS in the community include street verges, waterside, open camps, brownfields, semi-community gardens, lots and gaps. These IGS are dispersed and spatially distributed across the landscape of Funda. In all, nine different types of IGS were identified in Funda. Open camps are spatially distributed across the communities while the waterside – the largest IGS – is located at the north-eastern section of Funda (Figure 8.2).

Residents' Use of and Benefit from Informal Green Spaces

The use of IGS forms an intricate part of the daily lives of the residents of Funda. Given that the community is a low-income peri-urban area, located around the so-called Luanda "green belt" where agricultural cultivation is a mainstay, there is a strong connection between community residents and IGS. The waterside, for example, is used frequently by residents as a source of water, a place to socialise with other community members, subsistence fishing and other leisure activities (Figure 8.3). Children were also observed playing in brownfield sites or lots where sufficient space afforded collective games such as football. However, tree rings and street verges provided shaded spaces where adults usually undertook street vending, relaxation and socialisation. Respondents recounted:

(a)   (b)

Figure 8.3 (a) Children playing in an Open Camp (b) Residents doing laundry, fetching water and enjoying the Waterside.

"I go to the waterside on a daily basis. It is my favorite place to relax, meet other people. I also go there to access water and do laundry'. It's a nice place because there is green, cool winds and shade." (*Community respondent 4, female*)

"My kids also play around the lots and open camps. There are grass and trees which the children enjoy playing with. We do not have children parks and playing grounds, so this is useful for our kids to have outdoor activities" (*Community respondent 8, mother*)

The study reveals two main reasons for residents' dominant use of IGS in Funda: (i) the lack of properly planned UGS for residents (including children) and (ii) the neglect of IGS as a potential green resource in the planning and development of Funda community. In spite of this, the use of IGS has generated several benefits for residents in the community (Table 8.2).

Residents indicated that IGS was an important source of fruits and vegetables. Children obtained mangoes from mango trees along the street verges or the semi-community gardens. The semi-community gardens in particular, provided ready access to vegetables to community residents – and sometimes jobs to residents since "*IGS support entire families through subsistence farming and sale of vegetables to community residents ... (Community respondent 7, local farmer, female)*" and "*are literally ... [the] workplace ...*" for some residents *(Community respondent 17, female)*.

Table 8.2 Use and benefit of IGS in Funda

Type of IGS	Residents Use of IGS	Service/Benefits
1. Street Verges	Used as a form of shading or canopy for informal economic activities such as food vending	Regulatory (temperature control for climate comfort during hot days)
2. Lots	Children use lots as a playground (e.g. soccer)	Socio-cultural (leisure and relaxation)
3. Gap	Gaps are used as playground (depending on width) by children and also as passage to surrounding areas and buildings by most residents	Socio-cultural (accessibility and recreation)
4. Kitchen Garden	Mostly used as an orchard or for planting herbs and vegetables as a source of food, medicinal plants or as an orchard. Some farmers used them for teaching children about farming	Provisioning (source of food and medicine)
5. Open Camp	Used as multi-purpose space: "rent-free" spaces for commerce; playground for children; grounds for community meetings and cultural activities (e.g. funeral, weddings, etc); food vending; leisure; and study area; to prevent water run-off	Socio-cultural (religious activities/cultural rites), provisioning, supporting (water retention)
6. Waterside	Used as source of water, laundry, picnic, fishing, shaded space relaxation, and blind spots for drug peddling at night	Provisioning, socio-cultural and regulatory (tree canopies for micro-climate comfort)
7. Brownfield	Used as a soccer playground for children; commercial space for informal economic activities, grounds for physical exercise, place for hangouts and leisure.	Provisioning and socio-cultural (recreation)
8. Semi-community garden	Used for planting fruits, vegetables, and medicinal plants; an area for drying clothes in the sun, hang out to enjoy the pleasant views of the nearby natural environment	Provisioning, socio-cultural, and regulatory

Additionally, residents pointed to the medicinal value of leaves that were found in kitchen gardens, community gardens and street verges. Twenty residents out of the 23 interviewed alluded to regulating services from trees, grass and street verges. For them, shading was a major microclimate benefit, controlling high temperatures during the day while grass and tree rings helped to reduce flood damage and drainage problems during the rainy season. These assertions were corroborated by local opinion leaders and institutional respondents at the municipality office.

> "At specific seasons, the children pluck mangoes from the mango trees and eat together while they play. We adults also get vegetables like spinach and tomatoes from the gardens scattered around here. It is a major source of food. Of course, I should mention that most of the residents here boil the leaves of the trees as medicinal drinks to treat fevers and the like." (*Interview with opinion leader in Funda*)

> "Well, I know that peri-urban communities like Funda depend a lot on the spontaneous vegetation located where they live. They rely on them as a source of food and medicine. Often, these lots also are social spaces for gathering or other cultural events." (*Interview with Municipality Official*)

Residents' Management of Informal Green Space

Interviews with residents, community leaders, and staff of public agencies showed that there is no community-wide system for the stewardship and management of IGS. Rather, local churches were the main actors in the management of IGS. The Funda Seventh-Day Adventist church, in particular, were noted to organise clean up exercises on Sundays where their members cleared vegetation, tendered plants, and removed garbage from lots. Community-wide maintenance and stewardship was sporadic, occurring when the local administration entreats resident association to organise management activities. At times, individuals take lead roles in the maintenance and management of IGS in Funda. Typically, some young residents were devoted to creating awareness of the need for maintenance, planned activities and supported neighbors in managing IGS. During the interviews, a young undergraduate student, who considers himself an environmental activist, recounted:

> "On Saturdays I help neighbors with their kitchen gardens or clean up the lots or open camps. I do this because my father taught me how important it is to have a green environment; honestly, I love it, but I cannot do it alone. It is very difficult when people have no environmental awareness of IGS, even though they are benefitting from it. Convincing them that it is worth taking care of the IGS is a headache." (*Community respondent 10, male*)

Clearly, community-level management is spontaneous, amidst a seeming lack of residents' awareness of the need to effectively manage IGS in Funda. In this vein, two divergent perspectives were brought to the fore: (i) residents perceived that authorities at Funda municipality should take responsibility for the management of IGS, and (ii) staff at Funda municipality considered IGS as spontaneous and informal, and thus its maintenance lies in the hands of community members who were benefiting from its use.

Residents expressed willingness to support IGS management (21 out 23). However, few (4 out 23) were willing to contribute financially to support maintenance of IGS. The apparent lack of financial commitment was due to residents' socio-economic conditions such as lack of employment and low-paying jobs. Regardless of how one looks at it, residents' deposition demonstrates that their awareness and socio-economic disadvantages constrain effective IGS management despite their benefits. This sentiment is evident from one community leader:

> "I know that IGS is very critical to our survival in this community and we need to take care of it to enjoy its long-term benefit. I think most community members think so as well. But there is no management system in place. Each one must do it [maintenance] around their residence. We only do it [maintenance] when some churches or the municipality requests it. Maybe it is awareness. But remember most people here are low-income. They are most concerned about daily necessities and survival." (interview with community leader)

Factors constraining IGS in Funda

The study found that in spite of residents' dependence on the benefits of IGS in Funda, some factors constrain or limit the actualization of their full potential. The absence of community level management of IGS, such as the waterside, open camps and semi-community gardens, has made some of these spaces abodes for dangerous and/or wild animals (e.g. snakes, crocodiles, etc.) that pose a significant human threat and restricted use. This exposes users to sudden snake bite, especially to children. In addition, *"there are some poisonous plants in IGS as well, that can be dangerous if the user comes into contact with them or confuses them with edible plants/fruits"* Relatedly, some IGS were hang outs for criminals such as illegal drug dealers, gangs, and robbers. Criminal squatting in certain IGS at specific periods meant that there was a restriction in access to these spaces. These challenges are aggravated by the lack of proper lighting at night and the poor maintenance of IGS. These issues are confirmed by two responses who note that:

> "IGS is for everyone but nobody takes responsibility for it. The administration does not recognise it and the community does not maintain it together. The riverside is very dangerous because of the

> crocodiles. There is no effort to manage it well to prevent harm. The open camps and semi-vegetable gardens are common with snake bites. Very dangerous for children. Sometimes I wonder, would our IGS be managed very well if they were considered the same as the parks and gardens in the city center?" (*Student environmental activist, Male*)

> "Look, there's no streetlight here. How can we enjoy this camp at night? These young drug dealers seize the spaces and terrify [harass] people whenever they are there. Everybody is scared when they come around these spaces and so we all back off. No security." (*Community respondent 22, local farmer, male*)

Another limitation concerns the intersections of sanitation infrastructure and resident's behavior. Interviews with staff at the municipal office revealed that indiscriminate refuse dumping or littering was a major setback in Funda. Residents had a penchant for dumping household waste in lots, open camps and street verges (Figure 8.4). This was echoed by opinion leaders who reported that poor stewardship, such as garbage dumping, impairs the environmental quality of IGS and reduces their appeal to residents.

> "Some of these spaces (IGS) are being used as garbage sites. Unfortunately, germs and all sort of microbes can come from there, and they become a risk for public health around the areas they are located." (*Municipality staff, male*)

> "When there are no proper sanitation facilities and people have no attitude for environmental sanitation, these behaviours are common. If someone cares about the things which provide us so much benefit, these problems (indiscriminate garbage disposal) won't happen because people will invest in maintenance and it won't become a dump site for sure." (*Opinion leader, retired civil servant, male*)

Taken together, the challenges narrated above inadvertently created limited accessibility to IGS, especially for residents with special needs such as the elderly and the physically handicapped. For example, all respondents aged over 60 years reported that even though the riverside was a scenic place with aesthetic views for relaxation and socialising, they rarely used them because of poor mobility to these spaces, thefts, harassment and other criminal activities, and frequent attacks by wild animals.

Discussion

Funda has a rich diversity of IGS. The various types identified are defined by characteristics such as location, spontaneity, recognition, use and to

Figure 8.4 Open space used as garbage dump sites.

some extent vegetation. Their spatial distribution seemingly suggests a high degree of informality as most of the IGS identified are better described as spontaneous growth that often lacks recognition. This aligns with the classification and description found in earlier works on IGS (Rupprecht & Byrne, 2014a, 2014b). Residents of Funda do not conceive IGS simply as empty urban space, and akin to Adegun (2017) findings, residents view IGS as vital functional spaces that provide benefits to them. Such thinking resonates with global south theories that draws attention to the role of informal spaces in urban areas (Roy, 2005; Bolay, 2020). Indeed, Rupprecht et al. (2015) draw attention to the nexus between IGS and informality and how it is important that urban planning takes cognisance of these spaces in the planning and management of urban landscapes.

Informal Green Space provide different ecosystem services ranging from provisioning, regulatory, socio-cultural and supporting ecosystem services (Adegun, 2017). In Funda, IGS provides essential needs such as regulating micro-climate (e.g. temperature) through shading and drainage problems through water retention as well as socio-cultural benefits such as recreation and socialising spaces. Compared with studies that suggest IGS as anomalies in urban spaces (Jorgensen & Tylecote, 2007), IGS was rather the norm in Funda as formal UGS such as community parks were non-existing. Its uses were similar to those reported in the literature (Campo, 2013, Unt et al., 2014), especially in providing children with spaces to play and interact with nature (Platt, 2012). Undeniably, there is growing awareness of the importance of exposing children and youth to nature (Cheng & Monroe, 2012), as this is important for building their environmental experiences and consciousness as well as developing capacities for social interactions (Lekies & Beery 2013). In Funda, IGS provides conservation services and support food production akin to studies elsewhere (McLain et al., 2014). Also, IGS not only provide residents with fresh fruits and vegetables but also serve as a workplace for those who engage in their production. Indeed, in low-income peri-urban and informal communities, IGS provides immense benefits to support residents' everyday life in the absence of formal UGS and serve as important natural capital for addressing resident's needs (Kaoma & Shackleton 2014; Adegun 2019).

In Funda, both residents and municipal planners recognize the benefits of IGS unlike other places (Pincetl & Gearin, 2005; Platt, 2012). Despite all these benefits, there is little effort towards the active management of these spaces as IGS in Funda lacks proper planning attention from municipal authorities. Indeed, authorities from the urban management authority acknowledged resident's dependence on IGS but emphasised attention to other priorities in the current master plan on urban redevelopment projects as part of "planned future expansion" for real estate investment. This is not different from urban planning in other Africa cities, which pay little attention to IGS in peri-urban areas in spite of the vast expanse of their distribution, diversity, and relevance (Adegun, 2017; Shackleton et al., 2018). Evidently, the inherent manifestation of IGS as uncontrolled and unsafe spaces (Madge, 1997) and the negative view by planners as vacant urban spaces (Corbin, 2003) needing redevelopment require a critical rethinking. Additionally, the management of IGS in Funda is undertaken by local churches and individual environmental activists. There is at present no community-wide management system or a collective system of maintenance. This is underpinned by lack of formal recognition and behavioral attitudes by urban planners and residents, respectively. According to Rupprecht et al (2015), this signals a lack of care by its users and beneficiaries, and in this study, a lack of capacity by residents due to their socio-economic circumstances.

The challenges which constrain the use of IGS could be thematically organised around three main issues: ecosystem disservices, management, accessibility and criminality. Indeed, the IGS literature points to poor management, history of fear due to criminality and deficits in green supporting infrastructure as impediments to residents' access to the full benefits of IGS, especially in low-income communities (Adegun, 2017; Kim et al., 2018). Thus, while residents appreciate the benefits of IGS, their preference and use are influenced by its safety and services. Rupprecht and Byrne (2014a, 2014b) make a similar observation and draw attention to how risks affect the quality of IGS.

Subsequently, parents would be cautious about allowing their children to play in and near IGS because of the risk and safety issues associated with them. These perceived risks can become the basis for parents limiting their children's engagement with IGS which can deprive them of the mental, recreational and social interaction services that these spaces provide (Ward Thompson, 2012). In order to enhance access to the full benefits of IGS and thus promote sustainable development in peri-urban areas of Luanda, planning need to be cognisant of the unique dynamics of IGS in places like Funda to reflect how residents' use IGS to provide ecological services that urban planners have failed to provide. Wolch et al. (2014) therefore call for a re-evaluation of the mechanisms and goals for providing ecosystem services beyond parks as well as transcending existing planning tools – such as supplanting IGS with formal UGS (Campo, 2013) and its associated risks of eco-gentrification (Wolch et al., 2014). This is because such planning tools may not be effective in harnessing the potentials of IGS in providing UGS benefits to residents of low-income communities (Qviström, 2012). There is therefore a need for an inclusive approach to UGS planning that mainstreams the needs and preferences of residents, barriers to using these spaces as well as the integration of residents' collective action potentials into the planning of IGS as UGS for low-income communities (Cilliers & Timmermans, 2015; Rupprecht et al., 2015; Adjei Mensah et al., 2017). For this reason, there is a need to look beyond the natural value of these spaces (Mathey et al., 2018) to make the benefits of IGS tangible and real to those who use them.

Conclusion

This chapter has shown that IGS play a crucial role in the lives of residents in the low-income peri-urban community of Funda. In summary, the residents of Funda use and benefit from IGS in diverse ways such as source of food, plant-based medicine, shading, leisure and socialisation. In the absence of community-wide IGS management activities, church groups and individual environmental activists play key roles in the maintenance of IGS such as mobilising neighbours for cleaning and promoting social activities in IGS. Indeed, these benefits are important for ensuring urban sustainability for Funda but challenges such as poor management, sanitation infrastructure deficits, ecosystem disservices and criminality in IGS constrained access for children and the elderly limit its potential.

Subsequently, to harness the potential of IGS for urban sustainability, the following policy recommendations are suggested. First, there is a need for community-based systems for maintaining IGS. The existing work of churches and student environmental activists provides an avenue to galvanise support for community-based management of IGS. By bringing together community leaders, local government, students and churches, environment days could be introduced periodically (e.g. monthly) to organise residents for maintenance activities. Small local IGS maintenance units can be formed for residents to manage demarcated areas of IGS within or close to where they reside. To sustain local enthusiasm, this could be scheduled to coincide with national holidays such as independence days as well as building support through sensitisation initiatives. Second, it is necessary for the municipal government to provide enabling infrastructure that can make IGS safe to use such as street lights. By providing garbage collection containers or units, this will reduce the tendency of residents to use IGS as dumpsites and contribute to making IGS attractive sites. At the same, the municipal governments can erect barriers to restrict and control the movement of harmful animals in IGS. These could enhance safety, usability and the comfortability in the use of IGS.

Although IGS are not necessarily planned and equipped like formal UGS, the chapter has demonstrated that residents utilise and adapt these spaces in a manner that assure diverse socio-ecological benefits. The study contributes to efforts to improve access to UGS in low-income communities by demonstrating the potential of IGS in providing different ecosystem services for low-income and peri-urban settlements. These services represent the benefits of UGS that are important for promoting urban sustainability and improving residents' access to UGS as expected by the SDG 11 Target 7. Additionally, in view of COVID-19 restrictions on social gathering, non-essential travels and closure of indoor recreational spaces, improving the current conditions of IGS could contribute to the physical, mental and social wellbeing of informal residents who appear to be disproportionately affected. Thus, in line with the mantra of "leaving no one behind," this chapter provides insights for urban planners and policymakers to build on the potential of IGS and harness strategies that facilitate and support community-wide and collective management activities for sustainable urban development both now and in a postcovid19 context.

References

Adegun, O. (2013). *Sustainable Stormwater management in Johannesburg's informal settlement*. Master of Built Environment (Housing) Research Report. University of the Witwatersrand, Johannesburg.

Adegun, O. B. (2017). Green infrastructure in relation to informal urban settlements. *Journal of Architecture and Urbanism*, 41(1), 22–33.

Adegun, O. B. (2019). Green infrastructure in informal unplanned settlements: The case of Kya Sands, Johannesburg. *International Journal of Urban Sustainable Development*, 11(1), 68–80.

Adjei Mensah, C. (2014). Destruction of urban green spaces: A problem beyond urbanization in Kumasi city (Ghana). *American Journal of Environmental Protection*, 3(1), 1–9.

Adjei Mensah, C., Andres, L., Baidoo, P., Eshun, J. K., & Antwi, K. B. (2017). Community participation in urban planning: The case of managing green spaces in Kumasi, Ghana. *Urban Forum*, 28, 125–141. 10.1007/s12132-016-9295-7

Adjei Mensah, C., Gough, K. V., & Simon, D. (2018). Urban green spaces in growing oil cities: The case of Sekondi-Takoradi Metropolis, Ghana. *International Development Planning Review*, 40(4), 371–395.

Angel, S., Parent, J., Civco, D. L., Blei, A., & Potere, D. (2011). The dimensions of global urban expansion: Estimates and projections for all countries, 2000–2050. *Progress in Planning*, 75(2), 53–107.

Babbie, E. R. (2015). *The practice of social research*. Boston: Cengage Learning.

Bolay, J. C. (2020). *Urban planning against poverty: How to think and do better cities in the global south*. Cham: Palgrave Macmillan-Springer Nature.

Campo, D. (2013). *The accidental playground: Brooklyn waterfront narratives of the undesigned and unplanned*. New York: Fordham Univ Press.

Chen, W. Y., & Hu, F. Z. Y. 2015. Producing nature for public: Land-based urbanization and provision of public green spaces in China. Applied Geography, 58, 32–40. 10.1016/j.apgeog.2015.01.007

Cheng, J. C. H., & Monroe, M. C. (2012). Connection to nature: Childrenas affective attitude toward nature. *Environment and Behavior*, 44(1), 31–49.

Cilliers, E. J., & Timmermans, W. (2015). An integrative approach to value-added planning: From community needs to local authority revenue. *Growth and Change*, 46(4), 675–687.

Cilliers, S., Cilliers, J., Lubbe, R., & Siebert, S. (2013). Ecosystem services of urban green spaces in African countries – perspectives and challenges. *Urban Ecosystems*, 16(4), 681–702.

Cobbinah, P. B., & Darkwah, R. M. (2016). *African urbanism: The geography of urban greenery*. Paper presented at the Urban Forum.

Cobbinah, P. B., Erdiaw-Kwasie, M. O., & Amoateng, P. (2015). Africa's urbanisation: Implications for sustainable development. *Cities*, 47, 62–72.

D. Haase, N. Frantzeskaki, & T. Elmqvist. (2014). Ecosystem services in urban landscapes: Practical applications and governance implications. AMBIO, 43(4) 407–412, 10.1007/s13280-014-0503-1.

Darkwah, R. M., & Cobbinah, P. B. (2014). Stewardship of urban greenery in an era of global urbanisation. *International Journal of Environmental, Ecological, Geological and Geophysical Engineering*, 8(10), 671–674.

Del Tredici, P., 2010. Spontaneous urban vegetation: Reflections of change in a globalized world. *Nature and Culture, 5*, 299–315. doi:10.3167/nc.2010.050305

Diko, S., & Palazzo, D. (2018). Institutional Barriers to Urban Greenspace Planning in the Kumasi Metropolis of Ghana. *Urban Forum, 30* 357–376.

Dodman, D., Leck, H., Rusca, M., & Colenbrander, S. (2017). African Urbanisation and Urbanism: Implications for risk accumulation and reduction. *International Journal of Disaster Risk Reduction, 26*, 7–15.

Du Toit, M. J., Cilliers, S. S., Dallimer, M., Goddard, M., Guenat, S., & Cornelius, S. F. (2018). Urban green infrastructure and ecosystem services in sub-Saharan Africa. *Landscape and Urban Planning, 180*, 249–261.

Dubbeling, M. (2011). Integrating urban agriculture in the urban landscape, *Urban Agriculture Magazine, 25*, 43–46.

Gallaher, C., Mwaniki, D., Njenga, M., Karanja, N., & WinklerPrins, M. (2013). Real or perceived: The environmental health risks of urban sack gardening in Kibera Slums of Nairobi, Kenya, *EcoHealth, 10*, 9–10. 10.1007/s10393–013–0827-5

Geng, D. C., Innes, J., Wu, W., & Wang, G. (2020). Impacts of COVID-19 pandemic on urban park visitation: A global analysis. *Journal of Forestry Research, 32*, 1–15.

Gibbs G. R. (2007) *Analyzing qualitative data*. London: SAGE Publications.

Gillespie, T. (2016). Accumulation by urban dispossession: Struggles over urban space in Accra, Ghana. *Transactions of the Institute of British Geographers, 41*(1), 66–77.

Girma, Y., Terefe, H., Pauleit, S., & Kindu, M. (2019). Urban green spaces supply in rapidly urbanizing countries: The case of Sebeta Town, Ethiopia. *Remote Sensing Applications: Society and Environment, 13*, 138–149.

Gopal, D. (2011). Flora in slums of Bangalore, India: Ecological and socio-cultural perspectives: Master of Science Thesis. Institute of Botany and Landscape Ecology, Ernst Moritz Arndt University of Greifswald, Greifswald.

Gopal, D., & Nagendra, H. (2014).Vegetation in Bangalore's Slums: Boosting livelihoods, well-being and social capital, *Sustainability, 6*(5), 2459–2473. 10.33 90/su6052459

Güneralp, B., Lwasa, S., Masundire, H., Parnell, S., & Seto, K. C. (2017). Urbanization in Africa: Challenges and opportunities for conservation. *Environmental Research Letters, 13*(1), 015002.

Gwedla, N., & Shackleton, C. M. (2017). Population size and development history determine street tree distribution and composition within and between Eastern Cape towns, South Africa. *Urban Forestry & Urban Greening, 25*, 11–18.

Imai, H. (2013). The liminal nature of alleyways: Understanding the alleyway roji as a "Boundary" between past and present. *Cities, 34*, 58–66. doi:10.1016/j.cities.2012.01.008

Instone, L., & Sweeney, J. (2014). Dog waste, wasted dogs: The contribution of human–dog relations to the political ecology of Australian urban space. *Geographical Research, 52*, 355–364. doi:10.1111/1745-5871.12059

Jorgensen, A., & Tylecote, M. (2007). Ambivalent landscapes—wilderness in the urban interstices. *Landscape Research, 32*(4), 443–462.

Kaoma, H., & Shackleton, C. (2014). Collection of urban tree products by households in poorer residential areas of three South African towns. *Urban Forestry and Greening, 13*, 244–252. 10.1016/j.ufug.2014.02.002

Kim, M., Rupprecht, C., & Furuya, K. (2018). Residents' perception of informal green space – a case study of Ichikawa city, Japan. *Land*, 7(3), 102.

Kuruneri-Chitepo, C., & Shackleton, C. M. (2011). The distribution, abundance and composition of street trees in selected towns of the Eastern Cape, South Africa. *Urban Forestry & Urban Greening*, 10(3), 247–254.

Lategan, L., & Cilliers, J. (2016). Considering urban green space and informal backyard rentals in South Africa: Disproving the compensation hypothesis. *Town and Regional Planning*, 69(1), 1–16.

Lekies, K. S., & Beery, T. H. (2013). Everyone needs a rock: Collecting items from nature in childhood. *Children Youth and Environments* 23(3), 66–88.

Madge, C. (1997). Public parks and the geography of fear. *Tijdschrift voor economische en sociale geografie*, 88(3), 237–250.

Mathey, J., Arndt, T., Banse, J., & Rink, D. (2018). Public perception of spontaneous vegetation on brownfields in urban areas – results from surveys in Dresden and Leipzig (Germany). *Urban Forestry & Urban Greening*, 29, 384–392.

McConnachie, M. M., & Shackleton, C. M. (2010). Public green space inequality in small towns in South Africa. *Habitat International*, 34(2), 244–248.

McConnachie, M. M., Shackleton, C., & McGregor, G. (2008). The extent of public green space and alien plant species in 10 small towns of the Sub-Tropical Thicket Biome, South Africa. *Urban Forestry & Urban Greening*, 7(1), 1–13.

McGranahan, G., Mitlin, D., Satterthwaite, D., Tacoli, C., & Turok, I. (2009). *Africa's urban transition and the role of regional collaboration.* International Institute for Environment and Development.

McLain, R. J., Hurley, P. T., Emery, M. R., & Poe, M. R. (2014). Gathering "wild" food in the city: Rethinking the role of foraging in urban ecosystem planning and management. *Local Environment*, 19(2), 220–240.

McLain, R. J., Hurley, P. T., Emery, M. R., Poe, M. R., 2014. Gathering "wild" food in the city: Rethinking the role of foraging in urban ecosystem planning and management. *Local Environment*, 19, 220–240. doi:10.1080/13549839.2013.841659

M'Ikiugu, M. M., Kinoshita, I., & Tashiro, Y. (2012). Urban green space analysis and identification of its potential expansion areas. *Procedia-Social and Behavioral Sciences*, 35, 449–458.

National Statistical Institute of Angola. (2014) *Angola Census 2014 Report.* Luanda: NSIA.

Nero, B. F. (2017). Urban green space dynamics and socio-environmental inequity: multi-resolution and spatiotemporal data analysis of Kumasi, Ghana. *International Journal of Remote Sensing*, 38(23), 6993–7020.

Okyere, A., & Kita, M. (2015). Rethinking urban informality and informal settlements growth in urban Africa: A literature discussion. *Journal of Sustainable Development in Africa*, 17(2), 101–124.

Okyere, S., Diko, S., Hiraoka, M., & Kita, M. (2017). An Urban "Mixity": Spatial Dynamics of Social Interactions and Human Behaviors in the Abese informal Quarter of La Dadekotopon, Ghana. *Urban Science*, 1(2), 13.

Pieterse, E. (2017). The city in sub-Saharan Africa. In *A research agenda for cities.* Cheltenham UK: Edward Elgar Publishing.

Pincetl, S., & Gearin, E. (2005). The reinvention of public green space. *Urban Geography*, 26(5), 365–384.

Platt, L. (2012). "Parks Are Dangerous and the Sidewalk Is Closer": Children's Use of Neighborhood Space in Milwaukee, Wisconsin. *Children Youth and Environments*, 22(2), 194–213.

Rigolon, A., Browning, M., & Jennings, V., (2018). Inequities in the quality of urban park systems: An environmental justice investigation of cities in the United States. Landscape and Urban Planning, *178*, 156–169. 10.1016/j.landurbplan.2018.05.026.

Roy, A. (2005). Urban informality. Toward an epistemology of planning. *Journal of American Plan Association*, 71(2):147–158.

Rupprecht, C. D. D., & Byrne, J. A. (2014a). Informal urban green-space: Comparison of quantity and characteristics in Brisbane, Australia and Sapporo, Japan. *PloS ONE*, 9, e99784. doi:10.1371/journal.pone.0099784

Rupprecht, C. D. D., & Byrne, J. A. (2014b). Informal urban greenspace: A typology and trilingual systematic review of its role for urban residents and trends in the literature. *Urban Forestry & Urban Greening*, 13, 597–611. doi:10.1016/j.ufug.2014.09.002

Rupprecht, C. D., Byrne, J. A., Garden, J. G., & Hero, J.-M. (2015). Informal urban green space: A trilingual systematic review of its role for biodiversity and trends in the literature. *Urban Forestry & Urban Greening*, 14(4), 883–908.

Rupprecht, C. D., Byrne, J. A., Ueda, H., & Lo, A. Y. (2015). 'It's real, not fake like a park': Residents' perception and use of informal urban green-space in Brisbane, Australia and Sapporo, Japan. *Landscape and Urban Planning*, *143*, 205–218.

Seguin R., Flax V. L., & Jagger P. (2018) Barriers and facilitators to adoption and use of fuel pellets and improved cookstoves in urban Rwanda. *PLoS ONE*, 13(10), e0203775. 10.1371/journal.pone.0203775

Shackleton, C., Blair, A., De Lacy, P., Kaoma, H., Mugwagwa, N., Dalu, M., & Walton, W. (2018). How important is green infrastructure in small and medium-sized towns? Lessons from South Africa. *Landscape and Urban Planning*, *180*, 273–281.

Shackleton, C. M., Hebinck, P., Kaoma, H., Chishaleshale, M., Chinyimba, A., Shackleton, S. E., … Gumbo, D. (2014). Low-cost housing developments in South Africa miss the opportunities for household level urban greening. *Land Use Policy*, 36, 500–509.

Sikorska, D., Łaszkiewicz, E., Krauze, K., & Sikorski, P. (2020). The role of informal green spaces in reducing inequalities in urban green space availability to children and seniors. *Environmental Science & Policy*, 108, 144–154.

UNDESA. (2015). *World urbanisation prospects: 2014 revision.* New York: Routledge.

Unt, A. L., Travlou, P., & Bell, S. (2014). Blank space: Exploring the sublime qualities of urban wilderness at the former fishing harbour in Tallinn, Estonia. *Landscape Research*, 39(3), 267–286.

Venter, Z. S., Shackleton, C. M., Van Staden, F., Selomane, O., & Masterson, V. A. (2020). Green Apartheid: Urban green infrastructure remains unequally distributed across income and race geographies in South Africa. *Landscape and Urban Planning*, *203*, 103889.

Vollmer, D., & Gret-Regamey, A. (2013). Rivers as municipal in- frastructure: Demand for environmental services in in- formal settlements along an Indonesian river, *Global Environmental Change*, *23*, 1542–1555. 10.1016/j.gloenvcha. 2013.10.001

Ward Thompson, C. (2012). Places to be wild in nature. In *Urban wildscapes*. A. Jorgensen & R. Keenan (Eds., pp. 49–63). Abingdon: Routledge.

Ward Thompson, C. (2002). Urban open space in the 21st century. *Landscape and Urban Planning*, *60*(2), 59–72. 10.1016/S0169-2046(02)00059-2

Wolch, J. R., Byrne, J., & Newell, J. P. (2014). Urban green space, public health, and environmental justice: The challenge of making cities 'just green enough'. *Landscape and Urban Planning*, *125*, 234–244.

9 Collaborative Spatial Expressions of Sustainability: River Rehabilitation Projects in Durban, South Africa

Patrick Martel, Catherine Sutherland, Sylvia Hannan, and Fanele Magwaza

Introduction

The post-2015 global development frameworks, the New Urban Agenda (NUA, 2016), the Sustainable Development Goals (SDGs, 2015) and the Sendai Framework for Disaster Risk Reduction (2015) focus on the development of inclusive, safe, socially just, resilient and sustainable cities (UN-Habitat, 2013; Valencia et al., 2019). However, there is considerable debate in global urban policy, and in African cities in particular, about how sustainable cities should be defined, who should be defining them, and how best to achieve the SDGs in particular urban contexts (Barnett & Parnell, 2016; Cobbinah & Darkwah, 2016; O'Farrell et al., 2019). Sustainable urban development requires that social, economic, ecological and governance dimensions of development are taken into account in an integrated manner to meet the needs of current generations without compromising the ability of future generations to meet their needs (Cobbinah & Darkwah, 2016; WCED, 1987). In the Global South, the central sustainability challenge is how to eradicate urban poverty and inequality, and provide housing, services and employment, without degrading local, regional and global natural systems (Ahvenniemi et al., 2017; Cobbinah & Darkwah, 2016; Valencia et al., 2019). Given the strong influence of urban spatiality on sustainable development, planners are required to develop policy, spatial practices and instruments to deliver on the SDGs and the NUA (Barnett & Parnell, 2016). Planners are defined as those who link "knowledge to action" (Friedmann, 2011), with a strong spatial focus (Harrison & Todes, 2015), and who learn about their environment in order to change it (Barnett & Parnell, 2016). Both UN-Habitat and the United Nations Environment Programme (UNEP) call on planners to re-structure the space of cities through land use planning to reduce social and environmental risk and to produce healthy and green cities (Habitat III, 2016; UNEP, 2020). As the demands on planners are expanded, and as the transformation of urban space is increasingly being recognised as being critical for meeting the SDGs and the NUA, so the definition of "a planner" has become less clear (Barnett & Parnell, 2016). Planning has become more inclusive and open

DOI: 10.4324/9781003181484-9

through the involvement of public and private actors in the production and use of spatial knowledge and practices in urban processes, such as river rehabilitation projects. The "loosening" of political state control, with its associated codified spatial arrangements, is evident (Barnett & Parnell, 2016; Harrison & Todes, 2015; McFarlane, 2017; Sim et al., 2018). The spatial determinants of sustainable cities, and those who produce and implement them, are therefore now less fixed. Colonial and modernist forms of planning are no longer the dominant determinants of urban spatial form or urban sustainability, particularly in African cities (Sim et al., 2018). This chapter argues that river rehabilitation projects have become new spaces of planning, where multiple actors, as "planners," are taking action to transform the landscape.

Durban, or the eThekwini Municipal Area (EMA), is located on the east coast of South Africa, in the province of KwaZulu-Natal. It is South Africa's third largest city, with a population of 3.7 million people, a GDP growth rate of 0.4% in 2017, and the main economic sectors being finance, community services, communication and logistics and manufacturing. The city has high levels of poverty and inequality, with 42% of its residents considered poor, and 26% living in informal settlements (eThekwini Municipality, 2016/2017). It is however recognised as South Africa's best performing city in the 2016 Stats SA Community Survey in terms of its poverty headcount reduction, since 2011 (eThekwini Municipality, 2017). The EMA is located within the Maputaland-Pondoland-Albany biodiversity hotspot, one of only 36 biodiversity hotspots in the world. It therefore contains a wealth of natural capital, much of which exists within the Durban Metropolitan Open Space System (DMOSS). Eighteen major river catchments and 16 estuaries form part of the environmental assets of the city (Turpie et al., 2017a) (see Figure 9.1).

However, many of these rivers are impacted upon by human activities, raising concerns about river health in Durban and the uMngeni Catchment, which is the major water source for the city (Jewitt et al., 2020). Using the metaphor of rivers being "the veins and arteries of the city," this chapter argues that rivers reflect, hold, move and address multiple urban problems and challenges, through their hydrological and ecological processes and their relationships with their catchments. These challenges include rapid urbanisation; pollution; poor delivery of infrastructure and services; path dependencies created through hard infrastructure, which use rivers as buffers when engineering systems fail; the growth of informal settlements; sand winning; densification and hardening of catchments; poor storm water management, which is being exacerbated by climate change; and cycles of droughts and floods. If these "veins and arteries" are unhealthy and neglected, the entire system is compromised and the quality of life of urban residents, particularly the poor, declines (Anderson et al., 2019; Jewitt et al., 2020; Turpie et al., 2017b). The chapter presents the outcomes of research undertaken on

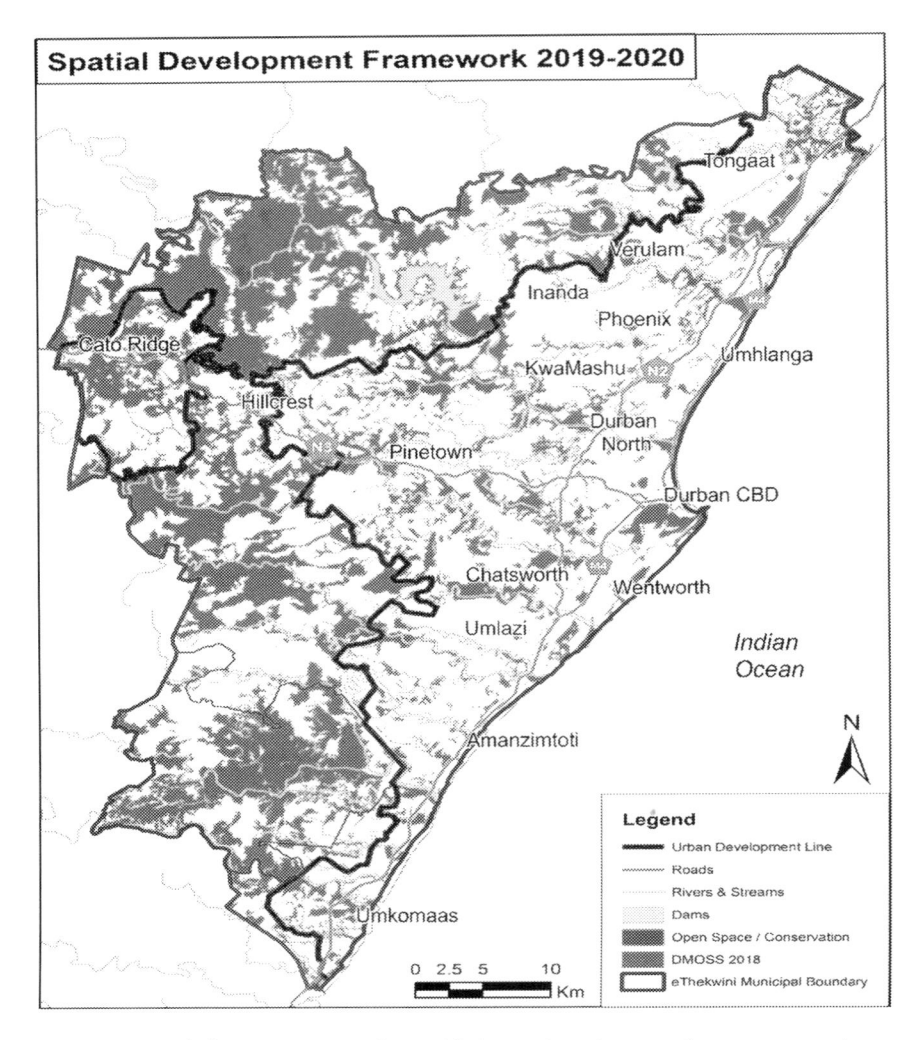

Figure 9.1 eThekwini Municipality with its major rivers and open spaces (map produced by Michela du Sart, EduAction).

four river rehabilitation projects in Durban. The argument is made that these projects are not merely passive spaces of "problems and opportunity, but ... [physical] spaces that hold creative concerted action" (Barnett & Parnell, 2016, p. 31).

The research therefore supports UNEP's (2020) focus on Green and Healthy Cities, which requires land use planning for urban ecosystems. However, it adopts Barnett and Parnell's (2018) broader view of planners and land use planning, which includes multiple actors with their particular knowledges and practices, co-producing spatial practices. As a result, it aligns with Lefebvre's (1968) claiming the right to the city by co-creating space. The chapter argues that Durban's river rehabilitation projects, with their multi-actor governance platforms, which by 2020 collectively contributed to the formation of eThekwini Municipality's "Transformative Riverine Management Programme," form valuable spatial "sustainable development" pathways in the city. The chapter first presents definitions of sustainable cities, river rehabilitation projects and ecological infrastructure (EI). It subsequently highlights the context of Durban with its particular social-economic, political and environmental characteristics. The methodology for the study, which identified spatial instruments of sustainability in the EMA, and produced the empirical data used in the analysis of the four river rehabilitation projects, is outlined. The chapter then provides a summary of the main spatial expressions of sustainability to provide the context within which river rehabilitation projects are emerging; and explains why and how these projects, with their multiple actors and different governance arrangements, have emerged as spaces of sustainable development. Finally, it reflects on the value of these projects in supporting sustainability transitions and transformations in Durban, and more broadly in other African cities.

Defining Sustainable Cities, River Rehabilitation Projects and Ecological Infrastructure

Cities comprise of complex social, economic and ecological systems that interact with one another in various ways (Liu et al., 2007). Cities become vulnerable if their subsystems are damaged or are unable to adapt to change (Coaffee, 2010). Unpredictable elements such as natural disasters, climate change, energy crises, political instability, socio-economic inequality, financial crises, food insecurity and terrorist attacks or crime pose a threat to urban development (Spaans & Waterhout, 2017; Zhang & Li, 2018). Romero-Lankao et al. (2016) contend that urbanisation and urban development profoundly alter the relationship between society and the environment, which impacts on urban sustainability. Simultaneously, cities are able to address sustainability concerns, due to their concentration of population, their social and human capital, which lead to social learning, and their ability to be innovative and scale up innovation, shift resource consumption and address environmental risks (Meerow et al., 2016; Nevens et al., 2013).

While sustainability and river rehabilitation are well-established concepts, there is a lack of consensus regarding their definitions and uncertainty about how they appear in reality. Urban sustainability conveys the interactions and dependencies between urban areas and the ecosystems on which they depend (Romero-Lankao et al., 2016). Sustainability is a normative concept focused on increasing quality of life with respect to environmental, social and economic considerations, for both present and future generations (Collier et al., 2013; Marchese et al., 2018). As a concept, sustainability grapples not only with expanded timescales, but also places increased value on collaborative and inclusive decision-making (Cobbinah & Darkwah, 2016; Nevens et al., 2013; Romero-Lankao et al., 2016; Valencia et al., 2019). Sustainability challenges are multiscalar, as urban areas both impact on, and are affected by, actions beyond their boundaries. They therefore require actors across various sectors and scales to work together through multi-level governance arrangements to formulate effective policies and actions (Cumming et al., 2017; Romero-Lankao et al., 2016). Despite the increased attention devoted to sustainable development as a result of the post-2015 global development frameworks (including the SDGs), the transformation towards more sustainable urban areas presents an enormous challenge to policy makers and scholars (Marchese et al., 2018; Roberts et al., 2020; Romero-Lankao et al., 2016).

River rehabilitation projects take on different forms (Keil, 1998). It is therefore important to reflect on how, and by whom, a rehabilitated river is conceptualised (Tooley, pers.com. 18/08/2019). Further critical questions include: what does a rehabilitated river look like? And what is the geographical boundary of river rehabilitation – the river or the catchment? River rehabilitation projects traditionally tend to focus on the ecological characteristics of rivers and endeavour to improve the ecological functioning of degraded ecosystems through the introduction of a variety of habitats (Grêt-Regamey et al., 2016; King et al., 2003). The degradation of aquatic ecosystems occurs as a result of physical, chemical and human disturbances and hydrological manipulations (King et al., 2003). Overall, river rehabilitation projects have tended to prioritise technical, scientific and engineering-based approaches which do not always consider the socio-economic and political relations in the catchment (Barraqué et al., 2008; Grêt-Regamey et al., 2016). Moore (2013) highlights that these scientific and technical approaches result in the governance context becoming opaque, resulting in a rigidity trap, where alternative paths cannot be imagined. Scientific and technical approaches often call for depoliticisation of solutions and therefore they neglect the social, political and institutional aspects associated with water (Moore, 2013; Steelman et al., 2015). However, water cannot be governed through technocratic management and engineering processes alone (Castro, 2007; Keil, 1998). Harrington (2017) states that with the increased range of actors involved in collaborative water governance at both the global and local scale, there is a growing need to consider political processes as being at the core of water issues.

River rehabilitation projects are therefore conceptualised in this chapter as having ecological, biophysical, social, economic and political dimensions with their influence extending beyond the physical boundaries of the river. In South Africa, the main approach to river rehabilitation includes improving water quality and quantity, investing in EI and supporting socio-economic development and poverty alleviation initiatives (Jewitt et al., 2020). Elsewhere in Africa, river rehabilitation projects are being developed to address the pollution of rivers, such as the "Adopt-a-River" projects in Kenya and Ethiopia, supported by a partnership between UNEP and Rotary Clubs (Rotary News, 2020) and ICLEI's Urban Natural Assets for Africa: Rivers of Life (UNA Rivers) programme funded by the Stockholm Resilience Centre (ICLEI, 2018). These projects have a strong focus on multi-actor partnerships and include the empowerment of the local state, training and involvement of communities in river rehabilitation, and the application of WASH principles. The ICLEI UNA Rivers programme focuses on mainstreaming biodiversity and ecosystem services in to land-use planning and government decision-making processes. The main lessons from the best practice case studies reveal an emphasis on community participation, urban flooding, multi-stakeholder engagement, with the need to build relationships between the state and citizens, and climate change adaptation supported by ecosystem services (ICLEI, 2018).

River rehabilitations are calculated activities which are planned to address various challenges and enhance the functioning of these systems in order to derive benefits. As linear systems, rivers hold and express many of the pressures of rapid urbanisation, acting as critical forms of EI, which capture, process and distribute the waste and pollution of the city. However, rivers reach tipping points or are flushed out by floods. The vast load they carry becomes evident in fish kills, nutrient overloads, and eutrophication, or solid waste arriving in large volumes on the beaches and in ports. As interventions which aim to address these challenges, river rehabilitation projects can be viewed as catalysts for local-level sustainable development, as they are spatial elements, running in the case of Durban from west to east, through the coastal zone to the Indian Ocean, taking many of the challenges and failures of the city with them.

The protection and enhancement of EI, with its associated ecosystem services, is recognised both globally and in South Africa, as being critical to river rehabilitation projects, which in turn improves water security (Daily & Matson, 2008; Jewitt et al., 2020). Due to the increase in produced capital stocks and the scarcity of natural capital, there has been growing interest in reinvesting in natural capital in the form of EI (Adamowicz et al., 2019; Salzman et al., 2018). Cumming et al. (2017, p. 253) posit that EI refers to "ecosystems that deliver services to society, functioning as a nature-based equivalent of, or complement to, built infrastructure." Jewitt et al. (2020) have expanded this definition, recognising that ecosystems both produce and deliver services. Li et al. (2017) define urban ecological infrastructure (UEI) as an organic integration of blue (water-based), green (vegetated), and grey (non-living) landscapes, combined with exits (outflows, treatment, or recycling) and arteries (corridors), at an ecosystem scale. They argue that as cities are "complex ecosystems driven by both socioeconomic activities and natural processes, urban ecosystems need more integrated, effective, comprehensive, and multi-functional ecological infrastructures" (Li et al., 2017, p. 13). Green and grey infrastructures with related landscape characteristics should therefore be integrated into cities at an ecosystem scale and be governed by multiple actors (Li et al., 2017). In South Africa, EI and its associated ecosystem services has been used for socio-economic development, supporting a suite of development imperatives through, for example, community ecosystem-based adaptation, which has been developed as part of Durban's response to climate change (Cartwright & Oelofse, 2016; Laros et al., 2013; Roberts et al., 2012; Sutherland & Mazeka, 2019).

Having briefly reflected on the definitions of urban sustainability, river rehabilitation projects and EI, the following section presents the context of Durban, or the eThekwini Municipal Area (EMA),[1] within which innovative river rehabilitation projects are emerging.

Durban's Socio-ecological and Political Context

Durban comprises of an urban core and a less dense rural periphery, with 43% of the municipal area governed by both eThekwini Municipality and traditional authorities, through a dual governance system (Roberts et al., 2020; Sim et al., 2018). The EMA's high biodiversity and unique biogeographical position supports a wide range of aquatic and terrestrial ecosystems with their associated EI (eThekwini Municipality, 2016/2017). In 2019, Durban was named "the greenest city in the world" according to the Husqvarna Urban Green Space Index (HUGSI), which is an index that records green spaces in urban areas. Durban has a well-developed open space system to protect its valuable environmental assets, DMOSS, which covers 33% of the municipal land area. DMOSS forms a layer of the municipality's Spatial Development Framework (SDF) (see Figure 9.1), with its policy and decision-making role being ratified by the eThekwini Municipality Council in 2016.

The city is endowed with an extensive network of rivers and streams, due to its high annual rainfall, topography, geology and biodiversity (see Figure 9.1). The 4,000 km's of rivers and nearly 80,000 hectares of land identified as forming part of DMOSS contribute significantly to the EI of the EMA (eThekwini Municipality, 2019/2020; Roberts et al., 2012; Turpie et al., 2017a). Turpie et al. (2017b)[2] found that DMOSS contributes R 4.2 billion worth of ecosystem flows per year and that the total asset value of these areas equated to R48 – 62 billion. While the value and impact of DMOSS on the sustainable development of Durban is well established and recognised, the broad benefits of rehabilitating rivers and their catchments is re-emerging as a critical sustainable development strategy, driven by a wide range of state and non-state actors.[3] This includes engineering, climate change and environmental planning departments in the municipality, university researchers, civil society organisations and in one case, the private sector, as this chapter will show. The establishment of experimental river rehabilitation projects is becoming increasingly important, given the impact of climate change on water-society relations in the EMA (Jewitt et al., 2020; Sutherland, 2020). Durban will experience more intense rainfall over shorter periods of time, followed by longer periods of low rainfall, in the face of a growing city with an increasing need for water-related services and greater impacts on the quality of rivers (eThekwini Municipality, 2015; Schulze et al., 2010). What happens in rivers and their catchments has significant socio-economic, political and governance impacts in Durban, as current water scarcity (Jewitt et al., 2020; Sutherland & Roberts, 2014), poor water quality, environmental degradation (Sutherland et al., 2016; World Bank, 2016) and the recent floods on 22 April, 2019 in the city have shown (Sutherland, 2020).

When examining the legislation governing water resources in South Africa, river catchments and their sub-catchments fall under Water Management Areas (WMAs) with their associated Catchment Management Agencies (CMAs). The National Water Act (No. 36 of 1998) requires the establishment of CMAs to govern water in South Africa. CMAs require engagement between state and non-state actors; and have a strong focus on the biophysical health of catchments as well as social transformation, supporting the principles of integrated water resources management (Meissner et al., 2017). Durban is located within the Pongola-Mzimkulu WMA, which does not have a functional nor influential CMA in place, which is the case in seven of the nine CMAs in South Africa (Meerow et al., 2016). As a result, smaller, more localised catchment management governance processes are emerging from the bottom up, taking the form of river rehabilitation projects. These projects have adopted different forms of governance, which reveal how their social, economic, political and environmental systems and their relationships are governed or "steered" through the establishment or use of institutional and organisational arrangements (Prakash et al., 2019). According to Prakash et al. (2019, p. 72) governance may be through: the act of government passing legislation, developing policy or providing information, private sector investments or interventions; collaborative efforts by local actors governing themselves through informal institutions; or the efforts of multiple actors, including the state, civil society and private sector in collaborative governance arenas. Through the lens of four river rehabilitation projects in Durban, this chapter reflects on the value of these projects and their governance arrangements as catalysts and spatial determinants of sustainability in the city. A brief background on each project is presented to provide the context of the case studies.

The Palmiet Catchment Rehabilitation Project

The Palmiet River is located in a sub-catchment of the uMngeni Catchment and flows into the lower uMngeni River. The Palmiet Catchment is situated in Durban's urban core and comprises a range of land uses, including high income residential areas, the industrial areas of Pinetown and New Germany, the Palmiet Nature Reserve, the University of KwaZulu-Natal Westville Campus and informal settlements, including Quarry Road West informal settlement. Given its steep and highly urbanised catchment, the Palmiet River is prone to flooding after storm events (Sutherland, 2020; Williams et al., 2019). The Palmiet Catchment was selected as eThekwini Municipality's proof of concept case study for assessing the value of EI in securing water in the uMngeni Ecological Infrastructure Project (Jewitt et al., 2020; Vogel et al., 2016). The Palmiet Catchment Rehabilitation Project (PCRP) was established in 2014 by local government officials and university researchers. Together, the Environmental Planning and Climate Protection Department (EPCPD) officials of the eThekwini Municipality and UKZN researchers were interested in exploring the convergence of water and climate governance through river rehabilitation and the value of EI in securing water quality in Durban. Funding for the project (until 2019) was through international and national research programmes awarded to UKZN[4] and Durban's Research Action Partnership (DRAP), which includes municipal funding. The PCRP has evolved into an innovative governance platform that is supporting a wide range of local government-led and community-based initiatives to support the resilience and sustainability of the Palmiet Catchment (Sutherland et al., 2019).

The Aller River Pilot Project

The Aller River is located in a sub-catchment adjacent to the Palmiet Catchment and flows into the lower uMngeni River. As part of Durban's "100 Resilient Cities" journey to develop the city's Resilience Strategy, the municipality initiated and funded several pilot projects, including the Aller River Pilot Project (ARPP), which focused on river rehabilitation and water governance in a local catchment (Martel & Sutherland, 2019). As with the PCRP, the ARPP stems from actions that are part of Durban's climate adaptation efforts. The ARPP was initiated by a civil society organisation, the eThekwini Conservancies Forum (ECF). There have been four phases of the ARPP since its inception in June 2016 which have been managed and implemented by the Kloof Conservancy (Martel & Sutherland, 2019). The project aimed to develop and implement community interventions to restore the health of a 5.6 km section of the Aller River which is characterised by poor water quality (Martel & Sutherland, 2019). The ARPP is part of ECF's broader Take Back our Rivers Programme; and uses the knowledge and resources of the conservancy movement to develop a community-based approach to river rehabilitation. By enhancing community ownership of the natural environment surrounding this river, it was envisaged that the ARPP would contribute to improved stewardship of eThekwini Municipality's water resources; enhance livelihood opportunities in low income communities; and strengthen resilience in the face of climate change (Martel et al., 2017). The design of the project focused on a number of interventions and activities (Kloof Conservancy, 2016), including project management; rehabilitation; monitoring; stakeholder engagement; capacity building of the Eco-Champs; community education and conservation awareness; and an external evaluation completed by the School of Built Environment and Development Studies from UKZN. The main strategy of the ARPP has been to recruit, train and stipend a group of Eco-Champs from local communities adjacent to the Aller River, with the goal of promoting water and environmental stewardship in the locality (Martel & Sutherland, 2019).

Sihlanzimvelo Stream Cleaning Programme

In 2011, the eThekwini Municipality Roads and Stormwater Maintenance Department initiated the Sihlanzimvelo stream cleaning programme. The objectives of the programme are the removal of litter/waste and invasive alien plant (IAP) species from waterways to reduce stormwater blockages and create employment. The programme focused on job creation and intended health benefits, which were aligned with the department's core mandate and functions (C40 Cities Finance Facility, 2019). With an operational focus, the initial design of the programme was to improve cost efficiencies in city service delivery (Martel et al., 2021). The project was meant to pool budget and resources from at least nine municipal departments to manage waterways – however the pooling of budgets did not materialise. Within the programme, community co-operatives have been established which employ local community members in their local area to collectively clean 300 km of stream banks and culverts from waste and IAP species. The streams are located in high density and low income settlements (in the north and south of the city) where poor river quality is associated with human health risks and flooding impacts (Martel et al., 2021). A consultant is responsible for managing the project, including appointing community assessors to monitor implementation and build local awareness (C40 Cities Finance Facility, 2019).

Wise Wayz Water Care

In 2009, severe flooding experienced in the Folweni area to the south of Durban was attributed to the dumping of solid waste into natural water courses. As a result, Durban Solid Waste (eThekwini Municipality) and the local community started to work together to clean up the area (Ward & Mudombi, 2018). Two communities are involved, from Folweni and Ezimbokodweni, to better manage a part of the Mbokodweni catchment, directly upstream from the AECI industrial complex (Ward & Mudombi, 2018; Water Research Commission WRC, 2017). Through funding from the AECI Community Education and Development Trust, the Wise Wayz Water Care (WWWC) Project was formed in 2016 to provide the volunteers with skills development and career path opportunities in water resource management (Water Research Commission, 2017).

The WWWC volunteers have adopted a 30 km stretch of river in the lower Mbokodweni catchment, which is faced with a myriad of challenges including illegal solid waste dumping and disposal, invasive alien plant infestations, poor aquatic health, effluent discharging directly into the river systems, freshwater leaks and illegal sand mining (Water Research Commission, 2017). Volunteers identified a number of interventions in the catchment: (1) water quality monitoring; (2) invasive alien plant removal and control; (3) community engagement on issues of solid waste, water leaks, infrastructure monitoring and education; (4) recycling and the development of buy-back centres; (5) community vegetable gardens with the potential to upscale to commercial agriculture; (6) solid waste removal from water courses; and (7) safety, health and environment. These volunteers have received training and mentorship support to develop their capacity in these areas of work (Water Research Commission, 2017).

Methodology

The city of Durban is used as a case study to reflect on the value of river rehabilitation projects, and their spatial expression, in improving the sustainability of African cities. The chapter draws on empirical research conducted on four river rehabilitation projects in Durban between 2014 and 2019, namely the Palmiet Catchment Rehabilitation Project (PCRP), the Aller River Pilot Project (ARRP), Wise Wayz Water Care (WWWC) and Sihlanzimvelo. The PCRP, ARPP and WWWC have clear spatial boundaries and are place-based; while Sihlanzimvelo is a stream cleaning project being implemented in various catchments across the city in high density and low income areas (see Figure 9.2).

The study used qualitative methods to collect data on these emergent spatial expressions of sustainability in the EMA. The annual eThekwini Municipality Municipal Spatial Development Frameworks (MSDF) from 2016 to 2020 were analysed using three framing questions to identify: the planning instruments and tools used to promote sustainability in the MSDFs; the spatial expressions of these instruments and tools; and the departments responsible for implementing them. This analysis produced the data used in outlining the main spatial determinants of sustainable development in Durban. An action research methodology was adopted

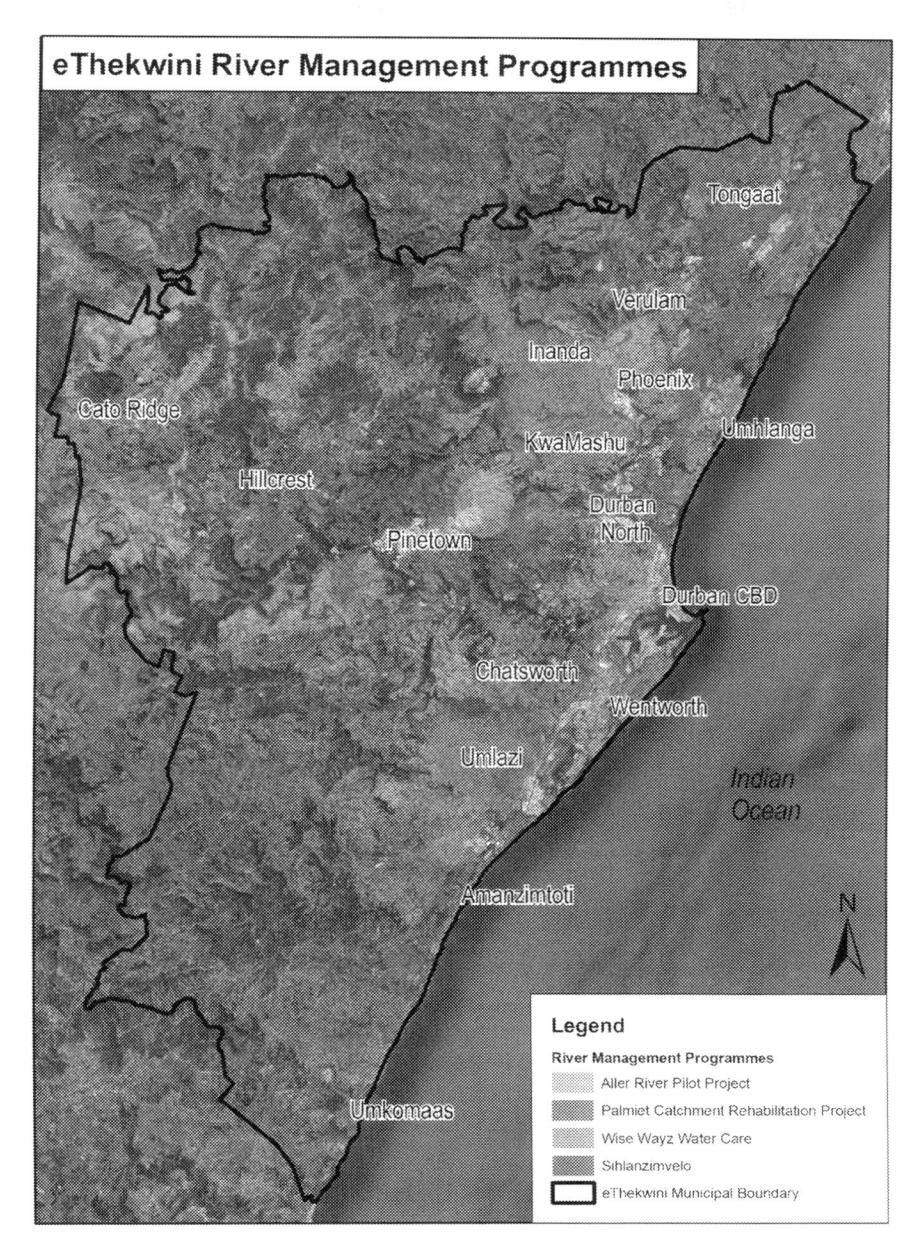

Figure 9.2 The location of the case study river rehabilitation projects in eThekwini Municipality (Map produced by Michela du Sart, EduAction).

to analyse the river rehabilitation projects, as two of the authors have been directly (PCRP, ARPP) or partially involved (Sihlanzimvelo Project; WWWC) in the establishment, review and analysis of these projects. The data for this study was collected through interviews with key stakeholders, a review of project-related documents and grey literature, and observations and notes from relevant project meetings over the last five years. Key themes have been identified across the four projects relating to biophysical, social, economic and governance aspects that are indicative of, or may contribute to, the promotion of sustainable development pathways and resilience in the city. The next section presents a discussion of the findings.

River Rehabilitation Projects as a Spatial Expression of Sustainable Development in the city of Durban

This section provides a brief summary of the main spatial expressions of sustainability in Durban, drawn from an analysis of the MSDF's from 2016 to 2020, to provide the context within which river rehabilitation projects are emerging. It then presents the analysis of the four river rehabilitation projects in terms of how they contribute to the sustainability of the city, acting as spatial expressions or determinants of sustainability, given their geographical nature.

Spatial Instruments Shaping Sustainable Development in Durban

Post-apartheid legislation in South Africa, which is globally recognised as being progressive and transformative, was promulgated in the mid to late 1990s, at the same time that sustainable development was gaining influence in shaping policy and practice across the world (Scott et al., 2015). As a result, sustainability discourses are embedded in South Africa's national legislation, informing local government policy and planning. The National Development Plan (NDP) 2030 (National Planning Commission NPC, 2012) recognises sustainability as an overarching framework for the development of the country with its focus areas being aligned with the SDGs. According to Cumming et al. (2017, p. 255):

> both the SDGs and the NDP place poverty reduction at the centre and aim to address job creation, inequality, water security, food security, climate change, disaster risk reduction, infrastructure development, human settlements, and health issues, as well as the sustainable use and conservation of biodiversity.

However, given the country's significant economic and social challenges, and the lack of recognition by many actors in government and the private sector, of the value of natural resources to a developmental state, the environment continues to be degraded (Scott et al., 2015; Swilling & Annecke, 2012).

The interpretation and implementation of sustainable development, and more recently the SDGs, play out in South African cities in contextually and geographically unique ways. South African metropolitan municipalities respond to, and shape, the spatial determinants of sustainability in their particular contexts with their own priorities, as they align themselves with national legislation and policy. The following section presents spatial instruments developed by eThekwini Municipality to support sustainable development as outlined in its MSDF (2019/2020). They reflect the efforts of a wide range of planners, defined more broadly, as those who take action to shape the environment for positive change (Barnett & Parnell, 2016). In the case of municipal plans and spatial instruments, a managerial governance approach is dominant, where the state is in control of the forms of engagement, with varying levels of participation by the private sector, civil society organisations and ordinary citizens (Sutherland et al., 2018). The Strategic Spatial Planning (SSP) department, which forms part of the Development, Planning, Environment and Management Unit of the eThekwini Municipality, is responsible for formal spatial planning in the city. Town and regional planners prepare the annual MSDF, which informs development and planning, with input from departments across the municipality. Durban's Long Term Development Framework guides the MSDF and the goals, priorities and budgets of eThekwini Municipality's Integrated Development Plan (IDP), which is prepared every five years as a requirement of national government. Durban's IDP (2019) is underpinned by global development frameworks including the SDGs and the NUA. This is evident in its six strategic priority areas (eThekwini Municipality, 2019) (Figure 9.3).

The 2017/2018 to 2021/2022 IDP states that in the context of wide ranging biodiversity threats and the projected impacts of climate change, eThekwini Municipality has committed to the protection, restoration and management of EI in the city, in order to enhance ecosystem resilience and the ability of citizens to adapt to change and short-term disasters (eThekwini Municipality, 2019). The IDP highlights the need for local government and society to work together to find practical and innovative solutions to manage threats to the city's natural resource base as a result of urban development (eThekwini Municipality, 2019). These resilience and sustainability principles take affect through the following spatial proposals: DMOSS, the Urban Development Line, Durban's densification strategy, a coastal erosion line for coastal planning and management, mapped areas of flood risk for disaster management and rural development strategies for the rural periphery (eThekwini Municipality, 2019).

DMOSS identifies open space areas and ecosystem service assets considered critical to maintaining Durban's biodiversity, and requiring protection and management. This includes rivers, wetlands, estuaries,

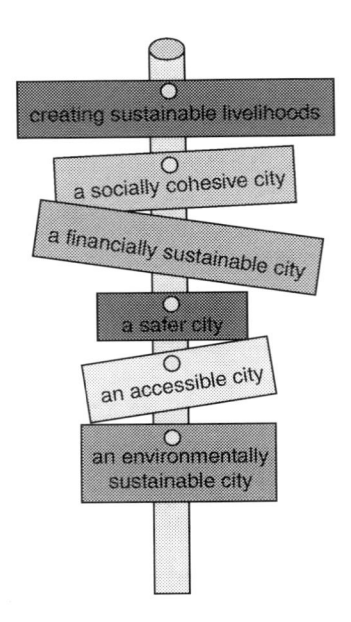

Figure 9.3 The six strategic priority areas of eThekwini Municipality's IDP (2018/2019).

grasslands, forests and coastal zone resources. The city's EPCPD attempts to secure these spaces using a variety of tools such as targeted land acquisition, supportive valuation and rating approaches, conservation servitudes, town planning mechanisms, education, awareness and incentives. The sustained provision of these services is important for the city's social and economic well-being, and is critical to sustainable development (eThekwini Municipality, 2019). In terms of management, less than 10% of DMOSS is formally protected, and below 7% is actively managed (Turpie et al., 2017b) (Figure 9.1), which reflects the challenges of implementing spatial and environmental policy.

The Urban Development Line (UDL), which is a major planning instrument in the MSDF, forms another spatial determinant of sustainability in the EMA (see Figure 9.1). This "urban edge" concept demarcates the urban and rural zones in the EMA based on the desire to achieve higher densities in the urban core, compacting the city, while protecting the "rural lifestyles" and environmental assets of the periphery (Sim et al., 2016; Sutherland & Roberts, 2014). According to Sim et al. (2016), the UDL has its power rooted in compact city, efficient service provision and resilience discourses. However, it remains a contested spatial determinant for sustainability in the city. Bond (2019) refers to the UDL as a class and race-based construct that legitimises the provision of different levels of urban development and services in the urban core and rural periphery, while obscuring its neo-liberal agenda. While the construction and implementation of this planning instrument remains contested, it has played a major role in defining living environments and sustainability across the EMA (Bond, 2019; Odili & Sutherland, forthcoming; Sim et al., 2016, 2018; Sutherland & Roberts, 2014). eThekwini Water and Sanitation Unit's (EWS) spatially differentiated service provision model is predicated on the UDL. Megaprojects and strategic economic development in the north of the city, the allocation of land by the traditional authority, and the absence of town planning schemes in traditional authority areas, undermine the UDL, and challenge the construct of a dense urban core and a more rural urban periphery. Durban's densification strategy, rural development strategies for the rural periphery and local area plans prepared by SSP also provide spatial determinants for sustainability. Environmental risk is addressed through a coastal erosion line for coastal planning and management and the mapping of areas of flood risk for disaster management.

Spatial expressions of sustainable development are not the sole responsibility of SSP. While the siloed nature of local government in South Africa and Durban is evident, with limited integration across departments, innovative programmes in eThekwini municipality ensure greater collaboration (Martel & Sutherland, 2019; Todes et al., 2009). Departments which focus on the environment, climate change and the SDGs, are increasingly working together as they recognise that sustainability challenges need to be addressed in an integrated manner (Douwes, 2017). Durban's EPCPD, its Sustainable and Resilient City Initiatives Unit and other environmentally concerned departments, such as EWS and Coastal Stormwater and Catchment Management are focusing their efforts on climate adaptation, sustainable sanitation, the protection of biodiversity and resilience building. Efforts to ensure greater sustainability in the city are being undertaken both through formal planning mechanisms, such as the IDP and MSDF, and innovative work streams, that are usually funded through external sources, enabling more flexibility and room to maneuver, in spaces of experimental governance. The Spatial Planning and Land-use Management Act (2013) requires that eThekwini Municipality undertakes a Strategic Environmental Assessment (SEA), as a tool for proactively integrating environmental sustainability into municipal plans, including the MSDF (eThekwini Municipality, 2019/2020). The SEA for the EMA is being conducted in phases, with the first phase, which focuses on the EMA's environmental status quo, completed in 2020. Climate change and Durban's commitments to the Paris Agreement and the Durban Climate Change Strategy (eThekwini Municipality, 2015) (eThekwini Municipality, 2015) are also shaping spatial determinants of sustainability in the city. The Climate Resilience Implementation Plan for Spatial Planning has been integrated in to the MSDF since 2017. This formed the basis for the development of Durban's C40 Climate Action Plan, which was produced in 2019. Localised climate studies, such as Cool Durban and the Urban Design Climate Lab are embedding climate change concerns in to spatial planning and land use schemes for local areas (eThekwini Municipality, 2019/2020).

Durban's Resilience Strategy was ratified by eThekwini Municipality's Council in 2017 and it is playing an important role in shaping resilience and sustainability in Durban, using six cross-cutting levers of change (Roberts et al., 2020; Sutherland et al., 2019) (see Figure 9.4).

Durban's Resilience Strategy has a strong spatial focus in its approach to building resilience. Two particular spaces in the city were selected to concentrate the municipality's resilience efforts: informal settlements and traditional authority areas (Roberts et al., 2020). The municipality's core resilience team determined that these spaces encapsulated the major resilience and sustainability challenges in the city. The team proposed that if the city focused on resilience building in these areas, then it would be able to scale up the outcomes of resilience building across the city from the learning and experience of these challenging spaces (Roberts et al., 2020). Durban's Resilience Strategy is therefore a spatial determinant for sustainability in the city.

This section has outlined the main spatial determinants of sustainable development undertaken by eThekwini Municipality in their administration of Durban. This chapter proposes that there are newly emerging spatial expressions of sustainability in the city that cut across the plans and programmes listed above. River rehabilitation projects are beginning to play a critical role in identifying sustainability challenges in the city, developing new governance approaches for sustainability, building state-citizen relationships and exploring alternative approaches to mitigating and adapting to environmental change in particular spaces as the results of this study show.

River Rehabilitation Projects as a Spatial Expression of Sustainable Development in Durban

Rivers and their associated EI, form a critical spatial determinant of, and opportunity for, advancing the sustainability of African cities. As linear systems, rivers are the locus of urban challenges, as they receive, move and process the impacts of human activities on the environment. Rivers and their associated EI support built infrastructure and provide ecosystem services to urban residents at multiple scales, enhancing quality of life and reducing urban impacts, as they act as buffers in multiple urban systems (Jewitt et al., 2020). The value of rivers and streams and the multiple services they produce is evident in the EMA in the recent establishment of the municipality's cross cutting Transformative Riverine Management Programme (Jewitt et al., 2020; Turpie et al., 2017b). Rivers and streams in Durban are becoming increasingly degraded, as they are exposed to chronic risks (e.g. ageing infrastructure, solid waste, industrial pollution, poor sanitation and failing waste water services) and more acute events (floods and

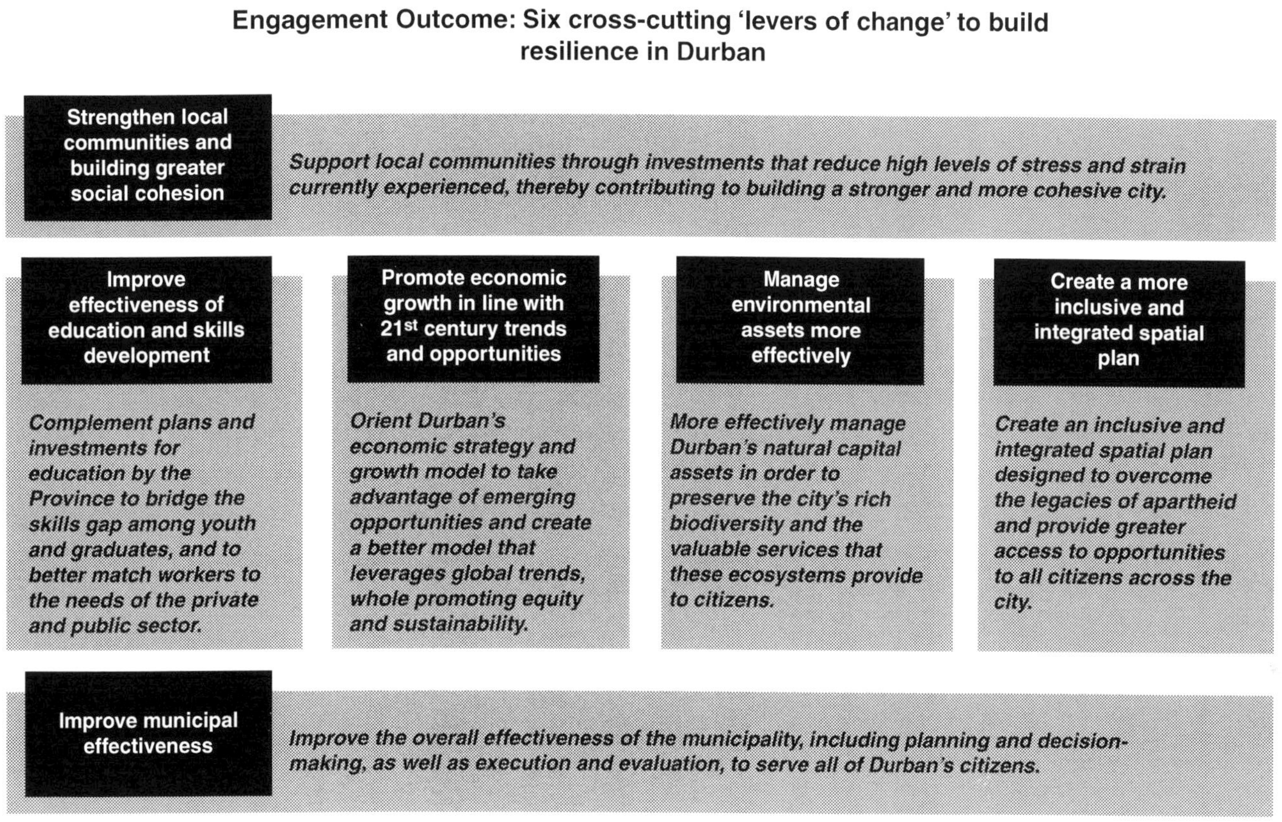

Engagement Outcome: Six cross-cutting 'levers of change' to build resilience in Durban

Strengthen local communities and building greater social cohesion

Support local communities through investments that reduce high levels of stress and strain currently experienced, thereby contributing to building a stronger and more cohesive city.

Improve effectiveness of education and skills development

Complement plans and investments for education by the Province to bridge the skills gap among youth and graduates, and to better match workers to the needs of the private and public sector.

Promote economic growth in line with 21st century trends and opportunities

Orient Durban's economic strategy and growth model to take advantage of emerging opportunities and create a better model that leverages global trends, whole promoting equity and sustainability.

Manage environmental assets more effectively

More effectively manage Durban's natural capital assets in order to preserve the city's rich biodiversity and the valuable services that these ecosystems provide to citizens.

Create a more inclusive and integrated spatial plan

Create an inclusive and integrated spatial plan designed to overcome the legacies of apartheid and provide greater access to opportunities to all citizens across the city.

Improve municipal effectiveness

Improve the overall effectiveness of the municipality, including planning and decision-making, as well as execution and evaluation, to serve all of Durban's citizens.

Figure 9.4 Levers for change for Durban's Resilience Strategy.
(Source: Roberts et al., 2020, p. 16).

drought). While all three spheres of government in South Africa (national, provincial and local) have responsibilities and mandates to protect and sustain rivers and their catchments, civil society organisations, research institutions and the private sector are now taking up this challenge. The institutional void created through the absence of functioning CMAs and the lack of capacity in local government departments has led to this action from below. This has resulted in the emergence of a range of river rehabilitation projects in Durban, shaped by environmental, development and poverty alleviation agendas and led by multiple actors, or planners (Barnett and Parnell, 2016) in different configurations or alliances (Martel & Sutherland, 2019; Martel et al., 2021). These projects are often experimental, operate in a learning-by-doing fashion and are driven by water security rationales. Each project has its own approach, governance arrangements and practices, which shapes their contribution to sustainability.

River rehabilitation projects have an "absolute" spatial expression as they are located within a biophysical boundary, a catchment. However, drawing on Harvey (1994) and Lefebvre's (1991) concept of relational space, river rehabilitation projects reflect hydro-social-spatial relations too, as they produce and assemble multiple socio-spatial relationships of urban life. They reveal: the relationships between the economy, society and water, in each particular context; the pressure on environmental resources, as the pro-growth and pro-poor discourses of South Africa are translated in to local spaces, and as inequality and informality in cities grow; the biophysical and ecological interactions between rivers and the land uses in their catchments; the value and limitations of the legislative and policy frameworks designed to manage rivers and their catchments; and they reflect governance and institutional arrangements, through the way in which they are governed in particular places. All these interactions influence these projects' ability to contribute to meeting the SDGs. Figure 9.5 presents the cross-cutting themes identified in the four river rehabilitation projects being analysed in this chapter.

Despite the variety of ways in which the river rehabilitation projects are being implemented in Durban, common elements in all four projects are evident which support the municipality's sustainability agenda. In terms of biodiversity, all four projects aim to improve and enhance the natural environment and associated EI; to improve water security; and to address chronic risks impacting local rivers and catchments. Their common characteristics in the economic theme reveal a focus on South Africa's national priorities of job creation and poverty alleviation, through the employment of youth from disadvantaged areas; as well as the provision of capacity development opportunities (Martel et al., 2021). The social theme highlights that the methods for changing human-environment relations are conceptualised as being dependent on co-producing knowledge; and educating, capacitating and empowering people who form part of the hydro-social relations in each particular catchment or on each river's edge, many

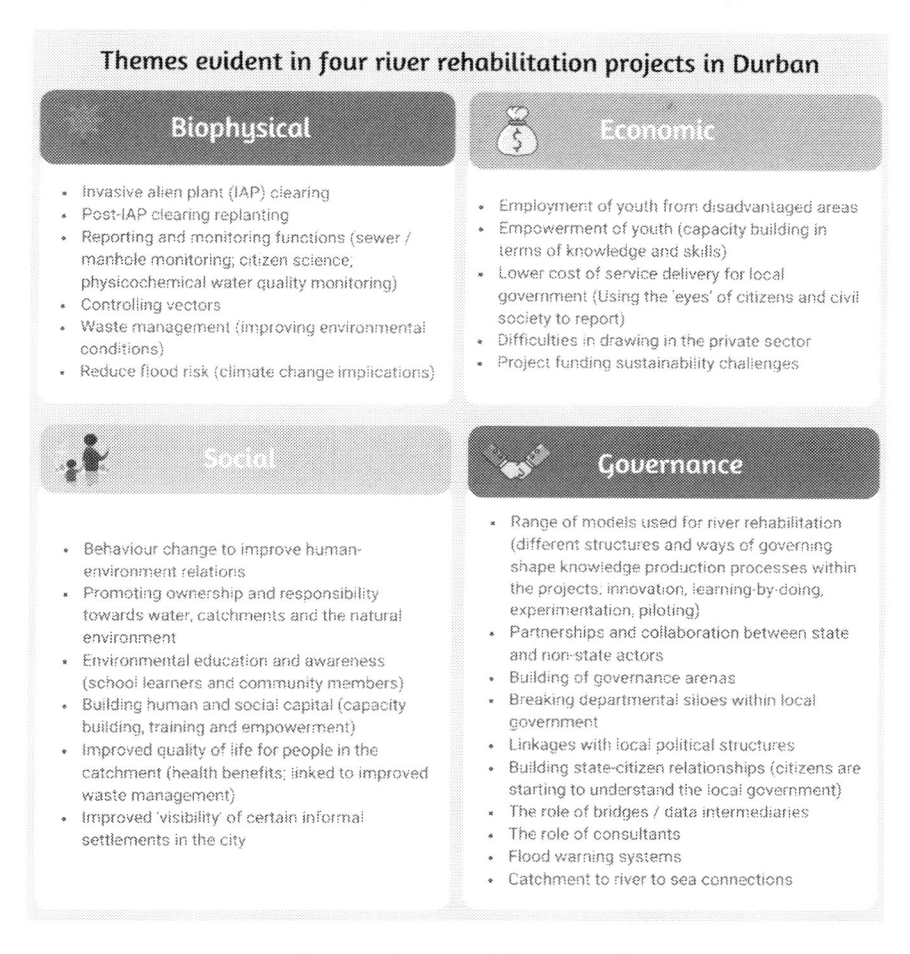

Themes evident in four river rehabilitation projects in Durban

Biophysical

- Invasive alien plant (IAP) clearing
- Post-IAP clearing replanting
- Reporting and monitoring functions (sewer / manhole monitoring; citizen science; physicochemical water quality monitoring)
- Controlling vectors
- Waste management (improving environmental conditions)
- Reduce flood risk (climate change implications)

Economic

- Employment of youth from disadvantaged areas
- Empowerment of youth (capacity building in terms of knowledge and skills)
- Lower cost of service delivery for local government (Using the 'eyes' of citizens and civil society to report)
- Difficulties in drawing in the private sector
- Project funding sustainability challenges

Social

- Behaviour change to improve human-environment relations
- Promoting ownership and responsibility towards water, catchments and the natural environment
- Environmental education and awareness (school learners and community members)
- Building human and social capital (capacity building, training and empowerment)
- Improved quality of life for people in the catchment (health benefits; linked to improved waste management)
- Improved 'visibility' of certain informal settlements in the city

Governance

- Range of models used for river rehabilitation (different structures and ways of governing shape knowledge production processes within the projects; innovation, learning-by-doing, experimentation, piloting)
- Partnerships and collaboration between state and non-state actors
- Building of governance arenas
- Breaking departmental siloes within local government
- Linkages with local political structures
- Building state-citizen relationships (citizens are starting to understand the local government)
- The role of bridges / data intermediaries
- The role of consultants
- Flood warning systems
- Catchment to river to sea connections

Figure 9.5 Cross-cutting themes of sustainability in Durban's river rehabilitation projects.

of whom experience development deficits. Promoting positive behaviour change and ownership of and responsibility towards the environment are crucial. Different forms of governance have developed across the four projects. In the case of Sihlanzimvelo, local government adopts a hierarchical style of governance to manage community co-operatives; in the PCRP and ARPP, it is the efforts of multiple actors, including local government, civil society organisations, research institutions and community members in collaborative partnerships which form the governance arena; and in the WWWC the private sector, local communities and local government interact with each other with the WWWC team members governing the project. In all cases, relationships that are built between local government and citizens have been critical in addressing the social, environmental and political dimensions of river rehabilitation and hence sustainability in the city. The economic dimension is less obvious, other than the impact of these projects on poverty alleviation, which to date has taken place mainly through the funding of community based eco-champs and community co-operatives but this funding has been minimal. However, the broader economic benefits of river rehabilitation projects, in terms of the services rehabilitated rivers and EI provide, and the costs of the degradation of rivers in Durban, are evident in research conducted on the value of EI in the uMngeni Catchment (Jewitt et al., 2020).

Conclusion

This chapter has focused on the role of river rehabilitation projects, which are focused on spatially defined areas within river catchments, and their associated EI in promoting spatial sustainable development pathways in Durban. They seek to address the multiple society-space-environment relations produced through urban processes in particular places which are concentrated and reflected in rivers. River rehabilitation projects represent catalytic spaces to address a range of challenges which impact on Durban's water bodies. The implementation of river rehabilitation projects in Durban has a broad focus, incorporating biophysical, social, economic and governance elements. The four river rehabilitation projects share many similar characteristics but they also differ in significant ways. They all have the goal of rehabilitating catchments, through addressing poor waste management, pollution and flooding, and building state-citizen relations, and improving monitoring and reporting mechanisms. They have a strong focus on supporting the development of sustainable livelihoods in the catchment and all draw on appointed local community members, who are provided with small stipends, to improve river health in a variety of ways.

All the programmes have actors who act as bridges or intermediaries between the municipality and the community: university researchers in the PCRP, the ECF and Eco-champs in the ARPP, a consultant in Sihlanzimvelo, and a consultant supported by AECI industrial complex in the WWWC. Funding comes from a variety of sources and the governance models in all four projects differ significantly. While one of the four projects analysed in this chapter (Sihlanzimvelo) has emerged through local government-led efforts focusing on local government-owned infrastructure, the other three have emerged, in part, due to the vacuum created by the absence of a CMA and poor water governance in the region. These projects have been established through state-citizen-research-private sector partnerships and are evolving as experimental spaces of governing for sustainable development in the city. As a result, these river rehabilitation projects, with their associated enhancement of EI, can be conceptualised as catalysts for transitioning to/promoting sustainable development pathways.

River rehabilitation projects reveal a more open and co-produced form of planning, which includes the knowledge and practices of multiple actors or "catchment planners," both from within and outside of the state. Here the spatial expression of sustainability is more collaborative and inclusive, emerging from the bottom up. Local authority officials, civil society groups, NGOs, researchers from universities and community members are working together to define and support sustainability at the local scale, claiming their right to the city (Lefebvre, 1968). This supports Barnett and Parnell's (2016) call for a diversity of definitions of the urban, each with their own associated spatial rationalities and spatial processes, which can bring about change in particular contexts. This is important, as the spatial expressions of sustainability in African cities are many and varied. While urban theory on sustainable cities and planning, largely developed in the north, provides useful concepts to understand and shape the patterns and processes of sustainability in African cities, theory from the south needs to be constructed. This chapter contributes to the development of southern theory and practices on the spatiality of sustainability in African cities. Rivers, and their associated EI, may be the ideal pathways for transformative sustainable development in African cities as they concentrate and reflect the positive and negative outcomes of urban processes; draw in networks of interested actors to shape sustainability in the city; and lead to volunteerism, experimental and multi-actor governance, transdisciplinary partnerships, innovation and learning-by-doing. To ensure sustainable development and transformation, river rehabilitation projects may need to be formalised, and included in urban spatial planning frameworks, as institutionalisation will result in prioritisation and a stronger consideration and protection of these vital arteries and veins of cities.

Acknowledgements

We would like to acknowledge the valuable comments of the reviewers of this chapter. We would also like to acknowledge the contributions of Sibongile Buthelezi and Duduzile Khumalo to this research, as well as all those engaged in catchment rehabilitation projects in Durban, from whom we have learnt so much. Wellcome Trust (SHEFS project) and the National Research Foundation of South Africa have provided funding for this research.

Notes

1 eThekwini Municipality is the administrative entity of Durban. The city of Durban and the EMA have the same geographical boundary and area. The city of Durban (or EMA) comprises of both an urban and rural zone.
2 The study focused on the direct values associated with the provision of natural resources, indirect use values associated with regulating services generated by ecosystem functioning, and the amenity values generated by ecosystem attributes (Turpie et al., 2017a).

3 In 2002 eThekwini Municipality launched the "eThekwini Catchments 2002: A Strategic Tool for Planning" project, which aimed to use research and tools developed on the health of catchments to inform environmental decision making and planning in Durban (Lubke, 2004). Lubke (2004) found that catchment discourses were being institutionalised in municipal planning, resulting in planners proposing that catchments become municipal administrative regions. However, these ideas did not gain broader traction due to a lack of political support and hence catchment discourses did not become institutionalised at the municipal level.

4 SANCOOP CLIMWAYS, Water Research Commission 2354, GCRF U-RES, City of Bremen-GIZ, NRF Community of Innovation, University of Manchester's SCI Urban Data Justice Project.

References

Adamowicz W., Calderon-Etter, L., Entem, A., Fenichel, E. P., Hall, J. S., Lloyd-Smith, P., Ogden, F. L., Regina, J. A., Rad, M. R., & Stallard, R. F. (2019). Assessing ecological infrastructure investments. *PNAS*, *116*(12), 5254–5261.

Ahvenniemi, H., Pinto-Seppä, A. H. I., & Airaksinen, M. (2017). What are the differences between sustainable and smart cities? *Cities*, *60*, 234–245.

Anderson, E. P., Kacson, S., Tharme, R. E., Douglas, M., Flotemersch, J. E., Zwarteveen, M. et al. (2019). Understanding rivers and their social relations: A critical step to advance environmental water management. *WIRES Water*, *6*(6), 1–21.

Barnett, C., & Parnell, S. (2016). Ideas, implementation and indicators: Epistemologies of the post 2015 urban agenda. *Environment and Urbanisation*, *28*(1), 87–98.

Barraqué, B., Formiga Johnsson, R. M., & Nogueira de Paiva Britto, A. L. (2008). The development of water services and their interaction with water resources in European and Brazilian cities. *Hydrology and Earth System Sciences*, *12*(4), 1153–1164.

Bond, P. (2019). Tokenistic water and neoliberal sanitation in post-apartheid Durban. *Journal of Contemporary African Studies*, *37*(4), 275–293.

Cartwright, A. and Oelofse, G. (2016). Reflections on the valuing of ecosystem goods and services in Cape Town, in Culwick, C. and Bobbins, K., (eds) *A framework for a green infrastructure planning approach in the Gauteng City-Region*, GCRO, University of Witwatersrand, Johannesburg.

Castro, J. E. (2007). Water governance in the twentieth-first century, *Ambiente & Sociedade*, *10*, 87–118.

Coaffee, J. (2010). Protecting vulnerable cities: the UK's resilience response to defending everyday urban infrastructure, *International Affairs*, *86*(4): 939–954.

Cobbinah, P. B. and Darkwah, R.M. (2016). Toward a more desirable form of sustainable urban development in Africa, *African Geographical Review*, doi: 10.1 080/19376812.2016,1208770.

Collier, Z., Wang, D., Vogel, J. T., Tatham, E. K., Linkov, I., (2013). Sustainable roofing technology under multiple constraints: a decision analytic approach. *Environment, Systems, Decisions 33*, 261–271.

Cumming, T. L., Shackleton, R. T., Försterc, J. Dini, J., Khan, A., Gumulae, M. and Kubiszewski, I. (2017). Achieving the national development agenda and the

Sustainable Development Goals (SDGs) through investment in ecological infrastructure: A case study of South Africa. *Ecosystem Services*, 27: 253–260.

C40 Cities Finance Facility (2019). Transformative riverine management projects in Durban: background and structuring.

Daily G. C. and Matson, P. A. (2008). Ecosystem services: From theory to implementation. *Proc Natl Acad Sci USA*, 105: 9455–9456.

Douwes, J. (2017). Exploring transformation in local government in a time of environmental change and thresholds: A case of eThekwini Municipality. Unpublished Masters Thesis, University of KwaZulu-Natal, Durban.

eThekwini Municipality (2015). Durban's Climate Change Strategy, Environmental Planning and Climate Protection Branch, eThekwini Municipality, Durban.

eThekwini Municipality (2016/2017). Spatial Development Framework, eThekwini Municipality, Durban.

eThekwini Municipality (2017). Durban Resilience Strategy, eThekwini Municipality, Durban.

eThekwini Municipality (2018/2019). Spatial Development Framework eThekwini Municipality, Durban.

eThekwini Municipality (2019). eThekwini Municipality Integrated Development Plan. 5 Year Plan: 2017/18 to 2021/22. 2019/2020 Review. http://www.durban. gov.za/City_Government/City_Vision/IDP/Documents/IDP2019_2020.pdf.

eThekwini Municipality (2019/2020). Spatial Development Framework, eThekwini Municipality, Durban.

Friedmann, J. (2011). *Insurgencies: Essays in planning theory*. Abington, United Kingdom: Routledge.

Grêt-Regamey, A., Weibel, B, Vollmer, D., Burlando, P. & Girot, C. (2016). River rehabilitation as an opportunity for ecological landscape design, *Sustainable cities and society*, 20, 142–146.

Habitat III (2016). Habitat III Issue Papers: Urban and spatial planning and design, United Nations Conference on Housing and Sustainable Urban Development, Quito.

Harrington, K. (2017). The political ontology of collaborative water governance, *Water International*, 42(3), 254–270.

Harrison, P. and Todes, A. Spatial transformations in a "loosening state": South Africa in a comparative perspective, *Geoforum 61* (2015) 148–162.

Harvey, D. (1994). The Social Construction of Space and Time: A Relational Theory, *Geographical Review of Japan*, 67(2): 126–135.

ICLEI (2018). Sustainable River-Based Urban Planning for Sub-Saharan Africa: Case Studies, Urban Natural Assets for Africa: Rivers for Life, ICLEI.

Jewitt, G. P. W., Sutherland, C., Browne, M., Stuart-Hill, S., Risko, S., Martel, P., et al, (2020). Enhancing water security through restoration and maintenance of ecological infrastructure: Global lessons from the uMngeni Catchment, South Africa. Water Research Commission Report K5/2354.

Keil, R. (1998). Greening the polis or policing ecology? Local environmental politics and urban civil society in Los Angeles. In M. Douglass and J. Friedmann (Eds.) *Cities for citizens: Planning and the rise of civil society in a global age*. Chichester: John Wiley and Sons.

King, J. M., Scheepers, A., Fisher, R. C., Reinecke, M. K. & Smith, L. B. (2003). River rehabilitation: Literature review, case studies and emerging principles. Report to the Water Research Commission, WRC 1161.

Kloof Conservancy. (2016). Aller River Pilot Project: A Proposal for a Community-Based Intervention to Improve River Health. Unpublished Proposal Submitted to eThekwini Municipality, University of KwaZulu-Natal, Durban.

Laros, M., Birch, S. and Clover, J. (2013). Ecosystem-based approaches to building resilience in urban areas: towards a framework for decision-making criteria. Background Paper, ICLEI-Africa, August 2013, CDKN & eThekwini Municipality.

Lefebvre, H. (1968). *Le droit à la Ville* [The Right to the City]. Paris: Anthropos.

Lefebvre, H. (1991). *The Production of Space*. London: Blackwell.

Li, F., Liu, X., Zhang, X., Zhao, D., Liu, H., Zhou, C., & Wang, R. (2017). Urban ecological infrastructure: an integrated network for ecosystem services and sustainable urban systems, *Journal of Cleaner Production*. Volume *163*, Supplement, 1 October 2017, Pages S12–S18.

Lubke, V. (2004). Environmental discourse in the eThekwini Municipality: The eThekwini Catchments Project. Unpublished Masters Dissertation at the University of KwaZulu-Natal.

Marchese, D. Reynold, E., Bates, M. E., Morgan, H., Clark, S. S. and Linkov, I. (2018). Resilience and sustainability: Similarities and differences in environmental management applications. *Science of the Total Environment*. 613–614 (2018) 1275–1283.

Martel, P. and Sutherland, C. (2019). Governing River Rehabilitation for Climate Adaptation and Water Security in Durban, South Africa. In P. B. Cobbinah and M. Addaney (eds.). *(2019). The Geography of Climate Change Adaptation in Urban Africa*, pp. 355–387.

Martel, P., Sutherland, C., Buthelezi, S. & Khumalo, D. (2017). Aller River Pilot Project External Evaluation. First External Evaluation. Unpublished Report Prepared for eThekwini Conservancies Forum, University of KwaZulu-Natal, Durban.

Martel, P., Sutherland, C., & Hannan, S. (2021). Governing river rehabilitation projects for transformative capacity development, *Water Policy*, 1–19. doi: 10.21 66/wp.2021.071

McFarlane, C. (2017). Learning from the city: a politics of urban learning in planning. In Bhan, G., Srinivas, S. & Watson, V. (Eds.). *The Routledge Companion to Planning in the Global South*. (pp. 323–333). Routledge.

Meerow, S., Newell, J. P., & Stults, M. (2016). Defining urban resilience: A review. *Landscape and Urban Planning*, *147*: 38–49.

Meissner R., Stuart-Hill, S., and Nakhooda, Z. (2017). The establishment of catchment management agencies in South Africa with reference to the Flussgebietsgemeinschaft Elbe: some practical considerations. In: Karar, E. (Ed) *Freshwater governance for the 21st Century*. Springer, Dordrecht.

Moore, M. L. (2013). Perspectives of Complexity in Water governance: Local Experiences of global Trends, *Water alternative*, 6(3), 487–505.

National Planning Commission (NPC). (2012). National Development Plan 2030: Our future - make it work. https://www.gov.za/sites/default/files/gcis_document/2 01409/ndp-2030-our-future-make-it-workr.pdf.

Nevens, F., Frantzeskaki, N., Gorissen, L., and Loorbach, D. (2013). Urban Transition Labs: co-creating transformative action for sustainable cities, *Journal of Cleaner Production*, *50*, 111–122.

Prakash, A., Cassotta, S. Glavovic, B., Hinkel, J., Karim, S., Orlove, B., Ratter, B., Rice, J., Rivera-Arriaga, E., Sutherland, C. (2019). Cross-Chapter Box 2: Governance of the Ocean, Coasts and the Cryosphere under Climate Change, *Special Report on the Ocean and Cryosphere in a changing climate*, IPCC.

Odili, A. and Sutherland, C., (2022). The shifting sanitation landscapes of Durban, South Africa through the lens of governmentality, in Cobbinah, P. and Addaney, M. (eds) *Sustainable Urban Futures in Africa*, Routledge.

O'Farrell, P., Anderson, P., Culwick, C., Currie, P., Kavonic, J., McClure, A., Ngenda, G., Sinnott, E., Sitas, N., Washbourne, C. L., Audoiun, M., Blanchard, R., Egoh, B., Goodness, J., Kotzee, I., Sanya, T., Stafford, W., and Wong, G. (2019). Towards resilient African cities: Shared challenges and opportunities towards the retention and maintenance of ecological infrastructure, *Global Sustainability*, 2, p. 1–6.

Prakash, A., Cassotta, S., Glavovic, B., Hinkel, J., Karim, S., Orlove, B., Ratter, B., Rice, J., Rivera-Arriaga, E., & Sutherland, C. (2019). Cross-Chapter Box 2: Governance of the Ocean, Coasts and the Cryosphere under Climate Change, *Special Report on the Ocean, Coasts and Cryosphere*, IPCC.

Roberts, D., Boon, R., Diederichs, N., Douwes, E., Govender, N., McInnes, A., et al. (2012). Exploring Ecosystem-Based Adaptation in Durban, South Africa: "Learning-by-Doing" at the Local Government Coal Face. *Environment and Urbanization*, 24(1), 167–195.

Roberts, D., Douwes, J., Sutherland, C. and Sim, V. (2020). Durban's 100 Resilient Cities journey: governing resilience from within, *Environment and Urbanisation*, in press.

Romero-Lankao, O. Gnatz, D.M., Wilhelmi, O. and Hayden, M. (2016). Urban Sustainability and Resilience: From Theory to Practice. *Sustainability*, 8(12), 1224.

Rotary News (2021). Rotary-UNEP implement Africa's largest river rehabilitation project, https://rotarynewsonline.org, accessed 21 January, 2021.

Salzman J, Bennett G, Carroll N, Goldstein A, Jenkins M (2018). The global status and trends of payments for ecosystem services. *Nat Sustain* 1:136–144.

Schulze, R. E., Knoesen, D. M., Kunz, R. P., & van Niekerk, L. M. (2010). Impacts of Projected Climate Change on Design Rainfall and Streamflows in the eThekwini Metro Area. Report Prepared for the eThekwini Municipality, University of KwaZulu-Natal, Pietermaritzburg.

Scott, D., Sutherland, C., Sim, V. and Robbins, G. (2015). Pro-growth challenges to sustainability in South Africa, in Hansen, A. and Wethal, U. (eds) *Emerging Economies and Challenges to Sustainability. Theories, strategies, local realities.* Routledge, London.

Sim, V., Sutherland, C., and Scott, D. (2016). Pushing the boundaries - Urban Edge challenges in eThekwini Municipality, *South African Geographical Journal*, 98(1), 37–60.

Sim, V., Sutherland, C., Buthelezi, S., and Khumalo, D. (2018). Possibilities for a hybrid approach to planning and governance at the interface of the administrative and traditional authority systems in Durban, *Urban Forum*, 29(4), 351–368.

Spaans, M., & Waterhout, B. (2017). Building up resilience in cities worldwide – Rotterdam as participant in the 100 Resilient Cities Programme. *Cities*, 61: 109–116.

Steelman, T., Nichols, E. G., James, A., Bradford, L., Ebersöhn, L., Scherman, V. et al., (2015). Practicing the science of sustainability: The challenges of transdisciplinarity in a developing world context', *Sustainability Science*, 10: 581–599.

Sutherland, C. (2020). Involving people in informal settlements in NHG based on South African experience, in Oxford Research Encyclopaedia of Natural Hazard Science, Oxford University Press, Oxford.

Sutherland, C. & Mazeka, B. (2019). Ecosystem Services in South Africa: Contemporary Changes and New Directions, In Knight, J. & Rogerson, C. (Eds.). The Geography of South Africa. Cham, Switzerland: Springer, Cham; 71–80. doi: 10.1007/978-3-319-94974-1_8.

Sutherland, C., & Roberts, D. (2014). Why Leadership Matters in Water and Climate Governance. Opinion Paper 12.

Sutherland, C., Sim, V., Buthelezi, S., and Khumalo, D. (2016). Social constructions of environmental services in a rapidly densifying peri-urban area under dual governance in Durban, South Africa, *African Biodiversity and Conservation*, 46(2), 1–12.

Sutherland, C., Scott, D., Nel, E., and Nel., A. (2018). Conceptualising 'the urban' through the lens of Durban, South Africa, *Urban Forum*, 29(4), 333–350.

Sutherland, C., Roberts, D. and Douwes, J. (2019). Constructing resilience at three scales: The 100 Resilient Cities programme, Durban's resilience journey and water resilience in the Palmiet catchment, *Human Geography*, 12(1), 33–49.

Swilling, M. and Annecke, E. (2012). *Just Transitions. Explorations of Sustainability in an Unfair World*, United Nations University Press, Geneva and UCT, Cape Town.

Todes, A., Sim, V. and Sutherland, C. (2009). The Relationship between Planning and Environmental Management in South Africa: The Case of KwaZulu-Natal, *Planning Practice & Research*, 24(4), 411–433.

Turpie, J, Letley, G., Chyrstal, R., Corbella, S. and Strecth, D. (2017a). Promoting Green Urban Development in Africa: Enhancing the relationship between urbanization, environmental assets and ecosystem services. Part 1: A spatial valuation of the natural and semi-natural open space areas in eThekwini Municipality. Report prepared by Anchor Environmental Consultants for AECOM on behalf of the World Bank.

Turpie, J, Letley, G., Chyrstal, R., Corbella, S. and Strecth, D. (2017b). Promoting Green Urban Development in Africa: Enhancing the relationship between urbanization, environmental assets and ecosystem services. Part 2: Evaluating the potential returns to investing in green urban development in Durban. Report prepared by Anchor Environmental Consultants for AECOM on behalf of the World Bank.

UNEP (2020). Sustainable Cities in Asia and the Pacific, United Nations Environment Programme, www.unep.org.

UN-Habitat (2013) State of the World's Cities, UN-Habitat, Nairobi.

Valencia, S. C., Simon, D., Croese, S., Nordqvist, J., Oloko, M., Sharma, T., Taylor Buck, N., and Versace, I. (2019). Adapting the Sustainable Development Goals and the New Urban Agenda to the city level: Initial reflections from a comparative research project, *International Journal of Urban Sustainable Development*, 11 (1), p. 4–23.

Vogel, C., Scott, D., Culwick, C. E., & Sutherland, C. (2016). Environmental Problem-Solving in South Africa: Harnessing Creative Imaginaries to Address 'Wicked' Challenges and Opportunities. *South African Geographical Journal*, 98(3), 515–530.

Ward, M. and Mudombi, S. (2018). Protecting and unlocking jobs through water stewardship: A case study linked to the Umbogintwini industrial complex eThekwini.

Water Research Commission (WRC) (2017). Wise Wayz Water Care Project: Community Water Stewardship.

Williams, D. S., Manez Costa, M., Sutherland, C., Celliers, L. and Scheffran, J. (2019). Vulnerability of informal settlements in the context of rapid urbanization and climate change, *Environment & Urbanization*, 31(1): 157–176.

World Bank (2016). Environmental Resources in eThekwini Municipality, prepared for eThekwini Municipality, Durban.

World Commission on Environment and Development (1987) *Our Common Future*. Oxford: Oxford University Press.

Zhang, X. and Li, H. (2018). Urban resilience and urban sustainability: What we know and what do not know? *Cities* 72(2018) 141–148.

10 Regulation of Physical Development in Ghana: Systems and Practices

Michael Addaney, Seth Opoku Mensah, and Florence Abugtane Avogo

Introduction

The global urban population is expected to increase by more than two thirds, with African and Asian urban centres taking about 90% (United Nations Population Division, 2015). This provides impulsion for monitoring land cover and land use change as rapid urbanisation is set to increase competition for space (Klopp & Petretta, 2017; Watson, 2016). Per paragraph 89 of the New Urban Agenda (NUA), African countries committed to "establish legal and policy frameworks, based on principles of equality and non-discrimination, to better enable prevailing governments to effectively implement national urban policies as appropriate and to empower them as policy and decision-makers, ensuring appropriate fiscal, political and administrative decentralisation based on the principle of subsidiarity" (McAuslan & Berrisford, 2017). This notwithstanding and with the increase competition for space, compliance with land use planning guidelines has been a major challenge.

Similar to most Anglophone West African countries, Ghana's urban land use planning is oriented on the British town planning legislation which specified procedures for controlling urban sprawl, for example, by seeking permission from the local council and by slum clearance (UK Parliament, 2016). After independence, comprehensive control of development started with the Town and Country Planning Ordinance (CAP 84, 1945) (Adarkwa, 2012). These have largely been ineffective in planning, controlling and monitoring physical development due to their colonial nature with little to no relevance in addressing contemporary planning issues. Since the promulgation of the CAP 84 in 1945 with its amendment in 1958, no revision was made for over five decades with a failure to meet the changing urban development situation in Ghana. These examples corroborate McAuslan and Berrisford (2017) assertion that "Africa's cities tend to be shackled to inappropriate, ineffective and redundant laws and policies for managing them. These laws run deeply through each country's social, economic and political systems and are often based on the assumption that there is a strong national government that is able to implement them."

DOI: 10.4324/9781003181484-10

Although research abounds to explore Ghana's urbanisation, there is a dearth of research that addresses the legal and regulatory frameworks for physical development planning in Ghana. This chapter therefore addresses this gap. This is in line with the call on African countries over the past two decades to reform their urban policies, practices and laws to make cities more efficient engines of economic growth and shift them from an extractive to a more developmental and inclusive system of urban governance (ibid). The chapter is divided into six. Following the introduction, Section two presents the method of data collection and research design. Section three discusses sustainable and inclusive physical development by analysing relevant concepts and themes. Section four further explores how sustainable and inclusive physical development could be realised in Ghana. This is followed by Section 5 which examines the legal and regulatory frameworks for physical development planning in Ghana, leading to conclusion.

Method of Data Collection and Research Design

The chapter used relevant, current and available literature on sustainable and inclusive physical development and its related issues. The literature was obtained from existing scholarship and policy documents and reports from global, national and local levels on the study variables. The global literature review focused on peer-reviewed articles, books and reports on land use, physical development and spatial planning (Acheampong, 2019; Amoateng et al., 2013; Leyzerova et al., 2016; McAuslan, & Berrisford, 2017; UN Habitat, 2008, etc.) using Google Scholar, WorldCat and Google search, SAGE Journals online, JSTOR and CABI. The chapter used policy documents and international organisations' development agenda such as Sustainable Development Goals (SDGs) and NUA. Also, development plans and legislation were reviewed. Examples of these included the Land Use and Spatial Planning Act, 2016 (Act 925), Local Government Act, 1993 (Act 462), National Development Planning Commission Act, 1994 (Act 479), the National Development Planning (Systems) Act, 1994 (Act 480), National Urban Policy of 2012, Town and Country Planning Act, 1945 (CAP 84) and Zoning guidelines and planning standards issued by the Town and Country Planning Department (TCPD). All literature was harmonised and streamlined using content analysis to deconstruct relevant evidences to the study variables. The content analysis provided the analytical framework to examine text data (Krippendorff, 2004) from legal and regulatory frameworks for physical development planning in Ghana. This was done in three stages: themes identification, descriptive accounts and interpretative analyses. The themes were then given meaning through descriptive accounts and interpretative analyses.

Sustainable and Inclusive Physical Development

Physical development involves carrying out of building, engineering, mining or other operations in, on, over or under land. It is the making of any material or substantial change in the use of any building or land (Acheampong, 2019; Amoateng et al., 2013; Keeble, 1969). Physical development is a major component of managing urban growth and expansion. Acheampong (2019, p. 2) conceptualises the fundamental goal of physical development planning in most countries, both developed and developing as:

> "the goals of coordinating the physical expressions of sectoral policies and safeguarding equity in the distribution of the outcomes of development between places while addressing the indispensable tensions between socio-economic development and environmental protection obligations are articulated and pursued through spatial planning."

This necessitate controlling the use of space and land which form the basis for physical development. Fuseini (2014) underscores land's socio-politico-religious functions that accord identity and sense of belonging to people. However, planned outcomes largely hinge on the existing land tenure systems, the nature of urban land market, planning legislation and the institutional arrangements for implementation. According to Amoateng et al. (2013), physical development manifests itself in the form of human activities or land uses in towns and cities. It can therefore be beheld as the rapid modification caused by human activities on land.

These human activities must create a balance in the social, economic and environmental requirements in order not to compromise the needs of future generations (Leyzerova et al., 2016) in physical development. Thus, sustainability in physical development calls on actors representing all sections of urban society to work together to develop the ability to reconcile varied interest for the common good. In particular, goal 11 of the Sustainable Development Goals (SDGs) underscores the necessity for sustainable cities and communities and calls for sustainability in the built environment to make cities and human settlements inclusive, safe, resilient and sustainable. Miljkovic et al. (2012) therefore calls for city governments to play central role in the development of inclusive and sustainable development strategies towards physical development. Sustainable physical development focuses on the control and the implementation of appropriate spatial and planning measures for the prevention of illegal and unplanned construction of structures (ibid). These are geared towards the ultimate objective of physical development to "sustain the improvement in the wellbeing of individuals and bestow benefits on all" (Amoateng et al., 2013).

Achieving Sustainable and Inclusive Physical Development in Ghana

The principle of sustainability features in the urban physical development process (Leyzerova et al., 2016). Sustainable and inclusive physical development advocates for the preparation of physical planning control tools and policies through a broad-based participatory process. In an attempt to achieve a sustainable and inclusive physical planning, a participatory and multi-approach to land use planning and management is very essential. In designing a plan to guide physical development, cities thus need to be integrally involved in all efforts to ensure sustainable and inclusive physical planning and development (ibid). Furthermore, to achieve sustainable and inclusive physical development, local governments have to include good initiatives such as parks, recycling of municipal waste, air pollution legislation in physical plans. Making cities more competitive and livable and social inclusiveness are the second and third of the three dimensional goal structure of Agenda 21 while the first is related to conservation and management of resources for development (Damodaran et al., 2015). Belsky et al. (2013) highlights five examples that can help to ensure inclusive and effective approach to planning for sustainable urban development in both developed and developing countries. These include clearly defined roles of their urban institutions from the national to local level, informed by public participation, and absence of political interference. Secondly, forecast growth patterns guide urban development to conform to metropolitan visions through long term (40–50 years) spatial plans that outline land use forecast that is disaggregated into 20-year plans and translated into local plans. Thirdly, availability of capable staff (adequate and qualified planners, architects, surveyors, engineers and analysts) and access to necessary software and resources. Fourth, plans are implemented transparently and consistently and city dwellers are given multiple opportunities to shape and inform metropolitan and municipal plans. According to Belsky et al. (2013), The New York City master plan employs public participation in socio-economic forecasts to develop long-term goals to achieve sustainable and inclusive physical planning.

Additionally, access to comprehensive spatial data, capable planning staff and a robust legal system provide insight into institutional planning frameworks which facilitate inclusive and sustainable development. Belsky et al. (2013) stated several constraints to achieving an inclusive and sustainable form of urban development that are common in developing countries as the political complexity of addressing informal settlements and activities, then the issue of a scarcity of revenue to invest in inclusive development, insufficient investment in strengthening community-based organisations and entrepreneurs and finally, the institutional, human, technical and financial resources to overcome capacity gaps are inadequate for regional, spatial and anticipatory planning and investment. These challenges affect inclusive and sustainable physical development. However, with the existence of efficient legal and regulatory frameworks and enforcement of development controls, city planning authorities can overcome the challenges towards achieving sustainable and inclusive physical development.

The physical development planning system and the accompanying practices in Ghana have evolved since 1945 through the Town and Country Planning Act (CAP 84). Since its inception, it has been known by three main terminologies; "physical planning," "land use planning" and "town and country planning" (Acheampong, 2019, p. 29). "Spatial planning" is a contemporary synonymous terminology. The public sector department that was established in 1945 and mandated to perform spatial planning functions is the TCPD. The new legislative framework associated with re-forming planning practice in Ghana merged the terminologies into "land use and spatial planning," apparently to mirror both the traditional regulatory function and the emerging strategic role that spatial planning is expected to play in developing countries. Despite recent and emerging developments in physical development planning practice, experience of planning controls in Ghana is not different from other African countries. The existence of legal and institutional frameworks and some control mechanisms suffer from weak enforcement including legislative bottlenecks, inadequate and/or lack of public participation, inadequate institutional capacity, cumbersome land acquisition processes, corruption, type of land ownership practised and overlapping and duplication of mandates in enforcement of development controls.

Legal and Regulatory Frameworks for Physical Development Planning in Ghana

The key features of the pre-independence planning system formally instituted in 1945 included a highly centralised planning system. This is evidenced by the fact that decisions regarding the preparation of a plan for an area under the jurisdiction of local government authorities were taken at the highest level of decision making by a Minister responsible for town planning. Despite being a highly centralised activity, land use and spatial planning in this era had an overall positive impact in terms of bringing about strategic infrastructure development, distributing national resources across regions and shaping the growth and development of major towns and cities (see e.g., Adarkwa, 2012; Fuseini & Kemp, 2015). The 1945 Act established the TCPD in Ghana and laid the foundations for the modern planning system. The Act which was the first of its kind to define the scope, purpose and legal basis for spatial planning set the ambitious objective to "… provide for the orderly and progressive development of land, towns and other areas, to preserve and improve their amenities and for related matters" (Town and Country Planning Act, 1945 [CAP 84]). In addition, the Act of 1945 defined development in relation to land to include "… a building or re-building operations and the use of the land or a building on it for a purpose which is different from the purpose for which the land or building was last being used" (Town and Country Planning Act, 1945 [CAP 84]). The regulatory and development control functions of spatial planning and the role it would play in the agenda of modernisation and social transformation were clearly expressed in its intent to bring about orderly and progressive development of human settlements in the country. Legal instruments provide support and regulatory powers to planning authorities to enable them carry out their functions without restrain. The last momentous period in the history of spatial planning is the reforms that were implemented between 2007 and 2010 under the Land Use Planning and Management Project (LUPMP). These reforms would once again bring spatial planning into mainstream policy and academic discourse and initiate a number of projects to experiment with various spatial planning models, introduce a new legislation and entrench a new system of hierarchical spatial planning at the national, regional and local levels of political administration (Acheampong, 2019, p. 31).

In Ghana each sector has its legislative instrument to support the functions of institutions. The Local Government Act 462 of 1993, Land Use and Spatial Planning Act 925 of 2016, National Development Planning Commission Act 479 and National Development Planning (System) Act 480 are among the legislative instruments provided to support planning authorities to manage growth in the built environment. The Local Government Act (Act 462) delegated substantial administrative powers to district assemblies at the local level and mandated them to ensure overall development of local government areas. In 1994, the National Development Planning (System) Act (Act 480) was promulgated to provide the legal basis for planning at all levels in Ghana. Thus, the Local Government Act (Act 462) and the National Development Planning (System) Act (Act 480) became the two most important legislation that will set out the institutional framework for planning and define the nature and scope of the activity for close to three decades. The local Government Act 462 complements the National Development Planning Commission (NDPC) by providing all planning activities at the district and local levels.

The NDPC was established in the same year with a mandate to undertake socioeconomic, environmental and physical planning as a single integrated task (Diaw et al., 2002). However, in practice, the spatial components of planning were largely de-emphasised. The tradition of "development planning" initiated by the National Development Planning (System) Act (Act 480), therefore, had a profound impact on spatial planning at all levels as well as on planning education in the country. Spatial planning was essentially neglected at the national and regional levels of political administration. At the level of MMDAs, a new department, the Development

Planning Unit (DPU) was established as a decentralised department to translate national goals formulated by the NDPC into local Medium-Term Development Plans (MTDPs). The MTDPs prepared under NDPC guidelines failed to incorporate spatial planning issues, in particular, the physical organisation of activities in towns and cities within their respective districts (Acheampong, 2019; Diaw et al., 2002). The TCPD, another decentralised department at level of MMDAs, provided spatial planning functions which was narrowly conceived as involving the designation of land uses and development control. On the other hand, was "land use planning" which was also narrowly conceived as encompassing the preparation of layouts for neighbourhoods, towns and cities and development control (Acheampong & Ibrahim, 2016).

Moreover, under this established notion of the "spatial" being distinctively separate from the "socio-economic," the activity of planning would become compartmentalised into the two separate decentralised departments at the local level (i.e. the DPU and TCDP with competence in development planning and land use or physical planning, respectively), with hardly any coordinated efforts leading to the identification of cross-cutting matters and dealing with them accordingly. Consequently, land use plans were prepared that had no bearing on the prevailing socio-economic realities of the day, except for assisting landowners to sell their land. Similarly, MTDPs were and continuous to be prepared without adequate consideration for the spatial implications of proposals. The significance of the decentralisation programme initiated in the late 1980s have profound impacts on the accompanying legal and intuitional arrangements governing spatial planning in contemporary times.

The roles of District Planning Authorities and validity period of permits are clearly indicated in the building code (Building code). Boamah et al. (2012) observed the loopholes in the legislative instruments where it was worth noting the contradiction in the Local Government Act 462 and L.I. 1630. For instance, Act 462 prevents any physical development without prior written approval by the planning authority while section 8(2) of L.I 1630 states an applicant not informed of grant or refusal of permit after three (3) months of application can commence development on the basis that the application is acceptable by the planning authority. This in itself makes it difficult for enforcement of development controls since there is a flaw in the legislative instruments. Currently, the Local Government Act (Act 462), Town and Country Planning Ordinance and the National Building Code L.I. 1630 are the main instruments used for the control of physical development in Ghana. Ahmed and Dinye (2011) argue that Ghana's legislation has been the concurrent operation of the Act 462 and the CAP 84 with regard to the approval of plans. While the Act 462 provides for the approval of plans to done by the Assembly, the CAP 84 provides that this should be done by the Minister in charge of Town Planning. The operation of the two legislation side by side has led to a situation where smart developers capitalise on some contradictions between the two legislation to frustrate the efforts of local planning authorities in their stab to manage physical development. An experience which is common with countries using different legislation without clear separation of powers and responsibilities. Generally, it can be argued that no country practice planning without any legal barking, though several different frameworks are in existence; they are all meant to protect planning authorities in undertaking decisions governing planning and development.

Institutional Arrangement for Physical Development in Ghana

Despite the establishment of the Town and Country Planning Department and its associated institutions, Ghana was still struggling to meet its town planning vision of creating liveable communities. It was often being observed that planning was sensitive within the institutional frameworks it operates. It therefore became necessary to identify some of the institutions involved in physical planning in Ghana as stated in several studies such as Boamah et al. (2012), Yeboah et al. (2010), Pogbekuu (2007) and Ahmed and Dinye (2011). In Ghana, local governments (i.e. MMDAs) are mandated by law to undertake the task of spatial planning. The spatial planning powers exercised by MMDAs and the various types of instruments and tools they use to realise their mandate in principle should reflect visions, goals and objectives articulated by national and regional spatial development frameworks. The local plans would, consequently, shape the development of cities, towns and rural areas within their respective jurisdictions of local governments. The local governments in Ghana are mandated to formulate and implement spatial planning instruments in the form of District Spatial Development Frameworks to influence the distribution of activities at district-wide level, and structure plans and detailed subdivision schemes to determine the physical layout and land use configuration for cities, towns and villages within the district.

Following the normative sequence of spatial planning preceding physical development, various tools and policies are to be deployed to manage development in conformity with the policies of existing plans. While the plan-led approach established by law is considered ideal for the primary reason that proactive planning provides the potential benefits to mitigate the negative effects of what would otherwise become haphazard and uncoordinated development of settlements, it is important to bear in mind that in some instances, local spatial planning does include reactive interventions aimed at managing development that has not necessarily emerged according to a formal land use plan (Acheampong & Ibrahim, 2016). As part of efforts towards managing and controlling the growth of settlements in Ghana, the Land Use and Spatial Planning Authority was established to replace the Town and Country Planning Department. The Spatial Planning Authority is responsible for the land use planning and management of physical development and growth of human settlements to enhance social and economic activities and the well-being of people in Ghana. This is pursued through the design of structure plans, detailed planning schemes and the administration of planning standards to guide and ensure orderly growth and development. The department also provides various forms of planning services to public authorities and private developers.

In terms of land use planning and administration, the Lands Commission currently operates under the Lands Commission Act 1994 (Act 483). The Commission is responsible for the management of public lands and any lands vested in the president or the commission on behalf of the government. The Secretariat provides Land Title Registry with records of all transactions on a given land before a land title registration certificate can be granted. The commission has the responsibility to manage public lands and any lands vested in the president or the commission on behalf of the government and to advise the government, local and traditional authorities on policies for the development of specific areas to ensure coordination between individual pieces of land and development plans for the area. Some constraints of the Lands Commission Secretariat include inadequate skilled personnel, frequent political interference in its activities, inadequate logistics and support services, poor remuneration and low morale among staff of the Commission.

The chiefs and other opinion leaders contribute greatly to sharpen the built environment especially in relation to the part played in land acquisition and development. Pogbekuu (2007) argues that the majority of developers in Ghana acquire lands from chiefs who are the traditional land owners. However, some developers also obtain land from other sources such as individual speculators. Kasanga and Kotey (2001) observe that about 80% of lands in Ghana are owned by traditional authorities. This makes the customary authorities very important players in land use planning and management and thus underscores the need for collaboration between all players in physical development towards achieving one specific goal. These are some of the most important institutions involved in planning and enforcement of regulations. Though the structures are in place to carry out development, certain institutional factors hamper their efforts to perform effectively in Ghana.

Preparing Planning Schemes for Sustainable and Inclusive Physical Development in Ghana

After decade-long discourse on the need for reforms in planning practice, the Land Use Planning and Management Project between 2007 and 2010 under the aegis of Government of Ghana ushered in a New Spatial Planning System through the adoption of the Land Use and Spatial Planning Act, 925 of 2016. The new Act seeks to develop a coherent, streamlined and sustainable land use planning and management system which is decentralised and based on consultative and participatory approaches in order to manage effectively human settlements development (Acheampong, 2019, p. 48). Ultimately, this initiative has introduced critical reforms in spatial and land use planning in Ghana including the restructuring of the institutional arrangements for spatial planning such as the establishment of a Land Use and Spatial Planning Authority (LUSPA) and the institutionalisation of the three-tier system of spatial planning instruments. The intent and purpose of new spatial planning law as stated in the Act is:

> An Act to revise and consolidate the laws on land use and spatial planning, provide for sustainable development of land and human settlements through a decentralised planning system, ensure judicious use of land in order to improve quality of life, promote health and safety in respect of human settlements and to regulate national, regional, district and local spatial planning, and generally to provide for spatial aspects of socio economic development and for related matters (Land use and Spatial Planning Act [Act 925], 2016).

The Act thus delineates the scope and purpose of spatial planning by using the combined terms "land use and spatial planning" to suggest a deliberate attempt to institute a new tradition of integrated and multi-scale planning that delivers wider socio-economic and environmental development imperatives with the traditional design and regulatory function of town planning. Most importantly, it recognises that effective planning is a precondition for judicious use of scarce resources such as land (Acheampong, 2019, p. 50).

Another important feature of the new planning law is its definition of planning areas. As was previously discussed, the 1945 Town and Country Planning Ordinance (CAP 84) adopted a piecemeal and centralised procedure whereby only specific areas determined to qualify for planning through a legislative instrument received the benefits of planning. The new planning law, in contrast, abandons this procedure and instead, declares all areas in the country as potential planning areas, subject to the provisions of the Act. Specially, a planning area in the Land Use and Spatial Planning Act is defined as:

> The territory of Ghana as defined under the Constitution of the Republic of Ghana including the landmass, air space, sub-terrain territory, territorial waters and reclaimed lands shall be a planning area and subject to the planning system provided under this Act and other relevant laws (Land use and Spatial Planning Act [Act 925], 2016).

Prior to the reforms, the authority and competence for spatial planning were vested in the TCPD which has offices at the national, regional and district levels of public administration. This three-tier institutional set-up is maintained under the Land Use and Spatial Planning Act (Act 925), although the names and functions of the institutions, especially those at the national and regional levels have changed. Under the new spatial planning law, the Land Use and Spatial Planning Authority (LUSPA) has been established to replace the National Head Office of the TCPD. According to the Act, LUSPA is a body corporate with perpetual succession headed by a Chief Executive Officer appointed by the president. Below the national structure, at the regional level, the Regional Spatial Planning Committee replaces the Old Regional TCPD while the authority and competence of spatial planning at the local level is now vested in the District Planning Authority, which replaces the former District TCPD.

The main tool employed in SPs is zoning – the practice of defining broad land uses including residential, commercial, industrial, mixed-use areas, major open spaces, agricultural areas and areas for upgrading and regeneration. The alignment and corridors of major transportation routes, major water, sewerage and power networks and other key features for managing the effects of development are to be delineated in SPs. The final SP consists of maps showing the designated land uses and infrastructure networks, identifying which parts of the network will need upgrading, which are additional to the existing network and which areas need repair. According to the planning model guidelines, at the MMDA level, the basic zoning classification will be included in the plan, while a SP for a sector of a town or for smaller areas may provide an additional layer of zoning ordinances that provide further information on permissible types of development and densities, the height and form of the building, site lines and setbacks and even use of construction materials. Local plans should be prepared when needed and the uses of land must be in conformity with permitted uses of the land in the designated zoning classification as identified in the approved SP. The local plan is also supposed to identify open areas unsuitable for development, including land where the slope exceeds what is permissible for construction and water bodies, including floodplains (though the latter may be designated for recreational areas) and areas where existing trees are to be preserved or new trees planted. Local plans are the primary instruments of development management at the level of towns, neighborhoods and specific sites and are as such legally binding documents. This also implies that where local plans exist, planning authorities are required to grant development and building permits in strict adherence to the plan unless a proposal for rezoning or revision of the plan has been accepted and the existing plan revised accordingly to accommodate any new proposals.

The preparation of the local plan may be funded and initiated by the District Assemblies, District Physical Planning Department, land owners, central government and any group of persons whose interest is directly affected by the presence or absence of a local plan. Institutions authorised to prepare and approve local plans are manned by qualified persons with appropriate academic and professional qualifications. A planning team consisting of staff of the physical planning department, the works department and the district planning coordinating unit and land use planning consultants. Base maps should be prepared by qualified surveyors and Geographic Information System (GIS) specialist. Boamah et al. (2012) also indicate that development plans and proposals require approval by planning and local authorities before their implementation according to planning regulations. This has been reported to take unnecessary long period of time and thus delaying developments in most of the local authorities in Africa. In most cases, developers have had to go ahead with their developments with no regard for submitted plans and many of such developments (petrol filling stations for instances) have health and environmental consequences on the life of the society (UN Habitat, 2008). Furthermore, UN Habitat (2008) argue that political interference is not uncommon in the local authorities. Political interference in the urban development control system has limited the local authorities' ability to fully regulate and control development. Powerful government officials have been known to enforce approvals which do not meet the stipulated requirements. High demand for space has led some authorities to overlook the standards required for various uses and abuse of development control especially open spaces. Lack of occasional court interventions affect activities of enforcing development control. Gyampo (2008) and Yeboah and Obeng-Odoom (2010) concur that strong political influence affect the approving of permits in the Ghanaian context.

The above discussions have succinctly been summarised by McAuslan and Berrisford (2017) that "any of the urban legal problems in Africa today are caused by inappropriate legislation." For decades, African countries have used laws that were inappropriate to their contexts, their development pressures, their implementation capacity and their political environments. As a result, citizens and officials became adept at sidestepping the law and introducing their own approaches, which were innovative and practical but often also unlawful. No law is perfect. All countries need to fine-tune, amend or even scrap urban legal interventions from time to time. This has not happened in most African countries which is one reason current urban legal frameworks are outdated and inappropriate. To prevent this from happening in future, it is necessary to establish a system to track whether a new legislation is achieving its intended outcomes. This system must identify indicators to measure the impact of the new law; clarify who is responsible for monitoring and evaluating the outcomes of the law and include efficient, workable templates for reporting, especially by local government."

In recognition of the limitations of the linear spatial plans in Ghana, the new legislation adopts a three-tier planning system involving the preparation of Spatial Development Frameworks – an indicative plan showing visions of future development over a 15–20-year period – Structure Plans and

Local Plans with due diligence to self-organisation. This law presents a new way of encouraging greater participation and a bottom-up approach to planning. The institutional arrangements specified in the new spatial planning law clearly is an attempt to address the isolation of the TCPD at the level of MMDAs highlighted previously by making the district TCPD an integral part of the local governance system. However, the new arrangement appears to fail to addressing this problem. The Decentralization Act, which has not been amended, still maintains that TCPD is not one of its decentralised departments. Secondly, the old arrangement whereby district TCPD works for and under one sector Ministry while the head office is responsible to a different sector Ministry has not be addressed by recent reforms in spatial planning and the new spatial planning law. Thus, the ability of the new institutional arrangements to respond effectively to the almost overwhelming challenges of sustainable land use planning and management that confronts human settlements of varying sizes remains to be seen.

Ghana can therefore learn from similar examples from Nigeria and South Africa and learn from their precedence. The Federal Urban and Regional Planning Decree (1992, updated in 1999) of Nigeria introduced a three-tier system of urban planning. It sets out the respective powers and institutional arrangements for federal, state and local government. However, as of 2015 only Lagos State had managed to put in place the required institutions to effect the provisions of the law (Urbanisation Research Nigeria, 2015). In 16 years, only 1 out of 36 states was able to implement the new system (McAuslan & Berrisford, 2017). Previously in South Africa, provincial governments drafted urban and regional planning laws to regulate municipal land-development decisions. The South African courts increasingly pointed out that decision-making powers lay with local government. Accordingly draft provincial laws became thinner and cities' bylaws became much thicker. The interpretation of the constitution determines the degree of uniformity in urban legal procedures across the country. Consequently, at least in theory, instead of one set of procedures for each province, there is now a set of unique procedures for each municipality. That is to say that there has been the evolution of the understanding of the constitutional distribution of planning powers between national, provincial and local government (De Visser, 2015). In all these learnings, McAuslan and Berrisford (2017) advised, a completely centralised or completely decentralised system is never going to be optimal. For each country, there is a need to divide powers between different levels of government, as determined by a range of political, geographical and economic forces. It is mostly not helpful to allocate an individual power or function to one level of government entirely. It is idea that the different levels should check each other and ensure accountability in decision-making.

Conclusion

This chapter explored sustainable and inclusive physical development in Ghana with a focus on the legal and regulatory frameworks for physical development. The analysis underscores that achieving sustainable and inclusive physical development is often interrupted by challenges in application and enforcement mechanisms including legislative bottleneck, lack of public participation, inadequate institutional capacity, land acquisition process and corruption etc. Ghana's urban land use planning is oriented on the British town planning legislation. This colonial nature of Ghana's urban land use planning has largely been ineffective in planning, controlling and monitoring physical development due to their little to no relevance in addressing contemporary planning issues. There are contradictions in these legal and regulatory frameworks that are counterproductive to the country's long-term sustainable development vision of sustainable and inclusive physical development. The effect is the seemingly "no clear land use regulator" with suitable administrative framework and sufficient powers for enforcement; an experience common with countries using different legislation without clear separation of powers and responsibilities. This is compounded by placing planning institutions under different parent institutions. The chapter therefore recommends that local government institutions in Ghana effectively perform their mandate as land use regulators and improve the capacity of their physical planning departments to deliver their legislative mandates effectively. Also, there is the need to fine-tune, update and harmonise physical development legal and regulatory frameworks in Ghana to make them appropriate and fit for purpose by strengthening planning institutions and ensuring effective coordination and collaboration between and among them.

References

Acheampong R. A., & Ibrahim, A. (2016). One nation, two planning systems? Spatial planning and multilevel policy integration in Ghana: Mechanisms, challenges and the way forward. *Urban Forum*, 27(1), 1–18.

Acheampong, R. A. (2019). *The concept of spatial planning and the planning system. In spatial planning in Ghana, 11–13*. The Urban Book Series. Springer International Publishing.

Adarkwa, K. K. (2012). The changing face of Ghanaian Towns. *African Review of Economics and Finance*, 4(1), 1–29.

Ahmed, A., & Dinye, R. D. (2011). Urbanisation and the challenges of development controls in Ghana: A case study of Wa Township. *Journal of Sustainable Development in Africa*, 13(7), 210–235.

Amoateng, P., Cobbinah, P. B., & Owusu-Adade, K. (2013). Managing physical development in peri-urban areas of Kumasi, Ghana: A case of Abuakwa. *Journal of Urban and Environmental Engineering*, 7(1), 96–109.

Belsky, E. S., DuBroff, N., McCue, D., Harris, C., McCartney, S., & Molinsky, J. (2013). Advancing inclusive and sustainable urban development: Correcting planning failures and connecting to Capital Joint Center for Housing Studies of Harvard University.

Boamah, A. N., Gyimah C., & Nelson J. K. B. (2012). Challenges to the enforcement of development controls in the Wa municipality. *Habitat International*, 36(1), 136–142.

Damodaran, A., Jorgensen, K., & Schreurs, M. (2015). Sustainable cities – inclusive, Green and competitive. *Indo-German Expert Group on Green and Inclusive Economy Policy Paper*.

De Visser, J. (2015). Local law-making in Cape Town: A case study of the municipal planning by-law process. *UN-Habitat urban legal case studies*, 4. http://unhabitat.org/books/local-law-makingin-cape-town-a-case-study-of-the-municipalplanning-by-law-process-urban-legal-casestudies-volume-4/.

Diaw, K. Nnkya, T., & Watson V. (2002). Planning education in Sub-Saharan Africa: Responding to the demands of a changing context. *Planning Practice and Research*, 17(3), 337–348.

Fuseini, I. (2014). *Land use competition: Its implication for food security in peri-urban Tamale, Ghana*. Saarbrücken: Lambert Academic Publishing.

Fuseini, I., & Kemp, J. (2015). A review of spatial planning in Ghana's socio-economic development trajectory: A sustainable development perspective. *Land Use Policy*, 47(2015) 309–320.

Gyampo, R. (2008). Direct election of district chief executives and mayors – a tool for effective decentralization and political stability in Ghana. *Ghana Policy Journal*, 38, 70–92.

Kasanga, K., & Kotey, N. A. (2001). *Land management in Ghana: Building on tradition and modernity*. London: International Institute for Environment and Development, Russell Press.

Keeble, L. (1969). *Principles of town and country planning*. London: The Estate Gazette Limited.

Keeton R., & Nijhuis, S. (2019). Spatial challenges in contemporary African New Towns and potentials for alternative planning strategies. *International Planning Studies*, 24(3–4), 218–234.

Klopp, J. M., & Petretta, D. L. (2017). The urban Sustainable Development Goal: Indicators, Complexity and the Politics of Measuring Cities. *Cities*, 63, 92–97.

Krippendorff, K. (2004). *Content analysis: An introduction to its methodology*. Thousand Oaks: SAGE Publications.

Leyzerova, A., Sharovarova, E., & Alekhin, V. (2016). Sustainable strategies of urban planning. *International Conference on Industrial Engineering, ICIE Procedia Engineering* (150 pp.), 2055–2061

McAuslan, P., & Berrisford, S. (2017). *Reforming urban laws in Africa a practical guide*. African Centre for Cities (ACC), Cities Alliance, United Nations Human Settlements Programme (UN-Habitat) and Urban LandMark.

Miljkovic, Z. J., Crncevic, T., & Maric, I. (2012). Land use planning for sustainable development of peri-urban zones. *Spatium International Review, No. 26*, 15–22. Doi: 10.2298/SPATi228015Z.

Pogbekuu, E. B. (2007). *Land use planning as a tool for environmental management: A case of the tamale metropolis*. Unpublished MSc. Thesis Submitted to the

University of Cape Coast, Cape Coast, from www.academia.edu/ Accessed 20/02/2015.

Town and Country Planning (Amendment) Act. (1960). *Act 33 The Thirty-Third Act of the Parliament of the Republic of Ghana.*

Town and Country Planning Act. (1945). CAP 84. http://www.epa.gov.gh/ ghanalex/acts/Acts/TOWN%20AND%20COUNTRY%20PLANNING%2 0ACT,1945.pdf.

Town and Country Planning Act. (1958). *Act 30 The Thirtieth Act of the Parliament of Ghana.*

Town and Country Planning Division. (1958). *Accra. A Plan for the Town. The Report for the Minister of Housing.*

UK Parliament. (2016). *Homepage of the Parliament of the United Kingdom (UK).* New Towns. Retrieved from: http://www.parliament.uk/about/living-heritage.

United Nations Centre for Human Settlements. (2008). *Reassessment of Urban Planning and Development Regulations in African Cities. The City Agency of the United Nations United Nations Centre for Human Settlements (Habitat).* From URL: http://habitat.unchs.org/home.htm Accessed 05/06/2015.

United Nations Population Division. (2015). World Urbanization Prospects: The 2014 Revision. United nations Department of Economic and Social Affairs. New York (ST/ESA/SER.A/366). From http://esa.un.org/unpd/wup/ Accessed 06/09/2020.

Urbanisation Research Nigeria. (2015). Urban land, planning and governance systems in Nigeria. UKaid/ICFI. Report available at: urn.icfwebservices.com Accessed 31 October 2020.

Watson, V. (2016). Locating planning in the New Urban Agenda of the urban sustainable development goal. *Plan Theory, 15,* 435–448.

Yeboah, E., & Obeng-Odoom, F. (2010). We are not the only ones to Blame: District Assemblies' Perspectives on the State of Planning in Ghana. *Commonwealth Journal of Local Governance.* From http://epress.lib.uts.edu.au/ojs/index.php/cjlg Accessed 07/10/12.

11 Spatial Expression of Climate Change in Rapidly Urbanising City of Tamale, Ghana

Enoch Akwasi Kosoe,
Patrick Brandful Cobbinah, and
Joseph Nyaaba Akongbangre

Introduction

The two critical and interrelated urban environmental phenomena in the 21st century are urbanisation and climate change (IPCC, 2014; Uitto et al., 2017). Urbanisation is a major force of global environmental change and interconnected to urban climate change (While & Whitehead, 2013). The attending climate change consequences of rapid urbanisation include increased risk exposure for urban residents and vulnerabilities for urban biodiversity and its capacity to provide ecosystem services in urban areas (Cobbinah et al., 2019; Solecki & Marcotullio, 2013). According to the Intergovernmental Panel on Climate Change [IPCC] (2018), extreme weather events are more frequent and intense as a result of climate change. These impacts go beyond the physical boundaries of cities, across spatio-temporal scales, increasing risk of exposure and limiting residents' capacity to cope with critical susceptibilities. Both urbanisation and climate change are dominant in the modification of the profile of risks and vulnerabilities of cities.

The cost of climate change has far-reaching implications and no country is immune (Atapattu, 2016); even though the degree of impact varies (Addaney & Cobbinah, 2019). Climate change is no longer a distant problem (Tripathi & Mishra, 2017) as it presents challenges to the survival of inhabitants in every region. In Africa, urban planning is generally blamed for its failure to exert a positive influence on managing climate change impacts in urban areas because of, *inter alia*, the lack of focus on climate change issues (Cobbinah et al., 2019). Despite being the least urbanised region in the world, Africa has the highest urbanisation rate of 3% per annum (Kumssa et al., 2015). It is projected that more than 1.2 billion Africans will be residing in urban areas by the year 2050 (OECD/Sahel and West Africa Club, 2020). This rapid urbanisation can be explained by both the natural growth of the urban population and increasing rural-urban migration. Urbanisation, if properly managed and planned for, could be an engine for economic growth and industrialisation. However, without a proper policy in place and implementation strategy, it may contribute to

DOI: 10.4324/9781003181484-11

urban poverty, proliferation of slums, regional inequalities, and degradation of urban infrastructure and environment. Therefore, delivering the vision of sustainable development especially in African cities is intrinsically linked to taking a holistic view of climate change adaptation and resilience in relation to unplanned urbanisation.

Climate change remains one of the greatest development challenges confronting cities, particularly those in Africa, due to their limited capacity to prepare for and to cope with its effects (Owusu & Nursey-Bray, 2018). Climate change impacts in urban areas are expressed by the degree of vulnerability. Among the urban populations that are particularly vulnerable to climate-shocks and risks are those living in dangerous locations (such as floodplains) and lacking protective infrastructure as well as those living in poor quality housing in informal settlements. While climate change affects all urban residents, it is believed that the impacts fall disproportionately on residents of slums or informal settlements mostly located in hazardous urban space (see Cobbinah, 2021). This trend is worrying as urban areas in Sub-Saharan Africa (SSA) are predominately informal settlements and are home to about 427 million people and this is expected to double by 2030 (Cobbinah et al., 2019).

At the regional levels, different studies have been conducted to analyse trends of temperature and rainfall (e.g., del Rio et al., 2013; Salma et al., 2012; Zahid & Rasul, 2011). These studies indicate that temperature and rainfall have increased and varied respectively and are expected to intensify globally with severe impacts on urban areas across formal and informal settlements (Khan, 2012). In recent times, satellite remote sensing data have been used to analyse changes in rainfall and temperature. However, studies that analyse the spatial expression of rainfall and temperature changes in urbanising regions, particularly in Ghana, and the impacts of climate change on urban dwellings are rare. Understanding the role of urbanisation in climate change is critical for the production of effective climate change mitigation and adaptation measures (Romero-Lankao & Qin, 2011), promotion of sustainable urban environments and transition towards increased urban resilience (Solecki, 2012). Also, appreciating and acting on the interface of urbanisation and climate change is the most pressing challenge of the 21st Century (IPCC, 2014). According to Mutunga et al. (2012), there is a strong correlation between urban population growth and climate change and the consequence thereof on sustainable development even though they are addressed separately at policy and programme levels.

At the global level, two policy instruments are advanced to support urban areas to overcome the challenges of development: the sustainable development goals (SDGs) and the new urban agenda (NUA) (Valencia et al., 2019). The SDGs provide renewed hope for urban development and planning. The SDG 11, in particular, promotes inclusive, safe, resilient and sustainable cities. This is in recognition of the fact that more than half of the world's population lives in urban areas and climate change is disrupting global economies and affecting livelihoods. Compounded by the impacts of global pandemics such as COVID-19, climate change impacts are distressing informal and densely populated urban areas in Africa. On the other hand, the NUA in 2016 offered hope of commitment to promote urban sustainability (Valencia et al., 2019), even though it lacks a formal implementation framework (McPhearson et al., 2016). These policies provide both synergies and trade-offs necessary to propel cities towards designing adaptive plans for tackling climate change and related impacts in urban areas, particularly those in Africa.

This chapter therefore uses Tamale, a rapidly growing city in northern Ghana, as a case study to examine the relationship between climate change and rapid urbanisation and the resultant implications of this relationship for sustainable urban development. Specifically, the chapter uses satellite images and spatial data to analyse the spatial expression of the two main indicators of climate change and variation: rainfall and temperature, and the consequences of rapid urbanisation on land-use change. The implications of this analysis for the future of the city are discussed in the context of sustainable development. The chapter consists of five sections with the introduction being the first. Section two explores urban planning capacity to deal with climate change impacts in Ghana. Section three presents the study area and methodology used. In Section four, the results and discussion are presented. The conclusion to the chapter is presented in Section five.

Urban Planning and Climate Change: A Focus on Ghana

Urban planning and management remains a central theme towards achieving the SDGs, particularly Goals 11 (sustainable cities and communities) and 13 (climate action). Within the development literature, it is argued that a well-planned urban centre is one that can anticipate and withstand natural disasters (Saghir & Santoro, 2018). However, urban areas in Ghana, despite serving as centers of innovation and growth, are beset with problems such as poor environmental conditions, poor infrastructure and service delivery, and uncontrolled growth such that their capacity to produce sustainable development outcome is threatened (Fuseini & Kemp, 2015). These challenges, among others, arise from or are exacerbated by climate change (Saghir & Santoro, 2018). As urban areas in Ghana continue to sprawl, the impacts of natural disasters resulting from climate change, poor urban planning and development deficits continue to have detrimental consequences on human survival and national development. Although integrating climate change into urban planning remains an essential pathway in managing risks, the reality suggests otherwise (Cobbinah et al., 2019). Similarly, many urban areas across Africa are characterised by weak and dysfunctional urban planning regimes (see Osumanu & Akomgbangre, 2020). For instance, scholarly opinion in Ghana (see Darkwah, 2016) indicates that weak urban planning regimes are producing and unleashing unguided urban growth across major cities and further contributing to increased climate risk. Ahmed et al. (2020) characterised Ghana's urban planning experience as planning chasing physical development. Unfortunately, the results have not been positive as sporadic spatial development has become widespread, infrastructure service provision is lacking, and climate change impacts are increasing in severity.

Studies (e.g. Cobbinah et al., 2017) show that the colliding force of climate change and unplanned urbanisation is threatening urban survival in Ghana. Nevertheless, little is known about how urban planning in the context of policy and practice is responding to the dual threats of climate change and urbanisation. Although some previous studies have focused on urban planning and climate change in developed countries (Bulkeley et al., 2011), it remains to be established whether urban planning can be considered as a potential pathway for managing these climate impacts in urbanising regions of Africa. In Ghana, the many policies, plans, and programmes aimed at assessing the spatial impacts of climate change on urban planning either show marginal success or are ineffective. Cobbinah (2017) argues that while existing planning legislation make provisions for inclusive approach to urban planning in Ghana, the situation is different in practice. Implementation challenges (e.g., inadequate funds, poor enforcement of planning laws, logistics and weak institutional capacity) have inhibited the integration of climate change issues into urban plans at both local and national levels. It is within this background that this chapter is based, particularly to understand how the interaction between urbanisation and climate change is shaping the future of African cities in general and Ghanaian cities in particular.

Study Area and Research Methods

Study Setting

This chapter uses Tamale, the regional capital of the Northern Region of Ghana, as a case study, to draw implications of the combined effects of urbanisation and climate change, and the spatial expression of these changes. Tamale is host to two local administrative assemblies: the Tamale Metropolitan Assembly and Sagnarigu District Assembly. The city has a total land size of 646.90180 km^2 (GSS, 2014). As the largest urban area in northern Ghana, Tamale has the third highest annual population growth rate after Accra and Kumasi Metropolitan Areas (Fuseini et al., 2017). The rainy season in the city occurs between May and November each year, when the Inter-Tropical Convergence Zone (ITCZ) or Inter Tropical Discontinuity (ITD) is in its northern position, with the prevailing moist south-westerly winds over the region. Tamale experiences severe north-easterly winds (*Harmattan*) in the dry season from November to February. In the rainy season, residents experience high humidity and slight sunshine, with heavy thunder storms, compared to the dry season which is characterised by dry harmattan winds and warming temperatures (GSS, 2014; Figure 11.1).

More recently, there is either prolonged dry season and a short but intense rainy season or the reverse. Tamale has unique characteristics in terms of history of, and vulnerability to climate-related events (e.g. flooding). Similarly, the city's rapid population growth and location as the traversing point for migrants, coupled with data availability and resource constraints (Cobbinah & Kosoe, 2019) make it appropriate for the exploration of climate and urbanization issues. Tamale has attracted migrants from the impoverished rural areas of northern Ghana and has experienced annual urban growth rate of 4% during the past decade (GSS, 2014). This rapid urbanisation has resulted in the competition for land use amidst the challenges for urban infrastructure and service provision. As the city grows, climate variability and change, manifested in the form of unpredictable rainfall patterns and high temperatures, continue to pose considerable threat. This chapter therefore focused on the the city of Tamale to further highlight climate change impacts and the implications on urban sustainability.

Research Methods

The study adopted a qualitative research approach to data collection and presentation. Data were obtained from both primary and secondary sources. The secondary data included climatic data (1986–2019) from the Ghana Meteorological Agency and National Disaster Management Organisation. Landsat images for 2000 (Enhance Thematic Mapper) and 2018 (Operational Land Imager) covering Tamale Urban (Path 194 Row 054) were downloaded from United States Geological Survey Department (USGS.gov) using the glovis web application. Training samples for the 2000 image were collected from true color high resolution google earth images and Bing Virtual Earth. However, training samples 2018 OLI were collected from the field using hand held GPS receiver.

Microsoft-excel was used to compute the average temperature and rainfall from 1986 to 2019. The python – a programming tool – was used to plot the various graphs used in the chapter. The study used Erdas Imagine 2015 to produce Land Cover/Land Use Maps for Tamale for the years 2000 and 2018. Administrative Vector Data of Tamale was acquired from Survey and Mapping Department of Ghana Lands Commission and used as the Region of Interest (ROI) to subset the images from the bigger scene downloaded. A supervised Classification based on the Maximum likelihood classifier was used to classify the images to four Land Cover/Land Use classes. Thus, Open Savannah vegetation; Close Savannah Vegetation, Built-Up and Water Bodies were classified. The classified

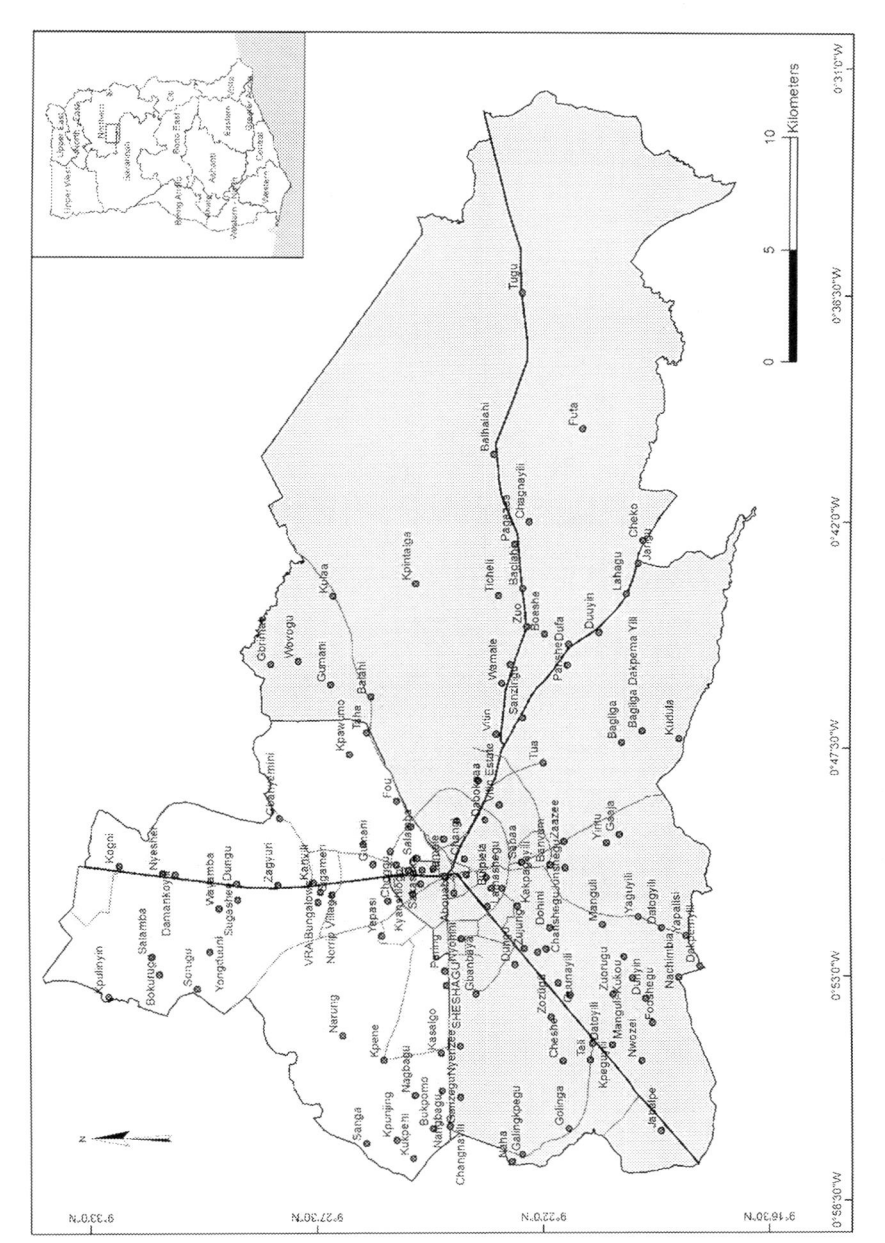

Figure 11.1 Geographical location of Tamale.

Table 11.1 Satellite images information

Date	Path	Row	Satellite	Sensor	Band	Coordinate System
23 February 2018	194	054	Landsat 8	Operational Land Image	10, 5, 4	UTM, WGS84
30 March 2000	194	054	Landsat 7	Enhanced Thematic Mapper	6, 4, 3	UTM, WGS84

Source: United States Geological Survey Department (USGS.gov).

images were exported into ArcMap 10.4.1 for final Land Cover/land Use maps composition. Table 11.1 provides detailed information of the satellite images used for the study.

To complement the spatial and secondary data, agency interviews with representatives of four institutions in Tamale were conducted to provide an understanding and explanation of the changing patterns of climate change and urbanisation influence in the city. These agencies included: Physical Planning Department of the Tamale Metropolitan Assembly, the Regional Town and Country Planning Department, National Disaster Management Organisation (NADMO) and the Ghana Meteorological Service. Representatives from these organisations were interviewed on the directions of urban growth of the city, climate vulnerable zones and initiatives to address climate change and urbanisation challenges. NVIVO 10 software programme was used to analyse the interview transcripts.

Results and Discussion

This section presents the findings from the study. It is organised into three sections: first, analysis of the influence of urbanisation on urban sustainability through land use/cover changes is presented. Second, an analysis of climate change evidence and the consequences thereof in the case study area is presented. Third, agency efforts and responses to managing climate change impacts and addressing rapid urbanisation are presented.

Influence of Urbanisation on Urban Sustainability: Land Use/Cover Analysis

Literature on urban studies in Ghana indicates that urban areas are experiencing rapid urbanisation with major cities including Tamale, expanding beyond their administrative boundaries. Similarly, these cities are faced with severe impacts of climate change especially flood and drought events. This situation is particularly worrying in Tamale given the city's strategic location in the northern part of Ghana, fueling rural-urban migration from neighbouring districts and regions, coupled with its distinctive climatic characteristics. To

Table 11.2 Land use/ cover changes

Land Use/ Cover	2000		2018		Change	Percent Change	Annual Rate of Change
	Ha	%	Ha	%			
Open Savannah	46,522.62	54.84	63,874.71	75.29	17,352.09	37.30	2.07
Close Savannah	35,038.79	41.30	14,526.81	17.12	−20,511.98	−58.54	−3.25
Water Body	96.69	0.11	37.26	0.04	−59.43	−61.46	−3.41
Built up Area	3,176.17	3.74	6,395.49	7.54	3,219.32	101.36	5.63
Sum	84,834.27		84,834.27				

appreciate the extent of influence of urbanisation on urban sustainability of the city, spatial data were used to assess the land use/cover changes over a nearly 20-year period. Findings from the satellite image analysis show that the built-up/bare land in Tamale expanded by 3219.39 ha between 2000 and 2018 from 3176.1 ha to 6395.49 ha. This is an indication that the built-up area more than doubled (101.36%) between 2000 and 2018 (see Table 11.2 and Figure 11.2). The increase in the built-up area mostly resulted from the conversion of the urban environmental resources including green spaces (close savannah), and water bodies. Finding answers to the rapid decline of urban environmental resources in less than two decades, agency interview data show that rapid population growth, characterised by increased rural-urban migration and natural increase between 2000 and 2018 contributed to demand for land for residential and related activities leading to an increase in the built-up area. With a population of 205,000 in 2000, Tamale's population nearly tripled by 2018, increasing to 582,000 in 2018 (Figure 11.3). Given that the rapid population growth of the city is commensurate with the increase in built-up area, it may perhaps be reasonable to argue that changes in the spatial extent of Tamale are largely dependent on population growth.

While rapid urbanisation was identified by the agency representatives as a leading cause of increase in built-up areas, the document review identified other important contributory factors: customary land governance system contributing to unregulated urban growth; religion and religiosity leading to non-adherence to planning requirements; weak planning systems distorting effective planning and management of the cities; and unregulated mushrooming of informal settlements contributing to sporadic growth of the city. Expectedly, while the population is growing rapidly (see Figure 11.3), the rate of urban expansion (built-up area) remains a reflection of the population dynamics. Table 11.2 shows how this pattern of urban growth threatens the ecological integrity of Tamale, which predisposes the city to increased climate risk.

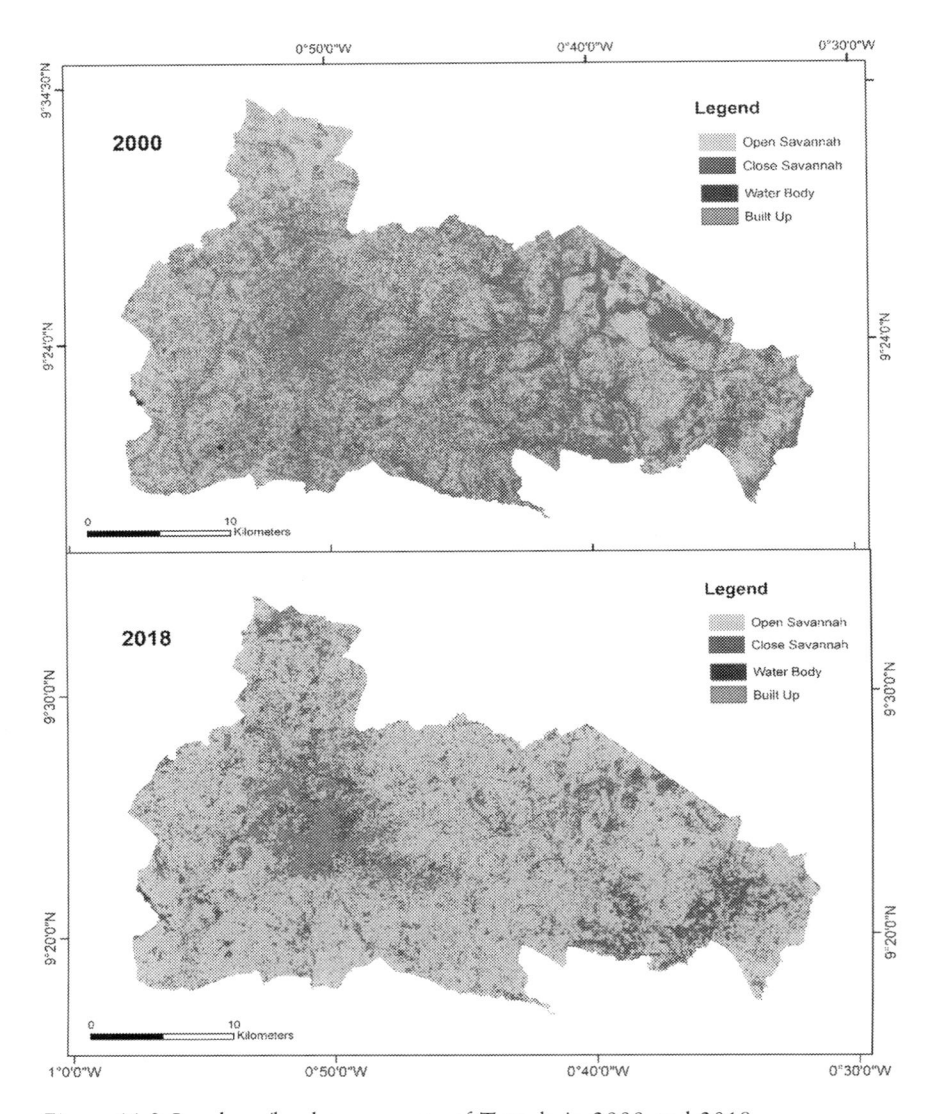

Figure 11.2 Land use/land cover maps of Tamale in 2000 and 2018.

Finding Evidence of Climate Change: Temperature and Rainfall Dynamics

As illustrated in Figures 11.4 and 11.5, there is evidence of climate change in Tamale with temperature patterns between 1987 and 2016 rising. The analysis of temperature data obtained from the Ghana Metrological Agency

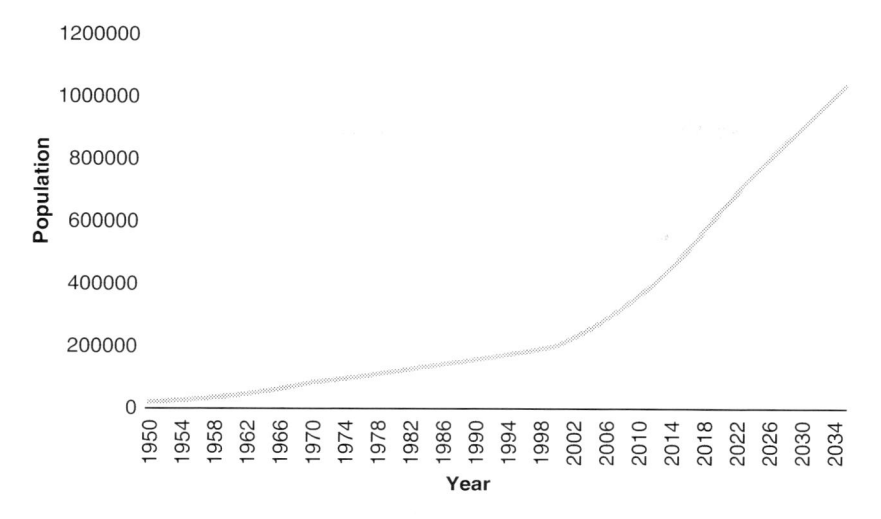

Figure 11.3 Actual and projected population growth (1950–2035).

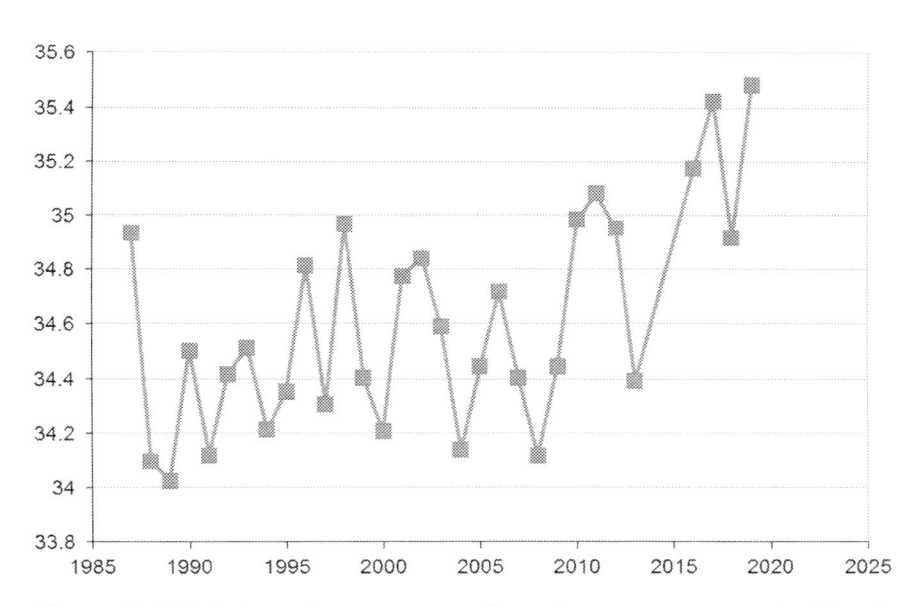

Figure 11.4 Variation of average annual maximum temperature in Tamale (1987–2019).

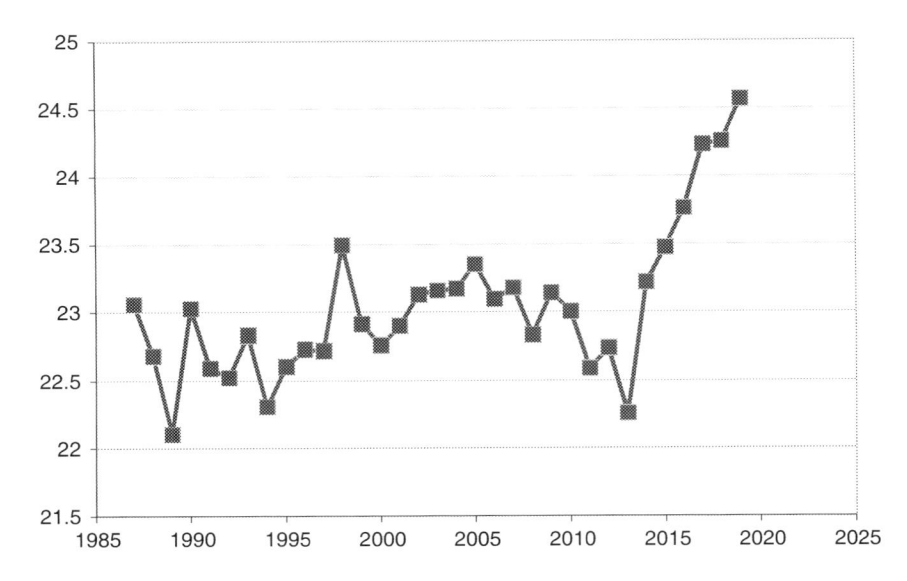

Figure 11.5 Variation of average annual minimum temperature in Tamale (1987–2019).

in Tamale over the past 30 years shows an erratic and a gradual increase in both the mean maximum and mean minimum temperatures.

Although there is an increasing trend in the average temperature, the data were highly variable. For instance, the year 2019 recorded the highest mean maximum temperature of 35.48°C whilst the year 1989 recorded the lowest mean maximum temperature of 34.02°C (see Figure 11.4). In addition, the highest mean minimum temperature of 24.56°C was recorded in the year 2019, whereas the lowest mean minimum temperature of 22.10°C was recorded in the year 1989 (see Figure 11.5). However, a careful look at Figure 11.5, reveals a steady rise in the mean minimum temperature for six years (2014 – 23.21°C; 2015 – 23.47°C; 2016 – 23.76°C; 2017 – 24.23°C; 2018 – 24.25°C; and 2019 – 24.56°C).

The rainfall data obtained from the Ghana Meteorological Agency in Tamale indicated the annual rainfall has been erratic, with the years 1991 (1579.8 mm), 1989 (1427.5 mm) and 1999 (1382.3 mm) recording the highest rainfall between 1986 and 2019. The lowest annual rainfall was recorded in the years 1992 (695.3 mm) and 2017 (696.6 mm). In addition, after the 1991 highest annual rainfall, a general trend of decreasing annual rainfall was observed (see Figure 11.6).

These changes in the meteorological data were further compared with perceptions and experiences of agency officials in an interview based on the research methodology. Related findings in terms of unpredictable precipitation patterns and warming temperatures and their associated

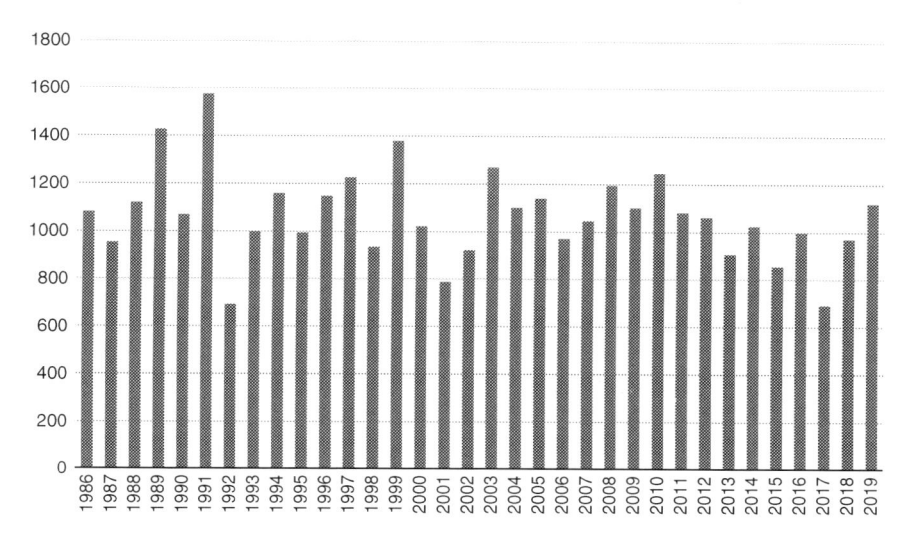

Figure 11.6 Annual rainfall variation over Tamale from 1986–2019.

consequences on urban planning and management were reported and extensively discussed by the agency officials during the interview conversations. Although the agency officials admitted that response to climate change in the city has not been encouraging, they were able to express and describe how changing weather patterns have impacted the functionality of the city. The interview data show that all the agency officials consider erratic rainfall pattern resulting in unexpected flood events as an evidence of changing weather patterns. There were others who mentioned increasing trend of warming as an indication of climate change. Exploring these issues further, the agency official from the Ghana Meteorological Service Department explained that weather patterns in the city, particularly rainfall, were easily forecasted with a high level of certainty in the past (in the mid-1950s to late 1980s), a situation which was important in planning and managing the city, especially its informal socio-economic activities and environmental resources. The official from the Ghana Meteorological Service Department commented that:

> … I have worked here for a very long time (over 20 years) and our reports (weather) have been useful for not only the city but farmers in the villages too but now, we can't forecast with certainty again as we used to, because it is very difficult, for example, to predict when the rainy season will start and end ….

Additionally, the agency officials from the Physical Planning Department mentioned rapid decline in urban environmental resources (e.g. water resources, green spaces) as an evidence of changing weather patterns. Although decline in urban environmental resources, occurring in the city of Tamale, is a result of pressures from rapid urbanisation and inefficient planning systems, the agency official reported that, recent cases of bushfires and droughts, coupled with rapid depletion of green spaces are due to changing weather patterns in terms of unpredictable precipitation and rising temperatures. As a consequence, the agency officials reported a decreasing trend of urban parks and open spaces and reduced availability of water resources (e.g. streams) in the city.

As climate change and rapid urbanisation continue to take their toll on the urban planning and management of the city of Tamale, the study findings suggest there are concerns amongst the agency officials about the certainty of the urban future in relation to addressing flood and drought events and loss of urban environmental resources. Given that the management of the city is plagued with many challenges including poor urban planning and management practices, agency officials indicated that it would only take providence to ensure the survival and sustainable functioning of the city should the current trend of changing weather patterns and unplanned urbanisation persists.

Agency Efforts and Responses Towards Urbanisation and Climate Change in Tamale

The agency officials identified community sensitisation programmes, tree planting exercises, and capacity building on climate change as ongoing responses and initiatives to addressing climate change and urbanisation challenges in the city. In relation to community sensitisation, all agency respondents reported an increasing trend of community sensitisation programmes. These programmes included awareness creation on flood and drought events via local community groups and media. With rapid expansion of the city and frequent climate events, all the agency respondents identified and considered community sensitisation programmes as the major initiative to support local adaptation efforts and manage pressures of urbanisation, particularly on the urban environmental resources. The agency interview data indicated that there has been a considerable engagement by city planning and management institutions in providing awareness at the local community level. However, some agency officials expressed concerns about the limited engagement of traditional and religious leaders of the local communities in the city in the sensitisation efforts. Although this limited local leadership engagement may not directly constrain the sensitisation success, the agency respondents claimed that the unplanned expansion and destruction of environmental resources in the city aredue largely to limited engagement of traditional and religious leaders. The NADMO official explained that:

... Everyone in this city (Tamale) knows it is a traditional city ... Residents respect and obey their traditional and religious leaders more than government officials ... So for me, I feel that we have not engaged adequately with these community leaders in our effort to make the city resilient and adaptable to environmental pressures. Yes, we've been using social and traditional media and sometimes community meetings to create awareness of climate change, but we need to involve the leaders more, in order to realize better outcomes ...

This finding supports those of other studies (e.g. Cobbinah, 2017; Osumanu & Akomgbangre, 2020) on weak urban planning and management regimes and their consequences on urban functionality. In addition to poor local leadership engagement, the agency interview findings revealed that climate change and urbanisation initiative of urban tree planting is hindered due to limited support from the residents. The agency respondents claimed that because the local leadership is not promoting the tree planting initiative, many residents do not consider it to be important and therefore are mostly not supportive. As a consequence, although this initiative has been ongoing for years, there is limited evidence of success as the land use/cover analysis shows rapid decline in urban green spaces. Though research indicates that rapid depletion of urban environmental resources in Tamale and many other cities in Ghana is a result of human population increase, weak urban planning response and climate change (Cobbinah & Kosoe, 2019; Fuseini et al., 2017), the agency respondents believed limited local leadership engagement is inherently fundamental to the changing weather patterns, rapid depletion of urban environmental resources and unplanned expansion of the city. It can be expected that the limited local leadership and unplanned destruction of urban environmental resources in the face of rapid urbanisation may further hamper agency initiatives to address the damaging impacts of climate change, especially flood events.

As a result of the poor local leadership involvement in urbanisation and climate change issues, the agency interview findings show there is an increasing number of agencies who are improving their traditional initiatives of community sensitisation and tree planting to capacity building. The majority of the agency respondents mentioned capacity building programmes for their staff to understand the complexity of climate change and urbanisation and to improve their response mechanisms including collaborating with local leadership groups. Given that the city of Tamale is the major metropolitan region in northern Ghana, the agency officials claimed that the challenges of unplanned urbanisation and the complexity of changing weather patterns have necessitated staff capacity building in the areas of community mobilisation and training; firefighting volunteering; workshops for all divisional chiefs on anti-bush fire campaign and prevention; Community-based Extension Agents (CBEAs) training to sustain farmer education/adoption of soil conservation technologies, including climate-smart strategy; training on basic concepts of climate change and disaster risk reduction for heads of decentralised departments in the city; training of communities on disaster prevention/early warning action system and resourcing them with logistics to operate; and constitution/animation of the city's disaster management teams and making them functional.

Agency respondents' capacity building responses and initiatives to address impacts of climate change and urbanisation were consistent with those reported in the literature (Chen et al., 2011; Cobbinah, 2017). For example, Cobbinah (2017) reported that Ghana has impressive legislation, policies and institutional structures to advance the production of functional urban spaces, yet implementation of planning and management decisions remain a hurdle. Thus, while it is interesting to note that planning and management agencies in Tamale are developing and proposing initiatives to address the impacts of climate change and urbanisation, the experience of poor implementation across the Ghanaian urban space raises doubts about the sustainability and effectiveness of these capacity building initiatives.

In discussing the sustainability and effectiveness of agency initiatives and responses, respondents were asked to identify major challenges limiting the realisation of their responses. As earlier mentioned, this question was important, considering that Ghanaian cities have a track record of poor implementation of planning decisions. The respondents identified the following as major challenges to their effort to manage the impacts of climate change and urbanisation: limited consideration of climate change and urbanisation issues in development plans and budgetary allocations; climate change policies as a development paradigm is yet to be embraced in the city; limited staff knowledge on the integration of climate change into planning practice; and coordinated institutional set up is yet to establish a management structure for formulation and implementation of climate change programmes. The Town and Country Planning official explained that:

> … Tamale is developing very rapidly and today; it is one of the major cities in Ghana … the reality of managing the rapidly expanding city with diverse populations is a great challenge. And unfortunately, climate change here is making things worse. As you may have read, Tamale has development and spatial plans but we are also behind schedule with implementation … the challenges are enormous ….

The agency respondents recognised the centrality of the city in the northern part of Ghana as encouraging migration which is compounding the already weak institutional mechanisms. They also maintained that their initiatives are hampered by climate change impacts, lending credence to Cobbinah's (2017) claim that despite the availability of planning regiments in Ghanaian cities, evidence on the ground suggests otherwise. In this case, it is reasonable to argue that the management initiatives outlined by the agencies may not be achieved, should the current weak planning system persist.

Conclusion

Although present and future impacts of unplanned urbanisation and climate change are widely reported, there is evidence from this chapter that current impacts are becoming more severe on growing cities in Africa. Both land use/cover analysis and meteorological data supported by agency experiences, perspectives and actions show that urbanisation and climate change are negatively impacting the natural environment and functionality of the city of Tamale. With limited urban planning and management interventions, Tamale is exposed and affected by uncharacteristically rapid urban population growth and unplanned spatial expansion as well as extreme and unpredictable weather events. Urban environmental resources – regarded as bastions and lungs of cities – are increasingly being threatened due to unplanned urbanisation contributing to haphazard urban development and changing weather patterns causing flash floods as well as occasional droughts and bushfires.

The population of Tamale has more than doubled between 2000 and 2018, mostly resulting from rural-urban transfers (see Figure 11.3). This demonstrates the rate of urban population growth in the city. This chapter has shown that this rate of urban population growth is accompanied by unprecedented increase in spatial expansion. The increase in the spatial extent (built-up area) of Tamale is twice the growth in urban population. While this phenomenon can be assumed to be a response to population growth, this chapter has revealed that poor planning and management of the city has contributed to uncontrolled and unplanned expansion of the city. More concerning is the contribution of this uncontrolled urban expansion to climate change impacts. Findings show that many of the urban environmental resources, especially green spaces and water bodies, have been depleted due to encroachment by developers. This situation has fueled climate change impacts of flooding and drought conditions in the city. The findings show gradual increase in both average minimum and maximum temperatures in the city over the past 30 years while rainfall remains highly variable. Evidence from this chapter confirms the views by other researchers and international organisations that rapid urbanisation and climate change are already threatening the survival of cities in developing countries, particularly in the world's most vulnerable regions (e.g., Cobbinah, 2021; Cobbinah & Addaney, 2019; IPCC, 2014).

Across the city of Tamale, agency responses and initiatives to unplanned urbanisation and changing weather patterns show that planning and management agencies are struggling to cope with urbanisation pressures and climate change impacts. Common agency responses and initiatives include increasing community sensitisation, facilitating tree planting efforts and developing capacity of institutions and local communities. While these responses and initiatives appear to be useful for restricting unplanned growth, conscientising local communities, and stimulating local commitment, they are largely ad-hoc, uncoordinated and with limited local community leadership involvement. This chapter shows that immediate support to strengthen planning and management institutions and encourage local communities to commit to, and engage in urban planning and climate change management interventions is urgent and tenable.

This chapter recommends strengthening of urban planning and management agencies in the city by the government in terms of logistics and personnel. This will improve the visibility of the agencies in the city in terms of addressing urbanisation and climate change challenges as well as promoting collaboration and coordination among the various agencies. Another important finding from this chapter relates to the limited involvement of local community leadership in planning initiatives. In response, this chapter recommends strong and improved relationship and engagement between planning and management agencies and local community leadership. Where possible, these local leaders should be involved in planning and management decisions and be regarded as channels of implementing planning decisions. In this regard, residents are more inclined to embrace and support planning decisions considering that their leaders are involved. However, research into the role and importance of local culture has also become an obvious area of consideration to help planning and management agencies to effectively deliver sustainable and adaptable urbanisation and climate change outcomes.

References

Addaney, M., & Cobbinah, P. B. (2019). Climate change, urban planning and sustainable development in Africa: The difference worth appreciating. In Cobbinah, P. B., & Addaney, M. (Eds.), *The geography of climate change adaptation in urban Africa*. Cham: Palgrave Macmillan.

Cobbinah, P. B., & Addaney, M. (eds.) (2019). *The Geography of Climate Change Adaptation in Urban Africa*. Cham: Palgrave Macmillan.

Ahmed A., Korah P. I., Dongzagla A., Nunbogu A. M., Niminga-Beka R., Kuusaana E. D., & Abubakari Z. (2020). City profile: Wa, Ghana. *Cities*, 97(2020), 102524

Atapattu, S. A. (2016). *Human rights approaches to climate change: Challenges and opportunities*. New York and London: Routledge.

Bulkeley, H., Schroeder, H., Janda, K., Zhao, J., Armstrong, A., Chu, S. Y., et al. (2011, June). *The role of institutions, governance and urban planning. Cities and climate change responding to an urgent agenda*(pp. 125–159).

Chen, J., Li, Q., Niu, J., & Sun, L. (2011). Regional climate change and local urbanisation effects on weather variables in Southeast China. *Stochastic Environmental Research and Risk Assessment*, 25(4), 555–565.

Cobbinah, P. B. (2017). Managing cities and resolving conflicts: Local people's attitudes towards urban planning in Kumasi, Ghana. *Land Use Policy*, 68, 222–231.

Cobbinah, P. B. (2021). Urban resilience in climate change hotspot. *Land Use Policy*, *100*, 104948.

Cobbinah, P. B., Asibey, M. O., Opoku-Gyamfi, M., & Peprah, C. (2019). Urban planning and climate change in Ghana. *Journal of Urban Management*. doi: 10.1016/j.jum.2019.02.002

Cobbinah, P. B., & Kosoe, E. A. (2019). Urban residents and communities responses to climate change impacts in Tamale, Ghana. In Cobbinah, P. B. & Addaney M. (Eds.), *The geography of climate change adaptation in urban Africa*. Palgrave Macmillan, Springer Nature Switzerland AG.

Cobbinah, P. B., Poku-Boansi, M., & Peprah, C. (2017). Urban environmental problems in Ghana. *Environmental Development*, *23*, 33–46.

Darkwah, R. M. (2016). *An analysis of urban resilience in selected communities in Kumasi and its Environs. A thesis submitted for the degree of Master of Science at the Department of Planning, Kwame Nkrumah University of Science and Technology Kumasi*. Retrieved from http://ir.knust.edy.gh/bitstream/123456789/9583/1/RHODA%20MENSAH%20DARKWAH.pdf Accessed September 2020.

del Rio, S., M. Anjum Iqbal, A. Cano-Ortiz, L. Herrero, A. Hassan, & A. Penas. (2013). Recent mean temperature trends in Pakistan and links with teleconnection patterns. *International Journal of Climatology*, *33*(2), 277–290. doi: 10.1002/joc.3423

Fuseini, I., & Kemp, J. (2015). A review of spatial planning in Ghana's socioeconomic development trajectory: A sustainable development perspective. *Land Use Policy*, *47*, 309–320. doi: 10.1016/j.landusepol.2015.04.020

Fuseini, I., Yaro, J. A., & Yiran, G. A. B. (2017). City profile: Tamale, Ghana. *Cities*, *60*, 64–74. doi: 10.1016/j.cities.2016.07.010

Ghana Statistical Service, GSS. (2014). *2010 population and housing census: District analytical report, Kumasi metropolitan*. Accra: Ghana Statistical Service

IPCC (Intergovernmental Panel on Climate Change). (2014). Climate change 2014: Impacts, adaptation, and vulnerability. Accessed 03/03/2014. http://ipcc-wg2.gov/AR5/images/uploads/IPCC_WG2AR5_SPM_Approved.pdf

Khan, A. Z. (2012). Climate change: Cause and effect. *Journal of Environment and Earth Science*, *2*(4), 48–53.

Kumssa, A., Mosha, A. C., Mbeche, I. M., & Njeru, E. H. N. (2015). Climate change and urban development in Africa. In Leal Filho, W. (Eds.), *Handbook of climate change adaptation*, 215–226. doi: 10.1007/978-3-642-38670-1_8

McPhearson, T., Parnell, S., Simon, D., Gaffney, O., Elmqvist, T., Bai, X., Roberts, D., & Revi, A. (2016). Scientists must have a say in the future of cities. *Nature*, *538*, 165–166.

Mutunga, C., Zulu, E., & De Souza, R. (2012). *Population dynamics, climate change, and sustainable development in Africa*. Nairobi, Kenya: AFIDEP. See http://www.afidep.org/images/downloads/pai_afidep_regional_reportsept2012.pdf

OECD/Sahel and West Africa Club. (2020). *Africa's urban dynamics 2020: Africapolis, mappingg a new urban geography*. Paris: OECD Publishing. doi: 10.1787/227f2b95-en

Osumanu, I. K., & Akomgbangre, J. N. (2020). A growing city: Patterns and ramifications of urban change in Wa, Ghana. *Spatial Information Research*. doi: 10.1007/s41324-020-00313-1.

Owusu, M., & Nursey-Bray, M. (2018). Socio-economic and institutional drivers of vulnerability to climate change in urban slums: The case of Accra, Ghana. *Climate and Development*. doi: 10.1080/17565529.2018.1532870.

Romero-Lankao, P., & Qin, H. (2011). Conceptualizing urban vulnerability to global climate change and environmental change. *Current Opinion in Environmental Sustainability*, *3*, 142–149.

Saghir, J., & Santoro, J. (2018). *Urbanisation in Sub-Saharan Africa: Meeting Challenges by Bridging Stakeholders* (Project on Prosperity and Development). Washington, D.C.: Center for Strategic and International Studies.

Salma, S., Shah M., & Rehman S. (2012). Rainfall Trends in Different Climate Zones of Pakistan. *Pakistan Journal of Meteorology*, *9*, 17.

Solecki, W. (2012). Moving toward urban sustainability: Using lessons and legacies of the past. In F. Zeman (Ed.), *Metropolitan sustainability: Understanding and improving the urban environment*. Oxford: Woodhead Publishing.

Solecki W., & Marcotullio P. J. (2013). Climate Change and Urban Biodiversity Vulnerability. In Elmqvist T. et al. (Eds.), *Urbanisation, biodiversity and ecosystem services: Challenges* and opportunities. Dordrecht: Springer.

Tripathi, A., & Mishra, A. K. (2017). Knowledge and passive adaptation to climate change: An example from Indian farmers. *Climate Risk Management*. doi: 10.1016/j.crm.2016.11.002.

Uitto, J. I., Puri, J., & Van den Berg, R. D. (Eds.). (2017). *Evaluating climate change action for sustainable development*. Cham: Springer Nature.

Valencia, C. S., Simon, D., Croese, S., Nordqvist, J., Oloko, M., Sharma, T., Buck, N. T., & Versace, I. (2019). Adapting the sustainable development goals and the new urban agenda to the city level: Initial reflections from a comparative research project. *International Journal of Urban Sustainable Development*, *11*(1), 4–23.

While, A., & Whitehead, M. (2013). Cities, urbanisation and climate change. *Urban Studies*, *50*(Special Issue), 1325–1331.

Zahid, M., & G. Rasul. (2011). Frequency of extreme temperature and precipitation events in Pakistan 1965–2009. *Sciences International* (Lahore), *23*(4), 313–319.

12 Planning for Sustainable Metro Express in Mauritius

Roopanand Mahadew, Michael Addaney, and Patrick Brandful Cobbinah

Introduction

African countries are faced with inefficient transport systems and infrastructure in addition to poor spatial planning, unplanned urbanisation, increased poverty and climate change risk. In fact, the importance of a purposeful infrastructure investment continues to be a recurring leitmotif in many discussions on Africa's urban development challenge. Although there is evidence of some infrastructural development programmes and policy schemes implemented over the past decades across the continent, significant infrastructure deficit remains. According to Popova (2017), Africa's infrastructure situation has two legs, namely, social infrastructure and economic/production infrastructure. The social infrastructure entails the common subsystems of healthcare, education, culture, tourism, etc., while the economic infrastructure comprises transport and transportation systems, telecommunication, electrical grid, water supply system, bridges, roads, etc. (Popova, 2017). Within these two legs of infrastructural shortfall, it is unsurprising that an estimated 60% of Africa's population lack access to these basic infrastructure systems (United Nations, 2015). Unfortunately, this situation undermines the continent's efforts towards achieving the UN sustainable development goals (SDGs) especially those relating to inclusive socio-economic development.

Sub-Saharan Africa is emerging as the fastest urbanising region with a population expected to be around 1.5–2 billion by 2050 (Ndebele et al., 2018). This rapid urbanisation aggravates the continent's urban development challenges. For instance, Africa's urban populations is projected to be growing at an average rate of between 4% and 5% annually, and thus heightens the demand for sophisticated infrastructure, particularly those relating to urban transport services, facilities and space (Pirie, 2013). The rapidly transforming African continent unquestionably presents new challenges to policy makers, governments, researchers and international organisations, as well as reinforces the need for a changing paradigm built on initiatives designed to facilitate and promote inclusive urban development. In this sense, public investment in various transport infrastructure has taken

DOI: 10.4324/9781003181484-12

centre stage and frequently regarded as one of the potential game changers, as it serves as a key driver of economic growth in many cities on the continent (Pirie, 2013).

Undoubtedly, high quality urban mobility in African cities has long been recognised as a fundamental cornerstone for major economic, environmental and social development (Ndebele et al., 2018; WEF, 2013). The wide-ranging benefits associated with improved accessibility to high quality, efficient and effective urban transport infrastructure are universally recognised. While there is evidence of African governments making strides to navigate the complex terrain of poor transport infrastructure, the challenge appears insurmountable across the continent. Perhaps, it may be reasonable to argue that poor economic management, corruption, institutional inefficiencies have contributed to the incapacitation of African countries to address urgent urban planning and development challenges particularly those relating to transportation. It is also worth acknowledging that there are exceptions, as some African countries (e.g., Rwanda) are making gradual and consistent progress towards sustainable urban development and management. But more efforts are required to position many African countries on sustainable development footing.

The purpose of this chapter is neither to provide a litany of urban planning and development challenges in Africa nor to discuss the factors contributing to the current urban development dispensation in the continent. However, this chapter offers an optimism towards resolution of some of these complex urban problems confronting the continent. Using qualitative research method and employing secondary data, with the Metro Express Project (MEP) as a case study, the chapter demonstrates the significance of targeted government initiatives in addressing critical urban planning challenges (e.g. traffic congestion and transport services). Research (e.g. Acheampong, 2018; Cobbinah et al., 2015) shows that spatial planning is lacking in many African countries as haphazard and uncontrolled urban development continues unabated across the region. The chapter therefore illustrates the centrality of such initiatives in advancing sustainable spatial planning in Mauritius. The chapter is organised into five main sections. Section 2 reviews relevant literature on the importance of spatial planning in Africa's urban dispensation and why transport infrastructure is critical. Section 3 provides background to the metro express project in Mauritius. Section 4 analyses the metro express project implementation and its relation to sustainable spatial planning. In Section 5, the conclusion of the chapter is presented.

Spatial Planning and Urban Transportation Development – A Focus on Mauritius

This section presents analysis of the literature on spatial planning and transportation development in Africa with a focus on Mauritius. It is worth mentioning that Africa is a huge continent with great diversity in culture, development and environment, as well as some similarities in development challenges. Although this section discusses spatial planning and transportation in Africa, it recognises the diversity across the continent, and further focuses on Mauritius as an example. Being influenced by the successes of some of the world-renowned urban transport systems such as Brazil and Bogota, some African cities are similarly reimagining their spaces and investing in urban transport development projects as part of unrelenting efforts towards spatial transformation and sustainable mobility. According to forecasts, in the African continent, it is estimated that about 55% of the inhabitants will be living in cities by the year 2050 (Acheampong, 2018). Undoubtedly, the growing population size in urban areas solicit equal distribution of opportunities, including employment, housing, transportation and social services and correspondingly, the promotion of social justice and inclusiveness (Acheampong, 2018). The development projects responding to these needs often create conflicts between economic, social and environmental policies and these are addressed via spatial planning (United Nations, 2008).

Spatial planning is concerned with "the problem of coordination or integration of the spatial dimension of sectoral policies through a territorially-based strategy" (Cullingworth & Nadin, 2006, p. 91). For instance, the 1976 Vancouver Declaration on Human Settlements (Habitat I Conference) adopted at the UN Conference on Human Settlements (UNCHS) underscores the pivotal role of spatial planning for future urban development. The declaration pointed out that "...it is the responsibility of Governments to prepare spatial strategic plans and adopt human settlement policies to guide the socio-economic development efforts" (United Nations Conference on Human Settlements, 1976, p. 6). In furtherance, in the European regional (spatial) planning in 1983 (Charter Torremolinos Charter), the concept of spatial planning was lengthily dealt with (Council of Europe, 1983). There are provisions for more stability and confidence for investment, proper identification of land in appropriate locations to meet economic development needs and equally ensures that land for development is well positioned in relation to the transport network and the labour force (United Nations, 2008).

In Africa, the discourse for the necessity to assimilate spatial planning and transportation design in terms of purpose, functionality and operations has gained prominence since the early 1990s (Berrisford & Kiato, 2008; Todes et al., 2009; UN Habitat, 2014b). Spatial planning instruments were recognised within these functional fields for their significance in enhancing planning, development and delivery in an integrated fashion. Studies (Collier, 2014; Middleton, 2016; Pirie, 2013; UN Habitat, 2013) offer strong empirical evidence of some of the key common features shared by African cities with respect to urban transport, including, old and decrepit transport infrastructure, traffic congestion, pollution and accidents, longer commuting and trip times, and the inadequate policies linking transport with land use. Sietchiping et al. (2012) state that urban planning efforts for diverse urban transport systems particularly in small or even medium-sized African cities are almost non-existent. The focus has largely been on the construction of more roads and freeways that encourage automobile-oriented cities which have no discernible assimilation with other forms of transport such as bus networks and trains. This practice has unfortunately led to the development of inefficient city spaces characterised by urban sprawl, chronic traffic congestion and other urban transport ailments as alluded to earlier. Land use and spatially-responsive transportation policies play a significant part in addressing these problems as prevailing institutional fragmentations in which land use and transportation issues are addressed do not permit broad integration. On the other hand, Sietchiping et al. (2012) question the few policy interventions and planning efforts that have been undertaken to address the apparent disconnect between spatial planning and urban transport design in African cities. This is however not surprising as Suzuki et al. (2013) point out that urban development that integrates transit and land use rarely takes place in both developing and developed countries. There is a need for integrated strategies which encompass land use measures that shape transit supportive urban structures, urban infrastructure development as well as measures that influence sustainable urban cultures (Doi & Kii, 2012).

The principle of sustainable development and the need for improved integration is not a novel consideration. For instance, the UN Habitat's Global Report on Human Settlements identified that the key urban mobility challenge hinges on the incorporation of land use and transportation planning; social dimensions and representativeness; environmental dimensions; economic dimensions, as well as institutional and governmental roles and responsibilities (UN, 2013). These principles are further directly and indirectly applied in various sources of the UN Habitat's International Guidelines on Urban and Territorial Planning (UN, 2014a). In Africa, the UN Habitat (2014b) identified assimilation of forces such as population, urbanisation, urban development, urban planning and resource management, urban culture and green urban development as the main agents for sustainable urban transformations and development. This implies the participation of various actors, professions and levels of government to manage and direct the planning, designing and implementation of urban transport systems. Many role players within the spatial planning purview have realised the delicate balance between environmental, human, economic, institutional, spatial planning and transportation planning in delivering on sustainable development in African cities. This balance is, however, difficult to achieve due to the poor application of planning instruments and tools by all spheres of government and professions involved in urban transportation planning and design. The reasons for this disconnection have been attributed to ecological degradation, widening of development inequality, segregation and compartmentalisation of planning and non-delivery (Berrisford & Kiato, 2008; Todes et al., 2009). This leads to spatial inefficiency and conflicts in planning and urban development priorities in developing African cities.

With effective spatial planning regime, the needs of the local communities are considered in development policies aimed at improving provision of facilities to new development location (United Nations, 2008). Spatial planning promotes proper use of land, buildings and infrastructure while protecting the environment and most importantly, it addresses issues with future probable environmental risks associated with the global environmental changes (United Nations, 2008). For instance, the Agenda 2030 is focused on people, planet and prosperity, and that the 17 Sustainable Development Goals (SDGs) were formulated by the United Nations (UN Sustainable Development Goals, 2015). The SDG 11 deals with sustainable cities and communities, such that given the growing trend of urbanisation in several countries across the globe, this SDG aim at making cities sustainable through the creation of career and business opportunities, safe and affordable housing, and building of resilient societies and economies (United Nations Development Programme [UNDP], 2020). In this sense, SDG 11 targets investment in public transport, the creation of green public spaces, and the improvement of urban planning and management (UNDP, 2020). Mauritius has adopted the 2030 Agenda for Sustainable Development in the year 2015 (Statistics Mauritius, 2018).

Mauritius – officially referred to as the Republic of Mauritius – is a small island nation located in the Indian Ocean about 2,000 km off the southeast coast of the mainland Africa. The island nation comprises the main island called Mauritius, Rodrigues, Agalega and St Brandon with Port Louis – the largest city – as the capital. The country spans 2,040 km². The estimated population of Mauritius was at 1,265,985, of whom 626,341 were males and 639,644 females as on July 2019. The population on the main island of Mauritius was 1,222,340, and that of Rodrigues island was 43,371; Agalega and Saint Brandon had an estimated total population of 274. Mauritius has the second highest population density in Africa. In the context of transport, public transport in Mauritius have been free of charge for students, people with disabilities and senior citizens since 2005. Mauritius faces a serious traffic problem due to the high number of road users, particularly car drivers. This situation makes sustainable transport and spatial planning imperative in Mauritius' development agenda.

Mauritius is committed to the implementation of all the SDGs in the Agenda 2030 and in its Roadmap for SDG Implementation dated 10 February, 2017, it is stated that there is a high degree of convergence between SDG targets and the national policies of Mauritius, 98 out of 107 SDG targets have been implemented and are found in its national policy documents (UNDP, 2017). However, it has been equally noted that for some SGDs, there are lacunas in their implementation in Mauritius and these include, *inter alia*, SDG 11 on sustainable cities and SDG 12 related to sustainable production and consumption (UNDP, 2017). Further highlighted in this report, Mauritius is inherently vulnerable as it belongs to the categories of Small Island Developing States (SIDS) by reason of its small land area, limited natural resources and it is environmentally sensitive, as such its exposure to seasonal natural hazards such as cyclones and tropical storms which cause flooding and infrastructural destruction (UNDP, 2017). Since there is an ongoing trend of climate change globally, this represents an additional risk for Mauritius.

The Metro Express Project in Mauritius: An Overview

Mauritius had been without a railway system following the closure of Mauritius Government Railways in the 1960s. With increased car usage and chronic road congestion, plans for a light railway system were proposed decades ago. The government of Mauritius embarked on the Metro Express project to help address the transport problems in 2017, and is led by an Indian company Larsen and Toubro after winning a tender from the Government of Mauritius. The Metro Express project is a light rail public transport system that starts from Port Louis to Curepipe, as seen in Figure 12.1.

For the realisation of the MEP, the government has proceeded firstly with the compulsory acquisition of plots of land which were found on the track length where the metro will be circulating. In total, 100 plots of land were concerned out of which 32 are residential areas, 67 are bare lands and lastly there is a warehouse on one (Parliamentary Debates, 2017). In fact, in the year 2014, the government has proceeded with the compulsory acquisition of properties found on the metro track and for this purpose the sum of 371 Million MUR (US$ 9,212,804) was disbursed (Defimedia, 2017b). As the government had already signed the contract with Larsen and Toubro and the properties which have already been compulsorily acquired were still in occupation by the respective former owners, the government then took a drastic step to demolish the aforesaid houses in order to handover the construction site to the main contractor. Through this action, several families were faced with difficult situations and they tried to save their houses through the formal Court procedures but in vain. While some families opted for an immediate equitable remedy in the form of an injunction which was granted only at the interim level, the remaining families could not obtain same since they did not have a lease agreement (Defimedia, 2017b). Finally, all the houses found on the metro track were demolished and the construction site handed over to the main contractor, Larsen and Toubro.

The Metro Express Project is over 26 km track of road length connecting the Immigration Square in Port Louis to Curepipe (Verdict Media Limited, 2020). For this stated track length, there will be 19 stations in

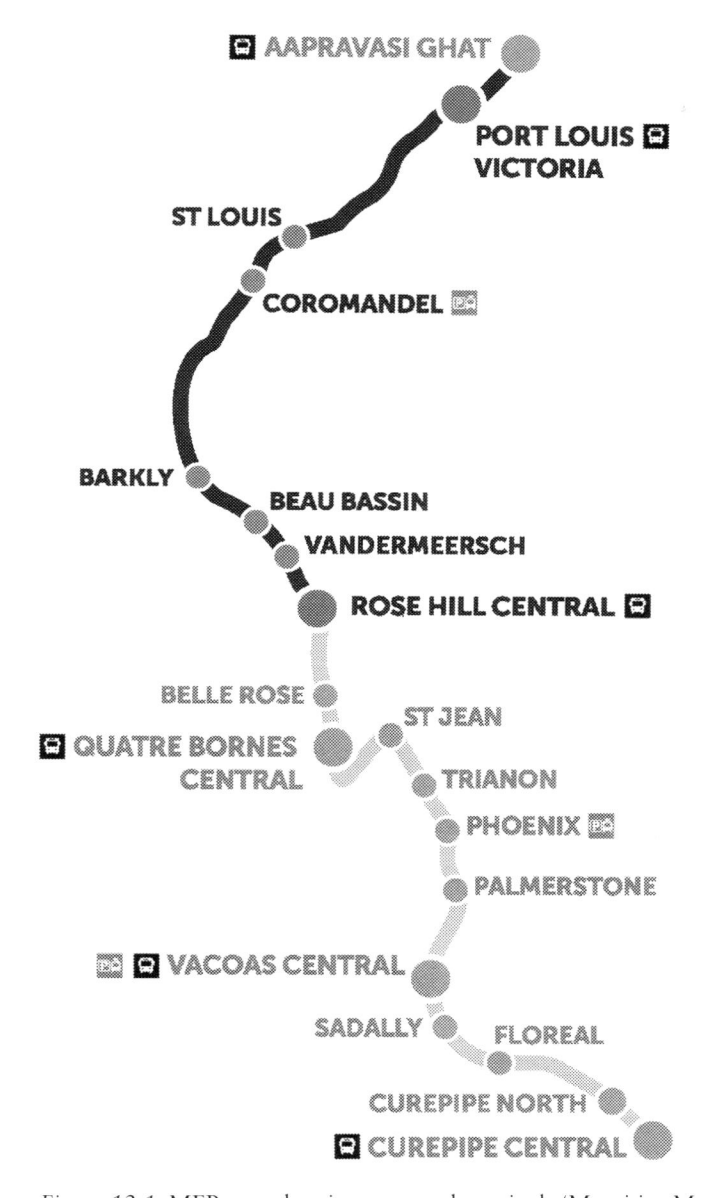

Figure 12.1 MEP map showing proposed terminals (Mauritius Metro Express, 2020).

total (VML, 2020) where travelers can have easy access to the metro. The MEP is not focused only on the vehicle but includes track works, the construction of stations, viaducts and bridges, installation of electric traction systems, ticketing and passenger information systems and other maintenance equipment (VML, 2020). The type of vehicle for the MEP are Light Rail Vehicles (LRVs). The Urbos 100 3rd generation LRVs, which are the innovative and high-quality trains, have been used and same were specifically designed by the Spanish railway manufacturer Construcciones y Auxiliar de Ferrocarriles (CAF) (Government of Mauritius, 2019a). Briefly, the width of the LRV train is of 2.65 m, the length is of 45.411 m and the height is of 3.25 – comprising of seven modules with five doors (Government of Mauritius, 2019a). The specifications of the LRVs include a "18 bi-directional, low-floor, air-conditioned trams with seven modules each" and the Urbos Trams go at a speed of 35–80 km/hour across the network (VML, 2020). Passengers have access to Wi-Fi facility when travelling in the metro and all the Urbos Trams are equipped with an advanced signaling system, automatic vehicle location system (AVLS), transit signal priority system (TSPS) and a driving simulator (VML, 2020).

The first phase of the MEP linking Port Louis to Rose Hill was inaugurated in October 2019 (VML, 2020). However, it came into commercial operation in December 2020 (Defimedia, 2019a). For the population to experience travelling in the metro, the government has launched a period of free travelling. In total, 432,000 tickets have been distributed freely in five municipalities and seven district councils and at three main metro stations that is at Rose-Hill, Port-Louis and Beau-Bassin (Lexpress, 2019). This free travel period was available to the public up to 5 January, 2020 (Lejournal, 2019). Currently, there are 12 LRVs which are in circulation servicing the route of Port Louis to Rose Hill and there are 6 more LRVs which was expected in June 2020 (Defimedia, 2020). In addition, a system of feeder busses for the metro express has also been set up in different locations in order to facilitate commuters and it will be available freely to the public for a lapse of two months as from the 10 January, 2020 (Radio One, 2020). The allocation of feeder busses despite being seen as an advantage, there has been several criticisms due to the fact that the demand for feeder busses was made quite late and this has caused disruptions in the usual bus lines schedules because 20% of the actual bus fleet is being used to service the feeder busses programme (Lexpress, 2020).

For the second phase of the MEP, construction works are estimated to be completed in 2021 (VML, 2020). Moreover, the first part of the second phase linking Rose Hill to Quatre Bornes was completed in 2020 with the route from Quatre Bornes to Curepipe expected to be completed in latter part of 2021 (Defimedia, 2020). The MEP is not only focused on the 26 km track length but in the future an expansion linking the north of the island to the south will be considered by the government to connect the airport to the north of the island (Verdict Media Ltd, 2020). Two track lines are being considered for the MEP with the first one being a line going from Rose Hill to the East which passes by Ebene and the second one from Port Louis going to the North (Defimedia, 2020). Concerning the east, the project is well-advanced and concerning the north, the extension could go as far as Pamplemousses, or even Goodlands (Defimedia, 2020). However, for the MEP to service the north of the island, this is not in doubt, but the eastern line could become a reality more quickly (Defimedia, 2020).

Governance and the Transport Industry in Mauritius: A Case of the MEP

Transport planning and policy require governance which is associated with the better allocation and practical usage of resources. Similar to other sectors, transportation has a unique set of characteristics about its governance due to the involvement of both public and private sectors. Governance as used here infers the ownership and management of assets and resources to realise goals through the exercise of authority and institutional resources (Slack & Rodrigue, 2020). The governance of transport infrastructure is particularly relevant because of the strategic, economic and social importance of transportation and the cross-territorial nature of urban transport infrastructures. The provision of public transport and modernised road infrastructural development have remained an important issue in Mauritius.

The innovation of the public transport sector features among one of the most important developmental projects of the Mauritian government. The Mauritian government has made massive investments for the construction of bypasses and link roads in addition to the metro express to improve public transport. It is vital to consider the element of governance of transport infrastructure due to its strategic, economic and social importance (Slack & Rodrigue, 2020). Indeed, "transport is not of mere convenience but a fundamental infrastructure that must systematically and constantly be available to its users" (Slack & Rodrigue, 2020). When a developmental project is under consideration, it is important to consider spatial planning as its core element. For example, when a modern bus station is being introduced, the government first considers the location that is the space to be used and how same can be built in a modernised way to help the citizens in an environmentally sensitive manner. Slack and Rodrigue (2020) elaborate that "... the capital intensiveness and the long-life span of transportation infrastructures underline the need for effective governance to ensure that the infrastructures are properly funded, maintained, operated and expanded." In similar way, the MEP as an innovative project includes a dose of governance for greater sustainability.

According to the report by the Japan International Cooperation Agency (JICA), there are three landslides prone areas in the network of the metro express (Defimedia, 2017c). This situation threatens the sustainability of the MEP, as in the event of landslide, lives and the MEP structures will be impacted. Also, due to a damaged pipe of the Central Water Authority, mud has gathered on the rails and as a result the metro express was forced to operate to only Coromandel (Defimedia, 2020a). Trams from Rose Hill station at 14 hr 15 to Coromandel required passengers to wait for more than 50 minutes before they could get a bus to reach Port Louis (Defimedia, 2020a). The problem of mud being gathered on the track was as a result of water accumulation, therefore in the event of flooding caused by heavy rainfall in this region, this problem will reoccur. Mauritius has recently experienced severe flooding in several regions over the island as it is exposed to seasonal natural hazards (UNDP, 2017). Further, the track of Port Louis to Rose Hill, the metro operates on bridges in places including Port Louis. This has complicated the road infrastructure in Beau Bassin and recently while the metro was available on a free travelling basis for the population, there was a minor accident in Beau Bassin. The tram captain had to apply the brake suddenly because of a car which turned into a prohibited direction at Beau Bassin (Lexpress, 2019a). The route of the tram is quite confusing and steps should have been taken to clearly indicate to road users about the changes which have occurred since the metro is passing on the road throughout the town of Beau Bassin.

Similar to other existing practice on transport planning in Sub-Saharan Africa which concentrate on narrow technical engineering issues and on roads, the planning of the MEP failed largely to incorporate the interests of and potential benefits to a wide sector of the Mauritian population. Spatially-sensitive transport planning requires a detailed understanding of the economic, social and political environments in which transport takes place and based on which interventions are made (Porter 2007). In addition, the number of passengers that travel in the metro is huge. For instance, during weekends, the number of passengers who are expected to travel by the metro is estimated between 2000 and 2400 per hour (Defimedia, 2020b). This development in terms of the patronage of the MEP concurs with the assertion by Dewar (2017) that the most important reason for building a rapid urban transport system is the enhancement of public transportation, reducing traffic congestion, and supporting land use planning policies. Flyvbjerg (2009) however argues that while the goal of traditional transport policy of improving accessibility is still useful, it must be considered in the context of other desirable goals such as improving safety and health, reducing vehicle emissions, improving equity, enhancing economic opportunities, improving community livability, and promoting mobility are all valid.

The MEP track of Port Louis to Rose Hill is a specific area which is being serviced by the metro express for now. An extension from Curepipe to the east is under consideration as well as extending the track to the north of the island of Goodland (Defimedia, 2020). Concerning the ecological aspects of the Urbos trams, they are designed to be eco-friendly and energy efficient and they cause neither pollution nor greenhouse emission

(Apec, 2018). The light rail vehicles possess their own energy saving devices for a lighting control system with occupancy sensors and timers and much more (Apec, 2018). Moreover, it can carry more passengers and provide a quick service compared to busses. Therefore, in some aspects, there will be a reduction in the dependence on fuel in the long run. It is worth noting that the installation of transformers on the track of Port Louis to Curepipe have cost the state approximately 400 Million MUR (US$ 9,891,177) (Business Mega, 2017). The focus is to integrate sustainability into the MEP planning, design and implementation process and that a clear merging between legal and policy requirements for planning, transportation and environmental sustainability has occurred. It can be argued that, despite the recognition of the need for greater incorporation of spatial planning principles at all levels of the project, some challenges and defects still remain. Specifically, this includes the lack of integration of urban and spatial planning principles inclusive of the application and/or use of demographic and socio-economic data in the MEP and related processes. This challenge may in part be addressed by assessing the existing policy and legislative framework and, more specifically, the opportunities created by the Planning and Development Act (2004) and the National Development Strategy and the National Planning Policy Guidelines (NPPGs). Several international and national policy documents such as the SDGs and the new urban agenda (NUA) recognise the need for configuring and strategically integrating inclusion and equity in urban development plans.

Conclusion

The introduction of various forms of Bus Rapid Transfer (BRT) systems across African cities is a fundamental shift in spatial transformation policy and indicates the bold steps being taken by transport planning authorities to challenge the status-quo and chart a sustainable development trajectory. This chapter provides an understanding of the metro express project in Mauritius. It explored its development and implementation phases and its spatial planning and sustainability implications. Findings show that MEP has significantly improved the transport infrastructure and services in the country. However, challenges remain. It further outlines some of factors such as landslides, feeder busses and traffic jam which still remain challenge in Mauritius and demonstrate that the MEP has not fully embraced the sustainability principles. More broadly, this chapter has established that there has been little progress made in improving the overall mobility level for many urban dwellers despite the documented effort of this public urban transport initiative in the country.

From the continental perspective, in many cities, policy responses to congestion have been through the construction of more freeways and rapid urban transport systems, which has hardly offered any relief from these challenges. Instead, it has only exacerbated the existing unstainable land use patterns of spread out development which often lead to spatial injustice and worsening mobility for majority of the urban populations. The integration of transport and land use activities is therefore a fundamental strategy in achieving the objectives of mixed land use typologies along the MEP as well as facilitating the achievement of sustainable and inclusive urban transport system in Mauritius. Finally, this chapter argues that urban transport infrastructure development opportunities should be anchored in spatial planning to respond to both current and anticipated challenges. It is thus critical to think creatively and imaginatively about urban futures based on a strong understanding of social, economic and spatial dynamics in African cities with a sense of what is strategically possible.

References

Acheampong, R. A. (2018). *Spatial Planning in Ghana Origins, Contemporary Reforms and Practices, and New Perspectives*. Cham, Switzerland: Springer.

Apec. (2018). *Ecological features of the Metro express Project*. Available at http://apec.mu/2018/07/06/ecological-features-of-the-metro-express-project/

Barrow, K. (2017). Mauritius light rail construction contract signed. *International Railway Journal*. Available at https://www.railjournal.com/passenger/light-rail/mauritius-light-rail-set-for-september-opening/

Berrisford, S., & Kiato, M. (2008). Local government planning legal frameworks and regulatory tools: Vital signs? In Van Donk, M., Swilling, M., Pieterse, E., & Parnell, E. (Eds), *Consolidating developmental local government. Lessons from the South African experience*. Isandla Institute. Cape Town: UCT Press.

Broekhof, S., & Van Marwijk, R. (2012). The role of spatial information for planning sustainable cities. *FIG Working Week 2012*. Available at https://www.fig.net/resources/proceedings/fig_proceedings/fig2012/papers/ts07g/TS07G_broekhof_vanmarwijk_5985.pdf

Business Mega. (2017). *Metro Express, CEB: Energy consumption of 11 megawatts*. Available at https://business.mega.mu/2017/09/26/metro-express-ceb-une-consommation-energetique-de-11-megawatts/

Chakwizira, J. (2013). Searching for sustainable urban transport solutions for Africa: A case study of the Greater Johannesburg region in South Africa. *WIT Transactions on The Built Environment*, *130*, 175–186.

Cobbinah, P. B., Erdiaw-Kwasie, M. O., & Amoateng, P. (2015). Africa's urbanisation: Implications for sustainable development. *Cities*, *47*, 62–72.

Collier, P. (2014). Attracting international private finance for African infrastructure. *Journal of African Trade*, *1*(1), 37–44.

Council of Europe. (1983). *European regional/spatial planning Charter Torremolinos Charter*. Available at https://www.are.admin.ch/dam/are/de/dokumente/internationales/dokumente/bericht/europen_regionalspatialplanningchartertorremolinoscharter.pdf.download.pdf/european_regionalspatialplanningchartertorremolinoscharter.pdf

Cullingworth, B., & Nadin, V. (2006). *Town and country planning in the UK* (14th ed.). London: Routledge.

Defimedia. (2017a). *Metro Express: Rs 572 M dépensées par l'ancien GM*. 15 April. Available at https://motors.mega.mu/news/metro-express-rs-572-m-depensees-par-lancien-gm-20170418.html

Defimedia. (2017b). *Protests derail Metro Express*. 8 September. Available at https://defimedia.info/protests-derail-metro-express

Defimedia. (2017c). *Metro Express: Should the route be reviewed?* 1 September. Available at https://defimedia.info/metro-express-should-route-be-reviewed

Defimedia. (2018). *Metro Express: The Rs 18.8 billion adventure begins!* 7 August. Available at https://defimedia.info/metro-express-rs-188-billion-adventure-begins

Defimedia. (2019a). *Metro: Rose-Hill /Port-Louis route in express mode*. 5 October. Available at https://defimedia.info/metro-trajet-rose-hillport-louis-en-mode-express

Defimedia. (2019b). *Landslide at La-Butte: The site of the collapse stabilized and filled*. 25 June. Available at https://defimedia.info/glissement-de-terrain-la-butte-le-site-de-leffondrement-stabilise-et-comble

Defimedia. (2020). *Metro Express: Extensions to the East and North under study*. 27 January. Available at https://defimedia.info/metro-express-des-extensions-vers-lest-et-le-nord-letude

Defimedia. (2020a). *Coromandel: Mud on the rails, the Metro Express stalls*. 13 January. Available at https://defimedia.info/coromandel-de-la-boue-sur-les-rails-le-metro-express-cale

Defimedia. (2020b). *Metro Express: 2,400 passengers per hour during the weekend*. 13 January. Available at https://defimedia.info/metro-express-2-400-passagers-par-heure-durant-le-week-end

Defimedia. (2020c). *Metro Express: Here are the places where you can take the Feeder Buses*. 15 January. Available at https://defimedia.info/document-metro-express-voici-les-endroits-ou-vous-pouvez-prendre-les-feeder-buses

Dewar, D. (2017). Transportation Planning in South Africa: A Failure to Adjust. *Transactions on The Built Environment*, 176, 27.

Doi, K., & Kii, M. (2012). Looking at sustainable urban mobility through a cross-assessment model within the framework of land-use and transport integration. *IATSS Research*, 35, 62–70.

European Commission. (1997). *European Compendium of Spatial Planning Systems and Policies 1997*. Available at http://commin.org/upload/Glossaries/European_Glossary/EU_compendium_No_28_of_1997.pdf

Flyvbjerg, B. (2009). Survival of the unfittest: Why the worst infrastructure gets built and what we can do about it. *Oxford Review of Economic Policy*, 25(3), 344–367.

Goodstadt, V., & Partidário M.R. (n.d.). *Spatial planning and environmental assessments*. Available at https://www.environment.gov.za/sites/default/files/docs/economicsof_ecosystems_spatialplanning_enviroassessment.pdf

Government of Mauritius. (2017). *Exact cost of the Metro Express project will be disclosed once contract is awarded, says Minister Bodha*. Available at http://www.govmu.org/English/News/Pages/Exact-cost-of-the-Metro-Express-project-will-be-disclosed-once-contract-is-awarded,-says-Minister-Bodha.aspx

Government of Mauritius. (2019a). *Metro Express Limited launches Free Passenger Service*. Available at http://www.govmu.org/English/News/Pages/Metro-Express-Limited-launches-Free-Passenger-Service-.aspx

Government of Mauritius. (2019b). *Average rating Metro Express Project: First light rail vehicle arrives in Mauritius*. Available at http://pmo.govmu.org/English/News/Pages/Metro-Express-Project-First-Light-Rail-Vehicle-arrives-in-Mauritius.aspx

http://www.r1.mu/actu/societe/les-feeder-buses-gratuits-pendant-deux-mois-p892399

https://mauritiusmetroexpress.mu/a-propos/

https://transportgeography.org/?page_id=6284

https://www.researchgate.net/publication/328492212_The_Concept_of_Spatial_Planning_and_the_Planning_System_In_the_Book_Spatial_Planning_in_Ghana_Chap_2

ION News. (2019). *Beau Bassin «étouffe» à cause du Metro Express, s'indigne un conseiller municipal* [Video file] (26 December). Available at https://www.youtube.com/watch?v=E2E33umoiPQ

Japan International Cooperation Agency. (2018). *Technical Cooperation Project: Landslide advisers for Mauritius*. Available at http://open_jicareport.jica.go.jp/pdf/12304226_01.pdf

Larsen & Toubro. (2020). About Larsen & Toubro. Available at https://www.larsentoubro.com/corporate/about-lt-group/

Lejournal. (2019, 23 December). Metro Express Limited launches Free Passenger Service. *Lejournal*. Available at https://lejournal.mu/2019/12/23/metro-express-limited-launches-free-passenger-service/

Le Mauricien. (2017). *METRO EXPRESS: Rien ne nous empêchera d'aller de l'avant, a déclaré le PM*. 1 August. Available at https://www.lemauricien.com/article/metro-express-rien-ne-nous-empechera-d-aller-l-avant-declare-pm/

Le Mauricien. (2018). *Nature under threat-The Key Roles and Functions of Trees as a Global Public Good*. 14 February. Available at https://www.lemauricien.com/article/nature-under-threat-the-key-roles-and-functions-of-trees-as-a-global-public-good/

Lexico. (2020). *Meaning of spatial in English*. Available at https://www.lexico.com/definition/spatial

Lexpress. (2018). *Metro Express: Blind work at Rose-Hill?* 2 November. Available at https://www.lexpress.mu/article/342198/metro-express-travaux-laveuglette-rose-hill

Lexpress. (2019). *Metro Express: 432,000 free tickets available*. 17 December. Available at https://www.lexpress.mu/article/366946/metro-express-432-000-tickets-gratuits-disponibles

Lexpress. (2019a). *Metro Express: Vehicle crosses in front of tram, injured*. 26 December. Available at https://www.lexpress.mu/article/367297/metro-express-un-vehicule-traverse-devant-tram-un-blesse

Lexpress. (2020). *"Feeder nozzles": RHT's Port-Louis-Rose-Hill service disrupted*. 21 January. Available at https://www.lexpress.mu/article/368473/feeder-buses-desserte-port-louis-rose-hill-rht-perturbee

Lexpress. (2020a).*Free feeder buses from this Friday*. 9 January. Available at https://www.lexpress.mu/article/367950/feeder-buses-gratuits-partir-ce-vendredi

Lexpress. (2020b). *Feeder Buses: The note promises to be salty… by the millions.* 27 January. Available at https://www.lexpress.mu/article/368839/feeder-buses-note-sannonce-salee-millions

Mauritius Times. (2018). *Metro works and traffic decongestion.* 3 December. Available at http://www.mauritiustimes.com/mt/metro-works-and-traffic-decongestion-2/

Metro Express Mauritius. (2019). *Metro Express Ltd.* Available at https://mauritiusmetroexpress.mu/about/?lang=en#mission

Middleton, L. *Freedom to move: Transportation in African cities: Policy Brief.* Available at https://www.urbanafrica.net/wp-content/uploads/2016/06/Mobility_ENG.pdf

Ndebele, R., Aigbavboa, C., & Ogra, A., (2018). Urban transport infrastructure development in African Cities: Challenges and opportunities. In Proceedings of the *InternationalConference on Industrial Engineering and Operations Management*, Johannesburg, South Africa, October 29–November 1, p. 833.

Parliamentary Debates. (2017). *Republic of Mauritius Sixth National Assembly Parliamentary Debates (Hansard).* Available at http://mauritiusassembly.govmu.org/English/hansard/Documents/2017/hansard0117.pdf

Pirie, G. (2013). *Sustainable urban mobility in 'Anglophone' Sub-Saharan Africa. Global Report on Human Settlements.* Un-Habitat.

Popova, Y. (2017). Relations between wellbeing and transport infrastructure of the country. *Procedia Engineering, 178*, 579–588.

Porter, G. (2007). Transport planning in sub-Saharan Africa. *Progress in Development, 7*(3), 251–257.

Radio One. (2020). *Metro-express: Les Feeder Buses gratuits pendant deux mois.* Available at

Russel Publishing Limited. (2019). Intelligent Transport. *Mauritius Metro project contract awarded.* Available at https://www.intelligenttransport.com/transport-news/24601/mauritius-metro-express-project-contract-awarded/

Sietchiping, R., Permezel, M. J., & Ngomsi, C. (2012). Transport and mobility in sub-Saharan African cities: An overview of practices, lessons and options for improvements. *Cities, 29*(3), 183–189.

Sitas, A. (2014). Rethinking Africa's sociological project. *Current Sociology, 62*(4), 457–471.

Slack, B., & Rodrigue, J. (2020). The geography of transport systems, the spatial organization of transportation and mobility-transport planning and governance. Available at

Slack, B., & Rodrigue, J-P. (2020). *The geography of transport systems* (5th ed.). New York: Routledge.

SPLC. (2014). *Agenda 21: The UN, sustainability and right-wing conspiracy theory.* Available at https://www.splcenter.org/20140331/agenda-21-un-sustainability-and-right-wing-conspiracy-theory

Statistics Mauritius. (2018). Sustainable development goals. Available at http://statsmauritius.govmu.org/English/StatsbySubj/Pages/SDGs.aspx

Suzuki, H., Cervero, R., & Luchi, K. (2013). *Transforming cities with transit: Transit and land-use integration for sustainable urban development.* Washington DC: The World Bank.

Todes, A., Sim, V., & Sutherland, C. (2009). The relationship between planning and environmental management in South Africa: The case of KwaZulu-Natal. *Planning Practice and Research*, 24(4), 411–433.

UNDP. (2017). Mauritius roadmap for SDG implementation. 10 February 2017. Available at http://www.sustainablesids.org/wp-content/uploads/2018/06/Mauritius-SDG-Roadmap.pdf

United Nations Conference on Environment and Development. (1992). *Agenda 21*. Available at https://sustainabledevelopment.un.org/outcomedocuments/agenda21

United Nations Conference on Human Settlements. (1976). *The Vancouver declaration on human settlements*. Available at https://mirror.unhabitat.org/downloads/docs/The_Vancouver_Declaration.pdf

United Nations Development Programme. (2020). *Goal 11: Sustainable cities and communities*. Available at https://www.undp.org/content/undp/en/home/sustainable-development-goals/goal-11-sustainable-cities-and-communities.html

United Nations Habitat. (2014a). *Towards the development of international guidelines on urban and territorial planning*. Nairobi, Kenya.

United Nations Habitat. (2014b). *The state of African cities. Re-imagining sustainable urban transitions*. Nairobi, Kenya.

United Nations Habitat (UN Habitat). (2013). Planning and design for sustainable urban mobility. *Global Report on Human Settlements*. Nairobi, Kenya.

United Nations Sustainable Development Goals. (2015). *Transforming our world: The 2030 Agenda for sustainable development*. Available at https://sustainabledevelopment.un.org/post2015/transformingourworld

United Nations Sustainable Development-Agenda 21. (1992). *United Nations Conference on Environment & Development*, Rio de Janerio, Brazil, 3–14 June 1992. Available at https://sustainabledevelopment.un.org/content/documents/Agenda21.pdf

United Nations. (2008). *Spatial planning key instrument for development and effective governance with special reference to countries in transition*. Available at https://www.unece.org/fileadmin/DAM/hlm/documents/Publications/spatial_planning.e.pdf

Verdict Media Limited. (2020). *Metro Express project*. Available at https://www.railway-technology.com/projects/metro-express-project/

World Economic Forum. *Strategic infrastructure in Africa. A business approach to project acceleration*. Available at https://www.weforum.org/reports/strategic-infrastructure-africa-business-approach-project-acceleration

Part III
Urban Informality, Regeneration and Tenure Security

13 Situating Everyday Urban Struggles Within the Context of the SDGs in an Informal Settlement in Accra, Ghana

Seth Asare Okyere, Louis Kusi Frimpong, Stephen Kofi Diko, Matthew Abunyewah, and Michihiro Kita

Introduction

The UN 2030 Agenda for Sustainable Development, commonly known as the Sustainable Development Goals (SDGs), was adopted in 2015 to provide a global development policy framework between 2015 and 2030. It comprises 17 goals, 169 targets and 230 indicators. The SDGs span social, economic and environmental issues and employ principles of integration and indivisibility (UN, 2015) to capture their interdependencies (Jiménez-Aceituno et al., 2019). The agenda is driven by an ambitious goal to "end poverty, protect the planet and ensure that all people enjoy peace and prosperity" – echoed by the mantra of "leaving no one behind" (UN-Habitat, 2015, p. 14). Notwithstanding its global orientation, achieving the SDGs requires extensive localisation (Satterthwaite, 2018; Smith et al., 2018), considering the interlinkages and overlaps among the goals in relation to local development realities (Stephens et al., 2018). The SDG identifies cities in Sub-Saharan Africa as one of its priority areas of action with special attention to people and places left out in past development frameworks (UN-Habitat, 2015). Apparently, this is fostered by rapid urbanisation and poorly managed urban growth (Turok & Borel-Saladin, 2018) persisting alongside sustainability challenges such as environmental pollution, underemployment, high crime rates, informality, and disaster risks (Myers, 2016; Okyere et al., 2017; Pieterse, 2017).

Socio-spatial inequalities exist (Klopp & Paller, 2019) and unequal development among neighbourhoods further complicates the sustainable development trajectory (Obeng-Odoom, 2015). Nowhere is this socio-spatial inequality as strikingly visible than in the informal settlements in African cities where about 60% of the urban population reside (Okyere et al., 2017; UN-Habitat, 2015). Informal settlements, especially those considered as slums (see Dovey, 2012; UN-Habitat, 2015), are often located in disaster-prone areas of the city and characterised by overcrowding, lack of tenure security, severe deprivations and infrastructure deficiencies (Ezeh et al., 2017; Okyere & Kita, 2015). Residents of

DOI: 10.4324/9781003181484-13

informal areas with slum-like conditions are often marginalised and ex-cluded through discriminatory urban policies that paradoxically aim to achieve sustainable urban development (Obeng-Odoom, 2013; Oteng-Ababio & Grant, 2019a; Watson, 2009, 2014). What emerges is a powerful and dominant narrative of the state, technocrats and elites, who construct the marginals as an impediment to sustainable urban devel-opment thereby subjugating and relegating the realities and experiences of those at the margins (Amoako, 2016; De Satgé & Watson, 2018; Obeng-Odoom, 2013).

In Ghana, sustainable development strategies are generally present in urban development policies and programmes. But their integration is ambiguous and limited in practice (Cobbinah et al., 2015; Oteng-Ababio & Grant, 2019b), as framings are not rooted in residents' experiences (Obeng-Odoom, 2013). The conditions of the marginals are also largely left to the market system (Gillespie, 2016) or individual/collective improvisations of survival (Okyere et al., 2017). The relegation of informal settlement residents' experiences has led to "formal" biases and endeared inequalities with negative repercussions on cities (Ulbrich et al., 2019). Therefore, there is a need to give an empirical space to the experiences of those at the margins through analysing and de-constructing their everyday realities as bottom-up magnifying lenses in the sustainable urban development discourse (Cirolia & Scheba, 2018; Okyere et al., 2019). This chapter therefore deconstructs the SDGs by engaging the idiosyncratic everyday urban realities of those at the bottom and margins of society (Pfeffer & Georgiadou, 2019; Ulbrich et al., 2019). It aims to advance literature on sustainable urban development for informal residents through the local lens of everyday urban experiences and the eminence of southern plan-ning theory (De Satgé & Watson, 2018). The analysis of everyday practices in southern urbanism (Myers, 2011; Pieterse, 2011) provides alternative ac-counts of lived experiences of the ordinary, temporariness, and mundane from the street level to unearth micro-scale and close-focused explorations of socio-spatial interactions and constraints of urbanity (Cirolia & Scheba, 2019; De Satgé & Watson, 2018). This chapter draws on a narrative account of ev-eryday urban struggles of informal dwellers of Accra to conceptualise and contribute to the ensuing debate on fostering the achievement of the SDGs for those at the margins. It is structured into seven sections. Section 2 provides a conceptual framework on the relationship between urban informal settlements and SDGs. Section 3 follows with an overview of Old Fadma settlement. The methodology and the results are in Sections 4 and 5. Finally, the discussion and policy implications are considered in Sections 6 and 7.

Informal Settlements and Sustainable Development: A Framework

In recent years, informal settlements have received considerable research attention including their morphology (Dovey, 2012; Dovey & King, 2011), development and sustenance (Gouverneur, 2015) and residents' social conditions and spatial dynamics and interactions (Lund & Stacey, 2016; Okyere & Kita, 2016; Okyere et al., 2017). Conceptually, the terminology of informal settlements is enmeshed within the theoretical contestations of urban informality in urban studies and planning (see McFarlane, 2012; Roy, 2005). Within this contestation, Marx and Kelling (2019) note that informal settlement as socio-spatial construct represents how urban informality has become variously known: as condition (e.g. levels of infrastructure and housing); as law (e.g. compliance with land use planning regulations, property rights); and as currency (e.g. activities/practices in space and how they are interpreted). In this sense, informal settlements, though considered to be a common spatial feature of urban space in most developing countries (Ezeh et al., 2017) constitute diverse socio-economic conditions and profiles including the rich and the poor, the slum and the non-slum – depending on settlement conditions, compliance with local planning laws and social constructs.

Indeed, according to Kita et al. (2020) and Okyere (2018), the terminology of informal settlements takes a generalist and linguistic form that encompasses slums, shanty towns and squatter settlements. Thus, while slums form a part of general informal settlement nomenclature, not all informal areas feature slum-like conditions or characteristics. Taking cognisance of these varieties of informal settlements, this chapter uses the term to refer to settlements with slum conditions via the lens of housing, basic infrastructure facilities and low socio-economic profiles of residents. In view of the above, informal settlements are places of makeshift buildings lacking adequate basic services and secure tenure (Turok & Borel-Saladin, 2018). The UN-Habitat (2015) emphasises distinctive features such as overcrowding, inadequate access to basic social and environmental services and poor-quality housing. Dovey and King (2011) provide a different perspective by noting that informal settlements are neighbourhoods or districts that develop and operate outside formal controls and regulations. They acknowledge variations within this generic terminology such that "a squatter lacks land tenure; a slum variously lacks space, durability, water and sanitation; and informality implies a lack of formal control over planning, design and construction" (Dovey & King, 2011, p. 11).

The growth and proliferation of informal settlements are attributed to varied factors: market inefficiencies facilitated by state neglect and urban regeneration and modernisation projects (Gillespie, 2016; Watson, 2009), ineffective governance systems (Obeng-Odoom, 2013), exclusionary colonial and postcolonial planning regimes (Fox, 2014; Njoh, 2008), "conflicting rationalities" between planning practice and local realities (De Satgé & Watson, 2018; Watson, 2009), uneven development between rural and urban areas and unplanned urbanisation (UN-Habitat, 2016; Wekesa et al., 2011). Other structural problems relating to unemployment in the formal labour market and lack of inclusive planning are also issues that facilitate the growth of informal settlements (UN-Habitat, 2015). In view of the foregoing, this chapter conceives informal settlements through the lens of the slum, as a complex manifestation of systemic neglect and/or institutional inefficiencies, conditioned by social, economic and ecological factors in urban development planning.

People living in such informal settlements are among those found within the low-income bracket (Smit et al., 2017). Even though most people living in informal settlements are engaged in some form of economic activities such as hawking, petty trading and artisanal works, income earned from these activities are often low and irregular (Chen et al., 2016). Unemployment and economic hardship persist in informal settlements, affecting some residents' ability to afford accommodation thus leading to homelessness (Omolabi & Adebayo, 2018). Buildings in informal settlements are characterised by overcrowding and are substandard and inadequate as they are built with wood, cardboard or plastics and offer less protection against disasters and crime. Moreover, infrastructure deficiencies (e.g. water and sanitation) significantly reduce the quality of life of its dwellers (Smit et al., 2017). They are often located on marginal lands or places of lowest environmental quality including wetlands, railway setbacks, places close to major drains and waste disposal sites (Douglas, 2018; Wekesa et al., 2011). The economic challenges of informal settlements often lead to social problems such as crime and social delinquency and sometimes tensions among different groups (Omolabi & Adebayo, 2018). Residents also face political, social and economic stigmatisation, discrimination and marginalisation that become a barrier to access economic opportunities (Owusu et al., 2008). Yet residents' collective vulnerability to economic and environmental shocks as well as state policies that threaten their existence have increased social capital among informal settlement dwellers (Dovey & King, 2011). This is typified by flexibility, pragmatism, negotiation around the myriad challenges they encounter and constant struggle for self-development and individual and collective survival strategies (Gouverneur, 2015; Okyere & Kita, 2016; Okyere et al., 2017; Oviedo et al., 2021).

The growth of informal settlements is occurring alongside increased wealth in most developing countries (Hove et al., 2013). African cities, for example, have been described as highly unequal (Lall et al., 2017) with rising inequality (Obeng-Odoom, 2015; Pillay, 2015). This raises critical issues about sustainable and inclusive urban development (Watson, 2009) for those facing socio-spatial deprivations. The reality of many informal settlements reveals that the path towards sustainable development is not straightforward for all groups, at least from a socio-spatial perspective. The proliferation of informal settlements questions the efforts on achieving the SDGs, as an agenda of sustainable development, especially in regions where informal settlements dominate (Teferi & Newman, 2018). Hence, conceptually situating informal settlements within the broader scope of sustainable development help to unearth its multifaceted and yet intersecting features.

Since its inception in the 1980s, the meaning of sustainable development has tended to mean fostering capabilities and creating opportunities to maintain or achieve desirable social, economic and ecological systems for current and future generations (Cobbinah et al., 2015). It provides integrated pathways for stimulating socio-economic development in an environmentally friendly manner (UN-Habitat, 2015). Functional urbanisation, poverty reduction and inclusive policies, investment in human capital, infrastructure and responsive governance offers potentials for sustainable development (UN-Habitat, 2016) by aligning issues that challenge urban life in developing countries, including those in marginal conditions, with sustainable development (Cobbinah et al., 2015). Thus, it is important to situate the granular experiences of informal settlements within the three dimensions of sustainable development: economy, equity (society) and ecology (see Figure 1). Here, economy refers to enhanced livelihoods, economic opportunities for all, improved living conditions and reduced poverty and income inequality (Gupta & Vegelin, 2016). Equity issues refer to opportunities for human development, social protection, political and civic engagement, shared opportunities for all and access to social services that enhance the dignity of all (Gupta & Vegelin, 2016). Ecology focuses on improved environmental conditions and management; reduced environmental pollution, reduced risk to environmental hazards and reduced consumption of finite natural resources (Gupta & Baud, 2015).

The three dimensions of sustainable development is expressed through all 17 SDGs. As shown in Figure 12.1, the challenges found in informal settlements are situated within and at the interface of the three dimensions of sustainable development. For instance, addressing SDG 1 which focuses on reducing poverty will require both improvements in the economy and equitable access to resources. Moreover, attaining SDG 11 which focuses on sustainable cities will also require improvements in the economy, the environment and equity within the urban space. The relevance of framing problems of informal settlements through the lenses of the dimensions of sustainable development and its interface with the SDGs is to provide a framework through which the potentials of informal settlements in helping attain the SDGs and its targets can be expressed (Figure 13.1).

Study Context: Old Fadama

Old Fadama is an infamous informal settlement located in the heart of Ghana's capital city, Accra. Geographically, it lies between latitude 5° 33' 25.44' and 5° 33' 17.28' north and longitude 0° 13' 10.56" and 0° 13' 36.48' west (Monney et al., 2013). It is approximately 1 km from the central business district and constitutes people from many ethnic groups and regions of Ghana as well as foreigners from neighbouring West African countries. It is bounded by Abossey Okai Road, the Odaw River and the Korle Lagoon (Oteng-Ababio & Grant, 2019a). Old Fadama had an

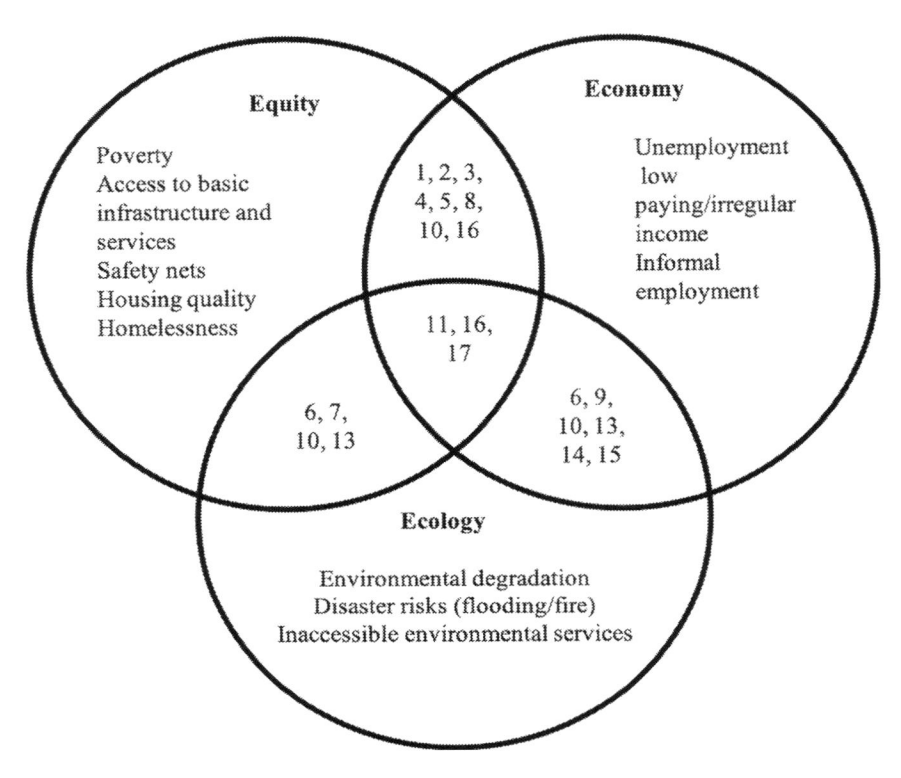

Figure 13.1 Conceptual framework linking the main features of informal settlements with sustainable development (3 E's) and the SDGs.

approximate total population of 80,000 in 2010 (Ghana Statistical Service, 2012) and a total land area of 0.313 square kilometers (Housing the Masses, 2010; Figure 13.2).

The settlement was originally an unused marshy area that was regarded by city authorities as uninhabitable for humans. Old Fadama became a known settlement in the early part of the 1980s where migrants mostly from the northern parts of Ghana settled to look for job opportunities. The size of Old Fadama increased significantly between 1990 and 1995 when the government in its bid to ease overcrowding and congestion in Accra to prepare the city for the Non-Aligned Conference temporary re-located street hawkers and the yam market to the area (Afenah, 2012; COHRE, 2004). The population swelled further when Ghanaians from the northern regions escaped the Konkomba-Nanumba tribal conflict in 1994/1995. Construction of wooden structures and shacks to accom-modate the rising influx of people apparently made Old Fadama a known residential area with low rental accommodation. The desire of people to

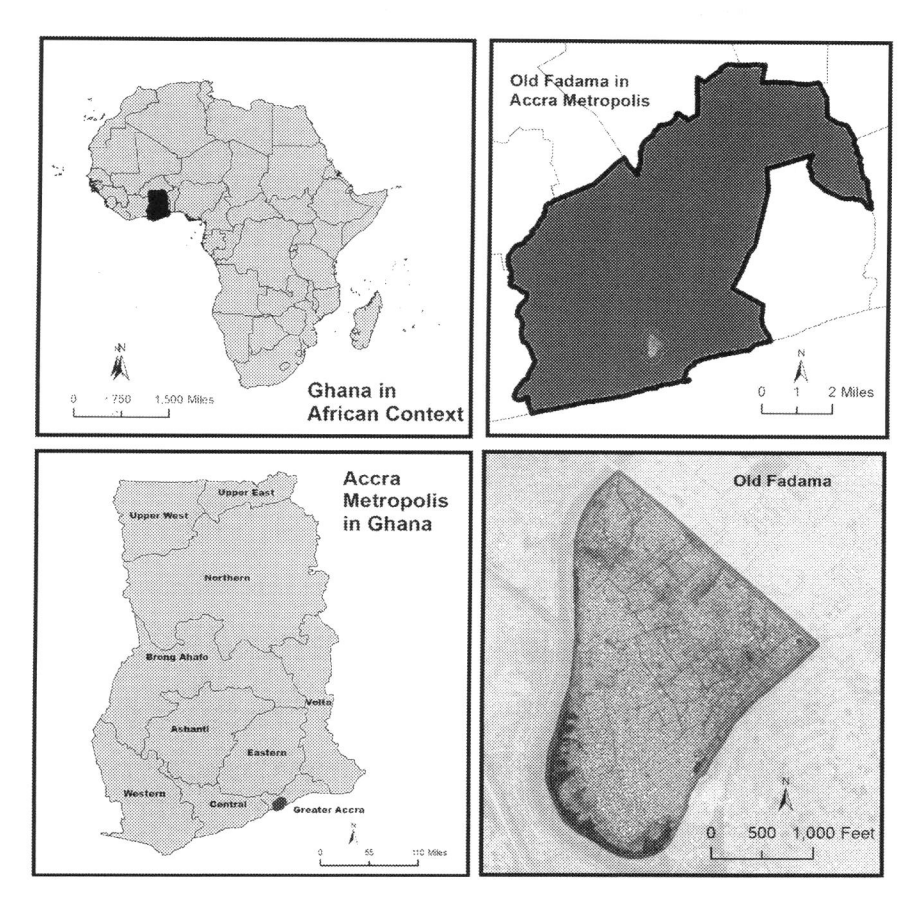

Figure 13.2 Study location.

Source: Authors Construct (using data files from ArcGIS online and January 12, 2018 Google Earth Imagery).

escape the rising cost of rent in the city and the state indifference towards informal housing increased population far more than what the land size could sustain (COHRE, 2004). The settlement has the largest commercial fresh produce market which attracts traders from all parts of Ghana and neighbouring West African countries (Oberhauser & Yeboah, 2011). The market together with the emergence of metal and e-waste market involving the importation of electronic appliances such as fridges and computers has exacerbated the congestion in the settlement. The resultant effect of overcrowding and enormous economic opportunities is the widespread prevalence of unsanitary conditions interspersed with inadequate infrastructure. The growth of e-waste market and the resulting burning of plastics has also exacerbated the environmental conditions in the settlement (Melara Arguello et al., 2013).

Further, environmental challenges have led to constant threats of eviction, beginning in July 1993, where people from 400 houses were evicted. Since then, the settlement has been under intensified threats of eviction – often after disasters. The most notable threat was in 2002, when the Accra Metropolitan Assembly (AMA) issued eviction notices on the grounds of (i) illegality of tenure and (ii) government plans in restoring the vital marine and river system of Korle Lagoon (Korle Lagoon Ecological Restoration Project [KLERP]). Residents of Old Fadama and some philanthropic organisations like the Centre for Housing Right and Eviction (COHRE) and the Centre for Public Interest Law (CEPIL) protested (du Plessis, 2005) and residents with the help of COHRE and CEPIL successfully petitioned the High Court for an injunction to prevent the government's eviction plans (Grant, 2006). The most recent eviction attempt occurred in June 2015, where a team of military personnel and public authorities demolished make-shift structures and displaced some of the inhabitants.

Method and Research Design

The research captures residents' everyday experiences to provide an alternative perspective of informality and its role in attaining the SDGs. It addresses two questions: (i) how does the everyday realities and struggles for those at the margins (informal residents), mirror and intersect the SDGs? and (ii) what kind of "policy-practice" implications do these ordinary, mundane and localised everyday idiosyncrasies of urban living provide in terms of the potential and challenge of achieving sustainable development for those at the margins in the contemporary African city? To answer these questions, this chapter adopted a case study design and combined multiple analytical methods to unravel the potential of informal settlements in attaining the SDGs. It utilised data from four in-depth interviews conducted in 2016 at Old Fadama informal settlement to document the daily realities of residents. Each interview lasted about 30–45 minutes and were conducted in the settlement. The core aspects of the interview focused on residents' background, livelihood experiences, accommodation, and personal and societal challenges encountered in Old Fadama. Interviewees were asked to describe and reflect on how a typical day in their lives unfolds as this was important in understanding their everyday realities.

The interviews were first transcribed and cleaned to ensure clarity. These interviews were complemented with field notes and visits to the settlement using non-participant observations. To analyse the interviews, the study employed a qualitative analytical method informed by Barney Glaser's Grounded Theory Methods (GTM) involving three stages of coding: open coding, selective coding and theoretical coding (Glaser, 2005; Urquhart, 2013). The first step of coding, *open coding*, entailed a line-by-line examination of the transcribed narratives of residents' everyday realities considering keywords and phrases derived from the characteristics and experiences of informal settlement residents in literature. This was followed by *selective coding* where the keywords, phrases and characteristics from the transcribed interviews are matched with keywords and phrases that capture the main themes embedded in the SDGs and their targets and formed the preliminary stage of unravelling the intersectionality of informality and the SDGs. Finally, the *theoretical coding* involved identifying the various intersections between informality and the SDGs and how they provide a basis to theorise about experiences of informal settlement residents and their potential for addressing the SDGs. Here, we determined meaningful connections (Urquhart, 2013) between informality and achieving the SDGs – the fundamental focus of this chapter. The notions of everyday experiences and sustainable development are thus the theoretical lenses through which the role of informal settlements in achieving the SDGs is unraveled.

This approach is thus "retroductive" as it began with examining the theoretical framework or concepts of informality and sustainable development (*Open coding*) and subsequently examined the everyday realities of the respondents in relation to the SDGs (*Selective coding*) and then using the intersectionality of informality and SDGs to theorise the role of informal settlements in attaining the SDGs (*Theoretical coding*). This process helped determined relationships and identified meaningful connections (Duminy et al., 2014) between informality and the SDGs. By focusing on the everyday experiences of respondents, the chapter highlights the characteristics and issues (Flyvbjerg, 2006) of informal settlements and draw implications for the SDGs.

Tracing Everyday Urban Struggles in Old Fadama

This section draws on empirical work conducted in Old Fadama. As much as possible, it provides an original account of the everyday urban experiences of four residents of Old Fadama informal settlement based on the in-depth interviews and non-participant observations.

Adiza[1]

Adiza is a 24-year-old head porter who works at the Agbogbloshie market. She moved to Accra in 2010 from Walewale in the Northern region of Ghana. Adiza discontinued her Junior High School (JHS) education in the first year because her family could not afford to support her schooling. She moved to Accra in search of opportunities to improve her life. Adiza has one child, who currently lives with her in Old Fadama. Adiza has engaged in kayayee (head porter) since moving to Accra. Initially, she worked at the Makola Market and slept on the street. Currently, she is a kayaye at the Agbogbloshie market, a busy trading area that enables her to get clients to carry their goods. This market is also closer to where she lives in Old

Fadama. She charges based on the weight of the item, from GH¢ 2 (US$ 0.50 cent) to GH¢ 4 (US$ 1) and makes between GH¢ 20 (US$ 3.50) to GH¢ 30 (US$ 5) a day.[2] Adiza works every day except Sundays and begins work early in the morning and closes between 6:30 pm and 7:00 pm. She lives in a rented wooden shack together with four other head potters because she cannot afford the full rent by herself. The rent is GH¢ 60 (US$ 10) per week and each person pays GH¢15 (US$ 2.60 cent) every week. This allows her to save for other expenditures such as food or remittances.

However, owners of shacks have the penchant of increasing the price of rent, which is a challenge for renters. Living in Old Fadama is the only option she has because the accommodation is affordable compared to other parts of the city, and closer to where she works. Adiza plans on saving money and starting a food vending business because it is profitable and has fewer health risks compared to a kayayee. According to Adiza, a few ladies have become paralysed after breaking their spine because of the heavy load they carried. She also plans to buy a shack and rent it out to residents in the community since it is a good source of extra income. Flooding is a perennial challenge in the community especially during the rainy season when the Odaw drain overflows. Adiza's shack is closer to the drain and has experienced flooding; her shack was destroyed by the rains and "she lost everything." Because of this experience, she plans on renting a room at the elevated parts of the community but the exorbitant prices have impeded her from doing so.

The wooden shack Adiza lives in has no housing facilities like baths, toilets or potable water. Again, the number of public baths is inadequate. Long queues to public baths and public toilets occur in the mornings. These facilities are usually provided by private individuals who reside in the community as profit-making ventures. She observes that inadequate toilet facilities are a reason people defecate indiscriminately along and into the Korle lagoon. Adiza notes that several young girls are sexually abused either by their boyfriends or men who they know casually. This situation is worse for those who are homeless. She narrates a personal experience

> "one time when I was not feeling well and alone inside my shack, I heard a male voice that asked me to open the door, and forcibly attempted to open the door. I suspect if he had opened the door to my shack, he would have raped me."

Eviction remains a constant threat to Adiza. After the 3rd June 2016 disaster, she recounts how structures along the Korle lagoon were bulldozed by city authorities and only halted because residents demonstrated against the decision. Threats of eviction has prevented her from investing in household and electrical appliances.

Salma

Salma is 20 years old and hails from Wrawra in the Volta Region of Ghana. She migrated to Old Fadama at age 17. She is a JHS graduate. Her motivation to migrate to Accra is informed by knowing people from her hometown who become economically successful after migrating. She currently assists a street food vendor who hails from her hometown. Typically, Salma's day begins at 4:30 am every day. She assists in the preparation of varieties of local staple foods, which are made ready for sale between 7:30 am and 8:00 am. They operate from a very small wooden structure erected close to the room rented by the street vendor as they have limited space for food preparation. Salma receives a daily wage of GH¢ 15 (US$ 2.60). From her savings, she intends to go through an apprenticeship to be a seamstress while working to assist the street vendor. Salma rents a small room together with another young lady who works at the nearby Kokomba market. The two share a monthly rent of GH¢ 200 (US$ 35). Prior to renting this room, she shared a single room with the owner of the food stall, her husband and three young children. She notes that rent for her present room is constantly increasing, as people keep arriving in the community in search for affordable accommodation. Those unable to afford have resorted to sleeping in open spaces. Salma elaborates:

> "Now we have a lot of people sleeping outside here. This is because more people are coming in and the cost of rent is also increasing. So, what people do is to sleep in front of people's structures or in groups in open spaces, and this is dangerous for females. But most of those who sleep outside are males."

There is no running water or standpipe in Salma's rental house. She pays to access the bath, toilets and water in the community. She does not pay for food and this helps her to save some money and remit her mother at Wrawra. According to Salma, social delinquency, prostitution and perennial floods are part of the living in Old Fadama. There is also a growing incidence of fire outbreaks. For Salma, these harsh realities at Old Fadama are better than staying in her hometown, which provides "*no future for her.*" To Salma, there are a lot of other people who have come to Old Fadama with the hope of getting money and doing something better with their lives.

Talata

Talata is a 22-year-old female head porter who lives in Old Fadama. She moved to Old Fadama in 2012 when she was 18 years. Talata is a JHS graduate from Dasabligo in the Upper East Region of Ghana. Talata came to Accra to join a friend who had moved to Accra a year before. She currently plies her trade at Makola market where she is a kayayee. Her father died before she completed JHS, and her mother is the only one taking care of her four younger siblings. She therefore came to Accra to find a job and support her mother. Before coming to Accra, Talata was aware that she would work as a head porter. She reports the work is tedious; earns between GH¢15–30 (US$ 2.60–5) a day, which does not commensurate with the heavy workload. She begins work around 5:00 am at one of the bus terminals together with her friends.

Talata decided to stay at Old Fadama due to cheap accommodation. The cost of rent in other parts of Accra is high and she does not have money for the usual "advance payment" of about two years rent demanded by landlords. She pays GH¢ 40 (US$ 7) per month as part of contribution to the GH¢ 200 (US$ 35) monthly rent for a shared wooden shack by five people. Already, the owner of the container has informed them that he will be increasing the price to GH¢ 300 (US$ 52) per month. Despite the increase in rent, she plans to stay due to the relatively cheaper accommodation and proximity to work. Talata recounts that there are three public toilets owned by private individuals. Despite the deplorable conditions and poor maintenance, she pays GH¢ 1.00 (US$ 0.20 cent) and GH¢ 0.50 (US$ 0.10 cent) for the public bath and toilet, respectively. There are also serious safety and security issues such as stealing, sexual harassment, and labour exploitation. She recalls the numerous cases of stealing. Usually, she locks the door of her shack and leaves for work, "praying that her things are not stolen." Talata discloses that the constant threat of eviction undermines her life:

> "I came to Accra to have a life, to support myself and to see if I can make a future out of it. That is why I live in Old Fadama because accommodation is affordable. So, if I am evicted, where do I go and start life from? We are pleading with the government to support us and make this place where humans can live. We are denigrated and demonized, and all this is to get us evicted."

Adams

Adams is a 23-year-old e-waste scavenger residing at Old Fadama. He moved to Accra from Tamale in the Northern region in 2015. Adams dropped out of school at primary four because of financial problems. Adams decided to come to Accra because he realised that when he stays in the north to help his family to farm, there will be little opportunity for him to make money and have a better life. Farming is seasonal (rainy season) and he is usually idle during the lean season. Adam scavenges in the south industrial area, Odornar and Adabraka. He also goes to Abossey-Okine to scavenge for scraps. His work starts at around 5:00 am as scavenging for scraps is competitive. Previously, electronic waste was given for free but now owners demand payment for the scraps. Adams makes GH¢ 35 (US$ 6) on average daily. Although most young people team-up, Adams scavenges alone. He initially scavenged with his cousin with whom he lodged at Old Fadama. He later got his own cart and now he is doing his own work. For Adams, scavenging for e-waste provides a major source of livelihood for several young migrants in Accra. However, potential dangers such as dangerous and reckless driving along the road are not uncommon.

Adam rents a room with a friend at Old Fadama. The structure is made up of a combination of bricks and plywood. He rents the room for GH ¢50(US$ 9) per week and considers the price and payment arrangements affordable. For Adam, it is important not to spend too much on rent as this allows one to spend on equally important necessities, especially remitting money to support his family. Flooding and fire are two critical issues that challenge his daily life in Old Fadama. He recalls:

> "In 2015 the whole place got flooded. People's belongings were destroyed by the flood. For me, my electrical appliances were destroyed; it was a painful experience. Because of this, I don't even have the desire to buy those things again. All that I need is my clothes. Almost every year we experience flooding. But we don't have many options. It is either you leave, or you stay. But when you leave, where will you go?"

Adams attributed frequent fires to the number of wooden structures and the illegal electricity connection people do. For the latter, this was the only way they can get access to electricity because only few residents are formally connected to the grid. He also considers the constant threat of eviction as a possible reason behind wooden structures or temporal building materials, which reduces their risks to potential loss from housing investment.

Tracing the Sustainable Development Dimension of Urban Struggles

This section traces the three elements of sustainable development – equity, economy and ecology – from the grounded realities of residents living in Old Fadama. It highlights the specific SDGs and their targets and their connections to residents' everyday experiences using the format of SDG Number: Target Number. For example, SDG 11:7 represents the *Goal* on sustainable cities and the *Target* to increase access to green and open spaces in urban areas by 2030.

Equity

The narratives from informants' show the multiple challenges that informal settlement dwellers go through to get a foothold in the city. It also highlights four important equity issues that managers of the urban space have either failed to interrogate or shown ambivalence towards: people's poverty conditions (SDG 1:1–2), share in development opportunities and benefits (SDG 1:4), levels of protection of and support to the marginalised and vulnerable within the urban space (SDG 1:3; SDG 10:4), and informal settlements residents' access to opportunities, infrastructure and services (SDG 1:4; SDG 10:1–3; SDG 11:1). From the narratives, there was limited opportunities for residents to build capacity and attain skills through education in the informal settlement (SDG 4: 1–7). This limited residents' opportunity in the formal sector which require some level of skill and knowledge (Smit et al., 2017). This has emerged because of the unbalanced regional development policies (SDG 9:1; SDG 11:11) and inequitable distribution of educational resources and infrastructure (Oteng-Ababio et al., 2017). The predicament of informal settlement dwellers is further worsened by limited access to basic services such as water and sanitation (SDG 6:1-6), basic healthcare services (SDG 3:3,5,9; SDG 8:8) and quality and affordable housing (SDG 11:1). Unfortunately, the quest to access some of these services has often led to economic exploitation and threats of sexual exploitation, especially from the experiences of females (SDG 5:2; SDG 16:1–2), calling into question how the safety and security needs of the vulnerable in society is safeguarded. The challenges mentioned clearly shows the lag in progress in meeting the SDGs, particularly Goal 1 (no poverty), Goal 3 (good health and well-being), Goal 4 (quality education), Goal 5 (gender equality), Goal 6 (clean water and sanitation), Goal 8 (decent work and economic growth), Goal 11 (sustainable cities and communities) and Goal 16 (peace, justice and strong institutions).

Further, residents' everyday experiences support Wekesa et al.'s (2011) argument that informal settlement dwellers are rarely involved in the planning processes, even though their daily activities contribute to the urban economy. The incessant threat of eviction from city managers questions the level of inclusiveness and participation within urban governance processes (SDG 11:3). Not only have this attitude from city managers failed to address the plight and social needs of the urban poor but also failed to appreciate the contributions of informal settlement residents in urban planning and development. For instance, in the wake of state neglect, some residents are stepping in to provide socio-economic services such as water and sanitation (Okyere et al., 2017). This shows that there is much potential for community and institutional collaboration in the planning and provision of basic services.

Economy

The economic dimension of the SDGs is one of the dominant themes in residents' everyday urban experiences in Old Fadama. Goal 1 (no poverty), Goal 3 (good health and wellbeing), Goal 8 (decent work and economic growth), Goal 10 (reduce inequalities), and Goal 11 (sustainable cities and communities) intersect with the residents' everyday experiences; specifically on issues of economic migration (SDG 2A; SDG 9:1; SDG 10:7; SDG 11A), informal sector employment (SDG 8:3), irregular incomes (SDG 10:1-2; SDG 2:3) and exploitation and lack of safety nets (SDG 1:3; SDG 5:4; SDG 10:4). The narratives indicate that easy access to informal economic activities is an important "pull" factor for youthful migrants seeking a foothold in Accra's vibrant informal sector. These are underpinned by two driving factors: (i) their low educational profiles and limited economic opportunities at their places of origin and (ii) absence of educational and skill barriers in most jobs in the informal sector for unskilled migrants in Accra (Oteng-Ababio et al., 2019). These contribute to the "meteoric rise" of inequality, including the territorial dimensions of north-south economic disparities in postcolonial Ghana (Obeng-Odoom, 2015, p. 551). Although migrants appear to be earning wages above the poverty line, the peculiarities of informal work engender marginality and unsustainable livelihoods with social and ecological externalities. For informal sector work in Accra, daily wage is not only low but erratic, linked to the fortunes of the market, clients, gender and power relations (Okyere & Kita 2016; Yeboah, 2017). Moreover, constant attacks and threats to street level work suggest the downward transition from informal work into unemployment is a constant reality (Obeng-Odoom, 2013; Roever & Skinner, 2016). It is hardly a wonder that urban multi-dimensional poverty is rather acute in low-income migrant communities as Old Fadama (Awumbila et al., 2014). These findings expose the ineffectiveness of sustainable development efforts in Accra for those in low-income urban communities, coupled with endemic mindsets and ideologies that conceive migrant spaces as marginal (Oteng-Ababio & Grant, 2019a). Indeed, the fragile livelihoods of those in the informal economy reflect the sustainability challenges of those at the margins (Obeng-Odoom, 2013).

Ecology

Residents of Old Fadama face a plethora of environmental challenges including insanitary conditions, congestion and disaster vulnerability and exposure. The actions and activities of informal settlement residents – such as combustion of plastics material and electrical wires and indiscriminate disposal of solid waste – creates environmental challenges which spotlights residents' limited access to safely managed sanitation services (SDG 6:2) and sustainable energy sources (SDG 7:1). Akin to many informal settlements across Africa (Douglas, 2018), Old Fadama is a disaster hotspot due to poor structural quality of housing, its location in the floodplains of the Korle Lagoon and indiscriminate disposal of solid waste into the drains (Abunyewah et al., 2018; Amoako & Inkoom, 2018; Williams & Webb, 2020). Dense housing, spontaneous physical layout, flammability of housing units and inadequate infrastructure facilities impede disaster response measures (Owusu et al., 2008). Unsurprisingly, fire and flooding are regularly disaster events in the settlement destroying the homes and property of many residents. The growing disaster vulnerability and exposure levels of informal settlements dwellers (Abunyewah et al., 2019, 2020) as well as their severity raises the urgent need for climate resilience and disaster management in informal settlements (SDG 13:1; SGD 11:1)

Conclusion

The chapter provides evidence that the urban experience for some of those living in Old Fadama remain far off from the sustainable development agenda. Economic, social, and ecological factors have constrained sustainable development for some. The following are some key policy imperatives necessary to reach those farthest behind in sustainable development. Firstly, the youthful and migrant status as well as the low socio-economic profile of residents in Old Fadama undermines the recent momentum around the "youth bulge" or the "demographic dividend": the potential role of Africa's young population to economic growth and productivity. While others (e.g., Oteng-Ababio et al., 2019, p. 1) have extolled the "informal exceptionalism" of young migrants in negotiating harsh urban life to address poverty, these might turn to "youth deficits" without effective development planning and policy innovations. Policy makers, in a collaborative manner, should devise actionable strategies for productive skills acquisition or training programs to enable young people engage in gainful and secured work in the informal sector (SDG 8:3,5,6). It means paying attention to manufacturing, sustainable agriculture and alternative livelihood support programmes that has been lagging or plagued by political apathy and negligence in places that act as the sources of migration (SDG 9:2–3). Relatedly, the disproportionate investment in Accra, against other areas is not a sustainable option in the long term. This requires urban planning that encapsulates sustainable development policy coherence (SDG 17:14) and principles of regional planning and rural-urban integration (SDG 1B; SDG 2A; SDG 4:5; SDG 9:1; SDG 11A).

Indeed, informal migrant workers have a role in the urban economy and environment (Roever & Skinner, 2016), requiring urban and state actors to soberly rethink informal work (SDG 8:5,6) and partner informal workers towards inclusive policies (SDG 17:16-17). This should start with a reversal of urban state's ambivalence and brutal attacks on informal workers (SDG 11:3). It warrants the need to move beyond mere recognition to protections for informal workers, the kind that guarantee economic well-being, reduce poverty and the uncertainties in informal work as well as creating access to socioeconomic opportunities, infrastructure, and services (SDG 1B; SDG 4A; SDG 5B, C; SDG 6B). Indeed, the examples of supportive state policies in Bogota and Lima suggest support for the informal sector can drive sustainable livelihoods for the urban poor (see Roever & Skinner, 2016).

Moreover, Accra's housing sector has been characterised as paradoxical trend of a boom in upscale residential units for the wealthy and shortages for the urban poor. As revealed from the interviews, housing prices and rental markets are insensitive to the economic conditions of urban migrants. Practical alternatives such as mixing informal settlement upgrading with affordable housing have not been actively taken up by policymakers. For example, the Amui Dzor Cooperative Housing Project is a notable case of affordable housing for informal residents (Gillespie, 2018) but has not witnessed any scaled-up interventions. The project is a key policy pointer that civil society, informal residents and local government can collaboratively develop workable solutions to address the woeful state of housing for the urban poor. Consequently, eviction-based bulldozing is not an inclusive strategy. Rather, planners should first recognise informal settlement residents' right to the urban space and innovate to improve their living conditions. This will require the provision and upgrading of infrastructure and services such as water and sanitation, electricity, and quality housing (SDG 6:1–6; SDG 7:1B; SDG 10:1). These strategies must be layered on tenure regulation programs that integrate popular participation (SDG 1:4).

Policy attention must also be given to the safety and security challenges in informal settlements. This can be addressed from two angles. The first involves reducing the conditions that propel informal settlement dwellers into committing crime and engaging in delinquent acts (SDG 3:5; SDG 5:2; SDG 16:1). These interventions must aim at skill acquisition and financial support for start-up businesses and other interventions to support livelihoods. The second angle involves reducing situations that make informal settlement dwellers, especially the most vulnerable, an easy target for perpetrators of crime. Interventions should include provision of streetlights to reduce night-time crimes, provision of a police post as a mark of police presence and strengthening collaboration between social/informal groups and the police. With regards to flood vulnerabilities, nature-based strategies can offer ways to tackle flooding, increase access to greenspaces, as well as treat and protect the polluted Korle Lagoon (SDG 6:3–6). However, this will require effective partnerships among residents, planners, designers, and engineers (SDG 6A, B).

Overall, the intersectionality of the SDGs with informality demonstrates the potential that informal settlements hold in promoting sustainable urban development by attaining the SDGs. It demonstrates that by tackling the everyday challenges of informal settlement residents, multiple SDGs can be attained beyond SDG 11:1 – the only framing of informality within the SDGs. Consequently, there is need for integrated development planning approaches. These should be built within reformed and effective institutional governance systems that prioritises the urban poor to foster progress towards sustainable urban development in Accra as well as other African cities.

Notes

1 The names of respondents have been changed to preserve their identify and ensure privacy.
2 The exchange rate at the time of data collection was estimated around US$1 = GH¢ 4.1 (12 December, 2016)

Reference

Abunyewah, M., Gajendran, T., & Maund, K. (2018). Profiling informal settlements for disaster risks. *Procedia Engineering*, *212*, 238–245. doi:10.1016/j.proeng.2018.01.031

Abunyewah, M., Gajendran, T., Maund, K., & Okyere, S. (2019). Linking information provision to behavioural intentions: Moderating and mediating effects of message clarity and source credibility. *International Journal of Disaster Resilience in the Built Environment*, *11*(1), 100–118. 10.1108/IJDRBE-08-2019-0059

Abunyewah, M., Gajendran, T., Maund, K., & Okyere, S. A. (2020). Strengthening the information deficit model for disaster preparedness: Mediating and moderating effects of community participation. *International Journal of Disaster Risk Reduction*, 101492. doi:10.1016/j.ijdrr.2020.101492.

Afenah, A. (2012). Engineering a millennium city in Accra, Ghana: The Old Fadama intractable issue. *Urban Forum*, *23*(4), 527–540. doi:10.1007/s12132-012-9155-z

Amoako, C. (2016). Brutal presence or convenient absence: The role of the state in the politics of flooding in informal Accra, Ghana. *Geoforum*, *77*, 5–16. doi:10.1016/j.geoforum.2016.10.003

Amoako, C., & Inkoom, D. K. B. (2018). The production of flood vulnerability in Accra, Ghana: Re-thinking flooding and informal urbanisation. *Urban Studies*, *55*(13), 2903–2922. doi:10.1177/0042098016686526

Awumbila, M., Owusu, G., & Teye, J. K. (2014). Can rural-urban migration into slums reduce poverty? Evidence from Ghana. *Migrating Out of Poverty Research Consortium Working Paper 13*, University of Sussex, School of Global Studies. Retrieved from https://opendocs.ids.ac.uk/opendocs/bitstream/handle/20.500.12413/14825/wp-13---awumbila-owusu-teye-2014-can-rural-urban-migration-into-slums-reduce-poverty-final.pdf?sequence=1

Baptist, C., & Bolnick, J. (2012). Participatory enumerations, in situ upgrading and mega events: The 2009 survey in Joe Slovo, Cape Town. *Environment and Urbanization*, *24*(1), 59–66. doi:10.1177/0956247811435888

Braun, B., & Aßheuer, T. (2011). Floods in megacity environments: Vulnerability and coping strategies of slum dwellers in Dhaka/Bangladesh. *Natural Hazards*, *58*(2), 771–787. doi:10.1007/s11069-011-9752-5

Chen, M., Roever, S., & Skinner, C. (2016). Editorial: Urban livelihoods: Reframing theory and policy. *Environment & Urbanization*, *28*(2), 331–342. doi:10.1177/0956247816662405

Cirolia, L. R., & Scheba, S. (2018). Towards a multi-scalar reading of informality in Delft, South Africa: Weaving the 'everyday' with wider structural tracings. *Urban Studies*, *56*(3), 594–611. doi:10.1177/0042098017753326

Cobbinah, P. B., Erdiaw-Kwasie, M. O., & Amoateng, P. (2015). Africa's urbanisation: Implications for sustainable development. *Cities, 47*, 62–72. doi:10.1016/j.cities.2015.03.013

COHRE. (2004). *A precarious future: the informal settlement of Agbogbloshie, Ghana*. Retrieved from https://www.mypsup.org/library_files/downloads/Report%20on%20the%20Informal%20Settlement%20of%20Agbogbloshie,%20Ghana.pdf

De Satgé, R., & Watson, V. (2018). *Urban planning in the Global South: Conflicting rationalities in contested urban space*. Cham: Palgrave Macmillan-Springer Nature.

Douglas, I. (2018). The challenge of urban poverty for the use of green infrastructure on floodplains and wetlands to reduce flood impacts in intertropical Africa. *Landscape and Urban Planning, 180*, 262–272. doi:10.1016/j.landurbplan.2016.09.025

Dovey, K. (2012). Informal urbanism and complex adaptive assemblage. *International Development Planning Review, 34*(4), 349.

Dovey, K. & King, R. (2011). Forms of informality: Morphology and visibility of informal settlements. *Built Environment, 37*(1), 11–29. doi:10.2148/benv.37.1.11

Duminy, J., Andreasen, J., Lerise, F., Odendaal, N., & Watson, V. (Eds.). (2014). *Planning and the Case Study Method in Africa: The Planner in Dirty Shoes*. London: Palgrave Macmillan.

du Plessis, J. (2005). The growing problem of forced evictions and the crucial importance of community-based, locally appropriate alternatives. *Environment & Urbanization, 17*(1), 123–134. doi:10.1177/095624780501700108

Ezeh, A., Oyebode, O., Satterthwaite, D., Chen, Y.-F., Ndugwa, R., Sartori, J., … Watson, S. I. (2017). The history, geography, and sociology of slums and the health problems of people who live in slums. *The Lancet, 389*(10068), 547–558. doi:10.1016/S0140-6736(16)31650-6

Flyvbjerg, B. (2006). Five Misunderstandings About Case-Study Research. *Qualitative Inquiry, 12*(2), 219–245. doi:10.1177/1077800405284363

Fox, S. (2014). The political economy of slums: Theory and evidence from Sub-Saharan Africa. *World Development, 54*, 191–203. doi:10.1016/j.worlddev.2013.08.005

Gillespie, T. (2016). Accumulation by urban dispossession: struggles over urban space in Accra, Ghana. *Transactions of the Institute of British Geographers, 41*(1), 66–77. doi:10.1111/tran.12105

Gillespie, T. (2018). Collective self-help, financial inclusion, and the commons: Searching for solutions to Accra's housing crisis. *Housing Policy Debate, 28*(1), 64–78. doi:10.1080/10511482.2017.1324892

Glaser, B. J. (2005). *The grounded theory perspective III: Theoretical coding*. Mill Valley, CA: The Sociology Press.

Gouverneur, D. (2015). *Planning and design for future informal settlements: Shaping the self-constructed city*. Abingdon, Oxon; New York, NY: Routledge.

Grant, R. (2006). Out of place? global citizens in local spaces: A study of the informal settlements in the korle lagoon environs in Accra, Ghana. *Urban Forum, 17*(1), 1–24. doi:10.1007/BF02681256

Gupta, J., & Baud, I. S. A. (2015). Sustainable development. In P. Pattberg & F. Zelli (Eds.), *Encyclopedia of global environmental politics and governance* (pp. 61–72). Cheltenham: Edward Elgar.

Gupta, J., & Vegelin, C. (2016). Sustainable development goals and inclusive development. *International Environmental Agreements: Politics, Law and Economics*, 16(3), 433–448

Hove, M., Ngwerume, E. T., & Muchemwa, C. (2013). The urban crisis in sub-saharan Africa: A threat to human security and sustainable development. *Stability: International Journal of Security and Development*, 2(1), 7. doi:1 0.5334/sta.ap

Jiménez-Aceituno, A., Peterson, G. D., Norström, A. V., Wong, G. Y., & Downing, A. S. (2019). Local lens for SDG implementation: Lessons from bottom-up approaches in Africa. *Sustainability Science*, doi:10.1007/s11625-01 9-00746-0.

Kita, M., Okyere, S. A., Sugita, M., & Diko, S. K. (2020). In Y. Ofosu-Kusi & M. Matsuda (Eds.), *Search of Place and Life in Indigenous Urban Communities: An Exploration of Abese Indigenous Quarter of La Dadekotopon, Accra*. Bamenda: Langaa.

Klopp, J. M., & Paller, J. W. (2019). Slum politics in Africa. *Oxford Research Encyclopedia of politics*. doi:10.1093/acrefore/9780190228637.013.985.

Lall, S. V., Henderson, J. V., & Venables, A. J. (2017). *Africa's cities: Opening doors to the world*: The World Bank. Retrieved from http://documents.worldbank.org/curated/en/854221490781543956/pdf/113851-PUB-PUBLIC-PUBDATE-2-9-2 017.pdf

Lund, C., & Stacey, P. (2016). In a state of slum: Governance in an informal urban settlement in ghana. *The Journal of Modern African Studies*, 54(4), 591–615. doi:10.1017/S0022278X16000586

Marx, C., & Kelling, E. (2019). Knowing urban informalities. *Urban Studies*, 56(3), 494–509.

McFarlane, C. (2012). Rethinking informality: Politics, crisis, and the city. *Planning Theory & Practice*, 13(1), 89–108.

Melara Arguello, J. E., Grant, R., Oteng-Ababio, M., & Ayele, B. M. (2013). Downgrading – an overlooked reality in african cities: Reflections from an indigenous neighborhood of Accra, Ghana. *Applied Geography*, 36, 23–30. doi:10.1016/j.apgeog.2012.04.012

Monney, I., Odai, S. N., Buamah, R., Awuah, E., & Nyenje, P. M. (2013). Environmental impacts of wastewater from urban slums: Case study – Old Fadama, Accra, *International Journal of Development and Sustainability*, 2(2), 711–728. Retrieved from https://isdsnet.com/ijds-v2n2-20.pdf

Myers, G. (2011). *African cities: Alternative visions of urban theory and practice*. London, UK: Zed Books Ltd.

Myers, G. (2016). *Urban environments in Africa: A critical analysis of environmental politics*. Bristol, UK; Chicago, IL, USA: Bristol University Press.

Njoh, A. J. (2008). Colonial philosophies, urban space, and racial segregation in British and French colonial Africa. *Journal of Black Studies*, 38(4), 579–599. doi:10.1177/0021934706288447

Obeng-Odoom, F. (2013). Degeneration for others. In M. l. E. Leary & J. McCarthy (Eds.), *The Routledge companion to urban regeneration* (pp. 189–198). London, UK: Routledge

Obeng-Odoom, F. (2015). The social, spatial, and economic roots of urban inequality in Africa: Contextualizing Jane Jacobs and Henry George.

American Journal of Economics and Sociology, 74(3), 550–586. doi:10.1111/ajes.12101

Obeng-Odoom, F. (2017). Urban governance in Africa today: Reframing, experiences, and lessons. *Growth and Change*, 48(1), 4–21. doi:10.1111/grow.12164

Oberhauser, A. M., & Yeboah, M. A. (2011). Heavy burdens: Gendered livelihood strategies of porters in Accra, Ghana. *Singapore Journal of Tropical Geography*, 32(1), 22–37. doi:10.1111/j.1467-9493.2011.00417.x

Okyere, S. A. (2018) A study on socio-spatial structure and community management system in Abese indigenous quarter of La, Accra, Ghana. *Rethinking urban informality and informal settlement improvement*. Doctoral dissertation, Osaka University. 10.18910/69602

Okyere, S. A., Diko, S. K., Abunyewah, M., & Kita, M. (2019). Toward Citizen-Led Planning for Climate Change Adaptation in Urban Ghana: Hints from Japanese 'Machizukuri' Activities. In P. Cobbinah & M. Addaney (Eds.), *The geography of climate change adaptation in urban Africa* (pp. 391–419). Cham: Palgrave Macmillan-Springer.

Okyere, S., Diko, S., Hiraoka, M., & Kita, M. (2017). An urban "mixity": Spatial dynamics of social interactions and human behaviors in the abese informal quarter of La Dadekotopon, Ghana. *Urban Science*, 1(2), 13. doi:10.3390/urbansci1020013

Okyere, A., & Kita, M. (2015). Rethinking urban informality and informal settlements growth in urban Africa: A literature discussion. *Journal of Sustainable Development in Africa*, 17(2), 101–124.

Okyere, S. A., & Kita, M. (2016). 'See, this is a very good place; we are doing many things': Resident activities and satisfaction in Abese informal settlement, La. *Journal of Sustainable Development in Africa*, 18(2), 77–100

Omolabi, A. O., & Adebayo, P. W. (2018). Regeneration – a pragmatic approach to informal settlement development of Abesan Lagos, Nigeria. *Sociology and Anthropology*, 6(9), 717–728. doi:10.13189/sa.2018.060904

Oteng-Ababio, M., & Grant, R. (2019a). e-Waste recycling slum in the heart of Accra, Ghana: The dirty secrets. In M. N. V. Prasad, M. Vithanage, & A. Borthakur (Eds.), *Handbook of electronic waste management: International* best practices and case studies (1st Ed., pp. 355–376). Oxford: Elsevier, Butterworth-Heinemann.

Oteng-Ababio, M., & Grant, R. (2019b). Ideological traces in Ghana's urban plans: How do traces get worked out in the Agbogbloshie, Accra? *Habitat International*, 83, 1–10. doi:10.1016/j.habitatint.2018.10.007

Oteng-Ababio, M., Masriwah, S., & Kusi, L. (2017). Is the underdevelopment of northern Ghana a case of environmental determinism or governance crisis? *Ghana Journal of Geography*, 9(2), 5–39 (special issue).

Oteng-Ababio, M., Tanle, A., Amoah, S. T., Kusi, L., Kosoe, E. A., & Bagson, E. (2019). 'Informal exceptionalism?' Labour migrants' creative entrepreneurship for sustainable livelihoods in Accra, Ghana. *Journal of Asian and African Studies*, 54(1), 88–103. doi:10.1177/0021909618789965

Oviedo, D., Okyere, S. A., Nieto, M., Frimpong, K. L., Yusuf, Y., Koroma, B., & Kita, M. (2021). Walking off the beaten path: Everyday walking environment and practices in informal settlements in Freetown. *Research in Transportation Business and Management*, in press.

Owusu, G., S. Agyei-Mensah, & R. Lund. (2008). Slums of hope and slums of despair: Mobility and livelihoods in Nima, Accra. *Norsk Geografisk Tidsskrift – Norwegian Journal of Geography*, 62(3), 180–190. doi:10.1080/0029195 0802335798

Pfeffer, K., & Georgiadou, Y. (2019). Global ambitions, local contexts: Alternative ways of knowing the world. *ISPRS International Journal of Geo-Information*, 8(11), 516. doi:10.3390/ijgi8110516

Pieterse, E. (2011). Grasping the unknowable: Coming to grips with African urbanisms. *Social Dynamics*, 37(1), 5–23. doi:10.1080/02533952.2011.569994

Pieterse, E. (2017). The city in sub-Saharan Africa. In J. R. Short (Ed.), *A research agenda for cities* (pp. 218–232). Cheltenham, UK: Edward Elgar Publishing.

Pillay, D. (2015). The global economic crisis and the Africa rising narrative. *Africa Development*, 40(3), 59–75.

Roever, S., & Skinner, C. (2016). Street vendors and cities. *Environment and Urbanization*, 28(2), 359–374. doi:10.1177/0956247816653898

Roy, A. (2005). Urban informality: Toward an epistemology of planning. *Journal of the American Planning Association*, 71(2), 147–158.

Satterthwaite, D. (2018). Who can implement the sustainable development goals in urban areas? In T. Elmqvist, X. Bai, & N. Frantzeskaki (Eds.), *The urban planet: Knowledge* towards sustainable cities (pp. 408–411). Cambridge: University Printing House.

Smit, S., Musango, J. K., Kovacic, Z., & Brent, A. C. (2017). Conceptualising slum in an urban African context. *Cities*, 62, 107–119. doi:10.1016/j.cities.2016.12 .018

Smith, M. S., Cook, C., Sokona, Y., Elmqvist, T., Fukushi, K., Broadgate, W., & Jarzebski, M. P. (2018). Advancing sustainability science for the SDGs. *Sustainability Science*, 13(6), 1483–1487. doi:10.1007/s11625-018-0645-3

Stephens, A., Lewis, E. D., & Reddy, S. (2018). Towards an inclusive systemic evaluation for the SDGs: Gender equality, environments and marginalized voices (GEMs). *Evaluation*, 24(2), 220–236. doi:10.1177/1356389018766093

Teferi, Z. A., & Newman, P. (2018). Slum upgrading: Can the 1.5 °C carbon reduction work with SDGs in these settlements? *Analysis and Policy Observatory*, 3(2), 52–63. Retrieved from https://apo.org.au/node/211936

Turok, I., & Borel-Saladin, J. (2018). The theory and reality of urban slums: Pathways-out-of-poverty or cul-de-sacs? *Urban Studies*, 55(4), 767–789. doi:1 0.1177/0042098016671109

Ulbrich, P., Porto de Albuquerque, J., & Coaffee, J. (2019). The impact of urban inequalities on monitoring progress towards the sustainable development goals: Methodological considerations. *ISPRS International Journal of Geo-Information*, 8(1), 6. Retrieved from 10.3390/ijgi8010006

UN-Habitat. (2015), *Habitat III Issues Papers 22-Informal Settlement*, New York. Retrieved from http://habitat3.org/wp-content/uploads/Habitat-III-Issue-Paper-22_Informal-Settlements-2.0.pdf

UN-Habitat. (2016). *World cities report 2016*. Nairobi, Kenya: UN Habitat. Retrieved from http://wcr.unhabitat.org/wp-content/uploads/2017/02/WCR-201 6-Full-Report.pdf

United Nations (UN). (2016). *Transforming our world: The 2030 agenda for sustainable development*. Retrieved from https://sustainabledevelopment.un.org/

content/documents/21252030%20Agenda%20for%20Sustainable%20Development%20web.pdf

Urquhart, C. (2013). *Grounded theory for qualitative research: A practical guide.* London: SAGE.

Watson, V. (2009). 'The planned city sweeps the poor away…': Urban planning and 21st century urbanisation. *Progress in Planning*, 72(3), 151–193. doi:10.1016/j.progress.2009.06.002

Watson, V. (2014). African urban fantasies: dreams or nightmares? *Environment and Urbanization*, 26(1), 215–231. doi:10.1177/0956247813513705

Wekesa, B., Steyn, G., & Otieno, F. A. (2011). Review of physical and socio-economic characteristics and intervention approaches of informal settlements. *Habitat International*, 35, 238–245. doi:10.1016/j.habitatint.2010.09.006

Williams, B. D., & Webb, G. R. (2020). Vulnerability and Disaster: Practitioner Strategies for Addressing the Needs of Vulnerable Populations. *Journal of Homeland Security and Emergency Management.* Retrieved from 10.1515/jhsem-2018-0063.

Yeboah, T. (2017). Towards Secure and Decent Work for Migrant Youth in Ghana. *IDS Policy Briefing 132*, Brighton: IDS. Retrieved from https://opendocs.ids.ac.uk/opendocs/handle/20.500.12413/12826

14 Connecting Solid Waste Management to Sustainable Urban Development in Africa

Enoch Akwasi Kosoe,
Issaka Kanton Osumanu,
and Francis Diawuo Darko

Introduction

Sustainable development is now a central theme in national and international discourse, with a focus on protecting the environment and promoting socio-economic development. Paragraph 218 of "the future we want," is dedicated to the development and enforcement of comprehensive national and local waste management policies, strategies and regulations, regarding a life cycle approach and the promotion of policies of resource efficiency and environmentally sound waste management (UNEP, 2015). Therefore, solid waste management is one of the important services provided by city authorities and a major environmental issue of our time. According to Goel (2017), waste is defined as any material that is discarded by the possessor or generator due to its lack of value to them. Therefore, solid waste is defined as any waste material that is neither in liquid nor gaseous state, that is discarded by the possessor or generator due to its lack of value to them. The last four decades have been marked by several incidents, highlighting problems with solid waste management (Goel, 2017). African cities are facing a growing and varied solid waste collection and management crisis (Godfrey et al., 2019). For instance, in Sousse, Tunisia; and Lagos, Nigeria; solid waste collection coverage is higher than 90% compared to Jimma, Ethiopia; where the collection rate is as low as 25% (see Figure 13.1). There are also variations in the collection rate of solid waste within countries. In Ghana for example, 28% of solid waste in Wa is collected whereas, in Accra, there is over 80% coverage of solid waste collection, as shown in Figure 13.1 (UNEP, 2018). These variations are the result of differences in local structures in terms of infrastructure, capacity and financing (Figure 14.1).

Across Africa, there is discrepancy in terms of waste collection coverage within cities. The inner cities' areas and wealthy neighbourhoods have good coverage whereas, the poor neighbourhoods are often left out (Kabera et al., 2019; Niekerk & Weghmann, 2019). In Nairobi, Kenya, many low and middle-income parts do not have any formal waste collection systems in place (Sunday, 2013; Wilson et al., 2017; Kabera et al., 2019; Niekerk & Weghmann, 2019). South Africa faces a similar situation of inequality in

DOI: 10.4324/9781003181484-14

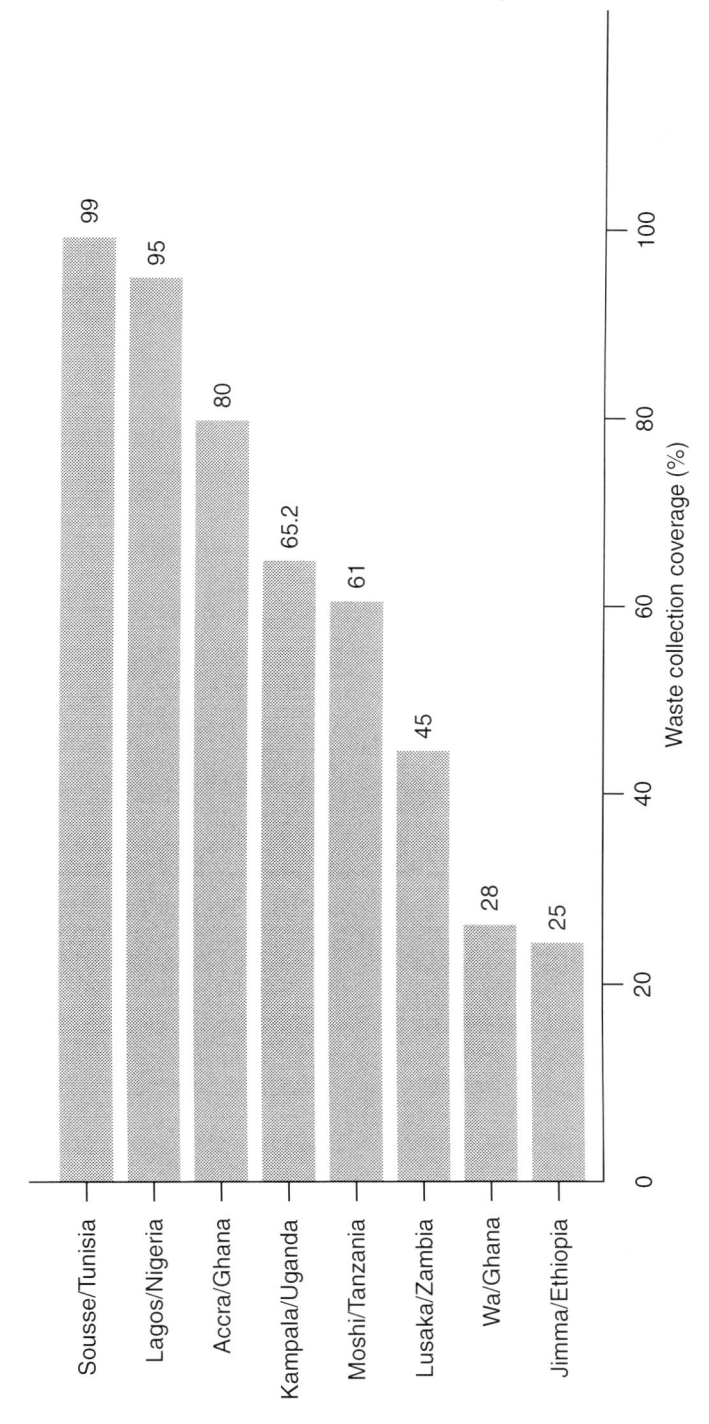

Figure 14.1 Waste collection coverage in selected cities in Africa.
Source: UNEP (2018).

the solid waste management services that are delivered in different areas, where the middle-class areas have a formal system of collection with trucks and many of the poorer areas have a more informal service, or a service that has been contracted out, or a very erratic and inadequate service from the municipality (Fakoya, 2014; Kawai and Tasaki, 2016; Niekerk & Weghmann, 2019; Tsheleza et al., 2019). In Dar es Salaam, Tanzania, privatisation of solid waste services has led to good coverage in the city area, while poorer neighbourhoods are left out, as private providers naturally only service areas where residents can afford to pay a fee for their waste collection (UN-HABITAT, 2010; Kirama & Mayo, 2016; Wilson et al., 2017; Kabera et al., 2019; Niekerk & Weghmann, 2019).

Consequently, residents in most part of Africa have witnessed relatively poor solid waste management practices characterised by indiscriminate dumping, which further exacerbates the already low sanitation level (Bello et al., 2016). Poor solid waste management has wider implications for sustainable urban development in Africa because waste management has become a development challenge in many African cities (Addaney & Oppong, 2015; Schlueter, 2017; Oteng-Ababio et al., 2018; Bundhoo, 2018). Following rapid population growth and urbanisation, rise in middle-income households and the accompanying increase in living standards and consumption, many cities in Africa generate large quantities of solid waste, which has become a development challenge (Elagroudy et al., 2016; Oteng-Ababio et al., 2018). Increases in human consumption patterns lead to the generation of different types of waste (United Nations, 2014; Jassim, 2017), the management of which affects the environment, health and economy (Lindell, 2012), thereby, drawing a direct link between solid waste management and sustainable development.

Africa's solid waste management problems are experienced at all levels – from households to neighbourhoods and city-wide (Osumanu, 2007; Osumanu, 2009; Amoah & Kosoe, 2014). But the problems occurring in and around the household are exacerbated by city-wide issues that usually reflect inadequate technical, technological and financial capacity. All too often, the impact of inadequate waste management, such as infectious diseases, land and water pollution, obstruction of drains and loss of biodiversity, are intensified by poor households' and neighbourhoods' low access to adequate waste management services. For many poor households living in inaccessible and marginal neighbourhoods (Porter et al., 2008), solid waste collection services are a rarity (Osumanu, 2008). Private sector participation in solid waste management in Africa is limited because it is regarded as a high-risk venture (UNEP, 2018; Niekerk & Weghmann, 2019). But in countries where there is private solid waste collection, residents pay the fee directly to the private operator. For example, in Lagos, Nigeria, the fee is paid directly to the private operator, but the amount is set by the local government. In Kigali, Rwanda, solid waste collection service bills are submitted directly to households, who are also expected to participate in the compulsory community scheme, *"Umuganda"* (Niekerk 2019). In Ghana, urban solid waste collection within the Metropolitan, Municipal and District Assemblies (MMDAs) is contracted to private service providers to enhance efficiency and improve quality of service delivery (Oduro-Kwarteng, 2011). Solid waste collection is generally serviced under the House-to-House (HtH) or Door-to-Door (DtD), and/or Communal Container Collection (CCC) systems. The HtH services are contractual agreements between the private waste collector and households whereby, households pay monthly collection fees set by the private company. The CCC service is largely provided by MMDAs in which, the service is paid for, on a pay-as-you-dump basis or not paid for at all, by households. In some poor neighbourhoods, solid waste is simply dumped in open spaces, from where it is removed occasionally, usually to uncontrolled dumping outskirts of the city.

The problems of solid waste management in cities of Africa are largely the result of inadequate governance and investment (Osumanu, 2009). In most cities, municipal governments, who are responsible for providing or contracting waste collection services, often have limited technical know-how, technology, institutional competence and capital to meet these responsibilities. Hence, little is done to monitor and regulate waste production, collection, treatment and disposal. The problem also occurs because of inadequate planning for population growth. City authorities are unable or reluctant to enforce the few regulatory controls they have (Osumanu et al., 2016), for fear of losing political power. As a result, solid waste from residential, commercial and industrial sources, increasingly contaminate African cities. However, household waste forms the greatest generator of solid waste. Regassa et al. (2011) estimate that the percentage of domestic waste generated is 76%, commercial waste constitutes 9%, hotel waste is 3%, industrial waste is 5%, street sweeping is 6% and waste from hospitals is 1%, as in the case of Addis Ababa city, Ethiopia. In a study in Lagos city, Nigeria, Aliu et al. (2014) estimated the average quantity of household solid waste generation in a week, to be close to 30.39 kg in a medium residential area and 22.75 kg in a smaller residential area. In Uganda, residential waste takes 52–80% of the total solid waste generated, followed by commercial, industrial and other sectors (Bello et al., 2016). In Kenya, 61% of the solid waste produced is from residential sources, with the rest coming from industrial and other sources, such as hospitals and markets (Bello et al., 2016), while 64% of Ghana's solid waste is from residential sources (Miezah et al., 2015). Variation in generation rates and characteristics is mostly dependent on the national economies, levels of industrialisation, waste management systems available and lifestyles of the country's residents (Simelane & Mohee, 2012).

Together, the Sustainable Development Goals (SDGs) and the New Urban Agenda (NUA), provide an opportunity for rethinking urban planning and development in all countries, with the three dimensions of sustainability (social, environmental and economic) in mind (Valencia et al., 2019). Solid waste management issues are critical in sustainable development of African cities. Sustainability in waste management is achieved by integrating aspects of economic, social, environmental and technological issues in the process (Hossain et al., 2015). The significance of sustainability in solid waste management is evident in its integration as a component of action for the achievement of at least 12 out of the 17 SDGs (Rodi'c & Wilson, 2017), and the NUA, which are founded on a safe environment. This underscores the recognition of waste management as a challenge for achieving sustainable development in Africa. In the context of urban planning process and practice, waste management in African cities needs to be well managed with a balance of meeting the needs of present and future generations. This has led to the rise of interest in sustainable urban development (Cobbinah & Darkwah, 2016), which seems to be the perfect alternative to addressing the many challenges of urban planning in Africa, especially in an era of global urbanisation and increasing urban poverty (Cobbinah et al., 2015).

This chapter focuses on solid waste management in African cities and what that means for sustainable development. The chapter draws on concepts of integrated solid waste management to rationalise and explain the enabling conditions, mechanisms and practices to articulate the critical role of municipal solid waste management, in achieving sustainable urban development. In doing so, it provides a variety of conventional and evolving theoretical and practical frameworks to inform the understanding and responses to the technical issues and technological challenges in solid waste management in African cities.

Data Collection Method

A systematic and inclusive literature search, focusing on six major databases subscribed by the University for Development Studies, was undertaken to access information, including Emerald Insight, Oxford Journals, Sage Journals, Taylor and Francis, Wiley Publications and the World Bank Database. In addition, published information and other documents were obtained from key organisations' websites, including the United Nations (UN), World Health Organization (WHO) and the United Nations Environment Programme (UNEP). Municipal solid waste management activities, related to sustainable development measures were taken as a precondition to consider studies that have been conducted on African cities. Combing the databases was done with all the likely blends of key words and their synonyms, to maximise the results. The titles and abstracts of retrieved publications were studied and a reference list relevant to sustainable municipal solid waste management used to identify supplementary materials. Publications obtained from the various databases were imported into Endnote Version 9 (Karimurio, 2013) and checked for duplications which were taken off the reference list. Papers related to solid waste management in African cities, explicitly referring to the attainment of sustainable development were reviewed. The Centre for Reviews and Dissemination's (CRD) guidelines (Khan et al., 2001) and systematic reviews of interventions (Higgins & Green, 2008), were employed to guarantee the quality of the literature analysis.

After explicitly stating the objective of the chapter, the literature review was conducted with a clear set of inclusion and exclusion criteria. The process was based on an understanding that the selected papers used qualitative, quantitative or mixed-methods research approaches, which is a common practice in solid waste management research. The NVivo Version 12 software (Di Gregorio, 2000), was used for qualitative extraction and analysis of the selected papers. The selected information was coded, using predefined themes related to the objective of the chapter. The major thematic areas used for the coding were literature, based on solid waste management practices in African cities, regulations, institutions, technical issues, technologies and sustainable development. Based on this, coding categories were generated and prearranged around the established themes, and each material was read in depth again and coded, whereby sections of the papers were manually assigned the appropriate code using the NVivo software.

State of Solid Waste Management in Africa

Solid waste management has been variously defined. According to Kumah (2007: 2), it is "the administration of activities that provide for the collection, source separation, storage, transportation, transfer, processing, treatment, and disposal of waste." Tchobanoglous et al. (1993: 7), provide a comprehensive definition of solid waste management as, "the discipline associated with the control of generation, storage, collection, transfer and transport, processing and disposal of solid waste in a manner that is in accord with the best principles of public health, economics, engineering, conservation, aesthetics and other environmental considerations and that is also responsive to public attitudes." Solid waste management involves six stages, namely; generation, on-site storage, collection, transportation, treatment and disposal of solid waste in an environmentally sustainable manner (Figure 14.2). If solid waste management is to be achieved in an efficient and sustainable way, the essential aspects and relationships involved in these stages must be identified and understood clearly (Tchobanoglous et al., 1993). Unfortunately, landfilling and incineration are the popular and common technologies for municipal solid waste management in most African cities although none of them is sustainable due to the significant environmental and financial costs involved (Nabavi-Pelesaraei et al., 2017). Moreover, residents often oppose these technologies because collecting and transporting waste for landfilling and incineration

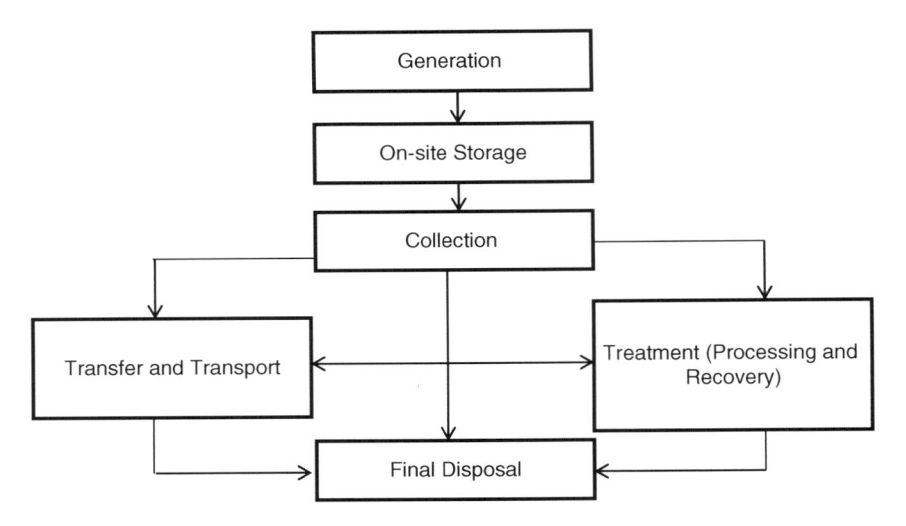

Figure 14.2 Key strategies for solid waste management.

produces greenhouse gases and causes great energy consumption (Seadon, 2010). Also, landfill sites produce gas and are expensive to maintain. Incineration causes air pollution if not well executed, and it is a massive inefficient use of materials if recyclable materials are not separated before combustion as in most African countries (Kaza & Bhada-Tata, 2018). These problems pose threats to future generations.

Solid waste composition has direct implications for the technology used for its management. Wastes of different composition have been noted in African cities, but one critical type of solid waste generated, is food waste (Thi et al., 2015). Available data (UNEP, 2018) reveal that 62.8% of municipal solid waste generated in Africa constitutes organic material from food waste (Table 14.1). This is a threatening factor, as many households and firms are producing this kind of waste on a daily basis (Halkos & Petrou, 2016). Moreover, solid waste consists of everyday items (Regassa et al., 2011), that are thrown away by industries, commercial units, households, schools, hospitals, hostels and businesses (Elagroudy et al., 2016). This implies that all the basic decisions on solid waste management in African cities should involve all the units of production and consumption, that are responsible for the production of solid waste.

Though practicing the complete functional components of solid waste management is the effective response to ensuring good sanitation, it remains a mirage for most African countries (Amoah & Kosoe, 2014). Technologies have mainly been on collection and disposal of solid waste, leaving out other essential elements of the process (Kasevea & Gupta, 1996; Kasevea et al., 2002). Reliable country data on waste generation,

Table 14.1 Composition of municipal solid waste generated in selected cities in Africa

City	Composition %					
	Organic	Paper/ Cardboard	Plastic	Glass	Metal	Others
Kampala, Uganda	77.2	8.3	9.5	1.3	0.3	3.4
Dar es Salaam, Tanzania	71.0	9.0	9.0	4.0	3.0	4.0
Ibadan, Nigeria	69.6	7.67	4.47	2.00	1.65	14.6
Accra, Ghana	65.0	6.0	3.5	3.0	2.5	20.0
Moshi, Tanzania	65.0	9.0	9.0	3.0	2.0	12.0
Sousse, Tunisia	65.0	9.0	9.0	3.0	2.0	11.0
Nairobi, Kenya	65.0	6.0	12.0	2.0	1.0	15.0
Lagos, Nigeria	62.6	10.7	4.2	2.5	2.2	19.7
Abuja, Nigeria	56.3	11.4	10.2	3.9	5.2	N/A
Cairo, Egypt	55.0	18.0	8.0	3.0	4.0	12.0
Tshwane, South Africa	53.8	11.5	9.5	6.7	1.8	16.7
Windhoek, Namibia	48.0	15.0	11.0	14.0	4.0	8.0
Average	**62.8**	**10.1**	**8.3**	**4.0**	**2.5**	**12.3**

Source: UNEP (2018).

collection, treatment and disposal required for vital statistics are inadequate in many African countries (Buenrostro et al., 2001; Niekerk & Weghmann, 2019). Where they exist, information on solid waste management is often inconsistent because they are often based on assumptions and originate from many sources which cannot be authenticated (UNEP, 2018).

To address the waste management data challenge in Africa, UNEP published the first Africa Waste Management Outlook in June 2018. The publication provides information on the state of solid waste management on the continent, including, waste governance and the related environmental, social and economic impact; and the prospects that waste offers through appropriate solutions and financing instruments. With an average waste collection rate of only 55% (i.e. 68 million tonnes) (Scarlat et al., 2015), almost half of all waste generated in Africa remains within cities, often dumped on sidewalks, open fields, storm water drains and rivers. Figure 14.3 shows the rate of solid waste collection by types of waste in African cities.

From the figure, the average solid waste collection rate in sub-Saharan Africa is lower (44%), but the rate varies significantly between cities, from less than 20% in some cities in Ethiopia, to above 90% in Tunisian cities (Godfrey et al., 2019). This is because waste collection technologies used in most African cities do not take into consideration the characteristics of the waste flow and a good understanding of local conditions, to form the basis for the choice of the management technologies and strategies. As noted by UN-HABITAT (2010), technologies employed in the developed countries

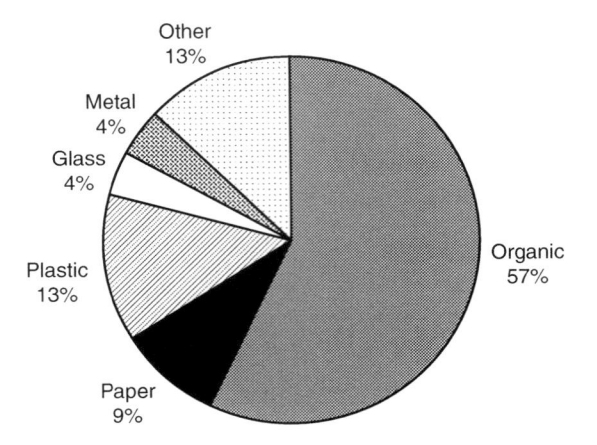

Figure 14.3 Municipal solid waste collection in Africa.
Source: UNEP (2018).

are designed for their own local circumstances, characterised by high labour costs, high technical capacities and waste rich in packaging materials. Ezeah and Roberts (2012) observed in Nigeria that the poor state of waste management in cities is the result of poverty, high population growth and urbanisation. They further attributed the problem to poorly trained waste management workers, insufficient and obsolete equipment, and the lack of clear policy strategies on sustainable waste management.

The lack of clear policy strategies in waste management is an issue in many African countries because governments are not fully prepared to integrate waste management into their development priority goals (Gutberlet et al., 2012). Available evidence (Regassa et al., 2011; Amoah & Kosoe, 2014; Osumanu et al., 2016) suggests that governments do not engage in proper planning of cities, which manifests in limited access to some neighbourhoods, poor conditions of final waste dumping sites and littering of waste around skips. This is also a reflection of non-integration of solid waste management into city-wide spatial planning because of the lack of cooperation between sector-specific planning and general planning.

Most African countries have responded to the need for effective solid waste management through efforts such as collaborations to minimise the harmful effects of waste. However, there is evidence of poor waste collection strategies that suggests that many countries are lagging behind in sustainable waste management strategies. Sustainable solid waste management is the collection, reuse, recycling, discovery, transportation and disposal of all kinds of waste, in a manner that does not jeopardize the environment, human health and future generations. The process is tangible when it minimises waste generation and disposal, so that resources are preserved for the future (Singh & Ordonez, 2016; Cucchiella et al., 2017). Hence, sustainable waste management strategies are the hierarchy of activities or plan of actions of waste management including waste prevention, minimisation, recycling and reuse, discovery, treatment and disposal.

Huge quantities of municipal waste in different cities across Africa are not managed in a sustainable manner, leading to public health issues and environmental challenges (Yoshida, 2018). Solid waste constitutes a significant proportion of the 33% of the world's open dumping of solid waste in Africa (Kaza & Bhada-Tata, 2018). This does not, however, suggest that the African continent is leading in waste generation. According to Niekerk and Weghmann (2019), waste generated in rural areas is less than that in urban areas and the total waste generated in Africa is lower than that in other less developed regions. This observation is plausible, given the fact that waste generation is a function of economic growth and urbanisation (Adipah & Kwame, 2019). For example, the average waste generation for Africa in 2012 was 0.8 kg per capita per day, compared with the world's 1.39 kg per capita per day (Niekerk & Weghmann, 2019).

In many African cities, solid waste management is a complex issue that has been a major feature on the priority list of governments, local authorities and researchers. Historically, city authorities have been responsible for providing waste management services in their areas of jurisdiction. For instance, the Accra City Council (ACC), according to Owusu-Sekyere et al. (2015), was able to manage refuse with the assistance of few community sanitary inspectors and also with the commencement of systematic waste collection and disposal services in 1925. Public dustbins, emptied by two pushcarts were later replaced with large carts, drawn by mules, introduced in the late 1930s. Due to the huge cost to local government and inefficiency of the public sector in the provision of solid waste management services, there was a policy shift towards private sector involvement in the 1990s (Osumanu, 2008). The private sector was to overcome governments' failure in public direct service delivery – too many workers, not enough supervisors, few incentives for better performance and limited finance (Cointreau-Levine, 1994, 2000; Post et al., 2003). With privatisation, companies were given particular zones to manage. The total cost of service provision is not pushed to beneficiaries (households and government agencies); government subsidises the cost. The service users usually pay between 10% and 20% of the total cost (Owusu-Sekyere et al., 2015). This means that financial resources which could have been used to develop other priority sectors of the national economies, are devoted to subsidising solid waste management.

Another form of private sector participation in solid waste management is the emergence of micro and small enterprises (MSEs), that work in waste collection and disposal in African cities. These waste collectors work in countless forms, based on local needs and capabilities. Therefore, they are characterised by the ability to adjust to local conditions and cultures (Wilson et al., 2006). There are several examples of MSEs in waste collection ranging from highly organised and registered companies, to unregistered and rudimentary cooperatives of scavengers that are organised in the hope of making a living or improving their socio-economic status (Adamoski, 2010). Solid waste management in Africa has followed what Oteng-Ababio (2014: 9), described as *"end-of-the-pipe approach,"* where waste is collected and disposed of or incinerated without any incentive to recover, recycle or re-use towards encouraging consumption within the waste stream. It is an unpalatable, yet widely practiced system, where solid waste collected is disposed of, in open dumpsites which, by far, remain one of the most practiced and economically viable methods of managing waste (Seadon, 2010). Final disposal sites are often located in environmentally and hydrologically sensitive surroundings and challenging neighbourhoods, including abandoned valleys, without proper leaching or recovery systems (Owusu-Sekyere et al., 2015). This usually results in local public health issues and global environmental problems, such as emissions of greenhouse gases (GHGs). This situation has brought about the need for national governments and municipal authorities to devise environmentally sound and sustainable solid waste management frameworks for their cities.

Solid Waste Management and Sustainable Urban Development in Africa

Sustainable development emerged from the World Commission on Environment and Development's (WCED) publication – *"Our Common Future,"* (the Brundtland Report), which defined the concept as, development that "meets the needs of the present without compromising the ability of future generations to meet their own needs" (World Commission on Environment and Development (WCED), 1987: 43). Sustainability has since become the model of development adopted at the global level, whereby governments, organisations and individuals act in accordance with its principles. In terms of urbanisation, Goal 11 of the SDGs and the NUA, recognises that urban areas still face numerous challenges in ensuring livable environments (United Nations General Assembly, 2016). The sustainable development concept relies on three pillars: economic, environmental and social. To achieve viable economic, environmental and social development, sustainable waste management strategies are highly desirable. In the context of sustainable development, waste management is an activity that shapes environmental protection (Izverciana & Ivascua, 2015). Among the human activities, waste management is one of the areas that needs close attention, in pursuit of sustainable development. Waste has direct adverse impact on urban environments, economic development and human health.

African countries are undergoing rapid development, with growth rates above four percent per annum and are now faced with huge amounts of municipal solid waste, which have direct effect on human health, safety, environment and economic development. Various governments across Africa have been faced with challenges in their attempts to implement sustainable waste management plans. While the quantities of solid waste generated in Africa are comparatively small, relative to other regions of the world, the mishandling of waste in African cities is already affecting human health and environmental quality (Godfrey et al., 2019). For instance, a recent study of Tomitha et al. (2020) on exposure to waste dumping sites and their impact on human health in South Africa, showed that people residing close to waste sites were significantly associated with asthma, tuberculosis, diabetes and depression. Meanwhile, Africa is set to experience major social and economic transformations over the coming decades, as its population increases, cities grow and residents' purchasing power goes up. The UNEP (2018), has projected an exponential growth in solid waste generation of 1,000 tonnes/day in sub-Saharan Africa, which is expected to place substantial stress on the already constrained public and private sector waste management services and infrastructure, and further aggravate the current state of solid waste management in cities. The situation is putting fears in development practitioners, that sustainable development objectives would not be achieved in Africa; which calls for integrated governance as highlighted in both the declaration of Agenda 2030 (United Nations, 2015) and the NUA (United Nations General Assembly, 2016), including, but not limited to, SDG 17, which expressly focuses on fostering partnerships among actors and across different levels or tiers of government institutions.

The SDGs and the NUA recognise the role of cities in achieving sustainable development. The NUA in particular, demonstrate governments' commitment to the promotion of urban sustainability (Valencia et al., 2019). However, GIZ (2017) has observed that there are concerns regarding African cities developing their capacities to manage solid waste, following the estimated amount of 2 billion tonnes of municipal solid waste generated annually. The fear is that some cities may lack the technical and technological capacity to respond to new ways of managing municipal solid waste in ways that will ensure sustainable development. Recent academic debates (e.g. Lindell, 2012; Giang, 2017; Kaza & Bhada-Tata, 2018; Yoshida, 2018; Adipah & Kwame, 2019) have reached a consensus on the broader objective of achieving sustainable waste management in cities. What appears different, are their observed varied efforts of different governance structures, institutional arrangements and countries' commitments to develop appropriate technologies for sustainable solid waste management. These studies contend that whilst the use of clean and modern technologies in solid waste management has worked well in some cities, the level of their adoption and application has differed in different institutional and governance systems.

One observation regarding sustainable waste management is the, "reduce, reuse, recycle, recover, and dispose" waste principle (Izverciana &

Ivascua, 2015). The principle states that waste materials must be; used repeatedly (reused); used to make new products (recycled); and used to produce energy (recovery) (Cucchiella et al., 2017). It emphasis changes in behaviour and ensures that waste generated is used as a resource for the production of further usable commodities. According to Jassim (2017), this is a way of reducing waste and turning it into other resources, by making use of sustainable technologies. For instance, solid waste recycling has been shown to be an effective technology that turns most substances considered as waste, into items that would have required different resources to produce (Jassim, 2017). The quest for sustainable development through waste management leads to what is currently advocated as the concept of "integrated waste management system" (Lindell, 2012: 45), which considers waste management as a multidimensional process that incorporates different sectors (e.g. economic, social and environmental) in the management of solid waste. Adipah and Kwame (2019) consider integration in the management of solid waste as a way of considering technical, semi-technical and non-technical aspects in waste management. In this context, waste management is seen as a technological process, where new knowledge is very relevant in the management process. Another form of integration in waste management is the consideration of the private sector, the public sector and communities to develop local solutions (Lindell, 2012; Kosoe et al., 2019). Besides, sustainable integration of waste management should cover a series of related activities from the complete life-cycle of waste generation, collection, transportation and treatment, to final disposal (Yoshida, 2018). Such a process should consider the technical issues and technologies along with institutional, economic and social components, if sustainable management is to be achieved.

In the view of Premakumara et al. (2011), integrated sustainable waste management should be based on reduction and reuse. Sallwey et al. (2017), also view integration as a process that builds on existing initiatives in the recycling and other resource recovery efforts, as well as institutional capacities in the management chain. This suggests that institutions have important roles in the management process of municipal solid waste in Africa. This is important as public institutions need to initiate and guide the integration of solid waste management by bringing different actors and sectors in the management process together. Citing specific examples from Kenya, Selin (2013), suggested that local authorities should be charged with the responsibility of mobilising both public and private sector actors, with assigned roles in the implementation of measures towards integrated solid waste management. Halkos and Petrou (2016) make a strong submission to the debate on sustainable waste management that appropriate combination of skills and knowledge of physical sciences is a basic requirement for sustainability to be achieved. This cannot be refuted since past (e.g. Premakumara et al., 2011; Hossain et al., 2015) and recent (e.g. Jassim, 2017; Kaza & Bhada-Tata, 2018) studies are consistent that technology has a role to play in the effective management of solid waste, as demonstrated in developed countries.

Available evidence from different studies (Premakumara et al., 2011; Simelane & Mohee, 2012; Owusua et al., 2013; Oteng-Ababio et al., 2013; UNEP, 2015) indicate that technologies for municipal solid waste management should be simple, low-cost and easy to follow, rather than the traditional landfilling and incineration technologies which are expensive, difficult to manage and pose a threat to the environment and health (Izverciana & Ivascua, 2015). From the perspective of Halkos and Petrou (2016), sustainable waste management strategies should encompass methodologies that use models of simulation to analyse financial viability (cost and benefits) and hence predict cost-effective practices. These suggest that the complexity and costs associated with technologies could be a hindrance to effective implementation of waste management strategies and hence should be considered in waste management planning. Wang and Nie (2001), for example, observed in China that environmentally-sound facilities for treatment and disposal of solid waste are in great shortage; suggesting that existing technologies have not been able to find solutions to waste management issues. Though Wang and Nie (2011), attribute the weakness to market economic failures, their observation does not guarantee an efficient solid waste management approach in control economies. This assertion brings to the fore, the controversy regarding which type of economic model (market or control) has more advantage in sustainable management of solid waste.

Many scholars (e.g. Lindell, 2012; Aliu et al., 2014; Addaney & Oppong, 2015; Joshi & Ahmed, 2016; Rodi'c and Wilson, 2017) are advocating partnerships between the public and private sector in the implementation of sustainable waste management strategies. According to Addaney and Oppong (2015), one way of achieving sustainable waste management through collaboration, is for state authorities to give the private sector the required training to build their technical and technological capacity in the waste management process. Capacity building for the private sector is a way of strengthening institutional and technological capacity, to discover and implement cost-effective technologies and strategies for solid waste management. This is consistent with the proposal made by Aliu et al. (2014), that public–private partnerships (PPPs) are often associated with the deployment of efficient technologies, service affordability, payment flexibility and a wider coverage, that enhances accessibility. However, collaboration of this kind in the management of solid waste is not done in a vacuum. It has been noted that efforts at achieving sustainable solid waste management have been successful when they are done through the application of specific technologies and management strategies, that take local content into consideration (Kosoe et al., 2019).

Similarly, Addaney and Oppong (2015) stipulate that achieving a sustainable and integrative municipal solid waste management, largely depends on a range of programmes and policies that will lead to the adoption of appropriate technologies. This should be guided by considering waste as an economic resource, which could be tapped for the production of finished and intermediate goods. Such technologies have been adopted by different institutions and the outcomes are studied and reported in scholarly debates. For example, Jassim (2017) has documented that solid waste recycling is an effective strategy that uses clean technology to turn waste into useful substances. Findings of Izverciana and Ivascu (2015) also support Jassim's (2017) argument that waste reduction and reuse should be achieved through best practices. In short, sustainable waste management can be achieved in African cities, through the application of the principle of "reduce, reuse, recycle, recover, and dispose" (Adipah & Kwame, 2019). But it appears that Africa is lagging behind other developing regions, in terms of the application of this principle. The majority of solid waste management efforts in Africa are devoted to collection, transportation, and disposal (UNEP, 2018). In Bangladesh, for instance, waste recovery technologies have been adopted and decentralised and have succeeded in promoting the recovery of economic and ecological resources from solid waste (United Nations, 2017). While the use of the principle of waste reuse is considered as a better way of solid waste management, Simelane and Mohee (2012) insist that African countries and their cities are yet to develop the required efficient technology for the conversion of waste into re-useable commodities.

The importance attached to waste separation at the source of generation, represents a greater effort in reducing the burden of waste management on municipal authorities (Vitharana, 2015). According to Owusua et al. (2013), waste separation at source would be successful, if municipal authorities provide free separation bins as economic incentives. In Ghana, Owusua et al. (2013) found that about 80% of households were willing to accept cash payment as incentive for participation in source separation. This implies that households that generate municipal solid waste are waiting for financial incentives from city authorities before participating in source separation, instead of considering participation as a basic responsibility. This is in line with Rodi'c and Wilson's (2017), contention that behavioral change interventions are lacking in solid waste management planning in Africa. Gutberlet et al. (2016) explained this from a different perspective, that municipalities can adopt the strategy of using scavengers and waste pickers (individuals and households) in informal settlements, who are key stakeholders in the solid waste management process. This strategy can also be a good option for waste separation at collection points.

Incineration as an energy recovery technology for municipal solid waste and a way of ensuring sustainable waste management, is strongly advocated (Kerdsuwana et al., 2015; Kaza & Bhada-Tata, 2018). The incineration technology has been used by both small- and large-scale energy producers in many countries. In their justification for the use of the incineration technology, Kaza and Bhada-Tata (2018) indicated that pyrolysis and gasification are two main associated technologies that are done through Advanced Thermal Treatment (ATT), which converts waste materials into gas or fuel. The advantages of this technology are it destroys toxic materials, reduces mass of volumes of waste quickly and results in the generation of energy for household use (Kerdsuwanaet al., 2015; Kaza & Bhada-Tata, 2018). This technology has been proven viable, as reported by Premakumara et al. (2011), in the city of Surabaya in Indonesia and in some cities in Mozambique (Sallwey et al., 2017).

Institutional and Regulatory Framework for Solid Waste Management

To have sustainable waste management systems for African cities, there should be integrated governance as highlighted in both the declaration of Agenda 2030 (United Nations, 2015) and the NUA (United Nations General Assembly, 2016). This means that an analysis of all aspects of the sustainable development, as well as demographic and cultural circumstances are very important. Taking into consideration the reality faced in African cities, a better approach would be one that brings together good service at low cost and the use of local resources (Kosoe et al., 2019). Local residents must be strongly involved to create awareness of the importance of waste separation and its benefits. Including MSEs (Adamoski, 2010), can also be a better way of joining efforts to implementing sustainable solid waste management systems but will require solutions that are more enforceable from different urban planning perspectives (Cobbinah & Darkwah, 2016). Private companies' participation represents a win-win situation for local authorities because it ensures efficient door-to-door waste collection and less public costs and, for city residents, a cleaner environment. Municipal authorities and planners have critical roles to play too, as they are the key elements to the effective functioning of local residents, MSEs and private companies, giving regulatory and better conditions for solid waste management.

To meet the present waste management requirements and maintain a clean environment for current and future generations, a set of waste management strategies that integrate the concept of sustainable development should be implemented to achieve the objective of protecting the environment, while yielding socio-economic benefits for city residents (Figure 13.4). The principle of "reduce, reuse, recycle, recover, and dispose," involves fewer stakeholders but needs even more enforcement of regulations, participation and agreements with municipal authorities, the private sector and local residents. The interaction of the various aspects (technical, technological, environmental, health, financial, economic, social, cultural, institutional and regulatory) in the integrated solid waste management framework is desirable to have a sustainable solid waste system that is most effective with a low cost solution (Figure 14.4).

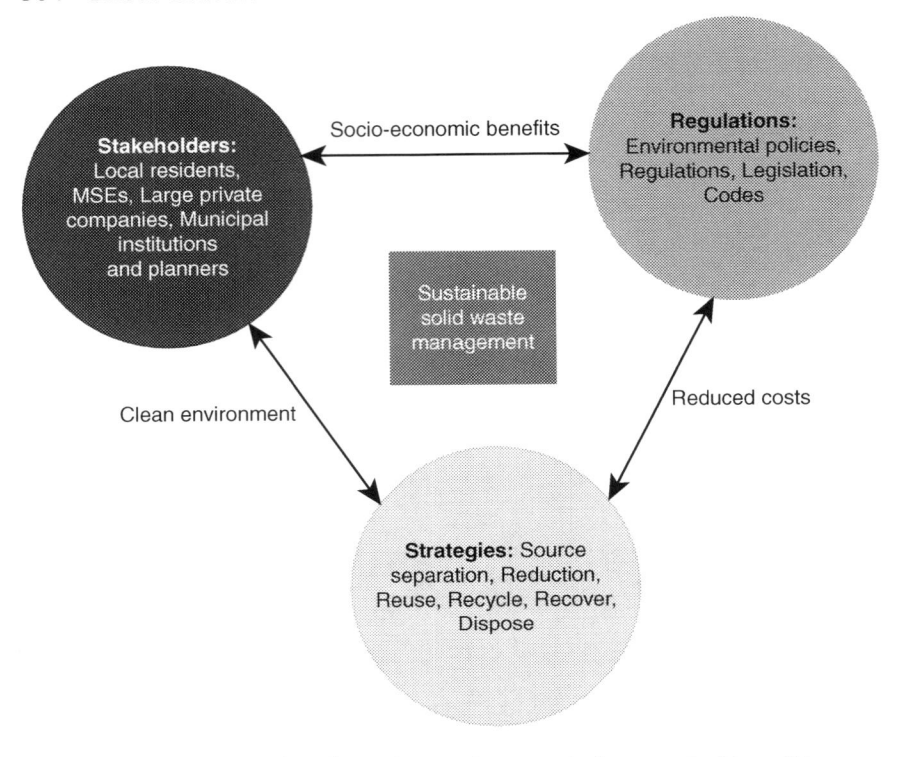

Figure 14.4 Institutional and regulatory framework for sustainable solid waste management.

Several African countries have regulations and policies on solid waste management (Bello et al., 2016), but regulatory frameworks for solid waste management are often fragmented and weak. In some cases, there are no clear distinctions between roles and responsibilities of municipal authorities, private service providers and city residents (Nwufo, 2010; NSWMP, 2011). In other instances, legislation has not been translated into practical action plans, which results in cities not meeting sustainable solid waste management objectives (DEA, 2012). National legislative frameworks on solid waste management places the state and municipal authorities as the key players and do not re-cognise informal waste collection which makes them inconsistent with prac-tices on the ground (Sentime, 2013). However, these agencies generally find it difficult to implement regulations due to their limited technical, technological, human, financial and logistic resources.

Conclusion

African cities are facing daunting challenges in achieving sustainable devel-opment as population increases, urbanisation and changing consumption patterns have escalated solid waste generation on the continent, with limited technical and technological capacity to manage this waste. This chapter discussed solid waste management in African cities, in relation to achieving sustainable development. The failure of African countries to adopt appropriate technologies in waste management through the principle of "reduce, reuse, recycle, recover, and dispose," suggests that municipal authorities are yet to get prepared for the implementation of sustainable waste management strategies. Technology for solid waste management in many African cities has been limited to costly and unfriendly technologies of landfilling and incineration. Weak institutional capacity, and poor coordination of waste management activities, thwart attempts to implement sustainable solid waste management efforts. This chapter concludes that population growth, urbanisation and changing lifestyles of urban residents are causing high rates of solid waste generation in all parts of Africa and this threaten the achievement of sustainable development. The future of solid waste management in African cities will remain a challenge, without efforts to discover and apply locally-appropriate technologies that incorporate the principle of "reduce, reuse, recycle, recover, and dispose."

References

Adamoski, M. (2010). *Waste management system for Western Africa – analysis of systems successfully applied in the world that may fit the reality faced in Western Africa*. Master Dissertation, Institutionen för Geovetenskaper, Uppsala University.

Addaney, M., & Oppong, R. A. (2015). Critical issues of municipal solid waste management in Ghana. *JENRM, 2*(1), 30–36.

Adipah, S., & Kwame, O. N. (2019). A novel introduction of municipal solid waste management. *Journal of Environmental Science and Public Health, 3*(2), 147–157.

Amoah, S. T., & Kosoe, E. A. (2014). Solid waste management in urban areas of Ghana: Issues and experiences from. *Journal of Environment Pollution and Human Health, 2*(5), 110–117.

Aliu, I. R., Adeyemi, O. E., & Adebayo, A. (2014). Municipal household solid waste collection strategies in an African megacity: Analysis of public private partnership performance in Lagos. *Waste Management & Research, 32*(9), Supplement, 67–78.

Bello, I. A., Ismail, M. N. B., & Kabbashi, N. A. (2016). Solid waste management in Africa: A review. *International Journal of Waste Resources, 6*(2). doi: 10.4172/2252-5211.1000216

Buenrostro, O., Bocco, G., & Vence, J. (2001). Forecasting generation of urban solid waste in developing countries: A case study in Mexico. *Journal of Air and Waste Management Association, 51*, 86–93.

Bundhoo, Z. M. A. (2018). Solid waste management in least developed countries: Current status and challenges faced. *Journal of Material Cycles and Waste Management, 20*, 1867–1877. doi: 10.1007/s10163-018-0728-3.

Cobbinah, P. B., Erdiaw-Kwasie, M. O., & Amoateng, P. (2015). Africa's urbanisation: Implications for sustainable development. *Cities, 47*, 62–72.

Cointreau-Levine, S. (1994). Private sector participation in municipal waste services in developing countries. Vol. 1, *The formal sector*. Washington, D.C.: The World Bank.

Cobbinah, P. B., & Darkwah, R. M. (2016). Toward a more desirable form of sustainable urban development in Africa. *African Geographical Review*, *36*, 262–285. doi: 10.1080/19376812.2016.1208770.

Cointreau-Levine, S., & Coad, A. (2000). *Guidance pack: Private sector participation in municipal solid waste management*. St. Gallen, Switzerland: Swiss Centre for Development Cooperation in Technology and Management Vadianstrasse.

Cucchiella, F., D'Adamo, I., & Gastaldi, M. (2017). Sustainable waste management: Waste to energy plant as an alternative to landfill. *Energy Conversion and Management*, *131*, 18–31.

DEA (2012). *National waste management strategy*. Pretoria, RSA: Department of Environmental Affairs.

Di Gregorio, S. (2000). Using Nvivo for your literature review: strategies in qualitative research. Paper presented at strategies in qualitative research: issues and results from analysis using QSR NVIVO and NUD*IST, conference at the Institute of Education, London – 29–30 September 2000.

Elagroudy, S., Warith, M. A., & Zayat, M. E. (2016). *Municipal solid waste management and green economy*. Berlin, Germany: Global Young Academy.

Ezeah, C., & Roberts, C. L. (2012). *Analysis of barriers and success factors affecting the adoption of sustainable management of municipal solid waste in Nigeria*. *Journal of Environmental Management*, *103*, 9–14. doi:10.1016/j.jenvman.2012.02.027

Fakoya, M. B. (2014). Institutional challenges to municipal waste management service delivery in South Africa. *Journal of Human Ecology*, *45*(2).

Godfrey, L., Ahmed, M. T., Gebremedhin, K. G., Katima, J. H. Y., Oelofse, S., Osibanjo, O., Richter, U. H., & Yonli, A. H. (2019). Solid waste management in Africa: Governance failure or development opportunity? *Regional Development in Africa*. IntechOpen, 10.5772/intechopen.86974

Giang, H. M. (2017). *A study on development methodology of sustainable solid waste management systems by using multi-objective decision making model – a case study in Hoi An City, Vietnam*. PhD Dissertation, Okayama University.

GIZ (2017). *Briefing circular economy and waste management*. Bonn, Germany: GIZ.

Gutberlet, J., Kain, J., Nyakinya, B., Oloko, M., Zapata, P., & Campos, M. J. Z. (2016). Bridging weak links of solid waste management in informal settlements. *Journal of Environment & Development*, *26*(1), 106–131.

Gutberlet, J., Kain, J. H., Nyakinya, B., Ochieng, D. H., Odhiambo, N., Oloko, M., & Zapata Campos, M. J. (2016). Socio-environmental entrepreneurship and the provision of critical services in informal settlements. *Environment and Urbanization*, *28*(1), 205–222.

Goel, S. (2017). Solid and hazardous waste management: An introduction. in S. Goel (ed.), *Advances in Solid and Hazardous Waste Management ‖ Solid and Hazardous Waste Management: An Introduction (Chapter 1)*, (1–27). Switzerland: Springer International Publishing. doi:10.1007/978-3-319-57076-1_1.

Halkos, G., & Petrou, K. N. (2016). *Efficient waste management practices: A review*. Munich MPRA Paper No. 71518, posted 22 May 2016 14:50 UTC. https://mpra.ub.uni-muenchen.de/71518/

Higgins, J., & Green, S. (2008). *Cochrane handbook for systematic reviews of interventions*. London: The Cochrane Collaboration.

Hossain, S., Al-Hamadani, M. Z. F., & Rahman, T. (2015). E-waste: A challenge for sustainable development. *Journal of Health & Pollution*, 5(9), 3–11.

Izverciana, M., & Ivascua, L. (2015). Waste management in the context of sustainable development: Case study in Romania. *Procedia Economics and Finance*, 26, 717–721.

Jassim, A. K. (2017). Sustainable solid waste recycling. *Skills development for sustainable manufacturing*. IntechOpen, 10.5772/intechopen.70046

Joshi, R., & Ahmed, S. (2016). Status and challenges of municipal solid waste management in India: A review. *Cogent Environmental Science*, 2(1), 1–18.

Kabera, T., Wilson, D. C., & Nishimwe, H. (2019). *Benchmarking performance of solid waste management and recycling systems in East Africa: Comparing Kigali Rwanda with other major cities. Waste Management & Research*, 37(1_suppl), 58–72. doi:10.1177/0734242x18819752.

Karimurio, J. (2013). *Using endnote to manage bibliographic information*. New York, NY: COECSA Research Training and Dessemination.

Kaseva, M. E., Mbuligwe, S. E., & Kasbenga, G. (2002). Recycling inorganic solid waste: Results from a pilot study in Dar es Salaam. *Resource Conservation and Recycling*, 35, 243–257.

Kasevea, M. E., & Gupta, S. K. (1996). Recycling – an environmentally friendly and income generation activity towards sustainable solid waste management: Case study Dar es Salaam city. *Resource Conservation and Recycling*, 17, 299–309.

Kawai, K., & Tasaki, T. (2016). Revisiting estimates of municipal solid waste generation per capita and their reliability. *Journal of Material Cycles and Waste Management*, 18, 1–13.

Kaza, S., & Bhada-Tata, P. (2018). *Decision maker's guides for solid waste management technologies*. Urban Development Series Knowledge Paper. Washington, D.C.: The World Bank.

Kerdsuwana, S., Laohalidanonda, K., & Jangsawangb, W. (2015). Sustainable development and eco-friendly waste disposal technology for the local community. *Energy Procedia*, 79, 119–124.

Khan, K. S., Riet, G., Glanville, J., Sowden, A. J., & Kleijnen, J. (2001). *Undertaking systematic reviews of research on effectiveness: CRD's guidance for carrying out or commissioning reviews*. New York, NY: NHS Centre for Reviews and Dissemination.

Kirama, A., & Mayo, A. W. (2016). *Challenges and prospects of private sector participation in solid waste management in Dar es Salaam City, Tanzania. Habitat International*, 53, 195–205. doi:10.1016/j.habitatint.2015.11.014.

Kosoe, E. A., Diawuo, F., & Osumanu, I. K. (2019). Looking into the past: Rethinking traditional ways of solid waste management in the Jaman South Municipality, Ghana. *Ghana Journal of Geography*, 11(1), 228–244.

Kumah, A. M. (2007). *The situation of solid waste in Ghana*. http://www.trend.wastsan.net

Lindell, A. (2012). *Achievement of sustainable solid waste management in developing countries – a case study of waste management in the Kavango region, Namibia*. Master Dissertation, Lund University.

Miezah, K., Obiri-Danso, K., Kádár, Z., Fei-Baffoe, B., & Mensah, M. Y. (2015). Municipal solid waste characterization and quantification as a measure towards effective waste management in Ghana. *Waste Management*, *46*, 15–27.

Nabavi-Pelesaraei, A., Bayat, R., Hosseinzadeh-Bandbafha, H., Afrasyabi, H., & Chau, K. W. (2017). Modeling of energy consumption and environmental life cycle assessment for incineration and landfill systems of municipal solid waste management: A case study in Tehran Metropolis of Iran. *Journal of Cleaner Production*, *148*, 427–440.

Niekerk, S., & Weghmann, V. (2019). *Municipal solid waste management services in Africa*. Public Service Organization Working Paper. Johannesburg, RSA: Public Service Organization.

NSWMP (2011). *National solid waste management programme (NSWMP) Egypt: Main report*. Cairo, Egypt: MoLD/EEAA/KfW.

Oduro-Kwarteng, S. (2011), Private Sector Involvement in Urban Solid Waste Collection: Performance, Capacity, and Regulation in Five Cities in Ghana, Leiden, The Netherlands: CRC Press, Taylor and Francis Group, 13–26.

Nwufo, C. C. (2010). Legal framework for the regulation of waste in Nigeria. *African Research Review*, *4*(2), 491–501.

Osumanu, I. K. (2007). Environmental concerns of poor households in low-income cities: The case of the Tamale Metropolis, Ghana. *GeoJournal*, *68*, 343–355.

Osumanu, I. K. (2008). Private sector participation in urban water and sanitation provision in Ghana: Experiences from the Tamale Metropolitan Area (TMA). *Environmental Management*, *42*, 102–110.

Osumanu, I. K. (2009). Urbanization challenges in Africa: Creating productive cities under globalization. In D. S. Graber, and K. A. Birmingham (eds.), *Urban planning in the 21st century* (pp. 129–140). New York, N.Y.: Nova Science Publishers.

Osumanu, I. K., Kosoe, E. A., & Dapilah, F. (2016). Residential housing in Ghana's low-income urban areas: An analysis of households living conditions in the Wa Municipality. *Journal of Geography and Regional Planning*, *9*(7), 139–153.

Oteng-Ababio, M. (2014). Rethinking waste as a resource: Insights from a low-income community in Accra. Ghana. *City, Territory and Architecture*, *1*(10). http://www.cityterritoryarchitecture.com/content/1/1/10

Oteng-Ababio, M., Annepu, R., Bourtsalas, A., Intharathirat, R., & Charoenkit, S. (2018). Urban solid waste management. In C. W. Rosenzweig, P. Solecki, S. Romero-Lankao, S. Mehrotra, S. Dhakal, & S. Ali Ibrahim (eds.), *Climate change and cities: Second assessment report of the urban climate change research network* (pp. 553–582). New York, N.Y.: Cambridge University Press.

Oteng-Ababio, M., Arguello, J. E. M., & Gabbay, O. (2013). Solid waste management in African cities: Sorting the facts from the fads in Accra, Ghana. *Habitat International*, *39*, 96–104.

Owusu-Sekyere, E., Bagah, D. A., & Quansah, J. Y. D. (2015). The urban solid waste management Conundrum in Ghana: Will it ever end? *World Environment*, *5*(2), 52–62.

Owusua, V., Adjei-Addoa, E., & Sundberg, C. (2013). Do economic incentives affect attitudes to solid waste source separation? Evidence from Ghana. *Resources, Conservation and Recycling*, *78*, 115–123.

Porter, R. B., Binns, T., Elliott, J. A., & Smith, D. (2008). *Geographies of development: An introduction to development studies* (3rd ed.). London: Pearson Education Limited.

Post, J., Broekema, J., & Obirih-Opareh, N. (2003). Trial and error in privatisation: Experiences in urban solid waste collection in Accra and Hyderabad. *Urban Studies*, *40*, 837–854.

Premakumara, D. G. J., Abe, M., & Maeda, T. (2011). Reducing municipal waste through promoting integrated sustainable waste management (ISWM) practices in Surabaya city, Indonesia. *WIT Transactions on Ecology and the Environment*, *144*(1), 457–468.

Regassa, N., Sundaraa, R. D., & Seboka, B. B. (2011). Challenges and opportunities in municipal solid waste management: The case of Addis Ababa city, Central Ethiopia. *Journal of Human Ecology*, *33*(3), 179–190.

Rodić, L., & Wilson, D. C. (2017). Resolving governance issues to achieve priority sustainable development goals related to solid waste management in developing countries. *Sustainability*, *9*(404). doi:10.3390/su9030404

Sallwey, J., Hettiarachchi, H., & Hülsmann, S. (2017). Challenges and opportunities in municipal solid waste management in Mozambique: A review in the light of nexus thinking. *AIMS Environmental Science*, *4*(5), 621–639.

Scarlat, N., Motola, V., Dallemand, J. F., Monforti-Ferrario, F., & Mofor, L. (2015). Evaluation of energy potential of municipal solid waste from African urban areas. *Renewable and Sustainable Energy Reviews*, *50*, 1269–1286.

Schlueter, R. (2017). *Solid waste management in the developing world: The role of local government in Kisumu, Kenya. Independent Study Project (ISP) Collection.* 2654. https://digitalcollections.sit.edu/isp_collection/2654

Seadon J. K. (2010). Sustainable waste management systems. *Journal of Cleaner Production*, *18*, 1639–1651.

Selin, E. (2013). *Sustainable municipal solid waste management - A qualitative study on possibilities and solutions in Mutomo, Kenya.* Master Thesis Submitted, Universitet UMEA.

Sentime, K. (2013). *The impact of legislative framework governing waste management and collection in South Africa. African Geographical Review*, *33*(1), 81–93.

Simelane, T., & Mohee, R. (2012). *Future directions of municipal solid waste management in Africa.* Pretoria, RSA: Africa Institute of South Africa.

Sunday, F. (2013) *Nairobi garbage collection business; a preserve of well-connected clique. Standard Digital.* https://www.standardmedia.co.ke/article/2000093445/nairobi-garbage-collection-business-a-preserve-ofwell-connected-clique

Singh, J., & Ordonez, I. (2016). Resource recovery from post-consumer waste: Important lessons for the upcoming circular economy. *Journal of Cleaner Production*, *134*(Part A), 342–353

Tchobanoglous, G., Theisen, H., & Vigil, S. (1993). *Integrated solid waste: Engineering principles and management issues.* New York, NY: McGraw-Hill Publishing Company.

Thi, N. B. D., Kumar, K., & Lin, C. (2015). An overview of food waste management in developing countries: Current status and future perspective. *Journal of Environmental Management*, *157*, 220–229.

Tomitha, A., Cuadros, D. F., Burns, J. K., Tanser, F. & Slotow, R. (2020). Exposure to waste sites and their impact on health: A panel and geospatial analysis of nationally representative data from South Africa, 2015–2018. *Lancet Planet Health 2020, 4,* e223–e234.

Tsheleza, V., Ndhleve, S., Kabiti, H. M., Musampa, C. M., & Nakin, M. D. V. (2019). *Vulnerability of growing cities to solid waste-related environmental hazards: The case of Mthatha, South Africa. Jàmbá Journal of Disaster Risk Studies, 11*(1). doi:10.4102/jamba.v11i1.632

UN-HABITAT (2010). *Solid waste management in the world cities: Water and sanitation in the world cities, 2010.* London: Earthscan.

UNEP (2015). *Global waste management outlook.* Nairobi: UNEP.

UNEP (2018). *Africa waste management outlook.* Nairobi, Kenya: UNEP.

United Nations (2014). *Resolutions and decisions adopted by the United Nations Environment Assembly of the United Nations Environment Programme at its first session on 27 June 2014.* Nairobi: UNEP.

United Nations (2015). *Transforming our World: The 2030 Agenda for sustainable development A/RES/70/1.* New York: United Nations.

United Nations (2017). *Sustainable development benefits of integrated waste management.* Washington, D.C.: United Nations.

United Nations Environment Programme (UNEP) & United Nations Institute for Training and Research (UNITAR) (2013) Guidelines for national waste management strategies. *Moving from challenges to opportunities.* Nairobi: UNEP.

United Nations General Assembly (2016). *New Urban Agenda: Quito declaration on sustainable cities and human settlements for all (71/256).* New York: United Nations.

Valencia, S. C., Simon, D., Croese, S., Nordqvist, J., Oloko, M., Sharma, T., Buck, N. T., & Versace, I. (2019) Adapting the Sustainable Development Goals and the New Urban Agenda to the city level: Initial reflections from a comparative research project. *International Journal of Urban Sustainable Development, 11*(1), 4–23.

Vitharana, A. D. (2015). The solid waste management for sustainable development: A case study of Hambantota Municipal Council Area in Sri Lanka. *Sri Lanka Journal of Economic Research, 3*(1), 79–111.

Wang, H., & Nie, Y. (2011). Municipal Solid Waste Characteristics and Management in China. *Journal of the Air & Waste Management Association, 51*(2), 250–263.

Wilson, D. C., Velis, C., & Cheeseman, C. (2006). Role of informal sector recycling in waste management in developing countries. *Habitat International, 30,* 797–808.

Wilson, D. C., Kanjogera, J. B., Soós, R. (2017) Operator models for delivering municipal solid waste management services in developing countries. Part A: The evidence base. *Waste Management & Research, 35,* 820–841.

World Commission on Environment and Development (WCED) (1987) *Our common future.* Oxford: Oxford University Press.

Yoshida, M. (2018). *Situation of municipal solid waste management in African cities – an interpretation of the information provided by the First ACCP Meeting.* Discussion Paper: The Second Meeting of African Clean Cities Platform (ACCP), June 2018, Rabat.

15 Urban Informality and Flexible Land Tenure Arrangements in Namibia: Lessons and Insights

Kennedy Kariseb and Ivone Tjilale

Introduction

There has been renewed calls for sustainable development that is dependent on secured land tenure (Amoateng et al., 2003; Cobbinah et al., 2015; Kleemann et al., 2017; Lall et al., 2017; Otto et al., 2019). It is therefore not surprising that the recognition of the importance of land tenure security as a determinant in the global developmental agenda has been on the rise for the last few decades. For instance, in its call for sustainable cities and communities in Goal 11, the Sustainable Development Goals (SDGs) underscore the importance of "enhanced inclusive and sustainable urbanisation and capacity for participatory, integrated and sustainable human settlement, planning and management in all countries." Given the immense informality of urban and peri urban spaces in Namibia caused predominantly by an unsustainable increase in population sizes as a result of urbanisation, urban informality has become an inescapable part of spatial surveying arrangements and land reform programmes. This is no surprise given the rise in urbanisation and the mushrooming of informal settlements in peri-urban and urban spaces. According to Alfonso (2015) and Banks et al. (2020), in Namibia, as in most parts of Africa, urban informality has become a reality due largely to weak land reform programmes and decentralisation framework. This has by necessary implication prompted a response from local authorities to address the imbalances brought about by such urban informality and the growing need for urban land. As a means to remedy these tenure shortcomings the government has introduced a system of flexible land tenure.

Flexible land tenure arrangements are relatively new to the conventional tenure arrangements in Namibia. Having been introduced in early 2012 in terms of the Flexible Land Tenure Act, these tenure arrangements seeks to "create alternative forms of land title that are simpler and cheaper to administer" as well as "provide security of title for persons who live in informal settlements or who are provided with low income housing." Accordingly, the flexible land tenure arrangements seek to provide affordable security of tenure to inhabitants in informal settlements in

DOI: 10.4324/9781003181484-15

Namibia. It is premised on the establishment of an interchangeable tenure registration system parallel and complementary to the current formal system of freehold tenure. In this regard, flexible tenure arrangements serve a dual purpose, which is to provide affordable housing and security of tenure thereof in informal settlements and further to complement existing and predominantly formal systems of (freehold) land tenure. While these are intended responses of flexible land tenure arrangements, in practice these arrangements fall short of addressing the rapid informality of urban spaces in Namibia. Therefore, there remains a need for a closer reflection, both from a theoretical and practical perspective, of the opportunities and implications of flexible tenure arrangements; a gap this Chapter seeks to fill.

By undertaking a comprehensive exploration of the (Namibian) flexible land tenure regime, as set out in the Flexible Land Tenure Act, 2012, this Chapter analyses the prospects and shortcomings of flexible land tenure arrangements in providing security of tenure to peri-urban and urban settlers in Namibia. This is undertaken against the backdrop of providing possible lessons and insight into such tenure systems for African countries, especially those contemplating to reform their urban and peri-urban informal settlements. This is because urban informality is increasingly becoming a cross-cutting issue in many African States, given the spatial and land reform inherent in these States (Potts, 2007). Namibia's experience of flexible land tenure arrangements, particularly the practical shortcomings derived from this tenure system, could provide valuable lessons and insights to African States on how best to phrase and implement similar or even advanced land tenure systems in their jurisdictions.

This chapter concerns itself with the central question of whether such tenure arrangements provide security of tenure to informal settlers in urban and peri-urban areas in Namibia. A key argument of this chapter, one based on comparative experiences, practices and trends in other jurisdictions such as Zambia, and Tanzania as a benchmark, is that flexible land tenure arrangements in practice fail to provide security of tenure predominantly because of the informal and relaxed nature of such arrangements. Therefore, African countries, more especially those contemplating to undertake a reform of their land tenure systems in general and flexible land tenure systems in particular, will have to reassess such systems by guaranteeing tenure security to their informal populace. To this end, besides this introductory background this chapter's contribution seeks to draw the intersectionality between urbanisation and urban informality, especially as it relates to informal settlements in Namibia. This will be done in Section two of the chapter. Section three outlines the nature and scope of flexible land tenure arrangements, and its feasibility in providing tenure security to peri-urban and urban settlers. Section four draws on the overall (legal) challenges of flexible land tenure arrangements while in Section five we draw some concluding reflections.

Data Collection Methods and Research Design

In order to fully appreciate the context and conclusions made in this analysis, it may be useful to briefly set out the use of sources and methods. The chapter is primarily based on a review of relevant scholarly literature and policy frameworks on flexible land tenure and sustainable urban and peri-urban developments in Africa. Thus, journal articles, books and monographs, policy documents on these areas were considered. As a primary source, reliance is made of the Flexible Land Tenure Act, 2012 in the analysis in this chapter as it is the basis of the flexible land tenure system implored in Namibia. The analysis is also informed and contextualised within the framework on the SDG's, particularly SDG's 1, 2, 5, 10 and 11. The chapter also undertakes a comparative analysis of flexible land tenure arrangements in other African jurisdictions in order to contrast and compare variances, insights and possible lessons Namibia's system can draw from. Zambia and Tanzania are to this end comparatively considered. Although a broad based analysis transplanting in other disciplines this chapter is primarily rooted in law. This legal perspective is informed by the fact that the basis of Namibian's flexible land tenure system is rooted in law. Moreover, the guarantee of tenure security which is the emphasis in this chapter contribution, can predominantly only be achieved through legal means.

Urbanisation and Urban Informality in Namibia and Beyond

According to Cobbinah and Darkwah (2016), urban growth is one of the issues constantly at the centre of debates across the world. It refers to the physical expansion and growing of cities (Shikangalah, 2005). In addition, Shikangalah (2005) argues, while several reasons may account for urban growth, it is commonly linked to increases of urban populations, which in turn necessitates stress on physical structures as a response to the demand for more infrastructure, economic development and social services. Urbanisation is the outcome of social, economic and political developments that lead to urban concentration and growth of large cities, changes in land use and transformation from rural to metropolitan pattern of organisation and governance (UNDP, 2014). According to a recent study by Saghir and Santono (2018), more than half of the global population now lives in urban areas. This figure is projected to increase to 75% by 2050, at a growing rate of 65 million urban dwellers annually. Urban areas in Sub-Saharan Africa currently contains 472 million people and will double over the next two and a half decades. It is also estimated that the global share of African urban residents is projected to grow from 11.3% in 2010 to 20.2% by 2050 (OECD/SWAC, 2020). According to Aryeetey-Attoh (1997), the rush to the cities is also caused in part by the attraction of opportunities for wealth generation and economic development.

Locally, Namibia like most parts of the world, experiences a kilometric growth of its urban population. Namibia has an urban population of 51% growing at an annual rate of 4.2% (World FactBook, 2020). In the case of Windhoek, the capital city, for example, the 2011 census shows that 62% of all the city's 324,470 residents are from other towns within Namibia (Census Report, 2011). The causes of urbanisation in Namibia are variant and multidimensional. They include amongst others poverty, environment and political history which defines the context within which people move (Indongo et al., 2013). Clearly, the proportion of people living in urban areas rises not only due to migration, but also due to the natural growth of the existing urban population. It is also worth stating that the exclusive bordering of urban Namibia to white settlers during colonialisation has also contributed immensely to the rapid rush into urban areas after independence as the economic market has been exclusively located in these areas.

An immediate outcome of such intense urban population growth has been what one may term the "informalisation" of such spaces as a result of progression of informal settlements. Such growth has caused tension between urban informal settlers and the authorities, leaving the latter with no option but to accommodate these dwellers within its urban habitat. The law has been an instrumental apparatus used by the authorities to control and address the growing urban population, especially in light of shortage in housing and general access to land. The Flexible Land Tenure Act is one such legal instrument that has been at the centre of controlling the settlement situation in urban and peri-urban Namibia. The above urban dynamics, both as indicative of Africa generally, and Namibia in particular, is a clear indication that urbanisation is a reality that requires peculiar consideration. Statistically all indicators point that urban sites will continue to expand, most likely with the increase of informal settlements leaving most urban spaces largely informal. How governments will address this reality, is not always settled but the laws and policies could be one of many variables that can be an aid in addressing the shortcomings of urban informality. In the case of Namibia, flexible land tenure is the legal and policy response introduced in the form of the Flexible Land Tenure Act, 2012. It is to this end, that we set out in finer detail this tenure regime in the discussions below.

Nature and Scope of Flexible Land Tenure Arrangements in Namibia

Rationale and Justifications for the Flexible Land Tenure System

Flexible land tenure arrangements are relatively new tenure arrangements in Namibia having been created out of the desire to respond to contemporary challenges facing the land reform programme. They are however not unique to Namibia. Similar arrangements have been made in a notable number of African States with a common history of colonial land dispossession. Occupancy licenses issued in terms of the Housing (Statutory and Improvement Areas) Cap 194 in Zambia since the early 1970s; residential licensing carried out in terms of the Land Act of 1999 in Tanzania and the permis d' habiter (permit to reside) licenses issued in Benin by virtue of decree 2.12 of 1964, are typical examples of these tenures. Though not original to Namibia, these tenure arrangements make a unique contribution to the land reform processes in Namibia which for the most part are in rural areas. By directing land reform efforts, more specially as it relates to access to land and housing in peri-urban and urban areas, flexible land tenure systems seeks to ease the contemporary challenges facing spatial habitation in urban localities.

That there is a need for flexible land tenure arrangements can be drawn from a wide variety of determinants, whether social, historical, economical and legal. For example, historically, tenure arrangements in Namibia are based on a pedigree of land tenure systems and consequential titles that claim their legitimacy from constructs of colonial racist administrations that illegally dispossessed the indigenous communities which deprived them of comprehensive titles to their land (Amoo, 2014). Urban policies, both under the German and South African colonial administrations, were based on a separatist land arrangement system pedigreed on exclusive white urban settlement whilst the Black majority were relegated to communal areas with limited access to urban areas. As a result of this tenure system, ownership of land was almost exclusively reserved for white settlers with the consequential impact of commercial and investment activity being restricted to such urban areas. The development of informal settlements was also strictly regulated by apartheid policy.

With the attainment of independence in 1990, colonial and apartheid (land use) policies and arrangements were abolished. Constitutional reforms and subsequent legal instruments were introduced to address shortages brought about by the land policies and arrangements of the previous regimes. Though these reforms marked a new dawn as far as governance and land reform is concerned, practically it did not address the situation in urban settlements. For example, freedom of movement and the right to ownership became entrenched in the Constitution. The formally denied Black majority flooded to urban areas in search of work and other opportunities. With a weak decentralisation policy that did little to centralise State services in rural areas, an increase in urban areas was inevitable. This increase was a direct result of the historical past that excluded the majority of the population from urban inhabitation. As a result, there has been a drastic increase of informal settlements and squatter camps in Windhoek and other urban areas. This systemic increase provoked responses from central government, one of which is the system of flexible land tenure.

The justification for the enactment of the system of flexible land tenure arrangements is multidimensional. First, the present land registration system is too bureaucratic, procedural and technical to accommodate the needs of the vast majority of the urban poor. The system has equally failed to provide a secure individual tenure. The pace of land registration under the current system is too slow. Another burden experienced under the current system is the fact that local authorities demand high standards for infrastructure. Second, a further dilemma with the current land tenures, especially freehold title is that, besides being costly, it requires high and complex expertise in as far as surveying and transfer of land is concerned. It is therefore not responsive to the needs and financial capabilities of the poor. The flexible land tenure arrangements seek to remedy this situation by introducing a parallel interchangeable land system, where the initial secure right is not only simple and affordable, but also upgradable over time. Equally, global urbanisation has repercussions on land accessibility and affordability. Without adequate land being delivered to cater for the growing urban population in an orderly fashion, only tensions can arise. Eventually the government has to tackle these challenges, through either re-planning, upgrading, rehabilitation and resettlement programmes. The Flexible land tenure system is therefore one such initiative aimed at suppressing the effects of land distribution, security and accessibility.

According to section 2(a) of the Flexible Land Tenure Act, the flexible land tenure system is predominantly aimed at creating an alternative form of land title that is simpler and cheaper to administer compared to existing forms of land title. Although what is meant by simplicity is not contextually defined, it may be safe to state that the simplicity of the tenure is anchored on the presumption that the costs of surveying and registration relating to the tenure in question will be solely borne by the state. It also presupposes that the titles will be reasonably affordable and accessible by those who cannot afford the luxuries of alternative land titles such as freehold titles. Hence, "simple and cheaper to administer" should be given a broad interpretation that places a burden on the state to meet the resource and capacity demands that go hand in hand with the proposed tenure. The tenure is also aimed at providing security of title for persons who live in informal settlements provided with low income housing schemes (section 2(b) of the Flexible Land Tenure Act) and as such the tenure takes due cognisance of existing patterns and practices of informal living. There is therefore a steady, yet coherent, transition of existing informal housing practices and the envisaged formal housing practices that will eventually come into play over time once there is a complete implementation of the flexible land titles. According to section 2(c) of the Flexible Land Tenure Act, by providing security over the tenure in question, the Act aims at empowering rural and peri-urban settlers economically by means of land rights through settlement formalisation and regularisation. Furthermore, the value of the flexible land tenure arrangements lies not so much in the alternative tenures it creates but rather in the fact that it crafts a less costly and efficient system of land registration that may be of a far reaching scope to the most vulnerable of society.

Basic Features of the Flexible Land Tenure System

The system of flexible land tenure provides for two forms of tenures: (a) starter titles and (b) land-hold tiles. These two titles combined are collectively referred to as the flexible land tenure system. The system has two basic operational features; namely its *parallelism* and *interchangeability*. Christensen (2004) rightly describes these features by lamenting:

> [T]he system would operate parallel to the existing registration system in the sense that parallel institutions will be responsible for the registration of different tenure types. This means that the same land parcel would be the subject of registration in both the starter and land hold title registry and the Windhoek Deeds Registry. However, the deeds registry would only reflect the ownership of the whole block erf of land and the fact that a starter and land hold title registry exists. Individual starter title and land hold title rights within that block erf would not be visible in the main registry but only in the starter and landhold title registry.

The system would be interchangeable in the sense that the different tenure types catered for in the parallel registries could be upgraded, over time, from an initial base offering basic security into individual full ownership or freehold title, as it is currently known to the common law and registration statutes of Namibia. In other words, starter title would be interchangeable in the sense that starter title rights could be upgraded in accordance with prescribed procedures to land hold title or freehold title. As far as a parallel land registration system is concerned, it may at this stage be regarded as a practical strategy, undertaken by the government with the aim of balancing the inequalities brought forward by the existing land tenure(s). A "balance" in the sense that it relaxes the often visible inequalities in social status and acquisition of land titles by citizens introduced by freehold and customary land titles. The tenures envisioned by this system, namely starter as well as land hold, looks promising in two respects. First, both tenures are relatively affordable; even to the poorest in the economic cycle. It, in the second instance, projects at providing security of title to the vast majority who under the current tenure regime have no security of title over land in the informal settlement areas.

Flexible Land Tenures Created

Starter and land titles are in nature group based tenure titles. The rationale being that the outside boundary of a block of land that is earmarked for titling under the flexible land tenure system is professionally surveyed and registered under the freehold tenure system in the Deeds Registry in Windhoek while individual rights or plots within the block are registered locally in the established Land Rights Offices. The ownership of the block piece of land can be with the Municipality, private developer or a community based organisation. The maximum number of households per starter title or land hold title is not limited to any quantity; however, there have been suggestions to limit a block to 100 households to avoid overcrowding. In terms of the steps outlined in section 11 of the Flexible Land Tenure Act, 2015 the relevant authority may on its own accord, or on application by the owner of a piece of land or one or more persons who reside on a piece of land, consider the establishment of a starter title scheme or land hold title scheme on that land. It is however not clear, in terms of this section, or any other provision of the Act, whether such person must have lawfully gained or acquired such piece of land. The presumption is that for purposes of legality such person must have acquired the piece of land lawfully and must as such be the lawful owner of that piece of land. Furthermore, before the establishment of a startle title scheme or land hold title scheme is considered, the land concerned must be subdivided or consolidated in such a manner that the scheme concerned would be situated on one portion of land registered as such in the deeds registry and any mortgage, usufruct, *fideicommissum* or similar right on that piece of land must be cancelled (section 11(2) of Flexible Land Tenure Act).

According to section 11(3) of Flexible Land Tenure Act, a relevant authority may prescribe a specified sum of money on the owner of a piece of land or the association to which a group of people occupying a piece of land belongs on which the establishment of a starter title scheme or land hold title scheme is considered. The use of these fees is primarily to cover the whole or part of the costs incurred by the relevant authority in establishing the scheme concerned. The relevant authority must also cause a feasibility study to be conducted in order to investigate the feasibility and desirability of creating a starter title scheme or a land hold title scheme on the piece of land concerned (section 11(6) of Flexible Land Tenure Act). Once these formalities are met, the names of the title holders are entered into the register at the Land Rights Office (LRO) and the title holders provided with a certificate of title which can be used as security over the tenure.

Starter Title

Although there are still some uncertainties as to the precise scope or meaning of a starter title, a cursory reading of the Flexible Land Tenure Act reflects that it is a statutory title scheme in respect of a specific blockerf which entitles persons to acquire some rights over that blockerf. By *blockerf*, on the other hand is meant a specified piece of land entitling a holder a starter title over the same (Christensen, 2004).

> ...[a] starter title is an individual type of tenure in that one person, as a custodian for a family or a household, is allocated a right to an unspecified site. It is, however, group based in that each household within a block erf must abide to the rules of the community laid down by a community association.

The rights in respect of a starter title are specified under section 9(1) of the Act. In terms of this section, the holder of such a starter title is entitled amongst others to a right to (a) erect a dwelling on the blocker at the specified location of the specified size and nature in terms of its deed; (b) to occupy any such dwelling in perpetuity (c) on his or her death to bequeath the dwelling to his or her heirs and to lease to another person; (d) to utilise any such services as may be provided by any local authority or any other person (e) to transfer his or her rights to any other person (whether that person is the heir of the holder of that rights or whether the transfer is another transaction recognised by law).

As envisaged in section 9(4) of the Flexible Land Tenure Act, starter title rights may be transferred by private agreement followed by occupation of the dwelling concerned by the person to whom the right has been transferred or any person assigned by him or her to occupy that dwelling. These rights may also be bequeathed to heirs and/ or legatees (Section 9(1)(b) of the Flexible Tenure Act). According to section 9(5) of the Flexible Land Tenure Act, it is however the duty of the transferor and the transferee and/or all other holders of rights in a starter title scheme to inform the Registrar of the property office in whose jurisdiction the scheme is situated of any transfer of rights, be it by private treaty or through bequeath to heirs or legatees. The land rights registrar must register any transfer of rights of which he or she has been informed or of which he or she has become aware, if he or she is satisfied that that transaction of transfer, occurred (Section 9(6) of the Flexible Tenure Act). As envisaged in Section 9(9) of the Flexible Land Tenure Act, no juristic person may hold any starter title right. The starter title is viewed as an inexpensive form of land registration. The starter title does not link the block of land to cadastre maps or site plans but only to registered names of beneficiaries. In practice, a group or the local authority informally designs a layout plan without proper surveying. The rights are recorded in the starter title register established by the Registrar of Deeds and located at a Land Rights Office. This way the registration is administered close to the affected communities and done in a decentralised manner.

The relevant authority in whose jurisdiction a starter title scheme is created or any other person may agree to provide services to the scheme as a whole under such conditions as may be determined by such authority or other person (section 9(2) of the Flexible Land Tenure Act). Where such services are provided, the deed of the Starter title scheme concerned must determine the rights and duties of every holder of rights in that scheme in respect of the services concerned and may provide for the forfeiture of such rights for any holder of such rights who does not fulfil his or her duties (section 9(1) of the Flexible Land Tenure Act). In terms of practical application and as envisaged in section 9(10) of the Flexible Land Tenure Act "no natural person may hold more than one starter title right and no person may acquire a starter title right if he or she is the owner of any immovable property or land-hold title right in Namibia." On face value, in the absence of a defending thesis or justifiable rational, the said section can have adverse inroads on Article 16(1) of the Namibian Constitution which provision empowers all persons the right in any part of Namibia to acquire, own and dispose of all forms of immovable and movable property individually or in association with others and to bequeath their property to their heirs or legatees.

The likelihood, if raised before a court of law, that section 9 be declared unconstitutional in the context of the constitutional entrenched right to acquire and own property is strong. The same applies to section 9(8) of the Flexible Land Tenure Act which stipulates "[e]xcept for persons who are married in community of property, a starter title right may not be held by more than one person jointly," which is an unjustified limitation on co-ownership. The holder of a starter title has the right to perpetual occupation of a site within a block erf. Such a holder may also erect and occupy a dwelling on such a starter scheme. There may be restrictions placed on the transfer or disposal, or donation of the right of the title holder. These restrictions may ensue from the group or associations constitution. Starter titles cannot be used as collateral to secure funds for possible improvement on the land in question.

Land-hold Titles

Land hold titles, like starter titles, are statutory land tenures entitling prospective holders' tenure in respect of a blockerf, with the only difference being that with land hold titles the land usually plots are surveyed and assigned numbers. The mere fact that land hold titles gives collateral rights gives it a strong resemblance of freehold titles. As envisaged in section 10(1) of the Flexible Land Tenure Act, the holder of land hold title rights has three *primary* rights:

a   all the rights in the plot concerned that an owner has in respect of his or her erf under the common law;
b   may subject to the provisions of this Act, perform all the juristic acts in respect of the plot concerned that an owner may perform in respect of his or her erf under the common law;

c   has an undivided share in the common property (irrespective of the exact size of the plot concerned).

These rights are not absolute and may be restricted in certain circumstances. For example, the rights of any holder of a land hold title may be limited by any servitude or other right in favour of the owner of any other property over the blockerf concerned held by such holder (section 10(3) of the Flexible Land Tenure Act). Land hold title holders are also barred from performing certain transactions without first registering same in the land hold title register at the land rights registrar. Section 10(5) singles out those transactions as follows:

a   transferring the land hold title rights to another holder;
b   creating or cancelling a mortgage or any other form of security for a debt executable on the plot concerned;
c   creating or cancelling a right of way in favour of any owner of land hold title rights in any plot on the same scheme as the plot concerned;
d   creating or cancelling servitudes relating to the provision of water, electricity, telecommunications or any similar services or the removal of sewerage from any plot on the scheme concerned.

Although land hold titles do not afford the holder entitlements that would necessarily ensue from a freehold title, the title nevertheless resembles freehold title schemes in that the title can be occupied in perpetuity, transferable, devisable and can be used as a collateral to secure any additional finances which can be used on improving or upgrading the title. Land hold title rights are recorded in the land hold title register at the Land Rights Office. The site of a land hold title is demarcated on a cadastral map which is held in the Land Rights Office. In this instance, the holder can enter into a limited range of commercial activities. Once tenure security is obtained, the holders of these titles can build their own houses and the local authority will be expected to provide other services. Land under land hold title may be sold, donated, inherited and mortgaged, and as such be sold in execution.

According to section 13(1) of Flexible Land Tenure Act, once the procedures laid out in section 11 of the Act are completed, the relevant authority may, once satisfied that the establishment of a land hold title scheme is desirable, approve the establishment of the scheme concerned. As soon as possible after the establishment of the scheme has been approved, the relevant authority must send a notice to the Registrar of the Land Rights Office in whose jurisdiction the blocker concerned is situated as well as to the Registrar of Deeds, who in turn must make an endorsement on the title deed of the blocker concerned to the effect that a land hold title scheme has been established on that blocker (section 13 (2-3) of Flexible Land Tenure Act). According to section 13 (4) of Flexible Land Tenure Act, once such an endorsement has been made the specific land hold title scheme is deemed to have been established on the date of such an endorsement.

Upgrading of Flexible Titles inter se or to Freehold

Flexible land tenure systems hold with them the material advantage of incremental tenure upgrading from one title to another. This means a starter title scheme may be upgraded to a land hold title scheme and subsequently to a freehold, provided that such a starter title scheme or land hold title scheme is situated within the area of an approved township (section 15(1) of Flexible Land Tenure Act). Once such an upgrading has taken effect the blockerf in respect of such starter or land hold title must be surveyed and subdivided in accordance with the applicable laws relating to the surveying and subdivision of land in Namibia (section 15(2) of Flexible Land Tenure Act). The upgrading of starter title scheme to land hold title scheme requires at least 75% of the holders of rights in a starter title scheme to consent to such upgrading and lodge an application in the prescribed form with the relevant authority for the upgrading of that scheme to a land hold title scheme. The same procedure relatively applies to the upgrading of land hold titles to freehold titles, entitling the holder full ownership. The costs of such upgrading must be borne by the holders of rights in the scheme concerned in the same proportion as the surface area of the plot or piece of land of such person bears to the surface area of all the plots or pieces of land on the scheme concerned (section 15(6) of Flexible Land Tenure Act). However, where under land hold titles only 75% of all land holders agree to the upgrading, the relevant authority may pay fair compensation to the holders of rights who did not agree and as a consequence of such compensation sell any such land that would have been allocated to them.

Administration of The Flexible Land Tenure System

Procedure for the Establishment of Starter and Land Hold Titles

According to section 11(6) of Flexible Land Tenure Act, before the establishment of a starter title scheme or a land hold title scheme is considered, the relevant authority must first cause a feasibility study to be conducted in order to investigate the feasibility and desirability of creating a starter title scheme or a land hold title scheme on the piece of land concerned. It is in this light that feasibility studies had preceded the promulgation of the Act in 1997, although these studies through pilot projects were not intended directly on establishing title schemes. The pilot projects addressed practical land surveying and related planning issues relating to the Act covering identification of different surveying and registration approaches for upgrading of tenure in different environ-ments. These projects also tested the absolute and/or relative accuracy of different survey methods under different environmental conditions, the material costs (including both human and capital costs) and the skills demand for each of the applied survey methods. The projects also gained tremendous input from informal settlement community members as well as community based organisations. The pilot programmes also evaluated present land registration systems in Namibia with regard to certainty of title as perceived by the users. Minimum requirements for the main-tenance of a viable property registration system were also assessed. These assessments indicated the feasibility of a flexible land tenure arrangement, especially in already proclaimed areas.

The prerogative of initiating title schemes is predominantly left in the hands of government authorities, i.e. town, village, regional councils. In order to satisfy itself of the desirability of establishing new schemes a relevant authority may (section 11(7) of Flexible Land Tenure Act):

a   inspect the blocker in question;
b   conduct a geological, environmental or any other scientific study relating to the blocker in question;
c   question or interview any person who is able to provide relevant information relating to the desirability of the establishment of the scheme in question;
d   require the owner of the blocker or the person who requested the establishment of the scheme in question to provide any information relevant to the desirability of the establishment of the scheme in question to the relevant authority;
e   consider all relevant legislation and any town planning scheme applic-able to the area in which the piece of land concerned is situated.

These considerations are essential in placing the relevant authority in ques-tion in a steady position aimed at making a decision that is just, reasonable, fair and in the public interest. If the relevant authority is satisfied, after due consideration and regard being had to any one or more of the above direc-tives, that the establishment of the scheme is desirable, it must cause a notice to be published in a newspaper circulating in the district in which the land concerned is situated, indicating that the establishment of the scheme is considered and inviting any person to provide information relevant to the establishment of the scheme to it section 5 (1) of Flexible Land Tenure Act). As a means to remedy the growing urbanisation problem in urban and peri-urban Namibia, parliament passed the Flexible Land Tenure Act, 2012 to ease the land issue by providing those with existing titles some form of security. It is generic truism that the vast majority of those settling in urban Namibia cannot afford basic housing and as a result opts for informal settlements, usually occasioned with poor sanitation and living conditions.

Establishment of the Land Rights Office

The Land Rights office is the primary administrative institution of flexible land rights together with the Ministry of Land Reform. Section 4 of the Act empowers the Minister of Land Reform, in consultation with the Minister of Regional, Local Government, Housing and Rural Development to establish a Land Rights office as the administrative organ of the Flexible Land Tenure system. Such establishment must be preceded by a notice in the Government Gazette. The establishment of such an office can be for each district in which FLTS operates or the Minister has the option of establishing one Land Rights Office for the whole country. The establishment of multiple Land Rights offices does not deter the Minister from altering the area of jurisdiction of a Land Rights Office, merging two or more Land Rights offices or alternatively withdrawing a Land Rights office if no land hold title scheme or starter title scheme exists in the area of jurisdiction of a Land Rights office. According to section 5 (1) of Flexible Land Tenure Act, the Minister also has the sole discretion to appoint a Land Rights Registrar and other officers of the Land Rights office. A registrar of Deeds must establish a land hold title register and a starter title register (section 6(1) of Flexible Land Tenure Act). The recording of such registers may be done on a computer system or in any other appropriate manner, on condition that it must be possible to readily retrieve any information relating to a specific title scheme.

The role of the Land Rights Registrar is extremely important in that due to the informal nature of the title schemes at play effective recording and maintenance of data is important. Hence, it is understandable why the Registrar has been given broad powers in terms of the Act (section 8 (1) of Flexible Land Tenure Act). The Registrar is, empowered to:

a　inspect land hold title schemes in order to determine whether the boundaries of plots are recorded accurately in the register;

b　inspect starter or land hold title schemes in order to determine any question that is relevant in him or her performing her duties and functions efficiently;

c　institute such enquiries or conduct such interview with any person as may be necessary in order to determine any question that may be relevant for the performance of any function assigned to him or her in terms of the Act;

d　conduct a formal hearing in order to determine any matter that is in dispute between two or more parties having a substantial interest in the determination of a matter relating to his or her duties, if it is necessary, or if he or she is requested by a party to a dispute; and

e　make any entry in the register which in his or her opinion is necessary in order to correct the register or to reflect the transaction concerned, when it is found that any information recorded in the register is inaccurate or does not reflect any transaction that has validly been concluded.

According to section 8(4) of Flexible Land Tenure Act, these powers may generally be delegated to any registration officer or land measurer. However, when the Registrar assigns such powers, he or she may give such instructions or guidelines relating to the exercise of such power or the performance of such function as he or she may deem necessary (section 8(6) of Flexible Land Tenure Act). The aim of these broad powers is to ensure that the Registrar is able to meet his or her duties in terms of the Act, which is primarily to ensure the accurate recording of information relating to the starter and land hold title schemes in the register. And to render assistance to any person or group who intends to transfer starter title or land hold title rights or who desires to create land hold title schemes or starter title schemes.

Flexible Land Tenure and Land Security

In light of the above exposition concerning the overall nature and scope of flexible land tenure arrangements in Namibia, a question worth considering is the feasibility of these arrangements in providing secure tenure. This in itself is not an automate question. Responding to it is even made worse by the fact that the implementation of these tenure arrangements is still not settled thus not providing a matrix upon which an assessment can be qualified. However, one may consider this question in light of past experiences, practices and trends in other (similarly placed) jurisdictions. A geography worth considering is Zambia. In 1974, the Zambian government under Kenneth Kaunda passed the Housing (Statutory and Improvement Areas) Act, Cap 194 in order to provide some form of security of tenure to people who occupied a piece of land without such title. This was done through the issuance of occupancy licenses. The aim of these licenses is twofold: first, to afford some form of security of tenure to the occupier and secondly to serve as a gateway for possible upgrading to leaseholds of 99 years once the specific area or improvement area is planned and surveyed. Section 37 of the said Housing (Statutory and Improvement Areas) Act, Cap 194 empowers the Minister for Land to declare any area of land within the jurisdiction of the local council as an "improved area." This takes place once the relevant line Ministry has identified a specific area as an "improvement area." Such an identification and declaration is made after a consideration of several factors such as:

a   if 60% or more of the land on which the settlement is located is publicly owned;
b   if the development for which the land is zoned on the development plan is not imminent;
c   if the settlement or specific area has been in existence since 1974; and
d   if 50% or more of the dwelling structures in the settlement or specific area are constructed of conventional materials.

The Ministry of Lands also further prepares a sketch plan for the specific area or settlement/improvement area which is lodged with the Commissioner of Lands and the Registrar of Lands and Deeds. The occupants of these areas are given an occupancy license of 30 years. This serves as a temporal title deed over the piece of land occupied by the occupants. An occupancy license is registered in the local property register.

The holders of occupancy licenses have several obligations towards the local council within its jurisdiction. These obligations include inter alia:

1 to pay for municipal services such as sewerage services, water supply etc.;
2 to pay a charge in lieu of rates based on the value of the average normal dwelling and out-building within the improvement area;
3 to occupy and use premises only for residential purposes;
4 to keep the improvement area or rather premises reasonably clean and tidy; and
5 not to sub-license or assign the premises without the consent of the local Council.

Like most flexible tenures, the right of occupancy licenses offered in Zambia do not offer any real substantive tenure security. Instead, it can at the very least be regarded as a drastic imminent measure aimed at temporarily redressing the pressures caused by urbanisation and colonial land dispossession. Gastorn (2013), correctly, states that flexible tenures are merely remedial and therefore unable to solve the problem of unplanned settlements either by planning the area or by giving the security of statutory tenure. The Zambian experience has not adequately solved the problems experience relating to security of tenure nor has it made any progress in dealing with the exuberating rural-urban migration, especially in the capital Lusaka. The same can be said of other flexible tenure mechanisms introduced in some other African countries. To take another standard example, according to Gbaguidi and Spellenberg (2004), in the early 1960s the Burundian government issued *permis d' habiter* (permit to reside) licenses to occupants in unplanned settlements, again with the primary aim of providing some form of security over tenure, which can eventually be converted into a freehold title. This noble initiative has failed. Chances are strong based on these comparative experiences that the implementation of flexible land tenure in Namibia will not yield the admired results of providing a tangible security over land to the urban and peri-urban poor in informal settlements.

In Tanzania, the issuance of residential licenses in unplanned settlements encourages squatting because people know that once settled on these settlements, pressure will mount on the government for them to be recognised. Therefore, these tenures have the tendency to encourage unlawful settlements. Gastorn (2013) argues that the creation of residential licenses is rather remedial than preventative in curbing further growth of unplanned settlements. By itself, it does not even have components of urban planning. It does not deal with the delivery of social services like roads, water systems or other infrastructure. He therefore concludes, convincingly so, by stating:

> ... [i]t is a process of recording who owns what, how and where in relation to real property. But it gives a solid basis upon which other urban planning schemes may be effected...even in terms of land tenure security, it is a half-way mechanism between the real right to land (the right to occupancy) and the unsecured right to land. It is therefore a saving mechanism for informal settlements to get 'refuge' before being completely obliterated.

Taking into account these sentiments, particularly the flexible tenure arrangements in Tanzania and Zambia, one may say that the implementation of flexible land tenures in Namibia may not yield the results it seeks. Similarly, Tanzania and Zambia, Namibia is a low income country faced with many economic hardships. It too inherited a skewed land system conceived by apartheid laws and colonial land dispossession. Because of these similarities, it can be predicted that if flexible land tenures are implemented, as is currently being done, in the long run one can expect growing land tensions because the tenures in question are not complete in form so as to give the much desired fruits derivable from a freehold title.

Based on the comparative experiences of flexible land tenure arrangements in other jurisdictions such as Zambia one can reasonable argue that these arrangements are only temporary safeguards, far short of ensuring long term security over land to poor and peri-urban poor. It is therefore true that although people, in this context, urban and peri-urban poor, have a high de facto, perception of their own tenure security as a result of flexible land tenure system; whilst their legal title, in other words, de jure situation, to the land is weak. Flexible land tenure arrangements are only the beginning, a weak beginning for that matter, of long journey to tenure security. They to some extent provide security of land to the occupants but these tenures fail to give immediate security of sound quality because in practice the settlement will still belong to the State and the tenures cannot be used as collateral. As long as flexible land tenures cannot provide collateral or serve as a mechanism for engaging credit or financial institutions, it cannot be truly said as providing a secure form of tenure. Hence, the sustainability of the incremental land reforms, such as flexible land tenure arrangements, are questionable, at least in their quest in addressing the challenges posed by urbanisation, especially security over land. It is also worth noting that flexible land tenure arrangements may not necessarily address urban informality posed by urbanisation. On the contrary, these tenure arrangements have the uneven likelihood of stimulating urbanisation because these arrangements legalise the de facto illegal occupation of unoccupied urban land.

Conclusion

Whilst it is inevitable that urbanisation has been a hallmark of globalisation and that nation-States, including Namibia cannot escape this reality, the effects of such urban growth has been tedious. For the most part, urbanisation in Namibia, as in most parts of the Africa and beyond has contributed tremendously to the informalisation of urban spaces. A manifestation of such informalisation has been the mushrooming of informal settlements and squatters' camps. Another consequence is the weakening of security over tenure. As was illustrated in the discussion, even though post independent land tenure arrangements, such as in the case of Namibia, flexible land tenure arrangements, have sought to provide cheaper means of acquiring land, such acquisition remains limited. In the instances that it occurs, it falls short of providing real security over property. Financial institutions, such as banks, refuse to provide financing for urban dwellers in informal settlements, because of the social stratification of those who live in those spaces and the shortage of security that can be tendered to enable financing. The comparative experiences from Zambia and Tanzania also corroborate this conclusion.

The long term effect of these developments is that those who live in urban areas under areas and tenure arrangements made in terms of flexible land tenure remain bound to be landless because they cannot afford to acquire the land they settle as it is demarcated as State land. It is therefore recommended that for flexible land tenure arrangements to work it must secure tenure for those in informal settlements. This would require the State to firstly cede the land to such dwellers, allowing them title over such ceded land and then only seek implementing the aspirations sought by such flexible land tenure arrangements (i.e. upgrading from starter to land hold titles etc.). As such there remains a need to completely relook the concept of flexible land tenure in Namibia given its shortcomings in providing tenure security. Tenured security remains crucial for an inclusive and sustainable urban growth and development in Namibia as envisaged under SDG 11. Secured land tenure supports sustainable development in diverse ways. Given that land title, especially in rural and peri-urban set ups provides a primary source of income, food security, cultural identity and shelter, tenure security to such land becomes extremely important. Secured land tenure may also serve as an incentive for economic empowerment because it provides for, and guarantees property rights. For instance, as a result of tenured land title, arbitrary expropriations and evictions are curtailed.

The more appealing question that remains to be answered is what lessons, insights or policy options can African States faced with urban informality draw from Namibia. This is not a tranquil question. Its complexity mainly derives from the geographical and economic variances that are prevalent in African States. No single African State identical to the other, whether historically, geographically, politically or economically. Therefore, though flexible land tenure arrangements may not yield the necessary result of providing tenure security to informal dwellers in urban and peri-urban spaces in Namibia and other comparable jurisdictions such as Zambia and Tanzania, as was indicated in this Chapter contribution, this cannot bluntly be interpreted to mean that it will be the same in other African countries. Possibly the outcomes could be different for other African States. What must however be stressed, and a point this paper strongly advance is that whatever the tenure arrangements and policy options African States opts for, its success or failure is dependent on the extent to which such arrangements can provide security of tenure. Such tenure security is a necessary and cumulative step in addressing the actual and prospective challenges urban informality may pose; one of them being the mushrooming of informal settlements.

References

Alfonso, A. (ed). (2015). *Informality and Urbanisation in African contexts: Analysing economic and social impacts*. Lisboa: Centro de Estudos Internacionais do Instituto Universitário de Lisboa.

Amoateng, P., Cobinah, P., & Owusu-Adade, K. (2003). Managing physical development in peri-urban areas of Kumasi, Ghana: A case of Abuakwa. *Journal of Urban and Environmental Engineering, 7*, 96–109.

Aryeetey-Attoh, S. (1997). *Urban geography of Sub-Saharan Africa*. In Samuel Aryeetey-Attoh (Ed.), *Geography of Sub-Saharan Africa Upper Saddle River* (pp. 183–222). New York: N.J Prentice Hall.

Amoo, S. K. (2014). *Property Law in Namibia*. Pretoria: Pretoria University Law Press.

Banks, N., Lombara, M., & Mitlin, D. (2020). Urban Informality as a Site of Critical Analysis *Journal of Development Studies, 56*(2), 223–238.

Christensen, S. F. (2004). The Flexible Land Tenure System– The Namibian solution bringing the informal settlers under the register. *Expert Group Meeting paper on Secure land tenure: New legal frameworks and tools*, UN-Gigiri in Nairobi, Kenya, 10–12 November 2004, pp. 1–10.

Cobbinah, P., Erdiaw-Kwasie, M. O., & Amoateng, P. (2015). Africa's Urbanisation: Implications for sustainable development. *Cities, 47*, 62–72.

Cobbinah, P. B., & Darkwah, R. M. (2016). Towards a more a desirable form of sustainable urban development in Africa. *Africa Geographical Review, 36*(3), 1–24.

Cobbinah, P. B., & Darkwah, R. M. (2016). African Urbanism: The geography of urban greenery. *Urban Forum, 27*, 149–165.

Flexible Land Tenure Act 4 of 2012.

Gastorn, K. (2013). Effectiveness of flexible land tenure in unplanned urban areas in the SADC region: A case study of Tanzania and experiences from Zambia and Namibia. *SADC Law Journal, 3*(1), 160–181.

Gbaguidi, A. N., & Spellenberg, U. (2004). Benin: Globalisaton and land tenure changes in peri-urban areas. Woodman, G. R. et al. (Ed.). *Local Land Law and Globalisation: A Comparative study of Peri-Urban areas in Benin, Ghana and Tanzania*. LIT Verlag.

Indongo, N., Angombe, S., & Nikanor, N. (2013). *Urbanization in Namibia: Views from semi-formal and informal settlements in Namibia*. Windhoek: University of Namibia.

Kleemann, J., Inkoom, J., Thiel, M., Shankar, S., Lautenbach, S., & Fürst, C. (2017). Peri-urban land use pattern and its relation to land use planning in Ghana, West Africa. *Land Scape and Urban Planning, 168*, 280–294.

Lall, S., Henderson, J., & Venables, A. J. (2017). *Africa's Cities: Opening Doors to the World*. New York: World Bank Publication.

Mandimika, P., & Matthaei, E. (2010). *The Flexible Land Tenure System in Namibia: Integrated Urban Land Rights into the National Land Reform Programme*. Windhoek: GIZ Publication.

Namibia Population and Housing Census Report (2011).

OECD/SWAC (2020). *Africa's Urbanisation Dynamics 2020: Africapolis, Mapping a New Urban Geography* (pp. 33–40). West African Studies: OECD Publishing.

Otto, O., Isinika, A., & Musahara, H. (2019). *Land Tenure Dynamics in East Africa: Changing Practices and Rights to Land*. Norway: Nordic Africa Institute.

Potts, D. (2007). The State and the Informal in Sub-Saharan African Urban Economies: Revisiting debates on dualism. *Working Paper No. 18: Cities and Fragile States*, 1–29. https://www.lse.ac.uk/international-development/Assets/Documents/PDFs/csrc-working-papers-phase-two/WP18.2-the-state-and-the-informal.pdf

Saghir, J., & Santono, J. (2018). *Urbanisation in Sub-Saharan Africa: Meeting challenges by bridging stakeholders* (p. 1). Washington: Centre for Strategic and International Studies. Retrieved from https://csis-website-prod.s3.amazonaws.com/s3fs-public/publication/180411_Saghir_UrbanizationAfrica_Web.pdf?o02HMOfqh99KtXG6ObTacIKKmRvk0Owd (Last accessed 12 May 2020).

Shikangalah, R. (2005). Challenges of delivery low-income housing. A case of the build together programme of Namibia. (Master's Thesis) Retrieved from: https://researchspace.ukzn.ac.za (accessed on 1 August 2020).

UNDP. (2014). *World Urbanization Prospectus*. New York: United Nations Population Division Publication.

World FactBook Statistics of 2020. Retrieved from https://www.cia.gov/library/publications/the-world-factbook/geos/wa.html (Last accessed 12 December 2019).

16 The Shifting Sanitation Landscapes of Durban, South Africa: Through the Lens of Governmentality

Anthony Odili and Catherine Sutherland

Introduction

Sanitation is a major global challenge with 1.7 billion people living without basic sanitation and only 54% of the world's population having access to safely managed sanitation (WHO/UNICEF, 2021). In sub-Saharan Africa, rapid urbanisation and steady economic growth is leading to significant demand for sanitation services in cities in a context of large sanitation backlogs. According to WHO/UNICEF (2021), 87% of urban dwellers in Sub-Saharan Africa have access to at least basic water services, but only 16% have access to a sewer connection. The provision of safe, affordable, accessible, reliable and dignified sanitation is essential to improve human health and well-being (Satterthwaite et al., 2019). However, meeting Sustainable Development Goal (SDG) 6: to ensure availability and sustainable management of water and sanitation for all remains a challenge for governments in Sub-Saharan Africa (Satterthwaite, 2016). The responsibility of providing water and sanitation services in cities in Africa falls largely on local governments, NGOs or citizens themselves.

In the case of South Africa, Water Service Authorities (WSAs) (in most cases, municipalities) are mandated to provide water and sanitation services. How they address the demand for improved sanitation provision in the face of ongoing urbanisation, inadequate infrastructure, limited financial resources and water scarcity becomes critical to the sustainability of South African cities. Adopting a technical approach alone which does not take into account the role of good governance will not lead to the solutions required. Foucault's concept of governmentality with its rationalities of government and technologies of rule (Li, 2007a) is used to explore shifts in sanitation governance and, hence, applied in the sanitation landscape in Durban. Rather than understanding the spatial determinants and outcomes of sanitation provision through a narrow, technical framing, the chapter reflects on the actors, their discourses or rationalities and their practices in shaping sanitation outcomes in the city. As a result, the chapter highlights "the alternative socio-technical tools and governance arrangements that are instrumental in moving beyond some of the dead-end roads of traditional

DOI: 10.4324/9781003181484-16

water engineering and sanitation provision" (van Vliet et al., 2011, p. 707). Sanitation governance is not merely a technical field that can be addressed through infrastructure provision and scientific expertise but a political one that involves human values, behaviour and organisation (O'Keefe et al., 2015). This chapter argues that identifying and analysing the various rationalities of government, governance arrangements and practices for the delivery of sanitation services in African cities, and their spatial expression, is helpful in identifying levers for change to support improved access to sanitation. It presents the approach adopted in Durban, by its WSA, eThekwini Water and Sanitation (EWS), to address sanitation backlogs in the context of a sprawling, rapidly urbanising city, with limited resources to extend centralised service provision.

Centralised sanitation systems which depend on good water supply, the provision of large-scale sewer systems and wastewater treatment plants, remain the most technically, politically and socially acceptable form of sanitation provision (Bhagwan et al., 2019; Satterthwaite et al., 2019). According to a World Resources Institute Report (Satterthwaite et al., 2019) which analysed sanitation practices in fifteen cities in the Global South, on-site sanitation services impact significantly on poor urban households, in terms of health risks and the high costs to households of servicing and maintaining them. The report recommends the use of centralised sanitation systems, connected to sewers, as the most cost-effective, safe and sustainable form of sanitation for the urban poor. However, this is not always possible due to the significant resource demands of centralised systems and rapidly increasing sanitation backlogs in cities in the South. Cities therefore need to develop, support and regulate on-site sanitation systems and make a variety of affordable sanitation services available (Mercer et al., 2018; Satterthwaite et al., 2019).

Study Area and Profile of the Sanitation Landscape of Durban

Durban is South Africa's third largest city on the east coast of the country, in the province of KwaZulu-Natal. eThekwini Municipality is the administrative entity for the city of Durban, or the eThekwini Municipal Area (EMA), which covers an area of approximately 2,300 km^2 with a population of 3.7 million (eThekwini Municipality, 2019/20). It is as classified as 55% urban and 45% rural. The city has high levels of poverty, unemployment and informality, with 42% of individuals considered poor (eThekwini Municipality, 2019). The EMA is located within a biodiversity hotspot, the Maputaland-Pondoland-Albany Region (eThekwini Municipality, 2019). eThekwini Municipality is recognised globally for its innovation in water and sanitation provision, most notably its water pricing, experimentation in sanitation technologies, context-specific and creative service delivery, and the participation of citizens in decision-making (Bond, 2020). In 2014, eThekwini Municipality was awarded the prestigious Stockholm Water

Award for its transformative and inclusive approach to providing water and sanitation services. In 2016, it became an engineering field testing (EFT) site for sanitation prototypes being developed as part of the Bill and Melinda Gates' "Re-invent the Toilet Challenge." However, EWS has also been criticised for its so-called tokenistic and neo-liberal approach to service delivery. According to Bond (2020, p. 276) "many of the innovations can be judged in retrospect as either failures on their own terms (such as the sanitation strategies), or as inadequate forms of 'tokenistic' social policy that regularly generate protest."

The municipality faces the challenge of expanding its waterborne sewerage network in the face of water scarcity, driven by both increasing demand and limited supply, and a fast growing and changing city, which is experiencing rapid densification in the rural periphery (Jewitt et al., 2020; Sim et al., 2018). Sanitation backlogs continue to increase in the EMA as the city becomes more informal and as poverty and inequality remains a critical challenge with 26.4% of residents living in the city's 566 informal settlements (eThekwini Municipality, 2019). In Durban, 94% of households have access to piped municipal water at least 200m from their dwelling and 73% have access to basic sanitation (eThekwini Municipality, 2018/2019). eThekwini Municipality is governed by both the municipal administration as well as the traditional authority. This results in a dual governance system in 43% of the municipal area (Sim et al., 2018). The municipality adopts an approach of managerial governance. Its politicians and officials engage with citizens but retains its position of being a "developmental local state" that provides water and sanitation services to its citizens through a top down approach (Sutherland et al., 2018). EWS has a strong and well-established partnership with the WASH Research and Development Centre (formerly known as the Pollution Research Group), University of KwaZulu-Natal (which includes Built Environment and Development Studies, UKZN); and this research relationship has enabled the local state to take a "fail safe and fail fast approach" in engaging in experimental learning by doing. The combination of a structured and spatially differentiated approach to sanitation delivery by EWS based on national legislation and local policy; EWS's responsiveness to the city's socio-economic and environmental context; research and experimentation; as well as the agency of other non-state actors have produced the sanitation landscape of Durban as this chapter will show.

Durban's approach to water and sanitation delivery post-1994 has a strong spatial expression. EWS provides universal access to basic sanitation across the EMA, but reproduces inequality, as backlogs in basic service provision, which include sanitation, are predominantly located in areas previously under-developed due to apartheid (Bond, 2020; Sutherland et al., 2014). The local authority, eThekwini Municipality, adopted a spatially differentiated approach to sanitation provision in

2000, providing different levels of services to residents in the urban core and rural periphery of the EMA and in formal and informal areas (Sutherland et al., 2014). Since 2014, this policy framework has been disrupted by the pressure of a growing and urbanising city; lack of capacity, both human and financial resources to meet sanitation demand; the involvement of a broader range of actors in sanitation provision; changing socio-technical and state-citizen relations; and the investment of a global philanthropic organisation in sanitation research in the city. This chapter presents and analyses the changing sanitation landscape of Durban, identifying the governmentalities that produced the city's sanitation landscapes between 2000 and 2013, and between 2014 and 2020. In so doing, it reveals Durban's approach to sanitation provision over time, shaped by clear spatial determinants, which in turn produce and re-produce a spatially differentiated service provision model.

The chapter draws on a wide body of research conducted by the authors on water and sanitation governance in Durban since 2010. It provides a review of the rationalities of government and technologies of rule adopted by the local state since 2000 to shape the sanitation landscape of Durban. It reflects on how these governmentalities have determined citizen's sanitation experiences and the state's response to national legislation and more recently the attainment of SDG 6. Foucault's concept of governmentality, which is the framework adopted for the analysis of sanitation outcomes, is presented. The analysis provides insight on potential levers for change for sanitation provision in Durban. This learning is applicable to other African cities with similar contexts and challenges.

The Governmentalities of Sanitation Provision

Foucault's concept of governmentality, or the "art of governing" (Foucault, 1991, p. 88), enables a political analysis of the outcomes of programmes of improvement by revealing attempts to shape the conduct of humans through calculated means (Li, 2007a). Governmentality can be a process of rendering problems technical, where those with the power to govern (in this case engineers and water authority managers), diagnose the problems and define the solutions for those who are positioned as subjects, requiring expert direction or technical solutions (in this case, citizens requiring sanitation) (Djama et al., 2011; Li, 2007a). Two central terms frame the analysis: political rationalities and the technologies of rule (Li, 2007a). The rationalities of government are a politics of truth, producing forms of knowledge and concepts that contribute to the "government" of domains of regulation and intervention, in this case sanitation systems and the citizens that use them, at different moments in time (Djama et al, 2011; Lemke, 2000). Gemechu (2018, p. 34) defines the rationalities of government as the element of government which "produces a discursive field in which the act of government becomes rational." This political rationality produces and legitimises multiple technologies of rule or practices and strategies of programme interventions. These in turn order or regulate the conduct of subjects (Lemke, 2000; Murdoch & Ward, 1997). The technologies of rule are the tactics, instruments, processes and practices used to manage the conduct of conduct, inscribed by the rationalities of government (Foucault, 1991). The problem with technologies of rule, as Li (2007a) suggests, is that they render challenges non-political and hence do not reflect or address the structural relations that produce inequality, which in the case of sanitation systems, has a strong spatial expression.

Governmentality therefore illuminates how society and its challenges are rendered governable. The state does not act on its own as the only source of power but rather a range of actors regulate and shape the way in which lives are lived or the way in which sanitation services are produced, delivered and experienced (Li, 2007a, 2007b; Rose, 1999; Sutherland et al., 2015). Subjects are not passive agents and they in turn act back on the development programmes and interventions designed to order their lives and manage their conduct of conduct, reshaping policies through different forms of social mobilisation (Dupont et al., 2016; Sutherland et al., 2015). Li (2007a) states that there are waves and waves of interventions embedded in particular political economies, discourses and contexts that lead to specific development outcomes. This chapter reviews and analyses two waves of interventions in sanitation provision in Durban which have produced particular sanitation landscapes.

Governmentality enables an analysis of the relations shaping the sanitation landscapes of Durban and the knowledge used in development interventions. The well-established and institutionalised practices of regulation, planning and engineering, which is the terrain of experts, translates the tensions over what is considered improvement and how it should be distributed into technical questions of sustainability and efficiency. The programmes or interventions which emerge from the will to govern are a combination of existing practices, established ways of doing things and accretion, as new ideas are added to the layers of what has gone before (Li, 2007a, b). The managerial approach to governance in Durban and the landscape of sanitation that emerged post-apartheid is reflective of the local state rendering what was, and is, intensely political (namely the delivery of sanitation in an unequal post-apartheid city) and the act of transforming a political issue into a technical issue (Bond, 2020; Sutherland et al., 2018). However, these managerial approaches and the practices they produce are continually disrupted by other actors re-shaping the sanitation services delivered by the state through protest, mundane responses, engagement with the state, new knowledge and self-improvement (Sutherland et al., 2015). The local state in turn has been responsive and supports social learning and experimentation as politicians and officials, NGOs, research institutions, civil society organisations and communities act in the production of sanitation services in the city. This is resulting in shifts in the sanitation landscape in Durban.

South Africa and Durban's State of Sanitation Provision

In 1994, South Africa adopted a developmental approach to government, namely the direct intervention of the state in the economic and social development of the country, to ensure transformation and to address the inequalities produced by apartheid (Edigheji, 2010). Given the low levels of access to sanitation for those marginalised by apartheid, sanitation was identified as one of the priority areas for development. Enshrined in the Constitution of South Africa (1996), the provision of water and sanitation was framed by a rights-based and socially just approach. This was further reinforced in the White Paper on Water Supply and Sanitation (1994), the Water Services Act (Act 108 of 1997) and the Strategic Framework for Water Services (2003). This legislations and policies support a pro-poor approach to basic service provision and includes the provision of free basic water and sanitation services to the poor.[1] Discourses of social justice, economic efficiency and environmental sustainability frame the provision of water and sanitation in the country.

However, the provision of water and sanitation to those marginalised by both apartheid and ongoing poverty and inequality continues to be a major challenge in South Africa's post-apartheid transformation. While 89.9% of South Africans now have access to piped water, 83% of South Africans have access to improved sanitation (StatsSA, 2020). Improved sanitation is defined as access to flush toilets connected to a public sewerage system or a septic tank, a ventilated pit toilet, or in the case of informal settlements, access to communal sanitation facilities (StatsSA, 2020). The national Department of Water and Sanitation's (DWS) mission is to ensure "dignity, equity, social-economic development and ecological sustainability by effectively and efficiently managing the nation's water resources and sanitation services" (DWS, 2017, p. 1). While the South African government met the targets for water and sanitation stated in the Millennium Development Goals by 2011, its own target of all citizens in South Africa having access to sanitation by 2014 (WSP, 2011) has not been achieved. Sanitation backlogs continue to be a major problem in both urban and rural areas, with improved sanitation often not meeting the rights and needs of communities in terms of accessibility, availability, safety and dignity.

The sanitation landscapes of cities, towns and rural areas in South Africa reveal the rationalities of government and its strategies, programmes, plans and practices in service provision as well as the agency of other actors in shaping sanitation outcomes in each context. Landscapes are the integrated spatial expression of "the essential infrastructure for wellbeing" (Egoz & De Nardi, 2017). In this case, the sanitation landscape refers to the system of sanitation infrastructure (built, technological and ecological) and its socio-political relations that are assembled through technical, socio-ecological, political and economic discourses, systems and practices. Under hydro-modernism, which is the dominant approach to water and sanitation provision in South Africa, water and sanitation services are provided at scale through hard infrastructure (dams, reservoirs, pipes, pump stations and waste water treatment plants) and standardised practices (Martel & Sutherland, 2019; Staddon & Langberg, 2014). The rapid growth of cities and the legacy of apartheid has placed pressure on built infrastructure and the traditional form of delivering sanitation services through centralised systems, requiring that alternative forms of sanitation are provided. In Durban, the sanitation system includes flush toilets, Communal Ablution Blocks (CABs) and waterborne sewerage networks, and in the absence of bulk infrastructure and sewer networks, improved ventilated pit latrines (VIPs), chemical toilets and Urine Diversion Dehydration Toilets (UDDTs).

Data Collection Method and Research Design

The chapter draws on empirical research undertaken by the authors on water and sanitation provision in Durban since 2010 as part of six water governance projects.[2] The data and the results from these studies formed the basis of the analysis of the governmentalities shaping Durban's sanitation landscape between 2000 and 2013 and 2014 and 2020. As such, the results presented in the chapter (section five) were produced by applying a governmentality framework to data and knowledge collected and produced on Durban's sanitation landscape over ten years. The chapter describes and analyses the relationships between the sanitation landscapes of Durban and the rationalities of government, technologies of rule, subjects and their agency, over two moments of water governance in the city. The shift from water governance to integrated water and climate governance in the city in 2014 led to the formation of the uMngeni Ecological Infrastructure Partnership (Sutherland & Roberts, 2014). This shift introduced progressive and more diversified socio-technical and socio-ecological approaches to resource management. It therefore marks the change from one moment or sanitation landscape to another.

Durban's Shifting Sanitation Landscape

The sanitation landscapes of Durban and the governmentalities that have produced them, have emerged out of particular socio-economic, political and environmental contexts at particular moments in time. The spatiality of the city (see Figure 16.1), which reflects its histories and geographies has shaped sanitation outcomes.

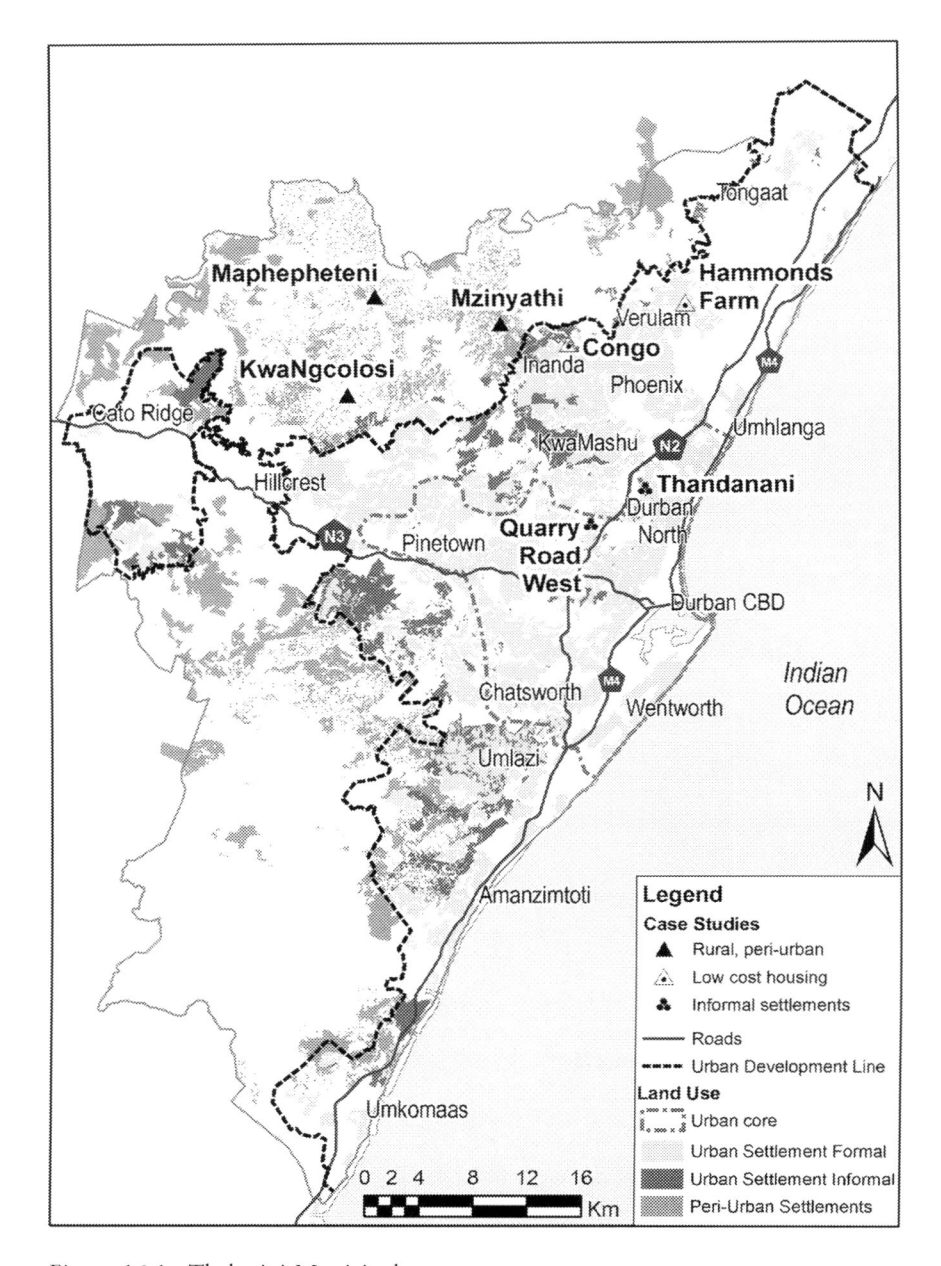

Figure 16.1 eThekwini Municipal area.

The main contextual factors and the governmentalities producing the two sanitation moments of sanitation provision in Durban identified in this chapter, are presented below.

The Sanitation Landscape of Durban: 2000–2013

In 2000, the sanitation landscape of Durban changed significantly as a result of a spatial intervention by national government. The national municipal demarcation process which created wall-to-wall municipalities across the country ensured the sharing of resources between urban and rural areas. This spatial restructuring aimed to fast track the country's transformation agenda by improving the delivery of public services through addressing decades of administrative, financial and socio-spatial marginalisation perpetrated by the spatial instruments of the apartheid government. These instruments had separated rural and urban areas; creating *bantustans* limiting access of African people to well serviced urban areas. For the newly created eThekwini Municipality (2000), this process resulted in a 68% increase in land area and an inheritance of 75,000 households in the rural hinterland urgently in need of water and sanitation services (Gounden et al., 2006). The majority of this additional land is located in the periphery of the EMA, a large percentage of which is held by the Ingonyama Trust, under the custodianship of the Zulu King. In 2000, the rural periphery was largely un-serviced as it had formed part of the homeland of KwaZulu during the apartheid era and hence suffered from underdevelopment. The EWS unit therefore had to respond to large service backlogs in these areas which lacked services and bulk infrastructure. The cholera outbreak of 2000–2002 in Durban provided further impetus to provide a basic level of water and sanitation to households without adequate services across the municipal area as quickly and efficiently as possible. Environmental health concerns, thus, supported the decision to provide a basic level of services to all across the EMA.

The EWS unit, mandated to provide water and sanitation services across the EMA, does so in a context of dual governance in the rural periphery where traditional councils with their *amakosi* and *isinduna*[3] govern Ingonyama Trust land. Land is allocated through a traditional communal land system and as a result, town planning schemes and planning and building regulations and controls are not implemented (Sim et al., 2018). The rapid densification of these traditional authority areas began in 2007. Citizens moving from both within and from outside of Durban began to realise the value of moving to the rural zone of the EMA, constructing the "city from below" (Sim et al., 2016). Residents obtained land through traditional systems and built houses outside of formal municipal processes (Mbatha & Ngcoya, 2019; Sim et al., 2016). The densification of the periphery, which has increased the demand for services, and in part has led to the privatisation of sanitation services, as wealthier households install their own sanitation facilities outside of formal building regulations, impacts on the sanitation landscape and ecological infrastructure.

Another major influence was a shift in policy towards housing the urban poor. Durban adopted a progressive approach to informal settlement upgrading from the early 1990s. In 2004, national government's Breaking New Ground Policy provided further impetus for informal settlement upgrading programmes. Informal settlements were, and continue to be, part of the solution to housing the urban poor in the EMA. The EWS unit provided basic provided basic water and sanitation services while informal residents waited for re-housing under the city's ambitious human resettlement programme of the mid to late 1990s and 2000s. This led to the establishment of the Interim Services Programme in the EMA. Under this programme, the CABs and communal tap points were provided to informal settlements not on the priority housing relocation list.

According to Roma et al. (2010, p. 1) the CABs were:

> a temporary service for those informal urban settlements that will not be upgraded by the Housing Department in the next 5–15 years. This initiative was started by the eThekwini Health, Architecture and Housing Departments in 2004. Since the end of 2008, the project was taken over by eThekwini Water and Sanitation (EWS).

The CABs, reconfigured "blue" shipping containers, with male and female toilet sections, showers, and washbasins, were and continue to be, installed across the city, usually on the edge of settlements due to bulk sewer connections. They reflect the investment of the state in communal sanitation facilities with community-based state funded caretakers to maintain the facilities.

A commitment to community engagement by the EWS, albeit through managerial governance, has played a major role in shaping the state's response to citizens in relation to sanitation services. The relationship between EWS and citizens of Durban is outlined in EWS's Customer Services Charter, Service Levels Standards and EWS policy (eThekwini Municipality, 2011, 2012). It is evident from the services charter that both the discourses of water and sanitation as a social good, and water and sanitation as an economic good, frame EWS's policies and practices. The EWS unit engages with the public on water and sanitation provision through the Sizakala Customer Service Units which are located across the city to engage with citizens in a formal and technical manner and through User Platforms and Focus Groups. The User Platforms were developed by EWS to engage citizens on water and sanitation issues and they continue to be the governance arena through which city officials formally engage with ward councilors and ward representatives on water and sanitation provision. However, service delivery protests, which are common, reflect citizens' more political responses to inadequate service provision in the EMA (Bond, 2020).

In summary, the spatial expression of sanitation delivery between 2000 and 2013 was shaped by the expanded municipal jurisdiction, the cholera outbreak, increasing informality, a managerial developmental state, the existence of a dual system of governance in the periphery of the city and the response of citizens through protest and mundane resistance to the local's states delivery of sanitation services. In addition to the dominant discourses of water as a social good, water as an economic good, and experimental governance, these contextual factors were internalised by the EWS and emerged as the rationalities of government in the state's governance of sanitation services (Sutherland et al., 2014) (see Table 16.1). These rationalities of government then informed and legitimised the strategies and practices, which produced the sanitation landscape of the EMA between 2000 and 2013.

The mandate of providing sanitation services was pursued by EWS from 2000 through different strategies and spatial practices. These did not all focus on improvement in access to bulk sewer infrastructure. Rather, the EWS focused on increasing indigent[4] access to basic water and onsite sanitation services through different service provision levels across the EMA based on the concept of an urban edge or Urban Development Line (UDL) (Sim et al., 2016). For, eThekwini municipality, the UDL was not intended to be a discriminatory servicing line as Bond (2020) suggests, but a "spatial tool for achieving compact and efficient urban growth over time. It prioritises areas with existing services and high accessibility (i.e. the integration zone) but also identifies the outer limits of urban growth as subsequent phases of development" (eThekwini Municipality, 2019, p. 395).

As the state implemented a spatially differentiated approach to sanitation delivery, with its alternative technologies and non-sewered systems, so non-state actors, most notably communities, began to act back through protest, mundane practices and engagement with the state, to re-make this form of sanitation delivery (Sutherland et al., 2015). The agency and self-conduct of citizens began challenging this particular sanitation governmentality and its spatial expression. Therefore, while the majority of peri-urban residents living beyond the UDL reported that they used their UDDTs every day, they also reported high levels of dissatisfaction with this form of sanitation largely due to smell and the challenges of emptying the chambers (Mkhize et al., 2017; Sutherland et al., 2014). Some residents converted their UDDT toilets, which are dry or waterless toilets to flush toilets and others converted them to store rooms or only used them for visitors (Sutherland et al., 2014). Meanwhile new residents moving into the traditional authority areas post-2007, building middle- and upper-income houses installed flush toilets with septic tanks, thereby privatising the sanitation landscape at the micro-scale.

Table 16.1 The governmentality of sanitation in Durban: 2000–2013

Context	Dominant discourses	Rationalities of government (local state aligned with national government)	Technologies of rule	Citizens as subjects or citizens as resistance
Post-apartheid transformation National municipal demarcation process created wall-wall municipalities: EMA (2000), 68% increase in land area of previous Durban Metropolitan Area, addition of 65 000 households in rural periphery without adequate access to water and sanitation.	Water and sanitation as a social good and as a human right	Rights based approach that addresses inequalities of the past. Provide citizens across EMA with universal access to acceptable, safe and affordable basic water and sanitation services. Provision of free basic water and sanitation to the poor. Sanitation ladder (incremental sanitation provision) to pave way for the progressive realization of the rights to water and sanitation as stipulated in the Constitution of South Africa.	Urban Development Line (UDL) (aligned with waterborne sewerage edge). Different levels of service provision in the urban core and rural periphery. Rural services beyond the UDL: one ground tank supplied with 300 litres of free basic water per day; UDDT. Roll out of 90 000 Urine Diversion Dehydration Toilets in the rural periphery to indigent households (2002 – 2019).	Citizens make use of UDDTs as state provided service. High levels of social dissatisfaction with UDDTs. UDDTs converted in to storerooms or only used for visitors. Citizens install pit latrines or flush toilets.
Cholera outbreak in Durban (2001-2002)	Sanitation services critical to human and environmental health in the EMA	Provision of basic level of sanitation services to address human and environmental health risk, limited by spatial reach of sanitation infrastructure.	Urban services within UDL: full pressure, billed household connections; waterborne sanitation or septic tanks.	

Increasing informality and growth in informal settlements	Progressive approach to informal settlements: focus on relocation and upgrading in the EMA	Interim Service Provision to support informal settlements not due for imminent (usually three + years) relocation. Informal settlements identified for relocation to receive basic services such as communal pit latrines and tap points. Interim service provision aligned with the national ladder of sanitation services and human settlements low cost housing programme in the EMA.	Provision of Communal Ablution Blocks as part of the Interim Services Programme. Located within 200 metres of served households. Provision of pit latrines and chemical toilets in settlements earmarked for relocation.	Caretakers and community members maintain CABs and insist on strict rules of use to manage state provided facilities. Caretakers and community members struggle to maintain CABs when municipal maintenance of infrastructure is poor: often linked to failure of outsourced service providers. Community members vandalise CABs as a form of resistance.
Managerial approach to governance of a developmental or interventionist state: state mandated to provide water and sanitation and ensure economic efficiency	Water and sanitation as an economic good	Services that are efficient and effective (the job is well done) and sustainable (services are financially, environmentally, institutionally, and socially sustainable) Customers that are not indigent pay for services; "user pays" principle.	Sizakala Customer Service Units. EWS's Customer Services Charter and Service Levels Standards.	Citizens contribute by paying for water and sanitation services. Low payment for water and sanitation services for those who do not qualify for free basic services. Water theft resulting in low revenue for the state from water and sanitation provision.
Progressive experimental governance within framework of a developmental state, led by innovative local government officials in	Learning by doing, experimental governance to address sanitation challenges	Innovation required to address social, economic and environmental constraints limiting provision of centralised	Partnership between EWS and PRG to test innovative sanitation solutions. Information sharing and	Limited participation of citizens in sanitation innovation. Focused mainly on the technical realm and information transfer.

(Continued)

Table 16.1 (Continued)

Context	Dominant discourses	Rationalities of government (local state aligned with national government)	Technologies of rule	Citizens as subjects or citizens as resistance
partnership with Pollution Research Group (PRG, UKZN)		sanitation systems across the EMA.	education about new technologies.	
Democratisation of South African society post-apartheid	Participation of stakeholders and beneficiaries in development interventions	Participatory governance and inclusion of stakeholders in decision making is essential to social and political acceptability of sanitation systems Focus on customer relations management: two-way communication between citizens and the state.	Participation legislated by a democratic state Participation of citizens of EMA in EWS decision making processes and practices Raising Citizens Voice (water dialogues) and User Platforms (focus groups used by EWS to engage citizens in ward committees). Education of users in roll out of sanitation services. Education programmes: raising community awareness. EWS Contact Centre for citizen reporting of technical problems.	Engagement of citizens and councillors in User Platforms. Service protests. Use of toll free call lines to report water and sanitation faults. Communicate through councillors to report water and sanitation faults, less effective that direct engagement by citizens with EWS.

Residents of informal settlements responded through mundane practices and protest to the provision of VIPs and CABs in their settlements: filling the VIPs with building waste so that they could not be used, taking care of the VIP by locking it so it could only be used by immediate neighbours, vandalising the CABs, or protesting against their poor maintenance. Resistance to and concerns about the use of the VIPs, UDDTs and CABs, and challenges associated with them, were raised at the User Platforms and focus groups and through state supported research. This led to further dialogue between the state and citizens and a change in practices of the state: such as the emptying of the UDDT toilets by the municipality in 2017 and an attempt to improve the relationship between the caretakers of the CABs, communities and the state. The sanitation landscape from 2000 to 2013 remained relatively stable once it had been established with adjustments being made as a result of community mobilisation, engagement and research. However, by 2014, global, environmental, political, social and economic factors further diversified and shifted the sanitation landscape of the city. This is explored in the following section.

The sanitation landscape of Durban: 2014–2020

South Africa is a water scarce country. Durban faces challenges of water insecurity as a result of demand exceeding supply in a fast growing city with high levels of non-revenue water due to leaks and illegal connections, cycles of drought and climate change (Hay, 2017). The 2015/2017 drought in KwaZulu-Natal which impacted significantly on Durban's water supply provided further support for the EWS's focus on using recycled water in its service delivery plans. This focus on developing alternative and innovative sanitation technologies, which built on the lessons learnt from the implementation of dry UDDTs, gained further momentum when Durban was selected as an engineering field-test site (EFT) for the Bill and Melinda Gates Foundation's Re-invent the Toilet Challenge in 2016 (Mercer et al., 2018). Sanitation prototypes from engineering institutes across the world have been tested in peri-urban areas and informal settlements in Durban. The rationale behind most of these innovative technologies includes reduction in the use of water in sanitation systems, resource reuse in a circular economy through source separation of urine and faeces, less dependence on bulk infrastructure such as wastewater treatment works, and with treated derived products to be used as fertiliser, biochar, and for electricity generation. The experimentation and social learning that has taken place in the city as a result of the introduction of decentralised, non-sewered, low water use systems by the EWS in partnership with Pollution Research Group (relaunched as the WASH R&D Centre in 2020), Water Research Commission and Bill and Melinda Gates Foundation through the EFT platform, is continuing to shift thinking about sanitation in the municipality (Sutherland et al., 2020).

Table 16.2 The governmentality of sanitation in Durban: 2014–2020

Context	Dominant discourses	Rationalities of government (local state aligned with national government)	Technologies of rule	Citizens as subjects or citizens as resistance
Water insecurity due to increasing demand, limited increase in supply (new dam supply already committed to sustain EMA), climate change and impact of 2015 – 2017 drought.	Water conservation and reduction in water use critical. Demand for water is exceeding supply. Alternative approaches to water security need to be developed. Reduction of water use in sanitation systems.	Development of innovative sanitation technologies to reduce water consumption. Value of ecological infrastructure in improving water security in uMngeni Catchment.	Investment in research to identify future systems that are environmentally sustainable, socially just, affordable, and not dependent on centralised sewer networks or large scale water supply. Testing and experimentation of innovative sanitation technologies that reduce or do not use water. PRG is testing and evaluating both a DEWATS plant (decentralised wastewater treatment system) and VUNA reactor. Restrictions on water supply.	Citizens engaged in experimentation with new sanitation technologies. Citizens committed to leaving a legacy through social learning in their everyday lived spaces to contribute to shifts in global sanitation. High level of awareness of water scarcity.
Increasing informality and growth in informal settlements.	Progressive approach to informal settlements: focus on in-situ upgrading in the EMA.	Incremental Service Provision as part of informal settlement upgrading.	Provision of Communal Ablution Blocks as part of the Incremental Services Programme.	Caretakers and community members maintain CABs and insist on strict rules of use to manage state

Social acceptance of basic sanitation services, particularly UDDTs remain low, recognition that UDDTs may no longer be appropriate form of sanitation for the poor in the rural periphery (reached their shelf life).

Sanitation systems developed post-apartheid to universally address sanitation backlogs and environmental health concerns may longer be appropriate or acceptable.
Need to develop a range of innovative sanitation technologies that can be applied in different contexts to address sanitation challenges.

Commitment to developing safe, socially acceptable, financially viable, environmentally sensitive sanitation systems that can be implemented in different contexts.
Universal provision of state provided sanitation systems at scale may longer be possible nor appropriate.
Engagement with citizens to assess willingness to pay for sanitation systems.

CABS provided to informal settlements within financial and infrastructural ability of the state: not dependent on housing relocation status.

Establishment of engineering field testing platform (partnership between EWS and PRG).
Implementation of municipal programme to empty all UDDTs in 2017/2018 to reduce social impact of UDDTs on citizens.
Inter-sectoral efforts across line functions to address river quality in EMA: the establishment of EM's Transformative River Management Programme.

provided facilities.
Caretakers and community members struggle to maintain CABs when municipal maintenance of infrastructure is poor: often linked to failure of outsourced service providers.
Community members vandalise CABs as a form of resistance.
Mundane resistance to UDDTs by transforming the form of sanitation.

(*Continued*)

Table 16.2 (Continued)

Context	Dominant discourses	Rationalities of government (local state aligned with national government)	Technologies of rule	Citizens as subjects or citizens as resistance
			Inter-sectoral efforts across line functions to address informal settlement upgrading in EMA: iQhaza Lethu informal settlement upgrading partnership.	
Financial resources of EM to provide free basic water and sanitation impacted by low level of payment for water and sanitation services, growing demand for services, high cost of provision of services, and limited access to funding from national coffers.	State can no longer afford to deliver free basic sanitation services in the face of rapid urbanisation, low city revenue and increasing environmental risk (particularly water insecurity).	New systems of sanitation provision need to be developed for the urban poor that are socially and environmentally acceptable and financially affordable. Willingness of the urban poor to pay for higher quality sanitation services.	Experimentation with sanitation technologies that reduce the use of water. Experimentation with sanitation technologies that separate faeces and urine to support the circular economy. Research to address high levels of non-revenue water in the EMA.	Citizens engaging in social learning and co-production of knowledge around new sanitation systems. Citizens resisting payment for inadequate water and sanitation services. Citizens increasing claims, both legitimate and illegitimate, for access to free basic services. Citizens engaging in unhealthy and undignified sanitation practices in absence of basic services.

Democratisation of decision making around urban services as the developmental state recognises that it can no longer justify nor afford to deliver services at scale, without higher levels of social acceptability and citizen self-responsibility.	Participatory approaches and the co-production of knowledge leads to more socially acceptable and sustainable forms of sanitation.	Participatory governance and the co-production of knowledge on appropriate sanitation systems for the urban poor will deliver more sustainable outcomes in service delivery.	Transdisciplinary research approaches adopted to test innovative sanitation technologies in the EFT.	Citizens taking over maintenance of CABs due to lack of support from the state. Citizens engaging in state-citizen partnerships to address water and sanitation challenges in the city.
Increasing recognition of the value of ecological infrastructure in supporting more resilient and sustainable sanitation services and ensuring increased water security.	Ecological infrastructure and its associated ecosystem services supports built or hard infrastructure in addressing sanitation challenges. Investment in the circular economy ensures more sustainable sanitation outcomes and turns waste in to resources.	Investing in ecological infrastructure is essential for water security and more resilient and sustainable water and sanitation management in the face of climate change.	Establishment of the uMngeni Ecological Infrastructure Partnership. Investment in research in the value of ecological infrastructure and the circular economy. Investment in eco-champs who live in local communities, are funded by the state, and educate their communities about ecosystem services and report sanitation failures.	Citizens engaged in social learning around the value of ecological infrastructure in supporting service provision and improved quality of life. Citizens impacting on the environment and reducing the value of ecological infrastructure due to the lack of basic services, lower levels of knowledge and a lack of citizenship.

The call for the implementation of decentralised sanitation systems in contrast to global support for centralised sanitation systems (Satterthwaite, et al., 2019) includes both localised physical infrastructure and operation and management systems. Since the development trajectory of cities in the Global South differs from cities in the Global North, it is imperative to develop innovative and flexible ways in which safely managed sanitation services can be effectively and efficiently provided to growing urban populations. One way is through decentralised wastewater treatment systems that create the possibilities for smaller wastewater treatment plants that can be scaled to service communities or smaller areas. Decentralisation can be achieved through onsite sanitation without any requirement for sewers. The Newlands Mashu Research Site, located in the Newlands East area of Durban is used to conduct research experiments and field-tests on innovative sanitation models. WASH R&D is testing and evaluating both a DEWATS plant (decentralised wastewater treatment system) and VUNA reactor. The DEWATS system can provide wastewater treatment options to spaces in the city that are located outside of the city's sewer network. The VUNA reactor recycles urine to recover nitrogen and phosphorus for use in fertilisers (Udert et al., 2016). The possibility of developing multiple technologies, most of which are off the grid, for safely managed sanitation services are therefore being considered as part of eThekwini Municipality's response to sanitation services backlogs.

The ongoing urbanisation of the city, the densification of the rural periphery and the growth in informal settlements continues to place pressure on Durban's sanitation landscape. Furthermore, ageing water and sanitation infrastructure is beginning to shape strategic decisions around water and sanitation provision in the municipality. After almost two decades of providing UDDTs and CABs, EWS is questioning their sustainability and seeking alternative solutions (Duncker et al., 2006; Mkhize et al., 2017; Roma et al., 2013), particularly given the high costs of providing and maintaining the CABs as well as aging bulk infrastructure. The environment continues to be a buffer for the failures in these systems (Martel & Sutherland, 2019) but many environmental systems are reaching their tipping points as a pollution event in the port of Durban on 10 May, 2019 revealed. According to Kockott (2019) "bathing, surfing and fishing have been banned in Durban due to raw sewage flowing into the water." Transnet National Ports Authority stated that the "severe sewage discharge stems from the failure of pumps at the eThekwini Municipality's Mahatma Gandhi Pump Station – one of the deepest and biggest waste treatment facilities in the city." Ongoing research on the value of ecological infrastructure and its associated ecosystem services for water security and the delivery of safe and sustainable water and sanitation services is playing a significant role in shaping the discourses of the Environmental Planning and Climate Projection Department, the EWS and Catchment and Stormwater Management Department (Jewitt et al., 2020; Martel & Sutherland, 2019; Sutherland et al., 2014). Partnerships between these sectors in local government have resulted in the emergence of Durban's Transformative River Management Programme which will influence sanitation governance in to the future (Martel et al., 2021).

In 2020, the COVID pandemic had a significant impact on water and sanitation provision in eThekwini Municipality. The pandemic highlighted the unequal access to adequate water and sanitation services in informal settlements as the global response to contain the spread of the virus was predominantly based on hand hygiene and social distancing. Both national government's Department of Water and Sanitation and the EWS responded by providing water tanks and chemical toilets to informal settlements as part of COVID-19 emergency responses. COVID-19 has both illuminated the inequality in access to basic water and sanitation services and the need for improved services that support hand hygiene in the face of ongoing epidemics. The EFT has been making progress in this regard and one such innovative technology that was successfully tested in Durban was the Eawag waterwall (Sutherland et al., 2020).

These more recently emerging rationalities of government are beginning to re-shape and re-order the sanitation landscape of Durban. Given the challenges facing the existing system of sanitation in the city and the opportunities provided by the research and experimentation that is underway, both globally and in Durban, new approaches are beginning to emerge. These are being developed in many cases in partnership with communities through the co-production of knowledge (Sutherland et al., forthcoming). Social assessments, which explore and reveal the social responses to the prototypes are being undertaken and this is informing the design of the technologies (Mercer et al., 2018; Sutherland et al., 2020). As a result, the distance between the government and its subjects continues to change, power relations are being reconfigured, with the technologies of rule reflecting both the state and its subjects' rationalities and preferences. This has opened up the space for transformation in the socio-technical sanitation regime of Durban from a managerial governance regime, to one which is more participatory in terms of the co-production of knowledge on sanitation services. While this change remains localised in spaces where experimentation is taking place, it is a positive start in transforming state-citizen relations around sanitation provision.

In 2021, the strategies and practices of the state, or technologies of rule, remain predominantly locked-in to the path dependencies of hydro-modernism, hard infrastructure, centralised systems, spatially differentiated and unequal service provision, universal basic service provision, and incremental services, which are not moving the urban poor up the sanitation ladder fast enough. The spatial expressions of these practices remain embedded in the landscape, producing much of the same sanitation landscape of the previous era. As Li (2007b) asserts, the programmes or interventions which emerge from the will to govern, are a combination of existing practices, established ways of doing things and new ideas. Innovation can be added on as new layers to what has gone before or as a complete break in practice. However, the shifting rationalities of government in Durban are starting to diversify this landscape and introduce a range of new practices with their spatial expression. Most notable is the emergence of pockets of innovative sanitation sites across the EMA. The field-testing of sanitation prototypes as part of the EFT, in three informal settlements, one school and a peri-urban area, have produced new sets of relations between sanitation systems, residents and communities. At the micro-scale these field tests have re-ordered space, producing a vision of what decentralised and localised sanitation landscape might look like. The response of communities to these localised systems and their participation in their design has also shifted their relations with the state and the university, breaking down the usual spatial barriers between those who produce knowledge and those who are on the receiving end of it.

The decentralisation of the provision and management of sanitation services also suggests a decline in the role of the state as it challenges the notion of sanitation being solely a public service and a state responsibility. This opens up the possibilities for greater self-conduct, which will alter the sanitation landscape, as individuals participate in solutions to their own sanitation needs. Given the experience of and learning from the rapid, unregulated provision of sanitation services in the peri-urban areas under traditional authority in Durban, this approach would need to proceed with caution. Decentralised sanitation systems would have to be compliant with the regulation and policy of both the local and national state. The potential of safely managing sewage onsite within communities redefines spatial planning and provides opportunities to rethink the single use zoning principles in planning and evaluate what it means to be an urban citizen. In this reinvention of space, it is crucial to evaluate the right to sanitation of an urban citizen; and who or what determines how these sanitation rights are shared. Sanitation facilities influence the reinvention of space and the formation of a sanitation identity that is marked by a reconfiguration of sanitary flows and networks. This change in sanitation landscape is also seen in East African cities. Letema, van Vliet and van Lier (2010) state that through decentralisation of both infrastructural facilities and the management of sanitation services; implementation of a mix of conventional and innovative sewerage systems; use of base-flow and population density as indicators for appropriate sanitation options; a shift from a traditional large treatment works model to innovative treatment options with a mix of scales; new land requirements, technological advancement, and decision making processes, sanitation services can be provided in a safe, appropriate and sustainable manner.

As opposed to the technical and top-down managerial approach taken by the municipality in the case of the roll out of the UDDTs, the pilot-testing of innovative onsite sanitation technologies have developed a strong socio-technical dimension to sanitation services (Mercer et al., 2018; Sutherland et al., 2020, forthcoming). The testing has revealed the social, political, cultural and technical entanglements that occur at the levels of individuals, households, communities, service providers (private or public), and the state. Through an approach of incremental services and experimental learning, a socio-technical feedback loop is created that offers varying perspectives on innovative sanitation technologies. Through individual and community participation, socio-cultural constructions regarding standards of cleanliness, convenience and hygiene are better understood rather than the imposition of institutional standards. Since "meanings" and "rationalisations" are socially constructed and are dynamic through their everyday interactions, citizens continue to engage, adjust, adapt and respond to sanitation technologies in ways that transform space and urbanity.

Conclusion

This chapter has explored the shifting sanitation landscape of a fast-growing African city, Durban, which has extensive experience in innovation in water and sanitation provision. It has used governmentality as framework through which to explore the changing rationalities of government and technologies of rule which are producing a new form of sanitation landscape in the city. The state has to date adopted a managerial approach to sanitation provision but this is beginning to shift as the introduction of new technologies has inspired the co-production of knowledge and greater acknowledgement of the value of tacit knowledge and user satisfaction in the acceptability and sustainability of sanitation systems. It has revealed that eThekwini Municipality is a responsive developmental state which has implemented sanitation services based on well-established and evidence-based rationalities of government and in response to the agency and self-conduct of citizens. However, these rationalities and their strategies and practices have produced an unequal and uneven sanitation landscape which continues to reflect class and race divides in a city with a strong transformation agenda. EWS acknowledges the challenges with current sanitation services for the poor but it faces significant physical, financial, environmental and time constraints in providing a high level of services to all. It recognises that its two main forms of sanitation provision for the urban poor, UDDTs and CABs, were only intended as interim services and may have reached their shelf-life. However, in the absence of other sustainable systems and in the face of rapid urbanisation and increasing informality, EWS cannot shift away from UDDTs and CABs as yet. Integrated sanitation solutions which are cognisant of local conditions, state capacity, social acceptability and technological reliability, and which adopt participatory processes in terms of implementation are being developed in cities in the South (Mercer et al., 2018; Sutherland 2015, 2020; van Vliet et al., 2011). However, the time required to test the prototypes and to ensure their commercialisation and provision at scale is lengthy while the need for sanitation services rapidly increases.

What is evident is that the new landscape of sanitation will be informed by a greater recognition of the value and scarcity of water; recognition that state managed centralised sanitation systems alone will no longer be able to address sanitation needs in the city. Sanitation services will need to be provided by a range of actors through decentralised systems provided by actors who ensure they are compliant with state policy and legislation. Sustainable sanitation systems should not be produced and implemented by the state alone but rather should be developed through extensive engagement and participatory governance where the knowledge of the beneficiaries of sanitation systems is included from the outset of the process. The two forms of governmentality identified in this chapter which has produced Durban's particular sanitation landscapes in Durban since 2000 have a strong spatial expression and in turn are produced by the spatiality of the city. Understanding the contextual factors, discourses, rationalities, technologies of rule and the response of beneficiaries, the governmentality of sanitation, and its spatiality is critical if we are to move towards more sustainable, socially just and transformative sanitation systems in Africa cities to meet the targets of SDG 6.

Acknowledgements

The authors would like to acknowledge the Bill & Melinda Gates Foundation for funding this research, and eThekwini Municipality (Water and Sanitation Unit), Khanyisa Projects, the University of KwaZulu-Natal (Pollution Research Group) for providing comments on the chapter. We would also like to acknowledge the valuable contribution of the external reviewers as well as the editors, Michael Addaney and Patrick Cobbinah, for their comments on the chapter.

Notes

1 In Durban, free basic water consists of at least a basic amount of 6 kl (6,000 L) of water per month per household or within 200 m of the household to indigent households. This amount may differ among municipalities. Free basic sanitation includes providing improved sanitation facilities within 200 m of a household.
2 (EU 7th Framework Chance2Sustain (2010–2014); NRF Sancoop Climways (2014–2017); eThekwini Municipality's Social Acceptance of Use and Emptying of UDDTs (2016–2019); Water Research Commission WRC 2354: the value of ecological infrastructure in securing water in the uMngeni Catchment; Engineering Field-Testing Platform for field-testing sanitation prototypes, Bill and

Melinda Gates Foundation's Reinvent the Toilet Challenge (2016–2020), Iqhaza Lethu upgrading informal settlements programme (2019–2020)).
3 Chiefs and headmen.
4 South African citizens who earn below the defined poverty threshold and live on a property valued less than R250000 (eThekwini Municipality, 2017, p. 152).

References

Bhagwan, J., Pillay, S., & Koné, D. (2019). Sanitation game changing: Paradigm shift from end-of-pipe to off-grid solutions. *Water Practice and Technology, 14*(3), 497–506.

Bond, P. (2020). Tokenistic water and neo-liberal sanitation in post-apartheid Durban. *Journal of Contemporary African Studies, 37*(4), 275–293.

Djama, M., Fouilleux, E., & Vagneron, I. (2011). Standard-setting, certifying and benchmarking: A governmentality approach to sustainability standards in the agro-food sector. In Ponte, S., Gibbon, P., & Vestergaard, J. (Eds.). *Governing through standards: Origins, drivers and limitations*. London, UK: Palgrave Macmillan.

Dupont, V. et al. (2016). *The politics of slums in the global south: Urban informality in Brazil, India, South Africa and Peru*. Oxford: Routledge.

Duncker, L., Matsebe, G., & Austin, L. (2006). Use and acceptance of urine-diversion sanitation systems in South Africa. *WRC Report No. 1439/2/06*. Pretoria: Water Research Commission.

DWAF. (1997a). *Water Services Act*. Pretoria: Department of Water Affairs and Forestry.

DWAF. (1997b). *White Paper on National Water Policy of South Africa*. Pretoria: DWAF.

DWAF. (1998). *National Water Act*. Pretoria: Department of Water Affairs and Forestry

DWAF. (2003). *Strategic Framework for Water Services*. Pretoria: DWAF.

DWS (Department of Water and Sanitation). (2017). *National sanitation policy*. Pretoria: Department of Water and Sanitation.

Edigheji, O. (2010). *Constructing a democratic developmental state in South Africa: Potentials and challenges*. Pretoria: HSRC Press.

Egoz, S. & De Nardi, A. (2017). Defining landscape justice: The role of landscape in supporting wellbeing of migrants, a literature review. *Journal of Landscape Research, 42*(10), 74–89.

eThekwini Municipality. (2011). Customer Services Charter, eThekwini Water and Sanitation Unit. Durban: eThekwini Municipality.

eThekwini Municipality. (2012). *Policies and Practices of the eThekwini Water and Sanitation Unit*. Durban: eThekwini Municipality.

eThekwini Municipality. (2016/2017). *Spatial Development Framework*. Durban: eThekwini Municipality.

eThekwini Municipality. (2017/2018). *Spatial Development Framework*. Durban: eThekwini Municipality.

eThekwini Municipality. (2019/2020). *Integrated Development Plan: 5 Year Plan2017/18 to 2021/22*. Durban: eThekwini Municipality.

Foucault, M. (1991). *Discipline and punish: The birth of a prison.* London: Penguin.

Gemechu, (2018). On water users' repertoire: Market rationality and governmentality in Peeth village's water supply, Rajasthan (India). *Geoforum, 94,* 33–40.

Gounden, T., Pfaff, B., Macleod, N., & Buckley, C. (2006). Provision of free sustainable basic sanitation: The Durban experience. In *32nd WEDC International Conference, Sustainable Development of Water Resources, Water Supply and Environmental Sanitation,* Colombo.

Hay, D. (2017). *Our water our future: Securing the water resources of the Umngeni River Basin.* Institute of Natural Resources.

HSRC (Human Sciences Research Council). (2004). *Assessment of the effectiveness of the education programme for households receiving sanitation and water.* Durban: HSRC.

Jewitt, G. P. W., Sutherland, C., Browne, M., Stuart-Hill, S., Risko, S., Martel, P., et al. (2020). Enhancing water security through restoration and maintenance of ecological infrastructure: Global lessons from the uMngeni Catchment, South Africa. Water Research Commission Report K5/2354.

Kockott, F. (2019). Massive pollution in Durban sea as waste treatment facility fails. *GroundUp, May 2019.* [Accessed 01/02/2020].

Lemke, T. (2000). Foucault, Governmentality, and Critique. *Conference paper, University of Amherst (MA).*

Letema, S., van Vliet, B., & van Lier, J. B. (2010). Reconsidering urban sewer and treatment facilities in East Africa as interplay of flows, networks and spaces. In van Vliet, B. et al. (Eds.), *Social perspectives on the sanitation challenge.* London: Springer.

Li, T. M. (2007a). *The will to improve: Governmentality, development and the practice of politics.* Durham: Duke University Press.

Li, T. M. (2007b). Practices of assemblage and community forest management. *Economy and Society, 36*(2), 263–293.

Martel, P., & Sutherland, C. (2019). Governing river rehabilitation for climate adaptation and water security in Durban, South Africa. In Cobbinah, P. B. & Addaney, M. (Eds.), *The geography of climate change adaptation in urban Africa.* Cham, Switzerland: Palgrave.

Martel, P., Sutherland, C., Hannan, S., & Magwaza, F. (2021). River Rehabilitation Projects, and their associated ecological infrastructure, as a spatial expression of a more resilient and sustainable Durban. Cobbinah, P. & Addaney, M. (Eds.), *Sustainable urban futures in Africa.* Routledge.

Mbatha, S., & Ngcoya, M. (2019). Peri-urban land transactions: The new geographies and cultures of peri-urban land in eThekwini Municipality. *Transformation: Critical Perspectives on Southern Africa, 99,* 1–36.

Mercer, S. J., Sindall, R., Cottingham, R. S., Buckley, C., Alcock, N., Zuma, L., & Gounden, G. (2018). Implementing an engineering field testing platform for sustainable non-sewered sanitation prototypes. Paper presented at the *41st WEDC International Conference: Transformation Towards Sustainable and Resilient WASH Services.,* Egerton University, Nakuru, Kenya.

Mkhize, N., Taylor, M., Udert, K. M. Gounden, T., & Buckley, C. A. (2017). Urine diversion dry toilets in eThekwini Municipality, South Africa: Acceptance, use and maintenance through users' eyes. *Journal of Water, Sanitation and Hygiene for Development*, 7(1), 111–120.

Murdoch, J., & Ward, N. (1997). Governmentality and territoriality: The statistical manufacture of Britain's 'national farm'. *Political Geography*, 16(4), 307–324.

O'Keefe, M., Messmer, U., Lüthi, C., & Tobias, R. (2015). Slum inhabitants' perceptions and decision-making processes related to an innovative sanitation service: Evaluating the Blue Diversion Toilet in Kampala (Uganda). *International Journal of Environmental Health Research*, 25(6), 670–684.

Republic of South Africa. (1996). *Constitution of the Republic of South Africa*. Pretoria: Government Printers.

Roma, E., Buckley, C., Jefferson, B., & Jeffrey, P. (2010). Assessing users' experience of shared sanitation facilities: A case study of community ablution blocks in Durban, South Africa. *Water SA*, 36(5), 589–594.

Roma, E., Philp, K., Buckley, C., Xulu, S., & Scott, D. (2013). User perceptions of urine diversion dehydration toilets: Experiences from a cross-sectional study in eThekwini Municipality. *Water SA*, 39(2), 302–312.

Rose, N. (1999). *Powers of freedom: Reframing political thought*. Cambridge: Cambridge University Press.

Satterthwaite, D. (2016). Missing the Millennium Development Goal targets for water and sanitation in urban areas. *Environment & Urbanisation*, 28(1), 1–20.

Satterthwaite, D., Beard, V., Mitlin, D., & Du, J. (2019). *Untreated and unsafe: Solving the urban sanitation crisis in the global south. Working Paper*. Retrieved from Washington, DC.

Sim, V., Sutherland, C., Buthelezi, S., & Khumalo, D. (2018). Possibilities for a hybrid approach to planning and governance at the interface of the administrative and traditional authority systems in Durban. *Urban Forum*, 29(4), 351–368.

Sim, V., Sutherland, C., & Scott, D. (2016). Pushing the boundaries – Urban Edge challenges in eThekwini Municipality. *South African Geographical Journal*, 98(1), 37–60.

Staddon, C., & Langberg, S. (2014). Urban water security as a function of the 'urban hydrosocial transition'. *Environmental Scientist – Water Security*, 23(3), 13–17.

Statistics SA. (2020). *Water and sanitation statistics, Republic of South Africa*.

Sutherland, C., Hordijk, M., Lewis, B., Meyer, M., & Buthelezi, S. (2014). Water and sanitation provision in eThekwini Municipality: A spatially differentiated Approach. *Environment & Urbanization*, 26(2), 469–488.

Sutherland, C., Odili, A., Khumalo, D., & Buthelezi, S. (2019). *Perceptions of emptying of Urine Diversion Dehydration Toilets (UDDTs). Phase 2. Post eThekwini Municipality Emptying Programme*. Retrieved from Durban, SA.

Sutherland, C., Reynaert, E., Dhlamini, S., Magwaza, F., Lienert, J., Riechmann, M. E., & Sindall, R. C. (2020) Socio-technical analysis of a sanitation innovation in a peri-urban household in Durban, South Africa. *Science of the Total Environment*, 143284. 10.1016/j.scitotenv.2020.143284.

Sutherland, C., & Roberts, D. (2014). *Why leadership matters in water and climate governance*. Opinion Paper 12.

Sutherland, C., Scott, D., & Hordijk, M. (2015). Urban water governance for more inclusive development: A reflection on the 'Waterscapes' of Durban, South Africa. *European Journal of Development Research*, 27, 488–504.

Sutherland, C., Scott, D., Nel, E., & Nel, A. (2018). Conceptualising 'the urban' through the lens of Durban, South Africa. *Urban Forum*, 29(4), 333–350.

Sutherland, C., Sim, V., Okem, A., Khumalo, D., & Buthelezi, S. (2016). *Perceptions on emptying of Urine Diverting Dehydration Toilets. Phase 1: Prior to eThekwini Municipality UDDT Emptying Programme, report produced for Khanyisa Projects, Pollution Research Group and eThekwini Municipality.* Retrieved from Durban, South Africa.

Sutherland, C., Sim, V., Buthelezi, S., & Khumalo, D. (2016b). Social constructions of environmental services in a rapidlydensifying peri-urban area under dual governance in Durban, South Africa. *Bothalia*, 46(2), 1–18.

Udert, K.M., Etter, B., & Gounden, T. (2016). Promoting Sanitation in South Africa through Nutrient Recovery from Urine. *GAIA*, 25(3), 194–196.

van Vliet, B. J., Spaargaren, G., & Oosterveer, P. (2011). Sanitation under challenge: Contributions from the social sciences. *Water Policy*, 13(6), 797–809.

Water and Sanitation Programme. (2011). *Water supply and sanitation in South Africa. Turning Finance into services for 2015 and beyond, Country Status Overviews*. WSP.

WHO and UNICEF. (2021). *Progress on Household Drinking Water, Sanitation and Hygiene 2000–2021: Five Years into the SDGs*. New York: WHO/UNICEF.

17 Transforming Urban Informal Settlements in Kenya through Adaptive Spatial Planning and Tenure Regularisation

Collins Odote and Philip Olale

Introduction

Urbanisation trends in African cities have become a centrepiece of any discourse on sustainable urban development. Indeed, urbanisation has become a strong global transformation force characterised by industrialisation, globalisation and rapid population growth (UN-Habitat, 2016; Saghir & Santoro, 2018). Thus, as the world's population continues to grow in number, sustainable urbanisation is germane to enabling improved living standards and development in urban areas (World Bank, 2016b; UN DESA, 2018). However, this is not the case as rapid urbanisation is outpacing the provision of critical infrastructure and social amenities such as affordable housing, water, sanitation and food. Given this worrying situation, the Sustainable Development Goal 11 seeks to make cities and human settlements inclusive, safe, resilient and sustainable. Specifically, target 11.1 provides that by 2030, parties should ensure access for all to adequate, safe and affordable housing and basic services and upgrading of informal settlements. In this regard, the SDG indicator for Target 11.1 is set to be measured by the urban population living in informal settlements by the year 2030 (UNGA, 2015; UN DESA, 2019a, 2019b).

There exists no universal definition of informal settlements that is generally agreed among scholars, policy makers and practitioners in the field of human settlements. In practice, the definitions adopted vary widely from one case to another and usually depend on a variety of defining parameters (UN-Habitat, 2003). In most instances, the defining parameters employed by analysts tend to dwell largely on the physical, social, or legal characteristics of the settlements in question, or a combination of these. The physical dimension is concerned with the quality of built structures, spatial organisation of built form and the level of infrastructure services available. The social dimension captures income levels and other socio-economic indicators such as educational levels of occupants whereas the legal dimension dwells on the question of property rights and entitlements of the residents (UN-Habitat, 2010). Durand-Lasserve and Clerc (1996) provide a fairly useful typology of informal settlements by arguing for three broad

DOI: 10.4324/9781003181484-17

categories, namely: slums, irregular subdivisions and squatter settlements. Based on this categorisation, slum is defined as a neighbourhood characterised by old dilapidated buildings, high population densities, poor levels of servicing, unauthorised occupation and some sorts of social ills (Durand-Lasserve and Clerc, 1996). Irregular subdivisions generally occupy privately-owned or communal land which has been divided up into plots without compliance to spatial planning standards and approvals. This is the type of informal settlements prevalent in the peri-urban areas of Sub-Saharan Africa where cities have expanded into land previously held under public or private tenure regimes (Durand-Lasserve and Clerc, 1996; UNCHS, 2003). Squatter settlements, *stricto sensu*, refer to settlements on land occupied without the permission of the legal owner, which limits the occupier or the state in provision of basic services or improvement of living conditions.

Within the above context therefore, all slums are informal settlements but not all informal settlements are slums. However, in discussions on settlements, the focus is on the category of informal settlements that are also referred to as slums. This chapter uses the two terms interchangeably on the premise that its focus is on the category of informal settlements referred to as slums. However, the former term does not capture the legality of the tenure which is the primary reason why slums mushroom – which results to lack of basic amenities and for which this chapter seeks to address. Consequently, the operational definition of informal settlement adopted by this chapter relates to the one advanced by UN-Habitat (2003) which combines a number of characteristics restricted to the physical and legal characteristics of the settlements and excludes the more difficult social dimensions. Thus, an informal settlement is defined as a dwelling place with inadequate access to safe water, inadequate access to sanitation and other infrastructure, poor structural quality of housing, overcrowding and insecure residential status (UN-Habitat, 2003). Whether they are established on public or private land, this chapter focusses on the definition of informal settlements from the point of view that they developed irregularly and often do not have critical public services such as sanitation that results in health and environmental hazards.

The quest for sustainable urbanisation and achievement of SDG 11 in relation to urban informal settlements is both a challenge and a commitment for the international community and countries across the world. To ensure that cities become a contributor and not detractor to sustainable development, it is important that they are well planned and governed through the application of spatial planning tools. According to Okeke (2015), spatial planning refers to a creative method of defining space use for sustainable land use management. Spatial planning stretches past "traditional" land use planning and outlines a strategic framework to guide impending development and policy interventions whether or not these are related to formal land use control (Okeke, 2015).

Therefore, spatial planning plays an important role in environmental and governance transformations in urban areas through preparation of plans to promote compatibility of land uses, efficiency in service delivery and effective connectivity of land use activities. Spatial planning provides urban areas with a framework for unleashing their transformative potential across African cities and ensuring that they attain the SDGs. The New Urban Agenda (NUA) agreed upon in 2016 in Quito, Ecuador during the third United Nations Conference on Housing and Sustainable Urban Development (UN Habitat, 2017) underscored this point and set out the pathways for realising that vision. The Quito Declaration on Sustainable Cities and Human Settlements for All adopted at that Conference committed to change the way cities are planned, designed, financed, developed, governed and managed (UN Habitat, 2017) so as to achieve the desired ideals under SDG 11.

With the SDGs tag line of "leaving no one behind," there is need to focus on inequalities in African cities to ensure that urbanisation addresses and does not exacerbate these inequalities. One of the important and overarching challenges to address in this context is that of slums. In a report released in 2003, the United Nations Human Settlements Programme catalogued the global challenges of slums and proposed policy responses to deal with what the then Secretary General of the United Nations, Kofi Annan, in the Foreword to the report described as "the worst of urban poverty and inequality" (UN-Habitat, 2003). Despite, the proportion of the world's urban population living in slums declining by 20%, from 28.4% to 22.8%, between 2000 and 2014 (UN DESA, 2018), the absolute numbers of those living in slums during this period actually increased with the majority being in Asia and Sub-Saharan Africa (UN, 2018).

Therefore, Sub-Saharan African cities, have to contextualise the SDG and NUA ideals to address the challenge of urban informal settlements in the path to sustainability and governance transformations. The priorities may differ but the focus must be on addressing the common challenges that face many processes of urbanisation worldwide. These range from environmental management, governance, socio-economic development, provision of basic services, informality, insecurity and unemployment. These have been summarised by some scholars, in the context of the African continent, as being fragmentation, conflicts, informal arrangements and fragile economic life (Simone, 1999). According to Cobbinah and Darkwah (2016), application of effective urban planning processes and practices in Africa has the potential of achieving sustainability and governance transformations through ensuring spatially integrated, economically viable, socially inclusive and environmentally sustainable urban environments. Nonetheless, the lack of appropriate spatial planning approaches, that addresses itself to the peculiarities of urban growth trends such as informality in most African cities, continues to be a major challenge.

In Kenya, the Government and other development partners have been implementing various settlement upgrading programmes. These programs usually involve either or both of two processes; physical upgrading and/or promoting sustainable livelihoods. Physical upgrading involves providing basic services such as water, electricity, sanitation, waste collection, storm drainage, access roads and footpaths, street lighting and regularising security of land tenure and housing. While promoting sustainable livelihoods involves providing social safeguards to the urban poor. Some of these social safeguards include provision of places of employment for youth and women, enabling access to micro-finance and saving schemes, cash transfers to the elderly and vulnerable among others. Despite these efforts, the challenges of proliferation of urban informal settlements in Kenya and many other African cities still persist due to application of a non-responsive spatial planning that has hindered several of these policy initiatives from achieving the target of sustainably upgrading informal settlements. These settlements have continued to occupy both poor and hazardous pieces of land or squat on public or private land with no appropriate spatial planning systems in place to provide affordable amenities. As argued by Kibwana (2000), urban informal settlements have continued to be a challenge largely because they have not been targets of land use planning policy, law and activity. This is in spite of the various benefits that such settlements provide to the city such as providing affordable housing to low-income employees and source of livelihood from informal sector activities.

Based on an assessment of past informal settlement upgrading initiatives in Kenya, this chapter argues for integrating adaptive spatial planning as a sustainable approach to ensuring improvement of the conditions of people in the informal settlements, integrating them into the wider city governance and delivering on the international commitments of making urbanisation sustainable and inclusive. Such an approach departs from the current system which views informality as an illegality and thus ignores it in planning processes as a basis for provision of basic services to a more nuanced and integrated approach where these informal settlements are seen as spaces where human beings live, human beings who are citizens and taxpayers, thus entitled to public services and whose localities must be captured in planning processes. This chapter is based on an analysis of existing literature on key themes including sustainable urban development, urbanisation trends, spatial planning and informal settlements. The search was done from google scholar and JSTOR from 1963 to 2020. The assessment of literature as the main source of data for this study focused on general scholarly literature contained in various journals, published reports by global organisations such as UN and policy documents and reports by the government of Kenya and other agencies. Over 30 published literatures were analysed to provide a framework for triangulating findings and arguments put forward in this chapter. Additional data for the chapter was generated from case law based on decisions from Kenyan courts on informal settlements.

Growth of Informal Settlements in Kenya and the Challenge for Spatial Planning

The total number of Kenyans in 2019 stood at 47.6 million up from 38.6 million in 2009 (KNBS, 2019). Of the total population, 14.8 million were urban translating to 31.2% (KNBS, 2019). Based on UN projections, Kenya is projected to become an urban country (at least 50% of the population living in urban areas) around 2050 (World Bank, 2011). Estimates of a World Bank review put the urban population at slightly more than 14 million people (World Bank, 2016a). By 2030, Kenya can expect to have over 22 million urban dwellers, and by 2050 about 40 million (World Bank, 2016a). Thus, while urbanisation continues to be a growing trend in the country, the population is still predominantly rural. Figure 17.1 illustrates key urban areas in Kenya.

The challenges of informal settlements continue to mark the growth patterns in Kenya's urban centers. As illustrated in Figure 17.2, Nairobi which is the capital city of Kenya and the most populated city has approximately 2.5 million slum dwellers in about 200 settlements. Kibera, which is one of the largest informal settlements in Nairobi houses about 250,000 of these people. The origin of these informal settlements traces its roots to the colonial period. During this period, Africans were barred from designated residential areas in the City (Nairobi then being the only city and main urban center) as these were reserved for Europeans and Africans (Amensty International, 2009). Africans, consequently resorted to creating informal settlements outside the planned areas (Mittulah, 2003). The initial spatial development plans for urban areas ignored these settlements, proceeded as if they did not exist because the areas were viewed as illegal. As a consequence, they were never served with roads or other basic services. This trend continued into independence and long thereafter. After independence, the colonial government bequeathed, to newly independent Kenya, a set of land laws and urban planning standards that were unable to reverse the inequitable colonial land distribution (Pamoja Trust, Shack/Slum Dwellers International, & Urban Poor Fund International, 2008).

Further proliferation of informal settlements in Kenya is largely driven by the prevailing insecure tenure. Informal settlements being the manifestation of a partial breakdown of the land tenure system – occurs because at such stage land tenure defines some people as landless – as having no recognised land rights (Kibwana, 2000). The informal settlement dwellers are, therefore, faced with tenure insecurity as they are not subject of land tenurial arrangements since the existing land tenure systems do not recognise them (Kibwana, 2000). Tenure defines the nature and content of property rights and determines how society allows individuals and groups to hold property

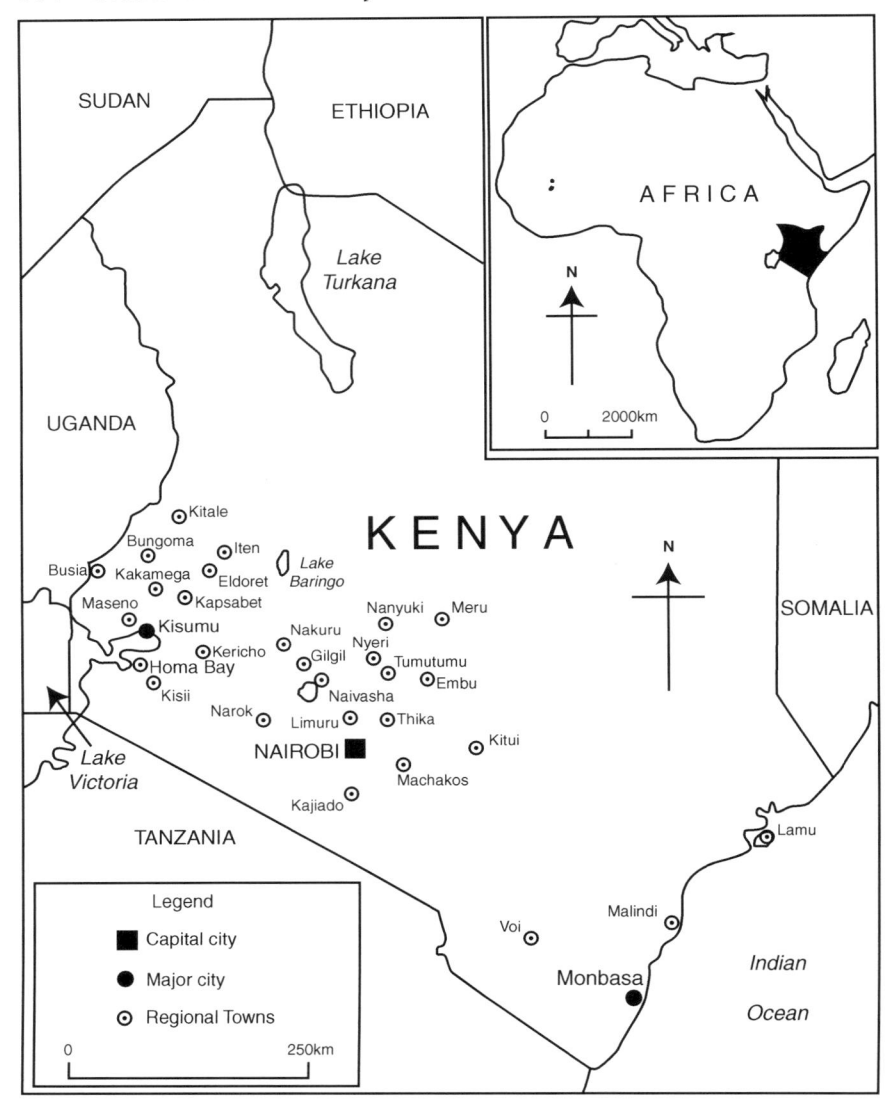

Figure 17.1 Key Urban Areas in Kenya.

Source: Otiso (2003).

rights in land or other resources and the conditions under which those rights are to held and enjoyed (Kameri-Mbote & Odote, 2016). Thus, land tenure security responds to an individual's perception of his/her rights to a piece of land on a continual basis, as well as the ability to reap the benefits of labour or capital invested in land, either in use or upon alienation (Mutangadura, 2007; Mahadevia, 2010).

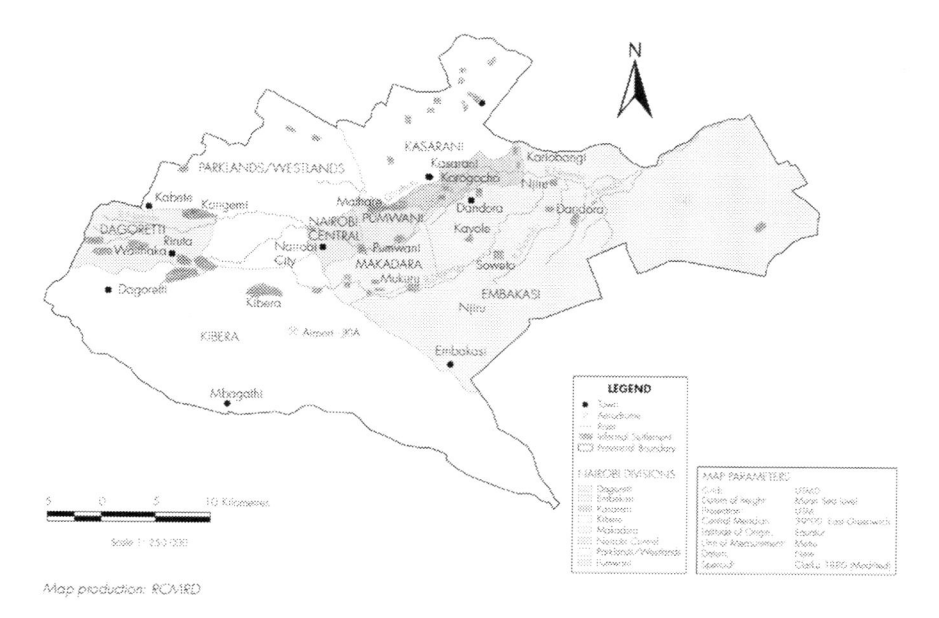

Figure 17.2 Informal Settlements in Nairobi Kenya.

Source: Regional Center for Mapping of Resources for Development (2016).

Informal settlement dwellers in urban areas in Kenya squat on public or private land characterised by no and/or limited tenure rights. In these settlements, land tenure is delivered mainly through informal subdivisions which often fall short of spatial planning requirements set by the approving authorities and thus cannot be registered. In some cases, land is availed through illegal occupation and informal settlement by squatters. Land provided through informal subdivisions is often short of essential services and social amenities (Republic of Kenya, 2004). Whatever they get is largely informal tenure which cannot be recognised or classified into the three tenure categories recognised by the Constitution of Kenya (Kameri-Mbote & Odote, 2016). As such informal tenure gives rise to settlement characterised by low if any provision of services. This low service provision including infrastructure such as roads often results in a settlement chocking on itself where the nature of structures is not only substandard but also highly organically organised. This is because infrastructure which is an urban spatial planning organising element is missing and supplied haphazardly based on demand. Figure 17.3 illustrates a section of an informal settlement in Nairobi that has encroached into a riparian reserve leading to pollution due to poor waste management.

In most towns in Kenya, the poor in informal settlements depend on water kiosks and pay far higher prices for water than those with house

Figure 17.3 Section of an informal settlement in Nairobi.

Source: Field Transect Walk (2020).

connections (Gulyani et al., 2008). In Nairobi, for instance, the price per m^3 at water kiosks is higher than Ksh 100 (US$ 1). In Eldoret, for instance, water kiosks retail water at Ksh 100 (US$ 1) per m^3, far above the purchase price of Ksh 10 (US$ 0.10 cent) per m^3 offered by the utility; and in Nakuru, water kiosks buy their water from the company at Ksh 15 (US$ 0.15 cent) per m^3 but retail at around Ksh 150 (US$ 1.50) per m^3. These higher prices do not reflect costs and are the symptoms of a non-competitive market for water given that water kiosks buy water from utilities at much lower prices, typically lower than the lifeline tariffs. High water prices in settlements where the majority live below the poverty line bring about substantial externalities because of the likely outbreak of water-borne diseases arising from the limited use of water by the poor. In the slums of Nairobi, Gulyani et al. (2008) point out that water use is about 23 litres per capita per day, emphasising that this is low compared to both previous use levels in Kenya and to current levels in other developing countries. This disproportionate high cost of basic services as compared to the utility derived from the services is what commentators such as Horn et al. (2020) have termed as "poverty penalty."

One of the demonstrations of the challenges that lack of appropriate spatial planning in informal settlements brings happened in 2011 in Sinai Slums, near Nairobi's industrial area. The slum is one of the numerous slums in Kenya. A leaking pipe due to a faulty gasket belonging to Kenya Pipeline Company resulted to death of 100 people and injury of 160 people who were living in the slum located on land belonging to Kenya Pipeline Company. One of the key challenges was the inability of the fire fighting and rescuing operations to access the area due to lack of access. The Member of Parliament for the area sued the Attorney General and the County Government of Nairobi seeking several reliefs including damages for loss. The Court declined grant the requested reliefs based on procedural failure by the applicants but ordered that Sinai Settlement be included as part of the Government's Slum Upgrading and Prevention Programme and to relocate or compensate the residents so as to clear the Kenya Pipeline wayleave.[1]

The end result of these challenges are that informal settlements have continued to proliferate and exist outside official policy recognition and support. This has led to these areas being unplanned, lacking in basic services and raising a range of social, economic, environmental and governance challenges. Housing and basic services are invariably provided by slumlords in a haphazard and unplanned manner. The ramification of these challenges has been witnessed during the ongoing COVID-19 pandemic. The lack of adequate water and sanitation facilities coupled with the high population densities in these settlements has made implementation of government directives on regular washing of hands and social distancing a challenge. Enforcement of curfew has also disrupted the livelihoods of majority of the informal settlement dwellers who depend on daily wages (Nyandera & Onditi, 2020). This brings to the fore the urgency of policy interventions. Post-independent government policies started with efforts geared towards eradicating slum's moved to upgrading the slums so as to improve their living condition's to conversations about tenure security or inclusion in planning processes. The next section discusses these upgrading strategies that have been applied as part of solving the informal settlements challenge.

Approaches Applied in Addressing Urban Informal Settlements in Kenya

Prior to the promulgation of the 2010 Constitution, interventions from the government and private land owners were geared towards forced evictions and slum clearance. However, over the years' interventions have focused more on improving the livelihoods of slum dwellers. Thus, the interventions are either focussed on, regularising tenure to enable the informal slum dwellers to legally access the land they occupy or on improving the living conditions of the settlements through infrastructure upgrading. Some of the options targeted at solving the challenges of informal settlements include: resettlement of the informal settlement dwellers to alternative land; compulsory acquisition of land from a private owner, allocation of public land;

purchase of land occupied at a subsidised rate; and court action and litigation based on adverse possession. These options are discussed below.

Forced Evictions and Slum Clearance

This was adopted in the 1970s through to early 1980s when it became evident that informal settlements were not about to disappear as predicted by economic models. As a result, agents of the state forcibly carried out mass evictions of slum dwellers, accompanied by razing down of their living quarters (Durand-Lasserve & Clerc, 1996; UN-Habitat, 2003). All over the developing world, slum clearance as a component of housing policy largely failed to ameliorate the proliferation of informal settlements, mainly because "it focused on the symptoms, rather than the root causes" of the problem (Arimah, 2010). If anything, it only succeeded in transferring the squatters from their old locations to some other new site in the city, as demolitions were seldom accompanied by the provision of alternative shelter to house the displaced victims. While evictions have been manifest in Kenya since the colonial period, majority of the eviction cases have targeted those in informal settlements (Angote, 2018). Their forced evictions without providing them with alternative shelter exacerbates their poor living conditions (Angote, 2018). It does not address the fundamental challenges of informal settlements, instead taking the erroneous policy position that they can be wished away. Experience in Kenya, demonstrates that in addition to the contestation over the legality of this approach, it results in creating greater socio-economic challenges than it resolves. Those evicted continue to suffer, either come back or go and establish other informal settlements within the country.

With the 2010 Constitution, and the provision of the right to property and the right to housing as entitlements to citizens within Kenya, forced evictions have been looked down upon and declared illegal by the Courts. In a Judgement that heavily borrowed the reasoning in the celebrated South African case of *Government of South Africa and Others v Grootboom and others,* Judge Isaac Lenaola in the case of Satrose *Ayuma & others v The Registered Trustees of the Kenya Railways Staff Retirement Benefits Scheme held* that forced evictions were against international law and also led to violations of the constitutional rights to housing. In the Judge's reasoning this was due to the fact that "wherever and whenever evictions occur, they are extremely traumatic. They cause physical, psychological and emotional distress and they entail losses of means of economic sustenance and increase impoverishment." Furthermore, the challenge of illegality of evictions has been restated by Kenya's highest court, the Supreme Court in a recent judgment in the case of *Mitu-Bell Welfare Society v Kenya Airports Authority and 2 others; Initiative for Strategic Litigation in Africa (Amicus Curiae).*[2] The Court stated that:

"The persistent problem is that its realisation depends on the avail-ability of land and other material resources. Given the fact that our society is incredulously unequal, with the majority of the population condemned to grinding poverty, the right to accessible and adequate housing remains but a pipe-dream for many. What with each successive government erecting the defense of "lack of resources? The situation is compounded by the fact that, for reasons incomprehensible, the right to housing in Kenya is predicated upon one's ability to "own" land. In other words, unless one has "title" to land under our land laws, he/she will find it almost impossible to mount a claim of a right to housing, even when faced with the grim possibility of eviction."[3]

Relocation of the Informal Settlement Dwellers to Alternative Land

The term resettlement is largely associated with migration policies since the second world war (Bamberg, 2018). One of the underlying principles for addressing the plight of refugees is that of resettlement, captured in the 1951 UN Convention relating to the Status of Refugees. The United Nations High Commission for Refugees (UNHCR), the agency that deals with refugee issues, developed a handbook, the *"Resettlement Handbook,"* which defines resettlement as the act or instance of settling or being settled in another place (UNHCR, 1996). Applying this to the context of those living in informal settlements, how and where they resettle when they are evicted becomes germane. Following criticisms on the inhumane treatment meted out on squatters during forced evictions and slum clearance, au-thorities mooted programmes of relocation and resettlement in which evicted households were assigned alternative locations on sites away from their former abode (UN-Habitat, 2003). Relocation programmes took two forms: households were either allocated new plots on a site-and-service scheme on which they were to begin the task of rebuilding their dwellings anew; or in certain cases, they were assigned newly constructed low-cost housing (van Horen, 1995; Arimah, 2010). The Dandora sites and services scheme was one such initiative implemented in Kenya. The project was designed in 1974 and construction of houses started in 1976 funded by the World Bank. This project was based on the idea of individual low-income families building their own houses, initially in simple materials, which could later be improved.

This approach ensured that when those living in informal settlements were evicted from their houses, alternative areas for resettlement had been identified for them. This ensures that their rights to housing are not com-promised. In pursuing a resettlement policy option in Kenya, the govern-ment is expected to comply with the provisions of the National Land Policy 2009, which requires in Paragraph 175, for the government to "establish criteria for the determination of who qualifies to benefit from resettlement programmes; ensure that it is carried out in a transparent and accountable manner; and provide those to be resettled with infrastructure and basic services" (Republic of Kenya, 2009). The implication of this option is that the Government is expected to among others provide alternative and appropriate land for the resettlement programme, give compensation and subsidies at early stage of the exercise to enable those affected to sustain themselves, enhance infrastructure construction, as well as initiate preferential policy on aspects such as tenure.

Unfortunately, relocation programmes also faced challenges. The authorities in most cases lacked the funds to either build low-cost housing or acquire and service sites in a magnitude that would appreciably reduce the problem of squatting. Moreover, the relocation sites were often on the urban fringe where the city authorities could acquire cheap land. This however meant that the relocated households could no longer access their old city-centre jobs without incurring huge expenses on commuting (van Horen, 1995; Basset, 2002). Sometimes, the absolute lack of livelihood opportunities meant that the beneficiaries were not able to service the costs of housing and infrastructure provision at their new homes as well as pay regular land rates and taxes that came along with formalisation. Given these problems, some beneficiaries often sold off their property and headed off to new squatter sites in locations more supportive of their lifestyles (Turner, 1967; Durand-Lasserve & Clerc, 1996; UN-Habitat, 2003; Arimah, 2010). As a consequence, this option did not lead to solving the challenge of informal settlements in urban areas. Instead it exacerbated the informality.

Settlement Upgrading

Owing partly to the criticism against earlier approaches, and also due to paucity of financial resources to sustain resettlement programmes, such strategies gradually waned in the 1970s and 1980s, giving way to strategies and programmes aimed at improving and consolidating the existing low-income housing stock (Mukhija, 2001). Consequently, upgrading programmes followed a number of approaches, employing locally-based improvement strategies designed to replace the various facets of informality, including the provision or improvement of basic services and physical infrastructure; provision of community services; as well as subsidised loans, appropriate technology and cheap building materials to improve dwellings (Arimah, 2010). Upgrading approaches also included for the first-time tenure regularisation as a substantive component of low-cost housing policy (van Horen, 1995; Basset, 2002). It is on this basis that the Kenya National Slum Upgrading Program (KENSUP) and the Kenya Informal Settlements Improvement Project (KISIP) were conceptualised to respond to the growing challenge of informality in urban areas in Kenya. The KISIP was initiated in 2011 to complement the Kenya

National Slum Upgrading Programme which was established in 2003. Both the KENSUP and KISIP targeted improving the living conditions in Kenya's informal settlements (Muraguri, 2011). However, while the KENSUP had a more focus on improving of housing, the KISIP was largely focused on securing tenure and improving basic infrastructure (Muraguri, 2011; Republic of Kenya, 2011).

The urban areas covered under KISIP included Nairobi, Machakos, Kitui, Embu, Thika, Nyeri, Mombasa, Kilifi, Nakuru, Naivasha, Kericho, Eldoret, Kakamega, Kisumu and Garissa (Republic of Kenya, 2011). One of the pilot projects under the KENSUP was implemented in Kibera. To carry out physical upgrading, the KENSUP adopted the use of "de-canting sites" where residents were temporarily relocated to allow the construction of permanent dwellings to proceed.[4] Although upgrading programmes have produced some impressive results, they too have been criticised on a number of grounds. Arimah (2010) summarises these criticisms as: low levels of investment that have been incapable of rectifying decades of neglect and deterioration; institutionalisation of project-oriented approaches that have failed to ensure the necessary follow-up and maintenance; hasty planning that allowed for little or no input from beneficiary communities, thereby resulting in beneficiary apathy, lack of project ownership and beneficiaries' reluctance to amortise project costs; inability to address the more fundamental supply constraints of land, finance and building materials; and the absence of any clear focus on livelihoods and poverty reduction.

Compulsory Acquisition of Land from a Private Owner

Compulsory acquisition arises from the state's sovereign powers and empowers it to take away property rights form a private entity and put it to public use subject to meeting laid down criteria. In Kenya, the constitution requires that to apply compulsory acquisition, the Government must require the land for public purpose or acquire it in the public interest, compensate the owner and allow one dissatisfied to challenge the acquisition in a court of law (Republic of Kenya, 2010). Compulsory acquisition of land by the government applies to informal settlements that are found on private land. This option requires that either the county government or the national government be convinced that acquiring and allocating the parcels of land under contestation to the inhabitants qualify to be a matter of public interest and that such land will be used for public purpose. The Land Act 2012 defines "public purposes" to mean *inter alia* the purposes of settlement of squatters, the poor and landless, and the internally displaced persons (Republic of Kenya, 2012). This, means that acquiring land for purposes of resettling squatters is legal and fits within the requirements of compulsory acquisition.

The responsibility of compulsory acquisition is given to the National Land Commission pursuant to Part VIII of the Land Act 2012. Section 107

(1) provides that whenever the national or county government is satisfied that it may be necessary to acquire some particular land, the respective Cabinet Secretary or the County Executive Committee Member submits a request for acquisition of public land to the Commission to acquire the land on its behalf (Republic of Kenya, 2012). The acquisition must meet the requirement of compulsory acquisition captured in the Constitution which are reiterated in Section 110 of the Land Act 2012. Should the intended compulsory acquisition pass the public interest test, the Government will still have to contend with other matters pertaining to the source of money for compensation and the modalities of proceeding with an allocation program for the beneficiaries. The legal position of these issues is provided under Section 135 of the Land Act 2012 which provides for a Land Settlement Fund to be administered by the National Land Commission to be used for the purpose of accessing land for squatters among others (Republic of Kenya, 2012). However, this fund is yet to be commissioned by the government. The challenge of resource availability makes this option difficult to operationalise to address the plight of squatters and informal settlements in Kenya. In addition, it is significant to note that such land acquired compulsorily and on the basis of use for public purpose should have its ownership retained by the public. The implication is that such land is changed from private to public land with beneficiaries given a negotiated bundle of land rights through the process of land regularisation. This can take the form of leaseholds for an agreed period of time. To guard against gentrification and resale of the land, the tenure system adopted should have stringent conditions on sale and transfer.

Allocation of Public Land

Informal settlement dwellers occupying public land have also engaged the government to formally allocate them the land. This has taken the form of negotiation between the community and the respective government agency legally holding the title to the land. Being public land, such negotiations are contemplated by the Land Act 2012. Section 12 of the Land Act 2012 provides that the National Land Commission may, on behalf of the National or county governments, allocate public land by way of among others, application confined to a targeted group of persons or groups in order to ameliorate their disadvantaged position (Republic of Kenya, 2012). Reliance on this section would enable the outcome of the negotiations to be translated to a formal allocation in accordance with the Land Act. Importantly, Section 12 (7) of the Land Act 2012 predicates the issuance of tittle through allocation on an approved spatial land use plan. It states that land shall not be allocated unless it has been planned, surveyed, serviced and guidelines for its development prepared (Republic of Kenya, 2012). As such, physical and land use development plans are prepared in order to provide for an orderly, harmonious development of the land as well as to ensure safety, convenience and aesthetics, therefore, providing a basis for provision of both physical and social infrastructure and amenities.

Purchase of Land Occupied at Negotiated Rate

Another option that has been pursued in dealing with informal settlements is by purchasing land occupied by squatters living in informal settlements and applying for individual titling. In this case, the squatters, either by themselves or through the government, negotiate with the land owner to purchase the land either at market rate or any other agreed formula. If the purchase is successful, then the community can then apply to the government to be issued with individual titles. This approach was implemented in 2015 in Mombasa where the government bought the controversial land to settle squatters after a 16-year battle between the over 1,000 squatters and the registered owner referred to as Mr. Evanson Kamau Waitiki (Nyassy, 2017). The subject land was a 943-acre land in Likoni area in Mombasa commonly referred to as the "Waitiki Farm" (Nyassy, 2017). The main challenge facing this option is that most times the squatters are not able to afford the money required from them to facilitate the purchase and transfer of the land.

Litigation Based on Adverse Possession

Adverse possession is a legal concept that prevents the true registered owner of land from claiming land against a squatter or another person who has been occupying his/her land (Transparency International Kenya, 2015). Gardiner (1998) argues that adverse possession is a method of acquisition of title to real property by possession for a statutory period under certain conditions that generally has five elements that a claimant must establish: the possession must be open, continuous for the statutory period, for the entirety of the area, adverse to the true owner's interests and notorious. This is supported by Gerstenblith (1988) who also identifies the elements of the doctrine of adverse possession as being required adverse, hostile, open, notorious, visible, exclusive and continuous possession to exist for a statutory period before the statute of limitations will bar the owner's suit to recover the property. Proponents of adverse possession argue that the rule forces landowners to maintain and monitor their land (Gardiner, 1998). Moreover, this policy discourages owners from hoarding their property rights for an indefinite period thus discouraging holding of land for speculation. Adverse possession promotes efficient and economic use of land, thereby serving important economic and social ends (Gardiner, 1998). Judge C.W. Meoli noted that adverse possession as a legal concept draws its principles from the historical importance of physical, factual possession of land, over documentary proof that, while conferring legal title does not directly imply that the owner will act on it (National Council for Law Reporting, 2016).

In Kenya, the doctrine of adverse possession has been used by various squatters as a basis of court action. One of the most notable cases is that of *Mtana Lewa v Kahindi Ngala Mwagandi* (2015) eKLR. The case was based on the argument that the doctrine of adverse possession as captured in the Limitation of Actions Act of Kenya was contrary to the Constitutional provision protecting the rights to property and should therefore be declared unconstitutional. The Court of appeal upheld the constitutionality of adverse possession. Even though they did so, one of the judges, raised the issue of its continuing relevance in Kenya when viewed against reforms to the doctrine in England and argued that there was no relevance for its continued application since invading one's land is a criminal offence in Kenya, and the Government with its powers of compulsory acquisition and also the creation of a Land Settlement Fund under the Land Act would help address the plight of squatters. In addition to the above challenges, discharging the burden of proof for adverse possession requires a squatter to demonstrate that they have been on the land openly, notoriously and exclusively for twelve years. Success requires enumeration and mapping to document their claim which needs financial resources which the squatters may not be able to afford.

The Place of Spatial Planning in Promoting Sustainable Development in Informal Settlements

The discussion on options to address urban informal settlements in Kenya has demonstrated a number of challenges. These options are complicated, expensive, time-consuming and more often than not have focused on regularising land tenure of structure owners at the expense of other socio-economic needs of the slum dwellers. Options such as allocation of public land, litigation, compulsory acquisition and purchase of land at negotiated rates all involve lengthy bureaucratic and legal process which are unaffordable to the slum dwellers. On the other hand, the option of settlement upgrading has continued to focus on provision of secure tenure through issuance of individual titles. The issuance of titles targets structure owners and not tenants who are usually the majority in the informal settlements. In Kenya, studies have consistently shown that the majority of squatters and slum residents are actually tenants as opposed to structure owners (Andreasen, 1996; Imparato & Ruster, 2003), often paying exorbitant rents to (absentee) "landlords" (Mwangi, 1997; Gulyani et al., 2008). In Nairobi's informal settlements, 92% of the households are rent-paying tenants rather than home-owning squatters, with 95% of all structure owners living off-site as absentee "slumlords" (UN-Habitat, 2003). Thus, various commentators have argued that this approach to upgrading of informal settlements through provision of freehold or leasehold titles may hinder community cohesion, dissolve social links (Gardiner, 1998) and induce or accelerate segregation processes through market eviction (Payne, 2004; Basset, 2005; Handzic, 2010).

These challenges have led to a phenomenon commonly referred to as slum gentrification where poor tenants are pushed out to make way for wealthier occupants and new commercial and service developments (UN-Habitat, 2003). The issue of gentrification is mainly caused by the inability of the majority tenant squatters to sustain the interventions proposed. According to Huchzermeyer (2008), the Kenya middle- and high-income buyers have moved into upgraded neighbourhoods and put up multi-storey rental tenements displacing the original beneficiaries. Therefore, if options for addressing urban informal settlements are to deliver their anticipated impacts especially of social inclusivity and right to the city, then policy makers must attend to the plight of tenants as a substantive target group in their own right (Andreasen, 1996; Gulyani & Talukdar, 2008). To address these challenges, UN-Habitat (2003) noted that cities should implement spatial planning policies that prevent the emergence of new slums as they also address the issues of poverty and exclusion. This has led to adoption of an adaptive spatial planning (ASP) approach for addressing the urban informal settlements. This approach capitalises on doctrines of participatory planning, flexibility and iterative planning process to innovate development conditions that support a city's capacity to respond to changing phenomena as opposed to the normally preferred rigid blueprint of conventional planning standards that seeks a predefined action (UN-Habitat, 2015; Rauws & Roo, 2016). Some proponents of the adaptive approach to spatial planning have argued that the development of low-income settlements is based to a great extent on a process led by the poor residents themselves (Imparato & Ruster, 2003). This presents a paradigm shift from the routine planning tasks where state planners single-handedly assume the entire process of project initiation, design and implementation (Otiso, 2003).

Adaptive spatial planning involves a two-fold approach. This first step includes the identification of risk specific indicators that impedes the planning, thus, existing vulnerabilities such as poverty and insecure tenure (Wendt, 2015). As such, the formation of conditions for settlement up-grading vis-à-vis its future integration with the wider urban context is taken into consideration (Batty, 2013; Rauws & Roo, 2016). Secondly, adaptive spatial planning exercises an adaptive government procedural system wherein the planning agencies and other stakeholders evaluate the spatial plans and strategies on the basis of their impacts upon implementation. This is so that there's realignment of such plans to particular risks they exhibit (Wendt, 2015). For example, obligation to evaluate existing land-use plans with regard to potentially new slums or squatter zones as well as expected coverage. These two steps of adaptive spatial planning also employ monitoring to keep track of the unforeseen impacts which enables planners to provide remedial solutions to address the impacts (Batty, 2013; Wendt, 2015; Rauws & Roo, 2016).

Thus, adaptive spatial planning requires a retreat from rigid planning guidelines that prescribed allowable dwelling types, densities and sizes and other urban infrastructure standards (UN-Habitat, 2003). This is because the fiscal and social costs of complying with conventional national or county government codes and standards of land use planning and design are prohibitive within the context of informal settlements (Mchome, 2017). Thus, standards should be rationalised in order to reduce production costs of habitable serviced land for housing to avoid rendering informal land and housing production processes illegal and to reduce procedures which have discriminatory or segregative effects. When carrying out regularisation initiatives through spatial planning, there should be concerted effort in formulating minimal/adaptive standards and major innovative strategies geared towards providing an acceptable level of infrastructure and services, urban layouts, and forms of delivery at minimal initial costs while permitting progressive improvements afterwards. Essentially, national government under the Directorate of Physical Planning should prepare policy guidelines while county governments should prepare and adopt detailed planning regulations through active community participation. This should focus on in-situ incremental upgrading where the informal settlement progressively transitions into a formal urban area.

Adaptive or rationalised standards approach have been used in various informal settlement upgrading plans in other countries such as Bolivia, Chile, Peru, South Africa and Tanzania (see Mchome, 2017). In respect to Kenya, the Physical and Land Use Planning Act 2019 has provided a framework for application of adaptive spatial planning through designation of a special planning area (SPA). This is an area with unique development potential or problems (Republic of Kenya, 2019). SPAs are created in situations where the established and conventional zoning and development control regulations do not adequately address local concerns. Thus, SPA allows uses, regulations and standards that would normally not be allowed under the prevailing regulations (Republic of Kenya, 2019). This approach has been used by the Nairobi City County (NCC), which in August 2017, officially declared Mukuru informal settlement as a SPA. By declaring Mukuru as a SPA, the County put a moratorium on any further development in the area for two years until an Integrated Development Plan for Mukuru was prepared and approved. Mukuru is a belt of three informal settlements in the industrial zone of Nairobi City (Horn et al., 2020). The three settlements that constitute Mukuru informal settlement are Mukuru Kwa Reuben, Mukuru Kwa Njenga and Viwandani located approximately 8 Km from the Nairobi Central Business District (CBD). The settlements are about 650 acres in size with Mukuru Kwa Njenga taking up 250 acres, Mukuru Kwa Reuben and Viwandani 200 acres each – see Figure 4.

The settlement provides a home to more than 100,000 households. The designation of Mukuru as an SPA emanated from collaborative research on living conditions in the settlement by the local community led by

Muungano wa Wanavijiji and involving non-governmental organisations such as Slum Dwellers international (SDI) Kenya, Akiba Mashinani Trust (AMT), the Katiba Institute and Universities of Berkeley, Nairobi and Strathmore. As a social movement of Kenya slum dwellers, Muungano wa Wanavijiji (loosely translated as confederation of slum dwellers), has had a long history of mobilising informal settlement dwellers to champion for land rights and improved living conditions through lobbying government to provide basic services. Arising from this lobbying, the county government accepted to enable the upgrading of Mukuru based on the SPA approach. According to the project website, it is reported that the SPA goes beyond providing a legal basis for upgrading an informal settlement towards an innovative, evolving approach to large-scale collaborative community planning, where Mukuru's residents, the County government, and around 42 organisations – civil society, academia and private sector – all work together to design an integrated spatial development plan for the area.

The Mukuru SPA is considered as a participatory process involving collection and analysis of data, consultations with the community and developing solutions that integrate community knowledge and aspirations with finance, legal and spatial realities. The areas of focus in the integrated development plan include housing, infrastructure and commerce; education, youth affairs and culture; health services; land and institutional frameworks; water, sanitation and energy; finance; environment and natural resources; and coordination and community organisation. According to Horn et al. (2020), the declaration of Mukuru as an SPA demonstrates a significant recognition by Nairobi City County that conventional planning processes cannot adequately address the complex challenges faced by informal settlements. Consequently, the SPA approach engineered an adaptive spatial planning framework which establishes partnerships between government, civil society, residents and other stakeholders; emphasises community participation in the planning process; and recognises that slum upgrading is a challenge for the whole city to unpack and resolve barriers to inclusive development through a multidisciplinary and multi-sectoral approach as envisaged by SDG 11 (Horn et al., 2020). In this context, the SPA provides an inclusive opportunity for input by residents through participatory planning and ownership of the upgrading process. This has enabled the County to proceed with the preparation of the settlement regularisation plan based on negotiated standards that seek to ensure inclusion.

Though not yet approved, the draft spatial plan has proposed relatively narrow accesses to promote predestination; use of common on-site service points for sanitation, water, parking and street lighting; and use of off-site services (health, schools, infrastructural networks) used collectively by the wider city. This approach is premised on the need to offer an immediate relief to the inhabitants through settlement regularisation and inclusion in the wider urban zoning as part of SDG 11 but also provide an opportunity for incremental upgrading of the settlement. The SPA process as an approach for informal settlement upgrading has not been widely used in Kenya and in the case of Mukuru is faced by challenges including the difficulty of rationalising the different needs and concerns of business owners and informal workers, of house owners and tenants, and of women, men, boys and girls (Dodman, 2017). Nonetheless, Horn et al. (2020) argue that the experience from the Mukuru SPA suggests that processes aimed at planning for informal settlement upgrading should be sensitive to context, flexible and adaptable in nature. This would lead to an adaptive spatial planning approach which is responsive to local and contextual realities without being limited by conventional spatial and land use planning standards as domesticated in statute.

Conclusion

Within informal settlements in African cities, infrastructure and other services are delivered mainly through informal processes, illegal occupation and squatting which often fall short of spatial planning requirements set by the approving authorities hence cannot be formally registered. This illegal occupation of land out of the formal regulations, more often than not limits the involvement of planning authorities from intervening so as to guide settlement layout and typology. Moreover, the insecure tenure discourages government, private investors and even the informal settlement dwellers themselves from fundamentally investing in the land further complicating the realisation of the SDGs. The adoption of the 2010 Constitution came in to solve some of these challenges. It introduced devolution whose essence was to ensure equitable distribution of resources across the country. It would also enhance the involvement of citizens in governance. The objects of devolution could have several consequences on urbanisation and the state of informal settlements. First, through resource distribution, these marginal areas too would be better served by Government services. Second, the pressure for rural-urban migration that results in informal settlements would be reduced. In addition, urban areas would arise in all the 47 Counties and across the entire country thus making urbanisation more inclusive and sustainable. In addition, and more importantly, Counties are expected to develop integrated plans for their areas of jurisdiction, a function that led the Nairobi City County government to develop the Nairobi Integrated Urban Development Master Plan 2014–2030, which recognised informal settlements and makes a commitment for service provision to these areas.

Preparation of adaptive spatial plans enables the regularisation of a settlement which had been hitherto excluded from services and development control due to their "informal" status to be now legally included within the urban areas zoning laws and ordinance. Consequently, such a plan when accompanied by appropriate development control standards provides a framework which can be used by respective county authorities in regulating development post the tenure regularisation and issuance of ownership documents. This ensures that as the settlements undergoes physical transformation due to secure tenure, it does so within a structured framework where all proposed new developments are subjected to approval processes and required to surrender land for provision of public utilities. Therefore, through adaptive spatial planning of urban informal settlements, policy makers are able to contribute to the realisation of SDG 11 commitments of ensuring access for all to adequate, safe and affordable housing and basic services and upgrading of slums. In addition, this will lead to actualisation of Kenya's constitutional provisions on the right to property and the right to housing as entitlements to all citizens.

Notes

1 See *Gideon Mbuvi Kioko alias Sonko vs The Honourable Attorney General and County Government of Nairobi*, High Court Petition Number 223 of 2011.
2 (2021) eKLR. Available at http://kenyalaw.org/caselaw/cases/view/205900/.
3 Ibid.
4 For a detailed assessment of the Kibera Informal settlement upgrading project see Rosa Amelia Flores Fernandez and Bernard Calas (2011), The Kibera Soweto East Project in Nairobi, *Les Cahiers d'Afrique de l'Est / The East African Review* [Online], 44; Available at https://journals.openedition.org/eastafrica/536.

References

Amensty International. (2009). Kenya-The Unseen Majority: Kenya-the unseen majority: Nairobi's Two Million Slum-Dwellerstwo million slum-dwellers Amensty International https://www.amnesty.org/en/documents/afr32/005/2009/en/

Andreasen, J. (1996). Urban tenants and community involvement. *Habitat International*, 20(3), 359–365.

Angote, A. O. (2018). Evictions in Kenya: Which way Under the New Constitution and Land Laws (Amendment) Act 2016. *Journal of CMSD*, 2(2), 56–85.

Arimah, B. C. (2010). *The face of urban poverty: Explaining the prevalence of slums in developing countries*. Helsinki: Working Paper, UNU-WIDER.

Bamberg, K. (2018). *The EU resettlement framework: From a humanitarian pathway to a migration management tool*. European Migration and Diveristy Program. Retrieved from http://aei.pitt.edu/94238/1/pub_8632_euresettlement.pdf

Basset, E. M. (2002). *Informal settlement upgrading in sub-Saharan Africa: Retrospective and lessons learned*. World Bank; Norwegian Trust Fund.

Basset, E. M. (2005). Tinkering with tenure: The community land trust experiment in Voi, Kenya. *Habitat International*, 29, 375–398.

Bassett, E. M., & Jacobs, H. M. (1997). Community-based tenure reform in urban Africa: The community land trust experiment in Voi, Kenya. *Land Use Policy*, 14(3), 215–229.

Batty, M. (2013). *The new science of cities*. Cambridge, MA: MiT Press.

Dodman, D. (2017). A special approach to slum upgrading: The Special Planning Area in Mukuru, Nairobi. *International Institute for Environment and Development*.

Retrieved from https://www.iied.org/special-approach-slum-upgrading-special-planning-area-mukuru-nairobi

Cobbinah, P. B., & Darkwah, R. M. (2016). Toward a more desirable form of sustainable urban development in Africa. *African Geographical Review*, *36*, 262–285 10.1080/19376812.2016.1208770.

Durand-Lasserve, A., & Clerc, V. (1996). *Regularization and integration of irregular settlements: Lessons from experience*. UNDP/UNCHS(Habita)/World Bank. Urban Management and Land Working Paper No 6.

Durand-Lasserve, A., & Selod, H. (2009). The formalisation of urban land tenure in developing countries. In Lall, S. V. et al., *Urban land markets: Improving land management for sustainable urbanisation*. Springer.

ESCAP, & UN Habitat. (2019). *The future of Asian and Pacific cities: Transfromers pathways towards sustainable development*. Bangkok: UN.

Gardiner, B. (1998). *Squatters' rights and adverse possession: A search for equitable application of property laws*. Retrieved from http://mckinneylaw.iu.edu/iiclr/pdf/vol8p119.pdf

Gerstenblith, P. (1988). Adverse possession of real property. *Buffalo Law Review*, *37*(1), 119–164.

Gulyani, S., & Talukdar, D. (2008). Slum real estate: The low-quality high-price puzzle in Nairobi's slum rental market and its implications for theory and practice. *World Development*, *36*(10), 1916–1937.

Gulyani, S., Talukdar, D., & Potter, C. (2008). *Inside informality: Poverty, jobs, housing and services in Nairobi's slums*. Report No. 36347-KE, Africa Water and Urban Unit 1. Washington, DC: Wolrd Bank.

Handzic, K. (2010, January). Is legalized land tenure necessary in slum upgrading? Learning from Rio's land tenure policies in the Favela Bairro Program. *Habitat International*, *34*(1), 11–17.

Horn, P. Kimani, J. Makau, J., & Njoroge, P. (2020). *Scaling participation in informal settlement upgrading: A documentation of community mobilization and consultation processes in the Mukuru special planning area, Nairobi, Kenya*. University of Manchester Global Development Institute.

Huchzermeyer, M. (2008). Slum upgrading in Nairobi within the housing and basic services market; A housing rights concern. *Journal of Asian and African Studies*, *43*(1), 19–39.

Hutter, M. (2016). *Experiencing Cities* (3rd ed.). New York: Routeldge Taylor & Francis.

Imparato, I., & Ruster, J. (2003). *Slum upgrading and participation: Lessons from Latin America*. Washington, DC: The World Bank.

Kameri-Mbote, P., & Odote, C. (2016). Innovating tenure rights for communities in informal settlements: Lessons from Mukuru. In C. Odote & P. Kameri-Mbote (Eds.), *Breaking the mould: Lessons from community land rights in Kenya*. Strathmore University Press.

Kibwana, K. (2000). Land tenure, sponteneous settlement and environmental management in Kenya. In S. C. Wanjala (Ed.), *Essay on land law: The reform debate in Kenya* (p. 105). Faculty of Law, University of Nairobi.

KNBS. (2019). *2010 Kenya population housing census: Vol 2. Distribution of population by administrative units*. Republic of Kenya.

Mahadevia, D. (2010, July). Tenure security and urban social protection links: India. *IDS Bulletin 41*(4).

Mchome, E. E. (2017, May). Assessement of space standards that are used to improve roads network in upgrading informal settlements: The case of Dar es Salaam City, Tanzania. *International Journal of Business and Social Science, 8*(5).

Mittulah, W. (2003). *Urban slums reports: The case of Nairobi.* Retrieved from understanding slums: Case studies for the global report on human settlements.

Mukhija, V. (2001). Upgrading housing settlement in developiing countries: The impact of existing physical conditions. *Cities, 18*(4), 213–222.

Muraguri, L. (2011). Kenyan government initiatives in slum upgrading. *Les Cahiers d'Afrique de l'Est/The East African Review [En ligne],* 44. Retrieved April 05, 2020, from http://journals.openedition.org/eastafrica/534

Mutangadura, G. (2007). The incidence of land tenure insecurity in Southern Africa: Policy implications for sustainable development. *Natural Resources Forum, 31,* 176–187. Retrieved from Natural Resources Forum 31 2007. http://agoralogin.research4life.org

Mwangi, I. K. (1997). The nature of rental housing in Kenya. *Environment and Urbanization, 9*(2), 141–159.

National Council for Law Reporting. (2014). *Mombasa Autocare Ltd v Japhet Pasi Kilonga & 9 others [2014] eKLR.* Kenya Law Reports.

National Council for Law Reporting. (2016). *Samuel Katana Nzunga & 102 others v Salim Abdalla Bakshwein & another [2013] eKLR; Civil Suit 40 of 2008.* Kenya Law Reports.

Nyassy, D. (2017). *State paid Sh1.2bn for Waitiki land, Kaimenyi says.* Nairobi: Business Daily Africa. Retrieved from https://www.businessdailyafrica.com/news/State-paid-Sh1-2-billion-for-Waitiki-land--Kaimenyi-says/539546-3947968-rinosvz/index.html

Nyadera, I. N., & Onditi, F. (2020). COVID-19 experience among slum dwellers in Nairobi: A double tragedy or useful lesson for public health reforms? International Social Work, 63, 838–841 10.1177/0020872820944997.

Okeke, D. (2015). Spatial planning as basis for guiding sustainable land use management. *WIT Transactions on State of the Art in Science and Engineering, 86,* 153–183.

Olima, W. H. (2001). *The dynamics and implications of sustaining urban spatial segregation in Kenya: Experiences from Nairobi Metropolis.* Retrieved December 18, 2013, from www.begakwabega.com/documenti/dynamics-implications-urban-segregation.pdf

Otiso, K. M. (2003). State, voluntary and private sector partnerships for slum upgrading and basic service delivery in Nairobi City, Kenya. *Cities, 20*(4), 221–229.

Pamoja Trust, Shack/Slum Dwellers International, & Urban Poor Fund International. (2008). *Nairobi slum inventory.* Retrieved from www.irinnews.org/pdf/nairobi_inventory.pdf

Payne, G. (2004). Land tenure and property rights: An introduction. *Habitat International, 28*(2), 167–179.

Rauws, W., & Roo, G. D. (2016). Adaptive planning: Generating conditions for urban adaptability. Lessons from Dutch organic development startegies. *Environment and Planning B: Planning and Design, 43*(6), 1052–1074.

Republic of Kenya. (2004). *Sessional Paper No. 3 of 2004 on National Housing Policy*. Goverment of Kenya, Ministry of Lands and Housing. Government Printer.

Republic of Kenya. (2009). *Sessional Paper No. 3 on National Land Policy*. Nairobi: Government Printer.

Republic of Kenya. (2010). *The Constitution of Kenya*. Nairobi: National Council for Law Reporting.

Republic of Kenya. (2011). *Operations Manual*. Nairobi: Kenya Informal Settlements Improvement Programme (KISIP).

Republic of Kenya. (2012). *Land Act, No. 6 of 2012*. Nairobi: National Council for Law Report.

Republic of Kenya. (2019). *The Physical and Land Use Planning Act, 2019*. Nairobi: Government Printer.

Saghir, J., & Santoro, J. (2018). *Urbanization in sub-Saharan Africa: meeting challenges by bridging stakeholders*. Washington, DC: Center for Strategic & International Studies (CSIS).

Simone, A. (1999). Thinking about African urban management in an era of globalisation. *African Soicological Review*, 3(2), 69–98.

Syagga, P. (2011). *Land tenure in slum upgrading projects*. Nairobi, Kenya.

Transparency International Kenya. (2015). *15 things youn need to know about lnad administration, ownership and tenure in Kenya*. Retrieved from Ti-Kenya.

Turner, J. C. (1967). Barriers and channels for housing development in modernizing countries. *Journal of the American Planning Association*, 33(3), 167–181.

UN. (2018). *The sustainable development goals report*.

UN DESA. (2012). *World urbanization prospects, the 2011 revision*. Department of Economic and Social Affairs: Population Division. New York: United Nations (UN).

UN DESA. (2014). *World urbanization prospects, the 2014 revision*. United Nations Department of Economic and Social Affairs: Population Division. New York: United Nations.

UN DESA. (2018). *World urbanization prospects, the 2018 revision*. United Nations Department of Economic and Social Affairs: United Nations Statistics Division. New York: United Nations (UN).

UN DESA. (2019a). *Sustainable development goals progress chart 2019*. United Nations Statistics Division, United Nations Department of Economic and Social Affairs. New York: United Nations (UN).

UN DESA. (2019b). *The sustainable development goals report 2019*. United Nations Statistics Division, United Nations Department of Economic and Social Affairs (UNDESA). New York: United Nations (UN).

UN Habitat. (2017). *The new urban agenda*. United Nations. Retrieved from http://habitat3.org/the-new-urban-agenda/

UNGA. (2015). Transforming our world: The 2030 Agenda for Sustainable Development. *UNGA Resolution A/RES/70/1. Resolution adopted by the United Nations General Assembly*. New York: United Nations (UN).

UN-Habitat. (2003). *The challenge of slums: Global report on human settlements 2003*. London: Earthscan.

UN-Habitat. (2010). *State of world cities 2010/2011: Cities for all, bridging the urban divide*. Earthscan.

UN-Habitat. (2015). Urban and spatial planning and design. In United Nations Task Team on Habitat III (Ed.), *Habitat III issue papers: United Nations conference on housing and sustainable urban development* (pp. 1–10). New York: UN.

UN-Habitat. (2016). *Urbanization and development: Emerging future, world cities report 2016*. Nairobi, Kenya: United Nations Human Settlement Programme (UN-Habitat).

UNHCR. (1996). *Resettlement handbook*. Geneva, Switzerland: United Nations High Commissioner for Refugess.

van Horen, B. (1995). *Informal settlements, upgrading and institutional capacity building in third world cities*. Vancouver, Canada: Asian Urban Research Network.

Wendt, W. (2015). Adaptive planning-needs and strategies for indicator based adaptive planning. *CUPUM 2015, Department of Information Management* (155-1–155-6).

World Bank. (2011). *Why do Kenyans want to live in cities?* Retrieved April 1, 2017 from http://blogs.worldbank.org/africacan/why-do-kenyans-want-to-live-in-cities

World Bank. (2016a). *Kenya Urbanization Review*. Report No: AUS8099. Retrieved from http://documents.worldbank.org/curated/en/639231468043512906/pdf/AUS8099-WP-P148360-PUBLIC-KE-Urbanization-ACS.pdf

World Bank. (2016b). *World Development Indicators 2016*. Washington, DC: World Bank. doi:10.1596/978-1-4648-0683-4

World Commission on Environment and Development. (1987). *Our Common Future*. Retrieved September 2014, 2014, from Report of the World Commission on Environment and Development. In World Bank. (2000). Poverty and the Environment: http://info.worldbank.org/etools/docs/library/36496/PovertyEnvironment.pdf; accessed 17 September 2014.

Index

Note: Page numbers in italics denotes figures; bold denotes tables.